1993
The Supreme Court Review

1993
The

"Judges as persons, or courts as institutions, are entitled to
no greater immunity from criticism than other persons
or institutions . . . [J]udges must be kept mindful of their limitations and
of their ultimate public responsibility by a vigorous
stream of criticism expressed with candor however blunt."
—*Felix Frankfurter*

". . . while it is proper that people should find fault when
their judges fail, it is only reasonable that they should recognize the
difficulties. . . . Let them be severely brought to book,
when they go wrong, but by those who will take the trouble
to understand them."
—*Learned Hand*

THE LAW SCHOOL

THE UNIVERSITY OF CHICAGO

Supreme Court Review

EDITED BY

DENNIS J. HUTCHINSON

DAVID A. STRAUSS

AND GEOFFREY R. STONE

 THE UNIVERSITY OF CHICAGO PRESS

CHICAGO AND LONDON

INTERNATIONAL STANDARD BOOK NUMBER: 0-226-36248-5

LIBRARY OF CONGRESS CATALOG CARD NUMBER: 60-14353

THE UNIVERSITY OF CHICAGO PRESS, CHICAGO 60637

THE UNIVERSITY OF CHICAGO PRESS, LTD., LONDON

© 1994 BY THE UNIVERSITY OF CHICAGO, ALL RIGHTS RESERVED, PUBLISHED 1994

PRINTED IN THE UNITED STATES OF AMERICA

The paper used in this publication meets the minimum requirements of American National Standard for Information Sciences—Permanence of Paper for Printed Library Materials, ANSI Z39.48-1984. ∞

FOR NANCY, JULIE, AND MOLLIE

"my future is in the shaping. . . ."

Hyman M. Spector (1928)

CONTENTS

LAURENCE H. TRIBE

THE MYSTERY OF MOTIVE, PRIVATE AND PUBLIC: SOME NOTES INSPIRED BY THE PROBLEMS OF HATE CRIME AND ANIMAL SACRIFICE

I. The Problem of Private Motive— Some "Hate Crime" Scenarios

One member of an all-white urban gang physically assaults the first affluent-looking passerby in order to rob the victim, indifferent to the fact that the victim, who is dressed in an expensive suit, happens to be black. A second member of the same gang assaults a black passerby in response to a dare to "attack the first black guy who walks by." A third gang member assaults a black passerby because he believes, as he puts it, that "blacks don't belong in this neighborhood." And a fourth individual, personally indifferent to race and not a member of the gang at all, assaults a black passerby in order to collect a reward the gang has offered to anyone who "sends the blacks a message that they're not welcome here."

Consider four ordinances: Ordinance A punishes all physical assaults equally, as felonies. Ordinance B doubles the punishment for a felony "motivated by the victim's race." Ordinance C doubles the punishment for a felony "motivated by the defendant's beliefs

Laurence H. Tribe is Tyler Professor of Constitutional Law, Harvard University.

Author's note: I would like to thank Melanie Oxhorn, J.D., 1994, for her excellent research assistance.

1

about race." Ordinance D doubles the punishment for a felony "motivated by the defendant's attempt to communicate a racist message."

Under Ordinance A, all four assailants would be punished equally; plainly, there is no constitutional problem with that.

Under Ordinance B, the latter three assailants—all of whom selected the victim based on the victim's race—are punished twice as heavily as the first; under the recent decision in *Wisconsin v Mitchell*[1]—unanimously upholding the constitutionality of a hate crime law prescribing enhanced penalties when the offender chooses his or her victim because of the victim's race, religion, disability, sexual orientation, national origin, or ancestry—all nine Justices would find that differential treatment constitutionally inoffensive.[2]

Under Ordinance C, the third assailant—the only one whose "beliefs about race" supplied the motive—is punished twice as heavily as any of the others. And under Ordinance D, the fourth assailant—the only one whose desire to communicate a "racist message" provided the motive—is punished twice as heavily as any of the others. Although *Mitchell* did not address the Ordinance C situation, I would think that the First Amendment presumptively bars any enhanced penalty in that case.[3] And although the Court

---

[1] 113 S Ct 2194 (1993).

[2] See id at 2199–01. In *Mitchell*, the defendant received an enhanced sentence under Wisconsin's hate crime law for his role in goading a group of young black men to assault a white teenager.

[3] But see pages 14–15. Many of the cases dealing with so-called "hate crimes," and many of the discussions of the subject, quite carelessly blur the distinction between an assault or other crime *motivated by the race of the victim* and an assault or other crime *motivated by racial bigotry*. In invalidating the hate crime statute in *Mitchell*, the Wisconsin Supreme Court mistakenly treated the two as equivalent. Although acknowledging that the state's hate crime statute could, given its text, apply to assaults not motivated by bigotry, the court regarded such cases as too anomalous to be of any concern. See *State v Mitchell*, 485 NW2d 807, 814 n 13 (Wis 1992) (concluding that "[t]he legislature may not subvert a constitutional freedom—even one as opprobrious as the right to be a bigot—by carefully wording a statute to affect more than simply that freedom"). However, during oral argument before the United States Supreme Court, Justice Kennedy challenged the assertion made by counsel for defendant Mitchell that the statute applies only to crimes motivated by bigotry. See Transcript of Oral Argument, April 21, 1993, at p 31 (observing that "it's mostly bigots who select people because of their race"; "[t]hat's just the way it happens to be, but that's not what the statute says"). The Court predictably and justifiably saw that the equation of Wisconsin's hate crime statute with a law targeting bigotry as such was indefensible. But see the majority opinion's misleading description of the statute in *Mitchell*, 113 S Ct at 2199 (asserting, incorrectly, that the Wisconsin "statute . . . enhances the maximum penalty for conduct *motivated by a discriminatory point of view*") (emphasis added).

has not yet addressed a situation precisely like that in Ordinance D, I would suppose that the recent decision in *R.A.V. v City of St. Paul*[4]—reversing a cross-burning conviction under an ordinance which made it a misdemeanor to place on property a symbol that "arouses anger, alarm or resentment in others on the basis of race, color, creed, religion or gender"—supports a First Amendment bar to enhanced punishment on those facts.[5]

II. A Variation—Punishing Private Conduct Motivated by Religion

Although this discussion, inspired by the facts of *Mitchell*, has revolved around the victim's race, the result would be no different had the case involved instead the victim's religion, sex, political party affiliation, or any other characteristic which might be protected by law.

To see why, consider a second set of scenarios, involving an all-Arab-American organization none of whose members are Christians or Jews. One member of the organization robs somebody who happens to be a Presbyterian minister, indifferent to the minister's religious vocation, in order to raise money for the organization's activities. A second member of the organization robs a Catholic nun in response to a dare to "get the first Christian who comes by." A third robs a passing Rabbi because, in his words, "I don't have any religious faith myself, but I hate Jews." And a fourth member of this group robs a passing Catholic priest because, as he puts it, "I have a sacred religious duty to prevent infidels from spreading the word of Satan. That's how the priest would've used every cent of the money I took."

Consider four statutes: Statute A punishes all robberies equally, as felonies. Statute B doubles the punishment for a felony "moti-

---

[4] 112 S Ct 2538 (1992).

[5] Id at 2541. The *R.A.V.* majority held that the government is forbidden to suppress selectively those fighting words that convey a particular viewpoint or message, even such a repulsive message as racial hatred. See id at 2545. Writing for the Court, Justice Scalia concluded that the ordinance singled out "symbols which will arouse 'anger, alarm or resentment in others on the basis of race, color, creed, religion or gender' " solely because "those symbols . . . communicate a message of hostility based on one of those characteristics." Id at 2548. See also *Police Dep't v Mosley*, 408 US 92, 95 (1972) (stating that "above all else, the First Amendment means that government has no power to restrict expression because of its message, its ideas, its subject matter, or its content").

vated by the victim's religion." Statute C doubles the punishment for a felony "motivated by the defendant's religious intolerance." Statute D doubles the punishment for a felony "motivated by the defendant's religious faith or fervor."

Under Statute A, all four robbers would receive the same punishment; there is no constitutional problem.

Under Statute B, the latter three assailants—each of whom chose the victim based on the victim's religion—receive double punishment; under the *Mitchell* decision, that differential treatment is perfectly constitutional.

Under Statute C, the third and fourth assailants—the ones whose "religious intolerance" was the motive—are doubly punished. And under Statute D, the fourth—the one whose "religious faith or fervor" was the motive—is singled out for heightened punishment. Again, although *Mitchell* did not address the Statute C situation, the First Amendment probably ought to bar that enhanced penalty for the third or fourth offenders.[6] And, although *Church of Lukumi Babalu Aye, Inc. v City of Hialeah*[7] dealt with animal sacrifice rather than human assault, the rationale that led all nine Justices to invalidate the local laws at issue in that case—laws which targeted the practices of adherents of the Santeria religion by punishing only religiously motivated animal killings—strongly supports a First Amendment bar to enhanced punishment for the fourth offender under Statute D.[8]

III. Mitchell, Babalu Aye, and R.A.V.: When Can Motive Matter?

At a superficial level, these results might appear contradictory. After all, if an actor's motive is a constitutionally *impermissible*

---

[6] See, e.g., *Abood v Detroit Bd of Educ.*, 431 US 209, 234–35 (1977) (observing that "at the heart of the First Amendment is the notion that an individual should be free to believe as he will").

[7] 113 S Ct 2217 (1993). This case was decided on the same day as *Mitchell*, supra note 1.

[8] See id at 2226. In invalidating Hialeah's "animal sacrifice" ordinances under the Free Exercise Clause, Justice Kennedy observed that the key question was whether the law "discriminates against . . . religious beliefs . . . or regulates or prohibits conduct because it is undertaken for religious reasons." Id. See also *Employment Div. v Smith*, 494 US 872, 877–78 (1990) (stating in dictum that the Free Exercise Clause is violated when the state bans an act only when it is performed for a religious purpose or only because of the religious belief reflected).

basis for singling the actor out for special punishment, as the analysis of Ordinances C and D and Statutes C and D might seem to indicate, then the outcomes under Ordinance B and Statute B seem anomalous. On the other hand, if an individual's motive is a constitutionally *allowable* basis for the imposition of special legal burdens, as the analysis of Ordinance B and Statute B suggests, then the outcomes under Ordinances C and D and Statutes C and D appear incongruous.

The contradiction dissolves, however, if we recognize that "motive" is by no means a unitary concept, and that the First Amendment has very different implications depending on what *aspect* of an actor's motive is being singled out for punishment, and on what is meant by motive.

Thus, if actions A and A' differ only in the respect that A was undertaken by the actor without awareness of, or with indifference to, an objectively discernible fact F about the situation confronted by the actor, whereas A' was undertaken by the actor by virtue of the actor's awareness of F, nothing about the First Amendment freedoms of belief and expression even presumptively precludes state action treating A' more harshly than A—provided there is a legitimate reason for government to treat A as more socially harmful when A is triggered by the actor's awareness of F than when A is not. Given such a reason, no strict scrutiny is called for. F might be a red light or a stop sign and A the act of driving past without stopping; or F might be the perceived race or religion of an assault victim and A an act of physical assault.

For example, it would be permissible for the state to provide that an actor is doubly guilty (i.e., subject to an enhanced penalty) if he or she went through a stop sign *because* the sign said "stop," but only normally guilty (i.e., subject to the ordinary penalty) if he or she acted *despite* the words on the traffic sign (as with reckless disregard), and not guilty at all if he or she was unaware of the sign.[9] Similarly, applying this analysis to the hate crime statute at issue in *Mitchell* suggests that it would be constitutional for the

---

[9] One might compare this with the Model Penal Code's treatment of the distinction between acting with "purpose" and acting with "knowledge": "Knowledge that the requisite external circumstances exist is a common element in both [acting purposely and knowingly]. But action is not purposive with respect to the nature or result of the actor's conduct unless it was his conscious object to perform an action of that nature or to cause such a result." Model Penal Code § 2.02 cmt 2 (1985).

state to treat an actor as doubly guilty if he or she committed an assault or other crime *because of* the victim's race or religion (the feature F in this case) but only normally guilty if he or she committed the assault *despite* the victim's race, religion, or the like.

Or, extending this analysis to anti-discrimination laws,[10] an actor could be treated as guilty *only* if he or she acted (e.g., by discharging an employee) *because* of that feature (the employee's race or religion). Thus, in *St. Mary's Honor Center v Hicks*,[11] an employee discrimination case decided the same month as *Mitchell* and *Babalu Aye*, the Court observed that "Title VII does not award damages against employers who cannot prove a nondiscriminatory reason for adverse employment action, but only against employers who are proven to have taken adverse employment action by reason of (in the context of the present case) race."[12] The *Hicks* Court upheld the district court's conclusion that "although [the employee] has proven the existence of a crusade to terminate him, he has not proven that the crusade was racially rather than personally motivated."[13]

Similarly, imagine that the ordinances in *Babalu Aye* provided for enhanced penalties where an animal had been selected for mistreatment *because* of the race, sex, or religion of the animal's owner, or because of the beliefs which the attacker ascribes to the owner regarding the animal (e.g., killing a particular animal because the attacker knows that it is sacred in its owner's religion). Under the *Mitchell* analysis, this would be perfectly constitutional. Such a penalty-enhancement law would not be the same, of course, as the ordinances at issue in *Babalu Aye*, since there are many crimes that may be "religiously motivated" but that have nothing to do with the religion, race, or sex of the victim (e.g., the defendant's religion advocates violence against meat-eaters, or the killing of furry animals). Likewise, there are many crimes that may be triggered by

---

[10] Federal anti-discrimination statutes make it unlawful to "refuse to hire or to discharge any individual . . . because of such individual's race." 42 USC § 2000e-2(g)(1) (1991). A typical hate crime statute imposes more severe punishment when "a person committed a felony or attempted to commit a felony because of the victim's race." Cal Penal Code § 1170.75 (West 1985 & Supp 1992). As the *Mitchell* Court concluded, selecting a victim for an adverse employment decision because of his or her race is no different from selecting a victim for an assault because of his or her race. See *Mitchell*, 113 S Ct 2194, 2200 (1993).

[11] 113 S Ct 2742 (1993).

[12] Id at 2756.

[13] Id at 2748 (quoting opinion of district court).

the religion of the victim but that have nothing to do with the defendant's own religious beliefs (e.g., attacking a Jew in order to carry out, for a fee, someone else's anti-Semitic designs even though one personally abhors anti-Semitism—where one cares more about money than about decency).[14]

In contrast, if actions A and A′ differ in the respect that, although *both* were undertaken by virtue of the actor's awareness of fact F, A′ but not A was committed as a reflection of, or in order to express, a particular belief B by the actor *about* F, then the First Amendment freedoms of belief and expression presumptively preclude state action treating A′ more harshly than A. Thus F might again be a stop sign and A the act of driving past without stopping, or F might be an assault victim's race or religion and A an act of physical assault, but if B represents, say, a philosophical objection to the traffic laws, or racial or religious bigotry, then serious First Amendment problems are posed by augmenting the actor's punishment in light of the views that A reveals or communicates.[15]

To be more concrete, imagine that the Wisconsin law in *Mitchell* drew a distinction, *within* the category of assaults in which the victim was selected based on his or her race, between (1) those selections which are made for *reasons unrelated to* the attacker's racial, sexual, or religious belief system or intended message (e.g., responding to peer pressure or a belief that members of a certain race are easy marks, or trying to win a bet), and (2) those selections which are made for reasons *growing out* of that belief system, or which are intended to convey a message. Punishing only those selections of a victim on the basis of the victim's race, religion, or sex, which were made *because of* the attacker's bigotry or intended racist or sexist message *would* presumptively violate the First Amendment. This conclusion is strongly supported by *Babalu Aye*, which held that the government generally may not distinguish within a category of conduct—for example, mistreatment or killing of animals—between those acts which are triggered by reasons *unrelated* to the offender's belief system (e.g., killing for food) and

---

[14] Of course, a person who selected a victim on the basis of the victim's religion in such circumstances would be guilty of a hate crime under a law like the Wisconsin statute upheld in *Mitchell*.

[15] These problems are not necessarily insuperable, however. See pages 14–15.

those acts which are taken specifically *because* of that belief system
(e.g., killing as part of a ritual sacrifice required by one's religion).

As the *Mitchell* Court recognized, the hate crime law at issue in
that case, by contrast, did not selectively penalize conduct on the
basis of the state's disapproval of any ideology (e.g., bigotry) as
such, or on the basis of the state's disapproval of any message
which the defendant sought to express or was perceived as expressing.[16] As the scenarios sketched above suggest, it makes no difference at all under such hate crime laws whether the deliberate selection of a victim of a certain race is or is not driven by ideological
adherence to a racist viewpoint, and no difference whether it is or
is not accompanied with expressions of racism. As the Supreme
Court observed in *R.A.V.*, "[w]here the government does not target
conduct on the basis of its expressive content, acts are not shielded
from regulation merely because they express a discriminatory idea
or philosophy."[17] Properly drafted hate crime laws do not punish
conduct because of what it expresses or reveals about the defendant's belief system but because of the harms it causes. Such harms
would occur from a defendant's discriminatory "motive" for selecting a victim regardless of whether the assault was motivated by or
conveyed a message of bigotry.

Of course, as an empirical matter, it is primarily bigots who
select victims for assault on the basis of the victims' race,[18] but it
is by no means a *requirement* of hate crime laws that the defendant
be bigoted or act upon his or her bigotry. Indeed, as the above
scenarios should make clear, a mercenary who harbored no racial
bias but agreed, in return for a sum of money, to attack a victim
on the basis of that victim's race would be every bit as guilty under
these hate crime laws as is the individual whose racist convictions
motivate such acts. In these cases, it is completely irrelevant *why*
an attacker is targeting a victim on the basis of the victim's race,
so long as that attacker's conduct is indeed triggered by awareness
of the victim's race.

Similarly, it may be true statistically that the vast majority of

---

[16] But see the Court's erroneous description of the statute, noted in note 3, supra.

[17] 112 S Ct 2538, 2546–47 (1992).

[18] In fact, most of those who violate certain federal criminal civil rights legislation are
likely to be motivated by racial, religious, or sex-based bigotry—attitudes that, however,
hateful, are fully protected by the First Amendment. For example, 18 USC § 245 makes
it a crime for an individual "by force or threat of force" to willfully intimidate another
person "on the basis of race, color, religion, or national origin." 18 USC § 245(b) (2) (1988).
Similarly, 42 USC 3631 makes it a crime to interfere willfully with any person in the

those engaging in certain conduct—for example, assaults—who select their victims on the basis of race *do* intend to express a racist message. But even if this is so, it would not follow that hate crime laws like the one in *Mitchell* are content-based or message-based restrictions—restrictions of the sort the First Amendment has long been understood to render suspect.[19] In contrast, the St. Paul ordinance was invalidated in *R.A.V.* because, even if the only speech that the legislature chose to outlaw consisted of constitutionally unprotected "fighting words," the First Amendment prevented the legislature from selectively targeting for prohibition those "fighting words that contain . . . messages of 'bias-motivated' hatred," just as it would prevent the legislature from selecting for prohibition unprotected fighting words critical of Congress, or unprotected obscenity that contains religiously offensive connotations. The *Mitchell* Court correctly concluded that the message-based government selectivity at issue in *R.A.V.* cannot be equated with the motive-based government selectivity at issue in *Mitchell*.[20]

In fact, in many cases it is not at all clear that a defendant who selects a victim on the basis of the victim's race will intend to convey a racist message. To see this, one need only focus on the commonplace situation in which the government has a difficult time proving that a defendant's conduct was in fact racially or religiously motivated: the defendant—for example, a real estate agent or an employer—may have tried mightily *not* to express, and indeed to conceal, the fact that he or she injured the victim on account of the victim's race or sex. Likewise, in practice hate crime statutes both punish some crimes that do not express racist ideas and fail to reach some crimes that do express such ideas. The statutes would apply to somebody who chose his or her victim on

---

acquisition or occupation of a dwelling because of that person's race, color, religion, sex, handicap, familial status, or national origin. See 42 USC §3631(a) (1988).

[19] See generally Geoffrey R. Stone, *Content Regulation and the First Amendment*, 25 Wm & Mary L Rev 189, 189–252 (1983) (discussing the distinction between content-based and content-neutral restrictions on speech).

[20] Indeed, failing to distinguish hate crime statutes from message-based restrictions would prove the undoing of much of civil rights and equal protection law. The refusal to hire a woman cannot be justified under 42 USC § 2000e-2 (1991) because it is the expression of the employer's viewpoint that women should not be in the workplace. Similarly, the exclusion of blacks from a jury is not exempted from the consequences of *Powers v Ohio*, 111 S Ct 1364 (1991), because it is an expression of the attorney's or client's viewpoint that blacks are incompetent. In such cases it is not the content of the speech that is prohibited, but the acts of discrimination. Regulation of conduct is not rendered suspect under the First Amendment simply because those likely to engage in that conduct will, in most cases, share a racist or otherwise bigoted viewpoint.

the basis of race, or whose crime was motivated by the race of the victim, even if the perpetrator was not seeking to express his or her views on race and perhaps even wished to hide those views. Clearly, then, such penalty-enhancement statutes do not apply in any selective way to conduct that is communicative.

Conversely, a person who happens to express a racist message in his or her attack (e.g., because the defendant believes that a racist message would be the most effective form of abuse) will not be punished under these laws if that person's motive for the attack or reason for selecting the victim was not the victim's race. Thus, these penalty-enhancement statutes also fail to apply to much communicative conduct. They would be both an overinclusive and underinclusive means of regulating the expression of racist ideas, in contrast to the ordinance in *R.A.V.*, which facially discriminated on the basis of the content of the expression.

Undoubtedly, even physical assaults might at times be considered expressive. For example, an assault where the defendant visibly selected his or her victim on the basis of the victim's race might be intended or perceived to express a message that the victim's race is inferior. Penalty-enhancement statutes will in fact tend, as a statistical matter, to punish those assaults that are most expressive, because in such cases the victims of the assaults are chosen as symbols of the broad class of individuals that the perpetrators seek to harm. Assaults motivated by the race or other specified characteristic of the victim will often be undertaken with the intent to convey a specific message, and the audience will almost always perceive this message.[21] However, unlike the ordinance in *R.A.V.*, the typical hate crime penalty-enhancement statutes are facially content-neutral. That is, on their face, such statutes ordinarily address the defendant's motive for committing the crime (i.e., the reason for selecting the victim), not the message communicated by the crime.[22]

---

[21] The *Mitchell* Court opined that assaultive behavior is not the type of expressive conduct that can count as protected speech. See *Mitchell*, 113 S Ct 2194, 2199 (1993). However, even if assaults as such fall outside the boundaries of expressive conduct, certainly other conduct reached by penalty-enhancement statutes, such as the cross-burning at issue in *R.A.V.*, do not.

[22] The *R.A.V.* Court observed, with respect to the St. Paul hate speech ordinance, that "[w]hat we have here, it must be emphasized, is not a prohibition of fighting words that are directed at certain persons or groups (which would be *facially* valid if it met the requirements of the Equal Protection Clause)." *R.A.V.*, 112 S Ct 2538, 2548 (1992) (emphasis in original). This suggests that a law which focused on the status of the victim (e.g., the

In short, although the concept of motive is complex, motive-based inquiries such as the one upheld in *Mitchell* should not be confused either with restrictions on ideology or viewpoint, or with message-based restrictions. The traditional First Amendment objections to restrictions of that sort have no relevance where the government merely identifies an external, objectively discernible fact about a situation and makes the culpability of an act depend on whether the actor was directly aware of this fact and acted because of it, or in spite of it. But, it is ordinarily *not* compatible with traditional First Amendment protections for freedom of thought[23] for the government to identify as the key to an actor's culpability something *purely internal* to the actor's thoughts and beliefs, even when that internal mental state has indirectly led to what the actor ultimately chose to do.[24]

IV. MOTIVE-BASED INQUIRIES AND THE FIRST AMENDMENT'S INTERNAL/EXTERNAL DISTINCTION

In part, this is just the familiar distinction between motive in the more-or-less superficial, external sense corresponding to the classic criminal law notion of intent or of *mens rea*, and motive in a deeper, more attitudinal or expressive sense—a sense that evokes the First Amendment norm that people shouldn't be penalized for the views, ideas, or opinions they hold or choose to express, however wrong-headed or hateful those views may be to the majority— even when those views accompany, or help to explain, actions that could be independently prohibited without violating the First Amendment.[25]

---

victim's race or religion) rather than on the expressive content of the defendant's conduct would be facially valid under the First Amendment.

[23] See, e.g., *Stanley v Georgia*, 394 US 557, 565 (1969) (stating that "[o]ur whole constitutional heritage rebels at the thought of giving government the power to control men's minds"); *Wooley v Maynard*, 430 US 705, 714 (1977) (holding that "[t]he right of freedom of thought protected by the First Amendment against state action includes both the right to speak freely and the right to refrain from speaking at all"). See also *Lamont v Postmaster General*, 381 US 301, 308 (1965) (Brennan, concurring) (asserting that the First Amendment includes the ancillary right to receive and process ideas).

[24] It may be another matter, though, when the mental state is one that is very likely to lead to repeated violations by the same actor whenever the external "facts" recur. See pages 14–15.

[25] See *R.A.V.*, 112 S Ct at 2544 (observing that speech or nonverbal expressive activity can be banned "because of the action it entails, but not because of the ideas it expresses").

Consider, for instance, the criminal law's references to "attendant circumstances" (for establishing culpability) and "aggravating circumstances" (for sentencing). In the terminology of the Model Penal Code, under a hate crime statute such as the one in *Mitchell*, the racial identity of the victim would be an "attendant circumstance of the crime."[26] Whether a person is guilty of a crime depends on whether he or she has the requisite state of mind with regard to all material elements of the crime.[27] To be guilty under a penalty-enhancement statute, the defendant must have acted "purposely" with regard to the attendant circumstance of the victim's racial identity. The defendant who selects a victim on the basis of that victim's race has such a state of mind, while a defendant who does not make this selection might know of, but is indifferent toward, the racial identity of the victim. But the criminal law does not ordinarily inquire into whether the defendant's purposeful action with respect to an attendant circumstance (e.g., the victim's race) was in turn motivated by his or her bigotry, or by an intent to communicate a racist message, or by peer pressure, or by a belief that victims of a certain race are less able to defend themselves, or by some other antecedent set of views or conditions.

Similarly, the fact that culpability or eligibility for an enhanced sentence may turn on the defendant's awareness of a fact F about the situation in which he acted is evident in the sentencing context and in the notion of "aggravating circumstances." For example, one aggravating circumstance under the Model Penal Code is that a "murder was committed for pecuniary gain."[28] But this "circumstance" has nothing to do with the actor's ideology or intended message. As with a victim's race or the writing on a stop sign, the criminal law has simply set forth the appropriate state-of-mind (*mens rea*) requirements (purpose or knowledge) with respect to the objectively discernible aggravators. Thus, to find a motive to commit a murder for pecuniary gain, it is necessary to show not merely that the defendant knew the murder would result in pecuniary

---

[26] See Model Penal Code § 1.13(9) (asserting that attendant circumstances can be elements of a crime). See also Eric J. Grannis, Note, *Fighting Words and Fighting Freestyle: The Constitutionality of Penalty Enhancement for Bias Crimes*, 93 Colum L Rev 178, 191–92 (1993) (discussing distinction between "purpose" and "knowledge" with regard to an attendant circumstance of a crime).

[27] See Model Penal Code § 2.02(4).

[28] See id § 210.6(3)(g).

gain, but rather that the crime was actually committed for the purpose of achieving such pecuniary gain. Again, this distinction turns entirely on the defendant's mental state with respect to a fact F (pecuniary gain resulting from the murder). For purposes of this aggravator, it's irrelevant *why* the defendant was motivated to commit the murder for pecuniary gain or what the defendant intended to express by committing this crime—whether, say, the defendant wanted to prove that such extreme greed is possible, or instead wanted to invest the resulting profit in helping flood victims. *Babalu Aye*—understood as a decision not necessarily limited to *religiously* motivated acts—reflects the principle that it is not permissible to make a punishment turn on motive in this deeper, more internal sense, and *R.A.V.* confirms that message-based punishment would similarly be prohibited. It matters only that the defendant acted purposely (or knowingly) with respect to that element of the crime.[29] This suggests that the First Amendment normally insulates from government burden and scrutiny just two aspects or dimensions of individual behavior: (1) what antecedent thoughts or beliefs ultimately *gave rise* to it, and (2) what thoughts and beliefs it *communicates*, but does not insulate from government burden or scrutiny (3) the mental state—in the limited sense of what "facts" the actor was perceiving—that triggered the actor's behavior. Both *Mitchell* and *Babalu Aye* appear to stand for the proposition that it's ordinarily none of the government's business, for purposes of targeting actions for special punishment, what particular racial, religious, or other ideology or belief system led to the conduct in which an actor engaged. Likewise, *R.A.V.* indicates that, in general, it's also none of the government's business whether the individual's action conveys a message of racial hatred, or instead conveys a different message or no message at all.[30]

---

[29] Of course, in determining whether a defendant in fact selected a victim on the basis of that victim's race, religion, or the like (or committed a murder because of the prospect of pecuniary gain), a court might find it relevant to know about the defendant's beliefs. In addition, deeper motive (e.g., a defendant's belief in violence) can perhaps be considered in connection with content-neutral sentencing factors (e.g., a defendant's lack of remorse). See *Dawson v Delaware*, 112 S Ct 1093, 1096–97 (1992); see also *Barclay v Florida*, 463 US 939, 949 (1983) (holding that the "Constitution does not prohibit a trial judge from taking into account the elements of racial hatred" provided it is relevant to the aggravating factors).

[30] The dichotomy I am suggesting here—that motive in the *mens rea* sense normally may be considered while motive in this more "internal" sense normally may not—evidently presupposes a distinction between "facts" and "values"—between objectively perceivable "realities" *in* the world, and subjectively held "ideas" *about* the world. The entire analysis, after all, depends on drawing a fairly bright line between a fact "F" which somebody

Apparent counter-examples may occur whenever the underlying "beliefs" or attitudes that are said to have given rise to a dangerous act translate directly into a demonstrably high probability of the act's recurrence whenever similar circumstances confront the actor. For example, I would suppose that a person who kills a law enforcement officer in the delusion that all police are emissaries of Satan, or out of the conviction that all police should be killed because all of law is inherently evil, could be deemed more dangerous and accordingly confined for a longer time (in a mental hospital, perhaps) or punished more harshly (if the "belief" is not excused as a manifestation of illness) than a person who kills a single police officer in the belief that one such killing would be just in light of a recent police killing of the killer's best friend. So too someone who assaults another physically out of a belief that assault is just a good form of aerobic exercise could be dealt with differently than someone who does so for reasons much less likely to suggest that further assaults will automatically follow. And a race-based assault motivated by racial bigotry might similarly be thought to be more indicative of further dangerousness than is an otherwise identical assault which is not so motivated.

In addition, the punishment of impossible attempts might present another instance in which the state may accord differential treatment to conduct on the basis of the defendant's beliefs. For

---

perceives, and but for which that person would have acted otherwise, and a belief "B" by virtue of which F played this causal role in that person's decision making. To be sure, there are many ways to describe the "F" but for which a given act would not have occurred. In *Mitchell* itself, for instance, one could say either that the assault would not have occurred but for the fact that "the victim was white," or that the assault would not have occurred but for the fact that "the victim belonged to the oppressor race." Invariably, beliefs and values shape what one perceives as a "fact" and how one conceptualizes it. Yet a distinction between what exists objectively in the world and how one evaluates various phenomena makes intuitive sense to most of us. Suffice it to say that this is anything but a self-evident line, and that the dichotomy it assumes is not universally acknowledged, but that it lies at the root of most efforts to provide a theoretical foundation for American constitutional law. See Roberto Unger, *Knowledge and Politics* 76–77 (1975) (arguing that liberal thought posits this fact/value distinction).

Even with some such line, it must be added that there are supposedly "objective" facts "F" that our constitutional system may put off limits as grounds for penalizing those who take certain kinds of action A by virtue of F, quite apart from any belief B. For instance, it would clearly be unconstitutional to make affectionate behavior A by an individual punishable depending on whether A is undertaken with indifference to, or by virtue of, the perceived race, F, of that individual's companion. See *Loving v Virginia*, 388 US 1, 12 (1967) (striking down a statute forbidding marriages between white persons and persons of other races). This much follows from the substantial freedom of private choice which the Constitution recognizes. Our Constitution guarantees us wide, although not unlimited, latitude to "discriminate" in deciding with whom we wish to associate.

example, the would-be poisoner who spoons what is in fact sugar out of an arsenic box into his aunt's tea might properly be found guilty of attempted murder. Even though such a defendant's conduct was harmless, he believed that it was not—and took action that made clear he was willing to translate murderous beliefs into concrete behavior. Although the defendants in these impossible attempt cases might be viewed as being punished for nothing more than "thought" crime,[31] a more realistic assessment is that they are being punished for *acting* in ways, and/or being *driven* by attitudes, that clearly show a propensity to dangerous behavior.

In sum, much of what might otherwise seem confusing or contradictory about the First Amendment doctrines emerging from the juxtaposition of cases like *R.A.V.*, *Mitchell*, and *Babalu Aye* can be clarified by drawing the distinction proposed here between motive in the fairly innocuous *mens rea* sense, and motive in the murkier sense that is thought likely to pose First Amendment difficulties because it entails more probing into the inner beliefs held, or the views expressed, by the actor. Whenever the latter is involved, the First Amendment should at least impose a heavy burden on government to justify, under a strict scrutiny standard, the assumption of heightened future danger which alone could warrant such probing.[32]

---

[31] See, e.g., *People v Dillon*, 668 P2d 697, 703 (Cal 1983) (noting that "[a]cts that could conceivably be consistent with innocent behavior may, in the eyes of those with knowledge of the actor's criminal design, be unequivocally and proximately connected to the commission of the crime"); *United States v Russell*, 255 US 138, 143 (1921) (noting that the congressional intent underlying Drug Control legislation was to abolish hypertechnical defenses, including the impossibility defense). But see *United States v Oviedo*, 525 F2d 881, 884 (5th Cir 1976) (applying impossibility defense to avoid "punish[ing the defendant's] thoughts, desires, or motives, through indirect evidence, without reference to any objective fact"). The Model Penal Code Provides that an actor need not satisfy the objective elements of the substantive offense to be liable for attempt; the defendant must engage in some conduct "with the kind of culpability otherwise required for commission of the crime," but the precise conduct that constitutes an attempt depends upon the *defendant's apprehension* of the situation—that is, upon "the circumstances as he believes them to be." Model Penal Code § 5.01(1) (Proposed Official Draft 1985).

[32] In defending such differential treatment of bigots against a constitutional challenge, presumably the government would have to establish a factual record demonstrating, for example, that a mercenary is less likely than a bigot to engage in further crimes that are motivated by the victim's race. Under *R.A.V.*, a law that draws upon a category of internal belief or expression is not per se invalid; rather, the government must satisfy strict scrutiny by demonstrating that the law is narrowly tailored to a compelling governmental objective and that there is no content-neutral alternative which would be as effective. See *R.A.V. v City of St. Paul*, 112 S Ct 2538, 2550 (1992) (holding that the cross-burning ordinance failed to pass strict scrutiny because there were effective content-neutral alternatives available, and the ordinance was not narrowly tailored).

V. The Connection Between Public and Private Motive

What I've had to say so far about private motive and about the respects in which government may take such motive into account when regulating private behavior contains quite a lot that sheds light on the seemingly distinct topic of how *government* motive does, or should, bear on the constitutionality of various legislative, administrative, or executive actions.[33]

We shouldn't be especially surprised to find parallels between the two topics. Certainly the epistemological problems of accurately *discerning* motive—of knowing "why" anybody did what they did—are to a degree independent of whether the action whose motives we're exploring is private or public, especially when the act in question is taken by a group, an organization, or an institution.

Then, too, many of the reasons—even apart from the difficulties of identifying actual or underlying "motive" or "motives"—for our reluctance to make legal consequences turn on states of mind apply whether the arguably relevant mental state is that of a real or of an artificial person, that of an individual or of a collectivity of individuals, that of a private or of a public person or group. There are, after all, structurally similar considerations in both sets of cases, all growing out of a systemic aversion to probing too deeply into the inner workings of others' minds.[34]

---

[33] It is not my intent here to engage in a comprehensive reassessment of the jurisprudence of government motive; I offer the following only as a supplement to that jurisprudence. See, e.g., Paul Brest, *Palmer v. Thompson: An Approach to the Problem of Unconstitutional Legislative Motive*, 1971 Supreme Court Review 95; J. Morris Clark, *Legislative Motivation and Fundamental Rights in Constitutional Law*, 15 San Diego L Rev. 953 (1978); Theodore Eisenberg, *Disproportionate Impact and Illicit Motive: Theories of Constitutional Adjudication*, 52 NYU L Rev 36 (1977); John H. Ely, *Legislative and Administrative Motivation in Constitutional Law*, 79 Yale L J 1205 (1970); Michael J. Perry, *The Disproportionate Impact Theory of Racial Discrimination*, 125 U Pa L Rev 540 (1977); Larry G. Simon, *Racially Prejudiced Governmental Actions: A Motivation Theory of the Constitutional Ban Against Racial Discrimination*, 15 San Diego L Rev 1041 (1978).

[34] The refusal to inquire into governmental motive in the "deeper" sense follows, at least in part, from the institutional concern that such an inquiry might impugn the integrity of, or intrude too deeply into, legislative and executive deliberative processes. The protection of government independence and deliberation from judicial interference is represented in the Constitution's Speech or Debate Clause. See US Const, Art I, § 6, cl 1 (providing that "for any Speech or Debate in either House, [Senators or Representatives] shall not be questioned in any other Place"). This clause, in many ways the government analogue to the Free Speech Clause, forbids certain sorts of inquiry into the acts and motivations that occur as part of the legislative process. See *United States v Brewster*, 408 US 501, 525 (1972). Like the First Amendment, which bars the government from imposing restraints or punishments based on an individual's beliefs, the Speech or Debate Clause creates substan-

Finally, many of the reasons for thinking that motive *ought* to matter despite these considerations are the same whether the motive in question is private or public. Just as everyone knows the difference between being sadistically kicked and being carelessly tripped over, so the harm suffered by one whose windows are broken by a neighbor or by a state official because one is a Jew— recall Kristallnacht—differs dramatically from that suffered by one whose windows are broken by a burglar or by a fireman trying to extinguish a fire. Not only is the harm *already* suffered different; so too is the probability of *future* harm of the same sort. And the same may be said of the harm suffered by one who is dragged off in the middle of the night whether by a police officer or by a mobster: whether the aggressor is responding to one's religion, to one's politics, or to one's suspected wrongdoing is likely to matter enormously to all concerned—and for much the same set of reasons whether the violator is a private individual or a government official.

It is plain, too, that government's motives, or the messages conveyed by its actions, may at times matter even *more* than those of a private individual. Indeed, virtually all of the considerations that support distinguishing state from private action—an enormous topic whose exploration is well beyond the scope of this essay[35]— are potentially relevant to the special question of when the Constitution might permit, or even mandate, inquiring into *why* a challenged government action was taken, or what it might symbolize or express, in circumstances where a similarly probing inquiry into the underlying motive or intended or perceived meaning of an otherwise comparable *private* action would be constitutionally intolerable, at least for the purpose of deciding whether or to what degree that action may be prevented or punished by the state.

VI. The Role of Motive in Constitutional Adjudication

Despite occasional statements to the effect that government's motives are or should be without any constitutional signifi-

---

tive and evidentiary barriers which presumptively place individual legislators' deliberations and speech off limits to judicial or executive scrutiny.

[35] See Laurence H. Tribe, *American Constitutional Law*, ch 18 (2d ed 1988) (addressing the problem of state action in general).

cance,[36] the law is often to the contrary, provided one means by "government's motives" nothing beyond the real-world effects the anticipation of which was the but/for cause of what government did.[37] For example, the well-settled constitutional rights not to be disadvantaged by government simply because of one's race or sex,[38] or in retaliation for the exercise of one's First Amendment[39] or other rights,[40] would be largely meaningless if courts were not free to inquire into whether a government official or body did in fact discharge a given employee, or arrest a particular individual, or take some other action adverse to the person involved, *because of* that person's race or other protected status, or *because of* the person's ideas, or *because of* the person's expressed views.

Recognizing that governmental motive in this sense may be important in constitutional adjudication, however, does not mean that it is relevant or should be an admissible consideration in all cases.

---

[36] See *United States v O'Brien*, 391 US 367, 383–84 (1968) (asserting broadly that a law's constitutionality does not depend on the motive that led Congress to enact it); *Edwards v Aguillard*, 482 US 578, 636–40 (1987) (Scalia dissenting) (criticizing the majority's rejection of creationism statute on grounds of legislature's improper motivation). The *O'Brien* Court held that, because the law prohibiting the deliberate destruction of draft cards did not on its face target expression or message, individuals who burn draft cards as a form of antiwar protest (as O'Brien did) should be no more able to challenge the government's motive than those individuals who burn draft cards for noncommunicative purposes, even if Congress's motive was in fact to suppress this form of antiwar protest.

[37] As in the context of private conduct, there are various ways to describe the "fact" but for which a particular governmental act would not have occurred. See note 30. However, the further one moves away from a naked description of real-world effects and toward an examination of the values and beliefs which led the government to seek those effects, the less constitutionally relevant public motive becomes.

[38] See, e.g., *Korematsu v United States*, 323 US 214, 216 (1944) (stating that "all legal restrictions which curtail the civil rights of a single racial group are immediately suspect"); *Weinberg v Wiesenfeld*, 420 US 636, 645 (1975) (noting that "the Constitution . . . forbids the gender-based differentiation that results in the efforts of female workers required to pay social security taxes producing less protection for their families than is produced by the efforts of men").

[39] See, e.g., *Sherbert v Verner*, 374 US 398, 406, 410 (1963) (holding that unemployment compensation may not be withheld from an employee who was denied employment because of religious beliefs, and observing that resting "the availability of benefits upon this appellant's willingness to violate a cardinal principle of her religious faith effectively penalizes the free exercise of her constitutional liberties"); *Pickering v Board of Educ.*, 391 US 563, 568 (1968) (holding that constitutionally protected speech is an impermissible ground for discharge from public employment).

[40] See, e.g., *United States v Jackson*, 390 US 570, 582–83 (1968) (holding unconstitutional a law which forced defendants to choose between guilty plea and trial by jury where jury, but not judge, could impose death penalty, and observing that the statute discouraged assertion of the Fifth Amendment right to plead not guilty).

That motive is sometimes but not always decisive reflects a fundamental distinction between two quite different kinds of constitutional principles—what I would call "output" and "input" principles. By "output" principles, I mean those that specify mandated,
allowed, or forbidden external "outputs" of government processes,
whether these "outputs" are procedural in kind, such as the right
to a jury trial or to procedural due process, or substantive in kind,
such as the right to use birth control free of government restriction,
to distribute leaflets in public streets and parks free of government
obstruction, or to make associational decisions free of government-
mandated racial separation. By "input" principles, I mean those
specifying the kinds of facts about the situation confronting the
government that government may not use to trigger certain otherwise acceptable actions or "outputs." Such principles, for example,
include those that prevent the government from using the race,
political attitudes, or religious beliefs of individuals to trigger the
distribution of benefits like public housing, to which no independent right exists.

Because they are concerned only with the effect or "output" of
the government's action, "output" principles do not call for inquiries into *why* the government acted as it did. Thus, if the output
of the government's conduct is to deny a defendant a speedy trial,
what motivated or led to this denial—what real-world effects the
government sought to bring about through such denial—is altogether irrelevant to the threshold question of a constitutional violation. An individual who suffers such a deprivation may establish
a prima facie constitutional violation without pointing to governmental motive—although, of course, government's supposed justifications or reasons for the deprivation will typically be relevant in
deciding the ultimate questions of constitutional validity.

In contrast, governmental motive (in the sense of the "but/for"
cause of the government's action) *is* relevant with respect to "input"
principles because they turn on what considerations went *into* the
government's action, and not merely on what impact that action
has on the world. The First Amendment, for example, includes
the "input" principle that public employees may not be hired or
discharged on the basis of their religious views, and this principle
requires that the government not have used the employee's religion
as the trigger for its employment decision. In those cases implicat-

ing "input-based" rules, the significance of governmental motive cannot be denied.[41]

Nor can this sort of inquiry into government motive—in the *Mitchell*-like[42] sense of identifying what external feature of the situation triggered the government's decision to injure a given individual or set of individuals—automatically be confined to executive, or law-enforcement, actions. For one thing, the Bill of Rights and the Fourteenth Amendment obviously apply with equal force to all state action; a statute that proscribes, say, "draft-card burning as a form of anti-war protest" is no less infirm under the First Amendment than is the arrest and prosecution of a draft-card burner "for the act of symbolic protest." For another thing, any distinction based on supposed ease of proof is illusory. One might think that we could be more confident about why a given officer arrested someone or why a given employer fired someone than about why a legislative body promulgated some rule. But that is by no means inevitable. In both cases, we are required to determine whether the actor's perception of a particular feature F was the "but/for" cause of the government actor's conduct with respect to a given individual or group of individuals,[43] and there is nothing inherently

---

[41] Note that a number of constitutional clauses, including the First Amendment and the Equal Protection Clause, cut across this dichotomy. For example, a law which prohibits individuals from speaking in public violates an "output" principle, and this violation does not depend on an inquiry into what may have motivated the government to enact the law. See *Schneider v Irvington*, 308 US 147, 163 (1939) (invalidating several ordinances that prohibited leafleting on public streets and other public places). On the other hand, a decision to fire a public employee on the basis of the employee's speech violates an "input" principle because the very process of establishing an abridgement of speech involves determining whether the employer's speech triggered the government's action. See *Pickering v Board of Educ.*, 391 US 563, 568 (1968) (holding that constitutionally protected speech is an impermissible ground for discharge).

Similarly, in the equal protection context, a law which prohibits individuals from associating with members of a certain race violates an "output" principle, and it is irrelevant why the government enacted the law. See *Loving v Virginia*, 488 US 1, 12 (1967) (invalidating a law against racial intermarriage). However, a decision to deny a zoning variance on the basis of race violates an "input" principle, making it necessary to examine governmental motive. See *Village of Arlington Heights v Metropolitan Hous. Dev. Corp.*, 429 US 252, 270 (1977) (stating that proof of racially discriminatory intent is required to show that a zoning decision violated the Equal Protection Clause). That most constitutional provisions are not governed exclusively by one or the other type of principle explains why, even within First Amendment law, or within Equal Protection jurisprudence, motive is sometimes but not always relevant to the analysis.

[42] See supra Parts II and III.

[43] See, e.g., *Personnel Administrator v Feeney*, 442 US 256, 279 (1979) (evaluating legislative motive, and stating that discriminatory purpose "implies that the decisionmaker selected or reaffirmed a particular course of action at least in part 'because of', not merely 'in spite of,' its adverse effects upon an identifiable group"); *Village of Arlington Heights v Metropolitan*

easier about performing this inquiry in the enforcement, rather than the law-making, context. Judicial analyses of motive certainly provide no indication that courts find this causal inquiry more or less manageable in cases of selective enforcement than in cases of laws or regulations challenged as impermissibly motivated.[44] Selective enforcement claims, no less than claims of impermissibly motivated laws or rules, might involve several government actors, and the burdens posed by an inquiry into their "collective" or "group" motive[45] do not seem different in kind from those posed by a similar inquiry into, for example, the motive of a large legislative body,[46] or into the motive(s) of several individuals alleged to have been

---

Hous. Dev. Corp., 429 US 252, 270 n 21 (1977) (zoning action sustained against equal protection challenge even improperly motivated if it would have been the same even without consideration of the improper motive); *Mount Healthy City Sch. Dist. Bd. of Educ. v Doyle*, 429 US 274, 287 (1977) (drawing distinction between illicit purposes that played merely some role in the actor's decision to fire an employee, and those purposes without which the action would not have been taken); *Givhan v Western Line Consolidated Sch. Dist.*, 429 US 410, 417 (1979) (public employee's dismissal, executed in retaliation for speech, can be sustained only if the government would have fired the employee even in the absence of the constitutionally protected speech).

[44] See, e.g., *Arcara v Cloud Books, Inc.*, 478 US 697, 708 (1986) (O'Connor concurring) (observing that "[i]f, however, a city were to use a nuisance statute as a pretext for closing down a book store because it sold indecent books or because of the perceived secondary effects of having a purveyor of such books in the neighborhood, the case would clearly implicate First Amendment concerns and require analysis under the appropriate First Amendment standard of review"); *Wayte v United States*, 470 US 598, 608 (1985) (recognizing in dictum that "the decision to prosecute may not be 'deliberately based'. . . on the exercise of protected statutory and constitutional rights"); *Cornelius v NAACP Legal Defense and Educational Fund, Inc.*, 473 US 788, 811 (1985) (stating that although "the government's posited justifications for denying [the NAACP Legal Defense and Educational Fund] access to the [Combined Federal Campaign] appear to be reasonable," "[t]he existence of reasonable grounds for limiting access to a nonpublic forum . . . will not save a regulation that is in reality a facade for viewpoint-based discrimination"); *Yick Wo v Hopkins*, 118 US 356 (1886) (statute requiring all laundry operators to apply for a permit unless their business was conducted in a brick or stone building held unconstitutional insofar as it was unfairly administered, effectively excluding Chinese laundry operators from the market).

[45] See, e.g., Seth F. Kreimer, *Allocational Sanctions: The Problem of Negative Rights in a Positive State*, 132 U Pa L Rev 1293, 1333–47 (1984) (discussing the problems inherent in discerning the motives of multimember legislatures); Cass R. Sunstein, *Interest Groups in American Public Law*, 38 Stan L Rev 29, 77 (1985) (stating that "[t]he problem [of determining motivation] becomes truly intractable when the issue is the 'motivation' of a multimember decision making body").

[46] In fact, the Court has shown a willingness to invalidate laws on the basis of the motive of just such legislative bodies. See, e.g., *Hunter v Underwood*, 471 US 222, 227–28 (1985) (invidious racial motive of large deliberative body, Alabama Constitutional Convention of 1901, may be determined and used to invalidate facially neutral state constitutional provision having racially disparate impact); *Wallace v Jaffree*, 472 US 38, 55–57 (1985) (moment of silence law held unconstitutional since Alabama legislature's motive was to further religion and return prayer to the public schools).

involved in a private conspiracy to deprive someone of his or her civil rights.[47]

However, although motive inquiries are not, and should not be, limited to government actions that involve administration or enforcement as opposed to law-making, there might be forceful reasons not to focus on motive at all—and few if any persuasive reasons to focus on motive—when analyzing legislative actions laying down *general rules of conduct*, or creating governmental institutions or practices, as opposed to legislative actions distributing benefits or opportunities—for instance, by setting criteria for voting,[48] employment,[49] housing,[50] and the like.[51] To the extent that the Bill of Attainder Clauses[52] already prevent legislatures from singling out the particular people who will be punished by legislative rules,[53] the case for applying *any* input-based constitutional principles to laws or regulations prospectively banning whole categories of acts seems quite weak.[54]

---

[47] See *Griffin v Breckenridge*, 403 US 88, 105 (1971) (holding that, to come within 42 USC § 1985(3), a complaint must allege that the private conspiracy was motivated by "some racial, or perhaps otherwise class-based, invidiously discriminatory animus").

[48] See *Hunter*, 471 US at 225 (unanimously striking down a provision of the Alabama state constitution that disenfranchised persons convicted of certain enumerated felonies and misdemeanors, when it was clear that the section's enactment represented an effort by the legislature to discriminate against blacks and poor whites).

[49] See *Washington v Davis*, 426 US 229, 240 (1976) (finding failure to establish that facially race-neutral employment recruiting procedures having a racially disproportionate impact were racially motivated, but stating that proof of such motive would trigger strict scrutiny).

[50] See *Village of Arlington Heights v Metropolitan Hous. Dev. Corp.*, 429 US 252, 270 (1977) (rejecting equal protection challenge to facially race-neutral city zoning decision without proof of discriminatory intent, but making clear that such proof would trigger strict scrutiny).

[51] Whether laws creating institutions or practices—e.g., establishing a practice of beginning the public school day with a moment of "silent prayer," see *Wallace v Jaffree*, 472 US 38 (1985)—should be treated as analogous to laws setting general rules of conduct rather than as analogous to laws distributing opportunities requires a closer analysis than this article has yet undertaken. See also note 80.

[52] Article I forbids passage of any bill of attainder by Congress, see Art I, § 9, cl 3, or by any state, see Art I, § 10, cl 1.

[53] See *United States v Brown*, 381 US 437, 442–44 (1965) (invalidating an Act of Congress making it a crime for any member of the Communist Party to serve as an officer of a labor union or to be employed by such a union except in a clerical or custodial capacity; the Court held that the ban on bills of attainder protects individuals or groups from being singled out for legislative instead of judicial trial, and that normally the Constitution requires Congress to proceed by general rulemaking rather than by deciding individual cases).

[54] In *Fletcher v Peck*, 110 US 6 Cranch 87 (1810), Chief Justice John Marshall recognized the broad principle that the judiciary may not look to government motive which does not bear on the law's application to individuals. The Court declined to overturn a Georgia statute on the ground that its enactment had been procured by bribing the legislators. See id at 130.

By contrast, laws or regulations *setting criteria for the distribution* of opportunities or benefits ought to be no less subject to input-based principles than are government actions *directly distributing* the same opportunities or benefits.[55] Thus, once one has decided that the Fourteenth and/or Fifteenth Amendments bar race-based state denials of jobs, housing, or the franchise, it would be untenable to hold racial motive on the part of the state irrelevant whenever the denials occur wholesale rather than retail—through *rules of distribution* put in place so as to filter out minorities rather than on a case-by-case basis.

But, setting to one side laws distributing benefits, if a government-enacted rule of conduct is constitutionally inoffensive both on its face and as applied to the particular individual challenging it, the fact that the rule would not have been promulgated (or the practice put in place) but for the enacting body's desire to achieve a constitutionally forbidden result tells us nothing more than that the government body engaged in an *unsuccessful attempt* to violate the Constitution.[56] So too, the fact that the rule would not have been promulgated or the practice established but for the enacting body's consideration of a factor the Constitution tells it never to consider—if there are such factors—hardly suffices to render the rule of conduct promulgated, or the practice put in place, constitutionally void.

Indeed, I can think of no input-based principles that, akin to such structural rules as the bicamerality and presentment requirements for legislative action by Congress,[57] should require invalida-

---

[55] Even in the context of challenges to laws setting criteria for distribution of benefits or opportunities, motive should be relevant only in the limited sense of identifying what real-world effects the government sought to bring about, not in the sense of characterizing the world view that led one or more government actors to seek those effects. Thus, the Court has often noted, although it has at times been less than lucid on the matter, that the inquiry into forbidden government motive that *is* sometimes relevant is *not* an inquiry into the underlying belief system or ideology that *led* to the state's attention to the racial, sexual, or religious impact of its action, but simply an inquiry into the *mens rea* type of "superficial" motive that may be explored without affront either to the personal privacy of individuals or to the institutional autonomy of government bodies. See, e.g., *Board of Educ. v Mergens*, 496 US 226, 248–49 (1990) (asserting that, even if some members of Congress intended solely to protect religious speech when they enacted the Equal Access Act, the Act must be upheld: the Court must consider the legislative purpose of the Act, not the subjective motives of the legislators).

[56] See pages 29–32.

[57] See *INS v Chadha*, 462 US 919, 945–52 (1983) (holding that all action taken by Congress that is "legislative" in "character" must be taken in accord with the "single, finely wrought and exhaustively considered procedure" set forth in the "explicit and unambiguous provisions" of article I, including the bicamerality and presentment rules).

tion of otherwise constitutional rules of behavior or institutional arrangements that a government body has put in place for *reasons* that violate those principles.

Although Supreme Court decisions in the *Lochner* era did strike down both state and federal laws in part on the ground that the responsible legislatures were pursuing ends illegitimate for them to seek,[58] and although the post-*Lochner* Court has on occasion rested on the supposedly illicit religious purpose of legislation in striking it down,[59] the decisions in question either seem wrong today[60] or, if right, seem defensible on non-motive grounds.[61]

There is one remaining possibility that needs consideration as an argument for judicially invalidating *any* government action—

---

[58] See *Lochner v New York*, 198 US 45, 57 (1905) (holding that the state's *"end itself* must be appropriate and legitimate," that the "act must have a more direct relation, as a means to an end," and that there "is no reasonable ground for interfering with the liberty of person or the right of free contract, by determining the hours of labor, in the occupation of a baker") (emphasis added); *Hammer v Dagenhart*, 247 US 251, 271–72 (1918) (striking down child labor law restricting interstate transportation of goods produced by factories in violation of the law because "[t]he act in its effect does not regulate transportation among the States, but *aims* to standardize the ages at which children may be employed in mining and manufacturing within the States") (emphasis added). Nor did this insistence that federal and state legislation pursue ends legitimate to the branch and level of government involved begin in the *Lochner* era. See, e.g., *McCulloch v Maryland*, 4 Wheat 316, 421 (1819) ("Let the *end* be legitimate, let it be within the scope of the constitution, and all means which are appropriate, which are plainly adapted to that end, which are not prohibited, but consistent with the letter and spirit of the constitution, are constitutional.") (emphasis added).

[59] See *Edwards v Aguillard*, 482 US 578, 583 (1987) (invalidating Louisiana's "Creationism Act"—which forbade the teaching of the theory of evolution in public schools unless accompanied by instruction in "Creation Science"—because the statute lacked a clear secular purpose); *Stone v Graham*, 449 US 39, 41–42 (1980) (per curiam) (striking down, after finding a "plainly religious" purpose for, a statute that required public schools to post in each classroom a copy of the Ten Commandments); *Epperson v Arkansas*, 393 US 97, 103 (1968) (holding a statute prohibiting the teaching of Darwin's theory of evolution in the state's public schools unconstitutional because it was motivated by the intent to "establish" a religious viewpoint).

[60] For the contemporary consensus, see *West Coast Hotel Co. v Parrish*, 300 US 379, 392, 397 (1937) (upholding minimum wage and maximum hours legislation as rationally related to the legitimate end of preventing economic exploitation); *Heart of Atlanta Motel, Inc. v United States*, 379 US 241, 258–59 (1964) (upholding the power of Congress, exercised in Title II of the Civil Rights Act of 1964, to prohibit racial discrimination in places of public accommodation, and denying that non-commercial ends are illegitimate for Congress to pursue under the Commerce Clause).

[61] See note 59. For example, the Establishment Clause cases might be understood as placing an output-based limitation on the government's ability to utter religious messages. The "endorsement" test advocated by Justice O'Connor and adopted by the Court in *Allegheny v ACLU Greater Pittsburgh Chapter*, 492 US 573, 595 (1980) focuses upon whether the government is reasonably perceived to be conveying a "message of endorsement" of religion. See note 72. This test does not depend upon a motive-based inquiry or on what factors the government considered.

whether an action promulgating a general rule of conduct, or an action putting in place an institutional practice—whenever it can be convincingly shown that the process leading to that government action was affected by an impermissible factor, such as a desire to suppress speech. It might be argued that striking down otherwise valid laws on the ground that the legislature had an illicit motivation would serve a function akin to the exclusionary rule.[62] Just as the Supreme Court has held that convictions tainted by the introduction of illegally obtained evidence should be reversed, so one might imagine a court holding that laws or regulations tainted by "admission" into the law-making process of some forbidden consideration should be set aside.

But even for those who remain strong proponents of the normal exclusionary rule,[63] this extrapolation from the rule would represent an extraordinary leap. First, it is more troublesome to talk about striking down government actions as a prophylactic measure in the context of federal or state legislation than it is in the context of police misconduct. Respect for the Congress as a coordinate branch, and for the sovereign state legislatures, is difficult to reconcile with such a strong prophylactic use of judicial review. Thus, although they might, with good reason, let "[t]he criminal . . . go free because the constable blundered,"[64] courts should be less willing to invalidate a law because the legislature "blundered" by considering an impermissible factor in its lawmaking.

Second, whenever a court excludes evidence, it can defend its action on non-deterrence grounds. Thus, admitting illegally obtained evidence is said to aggravate the original violation by making the victim suffer the additional deprivation of life, liberty, or property that occurs as a consequence of basing a conviction on the fruits of the unconstitutional search or seizure. Additionally, judi-

---

[62] See *Mapp v Ohio*, 367 US 643, 655 (1961) (holding that the fruits of unreasonable searches or seizures must be excluded at state trial); *Miranda v Arizona*, 384 US 436, 478–79 (1966) (requiring exclusion of confessions obtained in violation of procedural safeguards).

[63] See, e.g., *United States v Leon*, 468 US 897, 928–48 (1984) (Brennan dissenting) (arguing that the exclusionary rule is implicitly part of the Fourth Amendment, not a remedy for a Fourth Amendment violation); Laurence H. Tribe, *Constitutional Calculus: Equal Justice or Economic Efficiency?* 98 Harv L Rev 592, 606–10 (1985) (criticizing the Court's "reductive alchemy" with respect to Fourth Amendment rights, and arguing that the Court's relaxation of the exclusionary rule has involved "defining as benefits what we once deemed costs").

[64]*People v DeFore*, 150 NE 585, 587 (NY 1926) (Cardozo) (arguing against even such a result).

cial integrity is said to be tainted whenever courts admit such evidence, because they lend their imprimatur or approval to police misconduct and the violation of the defendant's rights.

No similar rationales beyond the merely instrumental apply where an otherwise valid general rule of conduct is being challenged. The refusal to strike down a law on the basis of illicit motivation does not itself constitute a further violation of anyone's individual rights. Moreover, not every judicial decision refusing to set aside a law as constitutionally invalid necessarily implicates or "taints" the judiciary in quite the same way as does a judicial decision upholding a particular conviction.[65] No such taint seems present, for example, with respect to a refusal to grant affirmative relief, whether declaratory or injunctive.

If applying an "exclusionary-like" rule to laws does not protect the rights of aggrieved individuals or the integrity of the judiciary, then all that remains is a weak deterrence justification for invalidating general legislative rules based on impermissible motive.[66] In short, exclusionary rule principles do not supply a plausible analogy for striking down otherwise constitutional rules of conduct on the basis of illicit legislative motive.

VII. Illustrating the Theory—Benignly Motivated Governmental Actions That Are Constitutionally Impermissible

It is axiomatic that an otherwise impermissible government action ordinarily cannot be saved from constitutional invalidation by the innocent, benign, or even exemplary motives or intentions that led the government to take that action. This will be so whenever the rights violated by the action in question do not depend on *why* that action was taken, apart from objective factors defining

---

[65] Compare *Korematsu v United States*, 323 US 214, 244–48 (Jackson dissenting) (arguing, in the context of dissent from a decision upholding a conviction for violation of a race-based military exclusion order, that "once a judicial opinion rationalizes . . . an [unconstitutional military] order, the Court for all time has validated the principle of racial discrimination in criminal procedure and of transplanting American citizens").

[66] The problem of further illegal searches and seizures escaping judicial review because no prosecution will be brought, or plea bargains may be struck, has no strong analogue in the context of improperly motivated enactments because non-motive-based judicial review remains available to protect individual rights should the legislature enact laws violating those rights in the future.

the action as falling within the rights-violating category. And, for nearly all rights, no such dependence exists. Suppose, for instance, that a law setting employment criteria, or an agency action discharging or declining to hire one or more public employees, explicitly discriminates against women in job opportunities but is shown to have been intended ultimately to make women better off, or to have been motivated by a sympathetic attitude toward the female sex. Despite an earlier line of cases upholding such rules,[67] it is now settled that the heightened level of judicial scrutiny applicable to such a law or other government action is not to be reduced merely because no overt misogyny is involved.[68] The same is true of benignly motivated race discrimination.[69] And the same should

---

[67] See *Bradwell v Illinois*, 83 US (16 Wall) 130, 139 (1872) (upholding a state law barring women from practicing law); *Muller v Oregon*, 208 US 412, 422–23 (1908) (upholding a state law setting maximum hours for women working in laundries); *Goesart v Cleary*, 335 US 464, 467 (1948) (upholding a statute which prohibited most women from obtaining a bartender's license).

[68] Even the Constitution's input principles are indifferent as to *why* the government in a particular case chose to discriminate, for example, against women, or against African-Americans, if it is the case that the government decided to take a step that in fact disadvantages women, or persons of African-American descent, where it would not have taken that step but for their sex or race. Put otherwise, apart from the question whether a challenged action was, in a causal sense, a negative response to some fact F to which the law forbids attaching negative consequences, it is typically immaterial what ultimately "motivated" that action. See *Washington v Davis*, 426 US 229, 240 (1976); *Village of Arlington Heights v Metropolitan Hous. Dev. Corp.*, 429 US 252, 265–66 (1977); *Personnel Administrator v Feeney*, 442 US 256, 279 (1979). See also Hearings on the Confirmation of Ruth Bader Ginsburg to the Supreme Court of the United States Before the Senate Committee on the Judiciary, 103d Cong, 1st Sess (July 21, 1993), available in LEXIS, Nexis Library, FEDNEW File (stating that "distinctions on the basis of gender should be treated most skeptically because of the history of regarding every classification that in fact limited women's opportunities as one that was cast benignly in her favor").

[69] See *City of Richmond v J.A. Croson Co.*, 488 US 469, 493 (1989) (holding that strict scrutiny applies to both "benign" racial classifications and racial classifications motivated by racial discrimination because "[a]bsent searching judicial inquiry into the justification for such race-based measures, there is simply no way of determining what classifications are in fact 'benign' or 'remedial' and what classifications are in fact motivated by illegitimate notions of racial inferiority or simple racial politics"); *Shaw v Reno*, 113 S Ct 2816, 2824 (1993) (citing *JA Croson* and stating that "[n]o inquiry into legislative purpose is necessary when the racial classification appears on the face of the statute"). Regardless of whether one approves or disapproves of these cases, it is hard to disagree that the mere invocation of a benign purpose should not lower the level of scrutiny for a facially discriminatory classification. See *Regents of Univ. of Cal. v Bakke*, 438 US 265, 361 (1978) (Brennan concurring in part and dissenting in part) (acknowledging that there is a "significant risk that racial classifications established for ostensibly benign purposes can be misused, causing effects not unlike those created by invidious classifications"). The strongest defense of race-specific, see *Metro Broadcasting v FCC*, 497 US 547, 565 (1990), or gender-specific, see *Califano v Webster*, 430 US 313, 317 (1977), affirmative action classifications is not that they are well-meaning albeit "discriminatory" but that, rightly understood, they are not "discriminatory" at all.

be true of government actions, legislative or otherwise, that are
(objectively speaking) directed against particular ideas, opinions,
or messages, or against those who hold or express those opinions—
regardless of how ideologically neutral, benign, or indeed welcom-
ing of alternative viewpoints the motives for those government actions might be.[70]

VIII. A FURTHER ILLUSTRATION—ILLICIT MOTIVATION "IN THE AIR"

Conversely, a facially neutral government action that does
not in fact burden or disadvantage a racial or religious minority, or
support or endorse a religious view, or otherwise violate anyone's

---

[70] See *Babalu Aye*, 113 S Ct 2217, 2240 (1993) (Scalia joined by Rehnquist, concurring in
part and concurring in the judgment) (observing that it would not matter "that a legislature
consists entirely of the pure-hearted, if the law it enacts in fact singles out a religious practice
for special burdens"); *Wright v Council of City of Emporia*, 407 US 451, 462 (1972) (holding
that the benign purpose of the city in establishing a separate school system was irrelevant
where the effect of the action would be to impede the process of dismantling a segregated
school system, and stating that "[t]he existence of a permissible purpose cannot sustain an
action that has an impermissible effect"). See also *City of Cincinnati v Discovery Network,
Inc.*, 113 S Ct 1505, 1516 (1993) (observing that "there is no evidence that the city has acted
with animus toward the ideas contained within respondents' publications," but concluding
that "[r]egardless of the *mens rea* of the city," it had enacted an invalid content-based regulation); *R.A.V.*, 112 S Ct 2538, 2549 (1992) (acknowledging that "the city's interests are
compelling, and that the ordinance can be said to promote them," but that the existence of
content-neutral alternatives "cast[s] considerable doubt on the government's protestations
that 'the asserted justification is in fact an accurate description of the purpose and effect of
the law' ") (citations omitted). In short, if the government's action targets an *external feature*
of a situation (e.g., the message that someone is communicating, or the belief on which
someone is thought to be acting) that is not supposed to trigger an adverse government
response, it should be irrelevant that the government's *internal motives* might have been
"pure."

Arguably, *Renton v Playtime Theaters, Inc.*, 475 US 41 (1988), might appear to suggest the
contrary. There, the Court upheld a facially content-discriminatory restriction on the location of adult theaters because the city's motivation was (purportedly) not to suppress speech
but to address the secondary effects of such theaters on the surrounding neighborhood. See
id at 48–49. At least in theory, however, although the zoning ordinance in *Renton* singled out
certain theaters based on the content of what they exhibit, the government was essentially
identifying an *external* feature of the situation (like the fact that the word on a sign said
"stop") for regulation that (supposedly) did not much affect any speaker's ability to communicate messages having that content to the speaker's audience. To be sure, the Court's
application of the "secondary effects" rationale in *Renton* was quite problematic, since the
zoning ordinance probably did create a significant access barrier between adult movie theaters and willing viewers of sexually explicit but non-obscene material. Nevertheless, the
Court's analysis does suggest that there might be a way of using content neutrally, such
that the law is actually a "time, place or manner" regulation that suppresses *no speech at all*
based on its content. For example, a library rule which required that all books about
philosophy be shelved in a certain location, although facially content-based, would generally
be unobjectionable.

constitutional rights or any constitutional principle (of the output *or* input variety), should not be rendered unconstitutional, or even suspect, just by virtue of the factors considered by, or the attitudes or intentions held by, the public officials responsible for that action—or by virtue of the misguided belief or hope of those officials that their action would turn out to have some forbidden effect.[71] An all-Catholic school board, for example, that insists on teaching trigonometry to first-grade children out of the misguided belief that the resulting exposure to triangles will incline the youngsters to accept the Holy Trinity might be foolish, but it will not have succeeded in violating the First Amendment's Religion Clauses— unless, as seems quite unlikely, the school board publicly portrays its curricular choice in such a way as to make it appear, to an objective observer, to be an endorsement of Christianity.[72]

---

[71] It should be noted that this proposition is in no way dependent on *Palmer v Thompson*, 403 US 217 (1971). In *Palmer*, the Court upheld the decision of the Jackson, Mississippi, City Council to close its public swimming pools after they had been ordered desegregated by a federal district court. The Court concluded that, since there was no proof of "state action affecting blacks differently from whites," id at 225, the city's decision could not be invalidated simply on a showing that one of the motives underlying it was "ideological opposition to racial integration." Id at 224. However, the effect of the pool closing was anything but racially neutral, for it seems clear that more whites than blacks had alternative places to swim in Jackson once the public pools were closed. Given the appropriate showing that the closings would have this racially unequal impact, the burden should have been placed on the government to show that its motive for the pool closing was racially neutral. For criticisms of *Palmer* see Brest, 1971 S Ct Rev at 116–17 (cited in note 33), and Tribe, § 16-16, at 1480–82; § 16-20, at 1504 (cited in note 35). See also *Hunter v Underwood*, 471 US 222, 232 (1985) (rejecting the application of *Palmer* and holding that equal protection violation could be established by proof that racial discrimination was a "substantial or motivating factor" in the enactment of a law with a disparate impact).

[72] Even though there ought to be *no* messages that private individuals are forbidden to utter, there *are* certain messages which the *government* should be forbidden to propagate. The most strongly rooted basis for distinguishing between private and government messages in this way appears to be the First Amendment's Religion Clauses. For example, the "endorsement" test advocated by Justice O'Connor to determine the constitutionality of a law under the Establishment Clause focuses on whether the "objective observer" would perceive of the government action as "convey[ing] a message of endorsement" of religion. See *Wallace v Jaffree*, 472 US 38, 69–70, 83 (1985) (O'Connor concurring); *Allegheny v ACLU Greater Pittsburgh Chapter*, 492 US 573, 595 (1980) (adopting Justice O'Connor's endorsement test for violations of the Establishment Clause); see also *Lee v Weisman*, 112 S Ct 2649, 2668–71 (1992) (Souter concurring) (arguing, in contrast to Justice Kennedy, that the Establishment Clause forbids not simply state coercion, but also "state laws and practices conveying a message of religious endorsement").

But the Establishment Clause may not be the only substantive constraint on what the government may say. The "endorsement" test of the Establishment Clause may have its parallel in the equal protection mandate of *Brown v Board of Education*, 347 US 483 (1954), and its prohibition against state messages of an entire group's racial inferiority or superiority. See *Brown*, 347 US at 494 (finding "separate but equal" public education facilities unconstitutional in part, at least, because the entire system sent a message of racial hierarchy); *Loving v Virginia*, 388 US 1, 10–12 (1967) (striking down statute forbidding marriages between

To this degree, Justice Scalia seems correct in criticizing those of his colleagues who have been inclined to make the ultimate intentions that led to the enactment of a rule of conduct decisive in assessing its validity.[73] Thus, what made the state action in *Babalu Aye* offensive to the First Amendment's Religion Clauses was not that the City of Hialeah *set out* to suppress religion; as Justice Scalia noted, such an effort would have been harmless had it not succeeded.[74] What made the city's action violate the First Amendment was that it *in fact* targeted, and punished, only those animal sacrifices which were religious in character. Governmental motive "in the air," as it were, should not be a justiciable matter.[75]

---

white persons and persons of other races because of its underlying message of White Supremacy); see also Charles R. Lawrence III, *If He Hollers Let Him Go: Regulating Racist Speech on Campus*, 1990 Duke L J 431, 462 (arguing that "*Brown* speaks directly to the psychic injury inflicted by racist speech in noting that the symbolic message of segregation affected 'the hearts and minds' of Negro children 'in a way unlikely ever to be undone' ") (quoting *Brown*, 347 US at 494). Moreover, even independent of its substantive nature or content (e.g., racist or religious), government speech might in some circumstances be restricted because of the danger that it will "drown out" private speech. See, e.g., Mark G. Yudof, *When Government Speaks*, 31–32 (1983) (describing "communications overload"); Steven Shiffrin, *Government Speech*, 27 UCLA L Rev 565, 607 (1980) (discussing the "drowning out" model and the need to ensure that "government speech will not unfairly dominate the intellectual marketplace"); Tribe, supra note 35, § 12-4, at 807 (observing that the government may "add its own voice to the many that it must tolerate, provided it does not drown out private communication").

[73] See *Edwards v Aguillard*, 482 US 578, 636 (1987) (Scalia dissenting) (arguing that "discerning the subjective motivation of those enacting [a] statute, is, to be honest, almost always an impossible task"); see also *Church of Lukumi Babalu Aye, Inc. v City of Hialeah*, 113 S Ct 2217, 2239–40 (1993) (Scalia, joined by Rehnquist, concurring in part and concurring in the judgment) (objecting to Justice Kennedy's inquiry into the Hialeah City Council's motives for enacting the discriminatory ordinances, and arguing that the Court should look exclusively to the text and objectively discernible effects of the ordinances).

However, Justice Scalia fails to draw what I believe is a necessary distinction between laws which lay down rules of conduct and laws which set criteria for the distribution of benefits or opportunities to individuals. See pages 22–23. Evidently, he would not permit any motive-based inquiries even in the context of legislative rules which set criteria for the distribution of benefits.

[74] See *Babalu Aye*, 113 S Ct at 2240 (Scalia, joined by Rehnquist, concurring in part and concurring in the judgment) (observing that "[h]ad the Hialeah City Council set out resolutely to suppress the practices of Santeria, but ineptly adopted ordinances that failed to do so, I do not see how those laws could be said to 'prohibi[t] the free exercise' of religion"). However, selective enforcement of such otherwise valid laws against adherents of Santeria or some other religion would violate the Free Exercise and Establishment Clauses.

[75] Compare *Palsgraf v Long Island RR*, 162 NE 99, 99 (NY 1928) (Cardozo) (stating that "negligence in the air," in the sense of risks that did not in fact materialize, is an insufficient basis for tort liability). See also *Price Waterhouse v Hopkins*, 490 US 228, 251 (1989) (observing that "[t]he plaintiff must show that the employer actually relied on her gender in making its decision," and concluding that "[t]his is not, as Price Waterhouse suggests, 'discrimination in the air'; rather, it is, as Hopkins puts it, 'discrimination brought to ground and visited upon' an employee").

There may be cases where there is a demonstrable discriminatory motivation behind a

It thus seems correct to say that a law neutrally banning a form
of conduct that is not intrinsically expressive or communicative or
religious cannot be condemned as an abridgement of free speech
or religion simply because it can be shown that the law would not
have been enacted in the first place had not some people chosen to
engage in the proscribed conduct as a form of protest or of worship.[76] Consider, for example, the local government of a lakeside
community which is willing to tolerate the noise and disruption
caused by jet-skiing—until some individuals on jet skis begin to
brandish signs bearing the slogan "Live Free or Die," or "Vote
Against the Crooked Mayor." Assume that this message represents
the last straw for this environment-loving community—and thus
becomes the "but/for" cause of the local government's decision
finally to enact an ordinance flatly banning *all* jet-skiing on the
lake. I very much doubt that individuals who wish to engage in

---

facially neutral action but no actual disparate impact on the plaintiff. For example, suppose
that in *Palmer v Thompson*, 403 US 217 (1971), rather than closing the pool to avoid having
blacks and whites swim together, Jackson decided to fire the only lifeguard (who happened
to be white) in the hope that this would make the pool less safe and discourage the public
from using it. As in *Palmer*, the white lifeguard would be able to show a racially discriminatory motive behind the government's decision to fire her. However, she would not have a
viable equal protection claim because, although the decision to fire her may have disadvantaged black members of the community, it has not disadvantaged *her* on the basis of race
or infringed on any concrete right belonging to her. Unlike the actual situation in *Palmer*,
this would be an example of discriminatory motive "in the air."

[76] See *Clark v Community for Creative Non-Violence*, 468 US 288, 289 (1984) (upholding the
National Park Service anti-camping regulations even though they were clearly enacted in
light of the fact that protestors were attempting to call attention to the plight of the homeless
by sleeping outside in a park across from the White House); see also Tribe, supra note 35,
§ 12-7, at 831 (stating that "so long as a law is not *aimed* at speech, the fact that it was
enacted *because* of speech should not suffice to subject it to the *strictest* scrutiny") (emphasis
in original).

Clark reversed the finding of a divided DC Circuit that the Park Service ban on sleeping
was invalid as a gratuitous abridgement of expression. See *Community for Creative Non-
Violence v Watt*, 703 F2d 586, 599 (DC Cir 1983) (ruling that "the Park Service cannot
mechanically apply its regulations to requests from groups seeking to exercise first amendment rights through sleeping"). Then Judges, now Justices, Ginsburg and Scalia engaged
in an interesting debate regarding the status of sleeping under the First Amendment. In her
concurrence, Judge Ginsburg extended First Amendment protection to the act of sleeping on
the basis of its facilitative, and not communicative, nature because sleeping in the park
allowed the demonstrators to continue their protest. See id at 607 (Ginsburg concurring in
the judgment). In contrast, Judge Scalia wrote a dissent in which he argued that the First
Amendment does not protect conduct that merely facilitates expression. He proposed that
if laws prohibit conduct generally and inhibit only nonspoken or nonwritten communication,
then they are subject only to minimal scrutiny unless they single out the communicative
aspects of conduct for regulation. See id at 622–23 (Scalia dissenting) (denying that "sleeping
is or can ever be speech for First Amendment purposes," but conceding that "[a] law directed
at the communicative nature of conduct must, like a law directed at speech itself, be justified
by the substantial showing of need that the First Amendment requires").

jet-skiing—for whatever reason—should be able to raise a First Amendment defense. Whatever event or perception triggered the passage of that law, one can hardly say that its existence genuinely burdens the freedom of speech, either of those whose jet skiing continues to be expressive in character or of those who engage in the now-prohibited sport just for fun.[77]

IX. A Possible Exception: When Motive "In the Air" Comes Down to Earth

The same might not seem to follow, however, when a law singles out for prohibition a category of acts that, while not inherently constituting "speech" or "worship" in the most literal and conventional sense, is *nearly always* engaged in solely as a means of conveying a message, or of engaging in a religious exercise. Obviously, such a category would not include overnight camping or jet-skiing, which are normally engaged in for non-expressive and non-religious reasons. But, in the case of those activities that are usually associated with or engaged in solely for the purpose of expressing certain messages or ideas, whether a law banning such activities in fact abridges or chills expression in any meaningful sense might be thought to turn, at least in part, on whether we can say with reasonable confidence that the law would not have been enacted but for the legislature's experience, or anticipation, of instances in which those acts would be undertaken in order to express a message that the lawmakers found unwelcome.

This could be so for at least two distinct but related reasons: First, the judgment that the specific category of conduct that the legislature chose to prohibit does in fact bear more than a haphazard and accidental relation to speech might itself seem more plausi-

---

[77] If one were to pursue the contrary theory that impermissible motive should invalidate an otherwise constitutional law, then anyone who violated that law—even an individual whose own situation did not implicate the factors making the law invalid on its face—would have a decisive constitutional defense. See generally Michael Dorf, *Facial Challenges to State and Federal Statutes*, 46 Stan L Rev 235 (1994). For example, a white person affected by a law could challenge it if it would not have been enacted but for the legislature's mistaken prediction that the law would disadvantage blacks. Likewise, on this view, the person who engages in jet-skiing purely for recreation or who spends the night in a municipal park for want of a better place to sleep should be no less able than the individual who engages in these activities as a means of expression to raise a First Amendment challenge to laws which would not have been enacted but for the fact that some individuals had been expressing themselves in these ways.

ble as an empirical matter if one is confident that the legislature chose to outlaw that particular conduct *only* because of the message(s) it was being used to convey. Second, if the public legislative history makes this causal connection evident to all ordinary observers, then the social meaning of the law in question is bound up with the public perception that the legislature did indeed undertake to abridge the freedom of speech, and a judicial refusal to reflect that reality in the course of adjudication is likely to undermine both the judiciary's efficacy as a guardian of constitutional values and the First Amendment's efficacy as an exemplar of the tolerant society.[78]

Take the famous example of Congress's statute criminalizing the deliberate destruction of draft cards. In upholding that law, the Supreme Court made the extravagant observation that it would *never* strike down a statute "on the basis of an alleged illicit legislative motive."[79] Such an unwillingness to probe motive makes obvious sense in a context like that of *Clark v Community for Creative Non-Violence*, where the conduct outlawed—overnight camping—would in the vast majority of cases be engaged in for non-communicative reasons. In a context like that of *O'Brien*, however, it may seem less clear that Congress's motive—at least in the *mens rea* sense of whether it would have enacted the challenged law but for the communicative significance of the action outlawed—can be ignored altogether in deciding whether Congress was indeed abridging the freedom of speech when it acted.

---

[78] See Lee C. Bollinger, *The Tolerant Society: Freedom of Speech and Extremist Speech in Society* 10 (1986) (arguing that the highest purpose of the Free Exercise Clause is that it enables society to cultivate the virtues of tolerance and self-restraint).

[79]*United States v O'Brien*, 391 US 367, 383 (1968). The *O'Brien* Court also reasoned that any inquiry into legislative motive is a "hazardous matter," because "what motivates one legislator to make a speech about a statute is not necessarily what motivates scores of others to enact it." Id at 383–84. See also *Edwards v Aguillard*, 482 US 578, 636–37 (1987) (Scalia dissenting) (asserting that "[t]o look for the sole purpose of even a single legislator is probably to look for something that does not exist," and stating that this problem is multiplied when one must divine how many members of a legislative majority had the "invalidating intent"). But this analysis seems misplaced, since the issue is only whether illicit considerations affected the outcome of the decision-making process; it is unnecessary to determine the consensus of the decision-making body in motivation analysis, or to decide exactly why any given legislator voted the way he or she did. Strictly speaking, it is irrelevant whether "a particular legislator . . . thought the bill would provide jobs for his district, or . . . wanted to make amends with a faction of his party he had alienated on another vote," or had any host of reasons for voting for a law. Id at 636. As in *Mitchell*, the motive inquiry in the *O'Brien* context, for example, need go no deeper than to ask whether the law would have been enacted but for the fact that draft-card burning was being used for protest. Cf Brest, 1971 S Ct Rev at 119 (cited in note 33) ("[I]t is inappropriate to ask which of several possible objectives was 'sole' or 'dominant' in the decisionmaker's mind.").

On closer inspection, though, this basis for looking at motive evaporates. For the only *reason* some of us might be tempted to pierce the veil of the purportedly neutral draft-card-burning law in *O'Brien* and inquire into Congress's motive—by looking, for example, at the circumstances of the law's enactment and the statements made on the floor of Congress—would be our sense that, although the law might *seem* on its face to be a general rule of conduct—applying to the odd soul who burns a draft card just to stay warm or to light up his campsite as well as to the more normal antiwar protestor—it is *actually* a prohibition on dissent which should be subject to the strictest First Amendment scrutiny rather than to the lesser scrutiny the Court in fact applied. Yet the sense that this is so would, in truth, be independent of *why Congress acted as it did*. It would seem better simply to say that such a law violates a First Amendment "output" principle that the government may not single out for restriction (at least not without a compelling justification) conduct that is almost always expressive of an anti-government position.[80] So long as *nearly all instances* of the conduct Congress outlaws in a particular statute are in fact instances of conduct intended and understood as expressions of a specific anti-government viewpoint (in *O'Brien*, opposition to our military role in Vietnam), the fact that one might *imagine* instances of the outlawed conduct that have no such meaning should be irrelevant to the First Amendment analysis and to the application of the output-based rule.[81]

---

[80] See also *Tinker v Des Moines Independent Community Sch. Dist.*, 393 US 503, 511 (1969) (striking down a high school prohibition on the wearing of black armbands, which were a symbol of anti-Vietnam-War protest). Although the Court referred to the school board's motivation, the ban in *Tinker*, like the draft-card-burning law in *O'Brien*, was best understood as a suppression of speech subject to a First Amendment output principle. From this perspective, no inquiry into governmental motive was necessary to invalidate the prohibition. See also Stone, 25 Wm & Mary L Rev at 222 (cited in note 19) (observing that "in practical effect, the [*O'Brien* draft card] statute had essentially the same content-differential effect as a law prohibiting any person from destroying a draft card 'as a symbolic expression of protest against government policy' ").

Although the distinction between laws which lay down general rules of conduct and laws which set criteria for the distribution of benefits might seem fairly clear in most cases, in a case like *Tinker* it might be possible to construe the restriction on conduct (there, the wearing of black armbands) as a deprivation of the benefit of education. To the extent that the ban has the effect of establishing criteria for the distribution of educational opportunities, a court might conceivably consider the motive of the government body that promulgated the rule. Compare *Pickering v Board of Educ.*, 391 US 563, 568 (1968) (holding that the decision to dismiss a public school teacher could not properly be motivated by constitutionally protected speech).

[81] It should be noted that one corollary both of this view, and of a view that would rely on forbidden legislative motive to trigger strict scrutiny, is that the laws in *O'Brien* and *Tinker* become unconstitutional *on their face*, assuming they cannot survive strict scrutiny, because virtually all instances of the activity restricted by the laws are expressive of an anti-government viewpoint. This means that the laws are unconstitutional even as applied

X. Conclusion

In sum, although it is almost never permissible for the government to punish private behavior on the basis of the disapproved *message* it communicates, and although the messages communicated by government action are only rarely decisive (or even relevant) in assessing the constitutionality of that action, the *motive* underlying—as opposed to the message expressed by—either public or private conduct quite often *is* a legitimate factor to consider in deciding how our polity should treat that conduct.

When the conduct is *private* in character, it ordinarily is appropriate as a constitutional matter for those assessing its harmfulness to society to evaluate why it occurred, at least in the sense of what underlying perceptions of fact were the "but/for" triggers of the actor's conduct. And when the conduct is *governmental* in character, the Constitution itself makes motive—again in the special sense of what factual perceptions were the "but/for" causes of the government's action—relevant to the validity of that conduct in those circumstances where the Constitution restricts the permissible *inputs* into various government decisions. The Constitution in turn imposes such input restrictions when government is allocating benefits or burdens among identified individuals or groups, but *not* when government is promulgating general rules of conduct or putting in place various practices or institutions.

The reason motive nonetheless often matters is that many of the rights of individuals and groups in our society—whether in the form of rights against the state recognized by the Constitution itself, or in the form of rights against privately inflicted injury recognized in legislation or common law—are indeed "input-based" rights whose very content is defined, at least in part, by reference to what "facts" the public or private actors who inflict that injury perceive about the situation in which they are acting and about the effects their action will have.

But even this justification for inquiring into motive stops short of a general invitation to unearth the inner belief systems that give to particular facts their motivating effect for private or public actors. It is true that, in relatively rare circumstances, one might be able to justify focusing on these belief systems in the private

---

to the unusual individual who burns a draft card to stay warm, or who wears a black armband to make a fashion statement or as a tourniquet. See supra note 77.

context as the only practical way of distinguishing isolated violations from violations that are likely to recur, and that one may thus be able to justify a differential response, on grounds of deterrence, to private acts motivated by different underlying beliefs. But few rights, if any, turn on the beliefs or values that make various perceptions *count* for the people who act on them. On the contrary, one of the presumptive rights people (and political entities) have under our constitutional system is that their values and beliefs ordinarily should not define what they are permitted to do, or shape the consequences that attach to how they choose to act.

CASS R. SUNSTEIN

STANDING INJURIES

In *Association of Data Processing Serv Org v Camp*,[1] the Supreme Court, in an opinion written by Justice William O. Douglas, revolutionized the law of standing. The Court rejected the old idea that a "legal interest" is a necessary basis for standing. Instead, it set out a new requirement: the plaintiff must show an "injury in fact."[2] The Court clearly thought that it was possible to identify "injury in fact" in an entirely law-free way. On the Court's view, judges should answer the question whether there was injury by looking at consequences, and without examining the relevant law.

The *Data Processing* Court did not make clear whether in setting out the "injury in fact" test, it was speaking of the Administrative Procedure Act[3] or the Constitution. But eventually the Court con-

---

Cass R. Sunstein is Karl N. Llewellyn Professor of Jurisprudence, University of Chicago, Law School and Department of Political Science.

AUTHOR'S NOTE: I am grateful to Thomas Brown for excellent research assistance.

[1] 397 US 150 (1970).

[2] Id at 153. The Court also suggested that the plaintiff's injury must be "arguably within the zone of interests" protected by the statutory or constitutional provision at issue, id at 156; but the Court meant this test to be quite lenient, and it is largely irrelevant for present purposes. If the discussion here is correct, however, the "zone" test holds some promise of refocusing standing law on the question of congressional instructions. The recent tightening of the "zone" test, see *Air Courier Conference of America v American Postal Workers Union*, 498 US 517 (1991), should be welcomed as an effort to return to the legal interest test, asking whether Congress has conferred a right to bring suit. I cannot discuss this issue here, though it should emerge from the discussion that there is an intriguing relationship between my reading of *Northeastern Contractors* and the possible tightening of the "zone" test.

[3] The relevant provision, which the Court purported to be interpreting, is 5 USC 702: "A person suffering legal wrong because of agency action, or adversely affected or aggrieved by agency action within the meaning of a relevant statute, is entitled to judicial review thereof." The interpretation was misconceived; the APA contains no "injury in fact" test. On the injury in fact idea and the APA, see Sunstein, *What's Standing After Lujan?* 91 Mich L Rev 163, 181–82 (1992).

cluded that an injury in fact is a constitutional prerequisite for standing under Article III of the Constitution.[4] Without injury, no one has standing. This is an extraordinarily novel development. Contrary to the Court's recent claims, the notion of injury in fact has no basis in the text or history of the Constitution.[5]

Indeed, the Court has never thoroughly explained the shift from "legal interest" to "injury in fact." But in *Data Processing*, the Court said that it wanted to make it unnecessary to investigate "the merits" in order to decide issues of standing, and it appeared to seek instead to make the standing problem turn on a law-free inquiry into the harm suffered by the plaintiff. Under this framework, whether the plaintiff had standing would not turn on the statutory or constitutional provision at issue.[6] Instead it would turn on a commonsensical, largely value-free inquiry into the question of harm. If you are harmed, you have standing; without an injury, you cannot sue.

All this seems very simple and straightforward. But how do we know whether an injury has been incurred? The question is much more vexing than it might appear. Consider the following cases.

1. Smith lives near a proposed project for developing a waterway; he thinks that the project would make the air dirtier. He believes that if the project is built, he will be injured. Is his injury an actual incidence of cancer? An increased risk of cancer? A diminished opportunity to enjoy days without sulfur dioxide in the atmosphere? A diminution in the value of his property?

2. Jones likes classical music, and she is unhappy that the Federal Communication Commission is going to award a license to a rock music station on 104.3 FM. Is her injury the actual unavailability of classical music in her area? Her diminished opportunity to hear classical music? The unavailability of classical music on 104.3 FM? Her offense at the presence of rock music on the airwaves?

3. Richardson wants the local prosecutor to initiate proceedings against the father of her child, who was born out of wedlock; she hopes that the proceedings will convince him to pay child support. But the prosecutor acts only in cases involving children born within

---

[4] See, e.g., *Simon v EKWRO*, 426 US 26 (1976); *Lujan v Defenders of Wildlife*, 112 S Ct 2130 (1992).

[5] See Sunstein, *What's Standing After Lujan?* 91 Mich L Rev 163.

[6] Subject to the qualification in note 2 supra.

wedlock. Is Richardson's injury the diminished incentive to pay child support? The actual absence of child support? The failure to have her child treated the same way as legitimate children?

4. Friends of the Planet (FOP) claim that they have suffered a procedural injury, consisting of an agency's failure to prepare an environmental impact statement before developing a waterway.[7] What sort of an injury must FOP allege in order to bring suit?[8] Must they live near the waterway? Must they show that the failure to prepare the statement will degrade their waters? What kinds of harms must they connect to any such degradation?

Questions of this kind may seem exotic, but they make all the difference. Take a recent example: People who live near Mexico think that if the North Atlantic Free Trade Agreement (NAFTA) is ratified, the air will become dirtier, and they will be injured. But what, exactly, is their injury?[9] If the injury can be characterized broadly—as, say, increased exposure to dirtier air—many people may have standing to contest NAFTA. If the injury must be characterized narrowly—as, say, cancers and respiratory diseases that would not otherwise occur—many and or perhaps all people will be deprived of access to court. They will lack the requisite injury, and they will be unable to show that any injury is due to the defendant's conduct or likely to be redressed by a decree in their favor. Few who are subject to dirtier air actually will be able to show that they will get some disease without court action.

Similar conclusions might be reached for our listeners to classical music. Such listeners will almost certainly be able to find their preferred fare elsewhere on the dial.[10] (It is unclear that their "offense" at rock music will count as a legally cognizable injury, a point that raises further complexities for the notion of a value-free inquiry into whether there has been "injury.") And as the Court

---

[7] Compare *The Fund for Animals v Espy*, 814 F Supp 142 (DDC 1993), granting standing to people interested in studying bison, in the context of a challenge to failure to complete an environmental impact statement. See also *Fund for Animals v Lujan*, 962 F 2d 1391 (9th Cir 1992), characterizing a similar injury as involving an "opportunity."

[8] See the discussion in *Lujan v Defenders of Wildlife*, 112 S Ct 2130 (1992).

[9] The issue arose in *Public Citizen v USTR*, 822 F Supp 21 (DDC 1993), in which the district court found standing without closely investigating the issues of injury and redressability. The court of appeals reversed on other grounds.

[10] Compare *Office of Communication of the Church of Christ v FCC*, 359 F2d 994 (DC Cir 1966); *Public Citizen v Friends of the Earth*, 5 F3d 549 (1993).

held,[11] it is highly speculative to suggest that prosecutorial action will necessarily lead a delinquent father to make good on past child support payments. Therefore—as the Court also held—no injury could be shown.[12]

It is astonishing but true that the Supreme Court has given very little guidance on a key issue in modern administrative law: how injuries should be characterized for purposes of standing. Its most serious and sustained confrontation with the issue came last term in *Northeastern Florida Chapter of the Associated General Contractors v Jacksonville* (hereafter *Northeastern Contractors*).[13] The result and the reasoning in the case are in conspicuous tension with other Supreme Court precedents, most of them quite recent. And the Court's distinctive approach, offered in an intriguing setting, has the potential to allow the Court to sort out much of the law in this area, and also to move standing doctrine in some generally salutary directions. This is so especially in light of the fact that, as we will see, the *Northeastern Contractors* case exposes the fundamental flaw in *Data Processing*—the view that it is possible to identify injuries without looking at law. One of the important legacies of *Northeastern Contractors* will be the understanding that in characterizing injury, it is the law that counts. In deciding whether there is standing, what matters is what the law says. There can be no law-free inquiry into the subject of injury. This will be my principal claim here.

I. The Case

A. DESCRIPTION

In Jacksonville and Duval County, Florida, there is an association of construction contractors, operating under the name of Northeastern Florida Chapter of the Associated General Contractors (hereinafter AGC). In 1991 AGC challenged Jacksonville's Minority Business Enterprise program, which requires that 10% of total city contract funds be set aside for minority business enterprises. A minority business enterprise is defined as one that is owned at least 51% by a woman or a member of a minority group.

---

[11] *Linda RS v Richard D*, 410 US 614 (1973).

[12] Id.

[13] 113 S Ct 2297 (1993).

AGC's members are mostly non-minorities under the program. They regularly bid and perform construction work for the City of Jacksonville. They complained, however, that they had been excluded from bidding on the contracts that had been set aside for minority business enterprises. They contended that many of the non-minority members of AGC would have bid on those contracts if not for the set-aside program. Invoking section 1983,[14] which provides a cause of action for people deprived of federal rights by state law, they claimed that they had been denied equal protection of the laws.

The United States Court of Appeals for the Eleventh Circuit held that AGC lacked standing.[15] The key point was that its members had not alleged that they "would have bid more successfully on any one or more of these contracts if not for the ordinance."[16] They therefore could not show injury in fact. In the court's view, it was purely speculative to say that if the program were invalidated, AGC's members would be awarded any additional contracts. The plaintiff's action thus ran afoul of a number of Supreme Court decisions holding that there must be a concrete and definable injury to the plaintiff, one that was attributable to the defendant's conduct and likely to be remedied by a decree in the plaintiff's favor.[17]

The Supreme Court reversed.[18] The centerpiece of the Court's decision consisted of a description of the injury not as a failure to receive a contract, but instead as an inability to compete. This description of the injury stemmed from the Court's understanding of the Equal Protection Clause. "When the government erects a barrier that makes it more difficult for members of one group to obtain a benefit than it is for members of another group, a member of the former group seeking to challenge the barrier need not alleged that he would have obtained the benefit but for the barrier

---

[14] 42 USC § 1983: "Every person who, under color of any statute, ordinance, regulation, custom, or usage, of any State or Territory, subjects, or causes to be subjected, any citizen of the United States or other person within the jurisdiction thereof to the deprivation of any rights, privileges, or immunities secured by the Constitution and laws, shall be liable to the party injured in an action at law, suit in equity, or other proper proceeding for redress."

[15] 896 F2d 1283 (1990).

[16] Id at 1219.

[17] For discussion of these cases, see Sunstein, *What's Standing After Lujan?* 91 Mich L Rev 163; text at notes 38–50 infra.

[18] 113 S Ct 2297 (1993).

in order to establish standing."[19] The injury in fact requirement was met by "the denial of equal treatment resulting from the imposition of the barrier."[20]

It was therefore sufficient for the plaintiffs to claim that they are ready and able to bid on contracts and that they were prevented from doing so as a result of the discriminatory policy. In so concluding, the most important precedent was the *Bakke* decision,[21] in which Allan Bakke was allowed to challenge an affirmative action program without showing that he would have been admitted without the program. And in an intriguing and seemingly offhand footnote, the Court added that because of this characterization of the injury, the redressability requirements were fully met.[22] By this the Court appeared to say that since the injury was the interference with the opportunity to compete, it was due to the defendant's conduct; and it also followed that any judicial decree in the plaintiffs' favor would remedy their injury.

The Court was aware that its decision was in some conflict with earlier outcomes, especially that in *Warth v Seldin*.[23] In the *Warth* case, the Court had denied standing to a construction association that was seeking to challenge an allegedly discriminatory zoning ordinance. In trying to come to terms with *Warth*, the Court made two points. First, the association in *Warth* did not contend that it could not *apply for* variances and permits on an equal basis; its complaint was that it could not *obtain* variances and permits. Second, there was no allegation in *Warth* that any members had actually applied for a permit or variance for a current project. Here, by contrast, actual applications were alleged.[24]

B. EVALUATION

It is not necessary to linger long over the question whether the Court's decision was correct. Section 1983 confers a cause of action on people whose federal rights have been violated by state law.

---

[19] Id at 2303.

[20] Id.

[21] See *Regents of the University of California v Bakke*, 438 US 265, 281 n 14 (1978).

[22] Id at 2303 n 5.

[23] 422 US 490 (1975).

[24] There was also a question of mootness, on which two justices dissented, id at 2305 (O'Connor, joined by Blackmun); but that question is not relevant for my purposes here.

The Equal Protection Clause is concerned to ensure an opportunity to compete on an equal basis.[25] If blacks who want to attend professional schools in Arkansas are not permitted to attend such schools in Arkansas, they have been deprived of their rights.[26] It does not matter whether any particular person can show that he would have been admitted under a nondiscriminatory policy. So too for the plaintiffs in *Northeastern Contractors*.[27] The appropriate remedy is a decree invalidating the discrimination, not a requirement of admission or award of a contract. Whether these things follow will depend on what happens when the discriminatory barrier is removed.

The Court's conclusion that standing existed because of the nature of the interest protected by the Equal Protection Clause is by itself highly notable, and it has general implications for the law of standing. The *Northeastern Contractors* case could not possibly have been resolved if the Court looked at the issue of "injury" independently of law. In order even to identify the relevant injury, the Court had to look at the law, that is, the Equal Protection Clause. So much for the attempt in *Data Processing* to ensure that courts would inquire into "injury in fact" without investigating law. In cases in which the issue is how to characterize the injury—that is, in every case—an exploration of "facts" will not be enough. Something has to be said, at least implicitly, about law as well. In the easy cases, the injury seems obviously present, but this is not because law is irrelevant. It is because there is agreement on the legal background.[28]

In any case, what sense would it make to require the plaintiffs to prove that they would actually have been awarded the relevant

---

[25] Of course this formulation does not imply a judgment about affirmative action; that question depends on what "equal protection" means, a question that is irrelevant here.

[26] The case may be different if there is absolutely no chance that the plaintiff could be admitted if he applied. But in almost all realistically imaginable cases, a prohibition on admission is enough. I do not discuss here the question whether someone must allege application for admission. Application may be discouraged by the discriminatory barrier—it would be futile—and in such a case a facial attack on the barrier would seem acceptable. This issue was not squarely presented in *Northeastern Contractors*, though the Court seemed to suggest an application would be required.

[27] This is so at least if we assume, as we must for purposes of the standing question, that their claim is correct on the merits.

[28] I cannot discuss some of the complexities underlying this claim. For general discussion, see Fletcher, *The Structure of Standing*, 98 Yale L J 221 (1988); Sunstein, *What's Standing After Lujan?* 91 Mich L Rev 163. See also text at notes 53–55 infra (discussing the ways in which any claim about consequences is in fact underlain by norms).

contracts? How would constitutional goals be served by such an odd requirement? It may be difficult or even impossible to reconstruct the facts sufficiently to assess the matter. Evaluation of what would have happened in a counterfactual world is often extremely difficult after the fact. Moreover, that assessment would seem to have no point. Because it would serve no ascertainable set of purposes, it would be a waste of judicial resources. Perhaps there would be some saving of judicial resources too, by avoiding the need to resolve disputes whose outcome may not result in an actual award of a contract to any party; but with respect to judicial resources, any gains seem likely to be small. In any event, no serious constitutional goal seems to require the plaintiff show that an actual contract would be awarded. At least this is what the Court in *Northeastern Contractors* seemed to assume. Some such assumption must be implicit in the Court's readiness to characterize the injury as involving an opportunity rather than a more discrete harm.

There is one possible line of response to this argument, suggested in the recent cases[29] though, surprisingly, not even discussed in *Northeastern Contractors*. Certainly courts ought to minimize the occasions for intervening with political processes; almost certainly this is especially so if we are dealing with a constitutional attack on state law. If the plaintiffs' interest is widely shared—and any "opportunity" is by definition likely to be widely shared—perhaps judges should refuse to interfere with the outcomes of electoral processes. And if the interest is as broad as the opportunity to compete, it is indeed going to be widely shared. On this view, the construction contractors in *Northeastern Contractors*—perhaps not incidentally, members of the white majority,[30] though this particular point need not be emphasized here—ought to have been forced to rely on the political process unless and until they could show that contracts would actually have been awarded to them. Without such a showing, all they had was a "generalized grievance," one that is best taken up before legislative bodies. Courts ought, in short, to require tangible, concrete harm, rather than injury to opportunities, as a way of minimizing the occasions for interfering

---

[29] *United States v Richardson*, 418 US 166 (1974); *Lujan v Defenders of Wildlife*, 112 S Ct 2130 (1992); *Allen v Wright*, 468 US 737 (1992).

[30] Compare J. H. Ely, *The Constitutionality of Reverse Discrimination*, 41 U Chi L Rev 723 (1974).

with political processes. It follows that the lower court in *Northeastern Contractors* was right after all.

In form, the Supreme Court has found this argument highly persuasive in other contexts.[31] In *Northeastern Contractors*, the Court should have addressed this underlying concern, especially in light of its prominence elsewhere in the law of standing. Here we find a significant gap in the Court's opinion.

The construction contractors burdened by the program were not, however, an electoral majority. While the possibility of political remedy may be relevant to an assessment of the merits of their claim,[32] it does not justify the view that the case should not be heard at all. The contractors are hardly in the same position as taxpayers or ordinary citizens; their injury, even if somewhat diffused, was not felt by all or most. In principle, the need to limit judicial interference with political processes is far too general to justify a restriction on standing when a discrete class of people has been precluded from competing with others on the basis of skin color. The dispute was hardly abstract or hypothetical. And if courts were to be made unavailable to the plaintiffs here, courts would be unavailable to a wide range of people making familiar constitutional or statutory claims. In the typical administrative law case,[33] for example, equally numerous plaintiffs are allowed to offer their claims; the same is true in many constitutional cases brought under (for example) the Equal Protection and Due Process Clauses.[34] A refusal to characterize the injury in terms of "opportunity"—if based on the numbers of people whose interests were at stake—would wreak havoc with too much established law. For all these reasons, the outcome in *Northeastern Contractors* is unexceptionable.

There is a further point. I have noted that in section 1983, Congress granted a cause of action to all those whose federal constitutional rights have been violated by state law.[35] In *Northeastern Contractors*, the plaintiffs alleged that the set-aside program violated

---

[31] *Allen v Wright*, 468 US 737 (1984); *Lujan v Defenders of Wildlife*, 112 S Ct 2130 (1992).

[32] See Ely, *The Constitutionality of Affirmative Action*, supra note 30.

[33] See, e.g., *Industrial Union v API*, 448 US 607 (1980); *NRDC v EPA*, 824 F2d 1146 (DC Cir 1987); *MVMA v State Farm*, 463 US 29 (1983).

[34] See, e.g., *Brown v Bd of Educ*, 349 US 294 (1955); *Griswold v Connecticut*, 381 US 479 (1965).

[35] See note 14 supra.

their rights under the Equal Protection Clause. The existence of a congressionally conferred cause of action should have been sufficient to establish standing. The Supreme Court neglected to emphasize this point—the creation of a cause of action for people whose federal rights have been violated—and here we have another major gap in the opinion. The Court did not refer to the particular source of federal law that conferred a right to bring suit on the plaintiffs. But if we attend to section 1983, the case seems relatively simple.

One final issue. In many cases since *Data Processing*, the Court has been faced with the implicit issue of how to characterize injuries in standing cases.[36] Often the question is whether to characterize an injury in terms that are familiar to the common law. At common law, a discrete wrongdoer typically imposes a discrete wrong on a discrete person at an easily identifiable time. This is the basic form of the common law allegation, and it can easily be transplanted to the administrative law setting, where we might ask whether the same framework is at work. In public law cases, however, it is possible that the common law understanding should be rejected, on the theory that it is poorly adapted to the goals and functions of the modern state. The alternative is to characterize an injury as involving (for example) an increased probability of harm, an injury to an opportunity, or a failure to have potential wrongdoers face the kinds of incentives that Congress (or the Constitution) seeks to impose on them. In many cases the Court has opted for the common law characterization, and thus denied standing, when the public law alternative was fully available. Strikingly, in *Northeastern Contractors* the Court seemed to think that a common law–like understanding, one that speaks in terms of discrete harms to discrete people, would make no sense; the Equal Protection Clause protects the opportunity to compete, not the award of contracts. We need not quarrel with this result in order to insist that the Court ought to have explained how this characterization of the injury fits, or fails to fit, with other cases. And it is here that the case leaves a conspicuous gap not only in logic but also for the future.

---

[36] See text at notes 38–50 infra.

II. PRECEDENTS AND PUZZLES

From what has been said thus far, it seems clear that *Northeastern Contractors* does not coexist easily with recent cases and trends in the area of standing. For this reason the case, though seemingly minor and technical, raises a host of complex and novel issues. It will be useful to begin by showing how the same analytic strategy used in *Northeastern Contractors* might have been used in a wide range of cases in which standing was denied. That strategy consists of recharacterizing the injury so as to ensure simultaneous compliance with the requirements of injury in fact and redressability.[37]

Consider, for example, *Linda RS v Richard D.*[38] It will be recalled that the case involved a complaint that the local prosecutor had failed to prosecute fathers of illegitimate children for failure to provide child support. The plaintiff claimed that the discriminatory prosecution policy was in violation of the Equal Protection Clause. The Court denied standing. On the Court's analysis, the problem for purposes of standing was that the plaintiff could not show that her injury would be redressed by a decree in her favor. Perhaps the father would simply go to prison. Structurally, this approach is the same as that of the Court of Appeals in *Northeastern Contractors*. The failure of redressability stemmed from the narrow characterization of the injury, just as the broad characterization of the injury in *Northeastern Contractors* eliminated any problem with redressability.

But it would have been equally plausible to say that the injury suffered in *Linda RS* involved not the absence of child support, but the opportunity to ensure that payments by the child's father were subject to the same incentives as everyone else similarly situated. *That* was the violation of the equality principle, and with respect to *that* violation, there was no problem with either injury or redressability—just as in *Northeastern Contractors*. Imagine, for example, if a local prosecutor initiated proceedings against white fathers

---

[37] There are really two such requirements: the injury must be due to the defendant's conduct, and the injury must be likely to be remedied by a decree in the plaintiff's favor. In most cases, these will lead to the same result. See *Allen v Wright*, 468 US 737 (1984).

[38] 410 US 614 (1973).

for child support, but not against black fathers. Suppose that in such circumstances a mother of a child whose father is black complains that the discrimination has made it impossible for her to support her child. Would there be any problem with standing? Certainly there should not be,[39] and *Northeastern Contractors* is a powerful precedent in her favor. The injury consists not of the absence of child support, but of the fact that her opportunity to receive child support is not subject to the same incentives as that of others similarly situated.

The only difference between *Linda RS* and *Northeastern Contractors* is that the former involved an action against a criminal prosecutor to enforce the law. It therefore raised the arguably distinctive considerations involved in a proceeding by a private party against the government to require it to proceed against another private party. In *Lujan v Defenders of Wildlife*,[40] the Supreme Court brought out this point, which had been largely implicit in several other cases.[41] In *Lujan*, the Court said that a case in which a plaintiff sought enforcement action was the weakest case for standing. In the Court's view, the injury in such cases is especially likely to be speculative. As we have seen, however, whether the injury is speculative cannot be decided in the abstract; *everything depends on how the injury is described*.[42] On that particular question, there is no difference between an ordinary action and one brought against the government for unlawful enforcement activity. On that particular question, it is utterly irrelevant whether the government is being asked to initiate proceedings. If the injury is characterized broadly, as it was in *Northeastern Contractors*, this difference should not make a difference. Certainly there is no Article II problem with a suit against a state or local prosecutor for unlawful discrimination.[43]

Perhaps Article II concerns should bear on standing in cases in which the federal executive is the defendant. But any such concerns should be analytically separate. They should not be folded into the inquiry whether the injury is "speculative." The merger of these two questions—both complex enough—is a recipe for confusion.

---

[39] See *Heckler v Mathews*, 465 US 728 (1986).

[40] 112 S Ct 2130 (1992).

[41] See, e.g., *Allen v Wright*, 468 US 737 (1984).

[42] See text at notes 22, 38–39 supra.

[43] See also Sunstein, *Article II Revisionism*, 92 Mich L Rev 131 (1993).

I conclude, then, that on the issue of injury, the strategy used in *Northeastern Contractors* could equally well have been used in *Linda RS*, so as to allow standing to be granted.

So much for *Linda RS*. Turn now to the key cases involving the redressability requirement, both arising under the tax code. In *Simon v Eastern Kentucky Welfare Rights Org.*,[44] the Supreme Court denied standing to indigent plaintiffs challenging a change in regulations implementing the Internal Revenue Code. The plaintiffs alleged that they had sought and been denied services at hospital emergency rooms. They contended (what was not controverted) that the new regulations decreased the incentives of hospitals to provide medical care to the indigent. According to the Court, the plaintiffs should be denied standing because they could not show that the change in policy was responsible for the particular denial of services of which they complained. In other words, they could not show injury, for they could not establish that if the previous policy had been in place, they would have received free services. For all we know, the denial of services might have taken place in any event. (Notice the structural similarity to the Court of Appeals ruling in *Northeastern Contractors*.)

But in *Eastern Kentucky Welfare Rights Org.*, the Court could have characterized the relevant injury quite differently. It could have said that the injury involved the interest in ensuring that hospitals are subject to the incentives that Congress sought to introduce through the relevant provision of the Internal Revenue Code. The plaintiffs could have complained that their "injury" involved the opportunity to receive medical services on the conditions and with the incentives for which the statute provided. Perhaps this seems odd;[45] but why would such a conception of the injury be any less appropriate than the parallel conception in *Northeastern Contractors?* The Court itself has offered no answer.

The second tax case is *Allen v Wright*.[46] In that case, parents of schoolchildren attending schools undergoing a process of desegregation complained about an IRS policy granting tax deductions to people who send their children to all-white private schools. Ac-

---

[44] 426 US 26 (1976).

[45] If it does, it is, I think, because of the persistence of common law thinking about injuries. See below.

[46] 468 US 737 (1984).

cording to the plaintiffs, the deductions were unlawful, and their existence jeopardized the desegregation process by encouraging "white flight." The Supreme Court denied standing. According to the Court, the parents could not show that their particular children would be affected in any way by a change in IRS policy.

As a factual claim, the Court's point seems quite reasonable; it is hardly clear that such a change would affect any particular child. But suppose that the plaintiffs had urged, not that any particular child would be affected in any particular way, but that each child had been injured in a legally cognizable fashion by the IRS's failure to ensure that the process of desegregation was not adversely affected by the grant of unlawful tax deductions. The plaintiffs might have described their injury as involving the opportunity to have a desegregation process unaffected by unlawful incentives for white flight. Here as well—the now-familiar punchline—the strategy used in *Northeastern Contractors* could easily have been used to authorize standing.

As a further example, consider *Lujan v Defenders of Wildlife*.[47] There the plaintiffs were people interested in the preservation of endangered species and planning to go abroad to see certain species at some unspecified future date. The plaintiffs complained about the relevant agency's failure to apply the Endangered Species Act extraterritorially, a failure that, in their view, injured their future prospects as professionals and tourists. The Supreme Court held that the plaintiffs lacked standing, since they could not show an injury. Their "abstract" interest in protecting and even in seeing members of the relevant species was not enough. If, on the other hand, the plaintiffs had acquired a plane ticket to places in which the endangered species were imminently at risk, there would indeed be a concrete harm.[48] Otherwise, no injury was at stake; any harm was speculative or merely ideological.

Suppose, however, that following the approach in *Northeastern Contractors*, the plaintiffs described their injury not as an inability to see a particular species at a particular time, but instead as a harm to their opportunity to see certain endangered species. Why

---

[47] 112 S Ct 2130 (1992).

[48] On this point see *Japanese Whaling Ass'n v ACS*, 478 US 221 (1986) (allowing standing to prospective whale watchers); *Animal Protection Inst. v Mosbacher*, 799 F Supp 173 (DDC 1992) (same, and characterizing injury as involving an opportunity).

would this description be illegitimate? Why would it be constitutionally inadequate? Is the plane ticket in *Lujan* the equivalent of formal bids in *Northeastern Contractors?* If so, why should we accept the conception of the injury entailed by these requirements?

Consider, finally, the most conventional of cases under the Administrative Procedure Act.[49] A company regulated by the EPA complains of agency noncompliance with the procedural requirements of the APA. Is there a hard standing issue if it is doubtful whether the agency would do anything different if the right procedures were followed? Surely not. The legally cognizable injury stems from the agency's failure to follow procedures that Congress has specified. It does not matter if an agency, having followed those procedures, nonetheless fails to do what the company wishes. The injury consists of the increased likelihood of harm, stemming from the failure to comply with procedural requirements.[50]

Northeastern Contractors shows, in short, that there is a large degree of manipulability in the characterization of the injury in standing cases. In nearly every case in which the Supreme Court has denied standing, it would have been possible to describe the injury in such a way as to meet all applicable requirements. It follows that *Northeastern Contractors* poses a large question of how to characterize the relevant injury. And on this question—the critical one for the future—the Supreme Court has offered no guidance.

III. A Proposal

A. POSITIVE LAW—AND THE DEMISE OF DATA PROCESSING

I suggest that when courts are deciding how to characterize injuries, the starting point is positive law. The key question—certainly the initial one—involves constitutional or congressional instructions. It follows that the question of standing is the same as the question whether the plaintiff has a cause of action.[51] The major

---

[49] 5 USC §§ 551 et seq.

[50] Compare the discussion of procedural injuries in *Lujan*, which seems to support this view: "This is not a case where plaintiffs are seeking to enforce a procedural requirement the disregard of which could impair a separate concrete interest of theirs (e.g., the procedural requirement for a hearing prior to denial of their license application, or the procedural requirement for an environmental impact statement before a federal facility is constructed next door to them)." 112 S Ct at 2130, 2142.

[51] To the same effect see Fletcher, supra note 28; Currie, *Misunderstanding Standing*, 1981 Supreme Court Review 41.

mistake in the last generation, made in Justice Douglas's opinion in *Data Processing*, was to split these questions apart. Always the issue is: Has the law entitled someone to bring suit? Courts should look to the underlying provision of law in order to identify the injury that it is designed to prevent. *Northeastern Contractors* was easy because it was clear that the constitutional provision protects the opportunity to compete on an equal basis, not merely the loss of a particular contract. *EKWRO* and *Allen* were much harder because in those settings, it is much harder to discern congressional instructions on how to characterize the injury.

This general approach suggests that it is quite hopeless to try to decide whether there is an "injury" apart from positive law. If courts must characterize injuries by looking at positive law—and where else might they look in order to do this?—it is necessary to reject the effort of the Court in *Data Processing* to abandon the "legal interest" test in favor of "injury in fact." As we have seen, the divorce of these questions was brought about explicitly and self-consciously by Justice Douglas in the (now-infamous[52]) *Data Processing* case. It is hopeless to divorce the two questions because we cannot know whether there is an injury without knowing what the law is. Before the enactment of the civil rights act in 1964, for example, a victim of racial discrimination lacked "injury"; there was no harm for courts to redress; any harm was purely ideological and no basis for a lawsuit. After enactment of the statute, the question of standing became trivially easy. Of course the injury requirement was met.[53]

To be sure, it is sometimes transparently clear that there is an injury—as, for example, when someone loses $10,000 or is put in jail. But even in such easy cases, an understanding of law does some important conceptual work. We see the loss of money or liberty as "injury" partly because our legal (not to mention social) tradition makes such matters clear. I do not deny that in some cases we can identify injuries as such without knowing much about the law. But as participants in the legal culture, even the easy cases are connected with shared understandings about the legal background; and when the cases become hard, an assessment of

---

[52] See Fletcher, supra note 28 (collecting authorities critical of *Data Processing*).

[53] See *Havens Realty Corp. v Coleman*, 455 US 363 (1982); *Trafficante v Metropolitan Life Ins. Co.*, 409 US 205 (1972).

law is indispensable to an assessment of whether, for legal purposes, there is harm.

There is a close relationship between this general point and the much broader claim that any social assessment of "consequences" is in fact mediated by social norms identifying which "consequences" matter, and helping us to decide how to characterize them.[54] People who purport to be pure consequentialists—in philosophy or law— may well be relying on a background normative theory, itself not purely consequential in character, that helps us see what counts at all, and exactly how those things that do count ought to be assessed in social decisions. Consequential approaches, in short, are rarely or perhaps never simply consequential. It is only in this way that we can understand, for example, the (probably correct) view that offense is not a legally cognizable harm under the Federal Communications Act, or for that matter under the Clean Air Act.

If injuries are a product of law, it follows that at least within broad limits (and perhaps across the board), it is for Congress to decide whether people are entitled to bring suit.[55] It also follows that the appropriate characterization of the injury should be based on an understanding of positive law. Especially intriguingly, *Northeastern Contractors* itself paves the way toward a repudiation of *Data Processing*, and explicitly so. In deciding on the relevant injury, the Court actually reasoned about the nature of the "legal interest" at stake under the Equal Protection Clause. We can therefore see *Northeastern Contractors* as at least a partial endorsement of the view that "legal interest," rather than "injury in fact," is the key issue in standing cases.

B. STATUTORY SILENCE

Positive law is a start; but it is only that. Frequently Congress does not attend with anything like particularity to the issue of standing; frequently it is not easy to make inferences from statutory text, structure, and history. Frequently the characterization of the injury will be far from simple. To be sure, the statutory structure and history might help. In *EKWRO* and *Allen*, for example, the Court might have been responding to the general idea that one

---

[54] See generally Elizabeth Anderson, *Value in Ethics and Economics* (1993).

[55] *Lujan v Defenders of Wildlife*, 112 S Ct 2130 (1992), imposes a limit on this understanding. Of course the Constitution might sometimes create causes of action and hence standing.

person ought not to be allowed to litigate the tax liability of an-other.[56] If this idea is in fact attributable to Congress' ordinary goals and understandings, both cases might be right—not because of absence of injury, but because this outcome is the best under-standing of the governing statutes. On this view, Congress did not say how the injury should be characterized, but Congress could be taken to have expressed a judgment about standing. That judgment excludes third-party actions in tax cases.

In other settings, however, there is no plausible congressional judgment with which to work. In such settings, the characteriza-tion of the injury will be a product of what we might call back-ground understandings on the part of the judiciary, rather than of anything realistically attributable to Congress. Two alternative approaches seem to be plausible candidates for judicial adoption.[57]

The first, a common law model of standing, favors narrow char-acterization of injury. This is so for two reasons: (1) any large group of citizens should presumptively be required to use the polit-ical process rather than the courts, and (2) there are special prob-lems, constitutional in origin, whenever citizens attempt to require the executive to undertake enforcement action on their behalf. The second candidate, a public law model of standing, favors broad characterization of the injury. It does so principally on the theory that broad characterization is most likely to fit with congressional goals and expectations.[58]

Of course broad-gauged models of these kinds cannot substitute for close engagement with particular statutes and facts. We cannot come up with a simple approach to unite the appropriate character-ization of injuries in cases involving consumers, radio listeners, victims of discrimination, environmentalists, purchasers of securi-ties, and many more. Any real case will require knowledge of the particular legal claim, and for these purposes abstractions provide at best broad orientation. But these alternative positions do seem

---

[56] See *EKWRO*, supra note 4, at 46 (Stewart concurring).

[57] The general standing provision is 5 USC 702, see note 3 supra, and it is of course binding. The problem is that it is uninformative on the question at hand. If it is taken to require an "injury in fact," the question remains how any alleged injury is to be character-ized. If it is to be taken to require a legal interest (as I think that it should), the question remains how to decide whether one exists. The APA provision therefore leaves a number of uncertainties.

[58] Related issues are discussed in more detail in Cass R. Sunstein, *Standing and the Pri-vatization of Public Law*, 88 Colum L Rev 1432 (1988).

to be the most important and most general candidates; ideas that draw on these positions are usually implicit in the cases. I devote the rest of this essay to a brief discussion of their merits.

1. *The common law model.* On one view, it is especially important to begin with a distinction between the objects of regulation (people subjected to governmental controls) and the beneficiaries of regulation[59] (people for whom statutes are enacted, like consumers, listeners to the radio, victims of discrimination, and so forth). Of course the objects of regulation have standing. Their common law interests are at stake, and the Due Process Clause may well protect their right to judicial review of interferences with those interests.[60] In any case, no one denies that the objects of regulation are entitled to standing. But perhaps courts should be reluctant to grant standing to beneficiaries of regulatory programs, at least when they are very numerous, and at least when they seek to require enforcement action of a certain kind or degree. We might think that the cases involving appropriate characterization of injuries, and especially those denying standing to regulatory beneficiaries, ought to be seen with these facts foremost in mind. Thus seen, the cases do not really turn on "injury"—that term is a smokescreen for the real concern—but instead on a particular understanding of the constitutional backdrop. That understanding calls for judicial caution when numerous beneficiaries ask the government to initiate enforcement proceedings.

This idea might be justified on various grounds. Perhaps numerous beneficiaries ought to be relegated to their political remedies. Perhaps an agency that (for example) fails to apply the Endangered Species Act extraterritorially, or to prepare an environmental impact statement before going forward with NAFTA, ought to be forced to defend itself before the public and in democratic arenas,

---

[59] A qualification is necessary here: The distinction between regulated objects and regulatory beneficiaries depends on some controversial assumptions. These include the decision to take the common law system as the ordinary or natural state of affairs, and to see departures from that system as regulatory impositions into an otherwise prepolitical status quo. See Sunstein, supra note 3, at 196–97. I stay with conventional usage here, but for ease of exposition, not because of acceptance of what underlies that usage. Note also that the "beneficiaries" of regulation could plausibly be (*a*) narrow interest groups of various kinds, including companies exempted from statutory requirements, or (*b*) people who are actually the "objects" of regulation, that is, people who can be imposed upon only because of what the law says. On the latter point, see Jeremy Waldron, *Homelessness and the Problem of Freedom*, 39 UCLA L Rev 295 (1991).

[60] See *Yakus v US*, 321 US 414 (1944).

rather than in court. This is a complex issue on which political deliberation ought to be strongly favored over adjudication. Of course courts should be available if there is a sharply focused injury, of the sort familiar to the common law; but if no such injury is at stake, standing should be denied.

There are, moreover, good reasons to be concerned about private conscription of public resources—a problem that is uniquely at issue in cases brought by regulatory beneficiaries. (When a company stops the government from regulating something, no such conscription is at work.) If beneficiaries are bringing suit against an agency on the ground that it has not enforced the law with sufficient intensity, perhaps there is a risk that some well-organized groups will be able to obtain enforcement resources at the expense of others. The problem is especially serious in light of the fact that an agency always has before it a wide range of possible claims to scarce enforcement resources. A suit brought by group X may make it harder for various social benefits—including law enforcement—to be granted to group Y. Environmental enforcement activity in Ohio may compromise efforts in New York; redress of discrimination in California may impair enforcement efforts in Illinois. This problem will rarely be visible to a court, which has only the particular problem before it. Considerations of this sort led the Supreme Court to conclude that agency inaction, unlike agency action, should be presumed unreviewable.[61]

Such considerations have special strength in the context of regulatory programs that must be coordinated with each other and over time. Typically an agency is charged with implementation of a variety of different statutes, and it has the large responsibility of bringing about a coherent overall scheme. Typically it must fit together provisions that were enacted at different periods and that must be implemented in a temporally rational manner. An agency is in an especially good position to decide which problems need to be addressed, and when. A court is most unlikely to have a sufficient overview to examine such issues.[62] This idea fortifies the view that courts ought to presume that Congress did not grant standing to beneficiaries alleging only an "opportunity-type" harm. At least in general, something more concrete must be claimed. It follows

---

[61] *Heckler v Chaney*, 470 US 821, 832 (1985).

[62] See the discussion of coordination in Breyer, *Closing the Vicious Circle* (1993).

that discrete harms—of the sort demanded in *EKWRO* and *Allen*—
must be shown in the typical administrative law case.

On the approach I am suggesting, ideas of this sort would not
have constitutional status. Congress could override the presumption against standing for "opportunity-type" harms by a clear statement. When it has done so, standing should be available for regulatory beneficiaries, however numerous, and however much courts
will be overseeing (for legality) enforcement action. This is one
way to understand things in the area of environmental law, where
beneficiary suits are plentiful, and where Congress has firmly endorsed them.[63] The common law model of standing would serve
only to provide the background understandings against which to
understand congressional silence. It would disallow suits by especially numerous beneficiaries unless Congress has said otherwise.
Narrow characterization of the injury would really be a proxy
for the relevant background understandings. In deciding standing
cases, we would really be talking not of "injury in fact," but of the
appropriate allocation of authority among Congress, courts, and
agencies.

This approach has the advantage of synthesizing a good deal of
current law. It helps reconcile *Northeastern Contractors* with the
cases that preceded it, most notably *Allen v Wright* and *Lujan*. It
explains why the strategy in *Northeastern Contractors*—broad characterization of the injury—would not make sense when regulatory
beneficiaries are seeking to compel enforcement action. The capacity for rationalization itself counts as a strong argument in favor of
this approach.

2. *The public law model.* A competing view would stress two
points. First, the common law model is untrue to the best understanding of Congress' goals and expectations. Second, the relevant
constitutional concerns are without force. Suits by regulatory beneficiaries produce no constitutional difficulties.

The initial point here is that regulatory statutes are rooted in
ideas quite foreign to the common law. Typically they are enacted
not to prevent discrete harms by discrete actors, but to restructure
incentives or to ensure against what we might describe as probable
or systemic harms. When Congress requires an environmental impact statement, for example, it is trying to restructure incentives

---

[63] See, e.g., 30 USC 1270; 42 USC 6305; 42 USC 7604.

by ensuring consideration of environmental effects, not to prevent identifiable harms to identifiable people. When Congress says that schools receiving federal funds may not discriminate on the basis of sex, it is creating an incentive for sex equality, rather than imposing particular results on particular schools with respect to particular students. When Congress imposes national occupational safety standards, it is trying to reduce systemic risks, not to eliminate particular incidences of cancer. When Congress requires motor vehicles to reduce levels of air pollution, it is not attempting to cure identifiable respiratory problems, but to produce air quality that produces lower aggregate risks.

This is the characteristic form of modern regulatory statutes. Risk management, rather than redress of grievances, is a conventional goal.[64] In many ways, this difference signals a fundamental departure from the more narrow right-duty relations characteristic of the common law. In the face of that departure, courts ought to be closely attuned to what Congress has done. The consequence—a public law model of standing—would be to allow standing to people complaining of opportunity-like harms, at least where Congress has not provided otherwise. Hence it should be presumed that listeners to radio, breathers of air in identifiable regions, victims of discrimination, and others should be allowed to bring suit to prevent the sorts of injuries that the regulatory scheme was designed to prevent. This understanding would be designed to ensure that agencies adhere to the will of Congress, and its conception of "injury" would track the best understanding to be attributed to the national legislature in light of its general goals and expectations.

Other considerations support this basic approach. The distinction between regulated objects and regulatory beneficiaries rests on shaky conceptual foundations.[65] The purported objects of regulation might well be counted as beneficiaries insofar as law—statutory and common—confers on them a wide range of rights that are advantageous to their interests. The so-called beneficiaries of regulation might well be regarded as objects insofar as it is

---

[64] Of course, risk management was a goal of the common law too; see Richard Posner, *Economic Analysis of Law* (4th ed 1992). But the common law judges lacked the tools to engage in the kinds of structural reform sought by modern regulatory agencies.

[65] See note 59 infra.

law—statutory and common—that allows people to intrude on interests that they would prefer to protect. As it operates in the cases, the distinction between beneficiaries and objects tends to take the common law as the normal or desirable state of affairs, and this judgment, however plausible it might be as a matter of theory, ought not to be made by courts in the face of conspicuously contrary views from Congress. This idea would be an effort to ensure that modern standing law is consistent with the post–New Deal shift in national legislation.[66]

Moreover, it is plausible to think that beneficiaries of regulatory programs are at least sometimes at a comparative disadvantage in the implementation process.[67] Often they are too poorly organized to exert continuing influence. Often they face large transactions cost barriers to exerting such influence; this is so even though "public interest" organizations can sometimes help overcome organizational problems. Often statutes enacted by Congress are defeated by a process of inadequate implementation, which can be the result of political pressure by regulated industries, pressure that is not adequately countered by those who seek vigorous implementation. Whether or not transactions cost barriers are severe, there is no reason to believe that regulated industries are at a universal or systematic disadvantage compared to regulatory beneficiaries. And if this is right, an asymmetry in the law of standing—of the sort that lies at the heart of the common law model—could be perverse from Congress' own standpoint. Such an asymmetry would immunize insufficient enforcement action from legal scrutiny, while at the same time subjecting aggressive enforcement action to judicial review.[68] This result is hardly likely to fit with Congress' goals in enacting regulatory statutes.

Nor is it entirely persuasive to say that the beneficiaries should be required to resort to political remedies. The beneficiaries will be able to win in court only if they can invoke a statute that entitles them to victory. This means that they can succeed only if they

---

[66] See Cass R. Sunstein, *Constitutionalism After the New Deal*, 101 Harv L Rev 421 (1987).

[67] See, e.g., *The Politics of Regulation* (James Q. Wilson ed, 1980); James Q. Wilson, *Bureaucracy* (1990). There is a complex set of influences here. See Kaye Schlozman and James Tierney, *Organized Interests and American Democracy* (1986).

[68] To say all this is hardly to argue that beneficiary suits are an important corrective to pathologies in the regulatory state. Those pathologies lie much deeper. See Stephen Breyer, supra note 62; Cass R. Sunstein, *After the Rights Revolution* (1990).

have—in the important sense—already won in the political process. To this extent, judicial review helps to fortify democratic processes by testing agency decisions against congressional instructions, which are the ultimate source of agency authority.

Perhaps these ideas do not apply when the Constitution is the source of the plaintiffs' claims. In such cases, perhaps courts should demonstrate the "passive virtues"[69] and allow the political process to deliberate as long as possible. It seems right to insist that courts will be cautious about allowing plaintiffs to obtain a constitutional ruling on legislative or executive action. For this reason, it is reasonable to say that courts should not readily assume that the Constitution creates private rights of action. Moreover, courts should generally require a discrete harm to a discrete interest before hearing a case based solely on the Constitution, without a statute creating a cause of action.[70] But statutory cases present a different issue. The argument for judicial refusal to hear the plaintiffs' claim is far weaker when plaintiffs are complaining not that the Constitution forbids legislative action, but that a democratically enacted statute requires a regulatory agency to take action of a particular kind. In a case of that sort, considerations of democracy point toward rather than against access to court. There is no special need to insulate administrative or bureaucratic deliberation from an attack based on a statute where an interest protected by that statute is at stake. In any event, the regulated entities are, by hypothesis, entitled to judicial relief; they need not resort to the political process. Here too it is important to avoid building an asymmetry into the law of standing.[71] None of this means that plaintiffs need not show an interest at all. But it does mean that in deciding whether a legal interest is at stake, the constitutional considerations do not counsel against granting standing to people who invoke "opportunity-type" harms.

The same considerations suggest the difficulty of invoking Arti-

---

[69] Alexander Bickel, *The Least Dangerous Branch* (1965).

[70] Compare *United States v Richardson*, 408 US 166 (1974), and *Valley Forge Christian College v Americans United for the Separation of Church and State*, 454 US 464 (1982), with *Bivins v Six Unknown Named Agents*, 418 US 166 (1974), and *Flast v Cohen*, 392 US 83 (1968).

[71] There are lurking questions here on the appropriate place of "protection by government" in the constitutional background. I cannot discuss those questions here. For relevant discussion, see Heymann, 41 Duke L J 507 (1991); Strauss, *Due Process, Inaction, and Private Wrongs*, 1989 Supreme Court Review 53. The New Deal of course bears on these issues. See Sunstein, *Constitutionalism After the New Deal*, 101 Harv L Rev 421.

cle II as a basis for denying standing to beneficiaries.[72] Article II
says that the President shall "take Care that the laws be faithfully
executed." Its basic purpose is to require executive implementation
of enacted law. To be sure, it forbids judicial execution of the
laws. But it does not forbid courts from saying that a regulatory
agency has failed to execute the laws, as it is constitutionally required to do. Of course there would be a problem if courts were
to require agencies to enforce the law as courts wished, or without
legal requirements to this effect. But nothing of this kind is at risk
in the cases at hand. Article II obliges the President to implement
the law. Suits by beneficiaries of regulatory statutes, complaining
of executive default on that fundamental obligation, do not undermine the allocation of power set up by Article II. At least this is
so if a genuine legal claim is at stake, and if recognition of a cause
of action is the best reading of legislative instructions.

*   *   *

I think that these considerations would justify several conclusions. First, *Warth* itself may well have been rightly decided. Because the plaintiffs' claim was constitutional in nature, it was probably right for the Court to require more particular allegations
before assessing that claim. In any case, there are important differences between constitutional and statutory claims for purposes of
standing. Second, *Allen* and *EKWRO* were wrong as "pure" standing cases. *Northeastern Contractors* shows that the relevant injuries
could well have been described in terms that would satisfy all
applicable requirements. The strongest argument on behalf of the
outcomes in these cases would rest on the peculiarities of judicial
assessment of the liability of one taxpayer in a case brought by
another. Perhaps Congress did not want to allow this result, and
in that event, both cases were right—not as a reading of "injury,"
but as a reading of the key issue, congressional instructions. Third,
Northeastern Contractors ought to stand for the general proposition
that when Congress has been silent, plaintiffs should be permitted
to characterize their injuries as involving increased risks or harms
to opportunities. It follows that in all of the cases with which I
began this essay, a creative plaintiff ought to be allowed to formu-

---

[72] See Sunstein, supra note 17, for a more detailed discussion.

late the relevant injury in such a way as to allow for a grant of standing.[73] It also follows that the public law model can be made to fit well with most of current law, seeing *EKWRO* and *Allen v Wright* as tax cases; emphasizing the difference between constitutional and statutory cases; and seeing *Lujan* as a narrow ruling, requiring a more definite plan on the part of the plaintiffs, rather like the equivalent of a bid in *Northeastern Contractors*.

If the public law model is to be resisted, it is because courts should adopt a clear statement principle, one that opposes standing at the behest of large numbers of regulatory beneficiaries seeking to require the executive to enforce the law. This principle would require an explicit congressional statement, on the basis of background concerns that are constitutional in nature, that seek politics first and adjudication last, and that insist on the need for presidential control over the enforcement process. I do not believe that this principle should be adopted, but it is certainly intelligible. Like its apparent adversary—the public law model of standing—this approach would have the large benefit of fitting *Northeastern Contractors* together with a set of cases with which it does not now easily coexist. In other words, both of the approaches that I have discussed here would serve to synthesize *Northeastern Contractors* with the complex body of law that preceded it.

Conclusion

Northeastern Contractors is the Court's first sustained encounter with a key issue in the new law of standing: the appropriate characterization of injuries. The Court's conclusion is unobjectionable, and there is nothing terribly wrong with the particular reasoning that underlay that conclusion. Section 1983 grants a cause of action to all those whose federal rights have been invaded by state law. The contractors in *Northeastern Contractors* complained that the set-aside program violated their constitutional rights. The Equal Protection Clause safeguards not particular outcomes, but general opportunities; and if the plaintiffs were correct on the merits, their legal rights had been violated.

The basic problem with *Northeastern Contractors* is conceptual,

---

[73] For some qualifications, see Sunstein, *Standing and the Privatization of Public Law*, supra note 58, at 1467–69.

and though it does not bear on the result in the case, that problem goes very deep. The case exposes, more clearly than any previous case, a fundamental problem in the modern law of standing—the assumption, key to *Data Processing*, that "injuries" can be identified without reference to positive law. This assumption is false. Whether there is an injury depends at least in significant part on what the law says. The Court's reasoning and result in *Northeastern Contractors* confirm the point; it would have been impossible to decide the case without reference to the meaning of the Equal Protection Clause. The case thus inaugurates a healthy return[74] to the view, vindicated by constitutional history[75] and by the Administrative Procedure Act, that the question of standing is the question whether some source of law has conferred a cause of action on the plaintiff.

Although a trend in this direction would be salutary, the Court has a large task of sorting out the relations among its previous decisions, nearly all of which ignore the issue of how to characterize injuries for purposes of standing. *Northeastern Contractors* fits poorly with the many cases in which the Court assumed or asserted a narrow characterization of the relevant injury. In all of those cases, the Court might easily have done what it did in *Northeastern Contractors*. It now remains to decide how the question of characterization is to be resolved.

I have suggested here that the answer lies in positive law; it depends on congressional (or constitutional) instructions. Recognition of this point would itself be a significant advance insofar as it would maintain fidelity with both the Administrative Procedure Act and relevant constitutional provisions. But often congressional instructions are unclear, and they must be constructed on the basis of an understanding of the legislative and constitutional background. In the modern regulatory state, statutes are typically designed to restructure incentives, to diminish risks, or to protect opportunities, rather than to guarantee particular results to particular people. If this is correct, a broad characterization of the injury is generally appropriate in administrative law cases. Hence the strategy used in *Northeastern Contractors*—recharacterization of the

---

[74] See also the discussion of the "zone" test, note 2 supra.

[75] See Sunstein, supra note 17, for details.

injury so as to ensure compliance with all standing requirements—
ought to be broadly generalizable.

An alternative view would suggest that in light of the Article II
background, and the need for judicial caution in overseeing enforcement programs, standing ought to be denied unless (*a*) Congress has expressly granted standing or (*b*) a common law–like
harm, one that can be described in discrete, individualized terms,
is at stake. This view would have the advantage of explaining both
Northeastern Contractors and a number of cases that deny standing
on apparently similar facts. And although I have urged that this
alternative is ultimately unsound, there is much to be said in its
favor, for it would also have the virtue of helping to correct the
fundamental flaw of *Data Processing*, and of reestablishing that it
is both desirable and inevitable for courts to focus on legislative
instructions, rather than to pretend to assess standing issues on the
basis of "injury in fact" alone.

JOSEPH L. HOFFMANN
AND WILLIAM J. STUNTZ

HABEAS AFTER THE REVOLUTION

The past few years have seen a series of Supreme Court decisions dramatically altering the law of federal habeas corpus.[1] Some of these decisions have significantly restricted access to habeas; others have declined to impose similar restrictions. No obvious pattern appears. The Court is fractured, and no one seems able to predict what will happen next.

Our purpose in writing this article is not to analyze or attack particular habeas decisions.[2] Rather, our goal is to suggest that the current state of confusion over habeas law involves more than the problem of how to decide particular cases or resolve particular issues. We believe that the present confusion exists primarily because the Court, along with most commentators, is not even thinking about habeas in the proper way. Both habeas law and habeas literature have failed to internalize the fact that habeas is a part of

Joseph L. Hoffmann is Professor of Law and Ira C. Batman Faculty Fellow, Indiana University at Bloomington. William J. Stuntz is Professor of Law and E. James Kelly, Jr., Research Professor, University of Virginia.

AUTHORS' NOTE: The authors wish to thank Barry Friedman, John Jeffries, Nancy King, Peter Low, and George Rutherglen for helpful comments on an earlier draft.

[1] *Teague v Lane*, 489 US 288 (1989); *Penry v Lynaugh*, 492 US 302 (1989); *Butler v McKellar*, 494 US 407 (1990); *Stringer v Black*, 112 S Ct 1130 (1992); *Keeney v Tamayo-Reyes*, 112 S Ct 1715 (1992); *Wright v West*, 112 S Ct 2482 (1992); *Herrera v Collins*, 113 S Ct 853 (1993); *Brecht v Abrahamson*, 113 S Ct 1710 (1993); *Withrow v Williams*, 113 S Ct 1745 (1993).

[2] Others have already done so. See, for example, Barry Friedman, *Habeas and Hubris*, 45 Vand L Rev 797 (1992) (analyzing and attacking *Teague v Lane*); James S. Liebman, *Apocalypse Next Time?: The Anachronistic Attack on Habeas Corpus/Direct Review Parity*, 92 Colum L Rev 1997 (1992) (analyzing opinions of Justice O'Connor and Justice Thomas, and attacking position taken by Justice Thomas, in *Wright v West*); Robert Weisberg, *A Great Writ While It Lasted*, 81 J Crim L & Criminol 9 (1990) (analyzing and attacking *Teague v Lane*).

the criminal justice system. This inattention to habeas's substantive legal context has prevented the development of a coherent intellectual framework for modern habeas law.

To put it differently, we think the current habeas confusion stems from a miscategorization. Habeas has long been viewed as a particular species of the genus of federal court remedies for violations of federal constitutional rights. Habeas issues have thus been seen as "of a kind" with issues that arise in Section 1983 litigation, the immunity of state governments and officials, *Younger v Harris* abstention, and the Eleventh Amendment. Specifically, the prevailing approach to habeas has focused the Court's attention on two competing ideologies that Professor Richard Fallon has aptly labeled "Federalism" and "Nationalism."[3] Federalists argue for greater state autonomy and less federal intervention; the Framing of the Constitution provides the historical anchor for this ideology. Nationalists, on the other hand, claim that federal interests require federal enforcement and that state courts cannot be fully relied upon to protect federal rights; the Reconstruction Era following the Civil War is the historical impetus behind the Nationalist view. Much of the law of federal courts today—whether in habeas, Section 1983, immunity doctrine, or the Eleventh Amendment— is the product of the struggle between these competing ideologies.[4]

That struggle, we believe, no longer provides a satisfactory framework for the habeas debate. A third historical event is more important to defining the proper scope of modern habeas law than either the Framing or Reconstruction: the Criminal Procedure Revolution of the 1960s and 1970s.

As far as the law of criminal procedure is concerned, the Revolution changed everything. Before the Revolution, the federal constitutional law that was relevant to state criminal cases (based primarily, though not exclusively, on the Due Process Clause of the Fourteenth Amendment) operated as a background limitation on the power of the states. Although it was federal law, and thus "supreme," the Due Process Clause left substantial room for the development and day-to-day operation of state criminal procedure

---

[3] Richard H. Fallon, Jr., *Ideologies of Federal Courts Law*, 74 Va L Rev 1141 (1988).

[4] Id at 1164–1224 (detailing influence of Federalist and Nationalist ideologies on development of several doctrinal areas within the law of federal courts).

doctrine. In other words, before the Revolution, federal constitutional law affected the handling of state criminal cases in much the same way that it affected other common kinds of state action, such as the regulation of property rights or the administration of public schools and universities.

During the 1960s and 1970s, however, the role of federal constitutional law in state criminal cases was completely transformed. Through incorporation of most of the specific criminal procedure guarantees contained in the Fourth, Fifth, and Sixth Amendments, the Court rendered state criminal procedure doctrine in such areas as search and seizure, interrogation, the right to counsel, jury selection, and double jeopardy essentially meaningless. Since the Revolution, the only criminal procedure law that matters on most issues—from the point of view of both state *and* federal courts—is *federal* criminal procedure law. Federal criminal procedure law has become in effect a detailed, national Code of Criminal Procedure that almost totally supersedes state law.

This transformation has not gone unnoticed by habeas courts and the academics who study them. But its implications have not been fully recognized. When criminal procedure issues appear in habeas cases and commentaries, they usually appear as an afterthought—as though all constitutional rights, and all constitutional litigation, are the same. But the constitutional rights of criminal defendants differ from other federal rights, both in their relationship to state law and in the ways they are enforced. And criminal litigation is not like other forms of constitutional litigation. These differences ought to matter to any sensible vision of habeas corpus.[5]

After the Revolution, it no longer makes sense to think about habeas primarily in terms of the ideological struggle between Federalism and Nationalism. The historical tension between state and

---

[5] Throughout this article, we discuss federal habeas corpus review of state criminal convictions. There is a parallel system of federal collateral review for federal criminal cases. That system, based for the most part on 28 USC § 2255, differs in some important ways from the law governing federal habeas for state prisoners. Perhaps the most important difference is in the treatment of claims previously adjudicated on direct appeal; unlike habeas courts reviewing state convictions, federal courts operating under Section 2255 generally may not reexamine previously litigated and rejected claims. See *Davis v United States*, 417 US 333, 342 (1974); James S. Liebman, *Federal Habeas Corpus Practice and Procedure*, § 36.7(e), at 569–70 (Michie Co 1988). We do not discuss this parallel system of federal collateral review for federal criminal cases, mainly because courts and commentators have focused much more heavily on federal habeas for state prisoners.

federal *law*, which still exists in most areas of federal constitutional law today, has been almost completely eliminated in the criminal procedure context. Because there is no longer a significant body of state criminal procedure law to conflict with the federal criminal procedure rights that are enforced through habeas, modern habeas issues should be resolved in light of the values and concerns that are relevant to criminal procedure, not those of federal courts law. We therefore propose a change in the terms of the habeas debate—a change that refocuses attention and energy on the task of identifying the most effective role for habeas to play within the criminal justice system.[6]

Our approach is fairly simple. We believe that habeas law should serve the basic goals of the criminal justice system: ensuring just outcomes for defendants, deterring unconstitutional behavior by government actors, and preserving needed opportunities for federal lawmaking. Yet these goals need not be addressed by a set of uni-

---

[6] On August 6, 1993, Joseph Biden introduced S. 1441, the Habeas Corpus Reform Act of 1993, in the U.S. Senate. Similar habeas reform legislation was also introduced in the U.S. House of Representatives. These reform initiatives would have made several important changes in the statute governing federal habeas corpus for state prisoners, 28 USC §§ 2241 et seq. Included among these changes would have been (1) the institution of a filing deadline for habeas petitions; (2) the codification of a general rule of non-retroactive application of new rules to habeas cases, along the lines of the Court's decision in *Teague v Lane*, 489 US 288 (1989); (3) a provision mandating de novo review on all matters of established federal law, including the application of law to facts, by habeas courts; (4) limitations on successive habeas petitions; (5) recognition of a right to habeas relief, even on a successive habeas petition, if a capital defendant could present sufficient new evidence of innocence or ineligibility for the death penalty; and (6) various provisions mandating the appointment of certifiedly qualified counsel to represent capital defendants during all state court proceedings and on certiorari to the Court.

In late 1993, these proposed habeas reforms were dropped from the packages of federal crime legislation that eventually passed the House and Senate, respectively, and were sent to a conference committee. As this article went to press, therefore, no habeas reform legislation seemed likely to emerge from Congress during 1994.

Although this article discusses primarily the Supreme Court's current view of the proper role of habeas, and explains why we think that view should change to reflect the dramatic impact of the Criminal Procedure Revolution, the article could just as easily be aimed at Congress in its consideration of the most appropriate role for habeas in the future. Whoever is making the relevant decisions about the nature and scope of habeas, we believe, should take into account the uniquely dominant role of federal criminal procedure law in the modern handling of state criminal cases. We think that Congress, like the Court, should try to identify and implement the most appropriate role for habeas within the criminal justice system, rather than engage in an outmoded debate about federalism, comity, the right to a federal forum, and the parity of state and federal courts. And it seems obvious to us that the proposed legislation, especially in its adoption of a de novo habeas standard of review, would represent a continuation of the same misguided approach to habeas that we criticize in the article.

tary, "one size fits all" habeas rules. We propose two "tracks" of habeas relief—one focused on the protection of innocents, the other focused on deterrence. On the first track, petitioners who can demonstrate a reasonable probability of innocence would receive de novo review of their federal claims, free of the restrictions currently imposed by the habeas doctrines of procedural default and retroactivity. On the second track, petitioners who cannot make a sufficient showing of innocence would have their federal claims (whether legal, factual, or mixed, and including those Fourth Amendment claims now barred in habeas under *Stone v Powell*) reviewed solely to determine if the state court acted reasonably in denying them; such deferential review is all that is needed for habeas to fulfill its deterrence role. By providing two separate roads to habeas relief, we can dispense with much of the complexity surrounding such doctrines as procedural default, the rule of *Stone v Powell*, and retroactivity. And this can be done without eliminating the ability of federal courts to make federal law where needed.

In Part I, we discuss the prevailing federal courts approach to habeas and explain why we believe that approach to be obsolete. In Part II, we develop the structure, and identify the basic values and concerns, of a habeas jurisprudence grounded in the criminal justice system. In Part III, we sketch some of the likely doctrinal implications of our proposed approach. Finally, in Part IV, we address the special context of death penalty cases, and suggest how our approach to habeas might produce a completely separate set of habeas doctrines applicable solely to capital cases.

I. Habeas and the Ideologies of Federal Courts Law

The statutory writ of federal habeas corpus for state prisoners can be categorized as one example of the general class of federal court remedies that have been created or recognized for the purpose of redressing violations of federal constitutional rights. This traditional classification of habeas has shaped the views of generations of lawyers, judges, and academics. For instance, although today a few criminal procedure casebooks include a smattering of habeas cases, for more than fifty years (dating back to well before Hart and Wechsler) habeas has appeared in law school curricula in federal courts courses, if it has appeared at all.[7] The traditional mind set has thus tended to see habeas issues as similar to other federal courts issues such as the scope of Section 1983, the availability of injunctions against state judicial proceedings, and the meaning of the Eleventh Amendment.[8]

The categorization of habeas as a member of the class of federal remedies for constitutional violations by state and local officials is not wrong; on the contrary, it is both correct and important. But it is also misleading, for habeas is part of another system as well—the criminal justice system. And the criminal justice system is quite different, substantively and procedurally, from the other settings in which federal constitutional law is enforced against state and local actors.

A. HABEAS AND THE FEDERAL COURTS DEBATE

The federal courts approach to habeas, like the federal courts approach to other federal remedies, has emerged from the tension between Federalism and Nationalism. Federalists tend to think of the Constitution as a document that preserves the balance between federal and state authority by carefully limiting federal power. In the judicial arena, Federalists view state and federal courts as equally competent and equally dedicated to the enforcement of federal rights—in other words, they believe in the "parity" of state and federal courts. For these reasons, when federal and state juris-

---

[7] For representative treatments of habeas in pre-Hart and Wechsler casebooks, see Felix Frankfurter and Wilber G. Katz, *Cases and Other Authorities on Federal Jurisdiction and Procedure* 476–95 (1931); Charles T. McCormick and James H. Chadbourn, *Cases and Materials on Federal Courts* 395–413 (1946) (McCormick and Chadbourn, *"Federal Courts"*). Treatises of the same period show habeas firmly located in the federal courts domain. See Armistead M. Dobie, *Handbook of Federal Jurisdiction and Procedure* 293–322 (1928). The Hart and Wechsler casebook, the first edition of which was published in 1953, expanded the coverage of habeas issues, see Henry M. Hart, Jr. and Herbert Wechsler, *The Federal Courts and the Federal System* 1232–1312 (1953), but it did not relocate habeas in the law school curriculum.

[8] The point is seen most clearly in older Federal Courts books, which did not have a separate unit on habeas corpus, but included the subject in a unit covering a variety of federalism issues. For example, McCormick and Chadbourn placed habeas in a unit titled "Conflicts between State and National Judicial Systems"; the unit also covered sovereign immunity, injunctions of state court proceedings, injunctions of state taxes, and the use of three-judge panels for constitutional challenges to state legislation. McCormick and Chadbourn, *Federal Courts*, at 298–413 (cited in note 7).

diction overlaps, Federalists tend to favor comity and deference to decisions made by state courts.[9]

Nationalism stresses national supremacy, federal interests, and federal enforcement of federal constitutional rights, at the expense of state sovereignty. Nationalists tend to think of the Constitution as a document built around the Fourteenth Amendment—as a charter that, first and foremost, protects individual rights against state infringement. And they believe only federal court enforcement of those rights can provide the necessary protection. From a Nationalist point of view, the federal courts are more trustworthy adjudicators of claims involving possible violations of federal rights; even the lower federal courts are generally superior to state courts in their ability to ensure the supremacy of federal constitutional law. For these reasons, Nationalists emphasize the importance of federal judicial review of federal constitutional claims, and discount the values of comity and deference to state court decisions.[10]

Of course, few cases have been decided solely on the basis of one or the other of these ideologies, and few judges consistently adopt either polar position. Rather, as Professor Fallon suggests, Federalism and Nationalism tend to serve either as rhetorical structures or as ideal models of the way the world should work.[11] Nevertheless, these two ideologies have done much to shape the law of federal courts. Disputed issues in a wide variety of areas have been analyzed and debated in terms of the values and considerations that are central to Federalism and Nationalism: comity, state sovereignty, the importance of federal enforcement of federal rights, and the relative competence and dedication of state and federal courts in enforcing those federal rights.

The pattern holds true for habeas doctrine as for other areas of federal courts law. In *Coleman v Thompson*, a recent Court decision about the scope of procedural default doctrine in habeas cases, Justice O'Connor began her majority opinion as follows:

> This is a case about federalism. It concerns the respect that federal courts owe the States and the States' procedural rules

---

[9] Fallon, 74 Va L Rev at 1151–57 (cited in note 3).

[10] Id at 1158–64.

[11] Id at 1145–50.

when reviewing the claims of state prisoners in federal habeas corpus.[12]

The opinion predictably proceeded to defer to the relevant state court decision dismissing the defendant's state habeas appeal.[13] Justice Blackmun's dissent in *Coleman* responded in kind:

> The majority proceeds as if the sovereign interests of the States and the Federal Government were co-equal. Ours, however, is a federal republic, conceived on the principle of a supreme federal power . . . . The ratification of the Fourteenth Amendment by the citizens of the several States expanded federal powers even further, with a corresponding diminution of state sovereignty . . . .[14]

Justice Blackmun went on to argue that federal courts must serve "as guardians of the people's federal rights,"[15] and so concluded that the dismissal of the defendant's state court appeal should not preclude federal court review of the merits of the defendant's federal claims.[16]

Coleman is a prime example of a common phenomenon. For the past four decades, Court opinions in habeas cases have resembled a tug-of-war between Nationalism and Federalism. In the 1950s

---

[12] *Coleman v Thompson*, 111 S Ct 2546, 2552 (1991).

[13] Id at 2561–66. In *Coleman*, there were two potential obstacles to this deference: the state court order dismissing Coleman's state habeas appeal had not specified the grounds for the dismissal, and Coleman's lawyer in *state* habeas proceedings had incompetently failed to file his appeal on time. Most of Justice O'Connor's opinion was devoted to establishing that the dismissal was apparently based on an adequate and independent state ground (the petitioner had filed his appeal one day late), and that the state court did not need so to specify in order for the default to "count" in federal habeas proceedings. Id at 2553–61. With respect to the attorney incompetence issue, Justice O'Connor fairly quickly concluded that absent a right to *any* counsel on state habeas—earlier decisions made clear there is no such right—there can be no claim of ineffective assistance of counsel in such proceedings. Id at 2566–68.

Throughout her analysis for the Court on both issues, Justice O'Connor treated habeas review of state criminal cases as something akin to a diplomatic faux pas: an affront to another sovereign, of the sort that ought to be avoided unless absolutely necessary.

[14] Id at 2570 (Blackmun dissenting).

[15] Id, quoting *Mitchum v Foster*, 407 US 225, 242 (1972).

[16] That is, Justice Blackmun concluded that absent a plain statement to the contrary, the Court should assume that the state court order rested on federal law, and hence lacked any adequate and independent state ground. Id at 2571–76. And he further argued that ineffective assistance of counsel should constitute "cause" for a procedural default even if the default occurred in state habeas proceedings. Id at 2576–78.

and 1960s, in cases like *Brown v Allen*[17] and *Fay v Noia*,[18] Nationalism prevailed; more recently, as in *Coleman*, the Federalists have won most of the battles.[19] But the relevant values—federalism, comity, the importance of enforcing federal rights in federal courts, and the relative dedication and competence of federal and state courts—have remained unchanged.

Scholars have responded accordingly. The late Paul Bator's famous article, *Finality in Criminal Law and Federal Habeas Corpus for State Prisoners*,[20] virtually defined the Federalist approach to habeas, emphasizing deference to state courts and the equal ability of state and federal judges to apply federal law. Well-known articles by Burt Neuborne[21] and Gary Peller[22] responded from a Nationalist orientation: Neuborne's article took issue with the assumption of parity among state and federal judges, while Peller emphasized habeas's place in the Nationalist tradition dating back to Reconstruction. More recently, as the Court's habeas decisions have become more Federalist, academics have tended to move in the opposite direction, as evidenced by the largely Nationalist writings of Larry Yackle,[23] Barry Friedman,[24] James Liebman,[25] and Ann Woolhandler.[26]

Some habeas commentary has not fit this pattern. Judge

---

[17] 344 US 443 (1953). *Brown* held that any federal constitutional claim could entitle a habeas petitioner to relief, notwithstanding that the constitutional claim was decided adversely to the petitioner by a state court that had jurisdiction over the case. The practical effect of *Brown* was to open up habeas to all possible constitutional claims, not merely those that might cast some shadow on the state court's jurisdiction.

[18] 372 US 391 (1963). *Fay* held that procedurally defaulted claims could be raised on federal habeas as long as the default was not "deliberate" (which, in the nature of things, it rarely is).

[19] For the leading examples, see *Stone v Powell*, 428 US 465 (1976); *Wainwright v Sykes*, 433 US 72 (1977); *Teague v Lane*, 489 US 288 (1989); *Brecht v Abrahamson*, 113 S Ct 1710 (1993).

[20] 76 Harv L Rev 441 (1963).

[21] Burt Neuborne, *The Myth of Parity*, 90 Harv L Rev 1105 (1977).

[22] Gary Peller, *In Defense of Federal Habeas Corpus Relitigation*, 16 Harv CR-CL L Rev 579 (1982).

[23] Larry W. Yackle, *Explaining Habeas Corpus*, 60 NYU L Rev 991 (1985).

[24] Barry Friedman, *A Tale of Two Habeas*, 73 Minn L Rev 247 (1988); Friedman, 45 Vand L Rev 797 (cited in note 2).

[25] James S. Liebman, *More Than "Slightly Retro:" The Supreme Court's Rout of Habeas Corpus Jurisdiction in Teague v. Lane*, 18 NYU Rev L & Soc Change 537 (1990–91); Liebman, 92 Colum L Rev 1997 (cited in note 2).

[26] Ann Woolhandler, *Demodeling Habeas*, 45 Stan L Rev 575 (1993).

Friendly's article *Is Innocence Irrelevant? Collateral Attack on Criminal Judgments*[27] focused on the relationship of habeas to the guilt-innocence determination. And many of Justice Harlan's opinions in habeas cases exhibited a special concern with how habeas could serve to deter misinterpretations of federal law by state courts.[28] These two jurists, along with some others, sought to analyze habeas as a part of criminal procedure. But their approach has been the exception. Most habeas opinions and articles have remained anchored in the Federalism-Nationalism debate.

Two particular types of habeas argument that have become increasingly popular in recent years are really disguised versions of that debate. The first is the argument from Congressional intent. Because federal habeas for state prisoners is based on a federal statute, this argument goes, the crucial question in deciding a disputed habeas issue ought to be: What does Congress think about the issue? Or, at least, what did Congress think when it last amended the statute in relevant ways?

Arguments from Congressional intent, however, face an enormous obstacle: the habeas statute simply does not speak to any of the key issues in habeas law. The statute does not define habeas's substantive scope,[29] nor does it dictate a particular rule of procedural default, harmless error, or retroactivity.[30] Consistent with

---

[27] 38 U Chi L Rev 142 (1970).

[28] See *Desist v United States*, 394 US 244, 256 (1969) (Harlan dissenting); *Mackey v United States*, 401 US 667, 675 (1971) (Harlan dissenting and concurring in the judgment).

In *Desist*, Justice Harlan expressed the view that habeas serves both to protect innocent defendants and to deter state courts from violating federal constitutional standards. 394 US at 262–63. But after a majority of the Court held that the Fourth Amendment's exclusionary rule applied in habeas cases, Harlan concluded that the protection of innocence must no longer be a principal purpose of habeas. Thus, in *Mackey*, Harlan wrote that the "primary justification" of habeas is to provide an incentive for state courts to "toe the constitutional mark." 401 US at 687.

[29] The statute provides that habeas courts "shall entertain an application for a writ of habeas corpus in behalf of a person in custody pursuant to the judgment of a State court only on the ground that he is in custody in violation of the Constitution or laws or treaties of the United States." 28 USC § 2254(a). This language suggests not that all federal claims must be considered, but that no non-federal claims may be considered. In addition, the statute directs habeas courts to decide petitions "as law and justice require." 28 USC § 2243. The combination of these provisions seems to leave substantive scope wholly undefined.

[30] Thus, the Court has dramatically changed its positions with respect to both procedural default and habeas retroactivity, even in the absence of major changes in the statutory language. Compare *Fay v Noia*, 372 US 391 (1963) (no procedural default bar to habeas relief absent "deliberate bypass"), with *Wainwright v Sykes*, 433 US 72 (1977) (procedural default bar to habeas relief unless petitioner can show "cause" and "prejudice"); compare

the statute, the habeas remedy could be—and has been—broad and fundamental, narrow and unimportant, or somewhere in between. Nor is there much evidence of what the 1867 Congress, or any of the Congresses that have amended the statute, thought about such issues. The ironic result is that arguments from Congressional intent almost invariably rest not on statutory language or legislative history, but on the parsing of Supreme Court opinions that supposedly formed the relevant backdrop to Congressional action.[31] And the Court opinions themselves focus heavily on (surprise!) comity, federalism, the importance of a federal forum for federal rights, and the relative trustworthiness of state courts—in other words, the standard litany of Federalist and Nationalist concerns.

The second argument, a cousin of the first, is the appeal to habeas history. This argument assumes that Congressional intent is unknowable; it looks instead to the broad traditions of habeas law since 1867. The hope is that, by examining habeas history, one can identify a consistent ideological perspective, at least with respect to a particular habeas issue, that can be attributed to Congress, the Court, or both. This ideological perspective can then, in turn, be used to decide the disputed case. The opinions of Justice Thomas and Justice O'Connor in *Wright v West*[32] are typical: Justice Thomas argued that the broad sweep of habeas history revealed a general Federalist pattern of deference to state court adjudications

---

Solem v Stumes, 465 US 638 (1984) (retroactive application of new rules to habeas petitions determined by balancing test of *Linkletter v Walker*, 381 US 618 (1965)), with *Teague v Lane*, 489 US 288 (1989) (new rules generally not retroactively applicable to habeas petitions). The Court has acknowledged its own "historic willingness to overturn or modify its earlier views of the scope of the writ, even where the statutory language authorizing judicial action has remained unchanged." *Sykes*, 433 US at 81.

[31] See, for example, *Keeney v Tamayo-Reyes*, 112 S Ct 1715, 1721, 1725–27 (1992) (O'Connor dissenting) ("[T]he fact that Section 2254(d)(3) uses language identical to the language we used in *Townsend* [*v Sain*, 372 US 293 (1963),] strongly suggests that Congress presumed the continued existence of *Townsend*"); *Wainwright v Sykes*, 433 US 72, 99, 106 n 7 (1977) (Brennan dissenting) ("Congress' grant of post-trial access to the federal courts was reconfirmed by its modification of 28 USC Section 2254 following our decisions in *Fay* [*v Noia*, 372 US 391 (1963),] and *Townsend v Sain*, 372 US 293 (1963)"); Liebman, 92 Colum L Rev at 2087–88 (cited in note 2) (concluding, based on analysis of both majority and dissenting Court opinions, that Congress's 1966 amendment to habeas statute "did not quite codify prior law" but instead "responded directly" to *Sanders v United States*, 373 US 1 (1963), and *Townsend v Sain*, 372 US 293 (1963), and thereby "*restored* prior law against some of the controversial changes the Court made").

[32] 112 S Ct 2482, 2484 (Thomas's plurality opinion); id at 2493 (O'Connor concurring in the judgment).

that had never been squarely rejected by the Court;[33] while Justice O'Connor argued that habeas history, at least with respect to applications of federal law to the facts of particular state criminal cases, showed a strong Nationalist preference.[34]

Habeas history arguments face a fundamental problem, too: they omit a key part of the history. For most of the habeas history to which Justices Thomas and O'Connor referred in *Wright v West*, federal criminal procedure doctrine was almost nonexistent.[35] Whether habeas review was "broad" or "restrictive" made very little practical difference, because there were so few colorable grounds for constitutional claims. Indeed, as a general matter, it can fairly be said that habeas's most persistent tradition has been its near-irrelevance—a tradition that was overturned (and dramatically so) only during the past thirty years. In light of this crucial difference between pre- and post-1960s federal criminal procedure, it seems pointless to try to draw elaborate lessons about the proper resolution of modern habeas disputes from forty- and seventy-year-old habeas cases (as the opinions in *Wright v West* purported to do[36]).

---

[33] Id at 2486–91 (Thomas's plurality opinion).

[34] Id at 2493–97 (O'Connor concurring in the judgment).

An unusually long and comprehensive example of this kind of argument appears in a recent article by Professor James Liebman attacking the apparent suggestion by Justice Thomas in *Wright v West* that a "reasonableness" standard of review might properly apply to mixed issues of law and fact on habeas. See Liebman, 92 Colum L Rev at 2041–94 (cited in note 2) (contending that, ever since 1867, habeas has been consistently defined as a virtual mirror image of the Supreme Court's appellate jurisdiction—and that a "reasonableness" habeas standard of review for mixed issues would be inconsistent with the direct-appeal analogy).

[35] This is at least true of the portion of criminal procedure law that applied to the states. For example, the Supreme Court's first involuntary confession case is in 1936, *Brown v Mississippi*, 297 US 278 (1936), and for the succeeding thirty years confessions law consisted of little more than an admonition to police not to be too brutal or offensive. So too, the Court applied search-and-seizure restrictions to the states only in 1949, *Wolf v Colorado*, 338 US 25 (1949), and for the following twelve years those restrictions consisted solely of the "shock the conscience" test. See *Rochin v California*, 342 US 165 (1952) (holding that pumping defendant's stomach to obtain evidence violated due process); *Irvine v California*, 347 US 128 (1954) (holding that repeated illegal entries into the defendant's home did not). There was no constitutional right to counsel until the 1930s, and even then it was designed to be exceptional. Compare *Powell v Alabama*, 287 US 45 (1932) (counsel required in capital cases) with *Betts v Brady*, 316 US 455 (1942) (for non-capital cases, counsel required only given some showing of special need). Plus, prior to the 1960s (and in some instances later), there were essentially no constitutional rules applicable to jury selection, discovery, self-incrimination (apart from police questioning), double jeopardy and mistrials, ineffective assistance, or burdens of persuasion.

[36] See 112 S Ct at 2487–88 (Thomas's plurality opinion), discussing *Brown v Allen*, 344 US 443 (1953); id at 2494 (O'Connor concurring in the judgment), discussing *Moore v Dempsey*, 261 US 86 (1923), and *Frank v Mangum*, 237 US 309 (1915).

Upon closer examination, the arguments from Congressional intent and from habeas history both serve merely to translate the claim, "This is what I believe about federalism, comity, federal enforcement of federal rights, and parity," into either, "This is what Congress believes about federalism, comity, federal enforcement of federal rights, and parity," or, "This is what we've all believed for a long time about federalism, comity, federal enforcement of federal rights, and parity." The difficulty with such arguments is that they are not based on the proper set of values. Federalism and Nationalism simply do not provide a satisfactory framework for the modern habeas debate.

B. THE CRIMINAL PROCEDURE REVOLUTION AND THE DISPLACEMENT
   OF STATE LAW

To see why Federalism and Nationalism should no longer frame the habeas debate, one must think about how dramatically criminal procedure has changed over the past thirty years. Before the 1960s, the states were relatively free to go about their business, making and applying state criminal procedure law (or simply acting according to the discretionary judgments and practices of state or local officials), so long as they did not run afoul of the broad limitations of the Due Process and Equal Protection Clauses. In this way, federal constitutional law operated in state criminal cases much as it does today in most other areas: it provided a vaguely defined "floor" of constitutional protection below which the states could not fall, but otherwise was not a significant presence in the day-to-day work of state officials and state judges.

When the Court incorporated most of the specific criminal procedure guarantees of the Fourth, Fifth, and Sixth Amendments into the Fourteenth Amendment's Due Process Clause, thus making those guarantees applicable to the states, it radically transformed the role of federal constitutional law in state criminal cases.[37] Through such landmark decisions as *Mapp v Ohio*[38] (extending the Fourth Amendment's exclusionary rule to the states), *Gideon v Wainwright*[39] (incorporating the Sixth Amendment's right to coun-

---

[37] The Court also, during the same period, expanded the range of rules based directly on the Due Process and Equal Protection Clauses of the Fourteenth Amendment.

[38] 367 US 643 (1961).

[39] 372 US 335 (1963).

sel), *Malloy v Hogan*[40] (incorporating the Fifth Amendment's self-incrimination privilege), and *Miranda v Arizona*[41] (requiring the states to give warnings, based on the Fifth Amendment, before interrogating suspects in custody), the Court converted federal criminal procedure law from a rarely invoked "background" limit on the states into a detailed set of rules that defined, on a day-to-day basis, the scope of state powers to investigate and prosecute crimes.

It is hard to overstate the effect of these cases. Thirty-five years ago, a police officer who wanted to search the glove compartment of a suspect's car for evidence would have looked primarily to state law for any regulation of his conduct, as would a state judge reviewing that conduct to determine the admissibility of the evidence; federal law was (for the most part) a concern only for a few extremely intrusive kinds of searches.[42] Today, by contrast, both the officer and the state judge would look to federal law, which provides a detailed set of rules governing the incidence and scope of car searches.[43] Similar examples can be found everywhere in the law of criminal procedure. Interrogation of suspects,[44] use of peremptory challenges,[45] rules governing mistrials,[46] potential conflicts of interest by defense counsel,[47] prosecutorial disclosure of

---

[40] 378 US 1 (1964).

[41] 384 US 436 (1966).

[42] Prior to 1961, only state searches and seizures that shocked the judicial conscience led to any federal sanction. *Rochin v California*, 342 US 165 (1952). *Rochin* itself was an extreme case—the government had ordered the defendant's stomach pumped in order to retrieve a pair of capsules containing morphine—and the Court made it clear that *only* extreme cases would be sufficiently "shocking." See *Irvine v California*, 347 US 128 (1954) (repeated illegal entries into defendant's home combined with eavesdropping of private conversations did not violate the *Rochin* standard).

[43] See, for example, *California v Acevedo*, 111 S Ct 1982 (1991) (car searches based on probable cause); *New York v Belton*, 453 US 454 (1981) (car searches incident to arrest of occupant); *Colorado v Bertine*, 479 US 367 (1987) (inventory searches of cars); *Michigan v Long*, 463 US 1032 (1983) (car "frisks" for weapons).

[44] See *Miranda v Arizona*, 384 US 436 (1966); *Massiah v United States*, 377 US 201 (1964). Both of these major interrogation cases have spawned many additional Court rulings. See, for example, *Edwards v Arizona*, 451 US 477 (1981) (invocation of *Miranda* "right to counsel" precludes further interrogation); *Maine v Moulton*, 474 US 159 (1985) (*Massiah* prohibits use of statements made by defendant charged with one crime to undercover police agents conducting investigation of other crimes).

[45] See *Batson v Kentucky*, 476 US 79 (1986), and its progeny.

[46] See *Illinois v Somerville*, 410 US 458 (1973); *United States v Jorn*, 400 US 470 (1971); *Downum v United States*, 372 US 734 (1963).

[47] See *Cuyler v Sullivan*, 446 US 335 (1980); *Burger v Kemp*, 483 US 776 (1987).

exculpatory evidence[48]—all these matters, and many more, were once governed entirely (or almost entirely) by state and local law; all now are governed, with rare exceptions, entirely by federal law.

In short, wherever federal criminal procedure law exists today, that law dominates the landscape. Federal constitutional criminal procedure law no longer serves as a vaguely defined "floor," above which the states are free to develop and administer their criminal justice systems with relative independence. Rather, federal law today serves as a floor and a ceiling and everything in between: federal law dictates, often in minute detail, the course of state criminal proceedings.

One might say that, in the criminal procedure context, the Nationalist view of federal-state relations triumphed, and the Federalists were routed. Today no one, not even the most ardent states' rights advocate, seriously contests the preeminence of federal constitutional law in determining how state criminal investigations and trials should proceed. Of course, this acquiescence was not immediate; in the 1960s, the Court was harshly criticized for usurping powers that had previously belonged to the states. But the efforts to undo the Warren Court's work—to overrule cases like *Mapp*, *Malloy*, and *Miranda* (and even to impeach Earl Warren)—failed. Justice Harlan's suggestion that incorporated rights might have a different, less intrusive meaning in state cases than in federal cases (a suggestion that might have allowed federal criminal procedure law to continue to play a "background" role similar to that of federal constitutional law in other settings) was given short shrift.[49] By the mid-1970s, Court opinions no longer mentioned the possibility that federal constitutional law might not constitute *the* law of criminal procedure, or that it might not mean the same thing in state and federal cases.

This enormous shift in perspective on the role of federal criminal

---

[48] See *Brady v Maryland*, 373 US 83 (1963), and its progeny.

[49] See *Williams v Florida*, 399 US 78, 117 (1970) (Harlan concurring in the result and dissenting in *Baldwin v New York*, 399 US 66 (1970)) (arguing that Sixth Amendment right to jury trial could be interpreted differently in state and federal cases).

By 1972, only one member of the Court, Justice Powell, was willing to adhere to Justice Harlan's view in *Williams*. See *Apodaca v Oregon*, 406 US 404 (1972); *Johnson v Louisiana*, 406 US 356 (1972). The last opinions explicitly opposing "jot for jot" incorporation of federal constitutional rights in state cases were those of Justice Powell, joined by Chief Justice Burger and Justice Rehnquist, in *Crist v Bretz*, 437 US 28 (1978), and *Ballew v Georgia*, 435 US 223 (1978).

procedure law in state criminal cases occurred so gradually that we have tended to overlook its implications for the law of federal remedies. Among the foundational premises for the law of federal courts, and for habeas law in particular, is the assumption that federal law is in some sense foreign to state courts—that it exerts its presence only rarely, and that it operates by trumping an existing body of state law that otherwise governs the relevant state action. This premise no longer holds true in criminal cases: there is no clear, institutional line of demarcation between federal and state law in criminal procedure. In those areas covered by federal constitutional criminal procedure, there are not two sources of relevant law that must be interpreted and applied by state courts in criminal cases, but only one body of law that applies to such cases: the law of the Fourth, Fifth, and Sixth Amendments, as defined by the Supreme Court, and as refined and applied by state and lower federal courts alike.

Indeed, in an important sense, the law of the Fourth, Fifth, and Sixth Amendments—our detailed, national Code of Criminal Procedure—today "belongs" to state courts as much as it does to their federal counterparts. Whether or not they agree with it, state judges no longer experience this body of federal law as alien or foreign. Instead, state courts deal with federal criminal procedure law the same way federal courts do—as the sole source of detailed rules that govern their criminal dockets.

This is not to say, of course, that state and federal courts always see eye-to-eye concerning the proper interpretation of the relevant constitutional provisions. Nor is it to say that state judges are necessarily as competent or conscientious as federal judges, or that the tasks of defining and applying these criminal procedure rules should be left to state courts without federal court supervision and review. Our point is only that, in the regular, day-to-day business of applying law to the facts of cases, federal criminal procedure law is virtually unique in the realm of federal constitutional law: it genuinely occupies the field, and thus is of immediate and primary, rather than remote and secondary, concern to state courts handling criminal cases.

C. FEDERALISM, NATIONALISM, AND HABEAS: THREE PROBLEMS

We are now in a position to see what is wrong with the current habeas debate. There are three main problems. The first has to do with the role federal constitutional law plays in criminal procedure. The Federalism-Nationalism debate presupposes disputes between federal and state *law*. Such disputes are, today, all but absent from criminal procedure; federal law is the only game in town. The second problem is that Federalists and Nationalists alike tend to ignore the special role of innocence and guilt in criminal justice. The third problem concerns the deterrent function of many criminal procedure rights. All constitutional rights serve a deterrent function, but that function substantially differs, and is implemented differently, in criminal procedure. We take up each of these problems in turn.

1. *Federal law and the need for a federal forum.* Both sides in the traditional habeas debate tend to view federal constitutional law as a means of policing the day-to-day administration of state law. Nationalists argue that criminal defendants have a powerful interest in adjudicating their federal rights in a federal forum: that forum is one in which federal law is natural, whereas in state court, state law is natural and federal law is foreign. Federalists, in rebuttal, raise the argument of parity: litigants' federal interests will be protected because state judges are just as good at applying federal law as are federal judges.

As far as criminal procedure is concerned, however, federal constitutional law is no more foreign or less natural in state court than in federal court. The Fourth, Fifth, and Sixth Amendments completely dominate the field in both; state actors, including state courts, look almost exclusively to these federal sources of criminal procedure law to govern the day-to-day administration of state criminal cases.[50]

Even the exceptions to this federal law occupation of the criminal procedure field are, in a sense, not exceptions at all. Some states have their own constitutional rules that go beyond federal law on some issues; in these states, state law still plays an important, though peripheral, role.[51] But these rules are "state law" only in

---

[50] This makes the traditional federal courts notion of entitlement to a federal forum lead, in one sense, to a reductio ad absurdum: if the day-to-day administration of state criminal cases is largely governed by federal constitutional law, and if litigants raising federal claims have a right to an adjudication of those federal claims in a federal forum, then (as a matter of simple efficiency) shouldn't all state criminal prosecutions be conducted in the first instance in a federal court? Or at least be removable to federal court?

[51] See *Symposium on State Constitutional Jurisprudence*, 15 Hastings Const L Q 391 (1988); William J. Brennan, *State Constitutions and the Protection of Individual Rights*, 90 Harv L Rev 489 (1977).

an odd sense. State courts that adopt criminal procedure rules more protective than the relevant federal constitutional doctrines commonly cite not state cases but Supreme Court dissents.[52] That is, state law criminal procedure decisions tend either to adopt federal constitutional rules mechanically (making the state law meaningless) or to adopt a minority position from the relevant Court cases. Either way, it is federal law that frames the debate and federal decision makers who craft the relevant rules.

Moreover, whenever state constitutional law provides more protection for a defendant than would the analogous federal constitutional provision, there is no genuine conflict between state and federal law. The relevant federal law—at least as applied to state actors in state criminal cases[53]—does not "trump" state law, because the criminal defendant simply gets the benefit of the more protective state rule. Thus, such situations provide no support at all for the traditional approach to habeas, which assumes the existence of a true conflict between state and federal law.

What has changed since the Revolution is that, for the most part, state courts no longer look primarily to state law for the rules

---

[52] See, for example, *Commonwealth v Upton*, 476 NE2d 548 (Mass 1985) (on remand from Supreme Court), adopting, under state constitution, view of dissenting opinion in *Illinois v Gates*, 462 US 213 (1983); *State v Opperman*, 247 NW2d 673 (SD 1976) (on remand from Supreme Court), adopting, under state constitution, view of Supreme Court dissenting opinion in *South Dakota v Opperman*, 428 US 364 (1976).

Justice Brennan, one of the most outspoken advocates of the use of state constitutions to protect the rights of criminal defendants, has also been relatively forthright in his call for state courts to base their state constitutional decisions on Supreme Court dissenting opinions (many of those opinions, of course, written by him). For example, in a recent article, he applauded the fact that "the state courts have responded with marvelous enthusiasm to many not-so-subtle invitations to fill the constitutional gaps left by decisions of the Supreme Court majority." William J. Brennan, *The Bill of Rights and the States: The Revival of State Constitutions as Guardians of Individual Rights*, 61 NYU L Rev 535, 549 (1986).

[53] There may be a problem with applying such state constitutional protections against federal actors, such as FBI or DEA agents, who routinely engage in criminal investigations jointly with state and local law enforcement officers. For example, if federal agents conduct a search that violates a state constitutional provision, but conforms with prevailing federal law (e.g., relevant Supreme Court Fourth Amendment decisions, or a federal statute authorizing the particular kind of search at issue), it is not clear whether the federal agent is bound by the state provision when acting in furtherance of federal law enforcement interests. This problem is a variation on the old "silver platter" problem that existed before the states were held subject to the exclusionary rule in *Mapp v Ohio*, 367 US 643 (1961). See *Elkins v United States*, 364 US 206 (1960).

that govern the day-to-day administration of criminal cases.[54] This means that even state supreme courts are, for the most part, no longer in the business of defining their own state criminal procedure rules. They act, in criminal cases, not as common law courts with plenary law-making authority, but as subordinate entities articulating and applying federal law within the confines of a large, multilayered, combined federal-state criminal justice system. As far as criminal procedure is concerned, state supreme courts operate as lower courts applying a common Nationalist code.

Today, federal criminal procedure law is as routine a part of state criminal litigation as it is of federal litigation. For purposes of applying the Fourth, Fifth, and Sixth Amendments, state courts, like lower federal courts sitting in habeas, are in the business of trying to follow (or distinguish) the relevant Supreme Court decisions.

Even more significant than this total federal occupation of the field of criminal procedure law is the fact that state courts—and everyone else, for that matter—have come to accept the dominance of federal law. There are several likely explanations. First, the idea of a national Code of Criminal Procedure seems to have worked out pretty well in practice. Second, the Burger and Rehnquist Courts have largely eliminated the perception, widespread during the Warren Court era, that the federal law was much too pro-defendant (or, at least, that the federal law was uniformly more pro-defendant than the state law it supplanted). Finally, we've simply gotten used to the idea of Nationalism in criminal procedure law—so much so that almost no one even thinks seriously, today, about the alternative.

In short, the criminal procedure arena has changed completely since the Revolution. Then, the battle involved competing sets of laws—state and federal. In the midst of that battle, habeas served as the Supreme Court's most powerful weapon, allowing it ultimately to prevail in reshaping the criminal justice systems of the states. During that difficult and painful period of transition, when federal law was seen by most state courts as a foreign invader

---

[54] The obvious exception is substantive criminal law, or the law of crimes and punishments, which is still mostly a matter of state law. But this exception is far less important than it may seem: a glance through any set of state appellate reports reveals that most disputed legal issues in criminal litigation, outside the special context of capital cases, have to do with criminal procedure and not substantive criminal law.

displacing entrenched state law, it made sense to think about habeas issues in terms of the Federalism-Nationalism debate.

Today, there is no debate over whether most criminal procedure
law should be state or federal. Instead, the debate is all about the
content of the federal law. State courts may still resist federal crim-
ial procedure law—but whenever they do, it is not because the
law is federal, but because they think the law is too pro-defendant.
Today's criminal procedure debate, in other words, is the same
debate that is inherent in any system of criminal justice, whether
or not that system is unitary.

It is pointless to worry about the traditional federal courts values
in such a setting. If the relevant governing law is totally federal,
and everyone accepts it as such, why should anyone defer to a
decision of a state court *qua* state court? And if federal law is as
natural to state courts as to their federal counterparts, why should
anyone have a right to a decision by a federal court *qua* federal
court? In criminal procedure law, the concept of institutional allegiance—the foundation for the traditional federal courts approach—is a relic.

This view of the institutional relationship between state courts
and federal criminal procedure law is quite separate from the question whether all, or most, state courts make decisions on criminal
procedure issues that are just as good as those made by their federal
counterparts. (For what it's worth, we think that they often do
not.) It does, however, bear on the parity debate. In the criminal
procedure context, the relevant question is not whether all, or
most, state judges are as good as federal judges at applying federal
law—it is pointless to ask that question, since no matter what the
answer, applying federal law will continue to be the bulk of their
job in state criminal cases. The important question is, instead,
whether habeas review of state court decision making on issues of
federal law, under certain kinds of habeas rules and procedures,
will significantly increase the protection of the values that federal
criminal procedure law is designed to protect.

The relevant question, in other words, involves the proper role
of habeas within the overall system by which federal criminal procedure rights are enforced in state criminal cases. In the criminal
procedure context, we should stop thinking about state courts and
habeas courts as if they belonged to two separate legal systems.
There is only one criminal justice system, enforcing one set of

criminal procedure rights, and that system includes both state and federal courts.[55]

2. *Drawing distinctions among rights—the primacy of innocence.* The most important concern of the criminal justice system is the protection of innocent defendants. Innocent defendants who are imprisoned suffer a horrible injustice that cries out for correction. All constitutional violations are important, but nowhere is the remedial role of habeas so important as in the case of an innocent person.[56]

There is little dispute about this point. Yet the conventional approach to habeas does not easily accommodate such a consideration. Within federal courts law, the content of the particular federal right to be enforced is mostly beside the point. All federal rights are supreme, and so warrant federal enforcement to the same extent—though the extent will vary depending on one's own views about federalism, comity, and parity. Thus, under the prevailing approach, the innocence of a habeas petitioner usually is "irrelevant," because it is unrelated to the primary questions of federal courts law: Should access to a federal forum be provided in order to vindicate federal rights, or can state courts be trusted to enforce those rights?

Of course, it is hardly novel to suggest that innocence ought to matter in habeas, or that some rights should be treated differently from others. Judge Friendly long ago suggested as much,[57] and *Stone v Powell*[58] (which essentially barred relitigation of Fourth Amendment claims on habeas) implemented his idea by differentiating one particular kind of non-innocence-related right from other rights. Since *Stone*, some individual Justices have espoused, in one form or another, the idea that distinctions should be drawn between different constitutional claims based on whether they go to

---

[55] This same basic observation led another commentator, over ten years ago, to propose replacing the present system of federal habeas review of state criminal cases with federal appellate review (either in the present federal courts of appeal or in a new U.S. Court of Appeals for the State Circuit). See Daniel J. Meador, *Straightening Out Federal Review of State Criminal Cases*, 44 Ohio State L J 273 (1983).

[56] This proposition is arguably anchored in the habeas statute. The statute directs courts to dispose of petitions "as law and justice require." 28 USC § 2243. To the extent that the injustice of punishing innocents is especially acute, this language would seem to require that innocence receive some weight in habeas doctrine.

[57] Henry J. Friendly, *Is Innocence Irrelevant? Collateral Attack on Criminal Judgments*, 38 U Chi L Rev 142 (1970).

[58] 428 US 465 (1976).

the basic justice of the defendant's conviction.[59] Yet most habeas opinions—written by "conservatives" and "liberals" alike—have minimized the significance of innocence in habeas law. *Stone* itself is now an orphan; this past Term, the Court once again refused to extend it beyond Fourth Amendment claims.[60] The law of procedural default has been framed without regard to the nature of the defendant's claim, the sole exception being the "fundamental miscarriage of justice" exception, an exception drawn so narrowly it seems never to apply.[61] So too with retroactivity,[62] exhaustion,[63] and abuse of the writ.[64] In all these areas the judicial debate is between those who argue for comity and federalism (and believe that state judges are the equal of their federal counterparts), and those who attach great weight to vindicating federal rights in a federal forum (and believe that state judges are not to be trusted). The accuracy of particular guilty verdicts seems little more than a detail.

This pattern of treating all constitutional rights alike might make sense in other enforcement settings, because elsewhere in constitu-

---

[59] Justices Powell, O'Connor, and Stevens have expressed this view. See *Kuhlmann v Wilson*, 477 US 436, 448 & n 8 (1986) (Powell for a plurality); *Withrow v Williams*, 113 S Ct 1745, 1758 (1993) (O'Connor concurring in part and dissenting in part); *Rose v Lundy*, 455 US 509, 543 (1982) (Stevens dissenting); *Brecht v Abrahamson*, 113 S Ct 1710, 1723 (1993) (Stevens concurring). See also *Reed v Farley*, 62 USLW 3356 (US S Ct No 93-5418, argued Mar 28, 1994) (involving whether *Stone v Powell* should extend to violations of Interstate Agreement on Detainers).

[60] *Withrow v Williams*, 113 S Ct 1745 (1993). But see *Reed v Farley* (cited in note 59).

[61] See note 84.

[62] Under *Teague v Lane*, 489 US 288 (1989), "new rules" may be declared or applied on habeas only if they fit one of two exceptions: (1) new rules placing certain conduct beyond the power of the criminal law to proscribe, such as the flag-burning case, *Texas v Johnson*, 491 US 397 (1989); or (2) "watershed" new rules of criminal procedure "without which the likelihood of an accurate conviction is seriously diminished." See *Teague*, 489 US at 313. This second exception, although related to "innocence," is defined categorically; the Court has not yet recognized a case-specific "innocence" exception to *Teague*'s general non-retroactivity principle, although such an exception has been suggested by at least a few commentators. See, e.g., Ellen Boshkoff, *Resolving Retroactivity after Teague v. Lane*, 65 Ind L J 651 (1990); Joseph L. Hoffmann, *Retroactivity and the Great Writ: How Congress Should Respond to Teague v. Lane*, 1990 BYU L Rev 183, 208 n 111.

[63] The test for whether a petitioner must go back to state court has no "innocence" component; rather, the law looks to whether the claim has been properly raised in state court. See *Rose v Lundy*, 455 US 509 (1982).

[64] "Abuse of the writ" doctrine covers cases in which a defendant raises a claim on a second federal habeas petition that might have been raised in his first petition. The law in such cases is essentially the same as in procedural default doctrine: the defendant must show "cause" for failing to raise the claim earlier, and "prejudice" from the failure. See *McCleskey v Zant*, 111 S Ct 1454 (1991). The only sense in which this test has anything to do with "innocence" is that, like the test for procedural default in state court, it includes a "fundamental miscarriage of justice" exception.

tional litigation the remedy awarded often reflects differences in the value of the constitutional claim. In a Section 1983 damages action, the degree of the plaintiff's injury determines the amount of damages; in actions for injunctive relief, the scope of the injunction is designed to remedy (or prevent) the relevant wrong. Different liability rules for different constitutional claims are unnecessary, because differences in plaintiffs' injuries are already taken into account at the remedy stage. And differences in levels of damages or breadth of injunctive relief (not to mention levels of attorneys' fees) may also correspond, albeit only roughly, to differences in the social value of the claims. Constitutional claims that generate million-dollar damage awards usually have greater value to society—meaning that it is worth more to society to have the claims brought, the victims compensated, and the violators punished—than constitutional claims that generate thousand-dollar awards. The penalty for the violation is thus likely to be at least roughly proportionate to the wrong done by the violator. (And where that is not so, punitive damages and attorneys' fees are available to correct the imbalance.) Remedies are the device for separating constitutional violations that are more harmful, or more socially important, from violations that are less so. This sorting process is far from perfect,[65] but it probably functions well enough that Friendly-style lines are unnecessary in most settings.

Habeas is different. The remedy for all successful habeas petitioners (except those challenging only their sentences—a group of petitioners who are almost never successful, outside of capital cases) is the same, regardless of the constitutional violation. Petitioners with winning claims have their convictions vacated (usually with the allowance of another trial, although if evidence has gone stale or the case is not important enough to the prosecutor, habeas relief may mean release). There is no grading of relief. The petitioner who may well be innocent is treated no differently from the petitioner who is very likely guilty. This means that if claims are not separated at the liability stage—that is, when the habeas court

---

[65] Professor Jeffries has pointed out that there are some important categories of Section 1983 litigation where the harm caused by the constitutional violation is not a good proxy for social interest in seeing the violation punished. John C. Jeffries, Jr., *Damages for Constitutional Violations: The Relation of Risk to Injury in Constitutional Torts*, 75 Va L Rev 1461, 1470–84 (1989). Our point is only that those categories are the exception rather than the rule; ordinarily, damages can be expected to track social injury fairly well.

determines whether to grant *any* relief—they will not be separated at all.[66] To put it differently, elsewhere in constitutional litigation the kind and severity of the victim's harm is reflected in the choice (money, declaratory or injunctive relief) and extent of the remedy. In habeas that is impossible. Guilt and innocence must either be taken into account when deciding whether to grant relief, or ignored altogether. And if guilt and innocence really are central to criminal justice, that centrality ought to be reflected in habeas law.

Prior to the constitutionalization of the day-to-day rules of criminal procedure, this was a minor problem. Before 1961, few federal constitutional claims were available to state criminal defendants; the only realistic avenue for habeas relief was a due process claim. But due process claims were granted only in extreme cases of fundamental injustice, meaning that most successful claims probably involved a likely-to-be-erroneous verdict.[67] In other words, refusing to treat innocence-related claims differently on habeas at the time of *Brown v Allen*[68] may have made sense, because successful habeas claims so often were innocence-related. The creation of detailed rules governing police and prosecutorial behavior ensures that this is no longer so. Today, constructing the law of habeas without reference to innocence and guilt means ignoring the central point of the criminal justice system.

3. *Deterrence and criminal procedure.* A major concern with any remedy for constitutional violations is its ability to deter future

---

[66] Harmless error rules of the sort at issue in *Brecht v Abrahamson*, 113 S Ct 1710 (1993), do not alter the point. Harmless error review ensures that the defendant's claim is plausibly related to the outcome of the proceeding. (The test under *Brecht* is "whether the error 'had substantial and injurious effect or influence in determining the jury's verdict.' " Id at 1722, quoting *Kotteakos v United States*, 328 US 750, 776 (1946).) But this relation to the outcome can be fairly tenuous or quite strong; relief is the same in either event. More important, this relation to the outcome need not have anything to do with the fundamental justice of the outcome. For example, improper police interrogation may affect the outcome of the defendant's trial by inducing the defendant to confess. But if the confession is credible (that is, if it is corroborated by other reliable evidence), then a conviction may nevertheless be "just." At the very least, conviction in such a case must be far more "just," as a relative matter, than conviction of a factually innocent defendant.

[67] Consider two examples. The first is police interrogation law, where defendants could obtain relief only if their confession was "involuntary," and findings of involuntariness tended to occur in cases of serious physical abuse of suspects. Such cases are, of course, precisely where it is most likely that the confession is false. The second is right-to-counsel doctrine, where the law did not require state-appointed counsel absent a showing of some special need by the defendant. See *Betts v Brady*, 316 US 455 (1942). This meant, in practice, that a defendant had to show a substantial likelihood that he was innocent in order to make out a viable right-to-counsel claim.

[68] 344 US 443 (1953).

violations. Habeas is, in this sense, no different from Section 1983 or the law of constitutional injunctions: one of the primary goals of habeas law should be to deter violations of the Fourth, Fifth, and Sixth Amendments. But deterrence works differently in habeas. The federal rights enforced through habeas arise primarily (although not exclusively) in criminal cases. This fact has two implications that distinguish habeas from other remedies for constitutional violations.

First, alleged violations of criminal procedure rights are much more likely to be litigated than other alleged constitutional violations. A would-be plaintiff with a possible Section 1983 claim must initiate the proceedings herself if she wants relief; this means finding a lawyer and proceeding through the process to trial if the defendants choose not to settle. The only tangible incentive for doing so is a possible damages award, and such awards are usually quite small.[69] A criminal defendant, on the other hand, is forced to defend himself against charges the state has initiated, and if, as is often the case, he cannot afford a lawyer, one is given to him free of charge. Moreover, the tangible incentive for pressing the claim is avoiding criminal punishment—a far bigger incentive than most damages awards—and the same incentive applies to any claim that may obtain the defendant's release.

This point has important deterrence consequences. Elsewhere in constitutional law, much official misconduct goes unnoticed (or at least unlitigated) and hence unpunished. Preserving access to federal court, and providing a system of remedies that includes potentially generous attorneys' fees, is thus critically important: if most violations are swept under the rug, the system must take very seriously the few claims that come to light through litigation. But in the criminal justice system, violations are constantly litigated in state courts,[70] because the litigants (criminal defendants) both have

---

[69] In a study of constitutional tort litigation in three federal districts in a one-year period in the early 1980s, Professors Schwab and Eisenberg found that the average total recovery (including attorneys' fees) in successfully litigated cases was $30,480. The median recovery was only $8,000. These figures include only cases taken to trial; the figures for settled cases are presumably a good deal lower. By comparison, in the same districts, the average recovery in non-constitutional tort cases against the United States was $77,300, and the median recovery was $20,000. Stewart J. Schwab & Theodore Eisenberg, *Explaining Constitutional Tort Litigation: The Influence of the Attorney Fees Statute and the Government as Defendant*, 73 Cornell L Rev 719, 736–38 (1988).

[70] For example, suppression motions are filed in approximately one-tenth of all state-court criminal cases. See Peter F. Nardulli, *The Societal Cost of the Exclusionary Rule: An Empirical Assessment*, 1983 Am Bar Found Res J 585, 594. This makes constitutional litigation in the course of state criminal proceedings vastly more frequent than constitutional tort litigation:

strong incentives to raise claims and bear minimal costs. It follows that the proportion of, say, *Miranda* violations that spawn suppression motions in state court must be far higher than the proportion of First Amendment violations that lead to Section 1983 litigation. (It also follows that there will be many more bogus *Miranda* claims, since criminal defendants have such strong incentives to raise claims, and they bear few costs when the claims are denied.) In short, habeas review supplements a state criminal justice system in which most constitutional violations are likely to be raised, while Section 1983 litigation is, in most settings, the sole (and infrequently used) path to adjudication of constitutional claims.

Second, habeas litigation of federal criminal procedure issues is invariably one-sided. Habeas courts review claims that the constitutional rights of defendants were not adequately protected in the state courts, but they cannot review claims by prosecutors that federal rights were erroneously overprotected by the state courts, thus leading to the defendant's acquittal.

The habeas literature has ignored this point, but its deterrent impact may be quite substantial. As Professor Kate Stith has explained, one-sided appellate review of many issues in criminal litigation skews the resolution of those issues at trial: trial courts tend to give defendants the benefit of the doubt on, say, contested jury instructions, because a pro-government error can mean reversal, while a pro-defendant error is usually unreviewable.[71] Habeas litigation is even more likely to produce this skewing effect. Prosecutors may sometimes appeal pro-defendant errors committed by state courts within the state court system: in some states, for example, the suppression of evidence can be appealed by the government before trial. And erroneous legal rulings that overturn a guilty verdict at trial or in an intermediate appeals court (if based on any ground other than insufficiency of the evidence) are generally appealable by the government. On habeas, however, the government cannot seek to overturn any adverse state court decision. Thus, to a greater extent than with any other federal remedy for constitutional violations, the threat of habeas relief must, at the

---

one study concluded that, *nationwide*, only about 2,000 constitutional tort actions are filed in federal court each year against police officers. Schwab & Eisenberg, 73 Cornell L Rev at 735 (cited in note 69).

[71] See Kate Stith, *The Risk of Legal Error in Criminal Cases: Some Consequences of the Asymmetry in the Right to Appeal*, 57 U Chi L Rev 1, 18–24 (1990).

margin, tend to push state courts toward greater protection of federal rights.[72]

These two observations suggest that, in the context of criminal procedure, a little deterrence goes a long way. Whatever opportunities may exist for habeas relitigation of federal constitutional claims, those opportunities will likely be used by state prisoners to a much greater extent than corresponding opportunities will be used by ordinary civil litigants. Moreover, habeas follows a state criminal process in which federal constitutional violations are more likely to come to light than elsewhere in constitutional litigation. And the one-sided nature of habeas review will tend to maximize the effect of pushing state courts in the direction of protecting the relevant federal rights.

II. HABEAS AND THE CRIMINAL PROCEDURE SYSTEM

What would the law of habeas corpus look like if one were to reconstruct it in light of the nature of contemporary criminal procedure doctrine? As with any other procedural device, the answer depends on one's views concerning the costs and benefits of the procedure. In the current system, the principal cost of habeas—leaving aside, for reasons we have explained, the supposed intrusion on state sovereignty—is the suspension of finality. Habeas occupies the time and energy of courts and prosecutors (and, in some instances, state-paid counsel for petitioners), and hence delays the conclusion of the proceedings.[73] These costs are not massive, but they are real, and should not be incurred unnecessarily.

The benefits must be assessed in light of the goals of constitutional criminal procedure, for that is the law that habeas enforces.

---

[72] Indeed, the one-sided nature of habeas suggests (independent of our arguments about the problems with the traditional federal courts approach to habeas) that Professor James Liebman's recently asserted analogy between habeas and direct appeal is inapt. See Liebman, 92 Colum L Rev 1997 (cited in note 2). The Court has regularly reviewed on appeal claims by the government that state courts erroneously over-protected criminal defendants under federal law; no such federal court review, on the other hand, is available at the request of the government via a habeas petition.

[73] We do not count privately paid defense counsel, because the defendant can make for himself the judgment whether that cost is worth the possible benefit. But, even if he has private counsel, the defendant still does not internalize most of the costs he imposes on the prosecutor and court.

We posit three goals: (1) that only the guilty be punished; (2) that police, prosecutors, and judges treat suspects and defendants fairly; and (3) that federal courts have adequate opportunities to make federal law. The key to any sensible reform of habeas law is to recognize that these goals need not all be achieved in the same way. Different kinds of constitutional claims may require different habeas rules.

A. PREVENTING UNJUST PUNISHMENT—THE PROTECTION OF INNOCENCE

As we have said, the possibility that a criminal defendant might be innocent of the crime for which he is being punished currently plays only a small role in the adjudication of his habeas petition. There are two ways to fix this: habeas courts can focus on the nature of the defendant's constitutional claim, or they can focus on prejudice to the individual defendant. We think the second approach is better than the first. The reasons are anchored in the nature of the rights established by the law of constitutional criminal procedure.

Stone v Powell[74] represents an example of the first approach. *Stone* effectively removed Fourth Amendment claims from habeas, partly on the ground that such claims were unconnected with the guilt/innocence determination.[75] When *Stone* was decided, it was widely viewed as the first step toward a broad restructuring of habeas, with the Court categorizing all constitutional criminal procedure claims as either innocence-related or not, and treating the former category more favorably on habeas than the latter. Instead, *Stone* has been limited to Fourth Amendment claims. Just this past year, in *Withrow v Williams*,[76] the Court declined to apply *Stone* to *Miranda* claims; Justice Souter's majority opinion in *Withrow* suggested that *Stone* is not subject to further expansion.[77]

Though *Withrow* may have come as a surprise to some observers, we think the Court got it exactly right: the categorical-"innocence"

---

[74] 428 US 465 (1976).

[75] Indeed, the point is stronger: criminal defendants with valid Fourth Amendment claims are *more* likely to be guilty than defendants as a whole, because the evidence they are seeking to suppress is by definition incriminating.

[76] 113 S Ct 1745 (1993).

[77] Id at 1750–55. But see *Reed v Farley* (cited in note 59).

approach of *Stone* does not work (at least not beyond the special category of Fourth Amendment claims) because it does not fit the general nature of criminal procedure law. In an across-the-board *Stone* regime in which innocence-related claims could be raised on habeas but other claims could not, *Miranda* claims, for example, would presumably be "out" and ineffective assistance of counsel claims, to take another example, would be "in." After all, *Miranda* aims primarily at deterring police misbehavior even if such misbehavior might turn up reliable evidence of crime, but if the defendant had an incompetent lawyer the guilt/innocence determination seems inherently untrustworthy.

This conclusion is, however, quite problematic. Improper police interrogation tactics can lead to false confessions.[78] And ineffective assistance claims need not have anything to do with the guilt/innocence determination: in *Kimmelman v Morrison*,[79] the Court held that defense counsel was constitutionally ineffective for not seeking to suppress highly probative incriminating evidence that apparently was illegally seized.[80]

These examples illustrate a general point: most criminal procedure rights protect multiple values, and they protect different values in different cases. Ineffective assistance claims are usually about ensuring reliable verdicts, but that is not always so. *Miranda* claims may primarily serve to deter police misbehavior of a kind that is unlikely to convict innocent defendants, yet they sometimes bear strongly on the reliability of a confession (and hence of any subsequent conviction).[81] The *Stone* approach tries to categorize rights as innocence-related or not. But most criminal procedure rights do not fit neatly into either of *Stone*'s boxes.

The alternative is to look not to the kind of claim the defendant

---

[78] For one recent example, see Roger Parloff, *False Confessions*, in *American Lawyer* 58, 59–60 (May 1993).

[79] 477 US 365 (1986).

[80] Id at 383–91.

[81] There are many other examples. The set of constitutional rules surrounding peremptory challenges in jury selection seems designed, in large part, to protect the interests of potential jurors in avoiding discrimination—an interest that has no necessary relation to the reliability of guilty verdicts. Yet in part, those rules also aim to prevent the government from "stacking" the jury in its favor by excluding groups that might be favorable to the defense, a goal that obviously has a great deal to do with the guilt-innocence determination. See Nancy J. King, *Postconviction Review of Jury Discrimination: Measuring the Effects of Juror Race on Jury Decisions*, 92 Mich L Rev 63, 75–100 (1993) (detailing the effects of race on jury decision making).

raises, but to whether the defendant can show *in his case* that the reliability of the guilt/innocence determination is seriously at issue. This was the original idea behind the "fundamental miscarriage of justice" exception to the procedural default rule of *Wainwright v Sykes*.[82] *Sykes* held that a defendant may not raise a defaulted claim on habeas unless he can show both cause for the default and prejudice resulting from it. The exception for fundamental miscarriage of justice permits habeas review of a defaulted claim, even without the required showing of cause and prejudice, if the defendant can show that he is probably innocent.[83]

The miscarriage of justice exception has the great virtue of not requiring the categorization of criminal procedure claims: in effect, a claim is "innocence-related" if a defendant can link it to a strong enough showing of innocence in his case, but not otherwise. This avoids the categorical over- and underinclusiveness of *Stone*. On the other hand, the exception seriously underprotects innocence. In practice, the burden of showing probable (more likely than not) innocence turns out to be too much to bear; the exception has become a virtual nullity, cited as evidence of the Court's concern with protecting innocence but almost never applied.[84]

The idea behind the miscarriage of justice exception is sound. But the Court's reluctance to distinguish among different habeas cases has led it to cabin the exception too severely. A defendant who can demonstrate a "reasonable probability" of innocence—not that he is "probably" (more likely than not) innocent, but that he "may well be" innocent, or can raise "substantial doubt" about his guilt—has made the kind of showing that should seriously undermine one's faith in the justice of the verdict in his case.[85] Whenever

---

[82] 433 US 72 (1977).

[83] See *Murray v Carrier*, 477 US 478, 495–96 (1986).

[84] In the wake of *Carrier*, a few cases actually found the miscarriage of justice exception applicable, though on grounds that went well beyond probable innocence. See *Power v Johnson*, 678 F Supp 1195, 1196–97 (EDNC 1988) (finding miscarriage of justice based on defense attorney incompetence); *Williams v Lane*, 645 F Supp 740, 748 (ND Ill 1986) (finding miscarriage of justice based on a showing of egregious prosecutorial misbehavior). The Supreme Court has since emphasized that only more-likely-than-not innocence will suffice to bring a petitioner's claim within the exception. *Dugger v Adams*, 489 US 401, 412 n 6 (1989). Accordingly, the exception as it stands today is very narrow indeed.

[85] This standard—essentially something midway between beyond a reasonable doubt and preponderance of the evidence—already exists in several areas of criminal procedure doctrine. See, for example, *Strickland v Washington*, 466 US 668, 693–96 (1984) (prejudice

such a showing of potential innocence is coupled with a claim of constitutional violation, it seems unacceptable to withhold habeas review of the constitutionality of the defendant's conviction.

We therefore propose that one branch of habeas law be premised directly on the recognition that habeas can provide a valuable layer of protection against the unjust punishment of innocent defendants. Under this first track of habeas review, a "reasonable probability of innocence" standard would apply to *all* constitutional claims (not simply defaulted or otherwise procedurally deficient claims), so that any defendant could obtain habeas review of the constitutionality of his conviction by (1) demonstrating a "reasonable probability" that he is innocent of the crime for which he was convicted, and (2) alleging a constitutional violation that resulted in his erroneous conviction. If the habeas court finds that a constitutional violation occurred, and that as a result the defendant was convicted even though he may well be innocent, habeas relief should be granted. If the defendant fails either to make the required showing of innocence or to prevail on the merits of his constitutional claim, habeas relief under this first track of habeas review should be denied.

Our approach would lead to habeas review on the merits of all claims that the government failed to disclose material exculpatory evidence, since our proposed "reasonable probability of innocence" standard is the same as that for showing "materiality" under existing *Brady* doctrine.[86] It would also mean habeas review of all innocence-related ineffective assistance of counsel claims: once again, the standard is the same.[87] And it would mean habeas review

---

standard for ineffective assistance of counsel cases); *United States v Bagley*, 473 US 667, 678–83 (1985) (plurality opinion) (prejudice standard for claims of prosecutorial failure to disclose exculpatory evidence). In these areas, the law has sought to craft a standard that provides relief when one's "confidence in the outcome" of the proceeding has been "undermine[d]," *Strickland*, 466 US at 694, but not otherwise. And in all, the Court has been quite careful not to use either "reasonable doubt" or "preponderance" language in formulating the relevant standard.

[86] See *Bagley*, 473 US at 682 (plurality opinion) ("The evidence is material only if there is a reasonable probability that, had the evidence been disclosed to the defense, the result of the proceeding would have been different").

[87] See *Strickland v Washington*, 466 US 668 (1984) ("The defendant must show that there is a reasonable probability that, but for counsel's unprofessional errors, the result of the proceeding would have been different").

of all *Jackson v Virginia* claims, which go directly to the sufficiency of the evidence of the defendant's guilt.[88]

With respect to most other constitutional claims, the "innocence" standard we propose would, under this first branch of habeas law, create an additional prerequisite to obtaining habeas review and possible relief. But the standard would actually benefit some defendants, since such a showing would justify habeas review of the merits of the defendant's federal claims without regard to any possible procedural deficiencies in state court. The contrary rule in existence today[89] rests on the notion that the state's interests in finality and the enforcement of procedural rules outweigh the interest of a potentially innocent defendant in avoiding punishment. This balance (with which we disagree in any event) reflects the current law's preoccupation with federalism concerns, a preoccupation that is out of place with the wholly nationalized body of law that state courts apply to resolve criminal procedure disputes.

Two other aspects of our proposed "innocence" habeas track deserve mention. First, habeas review under this "innocence" track would be de novo, with respect to both legal and mixed law-and-fact issues. We would not restrict habeas petitioners to case law that existed at the time of their state court trials and direct appeals, nor would we require habeas courts to defer to the prior rulings of state courts on legal or mixed issues. A defendant who can demonstrate a "reasonable probability of innocence," coupled with whatever the habeas court finds to be a constitutional violation under prevailing federal law at the time of the habeas adjudication, should get relief. The reasonableness of the state court's rulings under the federal law as it then existed is irrelevant, because the goal of habeas relief on this "innocence" track is not to send signals to the state courts but to prevent injustice to the defendant. Whatever impact *Teague v Lane*[90] should have on "non-innocence" habeas

---

[88] See *Jackson v Virginia*, 443 US 307 (1979) ("[T]he relevant question is whether, after viewing the evidence in the light most favorable to the prosecution, *any* rational trier of fact could have found the essential elements of the crime beyond a reasonable doubt"). This standard, of course, is much more restrictive than our proposed "reasonable probability of innocence" standard. Thus, habeas review of any credible *Jackson* claim would undoubtedly be de novo under our proposal—a *Jackson* claim could not possibly be credible unless the defendant was able to make a strong showing of innocence.

[89] Today, in cases involving defaulted claims, habeas petitioners must also show "cause" for the default. See *Wainwright v Sykes*, 433 US 72 (1977).

[90] 489 US 288 (1989).

claims (a question we will address in the next section), where a "reasonable probability of innocence" exists the *Teague* rule should *not* apply.

Second, we would not preclude habeas relief even for a "naked" innocence claim of the kind that was presented to the Court last Term in *Herrera v Collins*.[91] The petitioner in *Herrera* sought habeas relief simply on the ground that he was innocent. He alleged no constitutional violation. Herrera's claim was factually implausible,[92] so the Court did not need to rule out the possibility of such claims in order to deny Herrera habeas review and potential relief.[93] But in our view, habeas petitioners who can make a sufficiently strong showing of innocence, even without a separate constitutional violation, have negated the only good reason to keep them in prison (or, as in Herrera's case, to execute them). Relief should follow under the Due Process Clause, even if no other constitutional right is implicated.

Of course, there is much room for disagreement about what the

---

[91] 113 S Ct 853 (1993).

[92] Herrera was arrested on suspicion of killing two police officers, David Rucker and Enrique Carrisalez, in two separate shootings that occurred minutes apart along a highway in south Texas in late 1981. Carrisalez, before his death, identified Herrera as the person who had shot him. Another witness to the Carrisalez shooting also identified Herrera as the shooter, and identified the shooter's car as one that was registered to Herrera's live-in girlfriend. The witness testified that there was only one person in the car at the time of the Carrisalez shooting.

When Herrera was arrested, he was carrying a handwritten letter strongly implying his guilt in the Rucker killing. He was also carrying the keys to his girlfriend's car. His Social Security card was found alongside Rucker's patrol car. Blood and hair evidence tended to corroborate Herrera's presence at the scene of the Rucker murder. After being convicted of Carrisalez's murder and sentenced to death, Herrera pled guilty to the murder of Rucker.

Herrera's "newly discovered evidence" consisted of the affidavits of four persons. In 1990 and 1991, three of the four persons claimed for the first time that Herrera's brother, who had died in 1984, had told them before his death that he and not Herrera was the true killer of the two police officers. The fourth person, Herrera's brother's son, claimed that he was present at the time and place of the shootings and that Herrera's brother was the true killer.

All of these facts were detailed in the Court's opinion, and relied upon for the conclusion that "this showing of innocence falls far short of that which would have to be made in order to trigger the sort of constitutional claim which we have assumed, *arguendo*, to exist." 113 S Ct at 870.

[93] Indeed, a majority of the Justices indicated, in separate concurring and dissenting opinions, that a strong enough showing of even "naked" innocence might warrant habeas review and relief. Nevertheless, Chief Justice Rehnquist's majority opinion suggests that the Court might bar such claims altogether: "Federal habeas review of state convictions has traditionally been limited to claims of constitutional violations occurring in the course of the underlying state criminal proceedings. . . . History shows that the traditional remedy for claims of innocence based on new evidence, discovered too late in the day to file a new trial motion, has been executive clemency." 113 S Ct at 869.

proper standard for such "naked" innocence claims ought to be. Presumably it should be harder for a defendant to obtain habeas review by claiming innocence alone than by coupling an innocence claim with a claim of a constitutional violation of a kind that might have affected the reliability of the evidence or the accuracy of the verdict. Absent such a violation, there is far less reason for the habeas court to distrust the trial process that convicted the defendant. It follows that the showing necessary to obtain habeas review, and potential relief, in such a case should be far stronger—perhaps "more likely than not" innocence, or "clear and convincing evidence" of innocence. Both of these standards are fully consistent with our proposed approach to habeas, for the *Herrera* issue involves not the proper scope of habeas, but the meaning of substantive due process. Whatever one defines as the nature of substantive due process in cases involving claims of "naked" innocence, our "innocence" track of habeas law would implement that definition.

This leads to an important general caveat. Neither our proposal nor any other change in habeas law can sufficiently protect innocent defendants if the underlying criminal procedure doctrine is badly flawed. Some say, for example, that current ineffective assistance law is too restrictive, and that it is too hard for defendants to make the needed showing of attorney incompetence, which means that some innocent defendants cannot get relief because their lawyers, though inept, were not inept enough. If this claim is correct, then Sixth Amendment doctrine should be changed. But either way, our proposal does a better job of protecting innocent defendants by means of habeas review than does the existing system.

In short, adopting the approach Judge Friendly proposed many years ago—not as the exclusive route to habeas relief, but as one option available to habeas petitioners—would make habeas a more useful tool for preventing the most fundamental injustice the criminal justice system can produce. Currently, the unreliability of a defendant's conviction can be remedied on habeas only if the state court's decision was unreasonable under then-existing federal law, and then only if the defendant's claims are not defaulted (or otherwise procedurally deficient) or if he can show "more-likely-than-not" innocence. Our proposed approach would add significantly to the protection of innocent defendants, without adding to the

complexity of habeas law (indeed, as we will show in Part III, our approach would greatly simplify habeas doctrine). And our approach would fit in well with the nature of criminal procedure rights, which protect many values, of which innocence is the most important.

B. DETERRING CONSTITUTIONAL VIOLATIONS

Current habeas doctrine does a somewhat better job of fulfilling the second major goal of criminal procedure law: deterring misconduct by relevant state actors. In particular, the line of habeas retroactivity decisions beginning with *Teague v Lane* shows promise of developing into a sensible deterrence-based habeas doctrine. But the doctrine has not reached fruition yet, and the recent decision in *Wright v West*,[94] declining to adopt a "reasonableness" standard of habeas review for state court decisions on mixed questions of law and fact, indicates that the Court is not yet thinking clearly about habeas's deterrence function.

That function is necessarily different from the deterrence role played by other constitutional remedies. Section 1983 or *Bivens* litigation can occur immediately after the alleged constitutional violation. Plaintiffs need not exhaust other possible remedies, so there is no procedural filter through which the claim must pass before it gets to federal court. Federal habeas litigation, by contrast, always occurs after a trial (or guilty plea) and direct appeal, and also after any state collateral proceedings. And there are many, many more state court criminal procedure decisions (including rulings on suppression motions) than there are habeas decisions.[95]

Given this unique procedural setting, it is unrealistic to think of habeas as a significant *direct* deterrent of misconduct by state or

---

[94] 112 S Ct 2482 (1992).

[95] Of course, changes in habeas doctrine could alter this ratio, but not as much as one might think: the number of habeas claims has not fluctuated substantially with changes in habeas doctrine over the past twenty years or so. In 1970, the number of habeas petitions filed by state prisoners was 9,063; this figure declined relatively steadily until 1977, when it reached a low of 6,866; then it began to climb again, topping out at 10,545 in 1989. In no single year between 1970 and 1989 did the number of petitions vary by more than 1,000, in either direction, from the preceding year; and in only five of the nineteen years did the number of petitions vary by more than 500, in either direction, from the preceding year. See United States Department of Justice, *Sourcebook of Criminal Justice Statistics*, Table 5.25 (1980); United States Department of Justice, *Sourcebook of Criminal Justice Statistics*, Table 5.55 (1990).

local police and prosecutors. Those officials face a much greater threat of lost convictions in state court than they will ever face in habeas, and when habeas review does occur, it occurs later (sometimes much later) than sanctions applied by state courts. Police officers, for example, are unlikely to change their behavior because of what a federal habeas court might say about that behavior years after they question a suspect.

There is an appropriate deterrence role for habeas to play, but it is a role aimed more at state courts than at other state officials. For state judges, particularly trial judges, the grant of habeas relief resembles a reversal on appeal: the judge's decision is overturned in a way that (at least in some cases) suggests error on the judge's part, and if there are further proceedings the case usually returns to the same judge's docket. To whatever extent appellate review in general deters lower court judges from misapplying law, habeas review should exert a similar deterrent effect on state judges.[96]

Of course, state judges' rulings in turn deter state and local police officers and prosecutors from misapplying federal law; that is the theory on which the exclusionary rule and many other aspects of criminal procedure rest. But this indirect deterrent impact on primary actors, like police officers and prosecutors, is not the same as the direct deterrent impact of other federal remedies, such as Section 1983 litigation. In the habeas context, the goal is to create incentives for state courts carefully to scrutinize the conduct of primary actors, and thereby to transmit the deterrent effects of habeas review to those primary actors.

How can habeas law create those incentives? The temptation is to play out the analogy to appellate review. On legal and mixed law-and-fact questions, appellate courts reverse whenever they find error. This plenary standard of review not only ensures correct

---

[96] The empirical evidence on this point is sketchy, but there seems to be little disagreement among the members of the Supreme Court—regardless of their respective views about the proper role of habeas—that habeas review, and the threat of reversal, can exert at least some influence on the decisions of state judges. Perhaps the best available evidence in support of this proposition is the simple observation that state courts rarely refuse to abide by the legal rulings of the particular lower federal habeas courts that review their state criminal cases, even though the state courts are not obligated to do so. See Robert Cover and T. Alexander Aleinikoff, *Dialectical Federalism: Habeas Corpus and the Court*, 86 Yale L J 1035 (1977) (suggesting that state courts and lower federal habeas courts can engage in a "dialogue" about the nature of federal rights, because state courts are not obligated to abide by legal rulings of lower federal habeas courts).

outcomes in particular cases;[97] it also encourages lower court judges to take "super-care" to avoid errors, by imposing a kind of strict liability. Habeas law, some might argue, should do the same: provide for de novo review of legal or mixed law-and-fact decisions of state courts with respect to federal constitutional claims.

But the incentive effects of de novo review on habeas are different from the incentive effects of de novo review in ordinary appeals. Recall that habeas review, to an even greater extent than ordinary criminal appeals, is one-directional. Only state court errors that benefit the government can be the basis of habeas claims. Apart from the Supreme Court's rare use of its certiorari jurisdiction, state court errors that benefit defendants are not subject to any federal review at all.

State judges in criminal cases thus face asymmetric risks of reversal by federal courts. In this respect, they resemble individual defendants in Section 1983 actions. Most government officials get no direct reward for acting properly, but risk damages liability if they violate constitutional standards. The fear is that, as a consequence, such officials will be overdeterred and will avoid close-to-the-line behavior—officials will, for example, avoid making some good decisions in order to reduce the risk of liability for bad ones.[98] The response of Section 1983 law to this problem is the qualified immunity defense, which generally protects state actors from damages liability unless their conduct was clearly illegal.[99] By shifting the liability standard from "violation" (strict liability) to "clear violation" (a form of negligence), qualified immunity doctrine reduces overdeterrence.

State judges are in a similar position. Because of double jeopardy doctrine, they face a much lower risk of reversal on direct appeal for pro-defendant errors than for mistakes that favor the government. And they face no risk whatsoever of reversal on habeas for pro-defendant errors. If state judges care whether their decisions

---

[97] Though this is obviously a little artificial, since "correct" in this context means only that which the appellate court holds.

[98] For the standard discussions of this point, see Jerry L. Mashaw, *Civil Liability of Government Officers: Property Rights and Official Accountability*, 42 L & Contemp Probs 8, 29–33 (Winter 1978); Peter H. Schuck, *Suing Government: Citizen Remedies for Official Wrongs* 59–81 (Yale, 1983).

[99] See *Anderson v Creighton*, 483 US 635, 640 (1987) (in order to defeat qualified immunity defense, "in the light of pre-existing law the unlawfulness [of the defendant's conduct] must be apparent").

are reversed, this asymmetry should push their decisions marginally in favor of defendants.

This effect would not matter if the goal of criminal procedure law were to minimize errors favoring the government. But there is no *deterrence-based* reason to pursue such a goal. It is one thing to let ten guilty people go free to avoid sending one innocent person to prison. Basic principles of justice support tilting the risk of error heavily in the defendant's favor. It is quite another thing to prefer the mistaken suppression of ten (lawfully obtained) confessions by guilty defendants to the mistaken admission of one reliable (yet unconstitutionally obtained) confession into evidence. Assuming that the confession is reliable, the demands of justice do not dictate any particular allocation of errors with regard to *Miranda* questions. That is why the burden of persuasion for *Miranda* claims is not beyond-a-reasonable-doubt or clear-and-convincing evidence, but the preponderance standard.[100]

The logical solution for habeas doctrine is an analogue to qualified immunity doctrine: a rule requiring reversal on habeas only when a state court ruling was not just wrong, but unreasonably so—that is, when the decision was something other than a close call. Indeed, the case for such a negligence-type rule is stronger in the habeas context than in Section 1983 cases. Qualified immunity in Section 1983 cases may produce substantial underdeterrence: not only do Section 1983 defendants receive a favorable liability standard, but the small number of Section 1983 cases suggests they are unlikely to become defendants in the first place.[101] This last point is not true in the criminal procedure setting. The procedural setting in which the claims are raised—criminal litigation brought by the state, where the defendant receives appointed counsel, and where valid constitutional claims may lead to immunity from punishment—suggests that police officers and prosecutors cannot blithely flout criminal procedure rules in the belief that their violations will be overlooked. Violations of those rules *are* litigated in state court, with great regularity. Giving "close-call" state court decisions the benefit of the doubt on habeas would not change that.

In short, there is a strong argument for a general "reasonableness" standard of review on habeas—that is, for not granting ha-

---

[100] *Colorado v Connelly*, 479 US 157, 167–69 (1986).

[101] See note 70 supra.

beas relief unless the state court decision was unreasonable under federal law at the time it was made. As we have explained, this standard should not apply where the defendant can show a reasonable probability of innocence, for in such a case the potential for an unjust outcome warrants habeas relief apart from any deterrence concerns. But where deterrence alone is at stake, "reasonableness" review on habeas should suffice.

This conclusion holds true even if state judges generally are not the equal of federal judges, and even if some state judges sometimes engage in bad faith efforts to evade federal law. If particular state courts are either sloppy or inept, and if their incompetence manifests itself in plainly erroneous rulings in the government's favor, then habeas relief will follow, even under a "reasonableness" standard. The same is true if particular state courts are sometimes hostile to federal rights.

If, on the other hand, a particular state court makes a substantial number of errors on both sides of the line in "close call" cases, we can see no deterrence-based argument justifying habeas relief. A pattern of evenly distributed mistakes in marginal cases is perfectly consistent with properly functioning constitutional deterrence. The only scenario that would undermine our proposed "reasonableness" standard would be if a state court systematically erred in the government's favor in close cases. This scenario seems unlikely. The incentives to avoid reversal should, if anything, tend to push state courts in the opposite direction. And hostility to federal rights would likely manifest itself in plainly wrong rulings—the kind of rulings that habeas courts would, under our proposal, overturn.

We therefore propose a second "track" of habeas law that would use a "reasonableness" standard of review to achieve maximum constitutional deterrence of state courts at minimum cost. Implementing this second track of habeas review would be easy; the Court need only follow *Teague v Lane*[102] to its logical conclusion. *Teague* held that habeas review is ordinarily unavailable when granting the habeas petitioner's claim would require the adoption or application of a "new rule" of law.[103] The definition of "new

---

[102] 489 US 288 (1989).

[103] Id at 310, 315–16. Although the lead opinion of Justice O'Connor in *Teague* was only a plurality opinion, a majority of the Court has since adopted the views expressed in that opinion. See, for example, *Penry v Lynaugh*, 492 US 302 (1989). We will henceforth, therefore, refer to Justice O'Connor's *Teague* opinion as if it were a majority opinion.

rule" remains unclear, but recent decisions suggest that it encompasses any claim that a reasonable state judge could have rejected, based on the federal law at the time.[104] *Teague* thus adopts a "benefit of the doubt" or "reasonableness" habeas standard of review for purely legal issues.

In *Wright v West*,[105] however, the Court failed to extend this standard to mixed questions of law and fact (such as whether defense counsel was ineffective, or whether a confession was involuntary). The Court has not definitively resolved the issue, but several Justices and many commentators have expressed alarm at the idea of across-the-board "deference" to state court decisions on mixed issues in habeas.[106] This alarm is unwarranted. Habeas courts should not *defer* to state court decisions on mixed issues; such a notion of "deference" would be based on the same archaic Federalist arguments that we contend ought to be rejected. Rather, the real issue in cases like *Wright v West* is: what habeas standard of review is necessary to deter state courts from misconstruing or misapplying federal law? Given the frequency with which federal claims arise in state court and the one-sidedness of habeas review (and for the same reasons that support a qualified immunity defense in Section 1983 cases), an across-the-board "reasonableness" habeas standard of review, applicable to all issues, should ensure that state judges apply federal constitutional standards, on average, just about right.[107]

---

[104] See *Butler v McKellar*, 494 US 407 (1990); *Stringer v Black*, 112 S Ct 1130 (1992); Joseph L. Hoffmann, *The Supreme Court's New Vision of Federal Habeas Corpus for State Prisoners*, 1989 Supreme Court Review 165.

[105] 112 S Ct 2482 (1992).

[106] Id at 2493–98 (O'Connor, joined by Blackmun and Stevens, concurring in the judgment); id at 2498–2500 (Kennedy concurring in the judgment); Liebman, 92 Colum L Rev at 2012–33 (cited in note 2).

[107] There is a category of cases that this approach does not catch: cases in which the defendant never raises a valid constitutional claim because the government conceals the evidence on which the claim rests. One might argue that habeas review is necessary in such cases, notwithstanding the absence of any unreasonable state court decision, in order to deter fraudulent behavior by the government. We think such an argument is mistaken.

At the outset, we note that many (perhaps most) claims of concealment would be viable on habeas under our approach, because they involve claims of innocence. To take the most common example, a claim that the prosecution failed to disclose exculpatory evidence would receive de novo review on habeas as long as "exculpatory" is defined in the ordinary sense. So the question reduces to whether habeas review is necessary *for deterrence reasons alone* in "concealment" cases.

That question can only be answered by considering the contexts in which the claims are likely to arise. There are three major categories. The first is search and seizure cases where the claim is that the officer lied in the suppression hearing. It is impossible to allow litigation

C. FEDERAL COURTS AND FEDERAL LAW

One final aspect of the criminal justice system needs to be taken into account. In a system based on Nationalist criminal procedure rules, someone must make those rules. That "someone" is, ultimately, the Supreme Court. If a particular body of rules, such as those governing criminal procedure, is to be truly Nationalist, then the ultimate lawmaking authority properly must reside within the federal system. (This is so even if parity between state and federal courts exists; it is all the more so if federal courts are generally superior decision makers on federal issues.) There is a big difference between saying (as we do) that state and federal courts both apply federal criminal procedure law as their own, and saying (as we do not) that state courts should be given the authority to define, in the end, the content of federal law.

The Supreme Court has a limited decisional capacity. The Court may sometimes find itself incapable of ensuring, on its own, that federal criminal procedure law will develop in a sufficiently Nationalist manner. When such a situation arises, the Court needs to be able, in effect, to deputize an alternative federal lawmaker—namely, the lower federal courts sitting in habeas—who can perform a supporting role in creating and implementing a Nationalist body of law. That is essentially what happened in the 1960s: the Court dramatically expanded the scope of habeas just as the Criminal Procedure Revolution picked up steam. For the purpose of federal lawmaking, this expansion of habeas was appropriate, indeed probably necessary. Expansive habeas review of state criminal cases allowed the lower federal courts to help the Court craft,

---

of these claims without in effect allowing litigation of all Fourth Amendment claims: litigation of "concealment" would turn out to be indistinguishable from relitigation of the merits, since a decision that the officer lied is likely to be the same as a decision that the search was illegal. And reasonableness review is sufficient as a deterrent of bad merits decisions. The second category is police interrogation cases where, again, the claim is that the officer lied at the suppression hearing. Here, the defendant has the relevant information at the time of the state court proceeding—he is the one who was being interrogated. Thus, if the government makes false claims, the defendant is in a position to challenge those claims in the state court proceeding. The third category consists of grand jury discrimination claims in which the evidence of discrimination may have been concealed by the relevant actors. (Concealment is much less likely for petit jury selection, because defense counsel will ordinarily have the information needed to raise any available claims.) Here, the presence of multiple concerned parties means both that successful concealment is unlikely and that there is a reasonable prospect of non-criminal litigation raising the relevant claim. De novo habeas review does not seem to us necessary in any of these cases.

essentially from scratch, the detailed Nationalist code of criminal procedure that we know today.[108]

The need for federal lawmaking has been the basis of much criticism of *Teague* doctrine. *Teague* bars habeas relief anytime a petitioner's claim would require the adoption or application of a "new rule"; commentators have noted (correctly) that this means habeas courts are generally precluded from crafting such rules.[109] One can similarly object to the across-the-board "reasonableness" standard of review (which is really just an extension of *Teague*) that we advocate for our second track of habeas law. Does this standard of review too severely limit federal lawmaking?

The answer is no. What must be remembered is that habeas, as an alternative means of federal lawmaking, provides an opportunity for the Supreme Court to obtain the help of the lower federal courts *when needed* in performing a constitutional lawmaking role that belongs, first and foremost, to the Court itself. If the Court believes that it does not need the help, because it is confident in the lawmaking abilities of the state courts as constrained and guided by its own direct review, then that is the end of the argument. The Court is the ultimate federal constitutional lawmaker; it is entitled to decide whether or not to delegate its lawmaking authority. And, through the *Teague* line of cases, the Court has made plain that it does not currently need or want the help of habeas courts in shaping federal criminal procedure law.

Nor, for what it's worth, does the Court's judgment seem unreasonable. In the end, the need is for adequate opportunities for federal lawmaking, not limitless opportunities. And adequacy depends on context, especially on the scope and stability of the law already in place. In the 1960s and 1970s, much of federal criminal procedure law was a blank slate. Expansive habeas review, across the board, allowed the creation of the detailed federal criminal procedure rules that exist today. But those rules do exist today; the need for constitutional lawmaking has declined substantially. The Fourth Amendment, *Miranda*, grand jury discrimination, burden-of-proof instructions—all these areas, and many more, consist of relatively mature lines of doctrine. Today, in each of

---

[108] See Cover and Aleinikoff, 86 Yale L J 1035 (cited in note 96).

[109] See Richard H. Fallon, Jr. & Daniel J. Meltzer, *New Law, Non-Retroactivity and Constitutional Remedies*, 104 Harv L Rev 1731 (1991); Hoffmann, 1989 Supreme Court Review 165 (cited in note 104); Weisberg, 81 J Crim L & Criminol 9 (cited in note 2); Woolhandler, 45 Stan L Rev 575 (cited in note 26).

these areas, the Court either takes cases involving marginal issues, or almost never takes any cases at all. This suggests no great, continuing need for expansive habeas review as a means of federal lawmaking.

To be sure, this picture of doctrinal stability does not hold true throughout criminal procedure. Ineffective assistance law is still in flux, as courts try to give content to *Strickland v Washington*'s[110] vague "performance" and "prejudice" prongs. *Brady* doctrine, which requires prosecutors to turn over material exculpatory evidence, is also relatively undeveloped.[111] *Batson v Kentucky*[112] continues to spawn important new issues, so that the federal law of jury selection seems to change fundamentally on an annual basis.[113] And double jeopardy law seems to shift gears with surprising regularity.[114] Some of these areas (*Strickland* and *Brady*) involve the need to create interstitial law to give content to vague constitutional standards. Others (*Batson* and double jeopardy) involve important new rulings by the Court that require substantial lower court refinement. In such areas, the Criminal Procedure Revolution is ongoing, and the need to create federal law remains strong.

But this need is easily served within the two-track system of habeas review we have already proposed. De novo review of constitutional claims in all cases where the petitioner demonstrates a "reasonable probability of innocence" means substantial lawmaking authority for habeas courts in connection with almost all *Brady* claims and many *Strickland* claims. Meanwhile, *Batson* issues regularly arise in federal criminal prosecutions (and now in civil cases as well[115]), so that the lower federal courts have plenty of non-habeas

---

[110] 466 US 668 (1984).

[111] See *Brady v Maryland*, 373 US 83 (1963); *United States v Agurs*, 427 US 97 (1976); *United States v Bagley*, 473 US 667 (1985).

[112] 476 US 79 (1986).

[113] See, for example, *Powers v Ohio*, 111 S Ct 1364 (1991) (permitting *Batson* claims by defendants of different race than excluded jurors); *Georgia v MacCollum*, 112 S Ct 2348 (1992) (extending *Batson* to peremptory challenges by criminal defendants).

[114] See, for example, *Grady v Corbin*, 495 US 508 (1990) (adopting prosecution's-theory-of-the-case approach to defining double jeopardy implications of prosecution for complex crime); *United States v Felix*, 112 S Ct 1377 (1992) (suggesting traditional double jeopardy doctrines may not apply to complex crimes); *United States v Dixon*, 113 S Ct 2849 (1993) (overruling *Grady*, although no opinion declaring new double jeopardy rule to replace *Grady* garnered majority support).

[115] *Edmondson v Leesville Concrete Co*, 111 S Ct 2077 (1991). In addition, under *Georgia v MacCollum*, 112 S Ct 2348 (1992), *Batson* also applies to peremptories used by defense counsel in criminal cases.

opportunities for crafting new federal rules. The same is even more true of double jeopardy issues, many of which are triggered primarily by such complex federal crimes as RICO and CCE. There is thus little need for federal lawmaking on habeas in areas where a "reasonableness" standard of review would restrict it, while in areas where the need is great, there are many opportunities to satisfy it.

D. CONCLUSION: A TWO-TRACK SYSTEM OF HABEAS

We have tried to describe and justify the broad outlines of a habeas jurisprudence that aims at directly fulfilling the goals of criminal procedure, something habeas law does not currently do. The core of this jurisprudence is our proposal of two independent tracks of habeas review. We would grant habeas relief whenever a petitioner could show either (1) a constitutional violation (including substantive due process) coupled with a reasonable probability of an unjust outcome, that is, factual innocence, or (2) an unreasonable denial of a constitutional claim on the merits by the state courts. The first track protects against the imprisonment of innocent persons, which Judge Friendly rightly argued should be central to habeas.[116] The second track ensures that state judges "toe the constitutional mark"—that they adequately enforce the constitutional rules that govern police, prosecutors, and judges alike—which Justice Harlan viewed as habeas's core mission.[117] By creating a two-track system of habeas review, based on the values of innocence and deterrence, the criminal justice system can accommodate both Friendly's and Harlan's views about habeas in a way that also leaves more than adequate opportunities for federal lawmaking.

We also believe that these are the only justifications for federal habeas review of state criminal cases. Ensuring justice for potentially innocent petitioners, deterring unreasonable decisionmaking by state courts, and providing adequate opportunities for federal lawmaking are all that a habeas regime can realistically hope to accomplish. What remains is to discuss how habeas law might best play these roles.

---

[116] Friendly, 38 U Chi L Rev 142 (cited in note 57).

[117] See *Desist v United States*, 394 US 244, 256 (1969) (Harlan dissenting); *Mackey v United States*, 401 US 667, 675 (1971) (Harlan dissenting and concurring in the judgment).

III. Some Applications

Our proposed two-track system of habeas would do a much better job of handling claims of individual injustice than the existing system; it would also do at least as good a job of deterring unconstitutional conduct. These advantages flow, we believe, from the proposal's anchor in criminal procedure.

Our proposal has another advantage: it would dramatically simplify the law of habeas corpus. Current habeas doctrine is plagued by its complexity. This may well be an indirect consequence of the Federalism-Nationalism debate that has dominated habeas discourse. The battle between comity and federalism on the one hand, and federal court vindication of federal rights on the other, boils down to a battle between less habeas review (across the board) and more (again, across the board). Neither Federalism nor Nationalism is self-limiting: comity and federalism *always* offer an argument for further restricting habeas, just as the importance of a federal forum and the lack of parity *always* argue in favor of expanding it. Predictably, the Supreme Court has been unwilling to follow either argument to its logical end point. The result is a system of seemingly arbitrary compromises, limitations that go thus far and no further—Federalist rules boxed in by Nationalist exceptions, or vice versa. This describes the law of substantive scope (including *Stone v Powell* and its progeny, if that is the right word), the law of procedural default, and especially the ongoing debate about habeas retroactivity. In all these areas, habeas doctrine has achieved a Rube Goldberg quality that frustrates all efforts to give it logical coherence.

A two-track habeas system of the sort we have proposed would largely solve this problem. By abandoning the search for rules to govern "innocence" and "deterrence" claims alike, it is possible to avoid many of the doctrinal swamps in which habeas law is now mired. To illustrate, we explain below how our proposal might apply to several contentious areas of habeas doctrine.

A. SUBSTANTIVE SCOPE AND THE RULE OF STONE V POWELL

Stone v Powell[118] held that if a criminal defendant received a full and fair opportunity to litigate his Fourth Amendment claim in

---

[118] 428 US 465 (1976).

state court, that claim would not be available to him on federal habeas. Full and fair opportunity is defined broadly, so *Stone* amounts to an almost total exclusion of Fourth Amendment claims from habeas.[119] The decision once seemed likely to spawn a whole category of constitutional claims that would fall outside the scope of habeas, but that has not happened. *Stone* is today, as it was seventeen years ago, the sole exception to the rule that federal habeas review extends to all constitutional claims. We believe that the exception is probably a bad idea.

Two justifications seem to support the holding in *Stone*. The first is not terribly problematic: Fourth Amendment claims are unrelated to innocence and guilt, so habeas review is not necessary to prevent unjust outcomes.[120] We argued in Part II that the categorical approach to innocence and guilt does not work, that most rules of constitutional criminal procedure protect a mix of values that sometimes includes the reliability of the guilt determination. It follows that the categories of innocence-related rights and other rights do not exist; the relevant law does not usually fit neatly into either category. Fourth Amendment claims, however, are an exception (and a very large exception at that), since (1) they arise only when the defendant seeks to suppress incriminating evidence, and (2) unlike police misconduct in interrogation, police misconduct in search and seizure cases has no tendency to undermine the reliability of any evidence that is improperly discovered. If protecting innocent defendants were habeas's only role, in other words, *Stone* might well make good sense.

Yet even in terms of protecting innocents, a Friendly-style prejudice standard would accomplish the same thing as *Stone*, without the need for a special rule for search and seizure cases. If Fourth Amendment claimants are all guilty, because their claims arise in cases in which the police found the drugs or stolen goods on the suspect, then the claimants will never be able to show a reasonable probability of an unjust outcome. In innocence terms, *Stone* may be harmless, but if the system were to adopt an across-the-board prejudice standard tied to innocence, *Stone* would also be redundant.

---

[119] See Annotation, *What Constitutes "An Opportunity for Full and Fair Litigation" in State Court Precluding Habeas Corpus Review Under 28 U.S.C. §2254 in Federal Court of State Prisoner's Fourth Amendment Claims*, 75 ALR Fed 9 (1992).

[120] See *Stone*, 428 US at 489–91.

The real problem with *Stone*, though, flows from its second justification. *Stone* also rests on the assumption that habeas review is not necessary to get state courts to follow the governing Fourth Amendment law—that habeas deterrence has no role to play in this area.[121] But there is no deterrence-based argument for treating Fourth Amendment claims any differently from anything else in constitutional criminal procedure. If state courts are good enough to "toe the constitutional mark" in search and seizure cases, they should be good enough to adhere to *Miranda* doctrine, the rules governing peremptory challenges, double jeopardy law, and so forth. Thus, *Stone* really implies that habeas review should be limited to claims of factual innocence. If *Stone* is right, then the second "track" of our proposal is wrong: no deterrence-based habeas review is justified.

This could be the right bottom line. Anyone familiar with state court criminal procedure decisions of the 1960s and the 1990s would have to conclude that a dramatic shift has taken place. The notion that state courts as a whole are strongly pro-government in criminal procedure disputes seemed plausible thirty years ago, but it is a hard sell today, at least based on our own reading of scattered state cases. There is no good evidence (and it is hard to see how one would go about really testing the point), but it seems more plausible to believe that state court criminal procedure errors are distributed about equally on both sides of the constitutional line.[122]

Even if these happy conclusions are correct, however, the case for habeas deterrence remains fairly powerful. Habeas need not deter only pro-government decision making in state courts as a whole; it is enough if even some state court systems regularly tend to favor prosecutors and the police in deciding criminal cases. Again, we are unaware of any evidence that might support a confident judgment in either direction.[123] But it seems like quite a leap to conclude that just because state courts in general have improved,

---

[121] Id at 492–94. In making this assumption, Justice Powell necessarily relied on his belief in the parity of state and federal courts. See id at 493 and n 35.

[122] Note that this argument is quite different from Justice Powell's argument for parity: state courts may well err more than federal courts, yet those errors may not be systematically biased in the government's favor.

[123] Perhaps the most noteworthy recent effort to study this question is Craig M. Bradley, *Are the State Courts Enforcing the Fourth Amendment?* 77 Georgetown L J 251 (1988). Serious methodological problems, however, inherently plague such efforts; almost inevitably, such studies wind up relying on largely subjective judgments.

no particular state court system requires the policing of federal habeas courts. And because "toeing the constitutional mark" is so important, the burden of persuasion on this issue should be on *Stone*—that is, it should be up to those who wish to do away with habeas deterrence to show (not simply assert) that such deterrence is no longer needed *anywhere*. Until the showing is made, we think skepticism is justified.

And skepticism is not, in the end, especially costly. Deterrence-based habeas review does not mean de novo review; our argument suggests that across-the-board "reasonableness" review, akin to qualified immunity doctrine (or to a broad reading of *Teague v Lane*), would be enough to keep state courts in line. And if state courts in fact do a good job of following the relevant constitutional rules, "reasonableness" review will mean little in practice; most state court decisions will be reasonable, and most defendants will lose on habeas, absent plausible innocence claims. In short, if *Stone*'s assumptions about both innocence and deterrence are right, then—under the two-track system we propose—it is redundant. If the assumptions are wrong, it is destructive. The system would work at least as well, and more simply, if *Stone* were abandoned.

B. PROCEDURAL DEFAULT

Habeas doctrine has no messier thicket than the law of defaulted claims. Thirty years ago, *Fay v Noia* held that a defendant who fails to raise a claim in his state trial could still raise the same claim on federal habeas, as long as the defendant (or his attorney—it was never quite clear which) did not "deliberately bypass" the state courts.[124] Sixteen years ago, *Wainwright v Sykes*[125] virtually did away with *Fay*, holding that a procedurally defaulted claim—that is, a claim not timely raised in state court—cannot be raised on federal court unless there was "cause" for the default and "prejudice" from failing to raise the claim. After a decade and a half of extensive litigation, "cause" has come to mean, roughly, ineffective assistance of counsel (defined as gross incompetence) or some serious misconduct by the state (such as active concealment of informa-

---

[124] See *Fay v Noia*, 372 US 391 (1963).

[125] 433 US 72 (1977).

tion that would have given rise to the claim).[126] There may or may not be other things that count as "cause." The definition of "prejudice" is also unclear, though it appears to mean something akin to a reasonable probability that, had the claim been timely raised, the outcome of the state proceeding would have been different.[127] Both "cause" and "prejudice" have been, and continue to be, the subject of enormous amounts of litigation. On top of this cumbersome structure, the Court has now placed the fundamental miscarriage of justice exception, which permits one who is probably innocent to avoid the cause and prejudice requirements.[128]

This set of rules has two major problems. First, it permits potentially grave injustices. Almost all procedural defaults are the result of defense attorney mistakes. The narrow definition of "cause," however, means that most such mistakes will not excuse the default; anything short of truly awful attorney behavior will not suffice. Thus, defendants are routinely penalized for their lawyers' errors. And this includes defendants who may well be, but cannot show that they probably are, innocent. Second, procedural default doctrine is a morass; it requires lawyers and judges to work through the equivalent of a law school exam every time a defendant seeks to raise a defaulted claim.[129]

Both problems are easily solved, simply by separating out cases where the petitioner has a plausible claim of innocence from cases where he does not. If a habeas petitioner can show a reasonable probability that his conviction was unjust—that he is innocent of the crime charged—we believe it is wrong to deny him relief solely because his lawyer mistakenly failed to raise a claim. In the balance between justice for the defendant and the state's interest in enforc-

---

[126] See *Murray v Carrier*, 477 US 478, 488 (1986) ("[W]e think that the existence of cause for a procedural default must ordinarily turn on whether the prisoner can show that some objective factor external to the defense impeded counsel's efforts to comply with the State's procedural rule"). On the difficulty of showing ineffective assistance, see, for example, *Burger v Kemp*, 483 US 776 (1987) (refusing to find ineffective assistance of counsel based on conflict of interest when two members of same law firm represented co-defendants in capital murder case).

[127] See John C. Jeffries, Jr. and William J. Stuntz, *Ineffective Assistance and Procedural Default in Federal Habeas Corpus*, 57 U Chi L Rev 679, 684–85 and n 25 (1990) (arguing that this is in fact the standard). The Court has never defined "prejudice" in procedural default cases, so the process of giving content to that standard involves a good deal of inference-drawing. See id.

[128] See *Murray v Carrier*, 477 US at 495–96.

[129] Jeffries and Stuntz, 57 U Chi L Rev at 690 (cited in note 127).

ing rules against defense lawyers, the state's interest is surely the weaker. Current law acknowledges this point in principle, with the fundamental miscarriage of justice exception, but that exception is too narrow to do any good. We would accordingly broaden it a notch. Once that is done, procedural defaults should be ignored in cases involving potential innocence. The "reasonable probability" standard takes care of prejudice, and "cause" should be irrelevant.[130]

On the other hand, if the defendant is not raising a potential innocence claim, there is no reason to exempt him from the default. In cases where innocence and guilt are not at stake, habeas's proper role is to ensure that state judges are doing a reasonably good job of deciding constitutional criminal procedure claims. But if the relevant constitutional claim was defaulted, the state court system did not decide it. (Under current law, if the claim has been decided on the merits, it is no longer treated as "defaulted."[131]) There is no state court mistake to deter. Both "cause" and "prejudice" can safely be ignored.

In other words, our proposed two-track habeas system would permit the virtual abolition of procedural default doctrine. "Cause" would always be irrelevant—in potential innocence cases, because the defendant would get relief without it; in all other cases, because relief would be denied regardless of it. "Prejudice" would continue to matter in cases involving innocence claims; in all other cases that inquiry too would go by the boards. The only remaining rule would be that state courts would have to fairly apply their procedural rules, something they must do under present law anyway.[132] The resulting regime would treat claims of real injustice more fairly, and would preserve deterrence of state court misbehavior. It would also get rid of the *Sykes* thicket.

C. RETROACTIVITY AND THE HABEAS STANDARD OF REVIEW

With the nationalization of criminal procedure law in the 1960s came a flood of new constitutional rules. Almost immediately, the Supreme Court began to wrestle with the question whether (and

---

[130] For a more extended version of the argument made in this paragraph, see id at 691–93.

[131] See *County Court of Ulster v Allen*, 442 US 140 (1979).

[132] See Daniel J. Meltzer, *State Court Forfeiture of Federal Rights*, 99 Harv L Rev 1128, 1137–45 (1986) (citing and categorizing federal court decisions holding various kinds of state procedural grounds inadequate to bar federal review).

if so, to what extent) those rules should be applied retroactively on habeas—that is, applied to cases originally decided in state court before the new rules existed.[133] The Court has not stopped wrestling with the issue since.

The latest and most controversial installment in the Court's retroactivity saga is the line of cases spawned by *Teague v Lane*.[134] The plurality in *Teague* (since adopted by several Court opinions) went a step beyond prior retroactivity analyses: *Teague* concluded not only that habeas courts generally may not *apply* new rules retroactively, but that habeas courts generally may not *create* new rules either.[135] This makes the definition of "new rules" enormously important. On that score, the Court has not spoken clearly. Two years ago a pair of majority opinions described a new rule as anything not "compelled" by existing precedent.[136] As one of us has pointed out, this definition would turn retroactivity doctrine into a relaxed habeas standard of review for purely legal issues: as long as the state court decision was reasonable given the then-existing federal law—that is, the contrary position was not compelled by precedent—it cannot be overturned on federal habeas.[137] Yet in *Wright v West*, several Justices heatedly denied that *Teague* established a habeas standard of review for questions of law;[138] moreover, the Court in *Wright* declined to adopt a rule of "deference" to reasonable state court decisions concerning mixed questions of law and fact.[139] So it remains unclear how "new rule" is to be defined.

Of all the Court's recent habeas initiatives, we think—unlike

---

[133] See, for example, *Linkletter v Walker*, 381 US 618 (1965) (retroactive application to habeas cases of *Mapp v Ohio*, 367 US 643 (1961)); *Tehan v United States ex rel Shott*, 382 US 406 (1966) (retroactive application to habeas cases of *Griffin v California*, 380 US 609 (1965)); *Johnson v New Jersey*, 384 US 719 (1966) (retroactive application to habeas cases of *Escobedo v Illinois*, 378 US 478 (1964), and *Miranda v Arizona*, 384 US 436 (1966)).

[134] 489 US 288 (1989).

[135] Id at 315–16. *Teague* has two exceptions—one for claims of substantive unconstitutionality, and the other for "watershed" rules of criminal procedure seriously implicating innocence. Id at 311–14. The second exception is unlikely ever to apply; the real "watershed" rules are already in place. And the first exception will only very rarely apply outside the death penalty context, the one context where substantive constitutional restraints are common.

[136] *Butler v McKellar*, 494 US 407 (1990); *Sawyer v Smith*, 497 US 227 (1990).

[137] Hoffmann, 1989 Supreme Court Review at 180–84 (cited in note 104).

[138] 112 S Ct at 2496–97 (O'Connor, joined by Blackmun and Stevens, concurring in the judgment); id at 2498–99 (Kennedy concurring in the judgment).

[139] The Court left this issue open, though four of the seven Justices who expressed a view about it were critical of the idea of "reasonableness" review for mixed questions.

almost everyone else who has written about it—that *Teague* is potentially the most useful. Its chief problem is that, as in the rest of habeas law, the Court does not distinguish in *Teague* between innocence-related and non-innocence-related claims. For innocence-related claims, we see no reason to apply *Teague*'s general rule of non-retroactivity at all. But for non-innocence-related claims, there is every reason to extend *Teague* to its logical conclusion and require habeas courts to look generally, not at whether the challenged state court decision was right, but at whether that decision was reasonable. Once the distinction is drawn between innocence- and non-innocence-related claims, in other words, *Teague* can be seen for what it really is: not a retroactivity decision, but rather a decision about the appropriate standard of review in habeas cases.[140]

We have already explained why *Teague* should not apply to the proposed first track of habeas. If a defendant can show a reasonable probability of innocence, plus a constitutional violation—under the law in effect at the time of the federal habeas decision—that should suffice to justify habeas relief. The "reasonableness" of the state court's decision is not particularly relevant, since the point of habeas relief in such a case would not be to deter state court mistakes but to rectify injustice. The point is the same as in the procedural default context: it seems wrong to uphold a conviction in the face of both unconstitutional conduct (under today's law) and a substantial likelihood of an unjust outcome, solely because the state court is not blameworthy.

Under the proposed second track of habeas, however, where the defendant's claim is not that his conviction is unjust, but that habeas relief is needed for deterrence, an across-the-board "reasonableness" standard of review is appropriate. If the entire point of the second track of habeas is deterrence, and if the deterrence message is aimed at state courts, then the "reasonableness" of the

---

[140] This is why *Teague* seems to be so out of step with the rest of the Court's recent retroactivity caselaw. Outside the habeas context, in both criminal and civil cases, the Court has made clear that its decisions must generally be applied fully retroactively. See, for example, *Griffith v Kentucky*, 479 US 314 (1987) (criminal case); *James B. Beam Distilling Co. v Georgia*, 111 S Ct 2439 (1991) (civil case); *Harper v Virginia Department of Taxation*, 113 S Ct 2510 (1993) (civil case).

One of us previously has expressed some concerns about *Teague*'s deferential standard of review. See Joseph L. Hoffmann, *Starting from Scratch: Rethinking Federal Habeas Review of Death Penalty Cases*, 20 Fla St U L Rev 133 (1992); Hoffmann, 1990 BYU L Rev 183 (cited in note 62); Hoffmann, 1989 Supreme Court Review 165 (cited in note 104). These concerns

state court decision is precisely what should matter to the habeas court. It makes no difference, for deterrence purposes, whether the relevant constitutional issue is characterized as purely legal, purely factual, or a mixed issue of law and fact. The "reasonableness" standard (which, by the way, is surely sufficiently malleable to ensure that habeas courts can establish whatever standard of care they deem appropriate with respect to state court adjudication of federal issues) works just as well for all three kinds of issues.

A "reasonableness" standard of review for all non-innocence-related claims would greatly simplify habeas law while expanding the ability of defendants to raise claims of individual injustice. Under current habeas doctrine, habeas courts must first categorize an issue as legal, factual, or mixed. Review is then highly deferential on factual issues (under the federal habeas statute, state court findings of fact are generally presumed correct if the court's procedures were fair);[141] de novo on mixed questions of law and fact;[142] and on legal issues, under *Teague*, apparently available only for unreasonable errors of law by state judges, although *Wright v West* suggests this standard may not always apply.[143] This convoluted construct is indefensible. A "reasonableness" standard of review for all non-innocence-related claims is both logically defensible and much simpler.

A system such as the one we propose would mean that some constitutional violations would go unremedied on habeas. State court decisions that are erroneous, but not unreasonably so, and that do not lead to the conviction of a potentially innocent defendant, would not be subject to reversal by a habeas court. This supposed problem has prompted much of the criticism of *Teague*.

---

seem, in retrospect, to relate primarily to the application of a *Teague*-like rule of deference to prior adjudication of innocence-related claims.

[141] 28 USC § 2254(d); *Sumner v Mata*, 449 US 539 (1981).

[142] *Miller v Fenton*, 474 US 104 (1985).

[143] Compare *Butler v McKellar*, 494 US 407, 414 (1990) ("The 'new rule' principle . . . validates reasonable, good faith interpretations of existing precedents made by state courts even though they are shown to be contrary to later decisions") with *Wright v West*, 112 S Ct 2482, 2497 (1992) (O'Connor concurring in the judgment) ("*Teague* requires courts to ask whether the rule a habeas petitioner seeks can be meaningfully distinguished from that established by binding precedent at the time his state court conviction became final. . . . Even though we have characterized the new rule inquiry as whether 'reasonable jurists' could disagree as to whether a result is dictated by precedent, . . . the standard for determining when a case establishes a new rule is 'objective,' and the mere existence of conflicting authority does not necessarily mean a rule is new").

But the criticism misperceives the nature of the constitutional violations—that is, it misperceives the nature of modern criminal procedure. Violations of constitutional criminal procedure rules can inflict serious injury or slight harm on criminal defendants; they can
be case-specific or structural; they can bear directly on whether
the right person was convicted or have nothing to do with the
accuracy of the guilty verdict. Criminal litigation is used to enforce
rules in all these categories. It is used to protect both individual
defendants and other constituencies, like potential jurors or innocent citizens who might be targets of police searches. What it means
to "remedy" a given violation should depend on such factors, and
on the procedural setting in which the issue arises.

To put it another way, every right deserves a remedy, but it is not
true that every violation deserves every possible remedy. Where the
interest in avoiding the conviction of innocents is directly at stake,
habeas relief is necessary to avoid injustice. Where that interest is not
directly at stake, habeas has no real compensatory role to play. And
a "reasonableness" standard of review fully satisfies the habeas deterrence interest. Finally, Section 1983 actions are still available to compensate injuries other than wrongful conviction.

For the past twenty years, the Supreme Court has been seeking
some doctrinal device for separating habeas claims worth hearing
from those not worth hearing. *Stone v Powell*, procedural default
doctrine, and *Teague* are all products of that search. *Teague* is far
preferable to the other two: unlike *Stone* it does not require categorization of rights in the abstract, and unlike procedural default doctrine it responds directly to the reasonableness of state court decision making. Moreover, given a separate track of de novo habeas
review for potential innocence claims, *Teague*'s "reasonableness"
standard of review renders the other two doctrines completely unnecessary. The real problem with *Teague* is that it does not go far
enough: because of the Court's unfortunate decision in *Wright v
West*, we have been left with a hodge-podge habeas standard of
review. *Teague* needs not to be abandoned (as the critics have
urged), but to be expanded.

IV. Habeas and the Death Penalty

Since the revival of capital punishment in the mid-1970s,
habeas has been the primary battleground for death penalty litigation. One commentator has estimated that habeas relief is granted

in almost half of all death penalty cases,[144] as compared to a minuscule success rate on habeas in non-capital cases.[145] In these circumstances, it would be unthinkable to propose a new way of thinking about habeas law without considering its impact on the administration of the death penalty.

Under our general approach, habeas law should apply to capital cases in a manner that reflects the nature of the underlying federal constitutional rights that are enforced in those cases. Because the federal constitutional rights that are unique to death penalty litigation (namely, most of the intricate substantive and procedural rights that the Court has derived from the Eighth Amendment) may substantially differ from the rights that exist in non-capital cases, habeas law should perhaps differ as well.

The difference does not come into play in cases involving habeas's deterrence role. In cases where the primary purpose of granting habeas relief is to deter state court mistakes, there is no reason to treat the Eighth Amendment any differently from the Fourth, Fifth, or Sixth Amendments. If a state court acts unreasonably in construing or applying the Eighth Amendment in a capital case, habeas relief should be available. If the state court acts reasonably in interpreting and applying the relevant federal law, habeas relief should (to the extent deterrence alone is at stake) be denied.

The problem with death penalty cases is the difficulty of applying the concept of "innocence" to capital sentencing. The Court's modern Eighth Amendment law, and the fundamental values and concerns on which that law is based, clearly contemplate a notion of substantive justice in capital sentencing that extends well beyond the protection of defendants who are innocent of capital murder.[146] But how much further does this concept of substantive justice in capital sentencing extend? What is the analogue, in

---

[144] Professor James Liebman has determined that, between 1976 and 1985, the overall success rate for death penalty petitioners in habeas was 49 percent. See Liebman, *Federal Habeas Corpus* at 23–24 n 97 (cited in note 5).

[145] Professor Liebman notes that, in fiscal year 1985, only 1.2% of all habeas petitions decided by the federal district courts even received a hearing before final disposition, and only 15% of appealed habeas cases resulted in reversals or remands of the district court's disposition. Id.

[146] See, for example, *Lockett v Ohio*, 438 US 586 (1978) (recognizing constitutional right to present mitigating evidence, based on need for individualized sentencing to consider, inter alia, personal moral culpability of defendant); *Enmund v Florida*, 458 US 782 (1982), and *Tison v Arizona*, 481 US 137 (1987) (establishing minimum constitutional requirements of personal moral culpability for imposition of death penalty on non-triggerman felony murderer).

capital sentencing, of a defendant's claim that he is innocent of the crime?

The Supreme Court faced this problem in *Sawyer v Whitley*.[147] *Whitley* involved the scope of the "fundamental miscarriage of justice" exception to the procedural default/successive petition/abuse of the writ bars to habeas relief.[148] The specific question was, what kinds of capital defendants should be able to use this exception when challenging errors in capital sentencing proceedings? Only those defendants who claim to be innocent of their capital crime? Those who claim to be "innocent" of the aggravating circumstances that made them death-eligible? Those who contend that their death sentences are undeserved, despite their factual guilt? Or those who complain that, though they may deserve to die for their crimes in the abstract, other defendants of equal or greater culpability have not been sentenced to death?

In *Whitley*, the Court held that "fundamental miscarriage of justice," in the context of capital sentencing, requires a showing by clear and convincing evidence that no reasonable juror would find the existence of an aggravating circumstance that would render the defendant death-eligible. The Court concluded that any less stringent standard would be too subjective and would seriously undermine the cause-and-prejudice standard for procedural default by allowing capital defendants to obtain habeas relief upon a showing of "prejudice," whether or not they could show "cause" for the default.[149]

Whether one agrees with the Court's particular resolution of the "innocence" issue in *Whitley* will depend on one's own views about the administration of the death penalty. Some would argue that there is nothing seriously wrong with executing any defendant who commits a capital crime and also meets basic statutory requirements of aggravation that justify, in general, the imposition of the death penalty.[150] According to this position, the overriding concern

---

[147] 112 S Ct 2514 (1992).

[148] See *Murray v Carrier*, 477 US 478 (1986) (applying "fundamental miscarriage of justice" exception to procedural default rule of *Wainwright v Sykes*, 433 US 72 (1977)); *Kuhlmann v Wilson*, 477 US 436 (1986) (applying exception to successive petition rule); *McCleskey v Zant*, 111 S Ct 1454 (1991) (applying exception to abuse-of-the-writ rule).

[149] *Whitley*, 112 S Ct at 2521–25 and n 13.

[150] See, for example, Ernest van den Haag, *The Collapse of the Case Against Capital Punishment*, National Review (March 31, 1978), at 397 ("The Constitution, though it enjoins us to minimize capriciousness, does not enjoin a standard of unattainable perfection or exclude penalties because that standard has not been attained").

in administering a death penalty system is preventing the execution of a defendant who is *ineligible* to receive a death sentence. Beyond such eligibility concerns, some imprecision in actually meting out capital punishment to defendants is probably inevitable and generally morally acceptable.

Others would contend, however, that capital punishment must be reserved for those defendants who are truly the most deserving of death—and that even defendants who have committed aggravated capital crimes may properly claim injustice if they are given death sentences when others of equal or greater culpability receive prison terms.[151] On this argument, the death penalty cannot be imposed in a morally acceptable fashion unless a precise "fit" is achieved between those defendants who most deserve it and those who actually receive it.

Without trying to resolve this moral debate, we believe that our approach to habeas offers the best route to a solution. Whatever ultimately emerges as the most appropriate definition of "injustice" in capital sentencing—whatever turns out to be the most appropriate analogue in capital sentencing to a defendant's claim of innocence of a crime—should become an additional avenue for obtaining de novo review on federal habeas. If a capital defendant can combine an asserted federal constitutional violation with a sufficiently substantial allegation of "injustice" in capital sentencing (however that term may ultimately be defined), the habeas court should provide de novo review of the defendant's federal claim.[152]

In other words, habeas doctrine for capital cases should depend on the substantive goals of the constitutional criminal procedure rules that govern those cases. The goals themselves, and their proper relationship to just outcomes, are in dispute. But that dis-

---

[151] See, for example, Nathanson, *An Eye for an Eye?: The Morality of Punishing by Death* 62 (1987) ("If death is arbitrarily imposed on only some who deserve it, while others equally deserving are treated more leniently, then those who are executed are treated unjustly, even if they deserved to die").

[152] By analogy to non-capital cases, a capital defendant should be entitled to de novo habeas review of his constitutional claims upon a showing of a "reasonable probability" that an "injustice" (however that term may be defined) has occurred in his capital sentencing.

In addition, we reiterate here our view that a "naked" innocence claim of the sort presented to the Court in *Herrera v Collins*, 113 S Ct 853 (1993), if supported by a sufficiently strong showing of potential innocence (even stronger than a "reasonable probability of innocence"), warrants habeas relief in a non-capital case under substantive due process. By analogy, a capital defendant should be entitled to habeas relief upon a similarly strong showing of a potential "injustice" (however that term may be defined) in his capital sentencing. This result could be based on either the Due Process Clause or the Eighth Amendment.

pute ought to be addressed directly, not fought out through the proxy of habeas doctrine.

On the other side of the coin, habeas doctrine for non-capital cases should not be held hostage to disputes about the death penalty. As one of us recently argued,[153] battles over capital punishment have for too long distorted habeas doctrine ostensibly designed for all criminal cases. Unlike the Court, we see no reason to assume that the same habeas rules should govern both capital and non-capital cases. Just as innocence claims should, in our view, be treated differently under habeas law than non-innocence claims, so too should the special nature of substantive justice in capital sentencing give rise to a special way of obtaining de novo habeas review, and potential habeas relief.

V. Conclusion

The current debate about habeas is sterile. Judicial opinions and law review articles expound on the importance of federalism and federal rights, and debate the meaning of decades-old Supreme Court habeas decisions. But habeas is part of a criminal justice system in which federalism died a generation ago, when the Court nationalized the law of criminal procedure. In this system, as a practical matter, *all* criminal procedure rights are federal rights, and those federal rights are enforced routinely in state courts. In this system, there is no need to allocate power between state and federal spheres of sovereignty, because state law's sphere of sovereignty no longer exists. And the federal law that governs this system has changed so dramatically that forty-year-old Supreme Court habeas decisions might as well have come from another planet.

It is time to change the terms of the discussion. Habeas review can play several useful roles in the criminal justice system, but we can identify and implement those roles only if we start seeing habeas as a part of criminal procedure, rather than as simply a weapon in a battle between federal and state law. Seen as a part of criminal procedure, habeas can advance individual justice by giving special

---

[153] See Joseph L. Hoffmann, *Is Innocence Sufficient? An Essay on the U.S. Supreme Court's Continuing Problems with Federal Habeas Corpus and the Death Penalty*, 68 Ind L J 817 (1993); Hoffmann, 20 Fla St U L Rev 133 (cited in note 140).

status to constitutional rights coupled with substantial claims of innocence. Habeas review can also help ensure that the law of criminal procedure is obeyed by state and local actors, by overturning unreasonable interpretations and applications of that law by state judges. And habeas can do these things while still giving federal courts sufficient opportunities for federal lawmaking, at least in the context of a system where, in many areas, well-developed bodies of law already exist.

We propose two critical changes. The first is the realization that habeas need not operate on the principle that "one size fits all." Habeas is a remedy, and most remedies properly take account of the nature and magnitude of the wrong. In this context, that means treating innocence-related claims differently from other claims, a result that follows naturally from the fact that habeas is part of a system whose chief goal is to separate the innocent from the guilty. Habeas can provide a significant layer of protection for innocent defendants, but only if innocence-related claims are freed from the restrictions of the procedural default and habeas retroactivity doctrines.

The second is the recognition of the great opportunity presented by *Teague*. Though no recent habeas decision has received more criticism than *Teague*, it actually offers a way out of the habeas swamp: if followed to its logical conclusion, *Teague* could quickly lead to the establishment of a general habeas standard of review—for non-innocence-related claims—that would eliminate the need for *Stone v Powell*, procedural default doctrine, and even a separate habeas retroactivity doctrine. *Teague* offers the potential to untie all of these knots because, unlike *Stone v Powell*, *Wainwright v Sykes*, and all previous attempts to separate new rules from old ones, *Teague* focuses directly on the reasonableness of state court decision making. This is precisely the right focus for habeas in its deterrence role.

Protecting innocence, deterring unreasonable state court decision making, and providing sufficient opportunities for federal lawmaking—these are the goals that modern habeas law should strive to achieve. If we cast aside the debate about federalism, comity, the right to a federal forum, and the parity of state and federal courts, we can do a much better job of reaching these goals.

REBECCA L. BROWN

WHEN POLITICAL QUESTIONS AFFECT INDIVIDUAL RIGHTS: THE OTHER NIXON v UNITED STATES

The Supreme Court has banished another term from the Constitution to the twilight. The word "try" now lurks in the shadowy corner of the Court's separation-of-powers jurisprudence among a murky cluster of issues known as political questions. Like "war,"[1] "governing,"[2] and "republican,"[3] but unlike "legislative,"[4] "commerce,"[5] and "treaties,"[6] it will remain in the shadows, uninterpreted and unenforced in the judicial branch of the United States.

In *Nixon v United States*,[7] the Court chose not to illuminate this shadowy realm. Rather, it relied on a fairly mechanical political-

---

Rebecca L. Brown is Associate Professor of Law, Vanderbilt University.

AUTHOR'S NOTE: I am grateful to Barry Friedman, Robert K. Rasmussen, and Nicholas S. Zeppos for very helpful comments and discussions on the ideas in this paper.

[1] US Const, Art I, § 8, cl 11; see *Atlee v Laird*, 347 F Supp 689, 705 (ED Pa 1972) (three-judge court) (whether United States was at "war" in Southeast Asia presented nonjusticiable political question), aff'd, 411 US 911 (1973).

[2] US Const, Art I, § 8, cl 16; see *Gilligan v Morgan*, 413 US 1, 6 (1973) (organization of militia committed to Congress and beyond judicial review).

[3] US Const, Art IV, § 4; see *Luther v Borden*, 7 How (48 US) 1 (1849) (declining to resolve whether a state government is republican in form).

[4] US Const, Art I, § 1; see *INS v Chadha*, 462 US 919, 952 (1983) (defining constitutional meaning of "legislative power").

[5] US Const, Art I, § 8, cl 3; see, for examples, *Gibbons v Ogden*, 9 Wheat (22 US) 1 (1824) (defining commerce).

[6] US Const, Art II, § 2, cl 2; see *United States v Curtiss-Wright Export Corp.*, 299 US 304 (1936) (interpreting President's power to make treaties with the advice and consent of the Senate).

[7] 113 S Ct 732 (1993).

question test to determine an issue of justiciability without considering the consequences—either those involving the separation of powers or those related to individual rights. As a result, we now know that the courts will not review the adequacy of procedures used by the Senate in performing its constitutional function of "try"-ing impeachments, but we have no better understanding of why such a result serves the underlying objectives of the constitutional scheme.

In the narrow view, the holding of *Nixon* will have little effect on the political landscape of the future. Surely it is unlikely that the Senate will someday go on a rampage and seek to purge the ranks of judges and executive officials on invidious grounds or to determine their guilt by flipping a coin, employing thumb screws to extract confessions, or delegating the impeachment decision to a trial by ordeal. Thus, the question may fairly be asked: "So what if the Court closed the door to these unlikely claims?" What, after all, is the real difference between the majority's resolution of *Nixon*, which denies judicial review of Senate impeachment procedures altogether, and Justice White's approach in concurrence, which would have the courts review the procedures but then grant broad discretion to the Senate on defining the contours of permissible impeachment process?

The answer is that the difference is huge in terms of the vision that each expresses regarding the separation of powers. First, even from a pragmatic point of view, it is surely preferable to have a judiciary functioning appropriately in the constitutional system, rather than stumbling onto right answers most of the time by instinct or fortuity. There is no "safe" course for the Court in these cases: either it exercises its jurisdiction over the constitutional question or it does not. Either way, if it is wrong, it has done damage to the separation of powers. But the more substantive concern here is that the interest of an individual public official being tried under a bill of impeachment is not the only concern implicated in the *Nixon* case. At stake also is the Court's understanding of its own role with respect to its coordinate branches and its own obligation to protect individual rights. It is worth considering, then, whether there is a better way to understand the issue presented in *Nixon*, both in its own right and as a model for a broader group of cases involving judicial review of the actions of the political branches of government.

In this article, I suggest that there is a better way, a way that takes into account the purposes of separated powers and the consequences of identifying political questions in areas potentially involving individual rights. The Court would have more faithfully effectuated the constitutional design by permitting judicial review of the Senate action, even while perhaps granting substantial deference on the merits. The case does, in fact, raise an important question involving the conception of judicial review: the Court's approach demonstrates a troubling contempt for the place of judicial review in the constitutional system which, as a theoretical matter, is not confined to the relatively esoteric issue involved in this case.

If one accepts judicial review of legislative and executive acts as a norm in maintaining checks and balances, then one should also permit courts to entertain the constitutional challenge raised in *Nixon*—not merely to protect the procedural rights of the public official being tried, but more importantly to oversee the protection of judicial independence generally, and thus to serve the cause of individual rights as a systemic matter. In fact, the political-question doctrine itself—never really a doctrine in any meaningful sense—would be better abandoned at this point as a thorn in the side of separated powers, properly understood. The interests that such a doctrine might or should serve, such as judicial respect for the processes of the coordinate branches and efficient use of judicial capital, can be protected adequately by thoughtful adherence to the principles of standing.

I. THE NIXON DECISION

Former District Judge Walter L. Nixon sought to void his impeachment conviction on the ground that the Senate's reliance on a committee to receive and sift evidence for the entire Senate violated its constitutional duty to "try" all impeachments.[8] The committee, after hearing the testimony of ten witnesses, presented the full Senate with a transcript and a report that evaluated the evidence, reached conclusions on disputed issues of fact, and recommended Nixon's conviction. The full Senate received briefs and heard arguments from both sides, as well as a personal appeal by

---

[8] US Const, Art I, § 3, cl 6.

Nixon, but it did not hear any testimony.[9] At trial, Nixon showed that on one of the two counts on which he had been convicted, the committee had voted to convict by less that a two-thirds majority, and he argued (among other things) that had all of the Senators heard the evidence directly, the Senate might also have failed to convict by two-thirds, as required by the Constitution.[10] Briefly described, the Supreme Court's chain of reasoning went as follows: A controversy is nonjusticiable if the matter at issue is textually committed to another branch of government. The Constitution grants to the Senate "the sole Power to try all Impeachments."[11] "Sole" suggests that the power to try is committed to the Senate; and, in any event, "try" does not impose enforceable limits on the Senate's discretion. Therefore, the question whether the Senate breached its duty to "try" Nixon is a nonjusticiable political question. That is, the Court will not consider any case presenting an issue about whether the procedures used during an impeachment trial comported with any standard of adequacy associated with notions of what constitutes a "trial."

The court also offered a bit of embellishment from history, as it likes to do wherever possible[12]—historical evidence which apparently did not inform, but perhaps gave the comfort of validation to, the decision. Although all agreed that there were simply no historical data relating to the issue in the case, namely, whether courts should review impeachment procedures,[13] the Court nevertheless looked to the next best thing, historical evidence regarding the impeachment power itself. This inquiry led to the uncontroversial conclusion that the power of impeachment was designed as a check on the judiciary. But allowing judicial review of the Senate's impeachment procedures, the Court asserted, "would place final reviewing authority with respect to impeachments in the hands of the same body that the impeachment process is meant to regulate,"[14] and thus "would remove the only check placed on the Judi-

---

[9] 113 S Ct at 735.

[10] *Nixon v United States*, 744 F Supp 9, 11 (DDC 1990).

[11] Id.

[12] Rebecca L. Brown, *Tradition and Insight*, 103 Yale L J 177 (1993) (discussing Court's use of history).

[13] 113 S Ct at 737.

[14] Id at 739.

cial Branch by the Framers."[15] Because judges are potential targets of impeachment,[16] judicial "involvement in impeachment proceedings"[17] would "eviscerate the 'important constitutional check' placed on the Judiciary by the Framers."[18]

This conclusion works logically only if one grants to the Court a significant assumption: that judicial review of procedures is equivalent to judicial determination of outcome. Each step of the Court's analysis rests on that very critical assumption. The assumption is manifest in the Court's cramped interpretation of the term "sole": The Court took pains to point out that "[t]he common sense meaning of the word 'sole' is that the Senate alone shall have authority to determine whether an individual should be acquitted or convicted."[19] Whatever the theoretical value of a "common sense meaning" in the abstract,[20] this particular exercise in common sense propounds a relatively unexceptionable statement—but one that is irrelevant to the issue presented in the case. No one had asked the Court, instead of or in addition to the Senate, to decide whether Judge Nixon should be acquitted or convicted. But rather than precluding judicial review, the word "sole" might much more sensibly be read to distinguish between the two Houses of Congress:[21] ordinarily they act together in performing their constitutional functions, but in the case of impeachment one has the extraordinary "sole" power to bring a bill of impeachment,[22] and the other the "sole" power to conduct the trial.[23] The Court, even in its textualist quest for the meaning of "sole," ignored this symmetry in the constitutional language.

This "common sense meaning" of "sole" was then fortified with

---

[15] Id at 739 n 2.

[16] Federalist 79 (Hamilton), in Jacob E. Cooke, ed, *The Federalist* 532–33 (1961).

[17] 113 S Ct at 739.

[18] Id (quoting Federalist 81).

[19] Id at 736.

[20] See Nicholas S. Zeppos, *Legislative History and the Interpretation of Statutes: Toward a Fact-Finding Model of Statutory Interpretation*, 76 Va L Rev 1295, 1324 (1990) (suggesting pitfalls of common-sense reading of statutes, based on one court's assumption that a given reading of a statute presented a "metaphysical impossibility," while another court had read it exactly that way).

[21] See 113 S Ct at 742 (White concurring in judgment).

[22] US Const, Art I, § 2, cl 5.

[23] US Const, Art I, § 3, cl 6.

a fourth-tier definition from a 1971 dictionary: " 'functioning . . . independently and without assistance or interference.' "[24] "If the courts may review the actions of the Senate in order to determine whether that body 'tried' an impeached official, it is difficult to see how the Senate would be 'functioning . . . independently and without assistance or interference,' " the Court reasoned. (The quoted—now apparently dispositive—text is from the dictionary.) But judicial review to ensure a constitutional minimum of procedural requirements would still leave the Senate free to function as described. The Court simply proceeded on the unarticulated assumption that review of procedures is equivalent to a decision on the merits.

The assumption emerged for a fourth time in the opinion when the Court noted the historical evidence regarding why the Framers had not originally chosen the judiciary, instead of the Senate, to try impeachments. First, the judiciary in general would likely be involved in criminal proceedings arising out of the same charges that support the impeachment. Thus, the question arose for the Framers, "Would it be proper that the persons, who had disposed of his fame and his most valuable rights as a citizen in one trial, should in another trial, for the same offence be also the disposers of his life and his fortune?"[25] The Framers expressed some fear, consequently, that "the strong bias of one decision would be apt to overrule the influence of any new lights, which might be brought to vary the complexion of another decision."[26] The Court extrapolated that "[c]ertainly judicial review of the Senate's 'trial' would introduce the same risk of bias as would participation in the trial itself."[27] This conclusion makes sense only if one assumes that review of procedures is equivalent to making the ultimate decision on the merits. If there is truth to the assumption that drives the entire opinion, then review is properly denied, for of course the Court does not have the power to impeach its own members. And so the Court held.

---

[24] 113 S Ct at 736 (quoting *Webster's Third New International Dictionary* 2168 (1971)). See Zeppos, 76 Va L Rev at 1320–21 (cited in note 20) (discussing use of dictionaries to interpret statutes).

[25] Federalist 65 (Hamilton), in Jacob E. Cooke, ed, *The Federalist* 442 (1961).

[26] Id.

[27] 113 S Ct at 738.

The assumption that provides the necessary logical premise to each of the steps in the Court's analysis is antithetical to the system of separated powers and checks and balances embodied in the Constitution. It posits that when a court reviews the exercise of a power vested in one of the other branches, and evaluates that exercise for conformity with the requirements contained in the Constitution, the court is, in effect, exercising the power itself. In *Nixon*, that means that by reviewing the procedures used in convicting Walter Nixon, the Court would be effectively convicting Nixon itself.

A moment's thought reveals how implausible this claim is. When the Congress exercises its power to regulate commerce and passes a statute, say, outlawing race discrimination in public accommodations, which the Court reviews to determine whether it is, in fact, a regulation of commerce,[28] the *Nixon* assumption would suggest that the Court had exercised the legislative power to regulate commerce. When the Court considers whether an executive ban on drafting women violates the Fifth Amendment,[29] the *Nixon* assumption would suggest that the Court had acted as Commander in Chief. And so on. Were that suggestion to be embraced as a theory driving all of constitutional law, there could be no such thing as judicial review.

Admittedly, I have carried the Court's analysis to the limits of its logic, which perhaps exaggerates its intended meaning or consequences. At face value, it is fair to say that the Court's analysis does depend, implicitly, on an equation of judicial review with the exercise of the powers being reviewed, and thus casts doubt on the place of judicial review. Surely the Court did not mean to embark on a sinister attack on judicial review. It is much more likely that the rhetoric in the opinion, which tends to operate at a level of absolutes, flows from some unspoken sense that review of procedures does carry with it the power, and perhaps even the temptation, to shape outcome.

This is a legitimate concern. One can easily imagine instances in which a court may use procedural rules to promote its view of a preferred outcome. But that risk is one which is taken in many areas of the law. An appellate court reviewing a case in which a jury has reached a verdict is supposed to confine itself to examining

---

[28] See *Katzenbach v McClung*, 379 US 294 (1964).

[29] Compare *Rostker v Goldberg*, 453 US 57 (1981) (reviewing statute and executive policy).

factors that may have improperly influenced the jury, without ever placing itself in the position of a thirteenth juror. A federal court looks at the way in which an administrative agency exercised its statutory authority, without ever exercising that authority itself.[30] Courts decide whether procedures followed by federal and state bureaucracies are adequate under the Due Process Clause without, in most cases at least, second-guessing the merits of the particular decision. These are but a few examples of the judicial system's entrenched belief in a workable distinction between review of procedure and review of substance. There is, of course, always a danger that review of procedure will be used as a cover for reviewing the substantive determination,[31] but many bodies of existing law and practice are premised on the assumption that this does not happen routinely. And this assumption comports with a long- and deeply-held cultural commitment in this country to values of process as distinct from, and in some cases even more important than, result.[32]

An interesting question, then, is why Chief Justice Rehnquist should suddenly, but tacitly, question the legitimacy of this practice solely as it affects the judiciary's review of Senate impeachment procedures.[33] I can offer two possible answers to that question.

[30] See, for example, *Lincoln v Vigil*, 113 S Ct 2024 (1993) (holding that disputed matter was committed to agency discretion and thus unreviewable, but nevertheless considering and deciding separate issue of adequacy of agency's procedures in reaching decision); *Motor Vehicle Mfg. Ass'n. v State Farm Mutual Automobile Ins. Co.*, 463 US 29, 42–43 (1983) (agency action requires rational explanation; if agency failed to provide one, court will remand for reconsideration).

[31] The conflict is illustrated quite well by *Hampton v Mow Sun Wong*, 426 US 88, 114–17 (1976), in which Justice Stevens, for the Court, avoided a substantive equal-protection analysis, on the question whether aliens may be excluded from holding government jobs, by determining that the rule so providing had been promulgated by the wrong body and thus violated some due-process constraints. Justice Rehnquist, in dissent, saw the majority's procedural approach as a pretext for departing from settled law on the merits. See also *Vermont Yankee Nuclear Power Corp. v NRDC*, 435 US 519, 557–58 (1978).

[32] See Cass R. Sunstein, *Beyond the Republican Revival*, 97 Yale L J 1539, 1549–50 (1988) (discussing value of deliberation in political sphere); Robert K. Rasmussen, *Bankruptcy and the Administrative State*, 42 Hast L J 1567, 1578 (1991) ("Rather than focusing on the results of administrative decisionmaking, administrative law examines the process by which agencies reach their results and the deference this process should receive in the courts."); Cass R. Sunstein, *Factions, Self-Interest, and the APA: Four Lessons Since 1946*, 72 Va L Rev 271, 272 (1986).

[33] This is particularly curious in light of the fact that what the Court *did* do in this case—decide that the adequacy of Senate impeachment procedures is a nonjusticiable political question—may fairly be characterized as a decision on the merits as well. As Professor Henkin has made clear, the political- question determination itself is often inseparable from the merits. See Louis Henkin, *Is There a "Political Question" Doctrine?* 85 Yale L J 597 (1976).

First, it may be that he really was not concerned at all with the danger of judicial interference with impeachment. This would explain why he did not engage in any consideration of how great the danger would be, how one would identify the risks involved, and whether the risk was in some way compensated by corresponding benefits. Perhaps the Court was concerned about the appearance, in a world in which the judiciary is viewed as having a great deal of power, of its taking on the role of final arbiter of the fate of its own members. Perhaps it assumed that the distinction between review of substance and review of procedure would be lost on the general public, who would see, simply, headlines reading, "Supreme Court Orders Crooked Judge's Return to Bench" or the like.

A second possibility is that the Court saw no threat to individual rights in the facts of this case. Judge Nixon himself did not present a sympathetic portrait, having been convicted of taking bribes and having insisted on drawing his federal salary even while in jail for corruption. The Senate's vote to convict him seemed neither unexpected nor unfair. This case carried no overtones of racism or other invidious motivations either for the impeachment or for the underlying criminal conviction. A different picture might have been presented if the case to reach the Supreme Court had instead been that involving Alcee Hastings, a judge who alleged racist motivations for his prosecution,[34] and who was acquitted of the criminal charges brought against him,[35] but was nonetheless impeached by Congress.[36] As I discuss below, the Supreme Court has been quite consistent in preserving judicial review in situations in which there is a clear threat to an individual right, but in this case perhaps the Court perceived no such concern.

And so, it seems, the Court wrote an opinion which, if taken at face value, would call into question the entire system of judicial

---

In the *Nixon* case this is especially true. A significant portion of the opinion is devoted to rejecting, on the merits, the petitioner's argument on why he should have received better procedures in the Senate—all the while holding that the matter is nonjusticiable. See 112 S Ct at 736 ("[t]here are several difficulties with this position which lead us ultimately to reject it.").

[34] See Judith Resnik, *Housekeeping: The Nature and Allocation of Work in Federal Trial Courts*, 24 Ga L Rev 909, 951 n 164 (1990) (quoting from John P. MacKenzie, *The Virtue of Impeachment*, NY Times (July 28, 1988, at A26 col 1)).

[35] *United States v Hastings*, No 81-596 (SD Fla Feb 4, 1983).

[36] *Hastings v United States*, 802 F Supp 490 (DDC 1992), vacated and remanded, 988 F 2d 1280 (DC Cir 1993).

review. Obviously the Court is not laying a foundation for the elimination of judicial review, but I do think the *Nixon* opinion reflects what may be an unacknowledged contempt for judicial review, a contempt that results in the treatment of issues involving the role of the courts, through the political-question doctrine and otherwise,[37] in mechanical ways. This trend, if indeed it is a trend, threatens the separation of powers by remaining heedless of its underlying goal of protecting individual rights. Thus, what started out as a genuine effort, in *Baker v Carr*,[38] to reconcile the array of situations in which the Court had felt the need to exercise its "passive virtues"[39] with a fidelity to the protection of individual rights, has become more formalistic and less sensitive to that concern.

II. Separated Powers, Ordered Liberty, and Impeachment

In *Nixon*, the Court did not give a clue as to its real concern or the purpose of its inquiry; it delved immediately into the test for political questions articulated in *Baker v Carr* and began applying its terms.[40] Once satisfied that the test had been applied, the Court stopped, uncharacteristically brief in its disposition of a constitutional issue. Although we do not know, consequently, what the majority saw as the overarching objectives of its holding, it seems fair to say that the Court must have been motivated, at least in large part, by a desire to accord appropriate deference to Congress: the principal focus of the opinion was the danger of undermining a "textually demonstrable commitment to a coordinate branch," which has as its root a concern for comity among the branches.[41] And, indeed, although the scholarly literature devoted to the political-question doctrine over the years is far from homoge-

---

[37] See Cass R. Sunstein, *What's Standing After Lujan? Of Citizen Suits, "Injuries," and Article III*, 91 Mich L Rev 163 (1992).

[38] 369 US 186 (1962).

[39] Alexander M. Bickel, *The Least Dangerous Branch* 69–71 (2d ed 1986); see also Alexander M. Bickel, *Foreword: The Passive Virtues*, 75 Harv L Rev 40 (1961).

[40] 113 S Ct at 735.

[41] See id at 740 (Stevens concurring) (emphasizing need for respect for coordinate branches); id at 747–48 (Souter concurring in judgment) (political-question doctrine is essentially a function of separation of powers and designed to avoid unnecessary interference with political departments).

neous,[42] the one point of agreement among most authors seems to be that if there is a justification for the doctrine, it is the maintenance of proper balance among the separated powers of government.[43] Thus, the *Nixon* case presented an opportunity for the Court to think seriously about the separation of powers, invoking rich and compelling judicial and political traditions in an effort to resolve the conflicting policies that inevitably emerge in a case like this one.

Just as the political-question doctrine is, at bottom, a device designed to effectuate the separation of powers, the separation of powers is, in turn, a device intended to preserve individual liberty, avoid tyrannical concentration of power, and thus protect the rights of individuals from unwarranted interference by the government.[44] The formal structures housed in the Constitution provide an effective vehicle for achieving that end.[45] When contemplating a decision that requires drawing lines with respect to those separated powers, however, it is not enough for a court merely to employ those formal structures at their most superficial level, not considering what achieves the consequences most consonant with the objectives for which the structures were devised in the first instance. This approach, while advocated by some,[46] can lead to an utter evisceration of the very protections that the formal structures of the Constitution were designed to achieve.

The issue in *Nixon*, appropriately fleshed out to reflect the constitutional concerns, is whether the separation of powers, including its animating principle of protection of individual rights, supports

---

[42] See, for example, Gerald Gunther, *The Subtle Vices of the "Passive Virtues"—a Comment on Principle and Expediency in Judicial Review*, 64 Colum L Rev 1 (1964); Louis Henkin, *Is There a "Political Question" Doctrine?* 85 Yale L J 597 (1976); J. Peter Mulhern, *In Defense of the Political Question Doctrine*, 137 U Pa L Rev 97 (1988); Henry P. Monaghan, *Constitutional Adjudication: The Who and When*, 82 Yale L J 1363 (1973); Martin H. Redish, *Judicial Review and the "Political Question,"* 79 Nw U L Rev 1031 (1984–85).

[43] See, for example, Fritz W. Scharpf, *Judicial Review and the Political Question: A Functional Analysis*, 75 Yale L J 517, 538 (1966) (describing Court's view); Michael E. Tigar, *Judicial Power, The "Political Question Doctrine," and Foreign Relations*, 17 UCLA L Rev 1135, 1163 (1970); J. Peter Mulhern, 137 U Pa L Rev at 124–27 (cited in note 42).

[44] See Rebecca L. Brown, *Separated Powers and Ordered Liberty*, 139 U Pa L Rev 1513 (1991).

[45] See Martin H. Redish and Elizabeth J. Cisar, *"If Angels Were to Govern": The Need for Pragmatic Formalism in Separation of Powers Theory*, 41 Duke L J 449 (1991).

[46] See id; *Morrison v Olson*, 487 US 654 (1988) (Scalia dissenting) (criticizing Court's replacement of a "clear constitutional prescription" with a "balancing test").

a decision to preclude the Court from adjudicating whether the Senate "tried" Walter Nixon within the meaning of the Constitution. The way to approach questions involving the separation of powers is to consider explicitly the ramifications for the rights of individuals and to resolve the interpretive issue in the way most conducive to providing protections for those rights.[47]

An obvious argument in the *Nixon* case is that the public official being impeached has a personal interest in ensuring that the procedures used by the Senate to impeach are fair. Judicial review can be expected to increase the fairness and accuracy of the proceedings, and consequently it is consistent with the individual's interest to have the added protection offered by judicial review. Treating the targeted public official like any other individual target of adverse government action in that way, the individual-liberty model of separation-of-powers analysis might suggest that courts should provide judicial review of the Senate's procedures to protect the individual interest of the target and increase the accuracy of any determination made in the impeachment proceeding. Thus, the argument would go, consideration of the separation-of-powers issue with individual rights in mind requires judicial review.

But this solution may be a bit too glib. While it is true that the public official (here a judge) is an individual and is being singled out for subjection to the powers of the government, it is not necessarily true that the core purpose of the separation of powers—the protection of liberty—extends to the jobs of public officials accused of official misconduct in the same way that it encompasses attempted deprivations of private individuals' liberty. Public officials should in general to be subjected to political scrutiny whenever possible and forced to account to the public for decisions rendered in office—that much is clear from the tone of the Federalists and the language of the Constitution itself.[48] Impeachment is peculiarly designed to bring about that kind of accountability through the actions of the political departments of government, the House and the Senate. Moreover, the charging body's only goal in an impeachment is to remove the official from office; the Constitution explicitly ensures that impeachment will not result in the deprivation otherwise of any personal rights of the official as a private citizen.[49]

---

[47] I defend this position at length in Brown, 139 U Pa L Rev at 1557–58 (cited in note 44).

[48] Federalist 51 (Madison), in Jacob Cooke, ed, *The Federalist* 349–51 (1961).

[49] US Const, Art I, § 3, cl 7.

When evaluating the separation-of-powers issue, namely, the availability of judicial review, from the perspective of its effect on individual rights, it is not clear that the rights of the impeached official raise the concerns that I have argued are the underlying rationale for separated powers. It might be a mistake to assume that because the matter involves interests that under some circumstances give rise to procedural due process protections, the constitutional structure necessarily requires the protection of those interests as a matter of the separation of powers. Indeed, the assumption implicit in the Constitution—that it is preferable to let the guilty go free rather than to convict the innocent[50]—may not apply at all in the impeachment context. Perhaps for the welfare of the polity, it is better that occasionally a faultless public official be erroneously removed from office because of a lack of public confidence than that a corrupt public official be erroneously permitted to remain in office.[51] Thus, it is at best ambiguous whether the analysis of the structural issue points to a conclusion that judicial review of impeachment procedures is necessary, if we focus solely on the interests of the impeached official as the source of concern for liberty.

Broadening the perspective, however, does suggest the appropriateness of judicial review under these circumstances. Focusing on impeachment not as it affects random individuals in the executive and judicial branches, but rather as a legislative tool for exercising control over the judiciary as an institution, the individual-rights analysis takes on a different cast. Impeachment is a check on judges. Judges, at least in part, are the protectors in the constitutional scheme of individual rights.[52] Thus, if the legislature had an unchecked power to remove judges from office with no limits on its discretion and no possibility of review of the procedures used, then the independence of the judiciary could be threatened. As a structural matter, it is important that the judiciary operate free of the threat of the legislature's exercise of substantive control over its decisions.[53] And that structure is imperative to the protection

---

[50] Compare William Blackstone, 4 *Commentaries on the Laws of England* 358 (1765).

[51] Compare *O'Connor v Ortega*, 480 US 709, 721–25 (1987) (plurality opinion of O'Connor).

[52] *Marbury v Madison*, 5 US (1 Cranch) 137, 177–78 (1803); see Henry P. Monaghan, *Constitutional Adjudication: The Who and When*, 82 Yale L J 1363, 1366–67 (1973); Federalist 78 (Hamilton), in J. Cooke, ed, *The Federalist* 527–28 (1961).

[53] See *Ex Parte McCardle*, 74 US (7 Wallace) 506, 514 (1869).

of individual rights. Therefore, the structural question regarding the insulation of impeachment processes from judicial scrutiny must be answered by looking at the possible consequences of allowing unchecked, unreviewable discretion in the exercise of the impeachment power.

The answer seems straightforward: if the Congress set out to interfere with the independence of the judiciary, it could use an unchecked impeachment power to do so. If the independence of the judiciary were compromised by control of the legislature, there would be a clear implication for the enforcement of individual rights as a general matter. In other situations in which it perceived a threat to judicial independence, the Supreme Court has not shied away from protecting itself and has expressly justified that protection by referring to the judiciary's role in safeguarding individual rights.[54] It is consistent with the objective of the separated powers and the structure of the Constitution, therefore, to interpret the Constitution to permit judicial review of the exercise of the impeachment power as a means of self-defense for the judiciary. Justice White expressed the basic insight: "[T]he majority suggests that the Framers conferred upon Congress a potential tool of legislative dominance yet at the same time rendered Congress' exercise of that power one of the very few areas of legislative authority immune from any judicial review. [This] truly upsets the Framers' careful design."[55]

Further, it is part of the genius of the constitutional scheme that the legislature, feared for its potential to be carried away by faction and destructive passions, was rendered by and large incompetent to act with respect to individuals. One of the great protections for the liberty of the people was that generally whatever the legislature enacted would be applicable to all, creating a natural tempering of the majoritarian passion that might otherwise infect a representative body. Consistent with this view, the Constitution expressly disables the Congress from enacting bills of attainder and ex post facto laws.[56] Agents of Congress are prohibited by judicial decision

---

[54] See *Crowell v Benson*, 285 US 22, 57 (1932) (use of administrative fact finder could "sap the judicial power as it exists under the Federal Constitution, and to establish a government of a bureaucratic character . . . wherever fundamental rights depend . . . upon the facts"); *Northern Pipeline Constr. Co. v Marathon Pipe Line Co.*, 458 US 50, 58–60 (1982).

[55] *Nixon*, 113 S Ct at 743 (White concurring in judgment).

[56] US Const, Art I, § 9, cl 3.

from exercising a veto over individual decisions made by the executive branch,[57] and Congress is precluded from supplying the rule of decision in a pending case before the judicial branch.[58] These are all ways of structurally encouraging good lawmaking and ensuring that individuals—by definition without power to affect the legislative process because not aggregated with others of like interests—will not be singled out by the political process for unfavorable treatment. Yet, with much anguish and debate, and displaying deep ambivalence about the decision, the Framers placed the impeachment process—a trial of an individual—in the hands of the Congress.[59] Consistent with the effort to interpret issues involving the separated powers as a vehicle for the protection of individual rights, therefore, it would be prudent to read the one power granted to the Congress to act with respect to individuals in light of the general distrust of that role. "[T]he courts were designed to be an intermediate body between the people and the legislature, in order, among other things, to keep the latter within the limits assigned to their authority."[60] That perspective supports a decision to subject the exercise of this aberrational legislative power to judicial review.[61]

This analysis has proceeded on the basis of institutional generalizations. I have assumed that, institutionally, courts are better equipped to protect individual rights than is Congress. This does not mean, of course, that at any given point in history it will necessarily be the case that the courts are more avid proponents of individual liberty than Congress. One could imagine a hostile judiciary that refuses to give effect to statutes liberally protecting individual rights, and a Congress that sought to impeach judges for undermining the law in this way. In such a situation judicial review of impeachment procedures could actually become an obstacle to Congress' effort to remove these judges and thus to clear the

---

[57] *INS v Chadha*, 462 US 919, 959 (1983).

[58] *United States v Klein*, 80 US (13 Wallace) 128, 146–47 (1871).

[59] Raoul Berger, *Impeachment: The Constitutional Problems* 112–19 (1973).

[60] Federalist 78, in J. Cooke, ed, *The Federalist* 525 (1961).

[61] The Court has established a presumption, in interpreting statutes, that *executive* action is subject to judicial review—as a way to protect individual rights. *Abbott Laboratories v Gardner*, 387 US 136, 140 (1967); see William N. Eskridge, Jr., and Philip P. Frickey, *Quasi-Constitutional Law: Clear Statement Rules as Constitutional Lawmaking*, 45 Vand L Rev 593, 601 (1992).

way for a more effective enforcement of the rights it had created by statute. So hypothesized, these facts could suggest that individual liberty would be better served by an absence of judicial review. But the resolution of structural constitutional issues cannot depend on the personal proclivities of individuals who happen to hold the various offices at issue. The constitutional government was designed to function irrespective of who was in power at any given time, and, similarly, if one is to accept the methodology of resolving separation-of-powers issues by considering the effects on individual rights, one must also agree to accept generalizations about institutional tendencies.

Institutionally, federal courts are structured in such a way as to be able to exercise judgment largely independent of direct and current political pressure.[62] The Framers chose to allow political influence to have a role in determining the professional fate of individual judges, both prospectively, through confirmation, and retrospectively, through impeachment. Thus, where overwhelming political passions of one kind or another are directed at the judiciary, there will be consequences for the judiciary, no matter what the resolution of the *Nixon* issue. But the modest question here is whether the purposes of the separation of powers are better served by allowing that dominantly political impeachment decision to be a product of pure political will, or by holding that will to some standards of procedural fairness imposed by the judiciary. My claim is that the overall constitutional commitment to judicial insulation from political pressure—a principal reason that federal courts are institutionally competent to resolve matters affecting individual liberty—is best given effect by a scheme in which the departure from that principle of judicial independence is itself subject to review by a body free from direct political control.

Under any analysis of the separated powers animated by an understanding of the constitutional structure as a means to promote personal liberty, the Court's syllogistic reasoning in *Nixon* falls short. By both overemphasizing and undervaluing the constitu-

---

[62] See William N. Eskridge, Jr., *Politics without Romance: Implications of Public Choice Theory for Statutory Interpretation*, 74 Va L Rev 275, 305 (1988). For a different perspective, see Einer R. Elhauge, *Does Interest Group Theory Justify More Intrusive Judicial Review?* 101 Yale L J 31, 80–87 (1991) (arguing that interest-group influence permeates litigation process, judicial appointments, and judicial decision making to such an extent that there is no reason to believe judicially created policy is superior to policy generated by pure political process).

tional language, without regard to the implications for the principle
of separated powers, the Court too quickly embraced the option
of escaping an uncomfortable adjudication through the political-
question trapdoor, and thus did damage to the integrity of the
constitutional structure of government as well as to the individual
rights which it protects.

III. Ordered Liberty and the Political Question Doctrine

Precedent did not require the *Nixon* decision's devaluation
of individual rights in the name of the separation of powers. The
modern thinking about political questions began with *Baker v
Carr*,[63] in which the Court tried to make sense of the many decisions that recognized the need to abstain from certain kinds of cases
without sacrificing the essential role of the courts. In *Baker*, which
involved the justiciability of an equal protection challenge to a state
redistricting scheme, the Court derived several considerations,
some or all of which those prior decisions seemed to implicate, and
described them as "formulations which . . . may describe a political
question":[64]

> Prominent on the surface of any case held to involve a political
> question is found a textually demonstrable constitutional com-
> mitment of the issue to a coordinate political department; or a
> lack of judicially discoverable and manageable standards for
> resolving it; or the impossibility of deciding without an initial
> policy determination of a kind clearly for nonjudicial discretion;
> or the impossibility of a court's undertaking independent reso-
> lution without expressing lack of the respect due coordinate
> branches of government; or an unusual need for unquestioning
> adherence to a political decision already made; or the potential-
> ity of embarrassment from multifarious pronouncements by
> various departments on one question.

The Court never employed the word "test" to describe these observations, and it emphasized "the necessity for discriminating inquiry
into the precise facts and posture of the particular case, and the
impossibility of resolution by any semantic cataloguing."[65] Yet,
like so many efforts by members of the Court to control the future

---

[63] 369 US 186 (1961).

[64] Id at 217.

[65] Id.

use of their words, this proved unsuccessful. As time has passed, the "formulations" and "discriminating inquiry" have given way to invocation of "the *Baker* test" for political questions, by means of which one lists the six formulations, now more commonly referred to as "factors" or worse yet, "prongs," and plugs them into the facts of the case, in hopes that a ready answer will spew out. The formulations have lost their moorings, the specific cases which originally gave rise to them have long faded from memory, and the specific resolutions to which they in turn give rise are rooted in the concept of precedent or policy in only the loosest of ways. The courts have lost sight of the stakes.

The Court in *Baker* noted that political questions could endanger the enforcement of individual rights and should be found only where that was not a serious risk. It approved, for example, *Gomillion v Lightfoot*,[66] in which the Court employed the Fifteenth Amendment to strike down a redrafting of municipal boundaries which effected a discriminatory impairment of voting rights, in the face of what might have been viewed as a political question. Indeed, the court of appeals in that case had identified a sweeping commitment to state legislatures of the power to draw and redraw such boundaries, and thus had denied review of the claim.[67] To the *Baker* Court, *Gomillion* was evidence that the political-question doctrine had no place in denying the enforcement of individual rights.[68]

Whatever else may be said of the political-question doctrine, the result of applying the doctrine is the denial to a litigant of the opportunity to enforce a claimed right for reasons external to the nature of the injury. Assuming a case in which justiciability is determinative, the posture will likely be that the individual has suffered injury as a result of the government's violation of a constitutional limitation on its power, and the courts refuse a remedy out of concern for the autonomy of the political branches.[69] The

---

[66] 364 US 339 (1960).

[67] See *Baker*, 369 US at 229.

[68] See also Bickel, *The Least Dangerous Branch* at 191 (cited in note 39) (Fifteenth Amendment cuts across congressional authority in voting).

[69] There is no reason why, in theory, the case must involve a government violation of statutory or constitutional law. It happens, however, that political questions most often arise in cases in which the Court is asked to pass on the exercise of power by a coordinate branch.

nature of the political-question determination means that this individual and all others who have suffered or may in the future suffer
a similar injury will be unable to obtain judicial review of that
claim. Thus, a doctrine ostensibly rooted in the separation of powers necessarily conflicts with the very value for whose benefit we
have separated powers in the first place.

The problem with the doctrine is that, at least in theory, it has no
concern for the nature of the rights being claimed or the violation
allegedly committed.[70] It concerns itself only with the source of the
power exercised and the effects of judicial involvement on other,
exogenous, interests (such as political embarrassment and the like).
The six formulations from *Baker* take no account of the need—also
mandated by the separation of powers—to ensure that individual
rights are not swept up in the passions of the political branches
without recourse to an independent judiciary.[71] While the doctrine
of political questions speaks to some of the secondary or tertiary
concerns of the separation of powers—such as judicial respect for
political branches—it takes no account of why those concerns are
even worth protecting, especially at the cost exacted by the doctrine.

There is, however, another doctrine—standing—that is also
said to be a necessary adjunct to the separation of powers,[72] that
is receptive to the claims of individual rights, and that still is suited
to meeting the needs actually served by the political-question doctrine without threatening the core purposes of the separated powers. I speak of standing in its broadest sense, suggesting a means
of evaluating whether the claims of a particular individual are such
that the court can grant relief, and constituting, in effect, a preliminary inquiry into whether there really is an individual right at
stake.[73] There are different conceptions of what standing means in
any given case, and much has been written on the question of what

---

[70] See Redish, 79 Nw U L Rev at 1049–50 (cited in note 42) (criticizing effect of political-
question doctrine to allow violation of rights by political branches).

[71] Compare *United States v Muñoz-Flores*, 495 US 385, 393–94 (1989) (arguments about
individual rights are irrelevant to political-question inquiry).

[72] *Allen v Wright*, 468 US 737 (1984).

[73] Standing is an extremely complex theoretical notion, as well as a thorny practical one,
and I do not intend to enter that controversy here. I use the term comprehensively to
incorporate those inquiries that concern themselves with the nature of the plaintiff and the
injury alleged.

types of interest or injury should be cognizable in federal court. For purposes of this article, it is not necessary to adopt one or another of the formulations of standing, because my point depends only on what all theories of standing share in common.[74]

All models of standing ask that the claimant have a concrete injury allegedly caused by the defendant. This doctrine, however defined, seeks to determine whether the nature of the injury alleged is of the sort that is appropriate for judicial remediation. Because standing seeks to identify, preliminarily, cases that call for the exercise of judicial power based on the nature of the claim, it is well suited to carrying out the rights-protecting mission of the separation of powers. What the theories of standing have in common is a focus on the right being claimed. Thus, it would be a contradiction in terms for the standing doctrine to find nonjusticiable a claim in which an individual had been singled out for direct injury by a government violation of a specific constitutional limitation on its power. But the political-question doctrine, by its terms, could bar the adjudication of such a claim. Thus, the standing doctrine, although sibling to the political-question doctrine as an outgrowth of the separation of powers, does not create the same tension with the parent—the protection of individual rights, which is the basis of the separation of powers. Standing therefore presents a more appropriate alternative for attaining the objectives of separated powers without sacrificing the core interests.

As it turns out, the cases support this substitution—not necessarily in their rhetoric, but in their results. The Court has tacitly reacted to the conflict between the political-question doctrine and the enforcement of individual rights by not applying the doctrine in a way that would defeat a right—but never for reasons arising out of the doctrine itself.[75] It has done this by finding a matter to be nonjusticiable on political-question grounds only where the standing of the claimant, broadly conceived, or the concreteness of the claim can itself be said to be questionable or uncertain. When the standing of the claimant and concreteness of the claimed injury

---

[74] Because the standing considerations that I address below lie in the overlap with political-question cases, it will be most often the case that the type of injury claimed has to do with government violation of a constitutional or statutory limitation on power. This is the most common posture in which political-question concerns are raised. But I do not intend to suggest that only those situations constitute a legitimate "injury" under a standing analysis.

[75] See Scharpf, 75 Yale L J at 584 (cited in note 43).

are not in question, the courts have generally not found adjudication to be precluded by the political-question doctrine. Thus, at
least until *Nixon*, the courts have sensed, without often acknowledging, the need to temper the consequences of political questions
to protect individual rights. Even if the Court's views on standing
fall short of what one would like—and thus some good claims are
dismissed—it is still better for the Court to be asking whether an
individual has alleged an injury under the rubric of standing than
to be asking whether, despite the statement of a sound constitutional claim, the case should nonetheless be dismissed. It is only the
former question that comports with the appropriate effectuation of
the separated powers.

Consider, by way of illustration, a sample of cases in which the
Court actually dismissed claims on political-question grounds. I
discuss these cases in order to focus on whether the dismissal really
was occasioned by what I will term a "political-question-type" concern—that is, a need to decline to adjudicate a claim that is in all
other respects appropriate with respect to the plaintiff and injury
alleged—or instead appeared to be driven more by "standing-type"
concerns—those having to do with the directness or concreteness of the injury or the nature of the plaintiff's relation to the
case.

In *Goldwater v Carter*,[76] for example, a Senator brought suit
against the President to force him to obtain Senate consent before
abrogating a treaty that the Senate had initially approved pursuant
to its advice and consent function. A four-member plurality of the
Court found the case to present a nonjusticiable political question
because, although not textually committed by the Constitution to
another branch, the power to terminate treaties was not mentioned
at all in the Constitution. Thus the Court was left without standards to resolve a clash between two co-equal branches of government.[77] Yet, the Court's rationale suggested that it might just as
well have dismissed that case on the ground that the matter was
not a concrete controversy suitable for adjudication. The plaintiff,
a Senator who claimed only an institutional interest on behalf of the
Senate, and did not allege any infringement of individual liberty, is
not the kind of individual who implicates the core concerns of the

---

[76] 444 US 996 (1979).

[77] Id at 1002–05 (opinion of Rehnquist, joined by Burger, Stewart, and Stevens).

separation of powers. As then-Justice Rehnquist's plurality opinion noted expressly, the *Goldwater* case asked the Court "to settle a dispute between coequal branches of our Government, each
of which has resources available to protect and assert its interests. . . ."[78] This is a standing-type concern, not a political-
question-type concern. Moreover, there were questions about
whether this case was ripe for adjudication, in that there had as
yet been no real clash between the branches on the issue. Justice
Powell pointed out that, while "the political-question doctrine rests
in part on prudential concerns calling for mutual respect among
the three branches of Government," "[i]f this case were ripe for
judicial review, . . . none of these prudential considerations would
be present."[79] The real concerns about adjudicating that case,
therefore, were related to the lack of a clear claim that an individual
right had been violated, not the lack of judicial competence to
resolve a claim that such a right *had* been violated. This—and not
the plurality's political-question rationale—is an appropriate reason
to decline judicial review without undermining the integrity of the
separation of powers.

Similarly, in *Ange v Bush*,[80] the District Court held that a soldier
stationed in the Persian Gulf was precluded, on political-question
grounds, from challenging the President's unilateral deployment of
troops (without a declaration of war or other demonstration of
approval from Congress) because the court perceived "an explicit
textual commitment of the war powers not to one of the political
branches, but to both."[81] Again, as in *Goldwater v Carter*, the gravamen of the dispute was a matter of institutional prerogative between the executive and legislative branches. Unlike *Goldwater*,
however, this case involved an individual who was directly affected
by the conflict in a personal capacity, and thus the same standing
problems were not so clearly present in *Ange*. Although the court
went through the motions of reciting the test for standing and
determining that the plaintiff had met it—and in some sense he
clearly did meet it—the analysis of the political-question issue
demonstrated that the court was actually troubled by the fact that
the plaintiff had no concrete claim against the President. In addi-

---

[78] Id at 1004.

[79] Id at 1000 (opinion of Powell).

[80] 752 F Supp 509 (DDC 1990).

[81] Id at 514.

tion to a recitation of some standard political-question concerns, the court found that the matter was not yet ripe because the threat of executive bypass of congressional declaration of war was at that point purely speculative.[82] That, again, is a standing-type concern and not a political-question-type concern. The court would have been well advised to resolve the case only on ripeness grounds.[83]

The point—that what appear to be political-question concerns about justiciability are really better understood as concerns about standing—is supported as well by cases in which the Court considered, but rejected, a request for dismissal on political question grounds. In those cases, far outnumbering the cases in which the Court dismissed the action because of a political question,[84] it appears that the concern again was focused on the types of interest protected by standing. If the plaintiff has a real stake and articulates a real injury, the Court tends to adjudicate the case, even in the face of arguments that the case should be dismissed as a nonjusticiable political question. *Powell v McCormack*[85] is a good example.

That case raised the issue whether Adam Clayton Powell, who had been reelected to the 90th Congress as a Representative from New York, could be prevented from taking his seat for allegedly having committed financial improprieties during the 89th Congress. The House voted to exclude Powell and to notify the Governor of New York that the seat was vacant. He sued to invalidate the House action on the ground that it violated the Constitution. The Supreme Court considered the question whether it had the power to determine the constitutionality of the exclusion despite the constitutional language granting to each House the power to "be the Judge of the . . . Qualifications of its own Members."[86]

The mechanical application of *Baker*'s political-question formula-

---

[82] 752 F Supp at 515–16.

[83] Another judge of the same court did exactly that. See *Dellums v Bush*, 752 F Supp 1141 (DDC 1990) (relying on ripeness concerns in denying injunctive relief to members of Congress who sought to prevent President from initiating offensive attack against Iraq without congressional declaration of war).

[84] Apart from the *Goldwater* plurality opinion, the Court had, before *Nixon*, dismissed only one case on political-question grounds since the early Guarantee Clause cases. See *Gilligan v Morgan*, 413 US 1 (1973) (judicial evaluation of standards governing Ohio National Guard presents nonjusticiable political question). Consistent with my argument, that case, too, was afflicted with problems involving standing and mootness, as pointed out in the separate opinions. See id at 12 (dissenting statement of Douglas, Brennan, Stewart, and Marshall); and id at 12–14 (Blackmun and Powell concurring).

[85] 395 US 486 (1969).

[86] US Const, Art I, § 5.

tions adopted in the *Nixon* case would no doubt have made short work of Powell's claim, had the Court been inclined to follow that path of interpretation. An opinion written in that style would go like this: The constitutional language quoted above constitutes a "textual commitment" to each House of the question of its members' qualifications; the Constitution does not give the judiciary the power to judge the qualifications of members of Congress, and therefore the Court has no business reviewing the manner in which that committed power was exercised in the case of Adam Clayton Powell. It would no doubt be easy to find historical evidence to support the proposition that the Framers had no intention of investing the Judicial Branch with the power to determine the qualifications of members of Congress, which, in the style of *Nixon*, would suggest that the Court may not review the exercise of that power by the departments who were entrusted with it.

As the Supreme Court in fact decided the *Powell* case, however, there were other considerations. Significantly, the Court acknowledged the stakes: the case implicated the "'fundamental principle in a free government,' that restrictions upon the people to choose their own representatives must be limited to those 'absolutely necessary for the safety of the society.'"[87] "[T]his principle is undermined as much by limiting whom the people can select as by limiting the franchise itself."[88] Thus, the Court recognized that ultimately if it found the case to be a nonjusticiable political question, effectively leaving the House to exclude elected members at will, that decision would disserve the underlying goals of the constitutional structure itself and the individual rights attendant to it. Moreover, Justice Douglas's concurrence asserted that the case was infected with "racist overtones."[89] Although the majority opinion made no mention of them, these overtones might well have prompted the Justices in the majority to look beyond the mechanical application of the *Baker* test to ensure that judicial review would not, on grounds of deference to the political process, be denied to one who might have been the victim of an effort to obstruct that very process. These two aspects of the analysis are noteworthy because they suggest that even a Court ostensibly receptive to reli-

---

[87] 395 US at 543 (quoting 17 Annals of Cong 873–74 (1807)).

[88] Id at 547.

[89] 395 US at 553 (Douglas, J, concurring).

ance on a political-question doctrine could not bring itself to use the doctrine to defeat clear claims of individual rights violations, even though the terms of the doctrine might dictate that it do so. Some say the Court was wrong to reach the merits of Powell's claim because the political-question test was so clearly met; I suggest that the Court's mistake in *Powell*, instead, lay in concerning itself at all with reconciling its appropriate instinct for the vindication of individual rights with an ill-conceived obstacle in its path.

In *County of Oneida v Oneida Indian Nation*,[90] the Court rejected a political-question argument based on the "textual commitment" language of *Baker*. The Oneida Indian nation had brought a land claim on the ground that a long-ago conveyance of land violated a 1793 statute. Although the defendants sought dismissal because the Constitution explicitly commits to Congress, rather than the Court, the power to address Indian affairs, the Court found the case to be fully justiciable.[91] This was a case in which the plaintiffs had clearly suffered an injury, in that they claimed loss of land in violation of federal law, and the claim if successful would be remediable in federal court in the form of rental value of that land. Thus, the Court did not see any merit to the argument that Congress' possession of an express power precludes judicial action in the same area.[92]

The Court has consistently adhered to this principle—adjudicating cases in which a plaintiff had a clear claim of injury, despite the possibility that the political-question doctrine might be argued to defeat justiciability. Consider some cases in which the doctrine of political question was never mentioned, but one might have expected the Court to have had political-question concerns. For example, *In re Duncan*[93] involved a claim that a state legislature had enacted a particular statute invalidly. The proponent of this claim argued that the impropriety in the enactment procedures constituted a violation of the clause in the Constitution that guarantees

---

[90] 470 US 226 (1985).

[91] Id at 248–49.

[92] See also *Delaware Tribal Business Comm. v Weeks*, 430 US 73, 84 (1977) (even though power of Congress to abrogate Indian treaties has long been considered political, Court has not been deterred "from scrutinizing Indian legislation to determine whether it violates the equal protection component of the Fifth Amendment.").

[93] 139 US 449 (1891).

a republican form of government.[94] Every law student knows that a claim under the so-called Guarantee Clause is a political question—nonjusticiable because the Constitution vests in Congress, to the exclusion of the courts, the obligation and privilege of deciding whether a state government is complying with the republican mandate.[95] Time after time those who have attempted to bring actions seeking to invalidate legislation on this particular ground have been thwarted at the outset by judgments of nonjusticiability of their claims.[96] So one would expect exactly the same result for Duncan. Yet in that case, the Court outlined the contours of what the Guarantee Clause arguably ensures and concluded, on the merits, that no violation of those principles had occurred to the petitioner. No discussion of the justiciability of the claim was offered by the Court. The one feature of this case that the other Guarantee Clause cases lack? The state statute that Mr. Duncan challenged on federal constitutional grounds, based on the process by which it was enacted, was a capital murder statute under which he had been indicted. Under such circumstances, obviously Duncan had standing to challenge the statute, and the Court considered his claim on the merits without even a thought of nonjusticiability, while scores of similar claims brought by plaintiffs with less clear individual stake in the matter have been universally held to be nonjusticiable. Only one other time did the Court hold a Guarantee Clause issue to be justiciable, and in that case as well there was an unusual basis for an indisputable claim to standing.[97]

A more familiar example of the same principle at work comes from *Immigration & Naturalization Service v Chadha.*[98] In that case, the Court considered a claim by Chadha, the subject of a deportation proceeding who initially won an agency judgment suspending deportation by reason of extreme hardship, and then subsequently

---

[94] US Const, Art IV, § 4.

[95] *Luther v Borden,* 48 US (7 Howard) 1, 42 (1849).

[96] See *Pacific States Tel. & Tel. Co. v Oregon,* 223 US 118 (1912) (claim that initiative and referendum negated republican government held nonjusticiable); *Kiernan v Portland,* 223 US 151 (1912) (claim that municipal charter amendment passed by referendum negated republican government held nonjusticiable); *Mountain Timber Co. v Washington,* 243 US 219 (1917) (claim that worker's compensation violates republican government held nonjusticiable).

[97] See *Texas v White,* 7 Wall 700 (considering state's challenge to a congressional finding that its government was not republican in form).

[98] 462 US 919 (1983).

lost that suspension as a result of a one-house congressional veto of the Attorney General's order permitting him to remain in the country. As the target of adverse government action, there was no question that Chadha had standing to challenge the legality of that action.[99] The Court did consider an argument about justiciability of Chadha's claim, but notably the Court confined its analysis to the possibility that the case presented a political question by reason of the congressional power "[t]o establish an uniform rule of naturalization."[100] This argument, like that made in the *Oneida* case discussed above, would clearly prove too much and was easily rejected by the Court.

What the Court never considered was the possibility that the case should be considered nonjusticiable by reason of its challenge to a legislative process. Traditionally, the integrity of the means of reaching legislative decisions had been considered off limits to judicial review for reasons focal to the political-question doctrine. " 'The respect due to coequal and independent departments,' and the need for finality and certainty about the status of a statute contribute to judicial reluctance to inquire whether, as passed, it complied with all requisite formalities."[101] Thus, one might think that there would be at least the possibility that the internal decision-making process of Congress might also be beyond the reach of judicial review, especially when, as in *Chadha*, it is conducted according to statutory authority itself impeccably enacted and presidentially approved. Yet no such thought apparently impeded the court's journey to the merits of that case. It saw a plaintiff who alleged a real injury—deportation—and the political question presented no obstacle to the resolution of the controversy.

Similarly, in the classic separation-of-powers case of *Youngstown Sheet & Tube Co. v Sawyer*,[102] none of the members of the Court considered the possibility that the Court should decline to address the claim raised by individuals whose property had been seized by an allegedly illegal exercise of executive power. President Truman had seized the steel mills in order to avoid a steelworkers' strike which might interfere with supplies needed by American troops

---

[99] The Court disposed of Congress's contrary argument in one paragraph. Id at 936.

[100] US Const, Art I, § 8, cl 4.

[101] *Baker v Carr*, 369 US at 214 (citing *Field v Clark*, 143 US 649, 672, 676–77 (1892)).

[102] 343 US 579 (1952).

in Korea. It seems to me that a colorable argument could have been made that there was a lack of "judicially discoverable and manageable standards for resolving"[103] such a case (as demonstrated by the seven lengthy opinions and voluminous subsequent commentary generated by the case); or that the case required an "initial policy determination of a kind clearly for nonjudicial discretion" (such as decisions affecting the conduct of war on foreign soil); or the danger of "expressing lack of the respect due coordinate branches of government" (more than in the usual case of review of a coordinate branch's actions); or most plausibly an "unusual need for unquestioning adherence to a political decision already made" (in light of the tremendous political controversy surrounding this issue at the time[104]); or the "potentiality of embarrassment from multifarious pronouncements by various departments on one question." There was clearly no serious thought given to any of these possibilities, and I am suggesting it is because the plaintiff brought an unimpeachable traditional claim of injury—loss of property as a result of government violation of law—and thus, consciously or unconsciously, the Court's sense of its own core purpose hurtled it toward the merits. Perhaps if the issue had been presented in the form of a claim by a member of Congress that she had been deprived of the chance to approve the President's action, or by a commander in Korea who feared imminent loss of ammunition on the front lines, the specter of political question might have precluded resolution of the case.

In all of the sample cases, and all others of which I am aware— except *Nixon*[105]—the Court has stumbled onto a result that is consistent with the right analysis, without ever doing the right analy-

---

[103] The quotations are from *Baker v Carr*, 369 US at 217, which was, of course, not decided until after *Youngstown*. The standards set forth in *Baker*, however, were derived from existing case law and claimed nothing new in the way of a test for determining justiciability. See, for example, Field, *The Doctrine of Political Questions in the Federal Courts*, 8 Minn L Rev 485 (1924).

[104] For a comprehensive discussion of the events leading up to *Youngstown* and the political climate of the times, see Alan F. Westin, *The Anatomy of a Constitutional Law Case* (1958).

[105] Bickel insists that *Colegrove v Green*, 328 US 549 (1946), a leading early political-question case raising the vote-dilution issue under the Equal Protection Clause, "is in no sense a standing case." Bickel, *Least Dangerous Branch* at 191. And technically it is not, and neither are the other examples I discuss. But *Colegrove*, a difficult case, was essentially overruled by *Baker v Carr* and *Reynolds v Sims*, holding that a one-person-one-vote claim is justiciable.

sis.[106] It has either fudged or ignored what might otherwise be considered necessary dismissals in cases where individual rights were at stake; and it has dismissed cases on political-question grounds which could more appropriately have been dealt with on other grounds whose rhetoric is not so incompatible with the constitutional principle of separated powers. The Court tends not to acknowledge the conflict between the political-question doctrine and the need to enforce the provisions protecting individual rights, yet it persists in applying the doctrine in such a way as, most of the time, to do the least violence to those rights.[107] The result is a political-question "doctrine" that is mixed up and inconsistent with its own purposes. Sometimes, that kind of chaos is a sign that a doctrine needs to be strengthened, or that the Court should pay better attention to its animating principles. In this situation, the animating principle—protection of separated powers—is fundamentally at odds with the effect of the doctrine. In this situation, the chaos is a sign that the existence of the doctrine itself is highly suspect. It has no place in separation-of-powers jurisprudence.

Those who have promoted the doctrine of political questions have argued that it is needed to protect against several related evils. The judiciary should not interfere with the exercise of political judgment.[108] The judiciary should not expend capital in cases in which its directives will likely go unheeded.[109] The judiciary should not make decisions in areas that the Constitution commits to another branch.[110] Yet those injunctions about judicial behavior

---

[106] I do not go so far as to assert, as Professor Henkin has done, Henkin, 85 Yale L J at 600–601 (cited in note 43), that all applications of the political-question doctrine can be explained by considering only standard principles of judicial review. I find his discussion quite persuasive, but for my purposes it is sufficient to note the striking correlation between traditional notions of standing and the Court's use of the political-question escape hatch.

[107] See Scharpf, 75 Yale L J at 542, 584 (cited in note 43) (with a few specific and distinguishable exceptions, Court has consistently decided on the merits all constitutional issues arising out of cases involving foreign relations power; "where important individual rights are at stake, the doctrine will not be applied").

[108] Herbert Wechsler, *Toward Neutral Principles of Constitutional Law*, 73 Harv L Rev 1, 12 (1959).

[109] Bickel, *Least Dangerous Branch* at 184; Scharpf at 566–67; Finkelstein, *Judicial Self-Limitation*, 37 Harv L Rev 338, 344 (1924).

[110] See *Baker v Carr*, 369 US at 246 (Douglas concurring) ("Where the Constitution assigns a particular function wholly and indivisibly to another department the federal judiciary does not intervene.").

are not necessarily inconsistent with the protection of individual rights, and they need not subordinate the interest of that protection.

The rules of standing, at least as a core notion of limitation for judicial action, can accommodate the need to preserve judicial capital, but in the right sense. Judicial capital should be expended for the vindication of individual rights. It should not be expended in situations where adversity and injury are insufficient to present a clear controversy for judicial resolution. With regard to the judiciary's interference with political decisions, Chief Justice Marshall's comment from *Marbury v Madison* comes to mind: "[T]he president is invested with certain important political powers, in the exercise of which he is to use his own discretion, and is accountable only to his country in his political character, and to his own conscience."[111] That observation, far from creating a realm of shadowy issues that cannot ever be brought to the courts of law, can be better understood as simply a comment on the relatively uncontroversial fact that individual rights are not implicated when government performs acts that are wholly committed to political decision making. That is no reason for the court to deny review of such a claim, but only to accord substantial leeway for such decision making on the merits. The decision maker need only comport with whatever principles of individual rights, procedural or otherwise, may apply—as determined by a court. There need be no "doctrine" of nonjusticiability and its vague "exceptions," but only a conscientious effort to resolve every question in which an individual right is claimed to have been infringed. This had been the trend in practice, until *Nixon v United States*.

Nixon is the case that shows that rhetoric matters. Even if the Court is getting by and large the right results most, or even all, of the time, if it is not thinking about the right values there is cause for concern; a little hostility to judicial review can go a long way toward damaging the integrity of the separation between the branches. *Nixon* is such a case. Even though the claimant presented a clear claim to standing—including allegation of injury, causation, and redressability by the courts—the Supreme Court, for the first time in the face of those conditions, nevertheless required dismissal of the case on political-question grounds. The decision could be

---

[111] 5 US (1 Cranch) 137, 166–67 (1803).

read to suggest that even in the presence of a clear and concrete allegation of a violation of an individual right, the courts may elect not to adjudicate a claim out of concern for the separation of powers. That turns the separation of powers upside-down. By exposing the political-question doctrine as antagonistic to the constitutional scheme, maybe the other *Nixon v United States* was not such an unimportant case after all.

DANIEL R. FISCHEL
AND ALAN O. SYKES

CIVIL RICO AFTER REVES:
AN ECONOMIC COMMENTARY

Those who were involved in the enactment of the Racketeer Influenced and Corrupt Organizations (RICO) chapter of the Organized Crime Control Act of 1970[1] would be hard-pressed to recognize the statute today. Originally promulgated as a weapon to deter and penalize the infiltration of legitimate businesses by organized crime, the statute is now rarely used for that purpose. Rather, the statute has been used against defendants in a wide array of garden variety commercial disputes.[2] Because RICO awards successful plaintiffs their attorneys fees and contains a mandatory treble damage provision, plaintiffs have strong incentives to proceed under RICO whenever possible. Outside professionals such as law and accounting firms—perennial deep pocket defendants—have been sued routinely under the RICO statute.

Because of the divergence between the statute's purpose and how it has been interpreted, lower courts have continually attempted

---

Daniel R. Fischel is Lee and Brena Freeman Professor of Law, and Alan O. Sykes is Professor of Law, the University of Chicago.

Authors' note: The authors wish to thank Walter Blum, Richard Posner, and Stephen Schulhofer for valuable comments, as well as the participants in the University of Chicago Law and Economics Workshop. We are also grateful to the Olin Foundation for support.

[1] Pub L No 91-452, 84 Stat 922 (1970), codified at 18 USC §§ 1961–68 (1982 & Supp III 1985).

[2] The tension between RICO's statutory purpose and its application is discussed at length in Arthur F. Mathews, Andrew B. Weissman, and John H. Sturc, *Civil RICO Litigation* (2d ed 1992) (3 vols). Less than 10% of RICO litigation involves traditional organized crime activity. Id at 1–6.

to interpret RICO restrictively.[3] The Supreme Court, by contrast, has interpreted RICO broadly.[4] In fact, the Supreme Court has repeatedly rejected limitations on RICO's scope created by the lower courts.[5] While the Court has acknowledged that RICO has evolved in a manner at odds with its statutory purpose, the Court has generally reasoned that the statute's broad language, coupled with its liberal construction clause, require an expansive interpretation. Change, the Court has stated, must come from Congress, not the courts.

In *Reves v Ernst & Young*,[6] however, the Supreme Court changed course. *Reves* involved the interpretation of § 1962(c), the most important of RICO's civil liability provisions. Section 1962(c) makes it unlawful "for any person employed by or associated with any enterprise . . . to conduct or participate, directly or indirectly, in the conduct of such enterprise's affairs through a pattern of racketeering activity. . . ."[7] The question in *Reves* was whether an accounting firm which was found to have acted fraudulently in performing audits and other functions could be liable under this section. The Court, in an opinion by Justice Blackmun, held that RICO did not reach the conduct of the accounting firm because the firm was not involved in the "operation or management" of its client.

In reaching this result, the Court rejected various tests promulgated by the Courts of Appeals under which the nexus between the accounting firm and its client was sufficiently close to justify liability. Similarly, the Court rejected the position of the United States as amicus curiae and other amici who favored a more expansive interpretation of RICO.

Reves was immediately hailed as a major victory for professional defendants and a reversal of the Court's unbroken line of decisions

---

[3] Id at 1–25.

[4] For a discussion of how the Supreme Court has systematically rejected attempts by lower courts to limit RICO's scope, see Michael Goldsmith, *Judicial Immunity for White-Collar Crime: The Ironic Demise of Civil RICO*, 30 Harv J Leg 1 (1993).

[5] See, e.g., *HJ Inc. v Northwestern Bell Tel. Co.*, 492 US 229 (1989); *Sedima, SPRL v Imrex Co.*, 473 US 479 (1985); *Russello v United States*, 464 US 16 (1983); *United States v Turkette*, 452 US 576 (1981).

[6] 113 S Ct 1163 (1993).

[7] 18 USC § 1962(c).

broadly construing the RICO statute.[8] The case, however, raises a number of hard questions which will determine its importance as a precedent. What is the meaning of the Court's "operation or management" requirement? Does it mean that outside professionals are now effectively exempt from liability under RICO? And what is the logic of limiting liability of outside professionals who knowingly participate in, and thereby facilitate, a client's fraud? We analyze these questions, as well as the larger policy issues created by the RICO statute, in this essay.

I. The Factual Background of Reves

The Farmer's Cooperative of Arkansas and Oklahoma, Inc., was created in 1946. To raise money for its operating expenses, the Co-op sold promissory notes payable on demand. There were Co-op members elected annually as directors who in turn delegated management responsibilities to a general manager. Jack White served in this position until the Board of Directors removed him in mid-1982.

In 1979, White decided to build a gasohol plant. To do this he created another company, White Flame Fuels, Inc., which borrowed heavily from the Co-op to finance the construction and operation of the gasohol plant. These loans, which by 1980 totaled $4 million, were personally guaranteed by White. After being indicted for tax fraud, White persuaded the Board to purchase White Flame in such a manner as to relieve him of any personal liability for the loans.

Shortly after White was convicted in 1981, the Board hired an accounting firm which later became part of Ernst & Young to perform an annual audit of the Co-op. Joe Drozal was put in charge of the audit. The key accounting decision to be made was whether White Flame should be valued at its historic cost of approximately

---

[8] See, e.g., Marcia Coyle, *Back to the Law's Intent? RICO Limits Set for Professionals*, Natl L J (March 15, 1993), at 1; Pitt and Johnson, *Liberating Corporate Professional Advisers from the Taint of RICO Liability*, 17 RICO Law Rep 762 (Apr 1993); Linda Greenhouse, *RICO Suing of Accountants Is Limited by High Court*, NY Times (March 4, 1993), at D-1; Joan Biskupic, *Supreme Court Limits Use of Racketeering Law*, Wash Post (March 4, 1993), at A-1; Paul Barrett, *High Court Gives Accountants a Shield Against Civil Racketeering Lawsuits*, Wall St J (March 4, 1993), at A-3.

$4.5 million or its market value of less than $1.5 million. After consulting with White, now a convicted felon, Drozal decided that White Flame should be carried on the Co-op's at the $4.5 million figure. If Drozal had used the market value number for White Flame of less than $1.5 million, the Co-op would have been insolvent.

On April 22, 1982, the accounting firm presented its 1981 audit report to the Co-op's board. Although White Flame was valued at $4.5, the accounting firm in Note 9 of the Co-op's financial statements expressed doubt whether the $4.5 million investment in White Flame could ever be recovered. Note 9 also stated that White Flame was sustaining operating losses averaging $100,000 per month.

On May 27, 1982, the Co-op held its annual meeting for members. A representative of the accounting firm made a five-minute presentation and distributed condensed financial statements which included the $4.5 million figure but omitted the information contained in Note 9. Members were told, however, that White Flame had lost over $1 million and that copies of the full audit were available for review. The Co-op then hired the same accounting firm to perform its 1982 audit, which treated White Flame the same way as the previous year and contained a comparable footnote disclosure. The information in the footnote was again not presented to the members in the annual meeting.

In February 1984, the Co-op experienced a run in its demand notes and filed for bankruptcy. As a result, the demand notes were no longer redeemable by the noteholders.

The trustee in bankruptcy then filed suit against numerous individuals and entities on behalf of the Co-op and certain noteholders alleging violations of the federal and state securities laws and RICO. The district court certified a class of noteholders consisting of persons who had purchased demand notes between early 1980 and the time of bankruptcy in 1984. All defendants settled except Arthur Young, a predecessor accounting firm to Ernst & Young. The court then granted summary judgment in favor of Arthur Young on the RICO claim. In *Bennett v Berg*,[9] liability under § 1962(c) of RICO requires "some participation in the operation or

---

[9] 710 F2d 1361, 1364 (en banc), cert denied sub nom *Prudential Ins. Co. v Bennett*, 464 US 1008 (1983).

management of the enterprise itself."[10] Applying this standard, the District Court held that "Plaintiffs have failed to show anything more than that the accountants reviewed a series of completed transactions, and certified the Co-op's records as fairly portraying its financial status. . . . We do not hesitate to declare that such activities fail to satisfy the degree of management required by *Bennett v Berg*."[11] The case went to trial on the federal and state securities claims. The jury found that Arthur Young committed federal and state securities fraud and awarded $6.1 million in damages. After a complicated procedural history,[12] the Eighth Circuit affirmed in all major respects except with respect to damages. On the RICO claim, the Court of Appeals, like the district court, applied the "operation or management" test of *Bennett v Berg* and concluded that Arthur Young's conduct did not meet this requirement.[13] The Supreme Court then granted certiorari to resolve the conflict in the circuits on the "operation or management" requirement under RICO.[14]

II. The Supreme Court Opinions

A. JUSTICE BLACKMUN'S MAJORITY OPINION

The Court in *Reves* had to decide whether Arthur Young "conduct[ed] or participat[ed] in the conduct of" the Co-ops affairs as required by § 1962(c). Justice Blackmun's opinion for the Court resolved this question by focusing on the language of the statute. The word "conduct," which is used in the statute as both a noun and a verb, was interpreted to indicate "some degree of direction."[15] Similarly, the Court interpreted the word "participate" to require

---

[10] Id.

[11] *Robertson v White*, Nos 85-2044, 85-2096, 85-2155, and 85-2259 (WD Ark Oct 15, 1986), App 198–200 at 199–200.

[12] The Court of Appeals initially reversed, holding that the demand notes were not securities under federal or state law. *Arthur Young & Co. v Reves*, 856 F2d 52, 55 (8th Cir 1988). This ruling was in turn reversed by the Supreme Court. *Reves v Ernst & Young*, 494 US 56, 70 (1990). The case was then remanded back to the Eighth Circuit.

[13] *Arthur Young & Co. v Reves*, 937 F2d 1310, 1324 (8th Cir 1991).

[14] 502 US (1992). Other circuits had rejected the "operation or management" test of *Bennett v Berg*. See, e.g., *Bank of America National Trust & Savings Assn. v Touche Ross Co.*, 782 F2d 966, 970 (11th Cir 1986).

[15] 113 S Ct 1163, 1170 (1993).

"some part in that direction."[16] The Court then defined the class of individuals or entities that have a sufficiently close relationship to the racketeering enterprise to fall within the scope of § 1962(c):

> Once we understand the word "conduct" to require some degree of direction and the word "participate" to require some part in that direction, the meaning of s 1992(c) comes into focus. In order to "participate, directly or indirectly, in the conduct of such enterprise's affairs," one must have some part in directing those affairs. Of course, the word "participate" makes clear that RICO liability is not limited to those with primary responsibility for the enterprise's affairs, just as the phrase "directly or indirectly" makes clear that RICO liability is not limited to those with a formal position in the enterprise, but some part in directing the enterprise's affairs is required. The "operation or management" test expresses this requirement in a formulation that is easy to apply.[17]

The Court then concluded that the "operation or management" test found "further support" in the legislative history of § 1962(c). Congress, the Court stated, intended liability under § 1962(c) to be limited to those who have "participated in the operation or management of the enterprise itself."[18]

Because the Court found the language and legislative history of the statute to be clear, it found no inconsistency between the "operation or management" test and RICO's liberal construction clause.[19] That clause is meant to ensure that Congress' remedial intent was not frustrated by overly narrow interpretation, "but it is not an invitation to apply RICO to new purposes that Congress never intended."[20]

Finally, the Court applied the "operation or management" test to the facts of *Reves*. Arthur Young relied upon existing Co-op records in preparing the 1981 and 1982 audit reports and disclosed to the Co-op board that the value of White Flame was calculated based on historic cost. "Thus," the Court stated, "we only could

---

[16] Id.

[17] Id.

[18] Id at 1170–72. Justices Scalia and Thomas did not join section IV-A of the Court's opinion discussing legislative history.

[19] RICO provides that the "provisions of this title shall be liberally construed to effectuate its remedial purposes." Organized Crime Control Act of 1970, Pub L No 91-452, tit IX, § 904(a), 84 Stat 941, 947 (1970).

[20] 113 S Ct 1163, 1172 (1993).

conclude that Arthur Young participated in the operation or management of the Co-op itself if Arthur Young's failure to tell the
Co-op's board that the plant should have been given its fair market
value constituted such participation."[21] The Court held that Arthur
Young's failure to so inform the Co-op board of the value of
White Flame was insufficient to satisfy the "operation or management" test.

B. JUSTICE SOUTER'S DISSENTING OPINION

Justice Souter, joined by Justice White, dissented. First, the dissent disagreed with the majority's conclusion that the "operation or
management" test is compelled by the statutory language. The word
"conduct," the dissent argued, can mean "carrying forward" or
"carrying out" without "any implication of direction or control."[22]
Moreover, § 1962(c) reaches those who indirectly participate in
the enterprise's affairs. Based on this alternative interpretation
of the statutory language, and the liberal construction clause, Justice Souter concluded that § 1962(c) has "a long arm, unlimited by
any requirement to prove that the activity includes an element of
direction."[23]

Second, the dissent argued that even under the majority's "operation or management" test, Arthur Young's involvement with the
Co-op was sufficient to warrant liability under RICO. This was
because Arthur Young went far beyond "the role traditionally performed by an outside auditor"[24] which is to opine on management's
financial statements. Rather, Arthur Young "took on management
responsibilities"[25] by creating the financial statements and decided
what value to place on White Flame. Thus, the dissent concluded,
"[b]y assuming the authority to make key decisions in stating the
Co-op's own valuation of its major fixed asset, and by creating
financial statements that were the responsibility of the Co-op's
management, Arthur Young crossed the line separating 'outside'
auditors from 'inside' managers."[26]

---

[21] Id at 1174.

[22] Id.

[23] Id at 1175.

[24] Id.

[25] Id.

[26] Id at 1178.

III. The Expansion of RICO Liability Prior to Reves

Congress promulgated RICO as a weapon to be used against organized crime. Because of concerns that a statute specifically targeted at the "Mafia" or similar groups might be constitutionally defective, however, Congress avoided defining the statute's scope in terms of status. Rather, Congress focused on conduct believed to be characteristic of organized crime. Thus, RICO imposes criminal and civil liability upon certain individuals or entities who engage in "racketeering activities" defined as "any act or threat" involving specified state-law crimes, any "act" indictable under various specified federal statutes, and certain federal "offenses."[27] All of these predicate acts are crimes under either state or federal law. Commission of these predicate acts, however, is not sufficient for liability under RICO. Defendants must engage in a "pattern" of racketeering activity and this "pattern" must be in a specified relationship with a racketeering "enterprise." Section 1962 of RICO has three subsections which render criminally and civilly liable "any person" who, from "a pattern of racketeering activity," either: (1) uses or invests income from such activity or acquires an interest in or operates an "enterprise," (2) through such activity acquires or maintains an interest in or control of an "enterprise," or (3) through such activity conducts or participates in the conduct of an "enterprise's" affairs, directly or indirectly.[28] The statute also punishes any person who conspires to violate any of these three subsections.[29] Section 1964 provides that any person injured "by reason of" a violation of the statute is entitled to treble damages.[30]

By limiting RICO's scope to certain specified crimes, and by requiring that there be a "pattern" of prohibited activities that has a relationship to an "enterprise," Congress hoped to achieve its objective of deterring the infiltration of legitimate businesses by organized crime. What has occurred, however, is far different from what Congress intended.

---

[27] 18 USC § 1961 (1988). Justice Marshall has stated that "[t]he single most significant reason for the expansive use of civil RICO has been the presence in the statute, as predicate acts, of mail and wire fraud." *Sedima, SPRL v Imrex Co.*, 473 US 479, 501 (Marshall dissenting).

[28] 18 USC § 1962(a)–(c).

[29] 18 USC § 1962(d).

[30] 18 USC § 1964(c).

From RICO's inception, the statute's reach has been controversial. While lower courts have consistently attempted to interpret RICO to situations involving the infiltration of legitimate businesses by organized crime, the Supreme Court has taken the opposite approach. The significance of *Reves*, which may signal a reversal of this trend, can only be understood in light of the Court's prior RICO jurisprudence.

1. *United States v Turkette*.[31] This was the Supreme Court's first RICO decision, and thus its first opportunity to assess the validity of a judicially created limitation on RICO's scope. Although *Turkette* was a criminal case, the Court's reasoning was a precursor of that employed in its subsequent civil cases.

The issue in *Turkette* was whether a group formed for purely illicit purposes could qualify as a RICO "enterprise." The Court of Appeals began with the premise that RICO was not a general anti-crime or anti-fraud statute but was designed to prevent the infiltration of legitimate enterprises by organized crime. Since the conduct in question was in connection with an illegitimate enterprise, the Court of Appeals held it was not within RICO's scope. The Supreme Court reversed, holding that RICO reaches both legitimate and illegitimate enterprises. The court based its holding on the statutory language and structure which did not distinguish between different types of enterprises. As for the contention that its interpretation of RICO would invade states' traditional areas of law enforcement, the Court stated that this is precisely what Congress intended to do.

2. *Sedima, SPRL v Imrex Co.*[32] *Sedima* is the best-known RICO case. It involved a dispute between two joint venturers to provide electronic parts. The parties had agreed to split the net proceeds after expenses, but one party believed the other received more than its share by inflating its expenses by $175,000. The controversy, in other words, was essentially a garden variety commercial dispute having nothing to do with organized crime. To interpret RICO as providing a remedy for this type of commercial dispute would create, in effect, a general federal anti-fraud provision. To avoid this result, the Second Circuit held that civil RICO suits required both a prior criminal conviction and proof of "racketeering injury."

---

[31] 452 US 576 (1981).

[32] 473 US 479 (1985).

The policy rationale for these limitations is clear. For RICO to apply, a defendant must be guilty of a crime. In a criminal case, this would require a prosecutor to decide that the offense was serious enough to prosecute and the evidence be sufficient to convict beyond a reasonable doubt. In civil RICO cases, however, these protections become meaningless. The decision to sue is made by a self-interested private litigant, and the proof beyond a reasonable doubt standard, and other criminal safeguards, are absent. The Second Circuit's prior criminal conviction requirement was intended to ensure that only cases involving actual crimes are brought under civil RICO.

The "racketeering injury" requirement was also intended to limit civil RICO's scope. Without such a requirement, any plaintiff injured by a predicate act could bring a RICO action. The "special injury" requirement limited RICO to those cases where a plaintiff suffered particular injury resulting from the pattern of acts related to a racketeering enterprise. Again, the goal was to limit RICO to activities of organized crime involving enterprises.

The Supreme Court reversed, rejecting both the prior conviction and racketeering injury requirements. As in *Turkette*, the Court primarily relied upon the statutory language and structure, finding no support for either limitation. The Court also emphasized both the liberal construction clause and the "remedial purposes" of Congress in creating a private remedy for those injured by racketeering activity.

The Court, however, was not wholly unsympathetic to the Second Circuit's goal of preventing civil RICO from becoming a generalized federal law against fraud rather than a tool to tight organized crime. But the Court stated that this argument must be directed to Congress, not the courts:

> Underlying the Court of Appeals' holding was its distress at the "extraordinary, if not outrageous," uses to which civil RICO has been put. Instead of being used against mobsters and organized criminals, it has become a tool for everyday fraud cases brought against "respected and legitimate 'enterprises.'" *Yet Congress wanted to reach both "legitimate" and "illegitimate" enterprises. The former enjoy neither an inherent incapacity for criminal activity nor immunity from its consequences. . . .*
> It is true that private civil actions under the statute are being brought almost solely against such [white-collar] defendants, rather than against the archetypal, intimidating mobster. Yet

this defect—if defect it is—is inherent in the statute as written, and its correction must lie with Congress.[33]

3. *HJ Inc. v Northwestern Bell Tel. Co.*[34] RICO requires that a defendant do more than commit a predicate offense: the defendant must also engage in a "pattern" of racketeering activity with a specified relationship to an "enterprise." Another way to narrow RICO's scope is to interpret the "pattern" requirement restrictively. This is what the Eighth Circuit did in *HJ Inc.*, holding that a defendant must be engaged in multiple illegal schemes to satisfy the patterns requirement. Adoption of such a restrictive interpretation of pattern would make it less likely that, with clever pleading, all commercial disputes could be transformed into RICO actions.

The Supreme Court again reversed, however, relying heavily on its reasoning in *Sedima* that RICO be construed broadly and flexibly consistent with its remedial purposes. Significantly, the Court also rejected the suggestion that the pattern requirement require proof that a defendant's activities "are characteristic either of organized crime in the traditional sense, or of an organized crime perpetrator."[35] Rather, the Court held that the pattern requirement is satisfied whenever there is proof of "continuity of racketeering activity, or its threat, *simpliciter*."[36] To go farther and rewrite the statute to target organized crime, the Court stated "is a job for Congress . . . and not for this Court."[37]

4. *Holmes v Securities Investor Protection Corp.*[38] "Racketeering activity" is defined in the statute to include "any offense involving . . . fraud in the sale of securities . . . punishable under any law of the United States."[39] RICO further authorizes any person injured by unlawful racketeering activity to sue for treble damages. For a plaintiff to have standing to bring an action under the antifraud provision of the securities laws, he or she would have to be a purchaser or seller of securities.[40] The question before the Court

---

[33] Id at 499.

[34] 492 US 229 (1989).

[35] Id at 243–44.

[36] Id at 241.

[37] Id at 249.

[38] 112 S Ct 1311 (1992).

[39] 18 USC § 1961(1)(d).

[40] *Blue Chip Stamps v Manor Drug Stores*, 421 US 723 (1975).

in *Holmes* was whether the purchaser/seller requirement limitation also applied to RICO claims which allege securities fraud as the predicate offense. More generally, the issue in *Holmes* was whether the various restrictions and limitations in state and federal fraud statutes also apply in civil RICO actions where these same state and federal statutes are relied upon as predicate offenses.

In deciding *Holmes*, the Court was faced with the familiar tension between the broad language of the statute which contains no purchaser/seller restriction and the policy goal of limiting RICO's scope. Unfortunately, the Court decided the case unanimously on other grounds, and did not resolve the issue.[41] Justices O'Connor, White, Stevens, and Scalia, however, in two concurring opinions stated that they would decide the issue and hold that the purchaser/seller standing requirement under the securities laws does not apply to RICO actions. In light of these concurring opinions, and the Court's holdings in Turkette, Sedima, and *HJ Inc.*, there seems little doubt that the full Court would have reached this result had it decided the issue.

IV. THE CONSEQUENCES OF RICO LIABILITY IN COMMERCIAL DISPUTES

As the last section indicates, decisions prior to *Reves* steadily expanded the reach of RICO into ordinary commercial settings. We now provide further detail on the consequences of this expansion.

Prospective plaintiffs in RICO cases gain a number of advantages not available under state or other Federal laws. These advantages include broader discovery, a longer statute of limitations, and broader venue and service of process provisions.[42] We will not dwell on these aspects of RICO, however, and instead focus on the dramatic effect of RICO on damages awards—the successful RICO plaintiff is always entitled to treble damages and to attorneys fees. Further, RICO may affect the scope of "vicarious" liability for punitive damages, and at times even create a new cause of action.

---

[41] The Court ruled unanimously that recovery under RICO was unavailable because the proximate cause requirement was not satisfied.

[42] See 18 USC § 1965.

A. THE AWARD OF ATTORNEYS FEES

Under the American rule, otherwise applicable to the commercial disputes on which we focus, each side bears its own attorneys fees. But under RICO, successful plaintiffs recover reasonable attorneys fees, while successful defendants bear their own fees as usual.[43] Thus, RICO imposes what Shavell once termed the "proplaintiff" rule for fee shifting.[44]

The effects of the pro-plaintiff rule relative to the American rule are well known. First, because the plaintiff enjoys a higher expected award, the incentive to file suit is greater. The pro-plaintiff rule may thus be expected to generate more filings.[45] Second, the pro-plaintiff rule may tend to reduce the likelihood of settlements relative to the American rule. Under any rule, the parties will always settle when the defendant is more optimistic than the plaintiff about the plaintiff's chances of success. But when the plaintiff is more optimistic, it can be shown that settlement will occur in general only if the parties' joint expected litigation costs exceed the difference in the parties' assessment of the plaintiff's expected award. Holding constant both parties' expenditures on litigation, and assuming that the plaintiff is the more optimistic about his chances for success, joint expected litigation costs fall under the pro-plaintiff rule relative to the American rule because the plaintiff has a higher subjective probability of avoiding his litigation costs than the defendant has of paying them. Subject to an important caveat below, therefore, settlement is somewhat less likely.[46]

The pro-plaintiff rule also has the effect of increasing the stakes

---

[43] See 18 USC § 1964(c).

[44] Steven Shavell, *Suit, Settlement and Trial: A Theoretical Analysis under Alternative Methods for the Allocation of Legal Costs*, 11 J Legal Stud 55 (1982).

[45] It is not uncommon to see RICO suits that yield little in damages but a large fee award—suits that likely never would have been filed under the American rule. See, e.g., *Northeast Women's Center v McMonagle*, 889 F2d 466 (3d Cir 1989) ($2,661 in damages after trebling, $64,946 in fees and costs); *Nu-Life Construction Co. v Board of Education*, 795 F Supp 602 (EDNY 1992) ($23,400 in damages after trebling, $193,266 in fees and costs).

[46] More precisely, let p denote the plaintiff's subjective probability of winning the suit, let q denote the defendant's subjective probability of losing the suit, let J denote the judgment, and let c_p and c_d denote the plaintiff's and defendant's attorneys fees, respectively. With risk neutral parties, the condition for settlement under the American rule is $c_p + c_d > (p - q)J$. Under the pro-plaintiff rule, the corresponding condition is $(1 - p + q)c_p + c_d > (p - q)J$. If $p > q$, the left-hand side of the first condition exceeds the left-hand side of the second, and thus settlement is more "likely" under the American rule. For a more general treatment, see Shavell (cited in note 44).

in litigation for both parties—if the plaintiff wins, the defendant pays more and the plaintiff collects more. In general, we expect parties to invest in litigation expenditures to the point where the marginal expected return equals the marginal cost. Because the returns to success rise for both parties under the pro-plaintiff rule, we thus expect greater litigation expenditures in most cases.[47] This effect is enhanced for the plaintiff by the fact that the defendant "subsidizes" the plaintiff's expenditures. That is, the expenditure of an additional dollar on litigation will cost the plaintiff nothing in the end if he is successful (subject to the reasonableness limitation in the law).

The increase in litigation costs provides the caveat to the proposition that the pro-plaintiff rule reduces the likelihood of settlement. Once the increase in costs is taken into account, the net effect of the pro-plaintiff rule on joint expected litigation costs when the plaintiff is more optimistic becomes ambiguous, and hence the overall effect of the pro-plaintiff rule on the settlement rate cannot be predicted on the basis of theory alone. What can be said with confidence is that it tends to increase the number of lawsuits and to increase litigation expenditures.

B. THE AWARD OF TREBLE DAMAGES FOR FRAUD

RICO liability extends to a wide range of predicate acts, all technically crimes under state or federal law. Our concern is with the intrusion of RICO liability into mainstream commercial contract and securities litigation, however, where the basis for pleading RICO counts is almost always some form of fraud—ordinary criminal fraud, mail fraud, or securities fraud.

These offenses often afford a basis for an action in tort for common law fraud (we discuss the securities cause of action below). The plaintiff must prove that the defendant made a false statement of fact, with scienter, and that justifiable reliance resulted in damages to the plaintiff.[48] Upon such a showing, the plaintiff may

---

[47] The analysis is actually a bit more complex because the expenditures of each party will likely depend upon the expenditures of the other. Under plausible assumptions, however, an increase in the stakes will increase the litigation expenditures of both parties in equilibrium. See Robert Cooter and Daniel Rubinfeld, *Economic Analysis of Legal Disputes*, 27 J Econ Lit 1067, 1071–73 (1989).

[48] See, e.g., W. Page Keeton, Dan Dobbs, Robert Keeton, and David Owen, *Prosser & Keeton on Torts*, 727–29 (5th ed 1984).

recover compensatory damages equal to the loss suffered as a consequence of the fraud, and may ordinarily obtain an instruction allowing the jury to consider an award of punitive damages as well. The amount of the punitive award, if any, is a matter of discretion with the jury. The punitive award may be smaller than the compensatory award, or may be a substantial multiple of it.

The remedy under civil RICO is more predictable—treble damages plus attorney's fees. It does not alter the manner in which compensatory damages are computed prior to trebling. At first blush, it is not obvious whether plaintiffs do better or worse on average with the RICO remedy. But in fact, because of alternative pleading, a plaintiff can only benefit from adding a RICO count to the case. The jury will be instructed to compute damages on the common law fraud theory separately. Although the plaintiff will not be allowed "double recovery" of punitive damages, the plaintiff can nevertheless choose between the common law award and the treble award under RICO. Thus, the effect of RICO is to ensure the plaintiff of at least treble damages plus attorneys fees, an assurance that is not present otherwise. Plainly, the *expected* award can only rise.

The increase in expected damages under RICO also reinforces the effects of the pro-plaintiff rule noted above. Other things being equal, more suits will be filed because the expected return to suit is more likely to be positive. In addition, the increase in the stakes will stimulate greater litigation expenditures on both sides. Finally, under any rule for the allocation of legal fees, the pro-plaintiff rule included, an increase in the damages award can reduce the likelihood of settlement. For this to occur, it suffices that the increase in litigation expenditures on both sides be less than proportional to the increase in the stakes.[49]

C. THE SPECIAL CASE OF SECURITIES FRAUD

In several important classes of "fraud" cases, punitive damages are altogether unavailable in the absence of RICO. A plaintiff in a

---

[49] Continuing with prior notation, recall that the parties will settle under the pro-plaintiff rule if $(1 - p + q)c_p + c_d > (p - q)J$. Assume $p > q$, and consider the effect of trebling J. If c_p and c_d were to triple as well, holding p and q constant, there would be no effect on the settlement condition. But if c_p and c_d rise by less than a factor of three, settlement becomes less likely.

common law fraud action must demonstrate reliance on the allegedly false statement.[50] Under the "fraud on the market theory" routinely applied by courts in securities cases,[51] however, plaintiffs can recover for damages suffered from the purchase or sale of securities when the market price was distorted by fraud, even they did not rely on the fraudulent information. Similarly, the courts have extended the concept of securities fraud to encompass acts of "recklessness" that would not be actionable at common law because of the scienter requirement even if the plaintiff could prove reliance.[52] In these two groups of cases, therefore, plaintiffs can proceed under the securities laws but not on a theory of common law fraud. But the plaintiffs (in the absence of RICO) are limited to compensatory damages—punitive damages are not recoverable under the securities laws. Thus RICO's effect is to create a type of punitive damages remedy for conduct that is not actionable at common law and for which only compensatory damages are available under federal law.

In yet another important class of cases, plaintiffs may recover treble damages under RICO where there would be no other private remedy under federal law. The Supreme Court has held that only actual purchasers or sellers of securities can recover compensatory damages under Section 10b and Rule 10 b-5, the general antifraud provisions of the securities laws.[53] The rationale for the purchaser/seller requirement is to filter out fraudulent claims (those who allege they would have purchased or sold absent an alleged disclosure defect) and to prevent the resulting open-ended liability. The rationale of *Holmes*, however, suggests that the purchaser/seller restriction on liability is inapplicable in RICO actions. This result is perverse because it enables plaintiffs to recover treble damages in situations where no compensatory damages are available because the claims are too speculative. The effect of RICO in increasing expected awards is obvious.[54]

---

[50] For an extended discussion of the reliance requirement in common law fraud actions, see *Milkin v Wasserman* (Calif Supr Ct, Sept 9, 1993).

[51] See, e.g., *Basic, Inc. v Levinson*, 485 US 224 (1988).

[52] See, e.g., *McLean v Alexander*, 599 F2d 1190, 1197 & n 12 (3d Cir 1979) (noting cases from other circuits); *Rolf v Blyth, Eastman Dillon & Co.*, 570 F2d 38, 44–46 (2d Cir), cert denied, 439 US 1039 (1978).

[53] *Blue Chip Stamps v Manor Drug Stores*, 421 US 723 (1975).

[54] As we discuss below, even "compensatory" damages may be excessive in certain types of securities cases from an economic standpoint.

D. VICARIOUS PUNITIVE LIABILITY

Liability under § 1962(c) attaches to a "person" "employed or associated with" an "enterprise." This formulation is natural given the original conception of RICO as a statute to reach criminal infiltration of legitimate business enterprises, and to reach individual mobsters engaged in the direction of primarily criminal enterprises. The typical commercial disputes with which we are concerned do not fit either mold, but the statutory language nevertheless requires plaintiffs to pursue a "person," distinct from the "enterprise," under § 1962(c).

Reves is a typical case. There, the enterprise was the Farmer's Cooperative, and its general manager, Jack White, was one of the "persons" pursued under § 1962(c). Joe Drozal, the Ernst & Young accountant in charge of the audit, was another "person" under the complaint, as was his partnership. We term the potential liability of White and Drozal "personal liability," because it is the liability of an individual alleged to have been knowingly involved in the predicate acts. The liability of Ernst & Young as a partnership, and any other sort of derivative liability under RICO for the acts of an alleged wrongdoer, we term "vicarious."

At common law, employers and partnerships are not vicariously liable for the wrong of an employee or partner unless it is committed within the scope of employment. With many intentional torts, it can be difficult to reach the employer or partners under this standard. But in most of the cases that concern us here, the "fraud" may be said to occur within the scope of employment because it is plausibly motivated by an intention to serve the employer or partnership (such as to enable an accounting firm to collect its fees for an audit).[55] Thus, with the exception of the securities cases in which RICO may abolish the purchaser/seller requirement and create a new cause of action, it does not have much effect on vicarious liability for compensatory damages.

Vicarious liability for "punitive" or treble damages, however, is greatly expanded by RICO. As noted, RICO increases the personal liability of individuals accused of committing predicate acts by increasing the expected award in all cases, and by authorizing the award of treble damages in certain securities cases where only sin-

---

[55] See Keeton et al, *Prosser & Keeton on Torts* at 505 (cited in note 48).

gle damages would otherwise be available. Although the additional damages associated with trebling are considered "punitive," many jurisdictions do not distinguish at common law between vicarious punitive liability and vicarious compensatory liability, and thus hold employers and partnerships liable for both types of damages if the wrong is committed within the scope of employment. In these jurisdictions, therefore, the increased liability of employers and partnerships for "punitive" damages under RICO follows immediately from the increased personal liability of the individuals who commit predicate acts.

In other jurisdictions (and many federal common law decisions), vicarious liability for punitive damages is more limited. A few refuse to allow it altogether, while a number of others follow the Restatement of Torts in restricting it to the wrongs of managerial agents acting within the scope of employment.[56] Depending upon the circumstances, therefore, the employers and partners of individuals subject to personal liability under RICO would be protected at common law against vicarious liability for the "punitive" component of the award, even if the predicate act occurred within the scope of employment. This common law protection is destroyed by RICO to the extent that employers and partnerships become "persons" to which RICO liability attaches directly.

V. Does RICO Impose Excessive Liability?

The Supreme Court's expansive interpretation of RICO has encouraged plaintiffs to eschew pursuing traditional state law remedies for fraud and breach of contract in state court, and to litigate in federal court instead. This has led commentators to propose the repeal of civil RICO to ease the burden on overcrowded courts.[57]

The allocation of judicial resources is not the only issue. The discussion above shows that RICO significantly increases the damages award in ordinary fraud and securities fraud cases, and may also extend punitive liability to additional entities. This section inquires whether such an expansion of liability is economically desirable. It is not possible to give a single, definitive answer, but we suspect that for important classes of cases, the answer is no.

---

[56] Id at 11–12. The issues are discussed at length in *Johnson v Rogers*, 763 P2d 771 (Utah 1988); *Muratore v M/S Scotia Prince*, 845 F2d 347 (1st Cir 1988).

[57] See, e.g., William Rehnquist, *Remarks of the Chief Justice on Diversity Jurisdiction and Civil RICO*, 21 St Mary's L J 5 (1989).

Especially as to the "punitive" component of RICO damages, there are good reasons to fear overdeterrence from punitive damages in many of the commercial disputes to which RICO has been applied, and good reasons to doubt the wisdom of vicarious punitive liability even when punitive liability on the active wrongdoer might be justifiable.

A. BACKGROUND: PUNITIVE AWARDS AND THE UNITARY ACTOR

By "unitary actor," we mean an individual defendant who internalizes all of the benefits to the conduct that is subject to possible civil liability. The economic literature on punitive damages against unitary actors teaches that punitive liability is often undesirable, as it can induce overinvestment in precautionary measures and an inefficient contraction of valuable activities. This problem is especially likely to arise when the harm is accidental. If compensatory damages are equal to the social costs that result when an accidental harm materializes and the liability of the unitary actor is strict, compensatory liability alone will induce the unitary actor to internalize the social costs of harms in choosing the level of precaution against harm and the level of activity that risks harm. Punitive liability, by contrast, will produce overdeterrence on both margins.

The overdeterrence problem is potentially less acute when liability for accidental harm requires a showing of negligence because an actor can avoid all liability simply by exercising due care. But overdeterrence can still arise to the degree that the negligence system functions imperfectly. The due care standard will likely be set too high in some cases, and thus "negligence" is at times efficient—punitive liability will discourage it. More importantly, the due care standard is not always known ex ante, and the possibility of error exists ex post, so that punitive liability has the potential to induce actors to take excessive care to guard against findings of negligence. The commentators typically conclude, therefore, that punitive liability for accidental harms governed by a negligence rule is also undesirable in most cases.[58]

A caveat to these conclusions relates to administrative costs. Conceivably, the inefficiencies associated with overdeterrence may

---

[58] See, e.g., William Landes and Richard Posner, *The Economic Structure of Tort Law* 162, 302 (1987); Steven Shavell, *Economic Analysis of Accident Law* 127–28 (1987); Richard Posner, *Economic Analysis of Law* 209 (4th ed 1992).

be more than offset by a reduction in administrative costs due to a decline in the number of wrongs when punitive liability is imposed.[59] Because it is difficult to ascertain when this may occur, however, it is also difficult to rest arguments for punitive liability on this basis.

Another class of arguments for punitive damages invoke deficiencies in the compensatory damages regime. One possibility is that compensatory damages may understate the social harm (a common concern, for example, in wrongful death cases). "Punitive" liability may then be mislabeled because it corrects an undercompensation problem. A related possibility is that the wrongdoer does not expect to be caught or to be sued all the time. "Punitive" liability, in the proper magnitude, may then confront the wrongdoer ex ante with expected liability equal to actual harm. Hence, the earlier conclusions about the inefficiencies of punitive liability for accidental harms require qualification—the argument against punitive liability only applies to damages that are truly "punitive" and that do not have the effect of confronting actors with a certainty equivalent to the social harm that their activities may cause.

Now consider intentional harms, such as crimes against person or property. Assuming that such harms are socially unproductive in general, we need not worry much about overdeterring them with punitive damages. If actors can escape liability simply by refraining from some deliberate, unproductive act, there will be no excess of precaution or contraction of valuable activity. In this class of cases, therefore, the overdeterrence objections above to true "punitive" liability largely vanish. Any remaining overdeterrence issues relate mainly to the possibility of judicial error.

Of course, to say that punitive liability may not overdeter does not make an affirmative case for imposing it. One possible benefit of punitive liability is that it may at times substitute for a expensive computation of compensatory damages, but this argument does not apply if punitive damages are in addition to or a function of the compensatory award (as they are, for example, in a treble damages regime). Another benefit of punitive damages arises in a subset of intentional harm cases involving the coerced acquisition of property rights (as through theft). A transfer of property rights is assuredly efficient in some instances, but a voluntary market transaction will reveal whether the willingness to pay of the individual that acquires

[59] David Friedman, *An Economic Explanation of Punitive Damages*, 40 Ala L Rev 1125 (1989).

the property exceeds the reservation price of the individual that parts with it. Even though "efficient theft" is conceivable, therefore, punitive damages have the virtue of encouraging those who wish to obtain the property of another to use the market where transactions are cheaper than court proceedings and the possibility of error is avoided. Finally, in many intentional harm cases, we may infer that the actor perceives a good chance of escape or nondetection. Thus, the argument for some degree of supracompensatory liability to correct for underenforcement will often be compelling. But even then, the efficient level of liability will not be arbitrarily high—if nothing else, increases in the damages award will cause more resources to be devoted to litigation, an effect that is undesirable, other things being equal.

Notably absent from this economic perspective on punitive liability is any role for "punishment" per se. In general, there will exist an optimal level of damages in any category of cases that maximizes the net social gains to civil liability, taking account of the costs and benefits of activities that are discouraged, error costs, the costs of the judicial system, and so on. In reality, of course, "punitive" liability is not assessed with express reference to such matters—juries are encouraged to focus, inter alia, on the moral character of defendants' conduct. Some scholars argue that punitive damages in practice nevertheless provide in a rough way an economically appropriate supplement to ordinary compensatory damages.[60] Yet it is also possible that punitive damages in practice are higher at times than economic analysis suggests they should be. In the discussion to follow, it will be useful to distinguish at times between punitive damages that have sound economic justification, as when they correct for an underdetection problem, and punitive damages that exist simply to "punish" the wrongdoer—the latter we term "true" punitive liability.

B. IMPLICATIONS: PUNITIVE LIABILITY AND THE UNITARY FRAUDFEASOR UNDER RICO

Consider first a case of traditional common law fraud, with intention to deceive. True fraud is strictly unproductive. The social costs of fraud include the resources invested to perpetrate the fraud, and the marginal effect of fraud on the resources invested

---

[60] See, e.g., Landes and Posner, *The Economic Structure of Tort Law* 160–65, 184–85 (1987).

by potential victims to protect themselves. They also include the deadweight loss from any distortion of incentives caused by the misinformation transmitted through fraud, the costs that arise when any resources are not controlled by their highest valued users, and any marginal costs associated with socially valuable transactions that do not occur because of the fraud. These costs are difficult indeed to measure, and in any event are typically less than the gain to the fraudfeasor, much of which will be a transfer from the victim. Thus, to deter fraud, damages likely must exceed the deadweight loss as they must force the perpetrator at least to disgorge the gains.[61] Underdetection is also of considerable concern with fraud, which adds to the appropriate level of damages ex post. Fraud may also be analogized to the theft cases—there are obvious advantages to forcing transactions through a market uncontaminated with deliberately falsified or misleading information. For all of these reasons, there is much to be said for requiring the fraudfeasor to disgorge the gains and then some—perhaps quite a bit more than what the victim has lost. Hence, common law fraud tends to be a relatively attractive case for the imposition of "punitive" damages upon the fraudfeasor.

The requirement under RICO that certain individuals who commit common law fraud must pay treble damages plus attorneys fees, therefore, seems potentially unobjectionable. But RICO liability may extend to behavior that is not strictly unproductive, and it is here that a serious danger of overdeterrence arises.

As noted, RICO counts now appear routinely in securities fraud cases. These cases typically involve communications to the market that later prove to be incorrect, an outcome that can assuredly materialize in the absence of any fraud. For example, management's predictions about a firm's future earnings may have a reasonable basis when made yet turn out to be incorrect for any number of reasons such as changed market or industry conditions. In theory, such statements are protected from liability by the scienter requirement, but courts have interpreted the scienter requirement under the securities laws and RICO to be satisfied by a showing of "recklessness," notoriously difficult to distinguish from ordinary negligence. Further, mental state is traditionally viewed by the courts as a question of fact that can only be resolved at trial, where

---

[61] In this respect, fraud is similar to certain antitrust violations such as price-fixing. See Posner, *Economic Analysis of Law* at 315–19.

jury biases may play an important role in the outcome. The danger of a finding of "fraud" even in its absence, therefore, is considerable.

Hence, excessive damages in securities cases surely have the potential to cause overinvestment in precaution and undue contraction of valuable activity. Most obviously, firms may overinvest in verifying information as a defensive measure to reduce liability risk. Similarly, the liability risk will affect both the form and amount of information disclosed. Management that might otherwise make a prediction of future earnings, for example, may now say nothing or say that the difficulty of predicting the future makes it impossible to estimate future earnings. This response to liability risk imposes a cost to investors who may highly value management's beliefs because stock prices are determined by expectations of future performance, and management will frequently be in the best position to predict the firm's future performance, albeit with great uncertainty. Other perverse consequences may also occur, such as a decision by some firms not to go public.

The treble damages remedy of RICO is problematic because mere "compensatory damages" in securities cases likely exceed the amount required for optimal deterrence. Under the traditional "out-of-pocket" method for calculating damages in open market securities cases, damages are measured by the amount of "artificial inflation" caused by the alleged disclosure defect. Consider, for example, a hypothetical situation where a company's falsely positive earnings announcement causes its stock in the aftermarket to trade at $10. When the correct information about earnings is revealed, the price of the stock falls from $10 to $4 in response to the corrective disclosure. In this situation, all purchasers under the out-of-pocket method who purchased at $10 and held until the price fell to $4 can claim $6 per share in damages. In securities cases involving publicly held corporations with millions of actively traded shares, it is easy to see how this damages rule often produces damages claims in excess of $100 million. Commentators have criticized the out-of-pocket measure of damages, particularly in cases involving trading in the secondary market.[62] Because the $6 loss to purchasers in the above example is exactly offset by a $6 gain of

---

[62] See Paul Mahoney, *Precaution Costs and the Law of Fraud in Impersonal Markets*, 78 Va L Rev 623 (1992); Frank Easterbrook and Daniel Fischel, *Optimal Damages in Securities Cases*, 52 U Ch L Rev 611 (1985).

sellers, the loss to purchasers may bear no relationship to the net social loss caused by the alleged disclosure defect. Likewise, the loss to purchasers may bear no relationship to the gains of the wrongdoer from the challenged conduct, which in many cases are trivial if not nonexistent, especially in the aftermarket cases. Thus, damages under the out-of-pocket measure cannot be justified in general by the need to force a fraudfeasor to disgorge the gains. The strong suspicion arises, therefore, that damages in securities fraud cases are high enough even without RICO to produce serious overdeterrence problems.

Similar concerns arise with respect to RICO liability in cases such as *Sedima* that resemble ordinary breach of contract actions. Many breach decisions may be characterized by plaintiffs as the product of fraudulent behavior—"you never intended to keep your promise." Such allegations can raise difficult fact questions that courts will be reluctant to resolve on summary judgment, and the possibility that a jury may find a fraud where no fraud was present can at times be considerable. Thus, the applicability of RICO in these cases creates a distinct chance of punitive damages for simple breach of contract. The overdeterrence problem then arises because even though breach of contract is intentional much of the time, it can be socially productive. An actor who confronts accurately computed compensatory liability for breach of contract will weigh the social costs and benefits of breach, and commit a breach if and only if it is efficient. Punitive liability can distort the breach decision and lead to inefficient performance.[63] Punitive liability is also unlikely to be justified by any systematic undercompensation problem (since damages are generally economic) and only rarely by an

---

[63] This argument against punitive liability for breach of contract is, in fact, overstated, however, because the party who contemplates breach can always buy his way out the contract—all joint gains can be realized through renegotiation if the transaction costs are low enough (the Coase Theorem). Indeed, along the lines of the argument for punitive damages in theft cases, an argument might be made for forcing breach decisions "through the market" to avoid administrative costs and error costs associated with litigation. That argument has been advanced elsewhere in support of an expanded remedy of specific performance. See, e.g., Alan Schwartz, *The Case for Specific Performance*, 89 Yale L J 271 (1979). The case against punitive liability for breach of contract thus rests in considerable part upon the notion that the transaction costs of adjusting obligations voluntarily are high, including the costs of strategic behavior. A further argument against punitive liability applies to situations in which breach is not a deliberate choice, but a consequence of factors beyond the control of the party who may breach (failure of raw material supplies, for example, not covered by some excuse doctrine). As in tort settings, punitive liability can produce excessive incentives to take precautions against these eventualities.

underenforcement problem (because breach of contract does not go undetected, the only argument here would relate to excessive costs of suit in cases where damages are small).

C. PERSONAL LIABILITY OF OUTSIDE PROFESSIONALS

Many commentators have applauded the increased exposure of outside professionals under RICO.[64] The statute's scope, the argument runs, is not limited to members of particular groups such as the Mafia or Cosa Nostra but rather applied to any "person" or entity that engages in proscribed activities. Thus RICO provides no exemption for outside professionals or anyone else. While the argument that there is no blanket immunity under RICO for any group may be correct as a matter of statutory construction, there are important differences between accountants and members of organized crime, differences which suggest that the error costs associated with RICO liability may be far greater when it is extended to outside professionals.

Members of organized crime, by definition, have no reputational interest in honesty. They can only be deterred by legal sanctions, and it is difficult to imagine how the law will create serious problems of overdeterrence by assessing civil damages against individuals for a pattern of criminal activity that has resulted in multiple prosecutions and convictions.

The analysis plainly differs for outside professionals such as accountants. Corporations or other types of business associations of any size are frequently characterized by separation of the management from the risk-bearings functions. Those who have management skills run the firm while those who have capital and a willingness to invest bear risk. This separation of function benefits investors by allowing them to capture the benefits of specialization but subjects them to the risk that their funds will be used for managers' personal benefit. Investors will take this risk into account in deciding whether, and on what terms, to invest. To allay investors' concerns, those who raise capital have strong incentives to establish institutional arrangements that facilitate the monitoring of managerial performance.

---

[64] See, e.g., Michael Goldsmith, *Judicial Immunity for White Collar Crime: The Ironic Demise of Civil RICO*, 30 Harv J Leg 1 (1993); G. Robert Blakey, *Foreword: Debunking RICO's Myriad Myths*, 64 St John's L Rev 701 (1990).

Independent accountants are one such type of monitoring arrangements.[65] By examining a firm's financial condition and opining on whether management's representations reflect the true state of the firm, audits limit managers' ability to exploit investors. Other outside professionals such as investment bankers and law firms that vouch for management statements perform the same function. This explains why publicly traded corporations voluntarily contracted with independent accountants (and other outside professionals) long before there was any requirement to do so.

Now consider the case where an accountant or other outside professional acquires a reputation for dishonesty. In this event, firms that hire the accountant will not be able to allay investors' concerns that their funds will be expropriated. The opposite will be true and investors will discount management's representations to an even greater extent. Indeed, the retention of a professional with a reputation for dishonesty may be viewed as a signal that management is attempting to mislead investors. This will decrease the willingness of investors to commit capital or alternatively demand compensation of some type for the increased risk.

The above discussion illustrates why accountants have strong incentives to maintain a reputation for independence and why firms have equally strong incentives to retain accountants with such reputations. Accountants are selling monitoring services, and the price that firms are willing to pay for these services is a function of how much investors value the services provided. Unless accountants and other outside professionals who vouch for management maintain a reputation for honesty and independence, in other words, they have nothing of value to sell.

It is important not to overstate the above argument. Our point is not that outside professionals will never engage in fraud or that reputation is a complete deterrent to fraud. Sometimes the gains from fraud, particularly to individuals or small firms whose fortunes are tied to one client, outweigh the reputational loss. Other times an outside professional may conclude that the probability of detection is sufficiently low that it is worthwhile to participate in a fraud. But in many other cases, outside professionals will conclude that the reputational loss from engaging in fraudulent con-

[65] See Daniel Fischel, *The Regulation of Accounting: Some Economic Issues*, 52 Brooklyn L Rev 1051 (1987).

duct outweighs the prospect of receiving additional fees. This will be particularly true for large professional firms, the typical RICO defendant, that have many clients with no client being responsible for a large share of the firms' revenues.

The inference that we draw from this discussion is that allegations of "fraud" against outside professionals will often, though not always, be meritless. In securities cases in particular, it is easy to allege that an accountant either knowingly or recklessly omitted to correct some bit of misinformation in the financial statements, or conspired with management to conceal it . Likewise, outside professionals erroneously accused of fraud cannot be confident of exoneration, or that hard-nosed litigation tactics will cause the plaintiff to go away. The problem is a potentially serious one even without RICO liability, and the additional damages available under RICO simply heighten it.

These concerns are reminiscent of those discussed at length in the extensive literature on accountants' liability. The *Ultramares* rule,[66] followed today in many jurisdictions, bars actions against auditors for ordinary negligence absent special circumstances. Fears of overdeterrence due to error costs, litigation costs, and socially excessive damages have led a number of commentators to approve this "no duty" rule.[67] RICO liability may be distinguished by the presence of "fraud," yet as noted, the line between fraud and negligence can prove a fine one in the law, and a source of error in practice.

D. DID ARTHUR YOUNG ENGAGE IN FRAUD?

Our conclusion that allegations against outside professionals will frequently be meritless appears to be in some tension with *Reves* itself where the jury found Arthur Young liable for securities fraud. The jury further found that Arthur Young was responsible for the notes trading at artificially inflated prices and assessed damages accordingly. Whether Arthur Young's accounting decisions defrauded investors and caused them to suffer losses, however, is far from clear.

The principal allegation of fraud against Arthur Young was that

---

[66] *Ultramares Corp. v Touche*, 255 NY 170, 174 NE 441 (1931).

[67] See, e.g., Victor Goldberg, *Accountable Accountants: Is Third-Party Liability Necessary?* 17 J Legal Stud 295 (1988).

it valued White Flame in the Co-op's financial statements at historic cost and only disclosed in the footnotes that there was doubt as to the recoverability of this amount. Arthur Young was also alleged not to have fully disclosed its reservations concerning the market value of White Flame at the Co-op's annual meetings of its members since only summary financial information was disseminated without the key footnotes. The members were told, however, that White Flame was losing more than $1 million annually and that complete financial statements were available.

Were investors misled by Arthur Young's accounting decisions? One interpretation of Arthur Young's conduct (apparently accepted by the jury) was that Arthur Young made decisions deliberately designed to avoid having to record White Flame's market value on the Co-op's financial statements to make the Co-op appear to be solvent in an accounting sense. But even accepting this characterization, it does not follow that purchasers of the Co-op notes paid an artificially inflated price. The value of the Co-op notes was determined by the market value of the Co-op's assets, not how those assets were treated for accounting purposes. The case appears to have been litigated under the assumption that the only source of information about the market value of the Co-op's assets (and thus the value of the notes) was the treatment of White Flame in the Co-op's financial statements. But this assumption is implausible. White Flame was one of the major, if not the major, asset owned by the Co-op, and the losses it was incurring were a subject of heated discussion at the annual meetings with members. And, even from the perspective of accounting, there was disclosure of problems with White Flame in the footnotes to the financial statements. Thus the claim that investors were misled by Arthur Young's accounting decisions rests on the assumption that investors were sophisticated enough to be misled by the Co-op's financial statements, but not sophisticated enough to consider the footnotes to those statements.[68]

Ultimately, it is impossible to resolve with certainty the question of whether Arthur Young's accounting decisions misled investors and caused them to purchase notes at artificially inflated prices.

---

[68] If the notes were publicly traded, this premise would be even more difficult to accept. See Daniel Fischel, *The Use of Modern Finance Theory in Securities Fraud Cases Involving Actively Traded Securities*, 38 Bus Law 1 (1982).

But the jury's finding that Arthur Young committed fraud is sufficiently problematic that we are reluctant to reject the alternative
hypothesis that the outcome is better explained as the result of jury
bias and legal error. And, if this alternative hypothesis is correct,
the outcome in *Reves* reinforces our point that overdeterrence is a
serious problem facing outside professionals in securities cases.

E. VICARIOUS RICO LIABILITY ·

Vicarious liability for RICO damages raises additional issues.
To see why, consider a simple hypothetical. Suppose that the manager of a company commits traditional fraud, with scienter, to
induce a customer to purchase something that the customer would
not otherwise want. Profits from the sale benefit the manager indirectly, perhaps because compensation is linked to profits or to sales,
but much of the gains from the fraud (if it is successful) will be
shared with the residual claimants. Assume that the residual claimants have not participated in the fraud or encouraged the manager
to commit it.

In this example, the fact that gains are shared is of no great
significance as far as the liability of the manager is concerned. The
manager has engaged in strictly unproductive behavior, and it may
well be efficient for the manager to confront a prospect of personal,
punitive liability because of the underdetection problem or for the
other reasons noted previously. Any compelling objection to punitive liability on the manager must rest on the notion that such
liability cannot be appropriately confined and will create overdeterrence problems due to errors, or that it will add unduly to litigation
costs.

What about the liability of the residual claimants? The analysis
here is somewhat more subtle. Assuming that the residual claimants have some capacity to monitor the manager effectively, it is
important that they suffer a loss equal to the social costs of the
fraud to induce proper monitoring to prevent it. But because they
share in the gains from the fraud, much of which are a transfer,
liability equal to the social costs of the fraud will not usually be
sufficient to create this incentive (even if those costs could be accurately measured). Ideally, therefore, the residual claimants must
be forced to disgorge their gains from the fraud, plus its social
costs, to ensure that their net loss is equal to the social cost.

The compensatory measure of damages for fraud is simply equal to the damages suffered by the victim of fraud measured against a baseline of the status quo ante or against what was promised by the fraudfeasor (rescission is also allowed where the victim has transferred something of value).[69] The relation between this measure and the socially ideal measure for purposes of vicarious liability is uncertain, and indeed will vary from case to case. Consider, for example, a case in which an agent lies to a buyer about defects in a piece of real property, fraudulently inducing the buyer to purchase it for a vastly inflated price. Assume that the defects do not lead to an accident and that the buyer's ignorance of them does not exacerbate some decline in the value of the property. The social costs of the fraud then *may* be fairly small. Perhaps the property did not go to the highest valued user and must be reconveyed so that the fraud adds to transaction costs in the real estate market. Or perhaps the existence of such frauds makes buyers fearful in general and discourages some valuable transactions, so that the social costs of the fraud include its marginal contribution to this problem. Plausibly, a damages award that simply compensates the buyer for all losses suffered as a result of the fraud (measured against one of the two baselines) is roughly equal to the seller's gains from the fraud plus the social costs, which would provide some argument for limiting vicarious liability to the usual compensatory measure of damages. But the underenforcement problem remains to be considered, and if "punitive" liability is simply an adjustment for the underdetection problem it can be justified against the residual claimants using the familiar arguments. But where punitive damages represent "true" punitive liability as defined earlier, they will create an incentive for excessive monitoring of agents because the private returns to monitoring would exceed the social returns.

The implications of this example are fairly general: If the acts of an agent involve behavior that is strictly unproductive, such as traditional fraud, and ignoring the problem of judicial error, there is no harm and possibly a benefit in imposing punitive liability on the agent personally. But it is difficult to know exactly what the optimal level of liability is, and the possibility arises that it will exceed the amount required for efficient deterrence. Vicarious lia-

---

[69] Keeton et al, *Prosser & Keeton on Torts* at 766–68 (cited in note 48).

bility for "true" punitive liability will compound the problem by distorting another margin—the monitoring incentive. Thus, for example, where "punitive" liability corrects for an underdetection problem, vicarious liability for those damages is appropriate. But where punitive damages simply extract a pound of flesh from someone who is perceived to have behaved outrageously, vicarious liability seems quite undesirable.

Our conclusions are unaffected where RICO liability extends to "co-conspirators" or to "aiders and abettors," provided once again that the liability is only personal and that each actor has engaged in socially unproductive behavior. There, RICO liability becomes joint and several, and an issue arises as to how it will be shared, but the economics of the situation do not change importantly.

Likewise, the analysis does not change when the party who commits the predicate acts is not "employed by" the "enterprise," like our hypothetical manger, but is merely "associated with" it. The outside professional cases are again relevant. Suppose, for example, that an outside auditor conspires with a manager to perpetrate a fraud by doctoring the books or approving the results of an audit known to conceal important information. The objection here to punitive, personal liability on the outside auditor is the error and litigation costs problems, as argued above. But the extension of "true" punitive liability to accounting firms creates a further problem in the form of excessive monitoring.

We are particularly concerned that this problem will arise in securities fraud cases. As noted earlier, the social costs of securities fraud are likely considerably below the loss suffered by plaintiffs— especially in aftermarket cases, the plaintiffs' loss is largely offset by a gain to third parties. Further, any gains to outside professional firms from participation in the fraud are usually limited to fees collected, which are typically dwarfed by the plaintiffs' compensatory damage measure. In many cases, therefore, "compensatory" liability on the outside professional firm may already exceed the sum of gains to the firm plus social costs of the "fraud." RICO liability then compounds the associated overdeterrence problem unless it can be justified by the underdetection argument.[70]

---

[70] We note that it is not in general possible for the outside professional firms to protect themselves against this liability through indemnity agreements or actions. The individuals responsible for the fraud will usually have insufficient assets, and the client firm will often be in financial difficulty as well (recall the facts of *Reves*).

VI. Implications: The Extension of RICO Beyond Its Original Conception and the "Second Best" Approach of Reves

RICO may have been quite sensible when applied to the organized crime cases it was originally intended to address. Damages from ordinary criminal activity may at times be small in relation to litigation costs, and fear of reprisals from the targets of a lawsuit may deter claims even where damages exceed litigation costs. Conceivably, a trebling of the compensatory award, with the addition of attorneys fees, generates a valuable incentive for citizens to act as private attorneys general, supplementing the law enforcement efforts of public agencies.

We doubt that RICO liability may be justified in the commercial cases that concern us here, however, because of any comparable deficiency in the incentive to sue for commercial fraud. Indeed, it seems almost absurd that identical damages principles should govern both commercial fraud cases and suits against organized crime figures. The nature and magnitude of the social costs from the "predicate acts," the extent of any underenforcement problem, and the dangers of overdeterrence surely differ dramatically across these groups of cases. Thus, a strong suspicion arises that the extension of RICO remedies to garden variety commercial "fraud" litigation has been imprudent and ill-considered.

In a "first-best" world, therefore, perhaps RICO would be confined to the domain of serious organized criminal activity. As noted earlier, Congress had great difficulty in doing so when drafting the statute because of constitutional concerns, leading to the convoluted statutory language and structure. In light of that statutory language, perhaps the best that can be done judicially is to develop a clear notion of when the hefty sanctions of RICO are appropriate and when they are not, and thereafter to construe the statute where possible to confine RICO to sensible applications. *Reves* may accomplish just that to some degree—even though the "operation or management" test that it formulates is difficult to fathom as any sort of "first-best" solution to the overbreadth of RICO actions, it may be a "second-best" response given the constraints on the Court imposed by the statute and by its own prior decisions.

At first blush, the "operation or management" test sounds rather like the "control" test in agency law, which determines when an employee is a "servant" and thus in most cases whether the employer is liable for the employee's torts. The control test has some merit for this purpose, as it may function among other things to capture the degree to which vicarious liability will result in valuable monitoring of potentially insolvent wrongdoers.[71] But any similarity to the operation or management test is largely superficial. The operation or management test determines when *personal* liability will attach under RICO, and bears only indirectly upon the scope of vicarious liability. Further, the argument for the control test relates to the gains from the imposition of vicarious compensatory liability upon employers, whereas RICO liability is potentially punitive.

It is thus tempting to conclude that the operation or management test is unlikely to identify cases in which RICO liability is desirable (or less likely to be harmful). As to personal liability, the consequences of "punitive" damages turn, as indicated, on such factors as whether the acts in question are strictly unproductive and on the existence of an underenforcement problem. The question whether an actor has participated in the "operation or management" of the "enterprise," however, bears no immediate relation to either issue. Likewise, our analysis suggests that vicarious liability for truly "punitive" damages is never appropriate, and hence that vicarious liability for what the law calls "punitive" damages can only be justified by an undercompensation or underenforcement problem. Once again, it is difficult to see how the "operation or management" test captures anything of direct relevance here.

But perhaps the test accomplishes something else. If we focus on overdeterrence problems caused by the possibility of error in the imposition of RICO liability, certainly one factor to consider is whether the actor accused of a predicate act had a motive to engage in it. Plausibly, those engaged in the "operation or management" of an enterprise will on average reap more of the gains from causing the enterprise to engage in prohibited conduct. The operation or management test set forth in *Reves*, therefore, may serve crudely to filter out defendants who were unlikely to gain much from the challenged conduct and thus unlikely to have been active participants in any wrongdoing.

Finally, even if the "operation or management" test in *Reves* lacks

---

[71] See Alan Sykes, *The Economics of Vicarious Liability*, 93 Yale L J 1231 (1984).

convincing economic logic, it may nevertheless narrow the scope of potentially counterproductive RICO claims. By construing "operation or management" to afford some protection for outside professionals, *Reves* may help to avoid punitive liability for acts that are often more like ordinary negligence than classic fraud, and to limit potential liability in a class of cases where erroneous findings of fraud are of great concern. It may also help to avert the additional inefficiencies of vicarious punitive liability on outside professional firms. Further, because many of the outside professional cases involve alleged securities fraud by accounting firms, the result in *Reves* is appealing given the tendency of ordinary securities damages to overpenalize even without trebling.

VII. The Future Impact of Reves

We contend above that the extension of RICO liability into the sphere of ordinary commercial litigation raises serious concerns about overdeterrence and excessive litigation. As the first effort by the Supreme Court to stem this tide, *Reves* potentially is a very important case. On one level, *Reves* may dramatically lessen the exposure of professionals, the perennial deep pocket defendants in civil RICO actions. More generally, *Reves* is the first time the Court has opted for a narrow construction of RICO's scope. Thus the case may also mark a shift in the Court's attitude toward the statute. Whether *Reves* does in fact lessen the exposure of professionals, or represent a meaningful narrowing of RICO's scope, however, depends on how several issues left open by the decision are resolved in the future. What is certain is that Justice Blackmun's statement in his opinion for the Court that the "operation or management" test will be "easy to apply"[72] is surely incorrect.

A. THE MEANING OF THE "OPERATION OR MANAGEMENT" TEST

Reves clearly holds that outside professionals can be liable under RICO only if they "participated in the operation or management" of the RICO enterprise. What does this mean? On first reading, the opinion provides considerable comfort to professionals. Without

---

[72] 113 S Ct at 1170. The future implications of *Reves* are perceptively analyzed in Andrew Weissman and Arthur Mathews, *Whither Civil RICO in the Wake of Reves v Ernst & Young* (forthcoming).

question, the accounting firm in *Reves*, by creating the financial
statements and selecting the accounting treatment found to be
fraudulent, had greater involvement in management decision making than the typical accounting firm or outside professional. Indeed, Arthur Young's role in the fraud was sufficient for the Eighth
Circuit to affirm the jury's finding that it was liable for securities
fraud. This involvement was insufficient for RICO liability, however, because of the Court's focus on the importance of "direction."
Only those who have "some part in directing the enterprise's affairs" can be liable.

This language suggests that an outside professional can know
about a fraud, by its actions facilitate the fraud, but still not be
liable under RICO because it does not "direct the enterprise's affairs." Unless the outside professional is responsible for or in control of management decision making enabling it to "direct the enterprise's affairs," there can be no RICO liability.

While this interpretation of *Reves* will be advanced by professional defendants in future cases, there is sufficient contradictory
language in *Reves* to make the issue murky at best. For example,
the Court explicitly refused to define the participation requirement
as the ability to have control of an enterprise.[73] This interpretation
of the participation requirement, the Court stated, was too restrictive. Thus a defendant must do more than knowingly assist in a
fraud, but need not control the enterprise that commits the fraud.
It does not require great creativity to envision the line-drawing
problems created by the Court's distinction between playing some
role in directing an enterprise's affairs which is a prerequisite for
liability, and controlling those affairs which is not.

Even more confusing is the Court's discussion of the liability of
lower level employees of a racketeering enterprise. Before *Reves*,
courts had repeatedly held that lower level participants of RICO
enterprises, particularly criminal enterprises akin to organized
crime, could be liable under § 1962(c) because "the RICO net is
woven tightly to trap even the smallest fish, those peripherally
involved with the enterprise."[74] Concerned about the potential impact of *Reves* on its ability to prosecute such "small fish" in RICO

[73] 113 S Ct at 1170 n 4.

[74] See, e.g., *United States v Elliott*, 571 F2d 880, 903 (5th Cir), cert denied, 439 US 953
(1978).

cases, the Department of Justice, as amicus, argued that the Court should not limit RICO's scope to "upper management" of an enterprise.

Apparently sensitive to this concern, the Court made clear that "liability under § 1962(c) is not limited to upper management."[75] But if § 1962(c) is not so limited, how can lower level participants have the ability to "direct the enterprise's affairs," as the Court stated was required for outsiders to be liable? The Court glossed over this apparent tension by stating that: "An enterprise is 'operated' not just by upper management but also by lower-rung participants in the enterprise who are under the direction of upper management."[76] With this one sentence, the Court undercut much of its earlier emphasis on the importance of "directing" an enterprise's affairs. Now the "direction" requirement includes both those who direct, as well as those who take direction. For a Court that prides itself on the importance of the plain language of its statute, this contorted interpretation of the words "operated" and "direction" is, at the very least, paradoxical. This linguistic exegesis did not change the outcome in *Reves*, however, because, the Court stated, it was "clear that Arthur Young was not acting under the direction of the Co-op's officers or board."[77]

Why was it "clear" that Arthur Young was not acting "under the direction" of the Co-op's management? Presumably the Court was referring to the absence of any direct evidence of the Co-op management instructing Arthur Young to use fraudulent numbers. For Arthur Young's liability to turn on this point, however, is to exalt form over substance. The sale of the Co-op notes at inflated prices benefited the Co-op, not Arthur Young. Why else would Arthur Young knowingly participate and assist in the Co-op's fraud except at the behest of management? And even if Arthur Young somehow decided to participate in the fraud independently as opposed to being directed to do so by management, why should this be exonerating? The more the fraud can be attributed to Arthur Young and management as opposed to just management, the stronger the case for imposing liability on both.

The Court's discussion of Arthur Young not being directed to

[75] 113 S Ct at 1172.

[76] Id at 1173.

[77] Id at n 9.

participate in the management fraud makes sense only if the Court did not believe that Arthur Young was knowingly involved at all. Perhaps skeptical that a major accounting firm would risk its reputation with the resulting potential legal liability so that the Co-op could sell notes at inflated prices, the Court stretched to avoid finding Arthur Young liable. The Court, in other words, chose to disbelieve, at least implicitly, the jury and the Eighth Circuit which had found Arthur Young liable for knowingly participating in the management fraud. Since there was no direct evidence that Arthur Young was "directed" to participate in the fraud, it could not be liable.

Future courts will have to struggle with the alternative bases for liability under the Court's "operation or management" test. When outside professionals will be deemed either to play a role in "directing" an enterprise's affairs or be "directed" to act in a certain way by management is far from clear. Does a company's long-time outside lawyer, auditor, or banker who has the confidence of senior management, for example, play a role in "directing" the enterprise's affairs, directly or indirectly? What if the outside professional is a member of the board of directors? And if such an outside professional makes a recommendation which is rejected, and then goes along with whatever course is adopted, is that professional acting under the "direction" of management? Based on *Reves*, it is impossible to answer these questions.

B. THE MEANING OF "ENTERPRISE"

To determine whether a defendant played a role in directing an enterprise's affairs requires a definition of "enterprise." In *Reves*, the enterprise was the Co-op, but this is not the only possibility.

Section 1962(4) defines "enterprise" as including any "legal entity" such as a partnership or corporation and "any union or group of individuals associated in fact although not a legal entity."[78] In *Turkette*, the Court held that "a group of persons associated together for a common purpose of engaging in a course of conduct constitutes an enterprise."[79] The existence of an enterprise "is proved by evidence of an ongoing organization, formal or informal,

---

[78] 18 USC § 1962(4).

[79] 452 US 576 (1981).

and by evidence that the various associates function as a continuing unit."

Thus RICO's enterprise requirement can be satisfied by "a group of individuals associated in fact" even though not a distinct "legal entity." What if the plaintiff in *Reves* had alleged that an association in fact consisting of Arthur Young, Jack White, and the Co-op constituted the racketeering enterprise, and that Arthur Young directed the affairs of this "enterprise?"

Such an allegation might be sufficient if the plaintiff could demonstrate that the alleged association in fact was as *Turkette* requires, "ongoing" and functioned "as a continuing unit."[80] In other words, the alleged association in fact, even if not a separate legal entity, must have some separate existence apart from the alleged illegal acts. Otherwise, proof of the pattern of racketeering activity would also establish the existence of an enterprise. Whether the plaintiff in *Reves* could have adequately alleged an association in fact apart from the challenged fraudulent conduct is unclear. In future cases, courts' attitude toward association in fact enterprises will be critical in light of the obvious incentives of plaintiffs to allege such associations in fact to satisfy *Reves*'s "operation or management" test.

C. SECONDARY LIABILITY

Reves dealt with the question of whether Arthur Young violated RICO. Another important issue for the future is whether plaintiffs can limit *Reves* by alleging theories of secondary liability. What if plaintiffs in *Reves* had alleged, for example, that Arthur Young was liable as an aider and abettor and/or conspirator. Under either of these theories, arguably it would not be necessary for plaintiffs to establish that Arthur Young's conduct satisfied the "operation or management" test. So long as White played a role in directing the Co-op's affairs, as he clearly did, Arthur Young might be liable if it either aided and abetted White's violations or conspired with him.

Whether such an allegation of secondary liability against Arthur Young would be successful is again unclear. RICO is silent on whether it is unlawful to aid and abet a civil RICO violation by

---

[80] Id.

another party. For defendants such as Arthur Young that have been found liable for aiding and abetting the underlying securities violation, their liability for aiding and abetting a RICO violation would seem clear if such a cause of action exists. On the other hand, recognition of such a cause of action would effectively overrule *Reves* for defendants that are found liable for aiding and abetting the underlying securities violation or other predicate offenses.

Unlike aiding and abetting where the statute is silent, § 1962(d) of RICO does explicitly prohibit conspiracy to violate its substantive provisions.[81] The issue is whether a defendant such as Arthur Young in *Reves* that does not satisfy the "operation or management" test can be liable as a conspirator under § 1962(d). Lower courts are likely going to struggle with this question suggesting, once again, that the future impact of *Reves* is very unclear.

VIII. Should Civil RICO Be Modified or Repealed?

We have argued that the civil remedy under RICO is likely excessive in many of the commercial settings where predicate "fraud" can be alleged under RICO, and that *Reves* is likely to be only partly successful at confining the remedy to appropriate circumstances. The question arises whether there exists a better alternative, either through a different construction of the statute or through legislative changes.

Given the modest extent to which civil RICO claims are brought against individuals whose activities reflect "organized crime" in any conventional sense of that term, outright repeal of the civil provisions warrants consideration. To be sure, Congress may have reasonably believed that a civil action would provide a valuable supplement to enforcement activity against organized crime by public prosecutors, either because public resources are scarce or because the ability to recover damages might encourage certain individuals with private information to come forward with it. One can question whether this hope has borne out. Perhaps the fear of reprisals is powerful in these cases, or perhaps parties with the information necessary to make a case against organized crime figures are often in cahoots with them. In any event, as noted, the targets of civil

---

[81] 18 USC § 1962(d).

RICO actions are usually businesspeople or outside professionals who are not threatening figures, and the RICO action typically piggybacks on other civil remedies that we have no reason to believe are inadequate. Serious consideration ought thus be given to the possibility that the mine run of civil RICO litigation is an unfortunate and unintended consequence of the statute that outweighs any beneficial effects.

A less drastic legislative modification might aim at the particular cases on which we have focused—commercial litigation involving allegations of fraud. The deletion of securities fraud, mail fraud, and wire fraud from the list of predicate offenses would extinguish RICO claims in most securities and contract settings, alleviating the overdeterrence problems that concern us without affecting much the availability of the civil remedy in other contexts.

Another approach might be to strive to improve on the "definition" of organized crime that the statute implicitly embodies. Congress may well have been right in supposing that organized crime in the conventional sense differs in important respects from other forms of criminal activity, and that additional penalties may be valuable. In general, organizations like the Mafia arise because they increase the expected returns to criminal activity. The gains arise because collaborative criminal activity is valuable to criminals, and because criminals cannot draw upon the state to enforce their "contracts" for collaboration.

It is easy to see how collaborative criminal activity can increase the expected returns to crime. The expected returns may rise because effective collaboration aids in the concealment of crime (criminals can promise to supply alibis to each other, for example, or promise not to turn state's evidence if caught). The returns may also rise because certain crimes, such as extortion, require a credible threat of force that individuals cannot maintain in the face of a threat of arrest. Or gains may arise when experienced criminals plan crimes, but draw upon others with a lower expected penalty to commit them (juveniles, first offenders). The creation of a criminal organization is often essential to achieve these gains because contracts for collaborative criminal efforts are unenforceable, and the temptation to cheat on them can be great—the organization then substitutes internal means of disciplining its members and encouraging them to honor their commitments to each other. The criminal organization is thus similar to a legitimate business firm, which forms to economize on the costs of contracting in the open market.[82]

Because collaborative criminal activity can increase the returns to crime, it may be appropriate to adjust upward the penalty for collaborative crimes to maintain a given level of deterrence across collaborators and non-collaborators. This observation may help to explain why conspiracy is often a separate crime with a separate penalty. The next question is whether "organized crime" can be meaningfully distinguished from conspiracy, in a way that justifies still greater penalties. Perhaps the key distinction between, say, the mafia and an ordinary criminal conspiracy lies in the existence of a larger organization that uses extra-legal means to keep its members in line, and that provides additional services such as fencing of stolen merchandise, false alibis, and so on. In a mere conspiracy, for example, the arrest of the co-conspirators can create the Prisoner's Dilemma in the most classic sense. Knowledge of this possibility, ex ante, reduces expected returns. If members of an organized crime group anticipate that their confederates will not turn on them for fear of reprisal, by contrast, expected returns can rise.

By this reasoning, "organized crime" requires a broader criminal organization than simply the individuals involved in the crimes that are the subject of an instant criminal or civil action. Conceivably, the law might require proof of membership in such a criminal organization as a predicate to imposing criminal penalties for "racketeering," or to creating a special civil cause of action for "racketeering." This requirement might be created through statutory reform, or through a judicially imposed requirement of "racketeering injury" akin to that rejected by the Supreme Court in *Sedima*. Such a requirement would serve to dispose readily of the RICO claim in cases such as *Reves*. There was no suggestion in *Reves* that either the president of the cooperative or the accountants performing the audit were parties to a larger criminal organization extending beyond them.

Nevertheless, we question whether requiring proof of membership in a criminal organization as a prerequisite for RICO liability is workable. Such a requirement would add significant complexity because the characteristics of a defendant's affiliations over a broad

---

[82] See Ronald Coase, *The Nature of the Firm*, 4 Economica 386 (1937).

spectrum of activities would have to be considered in addition to the conduct at issue in a particular case. And, no matter how wide ranging the inquiry, the determination of whether an individual is a member of an organization which should be deemed "criminal" will inevitably be uncertain, with high error costs the result. In light of these practical difficulties, we suspect that the preferable approach to reform is legislative, and believe that a strong case can be made at least for the elimination of the predicate fraud offenses from the definition of racketeering activity.

JACK M. BEERMANN

THE SUPREME COURT'S NARROW VIEW
ON CIVIL RIGHTS

The right to choose abortion, although recently significantly cur-
tailed from its original scope,[1] is a federally protected liberty interest of women, and is at least protected against the imposition of
"undue burdens" by state and local government.[2] Some of the most
serious threats to women's ability to choose abortion have come not
from government regulation, but from private, national, organized
efforts to prevent abortions. In addition to seeking change through
the political system, some of these organizations, most notably
Operation Rescue, have focused on the providers of abortion, and
have attempted to prevent abortions by forcibly closing abortion
clinics and harassing and intimidating women and employees enter-
ing the clinics. These groups do not shy away from using illegal

Jack M. Beermann is Professor of Law and Associate Dean for Academic Affairs at Boston
University School of Law.

AUTHOR'S NOTE: William Zolla II's research assistance on this project was especially
important and helpful. Risa Sorkin, Hugh Hall, Carla Munroe, and Jennifer Walker also
provided valuable research assistance. Financial support was provided by a Boston University School of Law research grant. Hugh Baxter, Mark Brown, Ron Cass, Archibald Cox,
Betsy Foote, Barry Friedman, Fred Lawrence, David Seipp, Kate Silbaugh, Avi Soifer, and
Manuel Utset provided help with ideas and early drafts. Helpful comments were also received at
a Faculty Workshop at Indiana University—Bloomington School of Law. All errors are my own.

[1] Compare *Planned Parenthood of Southeastern Pennsylvania v Casey*, 112 S Ct 2791 (1992)
and *Webster v Reproductive Health Servs*, 492 US 490 (1989) with *Roe v Wade*, 410 US 113
(1973); *Doe v Bolton*, 410 US 179 (1973) and *Thornburgh v American College of Obstetricians &
Gynecologists*, 476 US 747 (1986).

[2] See *Casey*, 112 S Ct 2791 (1992). See also Jane Maslow Cohen, *A Jurisprudence of Doubt:
Deliberative Autonomy and Abortion*, 3 Colum J Gender & L 175 (1993). Professor Cohen
focuses on women's loss of deliberative autonomy inherent in the Court's approval of mandatory information and waiting periods. The waiting period also imposes considerable economic burdens which may make abortion significantly more expensive and thus difficult to
choose for poor women who do not live close to an abortion provider.

means to accomplish their goal.[3] In *Bray v Alexandria Women's Health Clinic*,[4] the Supreme Court rejected the consensus among lower federal courts[5] that private conspiracies to blockade abortion clinics were subject to federal court injunctions under 42 USC § 1985(3),[6] a provision of the Civil Rights Act of 1871.[7] *Bray* is the latest in a line of decisions that has rendered empty the forty-second Congress's promise of federal court protection against organized groups who interfere with individuals attempting to exercise their federal constitutional rights.

Bray involved Section 2 of the Civil Rights Act of 1871, often referred to as the Ku Klux Klan Act, now codified at 42 USC § 1985(3). The Ku Klux Klan Act was a direct response by Congress to widespread violence in the South against the newly freed slaves and their allies for equal rights.[8] The provision involved in *Bray* provides, *inter alia*, a cause of action in favor of parties injured

---

[3] See John Whitehead, *Civil Disobedience and Operation Rescue: A Historical and Theoretical Analysis*, 48 Wash & Lee L Rev 77 (1991); Alissa Rubin, *In God They Trespass: The Faces and Faith Behind Operation Rescue*, The Washington Post (May 16, 1993), p. c01.

[4] 113 S Ct 753 (1993).

[5] See *Volunteer Medical Clinic, Inc. v Operation Rescue*, 948 F2d 218 (6th Cir 1991); *National Organization for Women v Operation Rescue*, 914 F2d 582 (4th Cir 1990); *New York State National Organization for Women v Terry*, 886 F2d 1339 (2d Cir 1989), cert denied, 495 US 947 (1990).

[6] Section 1985(3) provides:

§ 1985. Conspiracy to interfere with civil rights

(3) Depriving persons of rights or privileges
If two or more persons in any State or Territory conspire or go in disguise on the highway or on the premises of another, for the purpose of depriving, either directly or indirectly, any person or class of persons of the equal protection of the laws, or of equal privileges and immunities under the laws; or for the purpose of preventing or hindering the constituted authorities of any State or Territory from giving or securing to all persons within such State or Territory the equal protection of the laws; or if two or more persons conspire to prevent by force, intimidation, or threat, any citizen who is lawfully entitled to vote, from giving his support or advocacy in a legal manner, toward or in favor of the election of any lawfully qualified person as an elector for President or Vice President, or as a Member of Congress of the United States; or to injure any citizen in person or property on account of such support or advocacy; in any case of conspiracy set forth in this section, if one or more persons engaged therein do, or cause to be done, any act in furtherance of the object of such conspiracy, whereby another is injured in his person or property, or deprived of having and exercising any right or privilege of a citizen of the United States, the party so injured or deprived may have an action for the recovery of damages occasioned by such injury or deprivation, against any one or more of the conspirators.

[7] See ch 22, 17 Stat 13 (1871).

[8] See Frederick M. Lawrence, *Civil Rights and Criminal Wrongs: The Mens Rea of Federal Civil Rights Crimes*, 67 Tulane L Rev 2113, 2140–46 (1993).

by conspiracies to "depriv[e] any person or class of persons of the equal protection of the laws, or of equal privileges and immunities under the laws."[9] The Court in *Bray* was called upon to address the applicability of this provision to Operation Rescue's efforts to prevent women, by blockading and otherwise temporarily closing abortion clinics, from having abortions.

Owing to inhospitable treatment by the Supreme Court, § 1985(3) has not, in its more than 120 years of existence, proven to be a useful tool in efforts to secure the enjoyment of civil rights.[10] For its first eighty years, § 1985(3) lay dormant, because soon after enactment, the Court held unconstitutional the criminal counterpart to § 1985(3), on grounds equally applicable to § 1985(3) itself.[11] Even after the clouds of unconstitutionality were carried away on the winds of constitutional change, the Court remained unsympathetic to the operation of § 1985(3).

In recent years, the Court has restricted the operation of section 1985(3) through a variety of limiting doctrines. In its first opinion construing the statute, the Court held that the statute's equal protection and equal privileges and immunities language meant that

---

[9] The statute also provides a cause of action against conspiracies entered into "for the purpose of preventing or hindering the constituted authorities of any State or Territory from giving or securing to all persons within such State or Territory the equal protection of the laws." The primary focus of the Court's decision in *Bray* was on the provision in text, because the Court did not believe that the plaintiffs had raised below a claim under the hindrance clause. The dissenters disagreed with this conclusion, but it is at least clear that the lower courts did not actually decide a hindrance claim, and this article will only raise the hindrance clause when relevant to understanding the main conspiracy provision.

[10] This is in line with the Court's generally conservative treatment of the Reconstruction-era civil rights statutes. For most of the period following the Civil War, the Supreme Court has been a conservatizing influence with regard to the enforcement of Reconstruction-era civil rights statutes, generally narrowing their reach and holding some statutes unconstitutional. See, e.g., *The Slaughter House Cases*, 83 US (16 Wall) 36 (1873); *The Civil Rights Cases*, 109 US 3 (1883) (holding the Civil Rights Act of 1866 unconstitutional); see generally Eugene Gressman, *The Unhappy History of Civil Rights Litigation*, 30 Mich L Rev 1323 (1952); Lawrence, 67 Tulane L Rev (cited in note 8). In recent years, the Court has also construed modern civil rights statutes very narrowly, provoking a response from Congress in the form of the Civil Rights Act of 1991. See note 155. The *Bray* decision has also prompted efforts in Congress to pass specific legislation protecting abortion clinics from activities like those carried out by Operation Rescue. This proposal, if enacted, would protect abortion clinics but would not amend section 1985(3) and thus would not address the issues concerning section 1985(3) discussed in this article. See proposed Freedom of Access to Clinic Entrances Act of 1993, S 636, 103rd Cong, 1st Sess (March 23, 1993).

[11] See *United States v Harris*, 106 US 629 (1883); see also *Baldwin v Franks*, 120 US 678 (1887). This was consistent with the nineteenth-century Court's treatment of other Reconstruction-era civil rights statutes which, as noted above, were either held unconstitutional or construed so narrowly as to be useless.

the statute was aimed primarily at conspiracies entered into by government officials.[12] This virtually eliminated any role for § 1985(3) in combating private activity that prevented the exercise of constitutional rights. The Court later expressed serious doubts concerning the correctness of this view,[13] but erected two limitations on the scope of section 1985(3) in its place, both of which serve to restrict severely the scope of the statute's remedy. First, the Court has required, relying on the use of the word "equal" in the statute, that the conspirators act out of class-based animus. The Court has not yet recognized any such animus beyond that based on race, and has expressed doubts that any non-racial classification can satisfy this requirement.[14] Second, while the *Griffin* Court recognized that the statute reaches private conspiracies to violate constitutional rights,[15] the Court subsequently held in *Carpenters* that a section 1985(3) action against a purely private conspiracy can reach only those few constitutional rights that are capable of violation by private actors.[16] These two requirements serve to severely restrict the utility of section 1985(3) against private conspiracies to deny constitutional rights.[17]

In *Bray*, these Court-imposed requirements doomed the plaintiffs' claim that Operation Rescue's blockades of abortion clinics

---

[12] See *Collins v Hardyman*, 341 US 651, 660–62 (1951). For a fuller explanation of this, see notes 61–82 and accompanying text.

[13] See *Griffin v Breckenridge*, 403 US 88 (1971).

[14] Id at 102 n 9. See also *United Brotherhood of Carpenters & Joiners v Scott*, 463 US 825, 836 (1983) ("It is a close question whether § 1985(3) was intended to reach any class-based animus other than animus against Negroes and those who championed their cause, most notably Republicans."); *Bray*, 113 S Ct at 759.

[15] *Griffin*, 403 US at 101.

[16] See *Carpenters*, 463 US at 831–34 (under § 1985, a private conspiracy cannot violate First Amendment rights, but only those rights guaranteed against private as well as public interference—rights under the Thirteenth Amendment and the right to travel). This may be even more restrictive than *Collins v Hardyman*, which at least allowed that an extreme private conspiracy could "work a deprivation of equal protection of the laws, or of equal privileges and immunities under laws." 341 US at 662. For example, private newspaper censorship is not a First Amendment violation, and a firing by a private company without a hearing does not violate due process. For state action doctrine generally, see *Moose Lodge No. 7 v Irvis*, 407 US 163 (1972).

[17] The Court found in *Bray* that a claim under the separate hindrance clause was not presented, but it addressed it anyway in response to the dissenters' that it was presented and made out. The Court, in a somewhat speculative vein, noted that the equality language appears also in the hindrance clause and that it would, in a properly presented case, import the class-based animus and state action requirements into a hindrance claim, thus rendering the hindrance clause also largely useless against private action directed against constitutional rights. 113 S Ct at 765–67.

could be enjoined by federal courts using § 1985(3).[18] The Court held that the class-based animus requirement was not met because opposition to abortion was not equal to animus against women[19] and because the class of women seeking abortions was not a proper class under § 1985(3).[20] The Court further held that Operation Rescue's activities did not violate either the right to travel or the right to abortion. The plaintiffs had relied primarily upon the right to travel since it is protected against private interference, and a large percentage of the women served by the clinics blockaded in *Bray* traveled from out of state to the clinics. The Court rejected both rights as bases for the § 1985(3) claim, the right to travel because women from out of state were treated no worse than women from within the state, and the right to abortion because it is not protected against private interference. Thus, a conspiracy to use illegal means to prevent women from exercising the federal right to have an abortion is not actionable under § 1985(3).

The Supreme Court has relied on two related bases for reading § 1985(3) so narrowly. First, the Court has expressed doubts about the constitutionality of a federal statute that would outlaw all private conspiracies aimed at depriving people of constitutionally protected interests. Second, the Court has stated that it is important to limit § 1985(3) so that it does not become a general federal tort law, displacing state law whenever a conspiracy exists. These two concerns, rooted in federalism, are closely related to grounds the Court has relied upon for reading other Reconstruction-era civil rights laws narrowly,[21] yet neither is a persuasive reason for the

---

[18] There is another interesting issue of whether injunctive relief is available under section 1985(3). The section itself provides only for a damages remedy, but as originally passed in the Civil Rights Act of 1871, the section allowed, in addition to the damages remedy, for the same remedies as provided in the Civil Rights Act of 1866. The Civil Rights Act of 1866, in turn, contemplated a civil action in federal district court, and did not specify the remedy available. See Civil Rights Act (Enforcement Act) of 1866, ch 31, 14 Stat 27, now codified at 42 USC § 1988. The lower court in *Bray* held that under the federal courts' general remedial discretion, injunctive relief was appropriate. The Supreme Court did not reach the issue. See 113 S Ct at 767 n 16.

[19] *Bray*, 113 S Ct at 759. The Court found it unnecessary to decide whether "women in general" constitutes a qualifying class under § 1985(3).

[20] Id at 759–60.

[21] See, e.g., *Monroe v Pape*, 365 US 167, 187–92 (1961) ("person" in § 1983 does not include municipalities); *Monell v Department of Social Services of City of New York*, 436 US 658 (1978) ("person" includes municipality but municipalities are not liable under ordinary tort rules of respondeat superior); *Pierson v Ray*, 386 US 547 (1967) (provision in § 1983 making all "persons" liable does not overrule common law government official immunities). In the criminal civil rights context, Professor Lawrence has referred to these concerns as the federalism and vagueness problems. See Lawrence, 67 Tulane L Rev at 2119 (cited in note 8).

limits the Court has imposed in this or other contexts. In short, there is no constitutional problem with federal court remedies against private individuals who conspire to deprive people of their constitutional rights even if the conspiracy is not motivated by racial animus, and § 1985(3)'s requirement that the conspirators act for the purpose of depriving their victims of constitutional rights (equal protection or equal privileges and immunities) eliminates the potential that § 1985(3) might displace large portions of state tort law.

This article explores the issues raised by *Bray* as follows. Part I explores the conditions that brought about § 1985(3), how those conditions shaped the statute, and how the statute was received in the Court soon after its passage. Part II analyzes, in light of that history, the development of current doctrine for applying § 1985(3), and traces that development to current § 1985(3) doctrine. Part III looks closely at the principal limiting doctrines, critiques how they were applied in *Bray*, and proposes rules in their place that would answer the Court's federalism concerns while making § 1985(3) a much more effective remedy against private conspiracies to prevent people from exercising constitutional rights. Part IV concludes with some observations regarding the Court's role, since the Civil War, in protecting civil rights.

I

Beginning in 1866, as part of the program of Reconstruction of the Union after the Civil War, the postbellum Congress,[22] through civil rights legislation, made several attempts to protect the rights of the newly freed slaves and their political allies both from government and private discrimination.[23] Many impediments to full participation in society for the newly freed slaves had arisen, and they were created by governmental units, government officials, and private resistance, most notably through the Ku Klux Klan, which enjoyed a very large membership among Southern white

---

[22] Sometimes over presidential veto; e.g., Civil Rights Act of 1866, ch 31, 14 Stat 29–30 (1866).

[23] These include Civil Rights Act of 1875, ch 114, 18 Stat 335 (1875); Ku Klux Klan Act, ch 22, 17 Stat 13 (1871); Enforcement Act of 1870, ch 114, 16 Stat 140, amended by Act of Feb 28, 1871, ch 99, 16 Stat 433; and the Civil Rights Act of 1866, ch 31, 14 Stat 27.

men at that time.[24] On the government side, some states attempted to restrict black ownership of property and discriminated in the provision of civil remedies, thus making it difficult or impossible for blacks to engage in economic activity. Further, restrictions were placed on the freed slaves' right to vote, and facially neutral criminal laws were enforced in a discriminatory fashion so that blacks were punished severely and those who victimized blacks were not punished at all. Finally, there were instances in which government officials assaulted blacks and their supporters. These attacks went unpunished, thus tending to provide the appearance of government approval to official and private mistreatment of blacks.

Private violence and discrimination against blacks was also viewed by Congress as a serious impediment to full integration into society for the newly freed slaves. There was widespread discrimination in public accommodations such as restaurants and hotels and discrimination in everyday economic transactions. It was also common for whites to act violently toward blacks, and there were several notorious examples of mob violence against blacks that were not adequately dealt with by state and local authorities.[25] The content of the statutes passed by Congress between 1866 and 1875 can be traced to particular problems that generally fall into these categories of both public and private hostility to equality for black citizens, and the combination of public and private violence makes it difficult to distinguish provisions motivated by one or the other.

The legislation attacked the problems that blacks were facing in the South just after the war through a variety of means, including creating civil and criminal penalties for private interference with voting[26] and the exercise of other rights;[27] creating remedies against official deprivations of federal rights;[28] creating substantive rights

---

[24] See *Collins*, 341 US at 662; see generally Ken Gormley, *Private Conspiracies and the Constitution: A Modern Vision of 42 U.S.C. Section 1985(3)*, 64 Tex L Rev 527, 534–36 (1985).

[25] See Lawrence, 67 Tulane L Rev at 2133–35 (cited in note 8) (discussing riots in Memphis, New Orleans, and Colfax, Louisiana); Gormley, 64 Tex L Rev at 543 n 40 (cited in note 24).

[26] The Enforcement Act of 1870, § 4, provides that a person who is hindered or otherwise intimidated while exercising the right to vote shall receive $500 from the offending party.

[27] The Enforcement Act of 1870, § 17, provides a criminal penalty against any public official who interferes with the Act's guarantee in § 16 that all persons shall enjoy the full and equal benefit of all laws, including the right to make and enforce contracts, to fully participate in court proceedings, and to receive equal punishment.

[28] Enforcement Act of 1870, § 17; Ku Klux Klan Act, § 1; Civil Rights Act of 1866, § 2.

such as granting all persons in the United States the same right as "white citizens" to make and enforce contracts, the right to own property, and the right to use public accommodations;[29] and making conspiracies to deny equal protection and equal privileges and immunities crimes and actionable for civil damages.[30]

These statutes have certain features in common.[31] They do not single out newly freed slaves as the only proper plaintiffs but rather grant rights generally to all potential victims of the specified deprivations.[32] Further, the statutes are largely directed at individuals, both government officials and private citizens, rather than at governmental units.[33]

While the form of civil rights legislation was influenced most heavily by the precise problems blacks were facing after the end of slavery, the decision to aim the statutes primarily at individuals rather than at governmental units appears to have arisen from pressure brought by some members of Congress to preserve as much of the original federalist structure as possible. The choice to employ primarily judicial remedies, both civil and criminal, and against individuals rather than governmental units, was arrived at after balancing several considerations, including effectiveness in protecting federal rights against both public and private violation, ease of administration, and respect for state and local government authority. Criminal and civil remedies against individuals might not be as effective as federal official intervention into the operation of state and local government, but they can be considerably less intrusive on government and thus were arrived at as an appropriate

---

[29] Enforcement Act of 1870, § 16; Civil Rights Act of 1866, § 1; Civil Rights Act of 1875, § 1 (held unconstitutional in *The Civil Rights Cases*). While the first two did not specify any remedy, the public accommodations provision of the Civil Rights Act of 1875 Act provided a $500 civil penalty to be recovered by the aggrieved party from the violating party.

[30] Ku Klux Klan Act, § 2 etc.

[31] See generally Lawrence, 67 Tulane L Rev 2113 (cited in note 8).

[32] The exceptions here are 42 USC § 1981 (derived from the Enforcement Act of 1870) and 42 USC § 1982 (derived from the Civil Rights Act of 1866). These provisions grant all persons the same right, *inter alia*, to make and enforce contracts, sue and be sued, and own property, as "white citizens." Despite the seeming illogic of applying the language to protect the rights of whites, the Court has allowed white persons to sue under § 1981 on reasoning that may apply equally to § 1982. See *McDonald v Santa Fe Trail Transp. Co.*, 427 US 273 (1976) (§ 1981 protects whites). See also *Jones v Alfred H. Mayer Co.*, 392 US 409, 437 (1968) (characterizing § 1982 as prohibiting "all racial discrimination . . . in the sale and rental of property.").

[33] Section 1983 is the exception, since it applies both to individuals and municipalities but, according to the Court, not to state governments. See *Monell*, 436 US at 658; *Will v Michigan Dept. of State Police*, 491 US 58 (1989).

method for ensuring that state and local governments recognized the rights of the newly freed slaves while at the same time not unnecessarily intruding on the authority of those governments.

From the start, this legislation did not fare well in the Supreme Court.[34] The Court developed a constitutional theory, rooted in concerns of proper federal-state relations, that confined some of the statutes to a relatively narrow sphere, and provisions that could not credibly be construed to meet the Court's requirements were declared unconstitutional. The basic doctrinal premise under which the Court operated (and still employs to a great extent) was that the Fourteenth Amendment addressed only state action, primarily state laws that were contrary to the Due Process, Equal Protection, and Privileges and Immunities Clauses.[35] The Court took very literally the language in the Fourteenth Amendment limiting its effect to state action. The Fourteenth Amendment itself did not reach private conduct at all, or, in the Court's words, "Individual invasion of individual rights is not the subject-matter of the amendment."[36] Along the same line of reasoning, the Court has stated that the Fourteenth Amendment does not create any individual rights but rather prohibits states from taking certain adverse actions against individuals.[37] This state-action-only theory of the reach of the Fourteenth Amendment still governs our understanding of the amendment today.[38]

---

[34] See, e.g., *The Slaughter House Cases*, 83 US (16 Wall) 36 (1873); *United States v Cruikshank*, 92 US 542 (1876); *The Civil Rights Cases*, 109 US 3 (1883); *United States v Harris*, 106 US 629 (1883). For a discussion of the "dreadful decade" from 1873 to 1883, in which most Reconstruction era civil rights legislation was sharply narrowed by the Supreme Court, see Gormley, 64 Tex L Rev at 541–46 (cited in note 24). While the Court's resistance to civil rights legislation might be chalked up to the prevailing views of the time, I view this more as an explanation than an excuse. Leaders in Congress, subject to the direct political pressure of periodic re-election, were much more progressive than the politically insulated members of the Supreme Court, a pattern that has repeated itself often since. Compare Randall Kennedy, *Race Relations Law and the Tradition of Celebration: The Case of Professor Schmidt*, 86 Colum L Rev 1622 (1986). In racial, political, and economic matters, the nineteenth-century Supreme Court was not a progressive institution.

[35] The Court first held that the Privileges and Immunities Clause would not federalize the great body of civil rights at the federal level—only a small subset of rights arising from national citizenship. *The Slaughter House Cases*, 83 US (16 Wall) 36, 79–80 (1873); *United States v Cruikshank*, 92 US 542, 554–55 (1876). The state action requirement was enunciated in *Cruikshank*, *United States v Harris*, 106 US 629, 637–39 (1883) and *The Civil Rights Cases*, 109 US 3, 26 (1883).

[36] *The Civil Rights Cases*, 109 US at 11.

[37] *United States v Harris*, 106 US 629 (1883).

[38] See, e.g., *United States v Price*, 383 US 787, 799 (1966); *Moose Lodge No. 7 v Irvis*, 407 US 163 (1972); *Great American Federal Savings & Loan Assn. v Novotny*, 442 US 366, 372 (1979) (§ 1985(3) does not create new substantive rights; the rights it vindicates must have

The primary theoretical justification the Court relied upon for its construction of the Reconstruction-era amendments and statutes was regard for the proper division of authority over personal relations between the states and the federal government. Under the view prevailing at the Supreme Court during and for a long time after the Reconstruction era, the only legitimate federal interests were abolishing actual slavery and voiding all state laws contrary to the Fourteenth and Fifteenth Amendments. Except for abolishing involuntary servitude, the regulation of relationships among private individuals, including crimes, tort law, and property and contract law, was a matter of state law, and federal intervention into these areas was a threat to the basic principles governing the allocation of power between the federal and state governments.[39]

This theoretical background is most clearly seen in the Court's discussion of the idea that Congress, legislating pursuant to the Fourteenth Amendment, could reach private conduct. The Court rejected any notion that the Fourteenth Amendment might "invest Congress with power to legislate upon subjects which are within the domain of State legislation. . . . It does not authorize Congress to create a code of municipal law for the regulation of private rights."[40] All aspects of relations among private individuals were seen as matters of private and, therefore, state law.

The Court's conclusion that the Fourteenth Amendment itself did not reach private conduct did not answer the question whether Congress intended, or had the power to, reach private conduct in the civil rights statutes of the immediate post–Civil War period. More particularly, that the Fourteenth Amendment itself reaches only state action does not answer whether Congress's enforcement power, granted in § 5 of the amendment, includes the power to reach private conduct that threatens Fourteenth Amendment interests. In the immediate post–Civil War era, the Court did not really separate the two issues, holding that § 5 of the amendment grants Congress only the power to enforce the actual effect of the substantive provisions of the amendment itself. Thus, congressional efforts

---

an existence of their own—First and Fourteenth Amendment rights do not exist without state action).

[39] This is what Professor Lawrence denominates the "federalism problem." See Lawrence, 67 Tulane L Rev at 2118–22 (cited in note 8). The Court probably also believed that no law, state or federal, should intervene into private social relations, but the dominant concern was the division of authority between state and federal governments.

[40] 109 US at 11.

under the Fourteenth Amendment to reach private civil rights violations were unconstitutional as beyond Congress's power.

The Court saw a difference between the enforcement power granted in the Fourteenth Amendment and other federal powers such as the commerce power. While Congress might have plenary power to regulate all aspects of matters falling within a power enumerated in Article I of the Constitution, the enforcement power of the Fourteenth Amendment was granted only for the purpose of enforcing the amendment's ban on certain state laws or practices, and therefore Congress could not legislate any further than the reach of the amendment. While some constitutional provisions, such as the Commerce Clause, granted Congress powers over a broadly defined subject area, the Fourteenth Amendment enforcement power was different. The Fourteenth Amendment enforcement power granted Congress only the power to remedy violations of the amendment. Thus, while Congress might legislate broadly over interstate commerce,[41] it may not legislate to protect generally Fourteenth Amendment interests. Rather, legislation may be directed only at actual violations of Fourteenth Amendment rights. Since private conduct could not violate the Fourteenth Amendment, public accommodations legislation directed at private innkeepers, for example, and even legislation directed at private conspiracies to prevent people from exercising constitutional rights, was held beyond Congress's power to enforce the Fourteenth Amendment.[42]

This construction of the Fourteenth Amendment was accompanied by a narrow view of the reach of the Thirteenth Amendment. Although the Court acknowledged that the Thirteenth Amendment addressed private conduct, the Court early on held that the Thirteenth Amendment's reach was confined to eliminating slavery. It was simply, to the Court, not slavery for a private individual to discriminate on the basis of race or even to beat or kill a person because of his or her race.[43] While the Court might concede that people have a right, in the abstract sense, to equal access to places

---

[41] In *The Civil Rights Cases*, the Court suggested that Congress might pass public accommodations civil rights legislation under its commerce power, but not under the Fourteenth Amendment. See 109 US at 18.

[42] 109 US at 11.

[43] Id at 24.

of public accommodation, this right was not granted to blacks by the Thirteenth Amendment but rather was "one of those rights which the states by the Fourteenth Amendment are forbidden to deny to any person."[44] Since, according to the Court, the "Thirteenth Amendment has respect, not to distinctions of race, class, or color, but to slavery," it did not grant Congress the power to pass public accommodations laws or laws regarding private violence against blacks.

It should be obvious that not all of the constitutional underpinnings to the Supreme Court's treatment of the Reconstruction-era civil rights statutes remain the law. While it is still accepted law that the Fourteenth Amendment reaches only state action, the Court has made it much easier for Congress to reach private action in legislation enforcing the Thirteenth and Fourteenth Amendments. Two key changes in Court doctrine have brought this about. First, the Court has construed the Thirteenth Amendment's reach more broadly than merely eliminating the actual relationship of slavery. The Court has characterized the amendment as abolishing all the badges and incidents of slavery, and these include both official and private acts of discrimination against blacks.[45] Congress now has broad power to identify and regulate the badges and incidents of slavery under its Thirteenth Amendment enforcement power, including the power to reach private action. Second, although it has expressed some doubts, it appears likely that the Court would allow Congress the power to legislate against private infringements of the interests protected by the Fourteenth Amendment. The Court has already recognized congressional power, with regard to government official conduct, to go far beyond the judicially recognized reach of the amendment. Under prevailing doctrine, Congress may create new rights and provide remedies to see that these new rights are recognized.[46] The Court has rejected its earlier view that the Thirteenth and Fourteenth Amendment en-

---

[44] Id.

[45] See *Jones v Alfred H. Mayer Co.*, 392 US 409 (1968) (§ 1982 bars all racial discrimination, private as well as public, and the statute is a valid exercise of congressional power to enforce the Thirteenth Amendment).

[46] That Congress could reach private conduct under § 5 of the Fourteenth Amendment was asserted in Congress during framing of the Civil Rights Act of 1871, but the Supreme Court has not yet so held. See Cong Globe, 42d Cong, 1st Sess 367–68, 607–08 (1871).

forcement powers are fundamentally different from other powers granted in Article I of the Constitution, and has subjected legislation under those powers to the minimal rational basis scrutiny applied to most legislation under Congress's Article I powers.[47] This test, which Reconstruction-era civil rights legislation would meet easily,[48] requires only that Congress might rationally have believed that an action would advance constitutionally legitimate goals.

Under this expansive view of Congress's power to legislate under the post–Civil War amendments, Congress could attack all impediments to full equality and rights. Congress would have broad authority to identify government and private practices that threaten the values underlying the amendments, prescribe substantive standards regulating those practices, and create remedies to enforce those standards. Thus, even though private conduct cannot violate the Fourteenth Amendment, Congress could regulate private racial discrimination and private racial violence to advance the Fourteenth Amendment value of a non-racist society.

This view of Congress's power fits neatly into twentieth-century developments regarding federalism limits on congressional power.[49] Congressional assertions of regulatory power are now subjected to only the most minimal judicial scrutiny, and Congress has not been shy about exercising extensive regulatory power in areas that nineteenth-century judges would have identified as areas within state control.[50] This expansion of federal regulatory power has en-

---

[47] See *Katzenbach v Morgan*, 384 US 641 (1966).

[48] It is not difficult to imagine how Congress in 1866, 1871, or 1875 might rationally have believed that in order to promote equality before the law it was necessary to protect persons and groups from private conspiracies against the exercise of constitutional rights.

[49] See *United States v Darby*, 312 US 100 (1941); *Heart of Atlanta Motel, Inc. v United States*, 379 US 241, (1964); *Garcia v San Antonio Metropolitan Transit Auth.*, 469 US 528 (1985).

[50] See Civil Rights Act of 1964, 42 USC § 2000 (1982) (prohibiting discrimination based on race, color, religion, sex, and national origin in public accommodations, restaurants, employment, housing, and education). The Court has recognized broad power to legislate regarding private discrimination under the commerce power. See *Fitzpatrick v Bitzer*, 427 US 445 (1976) (Congress has power, under the Commerce Clause and Fourteenth Amendment, to override state Eleventh Amendment sovereign immunity and subject states to liability for discrimination in employment); *Heart of Atlanta Motel, Inc. v United States*, 379 US at 258–61 (1964) (Title II of the Civil Rights Act of 1964, which prohibits discrimination in places of private accommodation, does not work a deprivation of liberty or property without due process of law, nor a taking of property without just compensation, and is within Congress's commerce power).

tailed a massive shift in governmental power from state government to the federal government, and to a great extent, judicial doctrine in other areas has been consistent with this shift.[51]

In the area of federal civil rights actions, the potentially radical implications of this view of federalism have not been realized.[52] The text, legislative history, and social context underlying § 1985(3) all indicate that the statute was intended to be part of a sweeping federal charter of liberty, granting remedies when private or public groups of individuals prevented people from enjoying their constitutional rights. Limiting doctrines, detailed in the following sections, rooted in the Reconstruction-era Supreme Court's constitutional dogma, have prevented § 1985(3) from becoming an effective tool for ensuring that people can actually enjoy their federal rights. The section that follows traces the doctrinal development of § 1985(3) under which *Bray* was litigated and asks whether the Court's understanding and application of the statute is consistent with contemporary understandings of congressional power and federalism.

II

The life of § 1985(3) can be divided into three stages. The first stage, from enactment until 1951, can be characterized as dormant because all indications were that the Court would find the statute unconstitutional for the same reason that it had struck down § 1985(3)'s criminal counterpart. The second stage, running from 1951 until 1971, is the period in which the Court construed the statute to reach public action only and to be inapplicable to private conspiracies. The final stage, which represents the doctrine prevailing since 1971, allows actions against private conspiracies, but limits the reach of the statute to those private conspiracies involving either joint action with public officials or constitutional rights that can be violated by private action, such as the right to travel. In addition, the Court held that the conspiracy must be motivated

---

[51] With the exception of some civil rights areas, in which the Court has been particularly sensitive to the federalism aspects of potential civil rights remedies. See *Younger v Harris*, 401 US 37 (1971); *City of Los Angeles v Lyons*, 461 US 95 (1983).

[52] See Jack M. Beermann, *A Critical Approach to Section 1983 with Special Attention to Sources of Law*, 42 Stan L Rev 51, 84–88 (1989) (discussing limits on § 1983 actions based on federalism concerns).

by racial or perhaps some analogous class-based bias, thus further restricting both public and private § 1985(3) actions. These stages are discussed below.[53]

A

The first case involving § 1985(3) reached the Supreme Court in 1951, eighty years after its passage. This is because in its 1882 term, in *United States v Harris*,[54] the Supreme Court declared unconstitutional § 1985(3)'s criminal counterpart[55] on grounds that would be equally applicable to the civil conspiracy provision.

The Court in *Harris* held that Congress lacked constitutional power to criminalize private conspiracies to deprive persons of due process and equal protection. The defendants in *Harris* were indicted for conspiring to assault, beat, and in one case kill people who had been arrested and were in custody awaiting trial. The Court construed the language of § 1985(3) (appearing identically in its criminal counterpart) to reach private conspiracies, and then considered whether § 1985(3) was a permissible use of Congress's powers under the Thirteenth, Fourteenth, or Fifteenth Amendment. On the Thirteenth Amendment, the Court held that, even though Congress might reach private conduct under the amendment, the statute went far beyond any conception of slavery—the Court noted that the statute reached even a conspiracy among blacks to deprive whites of equal protection, a result that could not be based on congressional power to outlaw slavery.[56] Similarly, the Court rejected the Fifteenth Amendment as a basis for § 1985(3) on the ground that the statute went far beyond voting rights.[57] These grounds are examples of the nineteenth-century Court's con-

---

[53] Other doctrines have also been created to limit § 1985(3)'s scope, largely involving the equal protection and equal privileges and immunities aspects of the statute. These additional limitations are addressed below in subsections B and C.

[54] 106 US 629 (1883).

[55] At the time, § 1985(3)'s criminal counterpart was codified at Revised Statutes Section 5519. Section 1985(3) itself has been codified in several different places: the Ku Klux Klan Act of 1871, 17 Stat 13; Rev Stat § 1980 (1878); 8 USC § 47(3); 42 USC § 1985(C) (1976); 42 USC 1985(3). For convenience, the current placement of the civil conspiracy provision at 42 USC § 1985(3) in the United States Code will be referred to throughout the text of this article.

[56] Harris, 106 US at 641.

[57] Id at 637.

sistently narrow reading of the amendments and Congress's power under them.

The Court also rejected, on state action grounds, the Fourteenth and Fifteenth Amendments as bases for Congress's power to enact § 1985(3). The Court characterized the Fifteenth Amendment as not granting to anyone the right to vote but rather as voiding any state law or practice that amounted to " 'discrimination in the enjoyment of the elective franchise on account of race, color, or previous condition of servitude.' "[58] With regard to the Fourteenth Amendment, the Court also stated, relying on several previously decided cases under that amendment, that the amendment restrains only state action, and Congress has no power to legislate beyond the bounds of the amendment itself.[59]

This reasoning was consistent with the fabric of the Court's treatment of the post–Civil War civil rights statutes, under which the Court consistently held that Congress lacked the power to reach private conduct through civil rights legislation.[60] And the Court's reasoning applied equally to the civil action for damages against conspiracies granted in § 1985(3). The Court in *Harris* did not rely at all on the criminal aspect of the case or the particular penalty provision of the statute. It relied only on Congress's attempt to go beyond the provisions of the Thirteenth, Fourteenth, and Fifteenth Amendments by regulating relationships among private individuals outside the context of actual slavery. Because the reasoning applied equally to civil and criminal actions, the civil provision was as ineffectual as if it had also been declared unconstitutional.

B

In the late 1940s and early 1950s, several civil cases were brought in federal court under § 1985(3), most arising out of politically motivated violence.[61] While the civil conspiracy provision that is

---

[58] Id, quoting *United States v Reese*, 92 US 214 (1875).

[59] Harris, 106 US at 638–39, citing *The Slaughter House Cases*, 83 US (16 Wall) 36 (1873); *United States v Cruikshank*, 92 US 542 (1876); *Virginia v Rives*, 100 US 313 (1879).

[60] In the years following the Civil War, the Court held other civil rights statutes unconstitutional for very similar reasons. See notes 10–11; see also *Collins*, 341 US at 657 n 10; *U.S. v Cruikshank*, 92 US 542 (1876); *The Civil Rights Cases*, 109 US 3 (1883).

[61] See *Hardyman v Collins*, 80 F Supp 501 (SD Cal 1948), reversed, 183 F2d 308 (9th Cir 1950), reversed sub nom, *Collins v Hardyman*, 341 US 651 (1951) (defendants, all private individuals, allegedly violently broke up a meeting of the plaintiffs' organization at which the Marshall plan was to be discussed and criticized); see also *Robeson v Fanelli*, 94 F Supp 62 (SDNY 1950) (defendants, including private individuals and government officials, allegedly conspired to disrupt a concert and gathering at which political issues were to be discussed);

§ 1985(3) had not technically been held unconstitutional along with
its criminal counterpart, there were several formidable obstacles in
the statute's text and nineteenth-century doctrine to the statute
becoming an effective tool against private conspiracies.

Ironically, the Court's invalidation of the criminal provision was
strong authority that as a matter of statutory text § 1985(3) reached
private conspiracies. Recall that the reason the Court held the criminal provision unconstitutional was that it reached private conspiracies[62] and that this was beyond Congress's power.[63] As one lower
court noted, the Supreme Court held that "a statute identical in
part with [§ 1985(3)] was directed 'exclusively against the action
of private persons.' "[64] The congressional intent to reach private
conspiracies was, to some, evident from the language describing
the potential defendants in § 1985(3) suits—the statute refers to
"two or more persons" either conspiring or going in disguise on
the highway. Government officials were obviously not the targets
of the "disguise" provision, and it would be incongruous to hold
that private parties may be sued under the disguise provision but
only government officials were the intended targets of the prohibition against other conspiracies.[65] Some courts, ultimately including
the Supreme Court, ignored these arguments and held that the
statute was intended only to reach actions of public officials.[66] One
argument for this was the statute's focus on conspiracies to deny
"*equal* protection of the laws or of *equal* privileges and immunities
under the laws."[67] In the most explicit discussions of the meaning
of the word equal, two different theories emerged, one that held
that the "equal protection" and "equal privileges and immunities"
language implied state action[68] (and thus private conspiracies were

---

Ferrer v Fronton Exhibition Co., 188 F2d 954 (5th Cir 1951) (defendants fired plaintiff jai alai
players in retaliation for their membership in an organization and hired illegal immigrants
in their places).

[62] This point was not really analyzed by the *Harris* Court but rather was taken for granted,
which, given how recent the statute had been passed, should be strong evidence that Congress intended the statute to reach private conspiracies.

[63] See *Harris*, 106 US at 639.

[64] *Hardyman*, 183 F2d at 311, quoting *United States v Harris*, 106 US at 640.

[65] *Hardyman*, 183 F2d at 311.

[66] See *Collins v Hardyman*, 341 US 651 (1951).

[67] Section 1985(3) (emphasis added).

[68] *Hardyman*, 80 F Supp at 506. Other courts holding that § 1985(3) did not reach private
conspiracies reasoned more generally, without relying on specific statutory language, that
the civil rights acts required action under color of law or state action. See *Love v Chandler*,
124 F2d 785 (8th Cir 1942); *Viles v Symes*, 129 F2d 828 (10th Cir 1942).

not redressable under § 1985 (3)), and another that held that the word "equal" meant no more than the violation of a right "which is enjoyed equally by other citizens" (thus allowing actions against purely private conspiracies).[69] A middle position allowed that private conspiracies might implicate "equal" rights but only if the conspiracy was an attempt to influence government officials to treat the victims of the conspiracy unequally.[70]

The other significant problem that advocates of private conspiracy based § 1985(3) suits had to face were the implications of the nineteenth-century Supreme Court's invalidation of the statute's criminal counterpart. Lower courts could not ignore the fact that the Supreme Court had held that there was no congressional power to reach private conspiracies directed at constitutional rights. To avoid the reach of *Harris*, a pair of lower court decisions developed a theory that granted Congress the power to protect a limited set of federal rights against private conduct.[71] The theory was that while most Fourteenth Amendment rights existed only with regard to the relationship between citizens and the states, § 1985(3) could be employed to attack conspiracies against the exercise of a special category of federal rights that implicated the relationship between citizens and the *federal government*. These included, *inter alia*, the right to assemble for the purpose of discussing national issues and petitioning the government for the redress of grievances. The idea was that the federal government has a special interest in constitutional rights that affect the relationship of citizens to the federal government, and this interest implies expanded congressional power.

The courts that allowed suits under § 1985(3) to challenge private

---

[69] *Hardyman*, 183 F2d at 312. The other principal case that allowed a § 1985(3) action against a private conspiracy expressed general agreement with this opinion. *Robeson*, 94 F Supp at 66–67.

[70] See *Ferrer v Fronton Exhibition Co.*, 188 F2d 954, 956 (5th Cir 1951). This was partially accepted by the Supreme Court in *Collins*, but only for extreme cases of private domination of government.

[71] See *Robeson v Fanelli*, 94 F Supp 62 (SDNY 1950); *Hardyman*, 183 F2d at 313. The theory here was that some rights uniquely concern rights with regard to the federal government, and so Congress had power (perhaps under Article I) to protect those rights even against private hindrance. Id at 314. Thus, in *Robeson*, the court dismissed claims based on officials' failure to prevent conspiracies to deny equal protection, but allowed claims based on a conspiracy to prevent discussion of national issues. The court reasoned that under *Harris*, the statute cannot constitutionally be read to reach a private conspiracy to deny equal protection. See *Robeson*, 94 F Supp at 67–69.

political violence during this period were in the minority. Most courts did not allow suits against private parties on the ground that the Fourteenth Amendment did not reach private conduct and thus neither could a civil rights statute passed under that amendment. Had they followed the Supreme Court's earlier construction of the same language, they might have held the statute unconstitutional as beyond Congress's Fourteenth Amendment enforcement power.[72] But since even under the more restrictive view of congressional power, § 1985(3) (and its criminal counterpart) could have some constitutional applications to state official conduct, at most it might have been appropriate for the courts to strike down § 1985(3) in part, only insofar as it purported to reach private conduct.

In *Collins v Hardyman*, the Supreme Court ignored the nineteenth-century Court's construction of § 1985(3)'s identically phrased criminal counterpart and held that the statute did not reach private conduct unless the conspiracy was so widespread that it might "dominate and set at naught" the lawful governments and "effectively deprive Negroes of their legal rights and to close all avenues of redress or vindication."[73] Because it treated it as an open question,[74] the Court apparently did not view *Harris* (its earlier holding regarding the criminal statute) as authority on congressional power to provide a civil remedy for private discriminatory violence.

The Court offered two justifications for its decision to construe § 1985(3) to reach, in the main, only public official action. First, the Court noted that construing § 1985(3) to reach private conspiracies

---

[72] A more expansive view of Congress's power under the Fourteenth Amendment did not emerge until *Katzenbach v Morgan*, 384 US 641 (1966). See also *United States v Guest*, 383 US 745 (1966). Implicit in the Supreme Court's holding in *Griffin v Breckenridge* that § 1985(3) reaches private conduct is that Congress has power to reach private conduct in a civil rights statute based on its Fourteenth Amendment enforcement power. See the post-*Griffin* case of *Action v Gannon*, 450 F2d 1227 (8th Cir 1977), which interpreted *Griffin* to hold that § 1985(3) applies to private conspiracies to violate Fourteenth Amendment rights and held that Congress has the power to reach private conduct under the Fourteenth Amendment. The seventh circuit disagreed with the eighth. See *Murphy v Mount Carmel High School*, 543 F2d 1189, 1194 (7th Cir 1976); *Cohen v Illinois Institute of Technology*, 524 F2d 818 (7th Cir 1975) (Stevens, J) (interpreting *Griffin* to require either state action or a right capable of violation by private parties). The Supreme Court, in *Carpenters* and *Bray*, adopted the seventh circuit's view of *Griffin*.

[73] *Collins*, 341 US at 662.

[74] Id.

would present important constitutional problems regarding federalism and Congress's power under the Fourteenth Amendment.[75] The Court hinted that if forced to construe the statute to reach private conduct it might agree with *Harris* and hold the statute unconstitutional. This justification has less to do with Congress's intent and more to do with the Court's attempt to avoid a constitutional question.

The Court also relied on the statutory references to "equal" rights and "equal" privileges and immunities to construe the statute to apply only to state action.[76] The Court's analysis here is interesting on two distinct scores. First, the Court interpreted the "equal protection" and "equal privileges and immunities" language to require that the object of the conspiracy be to affect the plaintiffs' legal rights, somehow either to influence the law, or "obstruct or interfere" with the operation of the law with regard to the plaintiffs' rights.[77] This is a refined version of the view that private parties are incapable of denying equal protection. It recognizes that private conduct can, in some circumstances, influence the operation of the law so as to prevent people from exercising their rights, but the conduct would have to influence the operation or availability of legal institutions.[78] The Court apparently did not think that private violence, based on a victim's group membership, could be characterized as a denial of equal protection or equal privileges and immunities.

The second significant aspect of the Court's state action analysis is its characterization of the statute as requiring a deprivation of equality and not reaching conspiracies to deprive people of just any right or privilege of a citizen of the United States.[79] The lower court had held that a civil action under § 1985(3) could be brought any time a conspiracy resulted in the deprivation of a federal constitutional right. The court of appeals had relied on the language in the remedial portion of the statute that grants the action for dam-

---

[75] Id at 659.

[76] Id at 660–61.

[77] Id at 661.

[78] Id at 662. This view was also adopted by some members of Congress during the debates on the statute. See Cong Globe, 42d Cong, 1st Sess, 456–82 (1871). See generally Stephanie M. Wildman, *42 USC § 1985(3)—a Private Action to Vindicate Fourteenth Amendment Rights: A Paradox Resolved*, 17 San Diego L Rev 317 (1980).

[79] See § 1985(3), as quoted in *Collins*, 341 US at 660.

ages to any person "injured in his person or property, or deprived of having and exercising any right or privilege of a citizen of the United States."[80] The Supreme Court held that this reference in the remedial portion of the statute to any federal right concerned only the result of the conspiracy, and that only conspiracies directed at equality of rights met the substantive requirements of the statute.[81]

Limiting the scope of the cause of action created by § 1985(3) to state action directed at deprivations of equality rendered the statute virtually useless as a tool for securing the full enjoyment of rights. To the framers of the Fourteenth Amendment and the Reconstruction-era civil rights statutes, preventing state deprivation of rights was not sufficient to guarantee the enjoyment of federal rights, because states might be "unable or unwilling"[82] to preserve those rights against both public and private attack. While they may have understood that the Fourteenth Amendment itself would operate only against state action, they thought that they had the power to ensure enjoyment of Fourteenth Amendment rights by legislating against private action interfering with the exercise of those rights, and by passing § 1985(3) they thought they had exercised that power.

c

The doctrinal framework under which *Bray* was decided was established by the Court in the 1971 decision of *Griffin v Breckenridge*.[83] That decision loosened up somewhat on the Court's earlier

---

[80] Section 1985(3). As noted above, the court of appeals did not think the equality language was important, holding that it meant that a person was deprived of a right possessed by all others. See *Hardyman*, 183 F2d at 312. Note that since this section contemplates damages for the violation of a right *or* for injury to property or person, damages under § 1985(3) should not be limited to damages for actual injury as in § 1983 cases. See *Memphis Community School Dist. v Stachura*, 477 US 299 (1986) (§ 1983 damages are limited to compensation for injuries recognized at common law; no damages for the mere deprivation of a right without further injury).

[81] Other provisions of the Reconstruction-era civil rights statutes, most notably § 1983, are more broad in that they grant remedies for violations of any federal right. See Neil H. Cogan, *Section 1985(3)'s Restructuring of Equality: An Essay on Texts, History, Progress, and Cynicism*, 39 Rutgers L Rev 515, 549–53 (1987).

[82] See *Monroe v Pape*, 365 US 167, 175 (1961) (discussing why Congress did not intend to limit § 1983 actions, derived from § 1 of the Civil Rights Act of 1871, to official conduct in conformity with state law).

[83] 403 US 88 (1971).

view that only the most extreme private conspiracies were within
§ 1985(3)'s reach,[84] but it established two other requirements that
have narrowed greatly the statute's scope. First, the *Griffin* Court
held that § 1985(3)'s equality language means that the conspiracy
must be motivated by "some racial, or perhaps otherwise class-
based, invidiously discriminatory animus[.]"[85] Second, by focusing
on the right to travel claims presented in the complaint, the *Griffin*
Court laid the groundwork for the principle that private conspiracies are actionable only when they violate constitutional rights that
are protected, as a constitutional matter, from private invasion.[86]

The changes in interpretation of § 1985(3) have not been justified
by the sorts of arguments that typically accompany abandonment
of prior statutory interpretation.[87] There is little indication in any
of the Court's opinions that the current interpretation of § 1985(3)
is based upon a better understanding of congressional intent than
prior Courts or commentators that have read § 1985(3) differently.[88]
The Court rarely refers in a serious way to the nineteenth-century
Congress's views. Rather, the interpretation the Court has settled
on for now was arrived at largely under the influence of constitutional considerations including the desire to avoid transforming a
great number of state torts and crimes into federal torts and crimes,
doubts about Congress's power under the Fourteenth Amendment
to reach private conduct, and the view that it is incongruous to
think of private action threatening rights protected by the Constitution itself only against state action.

i. The *Griffin* Court read § 1985(3)'s equality language to require
that offending conspiracies be motivated by class-based animus.
That Court rejected the *Collins* Court's holding that the equality

---

[84] This development is discussed below in Part IIIA.

[85] *Griffin*, 403 US at 102.

[86] See *Griffin*, 403 US at 105–6, as discussed in *United Brotherhood of Carpenters v Scott*, 463 US at 832–33.

[87] See generally Jay I. Sabin, *Clio and the Court Redux: Toward a Dynamic Mode of Interpreting Reconstruction Era Civil Rights Laws*, 23 Colum J L & Soc Probs 369 (1990) (discussing methods of interpreting Reconstruction-era civil rights statutes and advocating a "dynamic" approach).

[88] See Steven F. Schatz, *The Second Death of 42 USC § 1985(3): The Use and Misuse of History in Statutory Interpretation*, 27 BC L Rev 911 (1986); Sabin, 23 Colum J L & Soc Probs 369 (cited in note 87); Mark Fockele, Comment, *A Construction of Section 1985(c) in Light of its Original Purpose*, 46 U Chi L Rev 402, 417 (1979). Compare *Monell v Dept. of Social Services of City of New York*, 436 US 658 (1978) (overruling prior interpretation of § 1983 based on reevaluation of legislative history).

language signified a statutory state action requirement reasoning that only a conspiracy among state actors could work a deprivation "of equal protection *of the laws* or equal privileges and immunities *under the law*." In light of the overwhelming evidence that Congress intended to reach private conspiracies with § 1985(3), the *Griffin* Court rejected this state action interpretation of the equality language,[89] but read that same language to require that the conspiracy be motivated by racial or "perhaps" some other sort of class-based animus.[90] Both of these readings reject the court of appeals in *Collins*'s view that the only importance of the word "equal" was that the conspirators must have treated the victim differently than other citizens were treated.[91]

The opinion in *Griffin* documented thoroughly the textual and historical evidence of congressional intent to reach private conspiracies. The conclusion that the principal aim of § 1985(3) was action by government officials was plainly wrong in light of Congress's direct intention in § 1985(3) to attack the Ku Klux Klan and similar groups. Although many of these groups may have counted Democratic Party government officials among their members, they were private organizations and did not act under color of law. The most powerful pieces of evidence indicating that Congress intended the statute to reach private conspiracies, both relied upon by the *Griffin* Court, are the "disguise" and "hindrance" provisions of § 1985(3). The "disguise" provision, which extends the statute's reach to groups that go in disguise on the highway, is discussed above. The hindrance provision reaches conspiracies or action by persons in disguise that "hinder the constituted authorities of any State or Territory from giving or securing to all persons within such State or Territory the equal protection of the laws."[92] This provision is aimed at private parties hindering government authorities, and is thus not aimed at state action.[93] And there is no mention in the general conspiracy provision of any requirement that the conspirators be state actors, which would be expected if the conspiracy

---

[89] For a discussion of this development, see notes 92–95 and accompanying text.

[90] See *Griffin*, 403 US at 102, discussed at notes 92–100 and accompanying text.

[91] See *Hardyman*, 183 F2d at 312.

[92] Quotes are from § 1985(3).

[93] Since the hindrance provision achieves this independently, its existence should also rebut the suggestion that any private conspiracy reachable under § 1985(3) must have, as its aim, the disruption of government protection of rights.

section was to be so limited and yet stand alongside two provisions obviously aimed at private parties.

There is also plentiful evidence in addition to the text of § 1985(3) to support applying the statute to private conspiracies. The Reconstruction-era Congress addressed several statutes at government actors only, using the familiar "under color of law" formulation, the best example of which is 42 USC § 1983, which was passed as part of the same statute as § 1985(3). Congress did not, however, insert such language into § 1985(3).[94] Further, the historical background against which § 1985 (3) was drafted belies the notion that it was designed to reach only governmental action. The legislative history is replete with evidence that Congress was moved to act by several notorious instances of mob violence against blacks and their supporters, and that the drafting of the statute was carefully tuned to reach that type of private conduct.[95]

The *Griffin* Court thus rejected the earlier view that § 1985(3)'s equality language required state action, but in the place of this requirement the Court held that the equality language required that the conspiracy be motivated by some sort of class-based animus. In fact, the Court has not recognized any animus other than racial animus as satisfying this requirement for a § 1985(3) cause of action, and in *Bray* the Court characterized the *Griffin* Court's possible extension of § 1985(3) beyond race as "speculative."[96] While the class-based animus requirement is presented as an interpretation of the statute's equality language, it is justified primarily by the Court's professed concern not to create a "general federal tort law" under § 1985(3).[97] In fact, the Court does not pretend that the 1871 Congress intended to limit § 1985(3)'s reach to conspiracies with racial or closely analogous discriminatory motivations. Rather, it

---

[94] See § 1 of the Civil Rights Act of 1871, now codified at 42 USC § 1983, discussed in *Griffin*, 403 US at 99.

[95] See note 25 and accompanying text. See also Gormley, 64 Tex L Rev at 565 (cited in note 24); Schatz, 27 BC L Rev at 928–29 (cited in note 88); Alfred Avins, *The Ku Klux Klan Act of 1871: Some Reflected Light on State Action and the Fourteenth Amendment*, 11 St Louis U L J 331, 411–13 (1967). The *Griffin* Court also relied upon the hindrance clause, and the provision of the 1871 Civil Rights Act authorizing presidential use of military force if the local government authorities are overwhelmed by private lawlessness to establish that Congress addressed conspiracies directed at interfering with government in other provisions. See *Griffin*, 403 US at 99. This supports the argument that the conspiracy and disguise provisions were intended to reach purely private conduct.

[96] *Bray*, 113 S Ct at 759.

[97] See *Griffin*, 403 US at 101–02.

holds out the class-based animus requirement primarily as a way to avoid turning the statute into a "general federal tort law."[98]

The legislative history of § 1985(3) is mixed on whether Congress intended to require class-based animus for a § 1985(3) action, but there is little if any support for limiting eligible classes to racial or closely analogous ones. The most explicit discussion of the issue refers to Democrats, Vermonters, and other groups not racial or similar to racial groups in character, and states that members of such groups would be able to take advantage of § 1985(3) if their federal rights were attacked because of their group identity.[99]

The text of § 1985(3) also provides some evidence that Congress did not seek to impose a requirement of class-based animus at all. The statute reaches conspiracies directed at "any person or class of persons." By expressing itself in the disjunctive here, Congress provided that the conspiracy need not be directed at a "class" but could be motivated by the desire to deny rights to a single person.[100] It would be strange for Congress to state that the conspiracy could be directed at a single person in the first part of a phrase and then in the very next words in the same phrase completely contradict the earlier language by requiring class-based animus. Reading the word "equal" to require class-based animus reinserts what Congress specifically stated was not necessary—that the conspiracy be directed at a class of persons.

ii. Although the *Griffin* Court appears to have firmly rejected the state action requirement of *Collins*, the ghost of the *Collins* Court's views regarding Congress's power to reach private conspiracies still haunts § 1985(3) in the form of the Court's subsequent holding that private conspirators cannot be sued for interfering with rights protected constitutionally only against state action. Recall that the Court's primary justification for holding in *Collins* that the statute reached only government action was the constitutional question regarding congressional power that would arise if § 1985(3) were construed to reach private conduct that did not at least purport to

---

[98] Id at 102, quoted in *Bray*, 113 S Ct at 759.

[99] Senator Edmunds remarked that if there were a conspiracy against a person "because he was a democrat, if you please, or because he was a Catholic, or because he was a methodist, or because he was a Vermonter . . . then this section could reach it." Cong Globe, 42d Cong, 1st Sess, at 567 (quoted in *Bray*, 113 S Ct at 773, Souter, J, concurring in part and dissenting in part).

[100] Again, "equal" refers to the rights of the victim as opposed to the rights of non-victims.

be aimed at affecting government action.[101] In *Griffin*, after holding that § 1985(3) was intended to reach private conduct, the Court asked whether Congress had the power to do so,[102] since § 1985(3)'s criminal counterpart had been struck down by the Court on the ground that Congress lacked the power to reach private conduct in civil rights laws.[103] The Court in *Griffin* looked for constitutional power to reach the precise conspiracy alleged in the case and found that, since the conspiracy involved assaulting blacks who were riding in an automobile with a white civil rights worker from a neighboring state, the conspiracy could be reached under the Thirteenth Amendment and the right to travel.[104] The Court specifically stated that it was not reaching any question regarding Congress's Fourteenth Amendment enforcement power.

Contrary to the *Griffin* Court's language and disclaimer, the Court later characterized *Griffin*'s reliance on the Thirteenth Amendment and the right to travel as a holding that § 1985(3) does not reach private conspiracies against the exercise of constitutional rights that are capable of violation only by government officials. For example, the *Bray* Court rejected the plaintiffs' claim there that § 1985(3) was violated by Operation Rescue's conspiracy to deprive them of the opportunity to choose to have abortions on the ground that the right to abortion is not protected by § 1985(3) against a private conspiracy.[105] This is in accord with its earlier rejection in *Carpenters v Scott* of a First Amendment claim under § 1985(3) against a purely private conspiracy.[106] *Carpenters* marked a retreat from *Griffin*'s holding that § 1985(3) was intended to reach private conspiracies, and in practice it eliminates most of the potential reach of the statute. The Court is now basically in the same place it

---

[101] *Collins*, 341 US at 659.

[102] See *Griffin*, 403 US at 104.

[103] See *United States v Harris*, 106 US 629 (1883).

[104] The Court held that Congress's power to enforce the Thirteenth Amendment was broad enough to reach such a conspiracy under its new, more expansive view, that the Thirteenth Amendment power included power to "determine what are the badges and incidents of slavery, and the authority to translate that determination into effective legislation." See *Jones v Alfred Mayer Co.*, 392 US at 440, quoted in *Griffin*, 403 US at 105. The Court also held that the complaint raised the possibility that the plaintiffs' "right to travel interstate was one of the rights meant to be discriminatorily impaired by the conspiracy." *Griffin*, 403 US at 106.

[105] See *Bray*, 113 S Ct at 764.

[106] Id, following *Carpenters*, 463 US at 833.

was before *Griffin*, with § 1985(3) practically useless against private conspiracies that threaten constitutionally protected interests.

A close examination of the elements of a § 1985(3) civil action is necessary to understand why this is so. The elements of a claim against a conspiracy under the primary requirements of § 1985(3) are: (1) a conspiracy; (2) for the purpose of depriving "any person or class of persons of the equal protection of the laws or equal privileges and immunities under the laws"; (3) an act in furtherance of the conspiracy; and either (4a) an injury to the plaintiff's person or property or (4b) a deprivation of the plaintiff's "having and exercising any right or privilege of a citizen of the United States."[107] Element (1) is satisfied by a private conspiracy. Element (2) is satisfied, according to *Griffin*, if the conspiracy is motivated by "racial, or perhaps otherwise class-based, invidiously discriminatory animus" and if it is directed at preventing the plaintiffs, because of their race or perhaps other group membership, from enjoying legal rights such as free speech, association, and movement.[108] The *Griffin* Court appeared to conclude, then, that § 1985 (3), as a statutory matter, reached private conspiracies to deprive people of rights protected constitutionally only against state interference, such as speech, assembly, and association. Element (3) is satisfied by any overt act by the private conspiracy in furtherance of the conspiracy. Element (4) is satisfied either by an injury to the victim's person or property (which a private conspiracy can clearly accomplish) or by a deprivation of a right or privilege of a citizen of the United States. The second alternative of this last element may only be susceptible of satisfaction by state action except with regard to those few constitutional rights that can be violated by private action (like the Thirteenth Amendment and the right to travel), but any personal or property injury will satisfy the first alternative of this element anyway, so this is only a slight limitation on the statute's reach.

The Court in *Carpenters* misinterpreted the *Griffin* Court's reliance on the Thirteenth Amendment and the right to travel to uphold the constitutionality of § 1985(3)'s application to private conduct as a statutory requirement (perhaps under element (2)) that

---

[107] See *Griffin*, 403 US at 102–03, cited with approval in *Carpenters*, 463 US at 828–29. Quotes are from § 1985(3), as quoted in *Griffin*.

[108] See *Griffin*, 403 US at 102–03.

the private conspiracy violate a right susceptible of private violation. The *Griffin* Court never stated this as an element of the statutory cause of action, but the *Carpenters* Court appeared, in line
with the earlier Court's view in *Collins*,[109] to interpret the equal
protection language to require state involvement for causes of action founded on infringement of rights protected only against state
violation.[110] This reasoning marks a partial rejection of *Griffin*, and
an embracing of the reasoning in *Collins* that the *Griffin* Court had
appeared to reject.

Rather than re-institute state action as an element of most
§ 1985(3) actions, the *Carpenters* Court should have asked whether
Congress has constitutional power to reach conspiracies that have
as their purpose the prevention (perhaps by a protected group) of
the exercise of a right granted by the Constitution as recognized
by the Supreme Court. Even if private conspiracies cannot violate
the Fourteenth or First Amendments, Congress might have the
power under the Fourteenth to proscribe private interference with
those rights that the Court has held may not be denied by government.

While the debates in Congress and the language of the statute
are not crystal clear on this point, the only way to make sense of
a § 1985(3) that reaches purely private conspiracies is to construe
it to reach private conspiracies that threaten interests recognized
as constitutionally protected under the Fourteenth Amendment.
The Reconstruction-era Congress intended to reach private conspiracies, and it did not mean to reach only conspiracies that violated the right to travel or the Thirteenth Amendment. While the
debates show some consciousness of the issue, the forty-second
Congress could not have known what ultimately would become
the intricacies of Fourteenth Amendment state action doctrine, the
limited reach of the Thirteenth Amendment in its early years or
the fact that the right to travel would, almost 100 years later, be
recognized a right capable of violation by private individuals.[111]

---

[109] See *Collins*, 341 US at 651 (relying on equal protection and equal privileges and immunities language to hold that state action is necessary for a violation of § 1985(3)).

[110] See *Carpenters*, 463 US at 831–32.

[111] The state-action-only reach of the Fourteenth Amendment was recognized at least as
far back as *United States v Cruikshank*, 92 US 542, 554–55 (1876). See also *Virginia v Rives*,
100 US 313 (1879) ("these provisions of the Fourteenth Amendment have reference to state
action exclusively, and not to any action of private individuals"). The Court implied in
United States v Harris, 106 US 629, 641 (1883), that the Thirteenth Amendment reached

Congress was worried about private mob violence against protected groups, and it was concerned that mobs were thwarting the local justice system by taking the law into their own hands and depriving arrestees of the right to due process, a right that is protected constitutionally only against government deprivation. Congress was attempting, in § 1985(3), to ensure that federal judicial relief was available against private attempts to prevent people from exercising the rights that the Fourteenth Amendment granted them against public denial.[112] Whether Congress has the power to do that has not been resolved because of the *Carpenters* Court's misinterpretation of *Griffin*'s reliance on the Thirteenth Amendment and right to travel to uphold § 1985(3) as a statutory interpretation.

While it is beyond the scope of this article to address exhaustively Congress's power to reach private conduct that interferes with the exercise of rights recognized under the Fourteenth Amendment, there is strong support for such a power in the reasoning underlying the Court's recent jurisprudence on § 5 of the Fourteenth Amendment. The Court has, for the past thirty years, recognized much greater latitude for Congress than under its original view that Congress had power only to remedy actual violations of the Fourteenth Amendment.[113] The Court has allowed Congress not only the power to remedy violations of the Fourteenth Amend-

---

private conduct, and stated so more explicitly in *The Civil Rights Cases*, 109 US 3, 23 (1883). See also *Clyatt v United States*, 197 US 207 (1905). Not until *United States v Guest*, 383 US 745, 759–69 & 759n 17 (1966), did the Court hold that the right to travel extended to private conduct. See also id at 762–74 (Harlan, J, concurring) (arguing that right to travel should not apply against private interference). If the forty-second Congress knew that state action was required to make out a § 1985(3) action against a private conspiracy, it was knowingly engaged in virtually futile lawmaking.

[112] Congress meant by "equal protection of the laws or equal privileges and immunities" that all citizens should enjoy the same rights and freedoms as all others, and the mob should not be able to prevent any person from acting in accordance with those rights that were recognized as the rights of citizens under federal law. *Hardyman*, 183 F2d at 312–14.

[113] See notes 35–52 and accompanying text. As noted, the Court now equates the Fourteenth Amendment enforcement power with other legislative powers granted in Article I, and it has held that congressional judgments under the Fourteenth Amendment are entitled to the same judicial deference as legislation passed under Article I's Necessary and Proper Clause. Justice Brennan, concurring in *United States v Guest*, 383 US 745, 784 (1966), argued that "§ 5 of the Fourteenth Amendment appears as a positive grant of legislative power, authorizing Congress to exercise its discretion in fashioning remedies to achieve civil and political equality for all citizens. . . . [N]o principle of federalism nor word of the Constitution . . . denies Congress the power to determine that in order adequately to protect the right to equal utilization of state facilities, it is also appropriate to punish other individuals— not state officers themselves and not acting in concert with state officers—who engage in the same brutal conduct for the same misguided purpose."

ment but also the power to identify and define threats to the interests protected under the Fourteenth Amendment.[114] The Court has emphatically stated that Congress may legislate under the Fourteenth Amendment even where it is certain that the Court would not find a constitutional violation.[115] Under this reasoning, there is reason to believe that the Court would uphold Congress's decision, in § 1985(3), to protect constitutionally recognized interests against private interference.

There are at least two serious interpretive difficulties with this construction of § 1985(3) and Congress's power. The first is how to distinguish a violation of § 1985(3) from a mill run conspiracy against person or property. The Court has, in many different contexts within civil rights litigation, expressed concern that civil rights actions not displace state authority over tort law and criminal law. Protecting legitimate state authority over these areas has been the most commonly cited reason for construing civil rights legislation, and even underlying constitutional provisions, narrowly.[116] For example, if a gang steals an automobile, under the interpretation of § 1985(3) offered here, could the victim state a claim for a conspiracy to deprive the victim of property without due process of law?

The Court need not impose a strict state action requirement to prevent § 1985(3) from swallowing large portions of state tort law. Rather, this problem should be addressed by requiring, consistent with § 1985(3)'s language, that the defendants act with the purpose, in the sense of specific intent, to prevent the plaintiffs from exercising a constitutional right.[117] For example, Operation Rescue acts with the specific purpose or specific intent to prevent women from exercising their right to have an abortion. By contrast, the ordinary crime or tort is not motivated by a purpose or intent to prevent the victim from exercising a constitutional right. The mugger's

---

[114] See *Katzenbach v Morgan*, 384 US 641 (1966); *Fullilove v Klutznick*, 448 US 480 (1980).

[115] See *Fullilove*, 448 US at 476–81. The Court held that Congress, under the Fourteenth Amendment, may attack practices that did not involve discriminatory intent but that did tend, in Congress's opinion, to perpetuate the effects of past discrimination.

[116] See *Paul v Davis*, 424 US 693 (1976); *Carpenters*, 463 US at 834–35 (reason for class-based animus requirement is to ensure that § 1985(3) does not become a general federal tort law).

[117] Compare *United States v Guest*, 383 US at 753–54 (requiring "specific intent to interfere" with enumerated rights (relating to enjoyment of public accommodation) for criminal civil rights violation under 18 USC § 241).

purpose is not to prevent the victim from enjoying the right to due process before property is taken but is rather simply to appropriate the property. Similarly, the burglar does not have the purpose of avoiding the warrant requirement but rather simply to enter the home to steal valuables. But Operation Rescue, or a group intent on preventing a politician from speaking at a public rally, has a specific purpose to prevent the victim from exercising a right recognized under the Fourteenth Amendment.[118] While difficult boundary problems undoubtedly exist in distinguishing ordinary crimes and torts from those motivated by a purpose of depriving victims' constitutional rights, attempting to work those problems out would make § 1985(3) a more effective tool in preserving disfavored groups' ability to enjoy constitutionally recognized liberties.

The purpose requirement should also solve the paradox of private action impairing rights that can only be denied, as a constitutional matter, by the state. It is not that the private conspiracy itself deprives its victims of their Fourteenth Amendment rights, it is that private action prevents them from exercising rights that government is required by law to recognize. Thus, while Operation Rescue may not itself violate women's Fourteenth Amendment right to have abortions, it certainly has as its purpose interfering with women's exercise of that right. If a private individual kidnaps a person on their way to a hearing in court in order to prevent the hearing from taking place, and the kidnapper's purpose is to see that a default judgment is entered against the victim, the kidnapper has prevented the victim from having her day in court, that is, the kidnapper has at least indirectly deprived the victim of the opportunity to receive due process of law. Similarly, when a private individual assaults someone who is attempting to make a speech in a public forum, that private individual has prevented the victim from exercising his First Amendment right to make a speech in the public forum.[119] While the notion of a private conspiracy to

---

[118] The Court in *Griffin* stated that there is no requirement in § 1985(3) of a specific intent to deprive a person of a constitutional right. 403 US at 102, n 10. This statement was made to clarify that the racial animus requirement was distinct from the willfulness requirement for certain civil rights crimes. Id. The proposal in text is that the Court rethink this interpretation of the purpose requirement.

[119] One response to this argument might be that although the private individual should not be required to violate the Constitution, there should at least be a requirement that the conspiracy be directed at somehow preventing the state from recognizing a right that is protected constitutionally only against state interference. This is a good argument, but it makes § 1985(3)'s hindrance provision redundant. In any case, Operation Rescue certainly

violate rights protected only against government denial might seem puzzling, it is not conceptually difficult to imagine § 1985(3) functioning as a prophylactic against private efforts to undermine the actual enjoyment of rights that have been recognized as protected against government deprivation.[120]

The second problem with interpreting § 1985(3) to reach all conspiracies to interfere with the exercise of any federal constitutional right is that the most natural reading of the statute's equality language seems to require that the conspiracy be directed at a violation of equal protection or privileges and immunities. In other words, by its terms, a conspiracy does not violate the statute unless its purpose was to violate those constitutional provisions mentioned in the text of the statute and not just any federal right.

While there is some legislative history that supports the view that the conspiracy must be directed at creating legal inequality for its victims,[121] the genesis of the statute's equality language supports a much narrower understanding of its import. As originally proposed, the statute did not contain any reference to equality, and used language that reached all conspiracies to deprive people of constitutional rights if the conspirators engaged in conduct that was criminal under state law.[122] This proposal caused concern in Congress that a great deal of state criminal and civil jurisdiction would be shifted to federal courts. This was condemned as beyond Congress's power in that it created a general criminal and tort law.[123] While the supporters of § 1985(3) denied that it would have that effect, or that it was beyond Congress's power to punish and provide redress against private conspiracies in derogation of constitutional rights, the "equal protection" and "equal privileges and

---

meets this requirement, since one of its tactics is to close abortion clinics at least temporarily by overwhelming the local authorities who might otherwise attempt to preserve the right. And in at least one instance, the local authorities asked the abortion clinic to close during the Operation Rescue assault since the local authorities could not keep the clinic free of trespassers. See *Bray*, 113 S Ct at 780–82 (Stevens, J, dissenting).

[120] See Lawrence, 67 Tulane L Rev at 2213–18 (cited in note 8) (arguing for a similar intent test for civil rights crimes).

[121] See *Griffin*, 403 US at 100, quoting Cong Globe, 42d Cong, 1st Sess, App 188 (remarks of Rep. Willard), App 478 (remarks of Rep. Shellabarger "that he may not enjoy equality of rights as contrasted with his and other citizens' rights").

[122] See Cogan, 39 Rutgers L Rev at 557–58 (cited in note 81); Fockele, Comment, 46 U Chi L Rev at 412–14 (cited in note 88).

[123] See Cong Globe at App 153; Cogan, 39 Rutgers L Rev at 562–63 (cited in note 81); Gormley, 64 Tex L Rev at 537–38 (cited in note 24); Fockele, Comment, 46 U Chi L Rev at 417–18 (cited in note 88).

immunities" language was added to clarify that only conspiracies directed at federal rights were addressed by the statute.[124] Those that offered the amendment did not express the belief that the amendment made a substantive change.[125] Some Members of Congress adopted the state action interpretation and explained the statute as addressing conspiracies to use state instrumentalities to deny equal rights.[126] But it was not viewed that way by others, including a group in Congress that believed strongly in federal power to reach private conspiracies against constitutional rights. This group saw the equality language as merely providing a more explicit constitutional basis for the statute in the Equal Protection Clause.[127] But they did not think that by inserting the equality language the reach of the statute was being limited to a subset of constitutional rights or to conspiracies among public officials. Further, the framers of the statute had a different understanding of the meaning of equal protection and privileges and immunities than we have today, and the legislative history indicates that they used these phrases as shorthand for Fourteenth Amendment rights generally.[128] There is no indication, moreover, that the equality language was meant to limit the statute's application to conspiracies against blacks or other highly suspect classifications.

Insofar as the goal of preventing § 1985(3) from becoming a general federal tort law could be achieved by limiting the statute's reach to conspiracies motivated by a desire to prevent the exercise of federal rights, which is what the framers of the provision intended when they added the equality language, the fear of a general federal tort law is misplaced.[129] With § 1985(3) limited to cases in

---

[124] HR 320, Cong Globe, 42d Cong, 1st Sess, 317 (1871). For an in-depth analysis of the legislative debates preceding the Ku Klux Klan Act, see Cogan, 39 Rutgers L Rev at 556–69 (cited in note 81). See also Avins, 11 St Louis U L J at 331–32 (cited in note 95).

[125] Cogan, 39 Rutgers L Rev at 563–64 (cited in note 81). These people thought that equality referred simply to the fact that people unaffected by the conspiracy were free to act in ways that victims of the conspiracy were not.

[126] Fockele, Comment, 46 U Chi L Rev at 418 (cited in note 88).

[127] Cogan, 39 Rutgers L Rev at 562–65 (cited in note 81); Fockele, Comment, 46 U Chi L Rev at 418–20 (cited in note 88). See generally Janis L McDonald, *Starting from Scratch: A Revisionist View of 42 USC § 1985(3) and Class-Based Animus*, 19 U Conn L Rev 471, 481–83 (1987).

[128] See Avins, 11 St Louis U L J at 411–25 (cited in note 95) (discussing "equal protection").

[129] As it is in other contexts in which it is invoked. See Jack M. Beermann, *Government Official Torts and the Takings Clause: Federalism and State Sovereign Immunity*, 68 BU L Rev 277, 326–29 (1988).

which federal rights are under attack, there would be no general federal tort law developed, and the class-based animus requirement could be abandoned.[130]

III

The Court in *Bray* rejected arguments that a conspiracy to prevent women from exercising their right to have an abortion was class-based animus against women, that animus against the class of women seeking abortions was sufficient for the purposes of § 1985(3), that interfering with women who had crossed state lines to seek their abortion violated the right to travel, and that the private conspiracy interfered with the Fourteenth Amendment right to choose abortion. The Court did, however, reaffirm its earlier holding in *Griffin v Breckenridge* that § 1985(3) reached a broader set of private conspiracies than those tending to dominate state government.[131] This section looks more closely at the Court's rejection of the plaintiffs' claims in *Bray* and discusses whether, under the reinterpretation of § 1985(3) discussed above, the Court in *Bray* should have recognized the plaintiffs' claims.

A

In *Bray*, the plaintiffs claimed that Operation Rescue's purpose to prevent abortions was animus against women generally and if not, then the class of women seeking abortions satisfied the class requirement. The Court rejected both these arguments, holding that opposition to abortion was not animus against women, that the class of women seeking abortions was not a proper class for § 1985(3) purposes, and that it was still unclear, in any case, that § 1985(3) applied beyond the racial context.

While I have argued above that the class-based animus requirement should be abandoned, the Court is unlikely to do so. How-

---

[130] "Equal protection and equal privileges and immunities" would still have meaning in the statute. As expressed during the legislative debates, the equality language would refer to the fact that the victims of the conspiracy have unequal rights when compared to non-victims.

[131] See *Bray*, 113 S Ct at 758. In an uncharacteristically careless use of language, Justice Scalia stated that *Griffin*, "*reversing* a 20-year-old precedent" held that § 1985(3) reaches purely private conspiracies. Id. *Griffin* did not reverse *Collins*, nor did it overrule it. It did, however, state that it was no longer good law on the private conspiracy question.

ever, even with such a requirement, there is no good reason to confine § 1985(3) to conspiracies motivated by racial animus. Every indication is that Congress foresaw a broader reach for the statute.[132] Congress knew, when it used general, all-encompassing language, that it was not confining its Reconstruction-era civil rights statutes to protecting blacks, and it sometimes referred to race when it found it necessary or appropriate.[133] Further, the Equal Protection Clause itself has been extended far beyond race alone, and it would be ironic if a statute passed to enforce the Equal Protection Clause did not reach as broadly as the constitutional clause itself.

Under an only slightly expanded view of class-based animus, animus directed against women should satisfy the requirement, and preventing women from obtaining abortions should be viewed as animus directed at women. Only women can have abortions, and by targeting a right that only women can exercise, Operation Rescue is engaged in a conspiracy against women.

The Court relies on two justifications for rejecting the claim that Operation Rescue's efforts to prevent women from exercising the right to have abortions is class-based animus against women. First, the Court appears to rely on a definition of class-based animus that involves more than a decision to treat the victims unequally. Justice Scalia's opinion for the Court states that there are reasons for opposing abortion "other than hatred of or condescension toward . . . women as a class."[134] This view is further supported by the Court's observation that women are on both sides of the abortion issue— women opposing abortion, according to the Court, apparently could not be motivated by hatred or condescension toward women.

---

[132] See Schatz, 27 BC L Rev at 928–33 (cited in note 88) (nothing in language of statute or historical materials supports proposition that class-based animus was thought to be exclusively racial animus or that animus directed at groups defined by their economic views, or other non-racial, non-political characteristics, was excluded from the statute's coverage); Fockele, Comment, 46 U Chi L Rev at 402–03 (cited in note 88); McDonald, 19 U Conn L Rev at 484–85 (cited in note 127).

[133] See, e.g., Civil Rights Act of 1875, ch 114, 18 Stat 335 (1875); Enforcement Act of 1870, ch 114, 16 Stat 140, *amended* by Act of Feb 28, 1871, ch 99, 16 Stat 433; Civil Rights Act (Enforcement Act) of 1866, ch 31, 14 Stat 27. Also contrast with civil rights statutes from the 1960s which singled out certain classes for special protection.

[134] *Bray*, 113 S Ct at 760. It is difficult to understand how Operation Rescue, by not allowing women to make the abortion decision themselves, is not motivated at least by condescension toward them. See Cohen, 3 Colum J Gender & Law (cited in note 2), arguing that abortion regulation interferes with women's decision-making autonomy.

The Court's discussion here implies that some sort of ill-will or spite is required to establish class-based animus under § 1985(3).

The *Bray* Court thus appears to have tightened up further on the availability of the § 1985(3) action by requiring, under the class-based animus requirement, even more than what would be required to establish a violation of the Equal Protection Clause. The Court is looking for evidence that the conspiracy was motivated by a dislike for the victimized group. The Equal Protection Clause, by contrast, is violated by an intent to treat a group differently without sufficient justification. Equal protection jurisprudence focuses not on motivation but merely on intent to treat differently.

Justice Scalia also relies on the Court's holdings that classifications based on pregnancy do not constitute discrimination based on sex in violation of the Equal Protection Clause.[135] Besides the fact that the Court's view that discrimination on the basis of pregnancy is not sex discrimination was quickly rebuffed by Congress,[136] it is unclear why the constitutional definition of discrimination applies here with full force, but does not apply either to determine what motivation is required under § 1985(3) or to determine what classes satisfy the requirement of class-based animus. Justice Scalia illustrates that opposition to abortion is not directed at women as a class since not all women seek abortions with the example of a tax on wearing yarmulkes, which he states is a tax on Jews.[137] But just as not all women seek abortions, not all Jews wear yarmulkes,[138] and the reason a tax on yarmulkes appears to be a tax on Jews is that only Jews wear yarmulkes, just as only women can have abortions. Either Justice Scalia's example is wrong, or the Court is wrong to hold that preventing the exercise

---

[135] See *Bray*, 113 S Ct at 760, citing *Geduldig v Aiello*, 417 US 484 (1974). A growing scholarly opinion is that the best constitutional basis for protecting the right of women to have abortions lies in principles of equality. See Cass R. Sunstein, *Why the Unconstitutional Conditions Doctrine Is an Anachronism (with Particular Reference to Religion, Speech and Abortion)*, 70 BU L Rev 593 (1990); Ruth Bader Ginsburg, *Some Thoughts on Autonomy and Equality in Relation to Roe v Wade*, 63 NC L Rev 375 (1985).

[136] See PL 95-555, The Pregnancy Discrimination Act of 1978, 92 Stat 2076, amending Title VII of the Civil Rights Act of 1964 to prohibit sex discrimination on the basis of pregnancy and thereby overrule *General Electric v Gilbert*, 429 US 125 (1976).

[137] See 113 S Ct at 760.

[138] Some who wish to keep their heads covered wear other kinds of hats with or without a yarmulke underneath, and some Jews do not care about wearing a yarmulke at all.

of a right possessed by only a specific class of people is not discrimination against that group.

The *Bray* plaintiffs also argued that the group of women seeking abortions constituted a class under § 1985(3). The Court rejected this argument, based on the Court's rejection in *Carpenters* of the class of non-union workers who sued after they were assaulted by union members because of their lack of union membership. The *Carpenters* Court held that even if § 1985(3) were construed to reach a broad range of classes including political associations, it was not intended to reach discrimination based on economic views or status.[139] The *Bray* Court's analysis of this issue is as follows:

> Whatever may be the precise meaning of a "class" for purposes of *Griffin's* speculative extension of § 1985(3) beyond race, the term unquestionably connotes something more that a group of individuals who share a desire to engage in conduct that the § 1985(3) defendant disfavors. Otherwise, innumerable tort plaintiffs would be able to assert causes of action under § 1985(3) by simply defining the aggrieved class as those seeking to engage in the activity the defendant interfered with. This definitional ploy would convert the statute into the "general tort law" it was the very purpose of the animus requirement to avoid. As Justice Blackmun has cogently put it, the class "cannot be defined simply as the group of victims of the tortious action." *Carpenters, supra,* 463 U.S. at 850 (Blackmun, J. dissenting). "Women seeking abortion" is not a qualifying class.[140]

This reasoning is a significant extension of *Carpenters* because it appears to reject all classifications not based on immutable characteristics such as race. In *Carpenters*, the Court rejected only classifications based on economic views, status, or activities and left open the issue of whether § 1985(3) reaches political associations, religious groups, or state citizenship.[141] As noted above, there is support in the legislative history for holding that Congress intended for § 1985(3) to cover actions based on political associations and other non-immutable classifications.[142]

Contrary to Justice Scalia'a characterization, women seeking abortion are not a class defined merely because they wish to engage

---

[139] See *Carpenters*, 463 US at 837–39.

[140] *Bray*, 113 S Ct at 759 (citation omitted).

[141] See *Carpenters*, 463 US at 836–37.

[142] See supra note 128.

in conduct that Operation Rescue disfavors. Rather, they are defined as a class by their attempt to exercise a right that has been
recognized as constitutionally protected and fundamental. And
their efforts to exercise this right are threatened in much the same
way that the Ku Klux Klan threatened blacks who wished to work,
associate, and vote as free citizens, in an atmosphere of violence in
which local authorities are sometimes unable or unwilling to ensure
that the rights can be acted upon.[143] Only strong hostility to the
right to abortion could blind the Court to the difference between
everyday tort victims and women seeking to exercise their fundamental right to choose abortion.

B

As noted, the *Bray* Court rejected the arguments that a private
conspiracy could violate women's right to choose abortion and that
preventing both in-staters and out-of-staters from having abortions
violated the out-of-staters' right to travel. The rejection of the claim
that Operation Rescue interfered with the plaintiffs' right to have
abortions was premised on the *Carpenters* Court's categorical rejection of § 1985(3) claims against private conspiracies alleging violations of rights protected "only against state interference."[144] One
faulty basis for the *Carpenters* Court's decision is discussed above—
the Court equated *Griffin's* holding that the Thirteenth Amendment and the right to travel, both protected against private conduct, provided a constitutional basis for § 1985(3) actions against
private conspiracies with a holding that § 1985(3) reached private
conspiracies only when they violated such rights. As applied in
Bray, this reasoning led the Court to conclude that "the statute
does not apply . . . to private conspiracies that are 'aimed at a right

---

[143] Some localities have been very effective at dealing with Operation Rescue and keeping
abortion facilities open. See *Operation Rescue Suspends Protests in Buffalo*, Los Angeles Times
(April 30, 1992), p 33; *Operation Rescue's Mission to Save Itself Legal Challenges* . . . , The
Washington Post (Nov 24, 1991), p a01; *Clinics Poised to Combat Antiabortion Protesters*, The
Washington Post (July 10, 1993), p a03. Other communities have not been so effective,
mainly because they are overwhelmed by the numbers and tactics of anti-abortion protesters.
See *Bray*, 113 S Ct, at 781–82 (Stevens, J, dissenting); *Anti Abortion Group Shuts Down
Delaware Clinic*, Philadelphia Inquirer (July 11, 1993), p A01; *Operation Rescue Rally Closes
Santa Ana Clinic*, Los Angeles Times (Dec 9, 1990), p 48. Since the right to abortion is
imposed on the states from above, the Court's working assumption should be hostility to
the right on the part of the local authorities, just as Congress and some members of the
Court have remained hostile to the right.

[144] *Carpenters*, 463 US at 831–34.

that is by definition a right only against state interference.' . . . The right to abortion is not among them."[145]

The Court in *Carpenters* had also relied on the fact that under its jurisprudence, § 1985(3) does not create any rights but rather is designed merely to enforce the Fourteenth Amendment; the rights asserted in the § 1985(3) action must be found in the amendment itself, which does not protect against private conduct. The Court rejected equating § 1985(3) to statutes passed under the Commerce Clause that create rights.

The Court has not seriously considered the possibility of a middle position under which, while § 1985(3) does not create any new substantive rights, it does provide an action against private conspiracies to prevent its victims from exercising recognized constitutional rights. There is no logical fallacy in the idea that a private conspiracy might prevent people from enjoying rights protected only against the state. For example, when a person is lynched while awaiting trial, it is accurate to state that the victim was prevented from exercising the right to trial. While it is true that the right to a fair trial is protected constitutionally only against state deprivation, it does not seem strange to state that the action of the private lynch party interfered with that right. The vision of rights is not merely that the state does not interfere with certain actions, it is that people are generally free to exercise their freedoms.

It is easier to conceive of private interference with some constitutional rights than with others. It is more difficult, for example, to imagine private interference with the right to be indicted before being put on trial than to imagine private interference with the right to speak. The former is a procedural right that arises only in the context of one's relationship to the government, while the latter involves freedom of action that need not implicate government.[146] The right to abortion, like speech, involves an activity that is wholly separate from government, and it makes sense to say that

---

[145] *Bray*, 113 S Ct at 764, quoting *Carpenters*, 463 US at 833.

[146] Because the First Amendment right itself may be susceptible of violation only by government, this analysis goes against our usual Hohfeldian way of thinking about rights. See Wesley Newcomb Hohfeld, *Some Fundamental Legal Conceptions as Applied in Judicial Reasoning*, 23 Yale L J 16 (1913). Put succinctly, the argument is that a private person or group can interfere with a right that does not run against them in the sense of creating a duty to honor the right in the strictest sense. See id. See also Joseph William Singer, *The Legal Rights Debate in Analytical Jurisprudence from Bentham to Hohfeld*, 1982 Wisc L Rev 975.

a person is not fully able to enjoy the right to abortion if private parties prevent abortions from taking place.

This view of the role of remedial provisions in vindicating constitutional rights was adopted by the Supreme Court in construing a portion of the Civil Rights Act of 1866 that guarantees equal rights in the purchase of real property. In *Jones v Alfred H. Mayer Co.*,[147] the defendants argued that the statute's guarantee of equal rights did not apply to private discrimination, since only state actors could actually affect the "right" to own property. The Court rejected this argument and held that the statute prohibited private discrimination in transactions involving real property. The Court reasoned, as Members of Congress argued in support of the provision, that private interference could prevent blacks from enjoying the benefits of equal rights, and that this was a legitimate target of legislation.[148] The Reconstruction Congress recognized that the enjoyment of equal rights depended both on elimination of government discrimination and private interference.[149]

Thus, it makes sense to state that Operation Rescue interferes with women's right to have abortions. The problem that led to the passage of § 1985(3) was not state denial of rights, it was private interference with the ability of people to exercise their rights. Congress saw a significant risk that private resistance would frustrate full enjoyment of federally protected rights, especially for the newly freed slaves, fears that with hindsight we can say were justified. The Reconstruction-era Congress repeatedly acted against private conduct that interfered with the exercise of rights or discriminated against blacks, because the Congress recognized that full enjoyment of constitutional rights required that both public and private conduct be regulated. The Court's rejection of these efforts, based mainly on a narrow view of Congress's Fourteenth Amendment powers and more recently on crabbed readings of the Reconstruction-era statutes, has been a substantial barrier to fulfillment

---

[147] 392 US 409 (1968).

[148] See id at 432–44.

[149] See also *United States v Guest*, 383 US at 778–78 (Brennan, J, concurring). It may seem odd that private individuals' conduct in a situation not involving state action could raise concerns relating to rights protected only against government interference. But unless one adopts a very narrow view both of the nature of rights and of Congress's power under the Fourteenth Amendment, it should not seem strange that Congress would be concerned with the actual exercise of Fourteenth Amendment rights, especially in a period of intense private resistance to the recognition and exercise of those rights.

of Congress's vision and implementation of the plan of full enjoyment of rights for all. Once the Court recognized that § 1985(3) was plainly intended to reach private conspiracies, it should have given more thought to the universe of rights that Congress intended to protect.

The *Bray* plaintiffs, aware that the courts were unlikely to abandon the bar against actions challenging private conspiracies to vindicate rights constitutionally protected only against public deprivation, raised, in addition to the right to abortion, the right to travel, which the Supreme Court has held is subject to private deprivation. The lower courts accepted the plaintiffs' argument that the right to travel was violated by Operation Rescue since many people seeking abortions in the area that was the subject of the suit traveled from out of state to do so.

The Supreme Court rejected this argument on the ground that there was no indication that in-staters seeking abortion were treated better than out-of-staters seeking abortion. This conclusion makes sense in light of the Court's jurisprudence on the right to travel and also in light of the concern that otherwise the right to travel would be violated any time a tort or crime was committed against someone from out of state, or at least any time an out-of-stater was prevented from accomplishing the purpose of the interstate trip.[150] However, while there are hints to this effect in the *Griffin* opinion, that opinion could also be read to hold that the right to travel was violated as long as the plaintiffs were attempting to travel interstate, and the conspirators prevented them from doing so because of their status as blacks, or because they wished to associate with civil rights workers from out of state. There is no explicit statement in *Griffin* that the right to travel is not implicated unless the victims or white civil rights workers were chosen because the civil rights worker they associated with was from another state, that is, that had the civil rights worker been from the same state there would have been no assault.

The issues regarding the right to travel are not clear cut, and I do not pretend to resolve them here. The claims against Operation Rescue, in *Bray* and other cases, were brought under the right to travel only because founding the claim on the right to abortion was a lost cause. It is important for present purposes to note that the

---

[150] See *United States v Guest*, 383 US 745 (1966); *Zobel v Williams*, 457 US 55 (1982).

Court's decision in *Bray* to require a specific purpose to target victims because they traveled from out of state is similar in operation to the more general requirement proposed in this article that the requirement of a conspiracy to deprive the victim of equal protection or privileges and immunities be met whenever the plaintiff's purpose is to prevent or punish the exercise of constitutional rights. Just as a plaintiff in a right-to-travel case must prove that she was chosen because she had traveled interstate, so to should a plaintiff prevail if he shows that he was chosen because he was exercising a constitutional right.

c

The purpose requirement proposed above would preserve § 1985(3)'s effectiveness as a tool to ensure complete enjoyment of constitutional rights, would not displace a great deal of state authority over torts or crimes appropriately within state control, and would make more sense out of Congress's intent to reach private conspiracies with § 1985(3). The *Bray* plaintiffs would have to prove that Operation Rescue acted for the purpose of preventing them from exercising their constitutional right to have abortions, a showing that would be easy given the facts of the case. This purpose requirement would distinguish proper § 1985(3) actions from ordinary torts that happen to interfere with constitutionally protected interests. For example, a conspiracy to assault a person on the way to the voting booth would violate § 1985(3) only if it could be shown that the conspirators' purpose was to prevent the victim from voting, even if in either case the effect was to prevent the victim from voting.

Because the class-based animus requirement was created to avoid creating "a general federal tort law,"[151] it should be abandoned in favor of Congress's intent that a much broader class of plaintiffs than racial groups be able to use § 1985(3). The purpose requirement takes care of the "federal tort law" problem. In *Bray*, this would mean that it would be of no moment that discrimination against women is not racially motivated, or that discrimination against women seeking abortions might not be discrimination based

---

[151] See *Griffin*, 403 US at 101 (imposing class-based animus requirement to avoid creating a general federal tort law).

an immutable classification. Even if the Court adheres to its requirement of class-based animus, it should not confine the statute to racial classes, and should recognize that regulation of abortion is directed at women and that women seeking abortions are the sort of class that the 1871 Congress intended to protect.

It is unlikely, however, that the Court will take these steps. The Court is likely to perpetuate its Civil War ancestors' determination to prevent Congress from effectively dealing with state and private resistance to the full enjoyment of constitutional rights, and appears prepared even to resist more recent congressional efforts to address the continuing practice of discrimination.[152]

IV

The primary focus of this article has been the treatment of § 1985(3) by the Supreme Court, and has proceeded largely by examining the important cases and criticizing them on doctrinal grounds. The main point that has been arrived at through this analysis is that the federalism and other reasons the Court has given for its narrow readings of § 1985(3) do not sufficiently justify those readings. Specifically, if § 1985(3) plaintiffs were required to prove that the conspirators' purpose was to prevent them from exercising a recognized constitutional right, there would be no danger that § 1985(3) would become a general tort law and displace state authority over relations among private individuals. Such a purpose requirement would confine § 1985(3) actions to the sphere in which Congress has legitimate interest—ensuring that federal constitutional rights can actually be enjoyed, and that private resistance does not frustrate the goals of federal law.

Of course, there is plenty of room for disagreement about the desirability of the class-based animus requirement and the requirement that § 1985(3) actions against private parties involve a constitutional right that is capable of violation by private action. Section 1985(3)'s equality language and the references in the legislative history even support the notion that some group-based motivation must lie behind the conspirators' actions, although there is little support for limiting the statute to racial groups. However, it seems very unlikely that the explanation for the requirements the Court

---

[152] See notes 154–57.

has imposed that render § 1985(3) almost useless against private conspiracies lies in competing understandings of the language, history, or social context of § 1985(3).

The Court's treatment of § 1985(3) is part of a familiar pattern, dating back to the Reconstruction era, of resisting the aims and operation of civil rights legislation. The Reconstruction-era Congress, and Congresses during the more recent civil rights movement, attempted to work great changes in the legal aspects of civil rights, and their efforts have been thwarted at almost every turn by a Court that has either held their efforts unconstitutional or construed statutory language as narrowly as possible.

In fact, even under a narrow view of Congress's authority to reach private conduct, Congress might have wanted to legislate against both public and private threats to constitutional rights, and should have the authority to do so. Without such legislation, actual Fourteenth Amendment violations might go unremedied if state resistance to Fourteenth Amendment rights hides behind, or acts in concert with, private conduct. In addition, Congress might conclude that prohibiting private threats to rights protected only against government interference would safeguard those rights by creating a buffer zone around them.

It is perhaps understandable that the modern Court would be reluctant to apply nineteenth-century civil rights statutes broadly, since they represented a political consensus from the distant past and were written under a narrower understanding of the scope of rights upon which civil rights actions might be predicated.[153] And for a time, it appeared that the Court was much more receptive to more recent civil rights legislation, applying statutes like Title VII broadly to achieve their goals.[154] However, in recent years, the Court has repeatedly interpreted Title VII against plaintiffs, not only on new issues but also by retreating on prior, pro-plaintiff, decisions.[155] And even after Congress in 1991 sent the Court a

---

[153] For a theory on how to interpret old statutes in light of current conditions, see William Eskridge, Jr., *Dynamic Statutory Interpretation*, 135 U Pa L Rev 1479 (1987).

[154] See *Griggs v Duke Power Co.*, 401 US 424 (1971); *McDonnell Douglas Corp. v Green*, 411 US 792 (1973); *Texas Dept. of Community Affairs v Burdine*, 450 US 248 (1981) (burdens in Title VII). But see *St. Mary's Honor Center v Hicks*, 113 S Ct 2742 (1993). Compare treatment of § 1983 as not overruling the Eleventh Amendment in *Edelman v Jordan*, 415 US 651 (1974) with the Court's allowing Congress to override the Eleventh Amendment in the amendments to Title VII in *Fitzpatrick v Bitzer*, 427 US 445 (1976).

[155] The Civil Rights Act of 1991, PL 102-166, was designed to restore and strengthen civil rights laws that ban discrimination in employment. The bill was offered to specifically overrule aspects of the Supreme Court's decisions in *Patterson v McLean Credit Union*, 491

resounding message that it was out of touch with Congress's views on employment discrimination,[156] the Court has continued to chart its own, more conservative, course on Title VII.[157]

It is a strength of the separation of powers and judicial independence in the United States that allows a century-long pattern in the Supreme Court of resistance to civil rights to continue. It is a political reality, however, that judicial independence at the Supreme Court has not overall served the cause of civil rights well. I do not mean to suggest that the Court has never acted as a progressive force on civil rights or that all of its recent decisions have gone against civil rights plaintiffs or others asserting constitutional rights. But there is a pattern of unwillingness on the part of the Court to reach out to protect unpopular rights, and the Court seems to be at its most active when the rights of white men are at stake.[158] Rather than be part of the Reconstruction-era and later Congress's solution to the problem of civil rights, the Court has been part of the problem.

US 164 (1989); *Wards Cove Packing Co. v Antonio*, 490 US 642 (1989); *Price Waterhouse v Hopkins*, 490 US 228 (1989); *Martin v Wilks*, 490 US 755 (1989); *Lorance v AT&T Technologies*, 490 US 900 (1989); *Crawford Fitting Co. v J.T. Gibbons, Inc.*, 482 US 437 (1987); *Library of Congress v Shaw*, 478 US 310 (1986); *Evans v Jeff D.*, 475 US 717 (1986); *Marek v Chesny* 473 US 1 (1985). See also the Civil Rights Restoration Act of 1987, PL 100-259, designed to overturn the Court's decision in *Grove City College v Bell*, 465 US 555 (1984).

[156] See Civil Rights Act of 1991, PL 102-166.

[157] *St. Mary's Honor Center v Hicks*, 113 S Ct 2742 (1993) (burden of proof in Title VII cases).

[158] This could be thought to date back to the fact that the first case in which heightened scrutiny was applied to an equal protection challenge to a gender-based classification was a case involving discrimination against men. See *Craig v Boren*, 429 US 190 (1976). More recently, the Court has been at its most creative in creating new equal protection doctrine to protect white contractors discriminated against by minority set-aside plans and extending standing to white contractors in such cases who did not allege that the plan had actually caused them to lose any contracts. See *City of Richmond v Croson*, 488 US 469 (1989); *Associated General Contractors of America v City of Jacksonville*, 113 S Ct 2297 (1993) (standing). See also *Shaw v Reno*, 113 S Ct 2816 (1993) (white voters' challenge to redistricting). The federalism concerns that the Court relies on to justify its narrow reading of civil rights statutes do not appear to deter the Court from striking down state and local efforts to deal with the legacy of racial discrimination against blacks and other minority groups. See also Jack Beermann, Barbara Melamed, and Hugh Hall, *The Supreme Court's Tilt to the Property Right: Procedural Due Process Protections of Liberty and Property Interests*, 3 BU Pub Int L J 9, 29 nn 105–6 (1993) and accompanying text (comparing Supreme Court decision in which women were held to have sued too late to challenge a seniority system because they waited until it was applied to them when they could have sued when it was enacted, with decisions under which white firefighters who could have challenged an affirmative action plan when it was written were held to have a due process right to challenge it when it was applied to them).

PAMELA S. KARLAN

ALL OVER THE MAP: THE SUPREME COURT'S VOTING RIGHTS TRILOGY

So quick bright things come to confusion. Midway through the 1992 Term, the Supreme Court issued two unanimous decisions that clarified the role of federal courts in the decennial redistricting process. *Growe v Emison*[1] and *Voinovich v Quilter*[2] reflected the maturation of the voting rights system the Court had begun to construct three decades before with *Gomillion v Lightfoot*,[3] *Reynolds v Sims*,[4] and *Harper v Virginia Board of Elections*.[5] *Growe* and *Voinovich* recognized that state governments were largely capable of implementing the quantitative and qualitative constraints imposed by the Fourteenth Amendment and the Voting Rights Act and that minority citizens were now effectively integrated into the political process, at least in some jurisdictions.

Pamela S. Karlan is Professor of Law, University of Virginia.

AUTHOR'S NOTE: I thank Chris Eisgruber, Lani Guinier, Sam Issacharoff, Mike Klarman, Eben Moglen, Rick Pildes, Mark Rush, and Larry Sager for many thoughtful comments. I also received many helpful suggestions from participants in a roundtable sponsored by the American Political Science Association, the NYU Constitutional Theory Colloquium, and the Georgetown Constitutional Law Discussion Group. In the interest of full disclosure, I note that I served as counsel for amici curiae in *Voinovich v Quilter*, 113 S Ct 1149 (1993), and as counsel for one of the parties in several cases cited in the footnotes.

[1] 113 S Ct 1075 (1993).

[2] 113 S Ct 1149 (1993).

[3] 364 US 339 (1960).

[4] 377 US 533 (1964).

[5] 383 US 663 (1966).

But on the last day of the Term, in *Shaw v Reno*,[6] the Court plunged itself and the lower federal courts into a previously unexplored and particularly tangled precinct of the "political thicket." *Shaw* identified a new, "analytically distinct,"[7] constitutional cause of action: a reapportionment plan violates the Equal Protection Clause if, "though race-neutral on its face, [it] rationally cannot be understood as anything other than an effort to separate voters into different districts on the basis of race, and . . . the separation lacks sufficient justification."[8] But although the Court scattered its opinion with voting rights rhetoric, *Shaw* turns out not really to be a case about the right to vote, at least not the right the Court had identified in its earlier decisions. Rather, *Shaw* forms an integral piece of an ongoing struggle between the Supreme Court and the political branches over how to address the enduring problems of race in America.

The 1960s, 1970s, and 1980s together worked what has been called the "reapportionment revolution."[9] The revolution began with the declaration of a constitutional command to reapportion and with a set of quantitative constraints on permissible districting schemes. Soon, the Court and Congress turned their attention to the qualitative dimension of reapportionment, ultimately requiring that apportionments fairly respect the voting strength of identifiable racial and political groups. But as Robert Frost once remarked, "[T]he trouble with a total revolution . . . [i]s that it brings the same class up on top."[10] In this sense, *Shaw v Reno* may well be signaling the completion (or perhaps the abandonment) of the ongoing reapportionment revolution that has engaged the Court for the past thirty years.[11]

---

[6] 113 S Ct 2816 (1993).

[7] Id at 2830.

[8] Id at 2828.

[9] See generally Gordon E. Baker, *The Reapportionment Revolution: Representation, Political Power, and the Supreme Court* (Random House, 1966); Gordon E. Baker, *Whatever Happened to the U.S. Reapportionment Revolution?* in Bernard Grofman and Arend Lijphart, eds, *Electoral Laws and Their Political Consequences* (Agathon, 1986); Gordon E. Baker, *The Unfinished Reapportionment Revolution*, in Bernard Grofman, ed, *Political Gerrymandering and the Courts* 11 (Agathon, 1990).

[10] Robert Frost, *A Semi-Revolution*, in Edward Connery Lathem, ed, *The Poetry of Robert Frost* 363 (Holt, Rinehart & Winston, 1969).

[11] For one particularly neat example, compare *Reynolds*, 377 US at 562, 580 ("Legislators represent people, not trees or acres. . . . [P]eople, not land or trees or pastures, vote.") with *Shaw*, 113 S Ct at 2826 ("A reapportionment statute typically does not classify persons at all; it classifies tracts of land, or addresses.").

The 1993 voting rights trilogy raises fundamental questions about the American voting rights system. Part I of this essay sets out a framework for thinking about these questions. First, what does "the 'right' to vote" mean?[12] Despite Justice O'Connor's use of the singular person in *Shaw*, the right actually embodies a constellation of concepts: participation—the entitlement of individuals to cast ballots and have those ballots counted; aggregation—the choice among rules for tallying individual votes to determine election outcomes; and governance—the structure in which representative decision making takes place.[13] Reapportionment questions occupy a precarious position on the border between aggregation and governance.

Second, how should control over the voting rights system be allocated among various state and federal actors?[14] This question has both a vertical and a horizontal dimension. The former concerns the relationship between different levels of government, namely, federal and state. The latter concerns the relationship among different branches of government. It asks to what extent the judiciary may revise the choices reached by other branches, as well as to what extent the judiciary can intervene to resolve conflicts among other branches.

Using this framework, Part II examines *Growe* and *Voinovich*. These cases confronted the Court with a central failure of the existing system: its generation of pervasive, redundant, partisan litigation. The Court responded by adjusting the relationship among reapportionment institutions and by clarifying the prerequisites for federal intervention. *Growe*'s requirement that federal courts defer to state judicial proceedings serves two functions: it clearly establishes state courts as the primary judicial police of reapportionment and, by treating state courts as an integral part of an opaque state political process, manages to avoid federal involvement in state interbranch conflicts. And *Growe* and *Voinovich* together limited intervention under the Voting Rights Act to situations characterized by racial bloc voting and the ensuing process failure, thus providing a firm doctrinal basis for displacing the political process.

---

[12] *Shaw*, 113 S Ct at 2819.

[13] See Pamela S. Karlan, *The Rights to Vote: Some Pessimism About Formalism*, 71 Tex L Rev 1705, 1708 (1993).

[14] Compare Essay, *Voting Rights and the Role of the Federal Government: The Rehnquist Court's Mixed Messages in Minority Vote Dilution Cases*, 27 USF L Rev 627, 628 (1993) (drawing a distinction between the court's "right" cases and its "role" cases).

Shaw takes a diametrically opposite position, and in Part III, I focus on this turnabout. *Shaw* abandons the Court's previous circumspection about involving itself in questions of governance. The plaintiffs who challenged North Carolina's congressional districting raised neither participation nor aggregation claims. Instead, they raised what can best be described as a meta-governance claim. In order to address this claim, the Court turned its back on the entire fabric of standing law. The Court then proceeded to upset well-settled doctrines in equal protection law as well. Perhaps just as significant, *Shaw* may herald a new response to questions of how power over the voting rights system ought to be allocated among the branches of the federal government. Indeed, *Shaw*'s odd analytic path may represent the opening volley in a judicial attempt to control national, political resolution of the problem of minority exclusion.

I. The Voting Rights System

The current voting rights system is the product of three decades of judicial and congressional revision of the principles governing voting rights and the allocation of political power. This revision has proceeded antiphonally, as reconceptions of the meaning of the right precipitated more extensive federal involvement in state redistricting activity and the prospect of even greater federal involvement began to shape the contours of the right.

A. THREE RIGHTS TO VOTE

The "right" to vote actually embraces the separate, yet complementary, interests in participation, aggregation, and governance.[15] First, individual citizens have an interest in taking part in the formal electoral process by casting a ballot that gets counted. This ability to participate serves both a symbolic and an instrumental function. The symbolic function is to proclaim an individual's full membership in the political community. This aspect of voting, at least with regard to the core electorate—adult resident citizens— was firmly established as a fundamental individual right early

---

[15] This taxonomy is developed at greater length in Karlan, 71 Tex L Rev at 1709–20 (cited in note 13).

on.[16] The individualistic focus has an important corollary: out-come-independence. In determining whether an individual is entitled to participate, the Court has avoided asking what effect her participation might have on electoral results.[17]

But as soon as we move beyond this largely symbolic purpose, voting loses its purely individual character.[18] The instrumental purpose of voting—having one's preferences taken into account in choosing public officials—necessarily involves aggregating the votes of individuals to achieve a collective outcome. There are many ways to aggregate votes; an individual will of course prefer the electoral system most likely to result in the satisfaction of her preferences. Perhaps the most pervasive set of aggregation rules in American politics concerns the geographical allocation of voters among electoral jurisdictions. The way in which districts are drawn often determines which voters will be able to elect their preferred candidates and which voters will have their preferences go unsatisfied.

There are basically three ways in which geographic aggregation rules might impair a voter's ability to elect her preferred candidate—the euphonious trio of cracking, stacking, and packing.[19]

---

[16] Thus, restrictions on the franchise are subject to strict scrutiny. See, for example, *Dunn v Blumstein*, 405 US 330, 337 (1972); *Kramer v Union Free School Dist. No. 15*, 395 US 621, 626–28 (1969); *Harper v Virginia State Bd of Elections*, 383 US 663, 670 (1966). At least with respect to black voters, however, it was Congress' authorization of federal voting rights examiners, and not the Supreme Court's formal pronouncements about the centrality of the right to participate, that provided an effective right to participate. See Chandler Davidson, *The Voting Rights Act: A Brief History*, in Bernard Grofman and Chandler Davidson, eds, *Controversies in Minority Voting: The Voting Rights Act in Perspective* 7, 21–22 (Brookings Institution, 1992) (federal registrars registered more black voters in the South in the five years following passage of the Voting Rights Act than had been registered in the entire preceding century).

Although the formal entitlement to participation is well established, there remain significant barriers to full participation. The most pervasive of these are various registration requirements. See Frances Fox Piven and Richard A. Cloward, *Why Americans Don't Vote*, 178–80 (Pantheon, 1988). The desirability of removing the obstacle posed by these sorts of requirements has been a source of substantial controversy, as the tortured history of the so-called "Motor Voter" bill, which contains a variety of nearly automatic registration provisions, suggests. See Michael Wines, *Accord Reached on Easing Voter Registration*, NY Times (Apr 29, 1993), at A-16.

[17] See Karlan, 71 Tex L Rev at 1710 (cited in note 13).

[18] See id at 1713. In fact, Alex Aleinikoff and Sam Issacharoff go further in a recent article to argue that "an individual-rights based view" has very little relevance at all to voting rights issues since the very essence of voting in a democratic system is its group-oriented character. See T. Alexander Aleinikoff and Samuel Issacharoff, *Race and Redistricting: Drawing Constitutional Lines After Shaw v Reno*, 92 Mich L Rev 588, 600–601 (1993).

[19] For a more detailed account of these dilutive practices, see Frank R. Parker, *Racial Gerrymandering and Legislative Reapportionment*, in Chandler Davidson, ed, *Minority Vote Dilution* 85, 89–99 (Howard Univ Press, 1984).

Cracking occurs when a political group is split between two or more districts, in each of which it forms an ineffective minority. Stacking occurs when a group that would be large enough to form an effective majority in a district is placed within a multimember district in which hostile opponents constitute the majority and control election to all the available positions. Finally, packing occurs when a distinctive group is overconcentrated into a few districts; its opponents concede victory in those districts but leave group members in surrounding districts politically impotent.

The two major legal constraints on aggregation rules are the Fourteenth Amendment and the Voting Rights Act of 1965.[20] Unlike participation claims, which are subject to strict scrutiny under the fundamental rights strand of equal protection doctrine, constitutional aggregation claims are subject to strict scrutiny only when the plaintiffs can show both a discriminatory intent and a discriminatory effect.[21] In political gerrymandering cases, intent is essentially presumed, but the requisite effect—"consisten[t] degrad[ation of] a voter's or group of voters' influence on the political process as a whole"[22]—is in practice impossible to prove. By contrast, in racial vote dilution cases, the requirement that plaintiffs prove a racially discriminatory purpose often proves an insuperable obstacle even when minority voters have consistently been unable to elect their preferred candidates.[23]

Originally, the liability standard under the Voting Rights Act dovetailed with the constitutional standard. But in 1982 the Act was amended to eliminate the requirement that plaintiffs show a discriminatory purpose; proof of a dilutive effect is enough.[24] This

---

[20] There are two relevant substantive provisions of the Act. Section 2, which applies nationwide, forbids any state or political subdivision from using a voting procedure that results in minority voters having "less opportunity that other members of the electorate to participate in the political process and to elect representatives of their choice." 42 USC § 1973(b) (1988). Section 5, which applies only to specified jurisdictions with a history of depressed political participation (largely the Deep South, Southwest, and parts of New York City), requires jurisdictions to obtain federal approval, either from the Attorney General or the federal district court in Washington, D.C., before making any change in their existing election laws. To obtain such approval, they must convince the federal authorities that the proposed change will have neither the purpose nor the effect of diluting minority voting strength. See 42 USC § 1973c (1988).

[21] See *City of Mobile v Bolden*, 446 US 55, 112–14 (1980) (Marshall dissenting) (criticizing the court's failure to accord strict scrutiny).

[22] *Davis v Bandemer*, 478 US 109, 132 (1986) (plurality opinion).

[23] See Karlan, 71 Tex L Rev at 1715–16 (cited in note 13).

[24] The purpose behind the 1982 amendments is set out in Voting Rights Act Extension, Sen Rep No 97-417, 97th Cong, 2d Sess 15-30 (1982) ("Senate Report").

shift has had two effects. First, plaintiffs in racial vote dilution cases now normally seek relief under the more favorable statutory standard, rather than the constitutional one. Second, the relatively favorable treatment accorded racial vote dilution claims creates an incentive for partisan groups either to recast their claims to fall under the Voting Rights Act or to use plaintiffs protected by the Act as stalking horses.[25]

Even aggregation, however, serves only as a midpoint in the political process. Voters elect representatives with an eye toward having those representatives participate in official decision making.[26] Voting is a means for derivatively taking part in post-election *governance*. The extent to which a voter's policy preferences will be satisfied often depends as much on the overall composition of an elected body as well as on her direct election of a single representative to that body. Thus, although voters choose among candidates who then constitute elected bodies, rather than choosing among alternative elected bodies directly, a voter's preferences about the overall complexion of the assembly can be as important as her preference among candidates running from her district.[27]

Despite the individualistic, participation-oriented rhetoric, the slogan "one-person, one-vote" in fact reflects a concern with governance.[28] Plaintiffs in quantitative malapportionment cases do not invoke the participatory strand of the right to vote: they are not claiming that they are disenfranchised or that their ballots are ignored. Nor, in fact, are they really claiming that their aggregation interests have been impaired: they are not claiming that the candidates they support are being defeated at the polls. Their real complaint is that their voice is diluted at the post-election process of official decision making. Similarly, packing claims may ultimately be as much about governance as aggregation: after all, the group members who are packed into the conceded districts are able to

---

[25] See Karlan, 71 Tex L Rev at 1732 (cited in note 13).

[26] See *Reynolds*, 377 US at 565 ("[R]epresentative government is in essence self-government through the medium of elected representatives of the people, and each and every citizen has an inalienable right to full and effective participation in the political processes of his State's legislative bodies. Most citizens can achieve this participation only as qualified voters through the election of legislators to represent them.").

[27] See Jean-Pierre Benoit and Lewis A. Kornhauser, *Voting Simply in the Election of Assemblies* 27 (1991) (C. V. Starr Center for Applied Economics Working Paper); Pamela S. Karlan, *Maps and Misreadings: The Role of Geographic Compactness in Racial Vote Dilution Litigation*, 24 Harv CR-CL L Rev 173, 236–48 (1989).

[28] See Karlan, 71 Tex L Rev at 1717–18 (cited in note 13).

elect the candidate they prefer; only the group members left out of the packed district have a pure aggregation claim.[29]

The Court's entertainment of malapportionment and packing claims illustrates its willingness to consider governance interests if they can be achieved through the development of a rule about aggregation. But in general, the Court's voting rights cases have been quite reluctant to address questions of governance. In *Presley v Etowah County Commission*,[30] for example, the Court recognized that "in a real sense every decision taken by government implicates voting,"[31] but drew an explicit line between "voting" and "governance,"[32] holding that the Voting Rights Act provides no authorization for federal judicial intervention in post-electoral allocations of voting power. The background assumption seems to be that post-election judicial supervision is somehow too intrusive on self-government.

The process of decennial reapportionment lies on the boundary between aggregation and governance. How and where district lines are drawn will powerfully affect both which voters are able to elect the candidates of their choice (an aggregation interest) and the likelihood that those candidates will be members of elective bodies friendly to a group's legislative agenda (a governance interest). Ideally, a group will be able to achieve both goals simultaneously. For example, black voters might favor a plan that both creates majority-black districts in the urban areas where they live and draws districts in overwhelmingly white suburban and rural areas to favor the election of candidates likely to be sympathetic to black citizens' concerns. But aggregation and governance interests do not always point toward the same plan. A plan that maximizes the number of representatives a group directly elects could produce a generally unfriendly legislature. For example, the creation of majority-black districts may enable black voters to elect some rep-

---

[29] The fact that "packing" claims are often litigated by a class of minority plaintiffs some of whom live inside and some of whom live outside the packed district shows as much; if aggregation were the sole basis for such claims, presumably the voters who have been packed into the district would have no standing to sue, since they cannot claim that *their* ability to elect their preferred candidate has been impaired. Indeed, it has if anything been enhanced. The gravamen of their complaint is that their votes could be more influential elsewhere, where they might provide the margin of victory to a candidate who will otherwise lose.

[30] 112 S Ct 820 (1992).

[31] Id at 829.

[32] Id at 832.

resentatives to an assembly but may result in the election of hostile delegates from the remaining, majority-white districts; if the black community's representatives are consistently outvoted within the legislature, the black community may have achieved its aggregation interest at the expense of a real role in governance.[33] Thus, apportionment poses fundamental "choices about the nature of representation"[34] and the right to vote.

B. TWO ISSUES OF CONTROL

The problem of who is to control these fundamental choices has vexed the contemporary voting rights system since the very beginning. The Court's initial answer, in *Colegrove v Green*,[35] was to consign these issues entirely to nonjudicial actors—the state legislatures and, in the face of their default, Congress. Federal courts, Justice Frankfurter declared, "ought not to enter this political thicket."[36]

The Court's initial foray into the redistricting arena—the proclamation of one-person, one-vote in *Wesberry v Sanders*[37] and *Reynolds v Sims*[38]—attempted to respond to this danger by enunciating a straightforward quantitative rule that could be easily understood and applied. But the rule had the perverse effect of actually guaranteeing repeated visits to the "thicket." The requirement of decennial reapportionment meant the political system's answers to questions of how to allocate political power were necessarily subject to decennial reconsideration and attack.[39]

The thicket metaphor obscures as much as it reveals, for the Court's continued disclaimers that *this* judicial intervention would not plant the Court within the dread "political thicket" suggested the existence of neutral, apolitical standards for allocating political

---

[33] Some commentators have argued that interpretations of the Voting Rights Act that compel the creation of majority-black districts have had exactly this effect. See Abigail M. Thernstrom, *Whose Votes Count? Affirmative Action and Minority Voting Rights* 242–44 (Harv U Press, 1987); Carol Matlack, *Questioning Minority-Aid Software*, 22 Natl J 1540, 1540 (1990).

[34] *Burns v Richardson*, 384 US 73, 92 (1966).

[35] 328 US 549 (1946).

[36] Id at 556.

[37] 376 US 1 (1963).

[38] 377 US 533 (1964).

[39] See Karlan, 71 Tex L Rev at 1705 (cited in note 13).

power. But no such standards exist. Every rule has identifiable aggregative and governance consequences; every rule benefits some groups and disadvantages others. A judicial decision *not* to adjudicate voting rights claims will have distinctive political consequences, since it effectively freezes into place the resolution already obtained by a particular political faction.[40] The real question is not whether federal courts ought to enter the thicket but how they should treat the handiwork of the other denizens they discover there.

While announcing broad principles—such as the requirement of equipopulous districting or the prohibition of intentional political or racial vote dilution—the Court has sought to delegate the responsibility for putting those principles into effect to actors it views as more appropriately "political." The Court's first line of response has been to stress the primacy of state institutions in deciding apportionment issues. Originally, the Court treated its justiciability decision in *Baker v Carr*[41] and its announcement of one-person, one-vote in *Wesberry* and *Reynolds* as simply devices for triggering pre-existing state reapportionment mechanisms. The Court backed up this commitment by requiring that states be given an additional opportunity for self-apportionment even in the face of a voting rights violation.[42] Only when the state process fails completely ought federal courts step in and do the reapportionment themselves.

The Court's second line of response has been to recognize a prominent role for Congress and the executive branch in policing the voting rights system. *South Carolina v Katzenbach*,[43] *Katzenbach*

---

[40] This seems to have been Justice Clark's point in his concurrence in *Baker v Carr*, 369 US 186, 259 (1962) (noting that because of Tennessee's sixty-year failure to reapportion, "[t]he majority of the voters have been caught up in a legislative strait jacket. . . . the legislative policy has riveted the present seats in the Assembly to their respective constituencies, and by the votes of their incumbents a reapportionment of any kind is prevented.").

[41] 369 US 186 (1962).

[42] See *Wise v Lipscomb*, 437 US 535, 540 (1978); *Chapman v Meier*, 420 US 1, 27 (1975). See also *Tallahassee Branch NAACP v Leon County*, 827 F2d 1436, 1438 (11th Cir 1987), cert denied, 488 US 960 (1988). As Sam Issacharoff once noted, there is something more than a little ironic about deferring to the political branches' views in vote dilution cases since "the vindication of voting rights can hardly be trusted to the very representatives whose election is the result of the alleged vote dilution." Note, *Making the Violation Fit the Remedy: The Intent Standard and Equal Protection Law*, 92 Yale L J 328, 346 (1982). This point is of course less true in contemporary cases involving quantitative malapportionment: presumably the legislature's composition was constitutional at the time it was last redistricted.

[43] 383 US 301 (1966) (upholding federal voter registration, suspension of literacy tests, and imposition of preclearance on specified jurisdictions with a history of minority disenfranchisement).

v Morgan,[44] *Oregon v Mitchell*,[45] and *Thornburg v Gingles*[46] approved a system for safeguarding minority rights that explicitly went beyond what the Court itself was willing to guarantee. Section 5 of the Voting Rights Act confers on the Department of Justice practically unreviewable power to adjudicate voting rights controversies in large parts of the Nation;[47] *Mitchell* and *Gingles* effectively overruled, on statutory grounds, the Court's constitutional rulings regarding participation and aggregation rights.

But like the Court's different conceptions of the right to vote, its different conceptions of institutional deference can collide. In addition to empowering the federal executive to deal directly with state and local governments, Congress created a set of legally enforceable entitlements that require federal courts to review state reapportionment activities. Thus, the Court confronts a string of institutional questions. To what extent ought it recognize and enforce constitutional rights itself? To what extent ought it defer to congressional interpretations of constitutional provisions? To what extent ought it condone nonjudicial federal intervention in a state's internal process of self-governance? All these questions were presented by last Term's voting rights cases, and, as might be expected in light of a thirty-year track record of inconsistent approaches, the Court answered them in a somewhat confused fashion.

II. THE MEANS OF VOTING RIGHTS ENFORCEMENT: GROWE AND VOINOVICH

The round of reapportionment that followed the 1990 census was the first to be subject from the very outset to the overlapping constraints of one-person, one-vote and amended Section 2 of the Voting Rights Act.[48] It was also the first to involve widespread

---

[44] 384 US 641, 652–56 (1966) (upholding Congress' power under § 5 of the Fourteenth Amendment to suspend New York's English-language literacy test for citizens educated in certain Spanish-language schools).

[45] 400 US 112 (1970) (upholding nationwide suspension of literacy tests).

[46] 478 US 30 (1986) (implicitly upholding Congress' power to prohibit dilutive practices regardless of the intent behind their passage or maintenance).

[47] See *Morris v Gressette*, 432 US 491 (1977).

[48] After the passage of the 1982 amendments, plaintiffs did successfully use the new results standard to challenge post-1980 census congressional and legislative plans. See, for example, *Gingles*, 478 US 30 (North Carolina legislative districts); *Major v Treen*, 574 F Supp 325 (ED La 1983) (three-judge court) (Louisiana congressional districts); *Jeffers v Clinton*, 730 F Supp 196 (ED Ark 1989) (three-judge court), and 740 F Supp 585 (ED Ark 1990) (three-judge court) (Arkansas legislative districts), summarily aff'd, 498 US 1019 (1991).

use of sophisticated computer technology.[49] The combination turned out to be an infelicitous one for the operation of the voting rights system. Sophisticated redistricting software enabled interested groups to flood the market with plans that complied with one-person, one-vote, while at the same time enabling rather effective equipopulous political gerrymandering. The primary constitutional constraint thus had little constraining effect on the ultimate choice of a plan.

What it did do was provide a vehicle for short-circuiting the states' routine redistricting procedures. Immediately following the 1990 census, factions that foresaw defeat (or the denial of victory) within the state reapportionment processes rushed into court to challenge the pre-existing, 1980, apportionments.[50] A decade of population shifts had inevitably rendered *those* apportionments unconstitutional. The real point of these lawsuits, however, was not to establish the unconstitutionality of the 1980 plans. Rather, it was to maneuver one's faction into the best position for influencing the successor plans. At a minimum, filing a lawsuit would channel judicial review into the most favorable forum; a truly fortunate plaintiff might find a court whose judges would be moved to outright partisan activity.[51]

Once the existing plan has been struck down, the Voting Rights Act comes into play. In contrast to one-person, one-vote, the Voting Rights Act often does impose quite decisive constraints on the range of permissible plans. But in the context of partisan-driven litigation, it has often been conscripted into use as yet another weapon for factional advantage, used to knock out constitutionally acceptable but politically disadvantageous plans.

---

[49] See generally Samuel Issacharoff, *Judging Politics: The Elusive Quest for Judicial Review of Political Fairness*, 71 Tex L Rev 1643 (1993).

[50] For representative accounts of this phenomenon, see Ellen Spears, *The Republicans Go to Court: A Review of Republican Legal Strategies on Minority Rights in the Area of the Voting Rights Act* (S Regional Council, 1992); Leadership Conf Educ Fund, *Redistricting News Update*, Spring 1992.

[51] Federal District Judge James Nowlin, a former Republican member of the Texas House of Representatives, was one member of a three-judge court in a case involving the reapportionment of the Texas State Senate. Before the district court issued its plan, he contacted one Republican state senator *ex parte* and asked that senator to help him draw the new district lines. Ultimately, when this activity came to light, Judge Nowlin was reprimanded by the Fifth Circuit and, after lengthy litigation seeking his disqualification, recused himself. See Mark Langford, *Nowlin Withdraws from Texas Redistricting Case*, UPI (July 22, 1992), available in LEXIS, Nexis Library, Wires File; see also Issacharoff, 71 Tex L Rev at 1686 n 217 (cited in note 49) (discussing Judge Nowlin's behavior).

Both *Growe* and *Voinovich* confronted the Court with this messy reality. In particular, the litigation history of both the Minnesota and Ohio apportionments revealed a set of widespread assumptions about partisan partiality within the federal judiciary that sharply undercut the Supreme Court's conception of federal judicial intervention as a limited, principled incursion into the political process.

A. THE LIMITED DOMAIN OF THE FEDERAL COURTS

Minnesota's state legislative reapportionment offered a textbook illustration of dysfunctional political litigation.[52] Minnesota performs reapportionment through conventional lawmaking: the legislature passes a bill that is sent to the governor; if he vetoes the bill, the legislature must override the veto or the existing apportionment remains in effect. In 1991, the Democratic-Farmer Labor Party (DFL) controlled the Minnesota Legislature while a Republican occupied the governorship.

In January 1991—without waiting either for the release of final census figures or for the state legislature to begin the redistricting process—a group of voters allied with the DFL filed suit in state court claiming that the existing legislative districts were malapportioned ("*Cotlow*").[53] Within a month, the parties had agreed that

[52] The following account of the procedural background is based on information contained in the following sources: Brief for the United States as Amicus Curiae, *Growe v Emison*, 113 S Ct 1075 (1993); Brief of Appellants, *Growe v Emison*, 113 S Ct 1075 (1993) ("*Growe* Appellants' Brief "); Robert Whereatt, *State Redistricting Rift Goes Before U.S. Supreme Court*, Minneapolis Star Tribune (Nov 2, 1992), at 1B ("Whereatt, *State Redistricting Rift*"); Robert Whereatt, *Federal Judges Tell State Panel to Stop Its Work on Redistricting*, Minneapolis Star Tribune (Dec 6, 1991), at 2B ("Whereatt, *Federal Judges Tell State Panel to Stop*"); Robert Whereatt, *DFL Wins Round in Redistricting Fight; 3 Judges Say Revised Map Must Be Based on '91 Law*, Minneapolis Star Tribune (Oct 2, 1991), at 3B ("Whereatt, *DFL Wins Round*").

[53] Subsequently, a group of plaintiffs claiming to represent Republican interests intervened in *Cotlow*. See *Growe* Appellants' Brief (cited in note 52). These intervenors were represented by the same counsel who represented the plaintiffs in *Emison*. See id.
The *Cotlow* plaintiffs also challenged the existing configuration of Minnesota's congressional districts. Both the legislative and the congressional lines had been drawn by a federal district court following the state's failure to enact acceptable plans following the 1980 census. See *Lacomb v Growe*, 541 F Supp 145, 147–48 (D Minn) (three-judge court) (congressional districts), aff'd 456 US 966 (1982); *Lacomb v Growe*, 541 F Supp 160, 162 (D Minn 1982) (three-judge court) (state legislative districts). Minnesota seems to have been going for a triple crown of sorts—its post-1970 reapportionment also landed in federal court. See *Beens v Erdahl*, 336 F Supp 715 (D Minn) (three-judge court), vacated sub nom *Sixty-seventh Minnesota State Senate v Beens*, 406 US 187 (1972).
In the text of this article, I focus on the litigation concerning Minnesota's state legislature rather than its congressional districts for three reasons. First, Voting Rights Act considerations apparently played no part in the congressional case since it was impossible to draw a majority nonwhite congressional district. Second, the federal district court enjoined the state court's activities with respect to congressional redistricting at an earlier stage, and thus

the existing apportionment was now unconstitutional, whereupon the Minnesota Supreme Court appointed a three-judge special panel (two of whose members had DFL backgrounds) to preside over the remedial process. Shortly thereafter, a second group of voters, affiliated with the Republican Party, filed a separate lawsuit, this time in federal court ("*Emison*").[54] The *Emison* plaintiffs argued both that the existing plan was malapportioned and that it diluted the voting strength of blacks in Minneapolis and Native Americans on two reservations.

The *Cotlow* court acted first. It asked the parties to propose new plans, but it directed them to use a 1991 DFL-generated, Republican-opposed plan as their starting point.[55] The state court then released preliminary versions of its plans and announced its intention to put them into effect unless the legislature acted by mid-January 1992.

The federal panel viewed the state court's action as an attempt to end-run the political process: "The premature issuance of [a judicially created] plan prevented the occurrence of any possible compromise or negotiation which might have brought a divided state government to some form of agreement on redistrict-

---

there was no state judicial plan actually on the table. Finally, the Supreme Court's opinion in *Growe* largely focused on the shared issues by discussing the legislative redistricting.

[54] Of the seven original named plaintiffs, three were white, one was black, one was a Native American, one was Hispanic, and one was "Asian" (presumably an American citizen). They came from counties across the state. See *Emison v Growe*, 782 F Supp 427, 429 (D Minn 1992) (three-judge court), rev'd 113 S Ct 1075 (1993). They filed the lawsuit on behalf of all similarly situated voters, but what these voters had in common beyond their dissatisfaction with the likely outcome of the state redistricting process is unclear. The *Emison* plaintiffs were represented by the same lawyers who represented the Republican intervenors in *Cotlow*. To complete the circle, the *Cotlow* plaintiffs also intervened in *Emison*.

[55] The DFL had managed to enact that plan, over heated Republican opposition and a botched veto attempt by the governor. But the plan was so riddled with technical errors, such as noncontiguous districts and double representation, that it would have been unconstitutional to use it.

The *Cotlow* opinion thus served as a sort of *deus ex machina* for the DFL's otherwise unusable plan. See Whereatt, *DFL Wins Round* (cited in note 52) ("John French, a lawyer for the DFL-controlled House and Senate, said, 'In a preliminary and tentative way, it's a favorable result from the standpoint of the Legislature.' But others were more direct. 'It's all over. We won,' said Todd Johnson, a DFL House staff member who worked on the original redistricting plan and has followed the complex lawsuit."). Compare the reactions when the federal court enjoined further state activity. See Whereatt, *Federal Judges Tell State Panel to Stop* (cited in note 52) (The attorney who represented DFL interests "called the injunction stopping the state court action 'a political decision' that 'shows a gross disrespect for the federal system and the integrity of a coequal sister court. Were this permitted to stand, the losers would be the citizens of this state who did not elect these two judges,' while a Republican legislator termed the action 'a great victory for the people of Minnesota'.").

ing."[56] In order to protect what it saw as Minnesota's inter-branch allocation of redistricting authority, the federal court granted the *Emison* plaintiffs' request to enjoin all further state court proceedings and stayed all of the orders issued by the *Cotlow* court.[57]

After a DFL-sponsored plan was again passed by the Legislature but this time effectively vetoed by the Republican governor, the state court—reasoning that the legislature had not managed to enact a plan—issued a final order adopting its own previously announced plan. Two days later, the federal court held that the state court's failure to create a majority nonwhite state senate district in Minneapolis violated Section 2 of the Voting Rights Act. Moreover, it declined even to use the DFL-sponsored/state court adopted scheme as its starting point because the governor's veto showed that it had "been rejected as state policy" by an executive official who "has a constitutionally recognized role in redistricting in Minnesota."[58] Accordingly, it adopted plans created by its own special masters and permanently enjoined interference with their implementation.[59]

A unanimous Supreme Court reversed. Federal courts, Justice Scalia's opinion declared, must "defer consideration of disputes involving redistricting where the State, through its legislative *or* judicial branch, has begun to address that highly political task itself."[60] In holding that the district court "erred in not deferring to the Minnesota Special Redistricting Panel's proceedings,"[61] the Court meant two things. First, federal courts must defer in the sense of "stay[ing their] hands"[62] or "postponing consideration of [the] merits"[63] as long as some state entity is addressing the responsibility to redistrict. Second, as the Court's discussion of "what ought to have happened" shows,[64] federal courts must defer in

[56] *Emison*, 782 F Supp at 433.

[57] The Supreme Court vacated this injunction in January 1992. *Cotlow v Emison*, 112 S Ct 855 (1992).

[58] *Emison*, 782 F Supp at 442.

[59] Id at 448. Once again, the Supreme Court stayed the district court's injunction. See *Growe v Emison*, 113 S Ct at 1080 (stay granted by Blackmun in chambers).

[60] Id (emphasis in original).

[61] Id at 1080.

[62] Id (quoting *Railroad Comm'n v Pullman Co.*, 312 US 496, 501 (1941)).

[63] Id at 1080 n 1.

[64] Id at 1082.

the sense of *respecting* or *yielding to* the state court's choice among permissible plans, "rather than treating [the state court's scheme] as simply one of several competing legislative redistricting proposals available for the district court's choosing."[65] Thus, *Growe*'s statement that "state courts have a significant role in redistricting"[66] goes beyond their simply being responsible for enforcing the constitutional requirement of one-person, one-vote. *Growe* treated state courts as an integral part of the state political process, as well as an agent under the federal Constitution.

This approach has substantial appeal. If federal courts involve themselves at the outset of the apportionment process, they will often be left with no guidance on how to choose among acceptable plans in the event the state process does not coalesce behind a single one. The black-letter rule that federal courts must give defendants in reapportionment lawsuits a fair opportunity to develop a new plan does not answer the question of to *whom* a federal court should defer.[67] According deference to the Minnesota House of

---

[65] Id. This interpretation may also underlie the court's reference to "the mistaken view that federal judges need defer only to the Minnesota Legislature and not at all to the State's courts." Id at 1081. To recast a distinction once made by the Minnesota Supreme Court, *Growe* held that the state *process* to which federal courts must yield includes actions by all state *entities*, whatever the role accorded them by positive state law. See *Duxbury v Donovan*, 272 Minn 424, 432–33, 138 NW 2d 692, 698 (1965).

There is more than a little irony in Justice Scalia's celebration of the "legitimacy of state *judicial* redistricting," *Growe*, 113 S Ct at 1081 (emphasis in original), given his assertion in *Chisom v Roemer*, 111 S Ct 2354 (1991), that Section 2 of the Voting Rights Act should not apply to state judicial elections because judges are not "representatives" who act for the people. See id at 2372 (Scalia dissenting).

Moreover, the phrase "legislative redistricting proposals" contains a double entendre. Of course, Justice Scalia was referring to proposals for redistricting legislatures. But there is a long line of cases in which the Supreme Court has used the phrase "legislative plans" to refer to plans that are entitled to federal deference because they are plans that reflect legislative, that is, political, judgments. See, for example, *McDaniel v Sanchez*, 452 US 130, 138 (1981) ("we have recognized important differences between legislative plans and court-ordered plans"); *Wise v Lipscomb*, 437 US 535, 543–46 (1978) (White); id at 547–49 (Powell concurring in part and concurring in the judgment). This dual meaning may lead to problems in administering the preclearance scheme of Section 5 of the Voting Rights Act, because plans imposed by federal courts are not subject to preclearance. If redistricting litigation gets funneled into state courts in covered jurisdictions, are plans imposed by state courts "legislative" under *Growe* and therefore subject to federal preclearance or are they "court-ordered" and therefore exempt?

[66] *Growe*, 113 S Ct at 1081.

[67] See Karlan, 71 Tex L Rev at 1730 (cited in note 13). It is hard to advance any coherent reason why, for example, a court should defer to the nominal defendant in *Growe*—the Minnesota Secretary of State, who essentially performs ministerial functions connected with the electoral process. Under state law she plays absolutely no role in deciding legislative district boundaries. Why should the fortuity of litigation give her views greater weight?

Representatives and Senate would distort the reapportionment process by reducing the Legislature's incentive to compromise with the governor.[68] If a federal court cannot defer to either the legislature or the governor, what criteria would enable it to choose between the competing plans as long as both complied with one-person, one-vote and neither violated the Voting Rights Act?

B. THE CENTRAL ROLE OF THORNBURG V GINGLES

Having thus sharply limited federal judicial intervention, the Court turned to the substantive disagreement between the *Emison* and *Cotlow* courts—whether Section 2 of the Voting Rights Act of 1965 required creating a majority nonwhite state senate district in Minneapolis.[69] Here, too, the Court sought to clarify and limit

[68] As the *Emison* district court noted, the Legislature's knowledge that it could not obtain the legislative plan it wanted through the political process—because the governor would veto the plan—would encourage it to hold out and refuse to compromise. See *Emison*, 782 F Supp at 433; see also Whereatt, *Federal Judges Tell State Panel to Stop* (cited in note 52) (following the federal injunction against further state-court proceedings, one Republican legislator "said the federal panel's order will force DFLers who control the House and Senate to *negotiate* new congressional and district boundary maps") (emphasis added).

[69] The Court could have simply reversed the district court's judgment and remanded the case with instructions to dismiss the complaint. Instead, the Court apparently felt obliged to address the district court's reasoning—essentially for the purpose of reviewing the Minnesota Supreme Court's judgment. This may be because the Court ignored the larger implications of its requirement of federal district court deferral. *Growe* suggests that the Minnesota Supreme Court reached and resolved the Voting Rights Act implications of its plan. See *Growe*, 113 S Ct at 1079; see also *Growe* Appellants' Brief (cited in note 52) (claiming the state redistricting panel "reviewed [the DFL proposal] to ensure that it met the requirements of [Section 2]" and "[u]pon its own examination, . . . after full review of the parties' submissions, held that [it] did not violate the Voting Rights Act"). If this is correct, then there is a question under the *Rooker-Feldman* doctrine, see *District of Columbia Court of Appeals v Feldman*, 460 US 462 (1983); *Rooker v Fidelity Trust Co.*, 263 US 413 (1923), whether the district court would have been free to revisit that issue. *Rooker-Feldman* suggests that the sole forum for federal review of a state court determination is the U.S. Supreme Court, not the initiation of a new lawsuit in federal district court.

The *Rooker-Feldman* question is further clouded by the temporal relationship between the two Minnesota reapportionment cases. On the one hand, the fact that *Emison* was pending when the *Cotlow* court issued its judgment may suggest that the federal court was not precluded from reaching the Voting Rights Act issues. Otherwise, federal deferral will in fact become federal abstention despite Justice Scalia's footnote to the contrary. See *Growe*, 113 S Ct at 1080 n 1. On the other hand, the fact that *Cotlow* was already pending when the *Emison* complaint was filed, and the ability of the *Emison* plaintiffs to intervene in *Cotlow*, strengthens the case for precluding federal district court review, particularly since a contrary holding would vitiate *Growe*'s practical effect. (Parties dissatisfied with their prospects in state court could simply wait until the state court's proceedings were over and then file a new lawsuit challenging the now-in-place state court-created plan in federal court.) And even if *Rooker-Feldman* is not controlling, considerations of full faith and credit, res judicata, and collateral estoppel may lead to the same conclusion. (Indeed, one of the questions presented by the *Growe* appellants was "Was the federal court barred by the Full Faith and

the conditions that justify federal intervention. The mechanism it used was the extension of the *Gingles* test for assessing claims of dilution through submergence—in particular, the insistence on proof of racial bloc voting—to all claims of geographically based vote dilution.

Thornburg v Gingles[70] was the Supreme Court's first encounter with amended Section 2. There, the Court held that North Carolina's use of multimember state legislative districts unlawfully diluted black voting strength in several parts of the state. But rather than engaging in the multifactor, impressionistic, "totality of the circumstances" analysis that Congress had described, the *Gingles* Court articulated three "necessary preconditions" for finding dilution. First, the minority group must show that it is "sufficiently large and geographically compact to constitute a majority in a single-member district"; second, it must show that it is "politically cohesive"; and third, it must show "that the white majority votes sufficiently as a bloc to enable it . . . usually to defeat the minority's preferred candidate."[71] The critical concept underlying the test is one of causation: does the current system deny minority voters a fair opportunity to elect the candidates of their choice, and is there an alternative system which *would* provide that opportunity?[72]

In the half-dozen years following *Gingles*, the lower courts had come to treat the *Gingles* test as a bright-line threshold for weeding

---

Credit Act and the doctrines of collateral estoppel and mootness from adopting a legislative redistricting plan that was directly contrary to a prior state court legislative redistricting judgment?" See *Growe* Appellants' Brief (cited in note 52).)

Thus, the Supreme Court's conclusion that "[w]e must review [the *Emison* court's] analysis because, if it is correct, the District Court was right to deny effect to the state-court legislative redistricting plan," *Growe*, 113 S Ct at 1083, may well assume too much. *Emison's* analysis would in fact be sheer dicta if the district court had had no power to pass on the state court's plan in the first place.

[70] 478 US 30 (1986).

[71] Id at 50–51.

[72] See *Growe*, 113 S Ct 1084 (the first prong establishes "that the minority has the potential to elect a representative of its choice in some single-member district," while the second two prongs show "that the challenged districting thwarts a distinctive minority vote by submerging it in a larger white voting population"). See also *Dillard v Baldwin County Bd. of Educ.*, 686 F Supp 1459, 1461 (MD Ala) (the *Gingles* preconditions frame the inquiry into whether the difficulty a minority experiences in electing its preferred candidates is "in some measure attributable to the challenged election feature, or, to put it another way, that the minority has the *potential* to elect representatives in the absence of the challenged feature") (emphasis in original), aff'd, 862 F2d 878 (11th Cir 1988).

out "marginal" Section 2 lawsuits.[73] *Growe* endorsed that threshold approach,[74] at least with respect to the second and third factors, which, taken together, establish racially polarized voting.[75] Since the record was entirely barren of any evidence of bloc voting,[76] Section 2 provided no warrant for the federal courts to upset the state's apportionment.

Growe thus further tightened the test for assessing claims of racial vote dilution by extending *Gingles* to single-member districts—the most prevalent form of legislative and congressional districting— and by emphasizing the centrality of racial bloc voting even within the *Gingles* analysis.[77]

---

[73] *McNeil v Springfield Park Dist*, 851 F2d 937, 942–43 (7th Cir 1988) (Although "the *Gingles* criteria might conceivably foreclose a meritorious claim, in general they will ensure that violations for which an effective remedy exists will be considered while appropriately closing the courthouse to marginal cases. In making that trade-off, the *Gingles* majority justifiably sacrificed some claims to protect stronger claims and promote judicial economy."); see *East Jefferson Coalition v Parish of Jefferson*, 926 F2d 487, 491 (5th Cir 1991) (*Gingles* factors are "necessary preconditions"); *Neal v Coleburn*, 689 F Supp 1426, 1434 (ED Va 1988) (*Gingles* factors are "essential elements"). Compare *Solomon v Liberty County*, 899 F2d 1012 (11th Cir 1990) (en banc) (evenly divided on whether proof of the *Gingles* factors establishes liability outright or merely serves as a threshold determination), cert denied, 498 US 1023 (1991). See also Samuel Issacharoff, *Polarized Voting and the Political Process: The Transformation of Voting Rights Jurisprudence*, 90 Mich L Rev 1833, 1834–35 (1992) (describing the evolution of more bright-line dilution standards); Kathryn Abrams, *"Raising Politics Up": Minority Political Participation and Section 2 of the Voting Rights Act*, 63 NYU L Rev 449, 450–52 (1988) (same).

[74] See *Growe*, 113 S Ct at 1084 ("Our precedent requires that . . . a plaintiff must prove three threshold conditions.").

[75] The court explicitly left open the question whether a plaintiff could bring a so-called "influence" claim when the group to which she belonged was not large enough to actually control the outcome of an election but was sufficiently large so that an alternative to the present system would give it greater *influence* over the selection of public officials. See *Growe*, 113 S Ct at 1084 n 5; *Gingles*, 478 US at 46–47 n 12 (also leaving open that question). See also *Voinovich v Quilter*, 113 S Ct 1149, 1155 (1993) (assuming, without deciding, that such a claim may be brought). For more detailed discussions of influence district claims, see Bernard Grofman, Lisa Handley, and Richard G. Niemi, *Minority Representation and the Quest for Voting Equality* 117–18 (Cambridge U Press, 1992); J. Morgan Kousser, *Beyond Gingles: Influence Districts and the Pragmatic Tradition in Voting Rights Law*, 27 USF L Rev 551 (1993); Allan J. Lichtman and J. Gerald Hebert, *A General Theory of Vote Dilution*, 6 La Raza L J 1 (1993).

[76] See *Growe*, 113 S Ct at 1085. Indeed, there was substantial evidence before the district court showing that minority candidates had been elected from majority-white jurisdictions across the state. See *Growe* Appellants' Brief (cited in note 52). The plaintiffs' inability to meet the latter two prongs of the test enabled the court to leave open the question whether the first prong applies to all claims of racial vote dilution. See *Growe*, 113 S Ct at 1085.

[77] See generally Issacharoff, 90 Mich L Rev at 1845–91 (cited in note 73) (discussing the emergence and rationale for the centrality of the racial bloc voting inquiry).

C. THE BROAD DOMAIN OF STATE POLITICAL RESOLUTION

Growe answered the question of when a federal court could require majority-nonwhite districts. *Voinovich* addressed the converse
issue: when can federal courts prohibit them? Once again, racial
bloc voting emerged as the critical factor.

A heatedly partisan, Republican-controlled, reapportionment
process produced a plan ("the Tilling Plan") for the Ohio House
of Representatives that contained eight majority-black districts, an
increase of four over the 1981 plan.[78] It also produced a flood of
state and federal court litigation.[79]

The plaintiffs in the federal lawsuit were characterized by the
district court as "Democratic electors and state legislators, some of
whom are members of a protected class under the Voting Rights
Act."[80] Their complaint alleged that the 1991 plan violated the
Voting Rights Act, the Fourteenth and Fifteenth Amendments'
prohibitions of racial discrimination, and the Fourteenth Amendment's prohibition of political vote dilution through gerrymandering. After an extremely expedited process in which it gave each
party three hours to present its evidence, the federal district court
ruled that the Tilling Plan's deliberate creation of majority-black
districts violated Section 2 of the Voting Rights Act. The plan,
the district court held, unnecessarily and impermissibly "packed"
black voters into a few districts, wasting minority votes in the
packed districts and diluting minority voting strength in surrounding areas where black voting strength had concomitantly

---

[78] The following account is taken from *Quilter v Voinovich*, 794 F Supp 756 (ND Ohio 1992) (three-judge court), rev'd 113 S Ct 1149 (1993) ("*Quilter II*"); *Quilter v Voinovich*, 749 F Supp 695 (ND Ohio 1992) (three-judge court) (1992), rev'd 113 S Ct 1149 (1993) ("*Quilter I*"); *Voinovich v Ferguson*, 586 NE2d 1020 (Ohio 1992) ("*Ferguson II*"); *Voinovich v Ferguson*, 584 NE2d 737 (Ohio 1992) ("*Ferguson I*"); Brief for Appellants, *Voinovich v Quilter*, 113 S Ct 1149 (1993) ("*Voinovich* Appellants' Brief").

[79] The Ohio litigation was even more complex than Minnesota's. The Republicans filed an original-jurisdiction lawsuit before the Republican-dominated Ohio Supreme Court seek-ing a declaratory judgment that the Tilling Plan complied with Ohio law. The Democrats removed the case to federal court and counterclaimed, alleging the plan's invalidity under both the Ohio constitution and federal law. But when the case was remanded, the Democrats withdrew their counterclaims and filed their own lawsuit in federal court, alleging that the plan violated the US Constitution as well as the Voting Rights Act and the state constitution. The federal court sought, ultimately unsuccessfully, to enjoin the state court's proceedings; the state court judges went out of their way in their opinions to insist that they had resolved the federal issues as well and had thus foreclosed the federal court from addressing them.

[80] *Quilter I*, 794 F Supp at 695.

been diminished.[81] Moreover, the court explained, the process had been infected by a fatal legal error: while the deliberate creation of majority-black districts may be an "appropriate *remedy* under certain circumstances, [the Apportionment Board] here failed to make the requisite findings which demonstrate a violation of the Voting Rights Act, thereby permitting such a remedy."[82] The district court directed the state either to justify its deliberate creation of majority-black districts or to present a new, legally satisfactory plan. The state responded by slightly lowering the black concentrations in six house districts and presenting a variety of information designed to show that, under the totality of the circumstances as delineated in the legislative history to the 1982 voting rights amendments, its decision to draw majority-black districts was justified. The district court rejected the response, finding that the board's "analysis contains only meager information that was not previously before this Court."[83] In a later order, it noted "the absence of racial bloc voting, the [ability of black voters] to elect both black and white candidates of their choice," and the sustained electoral success of minority-sponsored candidates.[84] Thus, the district court held, "the Board fails once again to justify its wholesale creation of majority-minority districts, thus rendering the plan, as submitted, violative of the Voting Rights Act of 1965."[85] And it added an additional thought: "[W]e now proceed to decide that the plan as submitted is also violative of the Fifteenth Amendment of the United States Constitution."[86] That single sentence was the entirety of *Quilter*'s constitutional analysis.

Once again, the Supreme Court unanimously reversed. Justice O'Connor's opinion began by noting the importance of context in assessing districting schemes. Whether dispersal of a minority community among several districts constitutes impermissible "cracking" or concentration involves illegitimate "packing" will necessarily "depend[ ] entirely on the facts and circumstances of

---

[81] See id at 701.

[82] Id at 696 (emphasis added).

[83] *Quilter II*, 794 F Supp at 757.

[84] See *Voinovich*, 113 S Ct at 1154 (quoting from the unpublished order).

[85] *Quilter II*, 794 F Supp at 757.

[86] Id.

each case."[87] The appropriate composition of individual districts will depend on the demographic character of the minority community as well as the level of bloc voting.[88] Accordingly, apportionment architects must walk a sometimes narrow path between cracking and packing.

But the Court emphasized that "Section 2 contains no *per se* prohibitions against particular types of districts. . . . Only if the apportionment scheme has the *effect* of denying a protected class the equal opportunity to elect its candidate of choice does it violate § 2; where such an effect has not been demonstrated [Section] 2 simply does not speak to the matter."[89] Thus, Section 2 restricts state autonomy only to the extent necessary to correct the process failure caused by racial bloc voting.

The district court had found, however, that Ohio's political landscape was not blighted by racial polarization. It had stressed the

---

[87] *Voinovich*, 113 S Ct at 1156. For a more detailed explanation of these terms, see pages 249–50 above. Although majority-black districts give black voters an opportunity to elect their preferred candidates even in the face of racial bloc voting, a tipping point will eventually be reached at which putting additional minority citizens into already overwhelmingly black districts can diminish the overall voting strength of the minority community. For example, there might be enough black citizens within a given municipality to create two 97 percent black councilmanic districts. But using the same number of residents, it might also be possible to create three 65 percent black districts. Choosing the former configuration instead of the latter will not increase the electoral strength of any particular subset of black citizens and will diminish overall black influence on the composition of the council.

[88] With regard to the first question, the relatively greater dropoff between total population and voting-age population in black and Hispanic communities than in white ones, see, for example, *Whitfield v Democratic Party*, 686 F Supp 1365, 1380 (ED Ark 1988) (county was 53 percent black in total population but majority white in voting-age population), aff'd en banc by an equally divided court, 902 F2d 15 (8th Cir 1990), cert denied, 498 US 1126 (1991), combined with their lower rates of registration and turnout, see *UJO v Carey*, 430 US 144, 164 (1977), may require drawing a district with a nonwhite population "supermajority" to create a "toss-up" district on election day. See generally Grofman, Handley, and Niemi, *Minority Representation* at 120–21 (cited in note 75) (discussing the "so-called 65 percent rule" and the need for consideration of context). Thus, in a community blighted by pervasive bloc voting, a district that is less than, for example, 60 percent black, may never elect the black community's candidate.

By contrast, white crossover voting may mean that some majority-white districts nonetheless give minority voters a reasonable opportunity to elect the candidate of their choice. It is entirely possible, for example, that a 40 percent black district would give black voters an equal opportunity to elect candidates of their choice. If, for example, 90 percent of black voters vote for the candidate sponsored by the black community and 25 percent of white voters cross over, the black-sponsored candidate will win in a 40 percent black district (.90 × .40 + .25 × .60 = .36 + .15 = .51, or 51 percent of the votes), even though she would lose in a 30 percent black district (.90 × .30 + .25 × .70 = .27 + .175 = .445, or 44.5 percent of the vote).

[89] *Voinovich*, 113 S Ct at 1156 (emphasis in original).

"absence of racial bloc voting, the [ability of black voters] to elect both black and white candidates of their choice," and the sustained electoral success of minority-sponsored candidates.[90] In short, politics in Ohio was working. Blacks needed no more federal intervention than any other similarly sized group of citizens: in some places they elected representatives by themselves; in other areas, they built coalitions to attain a majority. Accordingly, the district court's inquiry under the Voting Rights Act should have come to an end.

Voinovich thus completed the ascension of bloc voting from one of seven optional "typical factors" indicating racial vote dilution[91] to one of three "necessary preconditions" in certain kinds of Section 2 cases[92] to the absolute centerpiece of Section 2 claims. This elevation promised to impose at least some order on Section 2 litigation, since it is at least possible to delineate fairly objective standards for assessing the degree and significance of bloc voting.[93]

In addition to identifying the district court's doctrinal misinterpretation, the Court also located a profound institutional failure in the district court's imposition on the state political process of a framework designed to curb federal *judicial* involvement. *Gingles*'s identification of conditions of process failure provided congressional warrant for federal judicial intervention. But "precisely because it is the domain of the States, and not the federal courts, to

---

[90] Id at 1154 (quoting unpublished district court order).

[91] See Senate Report at 28 (cited in note 24) (terming "the extent to which voting in the elections of the state or political subdivision is racially polarized" one of seven "[t]ypical factors" tending to show dilution, but cautioning that "there is no requirement that any particular number of factors be proved" and stating that "[t]he failure of plaintiff to establish any particular factor, is not rebuttal evidence of non-dilution," id at 29 n 118).

[92] See *Thornburg v Gingles*, 478 US at 50 (describing racial bloc voting as one of the "necessary preconditions" for multimember districts to operate to impair minority voters' ability to elect representatives of their choice"). See also id at 46 n 12 (noting that "we have no occasion to consider whether the standards we apply to [the] claim that multimember districts" violate Section 2 "are fully pertinent to other sorts of vote dilution claims, such as a claim alleging that the splitting of a large and geographically cohesive minority between two or more multimember or single-member districts resulted in the dilution of the minority vote"; since the first *Gingles* precondition still exists, this statement necessarily implies that it is the second and third—which together indicate racial bloc voting—that are uncertain).

[93] This is not to say, however, that the courts have in fact developed universally accepted standards. *Gingles* itself was divided on this point: Justice Brennan was unable to garner a majority for his analysis. None of the 1993 trilogy made any progress toward resolving this issue. For scholarly attempts to develop such standards, see Grofman, Handley, and Niemi, *Minority Representation* at 82–104 (cited in note 75); Issacharoff, 90 Mich L Rev at 1871–90 (cited in note 73).

conduct apportionment in the first place,"[94] states require no federal warrant to choose among districting plans. Essentially, the district court was hoist on its own petard. Rather than a Section 2 violation being a necessary precondition for a state's "remedy" of drawing majority-black districts, a Section 2 violation is a necessary precondition for the federal judicial remedy of overturning a state's affirmative choice to draw such districts.[95] In concluding that "surely Congress could not have intended the State to prove the invalidity of its own apportionment scheme" as a prelude to redistricting,[96] the Court rejected the lower court's attempt to "crosonize" the Voting Rights Act, that is, to require jurisdictions to set out a factual predicate for drawing majority-minority districts.[97]

Underlying that conclusion was the implicit recognition that *all* districts have a racial identity, at least in the sense that their racial composition can be readily described and readily perceived by any politically knowledgeable observer.[98] Thus, it is impossible to say that states must have a justification for consciously drawing racially identifiable districts without subjecting every state districting choice to federal review. But requiring special justification only for drawing majority-black districts reflects a deep normative indifference to racial vote dilution, for it assumes that majority-white districts have no racial identity even if black voters are submerged within them.[99] Since all districts in a biracial community must be either majority-white, majority-black, or evenly divided (and the last possibility will be attainable only if the starting point is an evenly split community), the state must either be compelled to draw districts which are all racial microcosms of the entire state or

---

[94] *Voinovich*, 113 S Ct at 1156.

[95] Because the court disposed of the Voting Rights Act issue in *Voinovich* on the question of racial bloc voting, it left open, as the *Growe* court had done, the question whether a protected group that is too small to form the majority in a fairly drawn single-member district can nonetheless prove a violation of Section 2. See *Voinovich*, 113 S Ct at 1155.

[96] Id at 1156.

[97] The reference is to *City of Richmond v J.A. Croson Corp.*, 488 US 469, 498–506 (1989). See Karlan, 71 Tex L Rev at 1735 (cited in note 13) (discussing the "crosonization" question). In light of the court's decision in *Shaw v Reno*, 113 S Ct 2816 (1993), Alex Aleinikoff and Sam Issacharoff have suggested that perhaps the court is attempting to "*Bakke*-ize" [perhaps "*Bakke*-slide" would be more appropriate] voting rights questions. See Aleinikoff and Issacharoff, 92 Mich L Rev at 609–18 (cited in note 18).

[98] See *Shaw v Reno*, 113 S Ct 2816, 2826 (1993) ("the legislature always is aware of race when it draws district lines") (emphasis omitted).

[99] See Lani Guinier, *Groups, Representation, and Race-Conscious Districting: A Case of the Emperor's Clothes*, 71 Tex L Rev 1589, 1591 (1993).

be free to draw districts with a variety of complexions. The former possibility is very likely unattainable and would, given residential patterns, require grotesque gerrymandering and carving up of geographically cohesive minority communities. And to pretend that the latter possibility can be achieved through non-race-conscious districting is to ignore reality: as long as politicians familiar with local circumstances draw districts, they simply cannot be unaware of the racial makeup of the districts they draw. Given the explicit race-consciousness of the Voting Rights Act,[100] its imperative cannot be race-unconsciousness.

This recognition that race-consciousness is not the same thing as intentional racial discrimination formed the basis for rejecting the district court's constitutional analysis. As it had with regard to the statutory influence–district/dilution claim, the Court assumed, without deciding, that the plaintiffs had advanced an actionable theory under the Fifteenth Amendment.[101] But, the Court concluded, the district court's "finding of intentional discrimination was clearly erroneous."[102] Evidence in the record actually contradicted the district court's finding. "Tilling and the board relied on sources that were wholly unlikely to engage in or tolerate intentional discrimination against black voters, including the Ohio NAACP, the Black Elected Democrats of Ohio, and the Black Elected Democrats of Cleveland, Ohio. Tilling's plan actually incorporated much of the Ohio NAACP's proposed plan; the Ohio NAACP, for its part, fully supported the 1991 apportionment plan."[103]

The Court's discussion raised as many questions as it answered. Some of those questions were explicit. For example, the Court "express[ed] no view on the relationship between the Fifteenth

---

[100] Section 2 expressly provides that "the extent to which members of a protected class have been elected to office . . . is one circumstance that may be considered" in assessing a dilution claim. 42 USC § 1973(b) (1988).

[101] It is unclear why the district court decided this as a Fifteenth Amendment claim rather than a Fourteenth Amendment claim, especially given the plurality opinion in *City of Mobile v Bolden*, 446 US 55, 64–66 (1980), that the Fifteenth Amendment does not reach claims of racial vote dilution and the fact that the Fourteenth Amendment clearly does reach claims of racial vote dilution, see id at 65; *White v Regester*, 412 US 755, 765–66 (1973). The Supreme Court's decision to treat *Voinovich* as a Fifteenth Amendment case of course left the coast clear for its Fourteenth Amendment constitutional analysis in *Shaw v Reno*, 113 S Ct 2816 (1993).

[102] *Voinovich*, 113 S Ct at 1158.

[103] Id at 1158–59.

Amendment and race-conscious redistricting,"[104] although that, of course, was precisely the gravamen of the plaintiffs' Fifteenth Amendment claim. The Court elided the issue by assuming that if there were no racially discriminatory *effect*, by which the Court seemed to mean no disadvantageous electoral consequences, then race-consciousness alone would not violate either the Fifteenth Amendment or Section 2. Other unanswered questions were implicit. If, for example, the approbation of the NAACP and a group of black elected officials was sufficient to "directly contradic[t]" a finding of discriminatory intent, what does this say about the propriety of allowing two white Democratic members of the Apportionment Board and "various Democratic electors and legislators,"[105] some of whom almost fortuitously happened to be "members of a protected class under the Voting Rights Act,"[106] to use the Act essentially as a weapon in a straight partisan wrangle over redistricting? What, to be more precise, gives white politicians elected from majority-white jurisdictions standing to claim a violation of black voters' rights in entirely distinct districts? At the same time, what role should this sort of evidence about minority groups' extensive "opportunity . . . to participate in the political process"[107] of reapportionment and, by extension, of governance, play in Section 2 cases generally? But what *Voinovich* did clearly establish was the Supreme Court's commitment to keeping the Voting Rights Act within its own domain—cases where well-defined evidence showed minority exclusion from the political process.[108]

---

[104] Id at 1159.

[105] Id at 1153.

[106] *Quilter II*, 794 F Supp at 695. This euphemism apparently refers to plaintiffs who are black, although that is nowhere stated in any of the courts' opinions. In fact, of course, *all* voters fall within that description, since Section 2 by its terms prohibits discrimination against white voters as well.

Had Justice O'Connor probed more deeply into the evidence before the district court, the essential absence of any black complainants from the case would have become even more obvious. The challenged plan actually involved *less* packing than its predecessor, which had been drawn by the Democratic plaintiffs' predecessors in interest. And the alternative plan proposed during the reapportionment process by the lead plaintiffs created only two fewer majority-black districts and only two more "influence" districts. Where the actual lines were drawn was thus no doubt a subject of intense *political* concern, but there seemed to be a consensus on the broad outlines of a fair *racial* allocation of legislative seats.

[107] 42 USC § 1973(b) (1988).

[108] Ultimately, the Court disposed of *Voinovich* on an issue connected with one-person, one-vote. The total deviation in the Ohio plan (the sum of the percentage by which the least populous district fell below the ideal, that is, equipopulous, district size and the percentage by which the most populous district exceeded the ideal) was over 10 percent.

III. THE ENDS OF VOTING RIGHTS ENFORCEMENT: SHAW V RENO

Growe and *Voinovich* offered a sensible response to attempted hijackings of Section 2 by the major political parties. *Shaw*, which came down the last day before the summer recess, was an entirely different story. The patent insufficiency of the Court's reasoning raises the question of the Court's real agenda in issuing such a confused and confusing opinion.

A. THE ROAD TO THE I-85 DISTRICT

Shaw concerned North Carolina's congressional reapportionment. By now it should come as no surprise that *Shaw* was not the only litigation challenging the state's new lines. Democrats controlled both houses of the General Assembly; the lack of a veto left the state's Republican governor a bystander.[109] The North Carolina situation, however, introduced two wrinkles absent from the Minnesota and Ohio experience. First, there was no point in trying to upset the process through state-court litigation: the North Carolina judiciary was firmly in Democratic hands.[110] Second, and more important, North Carolina was subject to the preclearance regime of Section 5 of the Voting Rights Act: it could not hold

---

Thus, under existing case law, the plaintiffs had established a prima facie case of malapportionment. See *Brown v Thomson*, 462 US 835, 842–43 (1983) (explaining that "as a general matter, . . . an apportionment plan with a maximum population deviation under 10% falls within [the] category of minor deviations" that are " 'insufficient to make out a prima facie case of invidious discrimination'," but that greater deviations among state legislative districts do require justification) (quoting *Gaffney v Cummings*, 412 US 735, 745 (1973)).

The *Quilter* court erred, however, in not giving the state the opportunity to show that the excessive deviation was justified as reasonably related to a rational and permissible state policy, in this case, preserving political subdivision boundaries. See *Voinovich*, 113 S Ct at 1159. Therefore, the Supreme Court remanded the case to give the state that opportunity. See id at 1159–60. But the Court was careful not to give the district court another opportunity for excessive intervention: "[W]e . . . remand *only* for further proceedings on whether the plan's deviation from equal population among districts violates the Fourteenth Amendment." Id at 1154 (emphasis added).

[109] See *Pope v Blue*, 809 F Supp 392, 394 (WDNC) (three-judge court), summarily aff'd, 113 S Ct 30 (1992).

[110] A majority of the state supreme court were Democrats, several elected after fierce partisan contests. And the Fourth Circuit was only six months away from holding that the state Republican Party and its members had stated a claim of unconstitutional political gerrymandering with regard to the configuration of North Carolina's trial bench—on which only two Republicans had sat in the last century. See *Republican Party v Martin*, 980 F2d 943, 948 n 10, 958 (4th Cir), cert denied, 114 S Ct 93 (1993). *Republican Party v Martin* appears to be the first post-*Bandemer* case in which the complaint has not been dismissed for failure to state a claim.

elections until it had obtained federal approval for the new district configurations.[111] As a practical matter, this meant that North Carolina required Department of Justice approval for its congressional reapportionment.[112]

The 1990 census entitled North Carolina to twelve congressional seats, an increase of one over its post-1980 delegation. The change in the number of districts meant, of course, that more than some simple tinkering with existing lines was required. At the same time, in significant part as a result of *Thornburg v Gingles*,[113] the size and influence of the black state legislative contingent had grown dramatically, and representatives of the black community were demanding that the state, which was roughly 22 percent black and which had not elected a black to Congress since the turn of the century, draw some majority-black congressional districts. Finally,

---

[111] Jurisdictions are designated for preclearance on the basis of a triggering formula contained in section 4(b) of the Voting Rights Act, 42 USC § 1973b(b) (1988). Coverage is mandatory if the jurisdiction used a literacy test broadly defined (to include, for example, the use of English language–only election materials in a significantly non-English-speaking community) and voter registration or turnout in the 1964, 1968, or 1972 presidential elections dipped below 50 percent of voting age population. Currently, nine states and parts of seven others are "covered jurisdictions." See 28 CFR Part 51 App (1993). Forty North Carolina counties are covered and thus, as a practical matter, all statewide redistricting activity requires preclearance.

[112] As a formal matter, Section 5 provides both an administrative and a judicial mechanism for obtaining preclearance. The administrative process resembles the Book of the Month Club. A covered jurisdiction submits its change to the U.S. Attorney General. If she does not object within 60 days, the change can be implemented. The judicial process requires bringing a declaratory judgment action in the United States District Court for the District of Columbia before a three-judge court. Theoretically, the standard for preclearance is the same whichever avenue a jurisdiction seeks. See 28 CFR § 51.52(a) (1993) (the Attorney General "shall make the same determination that would be made by the court in an action for a declaratory judgment under Section 5: Whether the submitted change has the purpose or will have the effect of denying or abridging the right to vote on account of race, color, or membership in a language minority group"). A jurisdiction that fails to obtain administrative preclearance is still entitled to seek a declaratory judgment. See 42 USC § 1973c (1988).

As a practical matter, however, jurisdictions that fail to obtain administrative preclearance rarely seek judicial preclearance. The process is time-consuming, costly, not all that likely to achieve the desired result, and requires holding the changes in abeyance during the course of the litigation. Thus, although there have been roughly 60 congressional and legislative reapportionments subject to preclearance, and the Department of Justice has objected several dozen times, there are only five reported preclearance lawsuits. See *Texas v United States*, 802 F Supp 481 (DDC 1992) (three-judge court) (post-1990 state senate); *South Carolina v United States*, 589 F Supp 757 (DDC) (three-judge court) (post-1980 state legislature), cert dism'd, 469 US 875 (1984); *Busbee v Smith*, 549 F Supp 494 (DDC 1982) (three-judge court) (post-1980 Georgia congressional reapportionment), aff'd, 459 US 1166 (1983); *Mississippi v Smith*, 541 F Supp 1329 (DDC 1982) (three-judge court) (post-1980 congressional reapportionment), appeal dism'd, 461 US 912 (1983); *Mississippi v United States*, 490 F Supp 569 (DDC 1979) (three-judge court) (post-1970 state legislature), aff'd, 444 US 1050 (1980).

[113] 478 US 30 (1986).

the Democrats were concerned to protect Democratic incumbents in a state where Republicans, although still a decided minority, were increasing.[114]

The General Assembly's first plan created one majority-black district in the northeastern part of the state. The district nicely reflected the political situation that produced it; it was contorted to favor both the interest of a nearby white incumbent Democrat in protecting his political base and the ability of the black community to elect a representative of its choice.[115] But when North Carolina submitted its plan to the Department of Justice for preclearance, the Department objected. It was unable to conclude that the state's plan had neither a discriminatory purpose nor a discriminatory effect in light of the state's failure to draw a second majority nonwhite district and the Department's suspicion that minority interests had been sacrificed to incumbent protection.[116]

Accommodating both two majority-black districts and the needs of incumbent Democrats required a bit more artistry.[117] Instead of drawing another majority-nonwhite district in the southeastern part of the state, which the Department had identified as a possible location for such a district, the General Assembly drew the now-infamous "I-85" district in the north-central part of the state. The district was 160 miles long and, in some places, no wider than a single point. The voting age population of the district was 53.34 percent black and 45.21 percent white.[118]

---

[114] See *Pope v Blue*, 809 F Supp at 394.

[115] As the Department of Justice noted in its objection letter, "The unusually convoluted shape of that district does not appear to have been necessary to create a majority black district and, indeed, at least one alternative configuration was available that would have been more compact." But the contortion provided no basis for objecting under Section 5, since the Department "concluded that the irregular configuration of that district did not have the purpose or effect of minimizing minority voting strength in that region." Letter from John R. Dunne, Assistant Attorney General for Civil Rights, to Tiare B. Smiley, Special Deputy Attorney General of North Carolina, Dec 18, 1991 ("DOJ Objection Letter"), reprinted in Appendix to State Appellees' Brief, *Shaw v Reno*, 113 S Ct 2816 (1993) ("*Shaw* State Appellees' Brief").

[116] See DOJ Objection Letter (cited in note 115).

[117] The late Philip Burton reportedly referred to his egregious gerrymander of the California congressional districts, see *Badham v Eu*, 694 F Supp 664 (ND Cal 1988) (three-judge court), aff'd, 488 US 804 (1989), as his "contribution to modern art." Larry Liebert, *Burton-Style Remapping May Be a Thing of the Past*, SF Chron (Jan 9, 1992), at A19.

[118] *Shaw* State Appellees' Brief (cited in note 115). House District 1, the other majority-nonwhite district, was 53.40 percent black and 45.49 percent white in voting age population. The ten remaining districts had black voting age population percentages of between 4.94 and 20.90 percent. Id.

"The Attorney General did not object to the General Assembly's revised plan. But numerous North Carolinians did."[119] Their first line of attack was a political gerrymandering challenge.[120] In light of *Bandemer*'s declaration that "unconstitutional discrimination occurs only when the electoral system is arranged in a manner that will consistently degrade a voter's or group of voters' influence on the political process as a whole,"[121] the district court had no trouble granting the state's motion to dismiss for failure to state a claim: the plan created a number of "'safe' Republican seats"; there was no allegation that Republicans in Democratic districts were unable to influence their Representatives; and although Republicans had been excluded from the "political process . . . of redistricting," there was no evidence to suggest that "they have been or will be consistently degraded in their participation in the entire political process [as opposed to] the process of redistricting."[122] The Supreme Court summarily affirmed.[123]

B. THE ROAD TO THE SUPREME COURT

At the same time that *Pope* was being litigated in the Western District of North Carolina, five voters who lived in the Middle District filed a lawsuit in the Eastern District against the federal and state officials who had been involved in North Carolina's congressional reapportionment. Their complaint was more than a challenge to the particular plan enacted by the General Assembly; it was an assault on the constitutionality of the Voting Rights Act as well.[124] The plaintiffs argued that the Equal Protection Clause

---

In the November 1992 elections, both the First and Twelfth Districts elected black representatives.

[119] *Shaw*, 113 S Ct at 2821.

[120] *Pope*, 809 F Supp 392.

[121] *Davis v Bandemer*, 478 US 109, 132 (1986) (plurality opinion). Given that three justices did not think political gerrymandering claims were even justiciable, see id at 144 (O'Connor, joined by Burger and Rehnquist, concurring in the judgment), a plaintiff must, at a minimum, meet the plurality standard.

[122] *Pope*, 809 F Supp at 397–98. These items largely point to governance concerns—with the responsiveness of elected officials and the control over delegation composition.

[123] 113 S Ct 30 (1992). Only Justice Blackmun would have set the case for oral argument.

[124] Much of this assault was deflected by the district court's conclusion that it lacked subject matter jurisdiction over the plaintiffs' challenge to Section 2's constitutionality because Congress had vested exclusive jurisdiction over such proceedings in the United States District Court for the District of Columbia. See *Shaw v Barr*, 808 F Supp 461, 466–67 (EDNC 1992). See also 42 USC § 1973*l*(b) (1988) ("No court other than the District Court

outlawed the intentional concentration of black voters in districts that are "in no way related to considerations of commpactness [*sic*], contiguousness and geographic or jurisdictional communities of interest,"[125] and that the Voting Rights Act was unconstitutional to the extent that it required such concentrations.

At the outset, the district court confronted what it termed a "puzzling" aspect of the plaintiffs' claim:

> They nowhere identify themselves as members of a different race than that of the black voters in whose behalf the challenged congressional districts allegedly (and concededly) were created. Nor, following this, do they plainly allege constitutional injury specific to their rights as members of a particular racial classification of voters. Indeed, in describing the constitutional injury allegedly caused by the race-conscious redistricting plan, they assert that it is injury suffered alike by "plaintiffs and all other citizens and registered voters of North Carolina—whether black, white, native American, or others."[126]

The district court repaired this "deliberate (and humanly, if not legally, laudable) refusal to inject their own race[s]" into the lawsuit by taking judicial notice of the plaintiffs' identity as white voters.[127]

But this repair in fact misled the district court into treating the plaintiffs' case as simply "some 'reverse' variety" of the traditional racial gerrymandering and vote dilution claims.[128] It enabled the court to make quick work of the plaintiffs' complaint. The claim that race-conscious redistricting was per se unconstitutional had been rejected by a fractured Supreme Court in *United Jewish Organi-*

---

for the District of Columbia . . . shall have jurisdiction to issue . . . any restraining order or temporary or permanent injunction against the execution or enforcement of any provision of [this Act]"). The court also concluded, in perhaps a surfeit of caution, that it should dismiss the federal defendants on 12(b)(6) grounds because the Department's preclearance decisions are discretionary acts immune to judicial review. See *Shaw v Barr*, 808 F Supp at 467.

The Supreme Court disposed of the claims against the federal defendants in one sentence. See *Shaw*, 113 S Ct at 2823 ("In our view, the District Court properly dismissed appellants' claims against the federal appellees."). But near the end of its opinion was the suggestion, despite the lower court's holding that it lacked subject-matter jurisdiction over a challenge to Section 2's constitutionality, see *Shaw v Barr*, 808 F Supp at 466–67, that the issue of Section 2's unconstitutionally "remain[s] open for consideration on remand." *Shaw*, 113 S Ct at 2831.

[125] *Shaw v Barr*, 808 F Supp at 465–66 (quoting complaint).

[126] Id at 470 (quoting complaint).

[127] Id at 470.

[128] Id at 469 n 7.

zations v Carey.[129] And when it came to an as-applied challenge, the plaintiffs had failed to allege either a discriminatory intent or a discriminatory effect. With regard to the former, they identified no "legislative intent to deprive white voters . . . of an equal opportunity with all other racial groups of voters—on a statewide basis— to participate in the political process and to elect candidates of their choice."[130] An intent to favor black voters was simply not the constitutional equivalent of an intent to injure white ones: "[t]he one intent may exist without the other."[131] And plaintiffs' concession that the state was simply trying to comply with the Voting Rights Act further fatally undermined any claim that it had acted with "the necessary invidious intent to harm [the plaintiffs]."[132]

With regard to the latter, the plaintiffs had alleged no discriminatory effect whatsoever. Only two of the five plaintiffs lived in one of the majority-black districts and neither, the district court held, would suffer any cognizable injury "if her or his particular candidate should lose by virtue of the district's racial composition."[133] Nor could the plaintiffs argue a general dilution of white voting strength: since whites constituted decisive majorities in 83 percent of the state's congressional districts (10 of 12), although they were only 75 percent of the state's population, "[t]he plan demonstrably will not lead to proportional underrepresentation of white voters on a statewide basis."[134] Only at the very end of its opinion did the

---

[129] 430 US 144 (1977).

In a brief paragraph, the district court also rejected the claim that race-consciousness was permissible only to the extent that the creation of majority nonwhite districts was required by the Voting Rights Act—essentially along the same lines the Supreme Court was later to use in *Voinovich:* the state's power to make districting decisions is not limited to remedying Section 2 violations. See *Shaw v Barr,* 808 F Supp at 472.

[130] Id at 472.

[131] Id at 473.

[132] Id. Compare *Voinovich,* 113 S Ct at 1158 (suggesting that "an inference of intentional discrimination" under the Fifteenth Amendment was rebutted by the finding that the race-conscious districting was undertaken in the belief it was required by the Voting Rights Act since "it demonstrates obedience to the Supremacy Clause of the United States Constitution.").

[133] *Shaw v Barr,* 808 F Supp at 473, relying on *UJO v Carey,* 430 US at 166 (plurality opinion) (stating that as long as white voters were fairly represented in the legislative body as a whole, individual white voters could not complain that they were unable to directly elect their preferred representatives, since "[s]ome candidate, along with his supporters, always loses"). In fact, nothing in the complaint alleged that any individual voter's aggregation interests were adversely affected by the redistricting plan.

[134] *Shaw v Barr,* 808 F Supp at 473.

district court, which had decided the orthodox questions entirely correctly, come to grips with the real heart of plaintiffs' challenge: the "political and social wisdom" of the General Assembly's plan.[135] Their real point had very little to do, in fact, with voting rights, at least not in the sense of being concerned with who votes or who wins. Rather, the plaintiffs sought "to participate in a process for electing members of the House of Representatives which is color-blind";[136] apportionment was simply one arena in which they were playing out a broader commitment to the ideal of the "color-blind constitution."

C. THE SHAPES OF THINGS TO COME?

At least at the outset, it looked as if the Supreme Court was uninterested in confronting the broad questions the *Shaw* plaintiffs had tried to raise. In response to a jurisdictional statement that squarely challenged the state's power to draw majority black districts and the Attorney General's interpretation of the Voting Rights Act, the Court wrote its own question:

> Argument shall be limited to the following question, which all parties are directed to brief: "Whether a state legislature's intent to comply with the Voting Rights Act and the Attorney General's interpretation thereof precludes a finding that the legislature's congressional redistricting plan was adopted with invidious discriminatory intent where the legislature did not accede to the plan suggested by the Attorney General but instead developed its own."[137]

The answer to this question was obvious and probably could have been answered unanimously by a two-sentence *per curiam*.[138] The Attorney General's imprimatur could not possibly immunize an unconstitutional plan from attack. Moreover, by its very terms, Section 5 provides no "safe harbor" against constitutional challenge

---

[135] Id.

[136] Brief for Federal Appellees, *Shaw v Reno*, 113 S Ct 2816 (1993) (quoting complaint), available in LEXIS, Genfed Library, Briefs File ("*Shaw* Federal Appellees' Brief").

[137] *Shaw v Barr*, 113 S Ct 653 (1992).

[138] That comes pretty close to what the Court did, in a paragraph buried toward the end of its opinion. See *Shaw*, 113 S Ct at 2831 ("Indeed, the Voting Rights Act and our case law make clear that a reapportionment plan that satisfies § 5 still may be enjoined as unconstitutional.").

to a precleared plan.[139] But as is often the case, a confusing answer is what a confused question begets.

To be sure, the Court's answer *seemed* simple:

> [W]e conclude that a plaintiff challenging a reapportionment statute under the Equal Protection Clause may state a claim by alleging that the legislation, though race-neutral on its face, rationally cannot be understood as anything other than an effort to separate voters into different districts on the basis of race, and that the separation lacks sufficient justification.[140]

But although reapportionment may be an "area in which appearances do matter,"[141] reality should matter more, and despite the Court's invocations of *Gomillion v Lightfoot*[142] and *Wright v Rockefeller*,[143] in reality, *Shaw* represents a dramatic departure from the prior case law.

Perhaps the most remarkable departure is one that no one on the Court seemed to notice: a complete disregard for standing requirements. What, precisely, was the "injury in fact" suffered by these particular plaintiffs that made them appropriate parties to challenge the districting scheme?[144] More particularly, what separated their criticisms from "a generally available grievance about government—claiming only harm to [their] and every citizen's interest in proper application of the Constitution and laws, and seeking relief that no more directly and tangibly benefits [them] than it does the public at large"?[145]

The plaintiffs did not claim that the reapportionment diluted

---

[139] See 42 USC § 1973c (1988) ("Neither an affirmative indication by the Attorney General that no objection will be made, nor the Attorney General's failure to object, nor a declaratory judgment entered under this section shall bar a subsequent action to enjoin enforcement of such qualification, prerequisite, standard, practice, or procedure.").

The Court's question contained a second misapprehension: the Attorney General does not "suggest" plans to covered jurisdictions. It is obviously the case that the tenor of her objections to a previously submitted plan may influence a jurisdiction to produce a new plan along particular lines more likely to obtain preclearance, but plans are always developed by jurisdictions rather than the Department of Justice. See *Shaw* Federal Appellees' Brief (cited in note 136).

[140] *Shaw*, 113 S Ct at 2828.

[141] Id at 2827.

[142] 364 US 339 (1960).

[143] 376 US 52 (1964).

[144] *Association of Data Processing Orgs. v Camp*, 397 US 150, 152 (1970).

[145] *Lujan v Defenders of Wildlife*, 112 S Ct 2130, 2143 (1992).

their votes.[146] Indeed, plaintiffs were in an ideological bind: it would ill behoove people seeking "a 'color-blind' electoral process"[147] to claim that their votes had been rendered ineffective because they were placed in too black a district.[148] Their argument thus had to be based on considerations unrelated to electoral outcomes, or at least to their ability or inability to elect the candidate of their choice. Thus, as the Court explained:

> [R]eapportionment legislation that cannot be understood as anything other than an effort to classify and separate voters by race injures voters in other ways. It reinforces racial stereotypes and threatens to undermine our system of representative democracy by signaling to elected officials that they represent a particular racial group rather than their constituency as a whole.[149]

Of course, if *all* voters are equally injured, then the *Shaw* plaintiffs are invoking "citizen standing," a concept several members of the *Shaw* majority have repeatedly condemned.[150]

Just as troubling, the "injuries" Justice O'Connor identifies as cognizable in *Shaw* very closely resemble interests to which she and her compatriots in the *Shaw* majority have usually been quite

---

[146] See *Shaw*, 113 S Ct at 2824 ("In their complaint, appellants did not claim that the General Assembly's reapportionment plan unconstitutionally 'diluted' white voting strength."). This enabled the Court to distinguish *Shaw* from its earlier decision in *UJO v Carey*, 430 US 144 (1977), as well. See *Shaw*, 113 S Ct at 2829–30.

The Court's suggestion that the plaintiffs' claim resembled the one advanced in *Gomillion v Lightfoot*, 364 US 339 (1960), see *Shaw*, 113 S Ct at 2825–27, is hard to take seriously. The purpose and effect of the notorious Tuskegee gerrymander was to strip virtually all of Tuskegee's black residents of their municipal citizenship (while keeping them subject to the city's police powers, see Tr of Oral Arg at 7, *Gomillion v Lightfoot*, 364 US 339 (1960)) and its few black voters (most eligible citizens having been effectively kept off the rolls) of their right to vote in municipal elections. Of course, none of the *Shaw* plaintiffs was deprived of the right to cast a vote in a congressional election. The sole question along those lines concerned in *which* district they would vote.

[147] *Shaw*, 113 S Ct at 2824.

[148] Compare David A. Strauss, *The Myth of Colorblindness*, 1986 Supreme Court Review 99, 111 (the argument that race should be treated differently from other group characteristics is race-conscious, not colorblind).

[149] *Shaw*, 113 S Ct at 2828.

[150] For one particularly pointed example, see Antonin Scalia, *The Doctrine of Standing as an Essential Element of the Separation of Powers*, 17 Suffolk U L Rev 881, 881–82 (1983) ("[C]ourts need to accord greater weight than they have in recent times to the traditional requirement that the plaintiff's alleged injury be a particularized one, which sets him apart from the citizenry at large."). Apparently, that was then, *Shaw* is now. For another, see Justice O'Connor's opinion for the court in *Allen v Wright*, 468 US 737, 751 (1984).

impervious. Viewing her opinion in *Allen v Wright*[151] in light of *Shaw* makes the two look uncomfortably like photographic negatives of one another. A group of white voters suffer cognizable injury from the "reinforce[ment]" of racial stereotypes[152] when a democratically elected state government accedes to the wishes of black citizens to draw a majority-black district, but a group of black parents suffer no "judicially cognizable injury"[153] when they claim "denigration" and "stigmatiz[ation]"[154] as a consequence of the Internal Revenue Service's complicity in invidious racial exclusion from private schools. The *Shaw* plaintiffs, but not the *Wright* plaintiffs, seem to enjoy standing based "simply on their shared individuated right" to a Government that obeys the Constitution.[155]

Nor can Justice O'Connor honestly claim, consistent with her position in *Davis v Bandemer*,[156] that the message race-conscious districting sends to elected representatives is "pernicious."[157] In *Bandemer*, Justice O'Connor agreed with the plurality's statement that "[a]n individual or a group of individuals who votes for a losing candidate is usually deemed to be adequately represented by the winning candidate and to have as much opportunity to influence that candidate as other voters in the district."[158] If this is so of Republican state legislators elected from districts deliberately drawn to ensure Democratic defeat, as she assumes it is in *Bandemer*, then she fails to explain anywhere in *Shaw* why it is not equally true of black Representatives elected from districts drawn in a way less likely to ensure white defeat and arguably drawn simply to give black and white voters an equal opportunity of seeing their preferred candidate prevail.[159] But if this is not so—if Representatives are in fact unresponsive to the interests of members of the

---

[151] 468 US 737 (1984).

[152] *Shaw*, 113 S Ct at 2827.

[153] *Allen*, 468 US at 753.

[154] See id at 749, 754 (internal quotations omitted).

[155] Id at 754.

[156] 478 US 109 (1986).

[157] *Shaw*, 113 S Ct at 2827.

[158] 478 US at 132 (plurality opinion); see id at 152–53 (O'Connor concurring in the judgment) (agreeing with this position).

[159] Nowhere in the Court's opinion, and buried in a single footnote in only one of the dissents, is any mention of the actual racial composition of House District 12. See *Shaw*, 113 S Ct at 2840 n 7 (White dissenting) (stating that the district is "54.71% African-American"). (Actually, 54.71 percent of the registered voters in the district are black; the district's total population is 56.63% black. See *Shaw* State Appellee's Brief (cited in note 115).)

racial minority within their district—then her earlier claim that "impermissible racial stereotypes" are at work becomes a bit more problematic, for now "the perception that members of the same racial group . . . think alike, share the same political interests, and will prefer the same candidates at the polls"[160] turns out to be true. And the decision not to draw any majority-black districts produces a congressional delegation in which *none* of the Representatives is responsive to the distinctive interests of this politically cohesive black community. The fact that Section 2 requires showing precisely this sort of political cohesion and racial bloc voting,[161] means, moreover, that the Court cannot simply decline to take account of such true racial generalizations—unless it is suggesting that Section 2 of the Voting Rights Act is unconstitutional. The Act reflects Congress' judgment that the continued election of all-white congressional delegations from states with significant, historically disempowered black communities "undermine[s] our system of representative democracy."[162]

Nor can Justice O'Connor sidestep this problem by claiming that only when districts are "obviously created solely to effectuate the perceived common interests of one racial group" will this message get through to elected officials.[163] As she earlier recognized, "the legislature is always *aware* of race when it draws district lines";[164] and if there is racial bloc voting, each elected official will similarly be aware of which voters support her and which oppose her. The message will be the same regardless of the shape of the envelope in which it is sent.

Thus, neither of the "injuries" Justice O'Connor explicitly identifies can support the *Shaw* plaintiffs' cause of action. Instead, their cognizable injury seems to stem from the Court's recognition of a new, "analytically distinct claim that a reapportionment plan [violates the Constitution if it] rationally cannot be understood as anything other than an effort to segregate citizens into separate voting districts on the basis of race without sufficient justification."[165] This new cause of action contains two components. First, the court must

---

[160] *Shaw*, 113 S Ct at 2827.

[161] See *Gingles*, 478 US at 50–51.

[162] *Shaw*, 113 S Ct at 2828.

[163] See id at 2827.

[164] Id at 2826 (emphasis in original).

[165] Id at 2830.

ask whether the plan "segregate[s]" voters on the basis of race. Second, it must ask whether there is "sufficient justification" for the segregation.[166]

If the Court had applied its newly discovered test to the undisputed record before it, it should simply have affirmed the district court's dismissal of the complaint for failure to state a claim. However race-conscious the General Assembly had been, and it concededly had drawn the plan with the intent to create two majority-black districts,[167] it had not in fact segregated the races into separate districts. Consider the racial composition of the two districts in which the *Shaw* plaintiffs lived. House District 2's population was 76.23 percent white and 21.94 percent black; House District 12's population was 41.80 percent white and 56.63 percent black.[168] To say that either district even remotely resembles "political apartheid"[169]—especially given that House District 2, where a majority of the *Shaw* plaintiffs lived, was a nearly perfect mirror of the state's overall racial makeup[170]—would be risible if it were not so pernicious.

Nor was the Court's discussion of the possible justifications more coherent. The Court identified several: compliance with Section

---

[166] I phrase the issue this way because it is not entirely clear how the Court proposed to allocate the burdens of pleading and persuasion. It seems that a plaintiff must allege both segregation and lack of justification, see *Shaw*, 113 S Ct at 2828 and 2830, but if she proves segregation, the burden shifts to the defendant to articulate, and perhaps to prove, a justification.

[167] The fact that North Carolina conceded race-consciousness raises the question why the Court devoted so much space to explaining how a district's "bizarre," 113 S Ct at 2825, or "irregular," id at 2824, shape may enable a court to determine that it was drawn for race-conscious reasons. See id at 2825–27. Presumably, if the state conceded that a perfect square was drawn for the purpose of creating a majority-black district, this would satisfy the first prong of the new cause of action.

If, however, the court's point is that only proof of bizarreness will do, then *Shaw* elevates form over substance. The court's insistence that compactness or regularity is not constitutionally required, see id at 2827; see also *Wood v Broom*, 287 US 1, 6–7 (1932) (finding that Congress had deliberately deleted these requirements from the reapportionment statute), means that the bizarreness and irregularity are at most evidence of some other transgression. Compare *Bandemer*, 478 US at 157–58 (O'Connor concurring in the judgment) (chiding the plurality for using proportionality as a measure of political vote dilution when it did not operate as an independent constitutional requirement).

[168] *Shaw* State Appellees' Brief (cited in note 115). The ten other districts ranged from 5.46 to 57.26 percent black. Id. Notably, no one seemed to object—at least not enough to file a lawsuit—to the creation of three 90 percent white districts.

[169] *Shaw*, 113 S Ct at 2627.

[170] Whites are 75.56 percent of North Carolina's population. *Shaw* State Appellees' Brief (cited in note 115).

5's "nonretrogression" principle;[171] compliance with Section 2's prohibition of minority vote dilution; eradicating the effects of past discrimination; and ameliorating the effects of racial polarization.[172] Notably absent from the Court's list was one quite plausible explanation for the configuration that had so troubled it: the General Assembly's partisan desire to protect white Democratic incumbents. This omission is somewhat suspicious. What would happen if, on remand, the state were to show that the shape of the challenged district[173] was the product of simultaneous desires to draw a majority-black district and to conduct a partisan gerrymander?[174] Even if political gerrymandering cannot serve as a justification for race-consciousness, proof that it played a role in the choice among configurations logically negates the first element of the plaintiffs' case, namely, showing that the legislation "rationally cannot be

---

[171] The principle forbids preclearance if a change renders minorities worse off "with respect to their effective exercise of the electoral franchise." *Beer v United States*, 425 US 130, 141 (1976). Given the precise holding in *Beer*—that a change from a city council plan with no majority-black districts to a plan with one could not be retrogressive—this justification seems clearly foreclosed in *Shaw*. Even the perpetuation of a ninety-year tradition of no majority-black districts would leave blacks no worse off than they were before.

[172] See *Shaw*, 113 S Ct at 2831–32.

[173] For some reason, although the Court early on described the First District as a "bug splattered on a windshield," *Shaw*, 113 S Ct at 2820 (quoting Wall St J (Feb 4, 1992), at A14), it proceeded on the assumption that the constitutionality of that district was not placed in issue by the *Shaw* complaint. It is not entirely clear why. If white voters in the Second District can challenge the configuration of the Twelfth District without claiming that they should somehow be part of it, there is no reason to suppose they cannot challenge the First as well. But compare *Davis v Bandemer*, 478 US at 153 (O'Connor concurring in the judgment) (arguing that voters in one part of a state should not be able to challenge the configuration of lines throughout the state because they can only vote in one district anyway and suggesting the implication of a contrary position would be that "members of a political party in one State should be able to challenge a congressional districting plan adopted in any other State, on the grounds that their party is unfairly represented in the State's congressional delegation, thus injuring them as members of the national party").
    In light of Justice O'Connor's reasoning in *Shaw*, though, it is unclear why even a resident of Virginia would have any less standing than a citizen of North Carolina to challenge the General Assembly's plan.

[174] Compare *Whitcomb v Chavis*, 403 US 124, 149–60 (1971) (suggesting that the use of a multimember district cannot be viewed as invidiously discriminatory under the Equal Protection Clause if the fortunes of the black community's candidates rise and fall along with those of other Democratic candidates).
    Incidentally, the court's distinction of districting schemes from at-large elections, on the grounds that "[a]t-large and multimember schemes . . . do not classify voters on the basis of race," *Shaw*, 113 S Ct at 2828, is yet another example of its historical ignorance. In fact, at-large elections and multimember districts were often adopted *precisely* because of their racially discriminatory effects, just as gerrymanders were. See J. Morgan Kousser, *The Undermining of the First Reconstruction: Lessons for the Second*, in Chandler Davidson, ed, *Minority Vote Dilution* at 27, 32–33 (cited in note 19).

understood as anything other than an effort to separate voters."[175] Given her endorsement of partisan gerrymandering in *Bandemer*,[176] Justice O'Connor, at least, should be reluctant to strike down an apportionment whose irregular lines are the function of political, rather than racial, concerns. The Court having already held that the North Carolina plan complies with the relatively toothless prohibition on political vote dilution,[177] the North Carolina Legislature's decision to draw an irregular majority-black district rather than a conventionally shaped one should be left to the state political process, where the *Shaw* plaintiffs were fully and adequately represented.

When it came to the possible justifications it *did* mention, the Court's discussion was cryptic, providing virtually no guidance to the district court on remand or to other lower courts faced with what promises to be a stream of such cases. The Court's repeated condemnation of the Twelfth District's shape suggests that black and Hispanic plaintiffs will be unable to satisfy the first prong of the *Gingles* test—"the minority group must be able to demonstrate that it is sufficiently large and geographically compact to constitute a majority in a single-member district"[178]—by drawing districts the courts find "bizarre" or "irregular" or "uncouth."[179] Moreover, the fact that plaintiffs in Section 2 actions might not be able to establish liability under *Gingles* through identifying such potential districts does not mean that if plaintiffs were to establish liability by providing a court with relatively regular illustrative districts the

---

[175] *Shaw*, 113 S Ct at 2828, 2830. In this sense, proof of partisanship resembles the sort of inquiry conducted under *Village of Arlington Heights v Metropolitan Housing Dev Corp*, 429 US 252, 266 (1977). There, the Court stated that proof that race played *a* role in governmental decision making required the defendant to show it would have undertaken the same course of action without regard to race; here, proof of partisanship might be held to require that the *plaintiffs* show that the state would have had to draw a bizarre shape even in the absence of partisan concerns.

[176] "The opportunity to control the drawing of electoral boundaries through the legislative process of apportionment is a critical and traditional part of politics in the United States, and one that plays no small role in fostering active participation in the political parties at every level." 478 US at 145 (O'Connor concurring in the judgment).

[177] See page 274.

[178] 478 US at 50. For extensive discussions of geographic compactness, see Karlan, 24 Harv CR-CL L Rev at 199–213 (cited in note 27); Richard H. Pildes and Richard G. Niemi, *Expressive Harms, "Bizarre Districts," and Voting Rights: Evaluating Election-District Appearances After Shaw v Reno*, 92 Mich L Rev 483, 527–59 (1993).

[179] What these terms mean remains anyone's guess. For an attempt to give them some meaning, see Pildes and Niemi, 92 Mich L Rev at 575–86 (cited in note 178).

defendant would be precluded from using an irregularly shaped district as a *remedy*, as long as the district provided minority citizens with a full and fair opportunity to participate in the political process and elect the representatives of their choice.[180] Thus, if Section 2 would obligate a defendant jurisdiction to draw *some* majority-black district—because racial bloc voting would otherwise unlawfully dilute the votes of a geographically compact, politically cohesive minority community—the jurisdiction's choice as to where to draw the lines should not trigger constitutional liability to white voters who would have preferred them drawn some other way.

In a similar vein, the Court never explained why a state's desire to dampen the effects of racial bloc voting does not override aesthetic considerations of compactness or regularity. The refusal of large numbers of white voters to vote for candidates sponsored by the black community results in the continuing exclusion of blacks from full participation in the political and governance processes. It may often reflect prejudiced or stereotypical thinking. In *Palmore v Sidoti*, the Court held that "[t]he Constitution cannot control such prejudices but neither can it tolerate them. Private biases may be outside the reach of the law, but the law cannot, directly or indirectly, give them effect. . . ."[181] In an analogous context, the Court has recognized that the government has "a fundamental, overriding interest in eradicating racial discrimination in education—discrimination that prevailed, with official approval, for the first 165 years of this Nation's constitutional history."[182] How this fundamental interest can be overridden by a preference for aesthetically pleasing districts in a system which tolerates all sorts of ugliness to benefit every sort of group but the original intended beneficiaries of the Fourteenth Amendment is hard to fathom.

D. COMING DOWN THE PIKE?

Shaw was not really a case about the right to vote, at least not as the Court had interpreted that right when the entitlements of

---

[180] For a particularly striking example of this, see *Dillard v Town of Louisville*, 730 F Supp 1546 (MD Ala 1990), where the court approved a defendant's proposal of a *non-contiguous* majority-black district. Indeed, as long as a defendant's plan fully remedies the proven violation, the plaintiffs' aesthetic preferences are irrelevant.

[181] 466 US 429, 433 (1984); compare *Terry v Adams*, 345 US 461 (1953) (holding, on an extremely fractured set of rationales, that a private, whites-only pre-primary violated the Fifteenth Amendment).

[182] *Bob Jones Univ. v United States*, 461 US 574, 604 (1983) (footnote omitted).

black citizens were before it. No one was denied the ability to participate in congressional elections. No one's ability to elect her preferred candidate was impaired.[183] No allegations were made that the plaintiffs had been hindered in any way from participating fully in the governance process of reapportionment.

Shaw is, instead, a meta-governance case, because it raises questions not merely about the composition of the North Carolina congressional delegation, but rather about the entire enterprise of the voting rights system. North Carolina's plan was the product of a General Assembly that, for the first time since Reconstruction, and as a direct consequence of prior litigation under the Voting Rights Act, contained significant numbers of legislators elected by black voters.[184] North Carolina's black citizens were also able to participate fully in the preclearance process. The political branches of the state and federal governments reached a political solution to a set of political concerns.

In *Shaw*, the same Supreme Court that had just told the lower courts not to interfere on behalf of the ostensible interests of black voters unless there was clear evidence that the political process had disregarded those interests thrust itself into the process on behalf of a group of voters who could not show that they had been discriminated against because of their race and who advanced no colorable claim that their right to vote had been impaired in any way. And by formulating a constitutional cause of action, the Court raised the specter that it was preparing itself for an all-out assault on the political branches' ability to preserve their resolution of competing claims. It is hard to escape the suspicion that the Court has learned a lesson from the sixteen times Congress has overruled its interpretations of civil rights statutes in the last fifteen years:[185] if it wants to impose its view of civil rights on the political branches,

---

[183] With regard to black voters' equal protection claims, the court has always required a showing of a discriminatory effect as well as some discriminatory intent. See Note, *The Constitutional Significance of the Discriminatory Effects of At-Large Elections*, 91 Yale L J 974, 976–77 (1982).

[184] Compare *Gingles*, 478 US at 40 (prior to *Gingles*, less than 4 percent of North Carolina's state legislators were black) with Joint Center for Political and Economic Studies, *Black Elected Officials: A National Roster, 1991* at xxx (Joint Center for Political and Economic Studies Press 1992) (in January 1991, over 11 percent of North Carolina state legislators were black).

[185] See Eric Schnapper, *Statutory Misinterpretations: A Legal Autopsy*, 68 Notre Dame L Rev 1095, 1099 (1993).

statutory interpretation is a weak tool. The Voting Rights Act
has already worked too well: minority enfranchisement and voting
strength has already given black Americans more influence in the
political processes of reapportionment than they enjoy with the
Supreme Court. *Shaw* at least raises the possibility that the Supreme Court will gut the Voting Rights Act and sharply limit
Congress's authority to empower the executive branch and state
governments to share in securing and enforcing the Fourteenth
Amendment's political rights.[186] And so, one-third of the way toward the next reapportionment, we find ourselves still within a
dark wood where the straight way is lost.

---

[186] *City of Richmond v J.A. Croson Co.*, 488 US 469, 486–91 (1989), distinguished Richmond's minority set-aside program, which the court found invalid under the Equal Protection Clause, from a virtually identical federal program upheld in *Fullilove v Klutznick*, 448
US 448 (1980), because Congress had acted under its special enforcement powers. This
distinction raises two questions. First, could *Congress* require states to engage in race-
conscious districting under specified circumstances? Second, if it could do so directly, could
it *delegate* the decision about how and when to do so to the states? See *Parker v Brown*, 317
US 341, 353–54 (1943) (in upholding a California raisin price-stabilization program against
antitrust attack, the Court assumed that Congress's passage of the Agricultural Marketing
Agreement Act of 1937 would have allowed the Secretary of Agriculture to devise such a
program and decided that "[f]rom this, and the whole structure of the Act, it would seem
that it contemplates that its policy may be effectuated by a state program either with or
without the promulgation of a federal program by order of the Secretary."); Note, *City of
Richmond v J.A. Croson Co.: A Federal Legislative Answer*, 100 Yale L J 451, 468 (1990) ("The
court's determination that a state's race-based program is unconstitutional does not preclude
congress from independently sanctioning a similar race-based program under its section 5
enforcement powers.").

KENNETH W. DAM

EXTRATERRITORIALITY IN AN
AGE OF GLOBALIZATION:
THE HARTFORD FIRE CASE

In *Hartford Fire*, the Supreme Court once again confronted the extraterritorial application of a statute.[1] This time it returned to the relatively familiar framework of a recurring mystery—the geographic reach of the Sherman Act. The *Hartford Fire* majority went further than ever before, arguably holding that once an intent to affect U.S. commerce and actual effect had been established, the Sherman Act was applicable—whatever the nationality of the defendants, wherever their acts occurred, and whatever the interest of a foreign sovereign that also sought to regulate the defendants— except in the rare case in which those acts were actually compelled by that foreign sovereign.

The case provided the opportunity for a murky and unsatisfactory doctrinal squabble between the Souter majority and the Scalia minority over the terminology and principles to be used in determining the extraterritorial applicability of a statute. As an anti-

Kenneth W. Dam is Max Pam Professor of American and Foreign Law, University of Chicago Law School.

AUTHOR'S NOTE: The author would like to thank his colleagues David Currie, Geoffrey Miller, Anne-Marie Slaughter Burley, and Diane Wood for their penetrating and helpful comments, as well as the Jerome S. Weiss Faculty Research Fund.

[1] *Hartford Fire Insurance Co. v California*, 113 S Ct 2891 (1993). Earlier Supreme Court cases on extraterritorial application of statutes will be cited as they are discussed in the text, but it is worth noting that *Sale v Haitian Centers Council, Inc.*, 113 S Ct 2549 (1993), decided just one week before *Hartford Fire*, held a provision of the Immigration and Nationality Act not to have extraterritorial effect, and that just two years previously the Court held Title VII not to apply extraterritorially even to employment of U.S. citizens by U.S. employees. *EEOC v Arabian American Oil Co.*, 111 S Ct 1227 (1991).

trust case, *Hartford Fire* illustrates the complex interactions that can arise in a matrix involving not only U.S. and foreign competition law but also U.S. and foreign regulatory schemes that each provide exemptions from their own competition laws. The practical implications of that matrix for foreign defendants under the far-reaching standard articulated by the majority are illustrated by the live possibility that, on remand from the *Hartford Fire* decision itself, the foreign defendants may be held liable under circumstances in which the domestic defendants could be ruled exempt.

Perhaps the greatest significance of *Hartford* lies in viewing it as an international economic policy decision. We normally do not think of the Judicial Branch as making such decisions. Yet when a private plaintiff, rather than the Executive Branch, brings the action, and where the Legislative Branch has not adequately confronted the question of extraterritorial application of a particular statute, then by default the policy decision falls to the courts. That being the inescapable if perhaps regrettable fact, the implications of the Supreme Court's Sherman Act approach for international economic policy as a whole are worth considering. The rule in *Hartford Fire*, if it proves over time to be as broad as it purports to be, is at odds with an emerging international consensus on how to deal with the fact that domestic microeconomic policies still conflict at a time when rapid technological change is promoting accelerating economic integration.

I

The facts of the *Hartford Fire* case itself illustrate some of the profound changes that have occurred in the international economy since the Supreme Court had last spoken on substantive Sherman Act extraterritoriality in 1962.[2] But before turning to the precise facts of *Hartford Fire*, it is worth asking about the general character of these changes. The U.S. and other major economies

---

[2] *Continental Ore Co. v Union Carbide & Carbon Corp.*, 370 US 690 (1962). Justice Souter cites the 1986 *Matsushita* case, but the cite is to a footnote which merely documents the fact that the case was about the artificially depressed level of prices in the United States and not the cartelization of the Japanese market; the case does not discuss the standards for extraterritorial application. *Matsushita Elec. Industrial Co. v Zenith Radio Corp.*, 475 US 574, 582–83 n 6 (1986). Substantive Sherman Act extraterritoriality should be distinguished from cases involving foreign discovery orders. See, e.g., *Société Nationale Industrielle Aérospatiale v United States District Court*, 482 US 522 (1987).

of the world have become increasingly interdependent. These economies have continued to penetrate one another, through both trade and private investment. From 1960 to 1992, U.S. exports of goods and services grew from a level of 4.5 percent to 11.6 percent of U.S. gross domestic product.[3] The *rate* of increase of U.S. exports was especially rapid beginning in the mid-1980s, reaching over 12 percent a year for the 1985–91 period.[4] Meanwhile, the volume of imports was even greater than that of exports, showing a growing dependence on imports as well to feed the U.S. consumer market and to provide capital goods for U.S. industry.[5]

The same patterns can be found in private foreign investment. During the postwar period, U.S. manufacturing firms have invested heavily abroad, with the ratio of the stock of U.S. foreign direct investment growing, measured as a percentage of OECD gross domestic product, from 7.7 percent in 1960 to 10.1 percent in 1990. This increasing role for foreign investment has in turn stimulated exports from the United States in view of the remarkable fact that some two-thirds of all U.S. exports are to affiliated corporations.[6] At the same time, investment has been pouring into the United States from Europe and Japan, providing goods for U.S. consumers and jobs for U.S. workers.[7] The rate of this investment interpenetration and the resulting degree of economic interdependence are accelerating.[8]

At the same time that the dependence on international trade has

---

[3] Emergency Committee for American Trade, *Mainstay II: A New Account of the Critical Role of U.S. Multinational Companies in the U.S. Economy*, Table App-2 (July 1993) (hereafter "*ECAT, Mainstay II*"). The data were based on U.S. Department of Commerce, Survey of Current Business, July and September 1992. Imports also rose during the same period, from 4.9 percent to 12.4 percent of GDP.

[4] Id, Table App-1 (based on OECD data).

[5] Id, Table App-2 (based on U.S. Department of Commerce data).

[6] Multinational companies accounted for approximately two-thirds of U.S. exports from 1982 to 1990. *ECAT, Mainstay II* 17. As a result, U.S.-based multinational corporations alone had a net balance of payments of over $129 billion in 1990, even after reinvestment of a portion of their overseas earnings. Id, Table App-16. During the 1960s and 1970s, U.S. foreign direct investment grew by 11.1 percent per annum, but that rate grew much more rapidly in the 1980s, reaching 53.6 percent. (The first figure is the annual rate of growth from 1961–70 to 1971–80; the second, the annual rate of growth from 1981–83 to 1986–88.)

[7] DeAnne Julius, *Global Companies and Public Policy* 54–57 (1990).

[8] United Nations, *World Investment Report* 51–64 (1992). For a study of U.S. and Japanese interpenetration, emphasizing the interrelationship of trade and investment and the role of multinational companies, see Dennis J. Encarnation, *Rivals Beyond Trade* (Cornell, 1992).

been growing, the nature of that trade has fundamentally changed. Relatively few final goods are created solely within one country. Trade in manufactures formerly was heavily in final products between firms at different levels in the distribution process (e.g., manufacturers to wholesalers) or firms in different industries (e.g, sales of final capital goods to consumer good producers). Today, however, such trade increasingly involves components and subcomponents to be incorporated in final products and therefore is increasingly intra-industry rather than inter-industry in character. The result, especially with the growth of private foreign investment, is frequently that the manufacture of a complete final product actually takes place in two or even more countries.[9] We may call this phenomenon "shared production."

These facts, so well known to those who work in business or who study the international economy, are often summarized in a single term—globalization.[10] An important question for public policy is how nationally based regulatory systems can best grapple with issues involving the rapidly increasing number of transnational transactions in an age of globalization.[11] A recent study for the Royal Institute of International Affairs points out that since foreign direct investment "has become a more important linkage than trade, so competition policy has the potential to overtake trade policy as the most contentious area of international economic relations" and points to the differences in competition policy among major developed countries as an important barrier to international competition.[12]

At the end of this essay, I shall return to the public policy

---

[9] Andrew W. Wyckoff, *The International Expansion of Productive Networks*, 180 OECD Observer 8 (Feb/March 1993); Graham Vickery, *Global Industries and National Policies*, 179 OECD Observer 11 (Dec 1992/Jan 1993). The more complex and "high tech" the product, the more likely this pattern is to predominate. Richard R. Nelson and Nathan Rosenberg, Technical Innovation and National Systems, in Richard R. Nelson, ed, *National Innovation Systems: A Comparative Analysis* 3, 14 (Oxford, 1993).

[10] The term "globalization" has achieved considerable recognition, at the international level, as a neutral term describing the phenomena discussed in the text. See, e.g., *Globalisation of Industrial Activities* (OECD, 1992), which reviews in great detail the rapid changes in trade and investment patterns in four key industries. See also the chapter on Technology and Globalisation in *Technology and the Economy* 209–36 (OECD, 1992).

[11] On the international economic policy agenda stemming from globalization, see generally Geza Feketekuty, *The New Trade Agenda* (Group of Thirty, 1992). Feketekuty, a Senior Advisor to the U.S. Trade Representative and Chairman of the OECD Trade Committee, wrote this essay for the Group of Thirty in his private capacity.

[12] Julius, supra note 7, at 100.

choices, but for now a summary conclusion would be that there is an overarching fundamental choice: Should a country prefer cooperation with other countries (such as by harmonizing their laws so that the question of which law prevails is unimportant or by allocating regulatory jurisdiction so that the law that prevails is known in advance)? Or should a country simply apply its own law to transactions that have an impact on its national economy, however much the same transaction may affect one or more other national economies?[13] This choice is squarely raised by how the courts deal with one of the oldest issues of economic regulation—namely, extraterritoriality. Here the focus will be on the light shed by *Hartford Fire* on whether the Supreme Court has adjusted its views on extraterritoriality in light of the changing underlying economic relationships in the world.

II

The *Hartford Fire* case involved insurance. Insurance is a service industry, not a manufacturing industry. Yet, as the facts of *Hartford Fire* vividly illustrate, the phenomena of interpenetration and shared production are found in services as well as goods. Reinsurance can be thought of as a component of insurance. It permits primary insurers to write more insurance by absorbing and spreading risks.[14] Retrocessional insurance, the reinsurance of reinsurance, is like a subcomponent, allowing reinsurance compa-

---

[13] On why the so-called extraterritoriality issue is really a question of conflicts of jurisdiction and the kinds of measures countries can take to reduce the resulting harm to international relations and the world economy, see Kenneth W. Dam, *Extraterritoriality and Conflicts of Jurisdiction*, Proceedings of the Annual Meeting, 77 Am Society Intl Law 370 (1983). For arguments for a harmonization approach by an economist, see Sylvia Ostry, *Governments and Corporations in a Shrinking World* (Cenn for Rel, 1990), and *The Domestic Domain: The New International Policy Arena*, 1 Transnational Corporations 7 (1992). For a political science analysis leading in the same direction, see Gavin Boyd, *Structuring International Economic Cooperation* (St. Martin's, 1990). President Clinton's Chairman of the Council of Economic Advisers advocated harmonization of competition policy in a book published just prior to her taking office. Laura D'Andrea Tyson, *Who's Bashing Whom? Trade Conflict in High-Technology Industries* 266, 279 (IIE, 1992). The jurisdictional allocation approach is used in the tax area through bilateral tax treaties. For one small step toward jurisdictional allocation in antitrust, see *Agreement between the Government of the United States of America and the Commission of the European Communities*, Trade Reg Rep (CCH) ¶ 13,504 (Sept 23, 1991), providing for consultation, coordination, and information sharing between the Commission and U.S. antitrust authorities.

[14] Justice Souter said that reinsurance allows a primary insurer "to sell more insurance than its own financial capacity might otherwise permit." 113 S Ct at 2897.

nies to write more reinsurance.[15] Extensive international trade takes place in reinsurance. Although U.S. primary insurers reinsure in part with U.S. reinsurers, they also rely heavily on British reinsurance companies, and that reinsurance is in turn covered by retrocessional insurance written in the London market. (For purposes of discussion of the Supreme Court's opinion, I shall simplify by treating both reinsurance and retrocessional insurance under the common heading of reinsurance.)

The pattern of U.S. primary insurance backed by British reinsurance came before the Supreme Court in *Hartford Fire*. The heart of the extraterritoriality branch of the controversy involved the extent to which the United States could regulate British reinsurers concerning reinsurance written by them in London relating to primary insurance written by U.S. companies in the United States in a situation where "Parliament has established a comprehensive regulatory regime over the London reinsurance market."[16] The Supreme Court held that so long as conduct in Britain by British companies was intended to, and did, affect U.S. insurance markets, the Sherman Act would govern the conduct unless British law *required* the conduct. That British law had "a strong policy to permit or encourage such conduct" was irrelevant because the only conflict that counted for the Supreme Court was compulsion by the British government of acts that were prohibited by U.S. law.

In so holding, the Supreme Court refused to modify the direction of Sherman Act decisions set in the *Alcoa* decision at the end of World War II.[17] Indeed, it plunged forward in applying the Sherman Act extraterritorially, whatever the foreign interests involved, despite the willingness of the Court to limit the extraterritorial reach of some other statutes.[18] The *Hartford Fire* Court essentially said that the United States would set the competitive ground

---

[15] Justice Souter explained that retrocessional insurance "does for reinsurers what reinsurance does for primary insurance." Id. The District Court called retrocessional insurance "insurance for reinsurers." *In re Insurance Antitrust Litigation*, 423 F Supp 464, 470 n 4 (N D Cal 1989).

[16] 113 S Ct at 2910.

[17] *United States v Aluminum Co. of America*, 148 F2d 416 (2d Cir 1945).

[18] For cases construing statutes as not applying extraterritorially, see *EEOC v Arabian American Oil Co.*, 111 S Ct 1227 (1991) (Title VII); *Foley Bros. v Filardo*, 336 US 281 (1949); and a trilogy of maritime cases relied on in Justice Scalia's dissent in *Hartford Five* and cited in note 60.

rules for the world economy, even where shared production was involved and even in a sector where the British—a world leader in reinsurance—had established what was conceded to be a comprehensive regulatory scheme for that industry and where the British government had objected, by way of amicus briefs, to the assertion of U.S. regulation.[19]

In so extending the reach of the U.S. antitrust laws, the Court turned its back on the increasing recognition by lower Federal courts that such an extraterritorial reach goes too far. In particular, the Court failed to consider the widely adopted and praised jurisdictional rule of reason created in the Ninth Circuit's 1976 *Timberlane* decision.[20] The term "jurisdictional rule of reason" refers to a judicially established list of factors to be weighed in determining whether a statute applies to a particular set of transnational facts. Since *Timberlane*, three other circuits had adopted a jurisdictional rule of reason, though with some differences in the factors to be weighed.[21] Although the Supreme Court normally does not cite a lower court case as precedent, it is nonetheless remarkable that it did not find it even necessary to consider whether there were legal and economic reasons for applying some kind of jurisdictional rule of reason—especially because the Court of Appeals below was able to apply such a rule of self-restraint and still find the Sherman Act applicable to the alleged facts. In ignoring any basis for self-restraint, the Supreme Court thereby signaled an apparent inten-

---

[19] Both the District Court and the Court of Appeals had accepted that characterization of the British regulatory scheme, and the Supreme Court, without questioning that characterization, said that it made no difference. 723 F Supp at 488; 938 F2d 919, 932–33 (9th Cir 1991); 113 S Ct at 2911.

[20] *Timberlane Lumber Co. v Bank of America, NT & SA*, 549 F2d 597 (9th Cir 1976) and 749 F2d 1378 (9th Cir 1984). Justice Souter's citations to *Timberlane* were not directed to the merits of a jurisdictional rule of reason.

[21] *Mannington Mills, Inc. v Congoleum*, 595 F2d 1287, 1297–98 (3d Cir 1979); *Montreal Trading Ltd. v Amax, Inc.*, 661 F2d 864, 869–70 (10th Cir 1981); *O.N.E. Shipping Ltd. v Flota Mercante Grancolombiana*, 830 F2d 449 (2d Cir 1987. See also *Restatement (Third) of Foreign Relations Law* § 403 (ALI, 1986) ("*Restatement*") for one version of the factors rendering exercise of extraterritorial jurisdiction in a particular case "unreasonable," including links to and interests of the forum state, expectations of the parties, the needs and traditions of the international system, the interests of "another state," and "the likelihood of conflict with regulation by another state." Two circuits have expressed reservations about any interest-weighing approach, albeit not in the context of the substantive reach of a statute. *Laker Airways, Ltd. v Sabena*, 731 F2d 909, 948–52 (DC Cir 1984); *In re Uranium Antitrust Litigation*, 617 F2d 1248, 1255 (7th Cir 1980).

tion to extend U.S. substantive law to its outermost extraterritorial limits, subject only to a sovereign compulsion defense.[22]

To add insult to the injury to official British sensibilities expressed through the British amicus brief, the Court explicitly raised the possibility that the British defendants would be denied access to an immunity that shielded, at least in part, the U.S. defendants—the McCarran-Ferguson Act, which provides a partial antitrust exemption for the business of insurance.[23] While formally leaving the immunity question for resolution by the Court of Appeals on remand and emphasizing that he expressed no opinion on the matter,[24] Justice Souter also made the availability of the immunity to the British defendants irrelevant to the question of Sherman Act extraterritoriality, thereby condoning the anomaly of holding the British defendants—at least potentially—to a higher standard than domestic defendants.[25] Although the Supreme Court's decision was taken by a narrow five-to-four margin, with Justice Souter in the majority and Justice Scalia in the minority on the extraterritoriality issue,[26] *Hartford Fire* states the standard to be followed by lower courts not just in government antitrust cases but in private litigation like the *Hartford Fire* case itself where no prosecutorial or other governmental discretion can ameliorate the extraterritorial

[22] The sovereign compulsion defense has turned out in the past to be very narrow, especially where the question was the reach of U.S. substantive law as opposed to the enforcement of procedural orders. For what appears to be the sole case in which a sovereign compulsion defense succeeded in a substantive context, see *Interamerican Ref. Corp. v Texaco Maracaibo Ind.*, 307 F Supp 1291 (D Del 1970).

[23] 15 USC §§ 1012–13 (1988). It is worth noting that the two courts below had avoided this differential treatment, the Court of Appeals by holding both subject to the Sherman Act and the District Court holding neither subject to it. 938 F2d at 928; 723 F Supp at 478–79.

[24] See 113 S Ct at 2902 (". . . even if we were to agree that foreign reinsurers were not subject to state regulation (a point on which we express no opinion)"); id at 2903 ("foreign reinsurers that, we assume for the sake of argument, were 'not regulated by states law' "); and see id at 2903 n 12.

[25] Of course, Justice Souter would have subjected all defendants to liability under his boycott theory; but the fact that that theory did not command the support of a majority of the court does not seem to have caused him to view the extraterritoriality issue any differently. Another possible explanation for Justice Souter's lack of concern about the possibility of differential treatment was that he possibly believed that on remand the *domestic* reinsurers would also be denied immunity, thereby creating a situation where foreign and domestic reinsurers would be treated alike. See his joint reference to domestic and foreign reinsurers, 113 S Ct at 2903 n 12.

[26] On another issue, the question of what constitutes a boycott under the McCarran-Ferguson Act, 15 USC § 1013(b), Justice Scalia's view triumphed 5–4 over that of Justice Souter.

consequences. The decision thus sounds a discordant note in an increasingly globalized economy in an era when the need for more outward-looking and cooperative economic policy measures has become increasingly obvious.

III

Before examining the merits of the majority and minority approaches, a closer look at the facts is warranted, if only to see that the Souter opinion goes out of its way to throw the extraterritoriality gauntlet down before the world economy and other governments without any necessity of going so far to reach the same outcome in *Hartford Fire* itself.

The origins of the controversy lay in the concerns of four large U.S. primary casualty insurance companies with regard to their exposure to "long-tail risks" under their commercial general liability insurance policies. The core of their concern was their liability to insureds under "occurrence-based" policies, which cover claims with regard to any occurrences during the period in which the policy was in force whenever the claim might later arise. Policies written on occurrence forms therefore subjected the insurers to liability that could not be quantified or even known until years or even decades after the policy had expired.[27] To deal with this problem, the insurers sought to eliminate the occurrence form not just from their own set of forms but for the industry as a whole. They sought to substitute an industry-wide "claims made" form. Under the latter form the policy covered only claims made during the policy period. Since such a form for newly written policies would otherwise expose them to retroactive and unforeseeable liability with regard to prior occurrences, they included in the claims-made industry form a cut-off date before which no claims would be recognized. In order to deal with other perceived problems, these

---

[27] The sensitivity of the insurers to this aspect of occurrence-based policies had been heightened by litigation over pollution and over hazardous waste sites where widespread claims had been made in the 1980s with regard to events that occurred in the 1960s and earlier under policies written in those earlier decades. The chief executive officer of a large U.S. casualty company once said to this writer, well before the *Hartford Fire* litigation arose, that the insurance industry was the only industry in which one did not know whether business had been profitable until decades later. Unlike the life insurance industry, moreover, the liability of the casualty industry depends heavily on changing and unforeseeable legal standards adopted years or decades after the occurrence policies expired.

U.S. insurers also sought to exclude certain forms of pollution from coverage under the new form.[28]

The four large U.S. primary insurers were successful in changing the industry over from occurrence forms to claims-made forms. The resulting elimination of long-tail coverage and the pollution exclusion were not popular with many insureds or with many others who had a view on the associated public policy issues concerning who pays for pollution and hazardous waste cleanup.[29] After lengthy investigations by insurance regulatory agencies in several states, nineteen states and numerous private parties brought actions, principally under the antitrust laws. Although the various complaints included a large number of diverse claims against a wide variety of defendants, the theories of the complaints and the facts alleged can be summarized to highlight the extraterritoriality aspects of the litigation.[30]

The four major U.S. primary insurers, no doubt for competitive reasons, wanted to be sure that the whole primary insurance industry would go along with the change in forms. The way in which they accomplished that objective laid the basis for the antitrust complaints. They sought assistance in bringing about an industry-wide change, not just from domestic reinsurers but also from British reinsurers doing business within the framework of Lloyd's of London.[31] A key to accomplishing the form change was to induce the Insurance Services Office (ISO) to withdraw its data collection and risk estimation support for the occurrence form. That support was essential to most primary insurers' ability to continue to offer

---

[28] In time all pollution coverage was excluded. 113 S Ct at 2898–99. Also involved in the case were efforts to include in the new form various other provisions, including an exclusion for seepage and a cap on defense costs, but these additional aspects of the litigation played no significant role at the Supreme Court level.

[29] The California complaint alleged, for example, that "pollution liability coverage [was] almost entirely unavailable for the vast majority of casualty insurance purchasers in the State of California." 113 S Ct at 2908.

[30] Such a summary is facilitated by the fact that the facts were not in dispute for the purpose of the rulings made. The District Court set the tone in the litigation by noting the failure of the plaintiffs to seek discovery prior to its ruling and therefore finding, in the context of a ruling for defendants, not just that it accepted the facts alleged in the plaintiffs' complaints but that there were "no factual disputes material to this ruling." 723 F Supp 464, 491. The Supreme Court merely held that since the case came to the Court on motion to dismiss, it took the allegations of the complaint as true. 113 S Ct at 2895.

[31] Not all of the British defendants operated within the framework of Lloyds and were therefore regulated under the Lloyds Act. These other British defendants were subject to a second regulatory scheme. See the District Court opinion, 723 F Supp at 488.

insurance under the occurrence form since they were unable to provide such support economically as individual companies. It was much cheaper to provide the support on an industry-wide basis. In order to help persuade ISO to withdraw those services, the four major U.S. insurers endeavored to induce the London reinsurers to promote the change. Those reinsurers joined the effort, refusing to reinsure henceforth except under claims-made forms. After the plaintiff states and several other states had approved the new form under their insurance regulatory systems, the ISO then withdrew its support for earlier forms.[32] All of these steps were alleged to have been taken by agreement between the U.S. primary insurers and, among others, the British reinsurers and to constitute Sherman Act conspiracies.

A key problem with the Sherman Act theory, however, was that the McCarran-Ferguson Act exempts the "business of insurance" from the Act.[33] This exemption is limited in two ways. First, the exemption is "inapplicable to any agreement to boycott, coerce, or intimidate, or act of boycott, coercion, or intimidation."[34] The plaintiffs argued that the refusals to insure and reinsure except under an agreed claims-made form constituted a boycott. The Supreme Court divided on this issue, with Justice Scalia winning five votes for his view that a boycott under the Act had to extend beyond a "concerted agreement to seek particular terms in particular transactions" and could only be proved by a showing that defendants refused to do business in "other, unrelated transactions" as leverage to achieve the terms they sought.[35] Even this broad interpretation of the exemption did not, however, entirely eliminate the defendants' antitrust exposure because Justice Scalia found that some of the conspiracy claims, including those against the foreign defendants, could be read to allege that "the defendants had linked their demands so that they would continue to refuse to do business on *either* form until *both* were changed to their liking" and that that "might amount to a boycott."[36]

---

[32] A final step was an agreement by domestic and London retrocessional insurers to use their "best endeavors" to ensure that all U.S. insurance and reinsurance business would be written only with the pollution exclusion.

[33] 15 USC § 1012(b).

[34] 15 USC § 1013(b).

[35] 113 S Ct at 2912.

[36] Id at 2916–17 (emphasis in original).

The British defendants were confronted with a second limitation to their McCarran-Ferguson Act immunity, which could result in their being held liable even if, after trial, they were to win on the boycott issue. That limitation was that immunity from the Sherman Act with respect to the "business of insurance" is not available under McCarran-Ferguson "to the extent that such business is not regulated by State law."[37] In the Ninth Circuit, Judge Noonan, while conceding that U.S. insurers might be exempt from liability on McCarran-Ferguson grounds, ruled that foreign defendants could not be exempt since a "state's regulation of insurance does not have extraterritorial effect [even] within the United States," since "[a] fortiori, regulation by the fifty states of foreign reinsurers is beyond the jurisdiction of the states," and consequently "McCarran-Ferguson Act immunity does not attach to the foreign defendants."[38]

Judge Noonan bootstrapped that conclusion with respect to the British reinsurers to remove McCarran-Ferguson Act immunity from the domestic defendants as well through his ruling that otherwise exempt domestic insurers lost their immunity by conspiring with nonexempt parties.[39] Justice Souter, however, rejected Judge Noonan's bootstrap theory. Justice Souter said that he did not have to address Judge Noonan's ruling because "even if we were to agree that foreign reinsurers were not subject to state regulation (a point on which we express no opinion)," it would not follow that domestic insurers would lose immunity by conspiracy with foreign entities.[40] The reason, according to Justice Souter, was that the precedents relied on by Judge Noonan had to do with exempt entities losing their exemption by conspiring with nonexempt entities, whereas the McCarran-Ferguson exemption explicitly had to do with exempting the "business of insurance," not insurance companies as entities.[41]

---

[37] 15 USC § 1012(b).

[38] 938 F2d at 928.

[39] Id at 928.

[40] 113 S Ct at 2902.

[41] Id. Having corrected Judge Noonan's methodology, Justice Souter went on to suggest that the Ninth Circuit could still hold the challenged activities of domestic reinsurers nonexempt: "As with the foreign reinsurers, we express no opinion whether the activities of the domestic reinsurers were 'regulated by State law' and leave that question to the Court of Appeals on remand." Id at 2903 n 12.

IV

Justice Souter had little trouble in disposing of the extraterritoriality issue. As summarized in his opinion, the complaints alleged "that the London reinsurers engaged in unlawful conspiracies to affect the market for insurance in the United States and that their conduct in fact produced substantial effect."[42] That was the long and short of it. The law, to Justice Souter, was clear: "[I]t is well established by now that the Sherman Act applies to foreign conduct that was meant to produce and did in fact produce some substantial effect in the United States."[43] He produced an impressive list of citations, nearly all antitrust cases to boot, for what I shall, for shorthand, call the "intent-plus-effects rule."[44]

As for comity, Justice Souter found no role in the case at hand. Despite apparent endorsement of comity in the legislative history of the Foreign Trade Antitrust Improvement Act of 1982, a Congressional enactment designed to stimulate exports by loosening antitrust limitations on collective action by exporters,[45] he said he did not have to decide the comity question. "[I]nternational comity," he concluded, "would not counsel against exercising jurisdiction in the circumstances alleged."[46] Why not? Because "[t]he only substantial question in this case is whether 'there is in fact a *true conflict* between domestic and foreign law.'"[47]

---

[42] Id at 2909.

[43] Id.

[44] Id. None of the intent-plus-effects cases cited holds that intent plus effects is enough no matter what the nature of the interests of other nations. Indeed, the grandfather of the intent-plus-effects principle, *United States v Aluminum Co. of America*, 148 F2d 416 (2d Cir 1945), stated that there was an international law canon of construction, to use Judge Scalia's phrase. Judge Learned Hand said that Congress must have "regard to the limitations customarily observed by nations upon the exercise of their powers; limitations which generally correspond to those fixed by the 'Conflict of Laws.'" 148 F2d at 443. This passage can be read simply as support for the proposition that the intent-plus-effects rule did not transgress international law under the facts of the *Alcoa* case, where no question of foreign regulatory systems was presented. However one reads *Alcoa* on this point, the fact is that many other countries and many scholars believed at the time that the *Alcoa* test violated international law. See, e.g., citations in James R. Atwood and Kingman Brewster, 1 *Antitrust and American Business Abroad* § 6.09 n 84 (McGraw-Hill, 2d ed 1981).

[45] 15 USC § 6a. A House Report stated: "'If a court determines that the requirements for subject matter jurisdiction are met, [the 1982 statute] would have no effect on the court['s] ability to employ notions of comity . . . or otherwise to take account of the international character of the transaction.'" HR Rep No 97-686, p 13 (1982), quoted in 113 S Ct at 2910.

[46] 113 S Ct at 2910.

[47] Id (emphasis supplied).

What then would be a "true conflict" for Justice Souter? If defendants had been compelled by a foreign sovereign to carry out the challenged acts, then, and only then, would a "true conflict" exist. The term "true conflict" has usually been used in choice-of-law cases to refer to a situation where both countries have an interest in applying their own law and those laws conflict, in contrast to a "false conflict" where, upon close inspection of the two laws and consideration of the interests involved, only one law is found to apply.[48] Justice Souter's "true conflict" is in truth a worst-case example of the former, where to apply both laws would be to impose sanctions simply because a party was caught between the commands of two sovereigns. Having narrowed the scope for mutual accommodation between two conflicting laws, the Souter opinion is troublingly vague about why the sovereign compulsion defense, and only the sovereign compulsion defense, should override his simple intent-plus-effects test. He relied for that exception on a minority opinion in *Aérospatiale*, a case that was not only not an antitrust action but not even one that raised a conflict of regulation.[49] Rather that case involved private negligence and breach of warranty claims arising out of an airplane crash. In fact, the issue in that case did not even involve jurisdiction to prescribe, as Justice Scalia termed the *Hartford Fire* extraterritoriality issue in dissent, but rather the circumstances under which trial courts may compel discovery abroad.[50]

Justice Scalia's dissent on extraterritoriality set out on a method-

---

[48] The terms "true conflicts" and "false conflicts" can be traced back to the writings of Brainerd Currie and have been variously defined. Larry Kramer defined false conflicts, in the extraterritoriality context, as "cases where the fact that conduct occurred in the United States creates no interest in applying American law, or the fact that conduct occurred abroad creates no interest in applying foreign law." Larry Kramer, *Vestiges of Beale: Extraterritorial Application of American Law*, 1991 Supreme Court Review 179, 211.

[49] *Société Nationale Industrielle Aérospatiale v United States District Court*, 482 US 522, 547 (1987) (Justice Blackmun concurring in part and dissenting in part).

[50] An important issue is whether the extraterritoriality test for substantive reach should be different from the test for foreign discovery. Certainly the substantive issue is best thought of as one of statutory interpretation, which implies deference to the legislative intent. Unfortunately, in the Sherman Act instance, both statutory language and Congressional intent give little guidance. In the case of foreign discovery, federal courts have traditionally assumed that, in the absence of special circumstances such as a foreign sovereign prohibition against compliance, a U.S. court with personal jurisdiction over a party may order discovery against that party even though the party or documents are located abroad. See *Restatement* §§ 441–42, cited in note 21 supra, and Gary B. Born and David Westin, *International Civil Litigation in United States Courts* 266–73 (Kluwer, 1991). As to the difference in this respect between parties and nonparties, see id at 271–73.

ological course of considerable interest. His basic point was that the issue was not one of jurisdiction in the Souter sense; rather, it was a substantive one of interpreting the Sherman Act. In short, the issue was one of legislative jurisdiction, not subject-matter jurisdiction.[51] Personal jurisdiction was not contested, and there could be no serious question of subject-matter jurisdiction, whatever the British defendants might have asserted in their motions. Plaintiffs had asserted "nonfrivolous claims under the Sherman Act," and therefore their claims were ones "arising under" a federal statute.[52] In short, there was federal question jurisdiction and therefore subject-matter jurisdiction.

But that, for Scalia, was beside the point: "[T]he extraterritorial reach of the Sherman Act . . . was a question of substantive law turning on whether, in enacting the Sherman Act, Congress asserted regulatory power over the challenged conduct."[53] The question was one of statutory interpretation. To be sure, substantive extraterritoriality was a question of jurisdiction, but of a wholly different kind from subject-matter jurisdiction. Substantive extraterritoriality raised an issue of "legislative jurisdiction" or "jurisdiction to prescribe." Granted that Congress had the Constitutional power to "make laws applicable to persons or activities beyond our territorial boundaries where United States interests are affected."[54] But the question in *Hartford Fire* was whether Congress had actually done so. To answer that question, Justice Scalia said, "[t]wo canons of statutory construction" interposed themselves.[55]

The first canon was that "legislation of Congress, unless a contrary intent appears, is meant to apply only within the territorial

---

[51] 113 S Ct at 2918. For a discussion of why it may make a practical difference whether the issue is posed as one of legislative jurisdiction, as opposed to subject-matter jurisdiction, see discussion infra at notes 75–79 and accompanying text.

[52] 113 S Ct at 2917. Moreover, Justice Scalia observed, the attempt by the Justice Souter opinion to "make adjudicative jurisdiction (or, more precisely, abstention) the vehicle for taking account of the needs of prescriptive comity" led him into the "breathtakingly broad proposition," contradicted by the trilogy of maritime cases, that U.S. law necessarily applies "unless compliance with United States law would constitute a *violation* of another country's law." Id at 2921–22 (emphasis in original). (For the three maritime cases, see infra note 60.) The Souter rule, he predicted, would "bring the Sherman Act and other laws into sharp and unnecessary conflict with the legitimate interests of other countries—particularly our closest trading partners." 113 S Ct at 2922.

[53] Id at 2918.

[54] Id.

[55] Id.

jurisdiction of the United States."[56] That presumption had been overcome, said Justice Scalia, citing some of the same intent-plus-effects cases that Justice Souter had cited: "[I]t is now well established that the Sherman Act applies extraterritorially."[57]

But wait, said the dissenting Justice, there is another, "wholly independent," canon of statutory construction, and it controlled. Reaching back nearly to the creation of the American political system, he found in an 1804 Marshall opinion the principle that "[a]n act of congress ought never to be construed to violate the law of nations if any other possible construction remains."[58] This second canon of statutory construction was:

> relevant to determining the substantive reach of a statute because "the law of nations," or customary international law, includes limitations on a nation's exercise of its jurisdiction to prescribe. . . . Though it clearly has constitutional authority to do so, Congress is generally presumed not to have exceeded those customary international-law limits on jurisdiction to prescribe.[59]

Justice Scalia proceeded to analyze three maritime cases where the Supreme Court had applied Scalia's second canon, and had found that the Jones Act and the National Labor Relations Act did not, as a matter of statutory construction, apply to certain extraterritorial fact situations because to construe the statutes otherwise would involve a violation of international law.[60]

It was an attempt by Justice Souter to rely on the Restatement for his expansive view of the extraterritorial reach of the Sherman

---

[56] Id at 2918, quoting *EEOC v Arabian American Oil Co.*, 499 US 244, 248 (1991), and *Foley Bros., Inc. v Filardo*, 336 US 281, 285 (1949).

[57] 113 S Ct at 2918. On the presumption against extraterritoriality, see Kramer, supra note 48, at 179.

[58] 113 S Ct at 1919, quoting *Murray v The Charming Betsy*, 6 US 64, 2 Cranch 64, 118 (1804).

[59] 113 S Ct at 2919.

[60] *Lauritzen v Larsen*, 345 US 571 (1953); *Romero v International Terminal Operating Co.*, 358 US 354 (1959); *McCulloch v Sociedad Nacional de Marineros de Honduras*, 372 US 10 (1963). What Justice Scalia did not satisfactorily explain is why the very cases he had just cited to explain that his first canon of statutory construction did not limit legislative jurisdiction in the case before him—namely, *Alcoa* and its higher court progeny—did not equally show that the second canon had been overcome. After all, if the prior cases could find sub silentio, without the slightest inquiry into the legislative history, that Congress had elected to apply the Sherman Act extraterritorially subject only to the intent-plus-effects criterion, then why could those earlier cases not have decided, equally silently, that Congress had chosen to ignore international law in extending the Sherman Act to the full extent implied by the intent-plus-effects rule?

Act that brought the sharpest attack in the Scalia dissent and that produced the lamest Souter response.[61] Justice Souter had cited a comment on a Restatement section for the proposition that the " 'fact that conduct is lawful in the state in which it took place will not, of itself, bar application of the United States antitrust laws,' even where the foreign state has a strong policy to permit or encourage such conduct."[62] Quoting from a comment to another Restatement section, he stated, "No conflict exists, for these purposes, 'where a person subject to regulation by two states can comply with the laws of both.' "[63] Justice Scalia, relying on a different part of the Restatement, to support his own position, charged the Souter majority with finding "literally the *only* support" for its position on extraterritoriality in a Restatement comment and then having "completely misinterpreted this provision."[64]

Justice Souter either did not deign to get into a struggle with Justice Scalia over how to read the Restatement or, possibly for the reasons suggested in the margin, had no answer to the Scalia interpretation.[65] His answer was a short, dismissive footnote:

---

[61] Several other points in the Scalia opinion, especially on the extraterritoriality question, are dealt with defensively in Justice Souter's footnotes and in turn answered by Justice Scalia. For example, Justice Souter tried to escape the question of prescriptive jurisdiction by observing that the parties did not argue it and that in any case, "it is well established that Congress has exercised such jurisdiction under the Sherman Act." 113 S Ct at 2909 n 22. The Scalia response, however, was that the defendants' failure to "make a clear distinction between adjudicative jurisdiction and the scope of the statute" was not controlling since "[p]arties often do not," yet have not for that failure of proper characterization been "punish[ed] with procedural default." 113 S Ct at 2921.

[62] 113 S Ct at 2910, citing *Restatement (Third) of Foreign Relations Law of the United States* ("*Restatement*"), cited in note 20, § 415, Comment j.

[63] 113 S Ct at 2910, citing *Restatement* § 403, Comment e.

[64] 113 S Ct at 2922. Justice Scalia relied on *Restatement* §§ 403(1) and (2). 113 S Ct at 2921.

[65] Justice Souter overlooked the fact that § 403(3), which is the subsection explicated by the second comment he relied on, begins with the introductory phrase, "When it would not be unreasonable for each of two states to exercise jurisdiction over a person or activity." This is the clearest possible indication that one does not get to the question of sovereign compulsion until one has established that prescriptive jurisdiction under, for example, the Sherman Act, is "reasonable." The preceding two subsections of § 403 deal with reasonableness. Subsection (1) makes clear that even where intent-plus-effect is present, "a state may not exercise jurisdiction to prescribe law . . . when the exercise of such jurisdiction is unreasonable." Subsection (2) contains a nonexhaustive list of factors to be used in determining when exercise of prescriptive jurisdiction is "unreasonable," which are similar to the factors set forth in *Timberlane* and similar jurisdictional rule-of-reason cases. On the other hand, Justice Scalia did not deal with the fact that § 415 purports to restate the rule that the United States laws apply; a Restatement note, seeking to bridge an obvious chasm between U.S. law and international law, gingerly points out that "other states (and the European Community) can apply, and to some extent have applied, the same principles in regulating similar activities." *Restatement*, § 415 (Introductory Note), cited in note 20. Clearly there is a tension between § 403 and § 415.

> Justice SCALIA says that we put the cart before the horse in
> citing this authority, for he argues it may be apposite only
> after a determination that jurisdiction over the foreign acts is
> reasonable. . . . But whatever the order of cart and horse,
> conflict in this sense is the only substantial issue before the
> Court.[66]

The interest of this footnote lies not so much in the question of
who was right about the Restatement, though one can read the
Souter footnote as a concession to the Scalia reading. Rather, by
rejecting any reasonableness qualification, the footnote underscores
Justice Souter's apparent determination to roll back any limitations
on the extraterritorial reach of the Sherman Act whenever intent
plus effects is presented, subject only to the sovereign compulsion
defense.

V

Does the *Hartford Fire* case mean what it says? Does it truly
lay down the extraterritorial gauntlet before the world trading and
investing community? Or will the *Hartford Fire* precedent prove,
when the facts are more compelling for the foreign defendants, to
have been an example of unnecessarily expansive language?

It is inevitable that efforts will be made by future litigants to
read the Souter opinion narrowly. The opinion itself offers several
suggestions. The first is Souter's reliance on the fact that the defendants failed to "question prescriptive jurisdiction," arguing instead
against subject-matter jurisdiction. Nothing in the Souter opinion,
however, gives any comfort for a belief that the outcome would
have been different if the case had been argued differently.[67]

Another approach to distinguishing *Hartford Fire* would be to
rely on Justice Souter's statements that "even assuming that in a
proper case a court may decline to exercise Sherman Act jurisdiction over foreign conduct . . . , international comity would not
counsel against exercising jurisdiction *in the circumstances alleged*
here" and that "[w]e have no need to address *other considerations* that
might inform a decision to refrain from the exercise of jurisdiction

---

[66] 113 S Ct at 2910–11 n 25.

[67] Quite to the contrary, Justice Souter said that there was "good reason" for not arguing
prescriptive jurisdiction—namely, that it was a losing argument. See id at
2909 n 22.

on grounds of international comity."[68] One can only speculate as
to what he might possibly have had in mind in inserting these two
caveats in an otherwise far-reaching opinion rejecting the more
moderate, interest-balancing approaches of the two court opinions
below. Certainly Justice Souter did not put any meat on these two
speculative bones.

One possibility is that he was alluding to the circumstance that
the alleged conspiracy was directly targeted on the U.S. market
alone and that it succeeded. This would distinguish conspiracies
aimed at more than just the United States. For example, if the
conspiracy had been directed at least as much at the British as at
the U.S. market, then the fact that British law exempted that activity might have weighed more heavily. Still another possibility is
that the British regulation in *Hartford* was passive in character,
essentially relying on self-regulation. One can imagine, particularly
if one looks to the Sherman Act "active supervision" state action
cases, that a more active regulatory scheme involving actual review
and approval of the challenged acts might have been treated differently.[69] However future Supreme Court cases may distinguish
Hartford Fire, the very opaqueness of Souter's two caveats may
simply reflect a situation in which Justice Souter's five votes
spanned differing, even contradictory, reasoning.[70] In that event,
legal realism suggests that the *Hartford Fire* precedent may not
prove as broad and categorical as it reads.

VI

The Souter opinion has several troubling implications for
policy and doctrine. On the policy dimension, it has one perverse
and no doubt unintended consequence. His ruling that only a sov-

---

[68] 113 S Ct at 2910 and 2911 (emphasis supplied).

[69] *FTC v Ticor Title Ins. Co.*, 112 S Ct 2169 (1992); *Patrick v Burget*, 486 US 94 (1988).

[70] For example, one or more members of the majority may simply have felt that Sherman
Act jurisdiction was reasonable under the circumstances alleged and did not choose to write
a concurring opinion taking issue with Justice Souter's approach. Given the prevalence of
concurring opinions in the Supreme Court, it might seem odd for such a Justice not to have
written a separate opinion. On the other hand, one must remember that *Hartford Fire* came
down on the final day of the term. Perhaps the language quoted in the text could have been
considered to reserve *Timberlane*-type analysis for future cases. But this is all speculation.
In any case, it is worth recalling that one of the five votes was that of Justice White, since
retired.

ereign compulsion defense can stand in the way of extraterritorial application of the Sherman Act (assuming intent plus effects) leads to the result that a foreign country cannot safeguard its citizens and corporations from Sherman Act liability for collusive behavior unless it compels collusion. This consequence, doubtless unintentional, is ironic when one is dealing with a statute, like the Sherman Act, that is based on free market principles. In an attempt to promote the Sherman Act's free market goals, *Hartford Fire* thus requires the most intrusive government regulation, substituting government direction for antitrust exemption.

The irony is clearest where the industry in question is one where governments throughout the world have elected not to impose antitrust style prohibitions but rather have permitted companies to collude within prescribed limits. That is the case with the insurance industry, where even the United States condones collusion through the McCarran-Ferguson Act.[71] Britain does the same. British law expressly exempts agreements among British insurers on rates and on terms and conditions of coverage from the British competition law, thereby essentially replicating the U.S. exemption.[72]

Since Justice Souter was interested in British regulation only to the extent that it compelled the British defendants to take the action challenged by plaintiffs, there is no exploration in his opinion of the extent to which the British regulatory system was truly com-

---

[71] One important qualification is that the McCarran-Ferguson Act may not exempt collusion of U.S. reinsurers because most states do not in fact regulate the business of reinsurers. Perhaps they do not do so because they consider such regulation beyond their constitutional power; even within the United States, reinsurers would normally be located outside the state in which the primary insurance was written and would take steps to insulate the insurance contract from that particular state's regulation. Compare the reference to arguments based on this premise in Justice Souter's opinion, 113 S Ct at 2903 n 12, with Judge Noonan's holding, after some back and forth, that the "American reinsurers" are "all . . . subject to regulation by the states." *In re Insurance Antitrust* 938 F2d 919, 927 (9th Cir 1991). See also the District Court opinion, finding that the state statutory schemes are broad enough to apply to reinsurers. *In re Insurance Antitrust*, 723 F Supp 464, 474 (N D Cal 1989).

[72] For a description of the British insurance regulatory system and the accompanying competition law exemption, see the District Court opinion, 723 F Supp at 488. The Souter opinion on extraterritoriality may thus lead to the result (assuming that on remand the boycott issue is decided for defendants and the issue of the applicability of the McCarran-Ferguson exemption to foreign reinsurers is decided for plaintiffs) that a different outcome will be reached where the facts involve both countries than where the events transpired solely within either one of the two countries, an anomaly that certainly does not encourage international economic integration. For an infamous example of this kind of anomaly, see *Marie v Garrison*, 13 Abb N Cas 210 (NY Super Ct 1883).

prehensive and whether, to the extent that it was a system with a large element of self-regulation, it can be considered sufficiently comprehensive to give rise to the kind of conflict that might tip the balance under a jurisdictional rule-of-reason approach.[73] Perhaps it suffices for present purposes to note the Court of Appeals' willingness to concede that a significant conflict in regulatory systems would be created by extraterritorial application of the Sherman Act: "The district court found that application of the antitrust laws to the London reinsurance market 'would lead to significant conflict with English law and policy.' . . . The British brief reiterates that conclusion; we do not doubt its accuracy."[74] Certainly the British insurance exemption from its own competition laws raises the sauce-for-the-goose question as to the probable U.S. reaction if Britain were to proceed against U.S. insurance companies for conduct that fell within the safe harbor of McCarran-Ferguson.

VII

On the doctrinal front, the Souter opinion makes a muddle of the distinction between subject-matter jurisdiction and jurisdiction to prescribe. He treats it as a distinction without a difference: "We see no need to address this contention here."[75] The distinction between subject-matter jurisdiction and jurisdiction to prescribe has a practical importance because these alternative approaches present the ultimate question of extraterritorial application vel non in sharply different postures.[76] The subject-matter jurisdiction approach puts the extraterritoriality question, at least in antitrust cases, in a "Why not?" posture. The Sherman Act has been applied extraterritorially in the past: Ergo, why not here? In short,

---

[73] Professor Lowenfeld has suggested that what was involved was largely self-regulation by the industry under the imprimatur of enabling legislation. Andreas F. Lowenfeld, *International Litigation and Arbitration* 137–38 (West, 1993). See the discussion of the Sherman Act state action cases, note 69 supra and accompanying text.

[74] 938 F2d at 933. See also the District Court opinion at 723 F Supp 487–89, analyzing the extent of conflict under the *Hartford* facts.

[75] 113 S Ct at 2909–10 n 24.

[76] In addition to the practical importance, the two approaches lead to different procedural conclusions. If there is no jurisdiction to prescribe, the complaint should be dismissed by a Federal court for failure to state a claim under Rule 12(b)(6), not for want of jurisdiction under Rule 12(b)(1). See Kramer, supra note 48, at 215 n 129; and Born and Westin, supra note 50, at 444–45.

a subject-matter jurisdiction line of inquiry leads ineluctably to the question: What are the circumstances that should lead the court, under principles of comity, to *abstain* in this particular case from applying U.S. law?[77]

The Supreme Court has sometimes looked with disfavor on abstention in domestic cases. Why then should abstention appeal to the Court in an international context? After all, as Professor Lowenfeld has put it, a decision not to apply the Sherman Act once the court has found the requisite intent and effect on U.S. commerce "looks like an act of grace, or diplomacy, or wisdom, but not one required by law."[78]

The advantage of the jurisdiction to prescribe approach is that it puts the question of extraterritorial reach up front. It asks at the outset whether the statute applies to the circumstances of the conduct presented in the particular case. Then the question is not one of grace but one of law: Does the statute apply to this transnational situation? Justice Souter no doubt thought posing the extraterritoriality issue first a dubious advantage at best in a Sherman Act case. The Sherman Act applied extraterritorially, he said, so why should he be concerned with purely formal questions: "[W]hatever the order of cart and horse," he ruled, there was nothing to debate, once intent and effect was alleged, unless sovereign compulsion was involved.[79]

The reason for that conclusion, he said, is that it has already been held that the Sherman Act applies extraterritorially. That

---

[77] See Justice Souter's version of this point, 113 S Ct at 2909 n 24.

[78] Lowenfeld, supra note 73, at 95. See Justice Scalia's criticism of abstention, 113 S Ct at 2820 n 9. Lowenfeld goes on to criticize the unfortunate associations of "the idea of subject matter jurisdiction [which] is derived from the half-forgotten constitutional battles in the United States in the 1920's and 1930's, when growing involvement in the American economy and society was challenged on the ground that it exceeded the powers delegated to Congress by the states. To say that 'subject matter jurisdiction' existed meant that the challenged regulation could be constitutionally supported, often through a variety of hooks—use of the mails, crossing state lines, failure to report income on a tax return—that might well not be centrally related to the problem at hand." Lowenfeld at 95. Significantly, the Restatement does not use the term subject-matter jurisdiction in discussing extraterritorial reach. See *Restatement*, note 21 supra, § 401, comment c: "Jurisdiction to prescribe with respect to transnational activity depends not on a particular link, such as minimum contacts . . . , which have been used to define 'subject matter jurisdiction' for constitutional purposes, but on a concept of reasonableness based on a number of factors to be considered and evaluated." The concept of subject-matter jurisdiction is, of course, also important in referring to the question whether a case can go forward in a court of limited jurisdiction, such as a Federal court, where ordinarily diversity or a Federal question is required.

[79] 113 S Ct at 2910–11 n 25. See discussion supra at notes 42–50 and accompanying text.

much is, of course, undeniable, and Justice Souter cites a number of such cases. But he totally overlooks the possibility that the cases do not hold that the Act *always* applies extraterritorially, even when intent plus effects are present. One can search the Supreme Court cases in vain for a case with such an actual holding,[80] and of course the lower court jurisdictional rule-of-reason cases are to the contrary.

Moreover, given Justice Souter's generalization from the prior Supreme Court extraterritorial reach cases, he gives no satisfactory rationale for his sovereign compulsion exception. Indeed, he totally fails to recognize that the case he cites for the sovereign compulsion exception did not involve the substantive reach of the Sherman Act; rather, it involved what the Restatement calls jurisdiction to enforce.[81] In the cited *Aérospatiale* case, the question was whether a District Court in ordering discovery against foreign litigants must employ the procedures of the Hague Convention or may alternatively apply the Federal Rules.[82] The majority held that the Federal Rules remained an option; the minority opinion by Justice Blackmun, on which Justice Souter relied, preferred a "presumption" that the Convention would govern, arguing that "courts are generally ill equipped to assume the role of balancing the interests of foreign nations with that of our own."[83] Although Justice Blackmun, in expanding on comity, did say that "the threshold question in a comity analysis is whether there is in fact a true conflict between domestic and foreign law"[84] (which is, of course, the nugget that Justice Souter mined from his minority opinion), Blackmun nowhere says that a "true conflict" exists only where compliance with U.S. law would constitute a violation of foreign law, as the

---

[80] Justice Souter relied on four Supreme Court cases. 113 S Ct at 2909. On the *Matsushita* case, see note 2 supra. *Continental Ore* is treated infra note 87. *Steele v Bulova Watch Co.*, 344 US 280 (1952), a trademark infringement case, actually cuts against the Souter position; since the Mexican courts had invalidated defendant's Mexican trademark, the Supreme Court, balancing the two countries' interests, held that "there is thus no conflict which might afford . . . a pretext that such relief would impugn foreign law." Id at 289. The fourth case, *United States v Sisal Sales Corp.*, 274 US 268, 276 (1927), held simply that a conspiracy "entered into by parties within the United States and made effective by acts done therein" is not immunized because of foreign "discriminating legislation"—there, the creation of a foreign monopoly.

[81] *Restatement* §§ 431–33, note 21 supra.

[82] *Société Nationale Industrielle Aérospatiale v United States District Court*, 482 US 522 (1987).

[83] Id at 552.

[84] Id at 555.

Souter opinion would have it.[85] In any case, Justice Blackmun's opinion did not even consider the question of the extraterritorial reach of a substantive statute but rather dealt solely with discovery.[86] Finally, Justice Souter, in overreading the Blackmun minority dictum to say that comity comes into play only where a foreign sovereign prohibition would be transgressed, overlooked the majority's view that comity requires the balancing of national interests: "[T]he concept of international comity requires in this context a more particularized analysis of the respective interests of the foreign nation and the requesting nation. . . ."[87]

If Congress had in fact decided in passing the Sherman Act that it should apply—regardless of foreign interests, comprehensive regulatory schemes, and the like—to all foreign activities that were intended to, and did, affect U.S. commerce, then the Supreme Court should of course apply the statute in all such situations. That would be true, under standard doctrine, even if that extraterritorial application violated international law.[88] Justice Scalia did not deny that point but on the contrary simply argued that a statute should not be construed to violate international law "unless a contrary intent appears."[89] There is no substantial evidence in the legislative history of the Sherman Act that Congress had such an intent.[90]

---

[85] Lower federal courts have in fact applied an interest-balancing approach in extraterritorial discovery cases. See *ABA Antitrust Section, II Antitrust Law Developments* 887 n 191 (3d ed 1992) for citations. And see *Restatement* § 442(1)(c), cited in note 21.

[86] Contrary to the implication of Justice Souter's quotation from *Aérospatiale*, Justice Blackmun's minority opinion did not argue that in those cases where his presumption in favor of the Convention had been overcome discovery should proceed unless the foreign party would violate local law by complying; quite the contrary, he pointed to the discretion in FRCP 26(c) as providing a mechanism "to ensure fairness to both parties." 482 US at 566.

[87] 482 US at 543–44. Justice Souter also cited *Continental Ore Co. v Union Carbide & Carbon Corp.*, 370 US 690 (1956), in support of his limitation of comity to a situation where foreign law would be violated. This Souter citation has the virtue of at least being concerned with substantive extraterritoriality, but the case unfortunately provides little support for the Souter position. In that case, unlike *Hartford Fire*, there was "no indication" that the foreign government had approved the challenged conduct or "would have approved" of it. Id at 706. Thus, although the Court did say that the challenged conduct had not been compelled by the foreign government, there was no proof of what the British government's brief sought to make clear and the courts below accepted, namely, that the British defendant's action was supported by a comprehensive British regulatory scheme. In short, in *Continental Ore*, there was no conflict even of policy.

[88] *Restatement* § 115(1); *Head Money Cases*, 112 US 580 (1884); *Whitney v Robertson*, 124 US 190 (1888); *The Chinese Exclusion Case*, 130 US 581 (1889).

[89] 113 S Ct at 2918.

[90] Indeed, the legislative history does little more than to make clear that Congress did intend, as the language of the Sherman Act itself states, that the Act shall apply to "commerce . . . with foreign nations," language that Justice Holmes found unhelpful in *American Banana Co. v United Fruit Co.*, 213 US 347 (1909), and which does not specify to what

And even if there were such an intent, there remains the question whether the Constitution places any limit on the extraterritorial application of Federal legislation. For example, the Due Process Clause might place such a limit in extreme cases.[91]

The upshot is that neither the legislative history of the Sherman Act nor the actual holdings of the decided Supreme Court cases resolve the applicability of the Sherman Act to fact patterns like *Hartford Fire.* In light of this silence, it is curious that Justice Souter is prepared to bow to general dicta in some Supreme Court extraterritoriality cases, especially when lower courts applying a jurisdictional rule of reason have not found prior Supreme Court cases to constrain them. Under these circumstances, the Supreme Court has to turn to something beyond its own prior cases to determine the ambiguous Sherman Act's jurisdictional reach.

VIII

In turning to a different approach, two different methodologies might be applied. One is an explicit choice-of-law framework, and the other is a jurisdictional rule of reason. A subsequent section of this essay examines in detail how such a reasonableness approach might work in practice. As for a choice-of-law approach, it suffices here to suggest the outlines of such an approach.[92]

Since the Sherman Act is ambiguous, we could look to its purpose. Since we do not know what, if any, purpose it has with

---

extent it applies to foreign, as opposed to purely domestic, conspiracies to restrain such foreign commerce. See Atwood and Brewster, supra note 44, at § 2.03. Earl W. Kintner, 1 *Federal Antitrust Law* § 7.2 (Anderson, 1980). Although it might be argued that Congress took care of this statutory ambiguity in 1982, when it amended the Sherman Act in the Foreign Trade Antitrust Improvements Act (FTAIA), 15 USC § 69, that amendment was intended to limit the jurisdictional reach of the Sherman Act in certain export commerce cases and to leave the jurisdictional reach of the Sherman Act untouched in other cases. See Justice Souter on this point, 113 S Ct at 2910; and see Eleanor M. Fox, *Extraterritoriality, Antitrust, and the New Restatement: Is "Reasonableness" the Answer?* 19 NYU J Intl Law & Policy 565, 589–90 (1987); P. M. Roth, *Reasonable Extraterritoriality: Correcting the "Balance of Interests,"* 41 Intl & Comp L Q 245, 259 (1992). And see the discussion of the legislative history of FTAIA approving comity and the *Timberlane* approach, supra note 45 and accompanying text. See, however, the District Court's opinion, 723 F Supp at 486–87 n 28.

[91] See *Tamari v Bache & Co.*, 730 F2d 1103, 1107 n 11 (7th Cir 1984). See Lea Brilmayer and Charles Norchi, *Federal Extraterritoriality and Fifth Amendment Due Process,* 105 Harv L Rev 1217 (1992).

[92] The literature on choice of law in conflict situations is so voluminous that it would transcend the bounds of this essay to do justice to the richness of that literature.

respect to foreign conspiracies, we should start with its domestic purpose—which, for shorthand, we may take in the *Hartford* context as the protection of consumers from horizontal conspiracies of upstream firms. Transposing that purpose to the international sphere, we see that applying the Sherman Act in the *Hartford* context would serve to protect U.S. consumers, and therefore a prima facie case for extraterritorial application can be made out.[93] But we also see that British law has the purpose of protecting British insurers and reinsurers by facilitating collusion and exempting it from the prohibitions of competition law. So we find a true conflict in the normal choice-of-law sense (though not in Justice Souter's sense).

To resolve that true conflict, we may apply one of several approaches. We might apply Professor Baxter's "comparative impairment" approach, and see which sovereign's policy would be more greatly impaired by having its law declared inapplicable to the circumstances.[94] This approach seems, however, to lead into a blind alley where both sovereigns lose equally, unless as suggested above one treats the U.K. law as too passive because there is not "active supervision" to balance the Sherman Act.[95] One could use the further Baxter idea of how these two sovereigns might allocate jurisdiction if they were to negotiate an agreement on the application of their respective laws in different transnational situations.[96] Certainly such an agreement should be negotiated, if possible on a multilateral basis, but it is hard to see how a Court could have enough information to predict the outcome of such a hypothetical negotiation.

Other refinements of the choice-of-law methodology are possible: a skeptic might say as many refinements as there are conflicts scholars. One strength of a choice-of-law methodology is that it tends to lay bare the underlying process in which courts often

---

[93] The domestic purpose of a statute is an important factor in interpreting the extraterritorial reach of legislation that is silent on its extraterritorial reach, at least where there are no offsetting policy considerations. See Larry Kramer, *Vestiges of Beale: Extraterritorial Application of American Law*, 1991 Supreme Court Review 179, 213–15; David P. Currie, *Flags of Convenience, American Labor, and the Conflict of Laws*, 1963 Supreme Court Review 34, 45 n 49; Brainerd Currie, *Selected Essays on the Conflict of Laws* 367 (Duke, 1963).

[94] William F. Baxter, *Choice of Law and the Federal System*, 16 Stan L Rev 1 (1963).

[95] See supra note 69 and accompanying text.

[96] See Larry Kramer, *Rethinking Choice of Law*, 90 Colum L Rev 277, 315 (1990).

implicitly engage without being explicit about what they are doing; in the *Hartford* case, Justice Souter did not explicate any particular process, apparently because he felt constrained either by precedent or the needs of creating a majority. In contrast to this strength, reliance on a choice-of-law methodology in *Hartford* has the weakness that we have in the cases today neither a coherent Federal doctrine specifying choice-of-law methodology in transnational cases nor enough agreement in the secondary literature as to a proper methodology to give much certainty as to probable outcomes.

For that reason, a *Timberlane* jurisdictional rule of reason seems preferable, at least for now. It exists, it has been endorsed in concept if not in all details by the Restatement, and it has been tried out in a number of cases. Moreover, it could be said to be one variant of a choice-of-law approach; certainly it shares a principal virtue of a choice-of-law approach in shining clearer light on foreign law and foreign interests. As we shall see in the next section, the uncertainty of a rule-of-reason approach, a weakness it shares with a choice-of-law approach, need not be so great in practice as is often assumed.

IX

How would a jurisdictional rule of reason work in a case like *Hartford Fire?* We have evidence on that point because both lower courts applied the *Timberlane* rule-of-reason criteria. Yet they reached opposite conclusions, showing that certainty is not necessarily a virtue of a balancing test. Of course, balancing tests, widely used in Supreme Court jurisprudence, rarely achieve certainty, and that is not their purpose.[97] In contrast, as we have seen, Justice Souter's test may provide more certain guidance, but it is the certainty of absolutism, a Lex Americana that applies U.S. law to all intent-plus-effects cases unless a foreign sovereign compels the challenged behavior. All interests, of whatever kind, of other sovereigns arc ignored.

A review of the lower court opinions in *Hartford Fire*, although illustrating the relative uncertainty of balancing tests, shows that

---

[97] Compare Antonin Scalia, *The Rule of Law as a Law of Rules*, 56 U Chi L Rev 1175 (1989), with Kathleen M. Sullivan, *The Justices of Rules and Standards*, 106 Harv L Rev 24 (1992).

the *Timberlane* criteria can be made to work. While the lower court found that the application of those criteria weighed against the "exercise of jurisdiction," and the Court of Appeals came to the opposite conclusion, the fact is that of the seven *Timberlane* criteria, the two courts agreed on three factors, disagreed on three factors, and—in one of the oddities of the case—the Court of Appeals completely overlooked the seventh factor. The District Court, in a nuanced review, found that this seventh factor—the "relative importance to the violation charged of conduct within the United States as compared with conduct abroad"—weighed against jurisdiction with respect to two claims and was neutral with respect to a third claim.[98] An analysis of the similarities and differences in the two courts' treatment of the first six factors leads to a rejection of any suspicion that a jurisdictional rule of reason would give a court uncontrolled discretion; on the contrary, it shows that the criteria can be applied evenhandedly and with reason, and that differences can be worked out, through normal adjudication, in the process of appellate review and Supreme Court resolution of splits in circuits.

The three criteria that the two courts agreed on were the "degree of conflict with foreign law or policy," the "relative significance of effects on the United States as compared with those elsewhere," and the "foreseeability" of an effect on U.S. commerce.[99] No uncertainty there! The three on which they disagreed were the "nationality or allegiance of the parties and the locations of principal place of business of [the] corporations," the "extent to which enforcement by either state can be expected to achieve compliance," and the "extent to which there is explicit purpose to harm or affect" U.S. commerce.[100] Despite the differences in outcome on these latter three criteria, the fact is that the two courts differed in ways that can easily be specified, and therefore the issues raised can be resolved through normal appellate processes.

On the nationality factor, the District Court, while conceding that the nationality of the parties alone tipped toward exercise of

---

[98] This seventh factor was the "relative importance to the violation charged of conduct within the United States as compared with conduct abroad. *Timberlane Lumber Co. v Bank of America*, 749 F2d 1378, 1385 (9th Cir 1984); *In re Insurance Litigation ("Hartford")*, 723 F Supp at 490. (Initial capital letters are deleted in this and subsequent quotations of *Timberlane* factors.)

[99] *Timberlane*, 749 F2d at 1384–85; *Hartford*, 723 F Supp at 487–90, 938 F2d at 932–34.

[100] *Timberlane*, 749 F2d at 1384–85; *Hartford*, 723 F Supp at 489–90, 938 F2d at 933–34.

jurisdiction because many of the foreign defendants were subsidiaries of American corporations, gave decisive weight to the fact that adjudication of the claims would require the testimony of witnesses and the production and analysis of documents which were likely to be unavailable because located in England;[101] the Court of Appeals, in contrast, ignored the discovery issues and looked at the parties alone. With respect to the enforcement factor, the District Court emphasized the inability to enforce the "requested injunctive relief against activities in London,"[102] while Judge Noonan, observing that damages against foreign defendants could be awarded and collected, believed that "substantial compliance" could be achieved by injunctions against the U.S. defendants.[103] On the final of the three factors, "explicit purpose," the District Court found that the alleged "purpose . . . to restrict the availability of certain types of . . . coverage" was "not inconsistent with the existence of a legitimate business purpose" of "reducing their exposure to certain risks and controlling losses," but the Court of Appeals held that for jurisdictional purposes the intent to affect U.S. commerce was more important than the intent to achieve a legitimate business purpose.[104]

We thus come away from this review of the *Timberlane* factors with three issues of law separating the two lower courts: the relevance, if any, of (1) unavailability of foreign discovery, (2) inability to give extraterritorial equitable relief, and (3) existence of a legitimate business purpose. Although these factors obviously have to be assessed under the facts of each particular case, their relevance

---

[101] 723 F Supp at 489. The documents would be subject to an English blocking statute. Id at 488.

[102] 723 F Supp at 489: "Indeed, the Protection of Trading Interests Act allows the British Secretary of State for Industry to forbid British nationals from complying with foreign antitrust judgments."

[103] "The decree of an American court setting out the obligations of the American insurers would undoubtedly be effective and surely would have an impact on the way the American insurers did business with the foreign defendants. Substantial compliance, in short, could be achieved." 938 F2d at 933. Judge Noonan apparently did not consider that his own argument demonstrated that extraterritorial equitable relief was unnecessary and therefore weighed against, not for, extraterritorial jurisdiction.

[104] 723 F Supp at 490; 938 F2d at 933–34. While the Court of Appeals approach may appear self-evidently correct, since the question of legitimate business purpose seems to be a substantive rather than a jurisdictional factor, two points can be advanced for the District Court's position. First, if Justice Scalia is right and the real issue is the substantive reach of the Sherman Act, then the business legitimacy of acts in London by U.K. nationals takes on importance. Second, *Timberlane* itself relied on the fact that defendants' acts were "consistent with customs and practices." 749 F2d at 1385.

is also in the final analysis a question of law. Thus, especially in view of the two courts' agreement on three other factors, we see that a balancing rule-of-reason test need not be an exercise in unfettered discretion but rather throws up clear questions of law that can be resolved, case by case, just like other questions of law, including those raised by other kinds of multifactor rules. If circuits come to different conclusions on particular legal questions, then the Supreme Court can resolve the split in circuits.

This review shows that although courts may differ depending upon their assessment of facts (here their assessment of the allegations), the uncertainty of a jurisdictional rule-of-reason test is not necessarily greater than the application of other kinds of legal standards to complex business facts. Indeed, in a Sherman Act context, a jurisdiction rule of reason is probably more certain than the application of the normal Section 1 substantive rule of reason. Of course, again in a Sherman Act context, there have been attempts to eliminate that substantive uncertainty by the adoption of per se rules. But certainty has proved illusive as conscientious courts have had to wrestle, with respect to one per se category after another, with when particular facts fall within or outside a particular per se category.[105]

In any event, the foregoing review of the *Hartford* lower court opinions throws doubt on Judge Wilkey's well-known criticism that "courts inherently find it difficult neutrally to balance competing foreign interests" and that "[w]hen there is any doubt, national interests will tend to be favored over foreign interests."[106] Perhaps such a skeptical view would be justified if balancing were to be done on a legal tabula rasa in each successive case. But it is definitely not the case where the factors involved lend themselves to

---

[105] A large share of Supreme Court antitrust decisions in recent years have involved the definition of practices acknowledged to be illegal per se. See, e.g., Tie-ins: *Fortner Enterprises, Inc. v United States Steel Corp.*, 394 US 495 (1969) and *United States Steel Corp. v Fortner Enterprises, Inc.*, 429 US 610 (1977); *Jefferson Parish Hospital District No 2 v Hyde*, 466 US 2 (1984); and see *Kodak v Image Technical Services, Inc.*, 112 S Ct 2072 (1992). Resale Price Maintenance: *Business Electronics Corp. v Sharp Electronics Corp.*, 485 US 717 (1988). Output Limitations: *NCAA v Board of Regents*, 468 US 85 (1984). Price-Fixing: *Broadcast Music, Inc. v Columbia Broadcasting System, Inc.*, 441 US 1 (1979).

[106] *Laker Airways Ltd. v Sabena*, 731 F2d 909, 951 (DC Cir 1984). It is important to note that Judge Wilkey was addressing himself to foreign discovery rather than substantive extraterritoriality. The same was true of Judge Marshall's complaint that "the judiciary has little expertise, or perhaps even authority, to evaluate the economic and social policies of a foreign country." *In re Uranium Antitrust Litigation*, 480 F Supp 1138, 1148 (ND Ill 1979).

case-by-case definition and resolution through normal adjudicatory processes.[107]

Taking then an optimistic view of the ability of courts to discipline themselves to apply a multifactor test consistently, one may conclude that a jurisdictional rule-of-reason test provides more certainty and workability than sometimes argued. Taking a less sanguine view, one may still find such a test preferable to the supposed certainty of the absolutism of *Hartford Fire*—a precedent that, as suggested earlier,[108] may collapse when the facts are more attractive from the standpoint of the foreign defendants.

X

Extraterritoriality is one thing when, for example, the Antitrust Division is considering bringing an antitrust action with extraterritorial aspects. Then law enforcement goals can be weighed within the Executive Branch against a variety of other factors, such as economic and foreign policy.[109] Law enforcement, economic, and foreign policy departments of the Executive Branch all presumably have a voice in weighing the relative advantages of sovereign

---

[107] For a jurisdictional rule of reason to work well, three additional steps are required of the Supreme Court, beyond simply resolving splits in circuits: (1) endorse a rule of reason approach; (2) specify what the factors to be considered are so that each circuit does not make up its own list or change the list arbitrarily à la Judge Noonan; and (3) avoid the temptation to write long general essays, unconnected to prior rule-of-reason decisions, thereby throwing lower court litigation into confusion. Compare Judge Easterbrook's view (expressed in a somewhat different legal context) that interest-balancing test would "call on the district judge to throw a heap of factors on a table and then slice and dice to taste," and that "a court's job is to reach judgments on the basis of rules of law rather than to use a different recipe for each meal." *Reinsurance Co. of America v Administratia Asigurarilor de Stat*, 902 F2d 1275, 1283 (7th Cir 1990) (concurring opinion). What is required for interest balancing to work in the Sherman Act context is for the Supreme Court to specify the recipe. Of course, there will remain problems in close cases. Obviously the final conclusion in any case should not be based simply on mechanical counting of factors—say, four for jurisdiction and three against. So judgment is still required, and some uncertainty will remain.

[108] See discussion supra notes 68–70 and accompanying text.

[109] The Antitrust Division's 1988 Guidelines set out a list of factors to be considered by it in bringing a case. Department of Justice, *Antitrust Enforcement Guidelines for International Operations* ¶ 5 n 170 ("*DOJ Guidelines*") in 4 Trade Reg Rep (CCH) ¶ 13,109–10. These factors look much like the jurisdictional rule-of-reason factors used by lower courts and the Restatement. See notes 98–104 supra and accompanying text. However, their application could be viewed as an exercise of prosecutorial discretion, especially in light of *Hartford Fire*'s reading of the Sherman Act. On prosecutorial discretion, see *Heckler v Chaney*, 470 US 821 (1985), and Cass R. Sunstein, *Reviewing Agency Inaction After Heckler v Chaney*, 52 U Chi L Rev 653 (1985).

cooperation and responsibility-sharing as against unilateral action in a particular case.[110]

Moreover, in an antitrust case under consideration within the Executive Branch, the arguments favoring unilateral application of the Sherman Act and the arguments made in this essay in favor of international cooperation could each receive a full hearing. Certainly the arguments for applying the Sherman Act extraterritorially are forceful where, as in *Hartford*, the conspiracy alleged was aimed only at the U.S. market and succeeded fully. Moreover, with increasing interpenetration of economies and with imports constituting an ever larger proportion of total domestic U.S. consumption, one can argue that it is more important than ever that the Sherman Act be available to strike down foreign conspiracies that have their intended economic effects within the United States. Under this line of argument, foreign conspiracies could perhaps be ignored when the U.S. domestic market was relatively isolated from imports, but with imports having gained a larger share of the U.S. market, their deleterious effect is likely to be greater.

Whatever the merits of these opposing lines of argument, the point is that the policy arguments concerning extraterritoriality would be heard and resolved within the Executive Branch prior to bringing a government case. Extraterritoriality is quite another thing, however, in private treble-damage actions where such economic and foreign policy considerations play no role in the private decision to bring the action.[111] Indeed, the existence of the contin-

---

[110] I say "presumably" because my State Department experience raises some concerns. U.S. attorneys are sometimes loath to hear counsels of restraint from the State Department or even from political appointee levels of the Justice Department, because the U.S. attorneys are, in their view, specifically responsible for seeing that the law is enforced. No doubt this problem is not as great in the antitrust field where practice acknowledges the right and duty of senior Justice Department officials to exercise prosecutorial discretion, at least up to the level of the Assistant Attorney General. Still the atmosphere of scandal and trial by media that pervades Washington makes it a dangerous adventure for someone outside the Justice Department to discourage an indictment or even a civil complaint. If, according to career officials, a violation of law has occurred, concerns about comity are unlikely to have a hearing on CNN and the evening television news when charges of impropriety are leaked. That practical constraint on sensible policymaking where foreign firms and extraterritoriality are involved is, from a legal standpoint, anomalous in view of the general understanding that it is completely legitimate for foreign policy to be taken into account in deciding when and whom to prosecute. See, e.g., Atwood and Brewster, supra note 44, at § 6.18, and *DOJ Guidelines*, supra note 109, at ¶ 5 n 171, referring to the 1984 termination, based on foreign policy concerns, of a grand jury investigation into U.S.-U.K. air travel.

[111] See *DOJ Guidelines*, supra note 109, at ¶ 5 n 167.

gent fee, as well as the absence in the United States of a general rule requiring the losing party to reimburse the legal costs of the winning party, virtually guarantee that private plaintiffs will take no account of such foreign and economic policy considerations.

Since *Hartford Fire* was a private case, the policy decision was implicitly but inevitably left to the judiciary. Hence, for better or worse, *Hartford Fire* constitutes international economic policymaking by the Supreme Court. The implicit suggestion in Justice Souter's opinion that he was not making policy but simply applying existing law will not wash. As we have seen, the Sherman Act does not specify its extraterritorial reach with sufficient precision to decide concrete cases like *Hartford Fire*. Nor do prior Supreme Court cases provide a conclusive answer.[112] The Souter majority made a choice and, whether they thought much about it, it was a deliberate international economic policy choice.

Indeed, the failure of the Court to discuss policy considerations, pretending that the case could be decided solely on principle and precedent, is out of keeping with recent Court practice. For example, the Court did not hesitate to take foreign and security policy considerations into account in the *Verdugo-Urquidez* case in construing an ambiguous Fourth Amendment as not applicable to a nonresident alien located in a foreign country:

> Some who violate our laws may live outside our borders under a regime quite different from that which obtains in this country. Situations threatening to important American interests may arise half-way around the globe, situations which in view of the political branches of our Government require an American response with armed force. If there are to be restrictions on searches and seizures which occur incident to such American action, they must be imposed by the political branches through diplomatic understanding, treaty, or legislation.[113]

Similarly, the Court has relied on foreign policy considerations and the needs of the international economic system in construing statutes. In *Lauritzen v Larson*, relied on by Justice Scalia, the Court pointed to the need for "rules designed to foster amicable and workable commercial relations"[114] in interpreting the extraterritorial

---

[112] See discussion supra at notes 80–87 and accompanying text.

[113] *United States v Verdugo-Urquidez*, 494 US 259, 275 (1990).

[114] 345 US 571, 582 (1953). See also *Romero v International Terminal Operating Co.*, 358 US 354, 382–84 (1959).

reach of the Jones Act. And in the *McCulloch* case it considered the need to avoid "retaliatory action" by other countries relevant for the same purpose in a labor law case.[115] Similarly, in a domestic context, the Court has repeatedly relied on economic policy considerations to interpret the scope of the antitrust laws.[116]

The conclusion to be derived from the foregoing discussion of the differences between government antitrust cases and private treble-damage actions and of the policy consequences of the courts not taking into account economic policy considerations in the latter through application of a jurisdictional rule of reason is not that the government cases should not be subjected to the same rule of reason. To be sure, the Antitrust Division would be happy to be free from judicial supervision over its extraterritorial assertions of jurisdiction.[117] While such freedom of action may make bureaucratic sense to the Antitrust Division, jurisdiction should not turn, whether one takes a subject-matter jurisdiction or a jurisdiction-to-prescribe approach, on the nature of the plaintiff. The conclusion rather is that the consequences of the courts not applying a jurisdictional rule of reason, or some other self-restricting principle, are likely to be especially grave in private actions where economic and foreign policy considerations will seldom have the slightest influence on the decision to bring the action.

XI

The fact that the Supreme Court made a policy choice in *Hartford Fire* is thus in keeping with tradition. The unusual part of the case is that both the majority and the dissent sought to avoid identifying the policy considerations involved. To understand the

---

[115] *McCulloch v Sociedad Nacional de Marineros de Honduras*, 372 US 10, 21 (1963). See generally on the use of international policy considerations in extraterritoriality cases, Harold G. Maier, *Extraterritorial Jurisdiction at a Crossroads: An Intersection between Public and Private International Law*, 76 Am J Intl L 280 (1982).

[116] For just a few examples, see *Matsushita Electric Industrial Co. v Zenith Radio Corp.*, 475 US 574 (1986) (predatory pricing); *Continental TV Inc. v GTE Sylvania Inc.*, 433 US 36 (1977) (vertical arrangements); *United States v Philadelphia National Bank*, 374 US 321 (1963) (mergers); and *United States v E I du Pont de Nemours & Co.*, 351 US 377 (1956) (monopolization).

[117] See *DOJ Guidelines*, supra note 109, at ¶ 5 n 167; the U.S. government amicus brief in *Hartford Fire* argued that "courts should not engage in any comity analysis in antitrust actions brought by the United States," but that such analysis is proper in private actions.

nature of the de facto policy choice in *Hartford Fire*, it is useful to examine the choices available to the Executive Branch in a situation where U.S. substantive law is different from the law of a particular foreign jurisdiction, and where the different foreign law is thought to be detrimental to the U.S. economy (or, more generally, to the U.S. national interest). In such a case, the United States can, in principle, follow one of four strategies. First, it may seek to change foreign law by persuasion—using sweet reason to argue, in effect, that "our rule is better than yours and you ought to follow ours." This strategy is *diplomacy* in its purest form. Second, the Executive Branch may pursue a *negotiations* strategy, seeking to change foreign law by offering the foreign government something of value in return. The recompense may be in the same field (as in trade negotiations), but the quid pro quo may be in quite different areas—say, security guarantees or financial assistance. A variant of this second strategy would seek to eliminate the adverse consequences of the difference in law by reaching agreement on harmonization of substantive law or by allocation of jurisdictional competence.[118] Third, the United States may pursue a *sanctions* strategy, threatening the foreign government that if the offending law is not changed, retaliation will follow. The prototypical example of this strategy is Section 301 of the trade laws, which has been used aggressively and sometimes effectively to open foreign markets to U.S. trade and investment.[119]

In addition to diplomacy, negotiations, and sanctions, there is a fourth, much simpler strategy. The United States may simply apply its own law directly to the transactions in question, taking punitive steps toward foreign corporations and persons with respect to their acts. In such a case the foreign law remains in place

---

[118] See discussion of harmonization and allocation negotiations, supra note 13 and accompanying text. For a comprehensive analysis of the need for harmonization, and the alternatives for achieving it, in the antitrust area, see Diane P. Wood, *The Impossible Dream: Real International Antitrust*, 1992 U Chi Legal F 277 (1992). See also Conferees Address Harmonization of US, EC Competition Regimes, 65 Antitrust & Trade Reg Rep 499 (BNA, 1993).

[119] Under Section 301 of the Trade Act of 1974, 19 USC §§ 2411–20, the United States makes a demand for change of foreign law—typically some barrier to U.S. exports or to U.S. direct investment—and if the change is not made, the United States retaliates by taking trade measures (such as the imposition of duties or quantitative restrictions on imports from the offending country) that harm the economic interests of that country. The hope is that the foreign country will capitulate and change its law before the retaliation takes place. See Alan O. Sykes, *Constructive Unilateral Threats in International Commercial Relations: The Limited Case for Section 301*, 23 Law & Policy Intl Bus 263 (1992).

but foreign entities will be forced to comply with the U.S. standard. Protests of the foreign government concerning the invasion of its sovereignty are simply ignored.

Where, under option four, the acts take place in the United States, no one would call the application of U.S. law extraterritorial. But to the extent that the acts take place outside the United States, and particularly within the country of citizenship (or place of incorporation of a corporation), the appellation "extraterritorial" may fairly be applied. On the other hand, the practice of most developed nations is increasingly to adopt the U.S. tendency to apply their law where the intent of the foreign actors was to have an impact on the local economy (including its exports and imports). In the antitrust field, the European Community, for example, has adopted the U.S. intent-plus-effects approach.[120]

Problems arise, however, where the two governments' policies are opposed. The flagrant use by the United States of extraterritorial measures, particularly in the antitrust field, has led to a variety of foreign retaliatory measures, such as blocking and claw-back statutes.[121] Such retaliation harms U.S. interests, both by interfering with U.S. law enforcement and, much more importantly, by destroying a spirit of cooperation and common purpose in solving international economic problems.[122]

The four options (diplomacy, negotiations, sanctions and extraterritorial application of U.S. law) constitute a hierarchy of increasing confrontation. Option three, the threat of sanctions, is often called aggressive unilateralism, but the hope behind the strategy is an amicable bilateral solution. Sometimes, of course, the sanctions strategy backfires and the foreign government counter-retaliates. Option four, the unilateral imposition of U.S. law, is still more aggressive and makes no effort to achieve either amicable relations or a change in foreign law. The conflicting national philosophies remain in place, laying the foundation for future discord and misunderstanding and perhaps more retaliation. If the goal is to pro-

---

[120] See e.g., *Åhlström Osakeyhtiö v Commission [Wood Pulp]*, [1988] ECR 5193.

[121] Blocking statutes have been used by some countries—notably the United Kingdom, Australia, and Canada—to impede enforcement of the U.S. antitrust laws by blocking discovery. See Gary B. Born and David Weston, *International Civil Litigation* 282–83 (1991), for discussion and citations. A claw-back provision appears in the U.K. Protection of Trading Interests Act. Directed at U.S. treble-damage actions, it creates a right to recover two-thirds of any U.S. antitrust award to a U.S. plaintiff. 21 Intl Leg Mat 834, 837–38 (1982).

[122] Kenneth W. Dam, *Economic and Political Aspects of Extraterritoriality*, 19 Intl Law 887, 890 (1985).

mote convergence of national laws to accommodate the high current level of economic interpenetration and to further it in the future in the aid of higher living standards, the fourth option is surely the least attractive of the four policy options. Yet it is precisely the option underwritten by the Souter majority.[123]

Unilateralism through extraterritoriality is doubly unattractive in the context of private treble-damage actions where there is in fact no governmental decision to pursue the fourth option. In *Hartford Fire*, the U.S. government filed an amicus brief arguing that notions of comity need not be applied where the United States was the plaintiff.[124] In such a case the U.S. government can weigh the options and make a governmental decision. But where private actions are concerned, the government has no opportunity to make a decision and indeed cannot even block the private action.[125]

Private extraterritorial enforcement resulted in a particular anomaly in *Hartford Fire* because of the regulation of insurance. If one compares the U.S. and British regulatory schemes, they are in essence quite similar. Both exempted the domestic insurance business from the national competition prohibitions against collusion. The means by which the exemptions were given effect were

---

[123] This is not to say that the fourth option may not meet contemporary international standards in some cases. We have seen that extraterritorial application of competition law has been accepted in the European community and some countries in some cases, particularly in a clear intent-plus-effects situation. To the extent that the alleged foreign conspirators had a clear goal to restrain competition within the United States and they succeeded, some countries would today accept it, particularly if the motive were not so much to reduce risk (as in *Hartford Fire*) but to increase cartel profits on sales to U.S. purchasers. Of course, an economist would say that there is no economic difference between collusion to reduce risk and collusion to increase profits. While analytically correct, this point merely shows that economics, law, and politics create different perceptions for policymakers, which in turn affect policy outcomes.

[124] For private cases, the U.S. government amicus brief supported the rule-of-reason approach, though preferring the slightly different set of factors set out in the *DOJ Guidelines*, at ¶ 5 n 170, cited supra note 109. The amicus brief, in contrast to Justice Souter, did not believe that a "true conflict" would arise only in sovereign compulsion cases; rather, frustration of clearly articulated policies of foreign governments also could give rise to such a conflict. The amicus brief came down on the side of the plaintiffs in the *Hartford* case itself on the ground that application of the Sherman Act would not frustrate British policy, but it at the same time argued that any relief should be limited to damages because comity might make an injunction inappropriate.

[125] It is worth remembering that the judiciary has no power to choose the first two of the Executive Branch options (diplomacy and negotiations), and only in the most unusual cases can it make even marginal use of the third option (sanctions). Only in option four (direct application of U.S. law) can it participate in foreign affairs and then only to the extent that U.S. statutory law admits of judicial discretion through statutory interpretation. In this light one can see the virtue of the emphasis on a broad sphere of Executive Branch discretion in foreign affairs articulated in *United States v Curtiss-Wright*, 299 US 304 (1936).

similar, differing only in detail. U.S. federal law delegated regulation of the insurance business to the states, fully anticipating and indeed perhaps intending that the states would condone collusion and seek only to regulate outcomes.[126] British law delegated regulation to a self-regulatory system, with essentially the same understanding as in the United States. Yet the outcome of private enforcement in *Hartford Fire* may well be that the United States applies to British companies a standard that it would never apply to its own companies.[127]

XII

How could such an apparently far-reaching and anomalous international economic policy choice have been made? Even taking the point that Justice Souter may have actually believed that he had no choice under the precedents, hardly a likely conclusion if he had simply read the two opinions below in the same case, one can see that the anomaly arose from the way in which the U.S. political system fragments policymaking. In *Hartford Fire* the issue was delegated not just to the courts, as is always true in part where economic policymaking arises under the guise of law enforcement, but also to private parties as plaintiffs. Private parties as plaintiffs were instrumental in applying the Sherman Act to British rein-

---

[126] On the antitrust exemption for the business of insurance, see Jonathan R. Macey and Geoffrey P. Miller, *The McCarran-Ferguson Act of 1945: Reconceiving the Federal Role in Insurance Regulation*, 68 NYU L Rev 13 (1993). Posner and Easterbrook argue that some collusion in insurance (and reinsurance) is essential because of the need to share information and pool risks; they conclude:

> The proper understanding of the McCarran-Ferguson Act may depend not on market failure but on antitrust failure. . . . In other words, the McCarran-Ferguson [Act] can be seen as a law that frees the insurance business of antitrust rules that would reduce it to a shambles. Congress also threw out rules that easily could have been applied to insurance, such as the ban on price fixing, but that may have been accepted in 1945 as part of the bargain.

Richard A. Posner and Frank H. Easterbrook, *Antitrust* 1045–46 (West, 2d ed 1981). In *Hartford Fire*, most states had in fact exercised regulation over outcomes by explicitly approving the new forms; however, they did not approve the dropping of the occurrence form, which happened after they approved the claims-made form.

[127] The text assumes no boycott. With regard to the applicability of McCarran-Ferguson to foreign reinsurers, see supra notes 69–74 and accompanying text. The text also passes over the point that domestic reinsurers may be in the same position as foreign reinsurers to the extent that the states do not regulate the business of reinsurance. See supra note 71.

surers, not a central Federal organ like the Antitrust Division.[128] To be sure, some of the plaintiffs were states, but they were suing on a parens patriae theory to enforce the Sherman Act rights of their citizens. Moreover, the states were not seeking to exercise any regulatory powers delegated to them under the McCarran-Ferguson Act; the states could presumably have done so under the power that statute gives to regulate insurance outcomes by, in one way or another, being sure that the alternative of occurrence-based insurance was preserved. Instead of using that form of regulation of their own state's economy, the states used the Federal judiciary, in effect, to exercise regulatory power over foreign commerce.

With respect to purely private parties (as opposed to states suing parens patriae), even if one is willing to use the oxymoronic phrase "private Attorneys General," it is clear that the Souter opinion allows them to participate in international economic policy decisions, not just without any substantial judicial supervision as a result of the Souter rule, but with none of the safeguards we have grown accustomed to with respect to public officials who make such decisions. Not only are Federal public officials not permitted to charge any fees that add to their salary (much less contingent fees), but they are subject to elaborate ethics, financial disclosure, and Congressional review procedures to assure that their personal interest is in no way involved in their decisions.[129]

So long as private antitrust treble-damage actions exist, it is incumbent on the courts to impose standards not just to prevent "private abuse" but to assure that the public interest (and, in international cases, the national interest) is taken into account. Courts use controls in such areas as the review of fees awarded in class actions. Surely it is reasonable to ask the court system to impose some limits on the reach of private cases where the international

---

[128] Indeed, it is perhaps significant that the Department of Justice elected not to bring an action despite the widespread protest against the insurance industry's action in eliminating the occurrence-based form. Moreover, it should be borne in mind that *Hartford* was not a case, unlike a large number of cases over the years, where private plaintiffs came in behind the Antitrust Division in order to collect damages.

[129] Private extraterritorial enforcement is doubly troublesome in the context of an injunction. In *Hartford Fire* an injunction would "impose a U.S.-style antitrust compliance programme on the underwriting of reinsurance in London." Joseph P. Griffin, *U.S. Supreme Court Encourages Extraterritorial Application of U.S. Antitrust Laws*, 21 Intl Bus Law 389, 391 (1993). Comity may reenter the equation at the remedy stage despite Justice Souter's blanket statement.

economy is involved. A jurisdictional rule of reason would be one modest step toward limiting the devolution to private parties of international economic policymaking. Such a rule, involving a list of criteria for balancing the interests of the United States and the foreign sovereign in regulating the conduct of the parties involved, might not have changed the actual result in *Hartford Fire*, where— according to the allegations—the conspiracy was aimed directly and only at the U.S. market and succeeded, and the British authorities played no role in considering the goals or activities under challenge. But it would make a difference in cases where a strong regulatory objective was served in the foreign country. Nor would it necessarily have prevented the anomaly that foreign firms may be subjected to higher standards than domestic firms, but it would at least have provided a framework for analysis of that problem.[130]

A second-best alternative would have been to accept Justice Scalia's second canon of construction, which would have placed international law limitations on the Sherman Act. The problem with that approach is unfortunately that international law provides little guidance in the absence of an international agreement. Yet the willingness of the *Hartford Fire* Court to underwrite unlimited U.S. jurisdiction, so long as intent plus effects is shown, is at best a disincentive for negotiation of such an agreement. Although it might give other countries, such as the United Kingdom, an incentive to attempt to reach, say, agreement on allocation of jurisdiction over transnational disputes, it puts the U.S. negotiators in the position of giving away law enforcement authority accorded it by no less an institution than the Supreme Court.

One can only conclude that it is unfortunate that both the Souter and the Scalia opinions ignored the *Timberlane* jurisdictional rule-of-reason approach. The opinions thereby obscure the fact that applying the Sherman Act extraterritorially may in fact constitute major international economic policymaking by the courts and by private parties in important cases. The *Hartford Fire* decision also probably puts off the day when a more rational international approach involving harmonization or allocation of jurisdiction will make extraterritorial law enforcement less compelling and less disruptive of international economic cooperation.

---

[130] The Court of Appeals applied a jurisdictional rule of reason and still held the foreign reinsurers liable, but avoided the anomaly by holding the domestic insurers liable as well. See discussion at note 71 supra and accompanying text.

DEAN ALFANGE, JR.

MARBURY v MADISON AND ORIGINAL UNDERSTANDINGS OF JUDICIAL REVIEW: IN DEFENSE OF TRADITIONAL WISDOM

I. INTRODUCTION

Writing thirty years ago, Alan Westin assayed a prediction that, contrary to the fate of so many confident assertions of what the future has in store, has proved to be entirely accurate. After noting that Chief Justice John Marshall's classic opinion asserting the power of judicial review in the seminal case of *Marbury v Madison*[1] "has come to draw argument as a cornflower draws bees,"[2] he expressed assurance that the debate over the legitimacy of judicial review "will continue to attract partisans and scholars in the coming decades" and added that, "[i]n 1990, I expect that it will still be one of the murky questions of our constitutional politics."[3] Now that 1990 has come and gone, it is clear that Professor Westin was right on both counts. Within the past four years, at least one article—by James O'Fallon[4]—and two books—by Robert Lowry

---

Dean Alfange, Jr. is Professor of Political Science, University of Massachusetts at Amherst.

[1] 1 Cranch 137 (1803).

[2] Alan F. Westin, *Charles Beard and American Debate over Judicial Review, 1790–1961*, Introduction to Charles A. Beard, *The Supreme Court and the Constitution* 9 (Prentice-Hall, 1962).

[3] Id at 33.

[4] James A. O'Fallon, *Marbury*, 44 Stan L Rev 219 (1992).

Clinton[5] and Sylvia Snowiss[6]—have appeared which challenge conventional understandings of the *Marbury* decision and its relationship to judicial review as it is practiced today, demonstrating that the case and the doctrine for which it stands still retain a largely undiminished capacity to attract the attention of partisans and scholars. And the fact that the new view of Marshall's opinion and its role in the establishment of judicial review that is presented in each of these works is entirely at odds with the views presented in the others is rather convincing proof that the question not only remains murky, but that additional murk is still being plentifully generated.

Professor Westin further predicted that, despite "those who hope to carry off a coup from the library stacks," "no one will uncover a crumbling diary or set of letters, or fashion a new thesis which will resolve this dispute once and for all,"[7] and there is nothing in these new works that would prove him wrong. All three authors downplay the significance of *Marbury v Madison* in the development of judicial review as it is understood today. Each sees it as simply a ratification or restatement of a concept already widely accepted at the time of the decision, and not, as Alexander Bickel described it, as the establishment of an institution that was " 'done' at a given time and by a given act."[8] But the widely accepted concept that each finds expressed in Marshall's opinion is a different concept from that found by the others. As Westin foresaw, each has tried to "fashion a new thesis" to explain to us "once and for all" why we have fundamentally misunderstood *Marbury*'s significance, but none purports to have uncovered any new documentary evidence. Instead, each claims to have found the overlooked answers in the same materials that have been sifted through, analyzed, and dissected by every major constitutional historian for over a century, including both critics and enthusiasts of judicial review and defenders and detractors of John Marshall. It would indeed be truly remarkable if, in the absence of the discovery of "a crumbling diary or set of letters" or some other hitherto unexamined material, someone replowing the field today could show persuasively that our knowledge of this central event of American constitutional history

---

[5] Robert Lowry Clinton, *Marbury v. Madison and Judicial Review* (U Kans, 1989).

[6] Sylvia Snowiss, *Judicial Review and the Law of the Constitution* (Yale, 1990).

[7] Westin, *Charles Beard* at 33 (cited in note 2).

[8] Alexander Bickel, *The Least Dangerous Branch* 1 (Bobbs-Merrill, 1962).

has been based on fundamental misconceptions resulting from the universal failure of historians to comprehend the meaning or significance of the available historical materials. Since this is the task each author has set out to accomplish, it is hardly surprising that they are all, to varying degrees, unsuccessful.

II. Three New Views of Marbury's Historical Significance

A. JAMES O'FALLON

James O'Fallon barely even alludes to *Marbury*'s role in the development of judicial review, for he regards it as an unimportant aspect of the case, and certainly not the focal point of Marshall's interest. In his view, "Chief Justice Marshall's concern with judicial review has been exaggerated by the desire of legal scholars for a strong foundation for this doctrine,"[9] and Marshall's discussion of it reflected little more than political rhetoric—"the hackneyed litany of the Federalists."[10] Marshall's conception of judicial review, as O'Fallon describes it, was "loyal to this [Federalist] vision" in which "the people were 'their own worst enemies'" who "would be driven by their passions to the election of demagogues (such as Jefferson) who would lead an assault on the rights of the stable and virtuous members of the community."[11]

While the Republicans, of course, did not share the Federalists' view of a readily corruptible people, and were profoundly distrustful of a federal judiciary in which Federalist partisans were entrenched, O'Fallon notes that many of their number in Congress had "acknowledged that courts could legitimately declare an act of Congress unconstitutional,"[12] which he regards as essentially negating "the claim that the establishment of judicial review was Marshall's primary objective in *Marbury*."[13] Precisely because it was not necessary to make a strong case for judicial review, O'Fallon sees Marshall's argument in support of it as "the almost rote

---

[9] O'Fallon, 44 Stan L Rev at 219 (cited in note 4).

[10] Id at 256.

[11] Id at 258.

[12] Id at 227. The Republicans, having hoped for judicial invalidation of such Federalist measures as the national bank, the carriage tax, and the Sedition Act, were not strongly situated to mount a principled attack on the institution of judicial review, per se. See Charles Warren, *Congress, the Constitution and the Supreme Court* 97 (Little, Brown, 1925).

[13] O'Fallon, 44 Stan L Rev at 227 n 30.

repetition of a party position, rather than a measured treatment of the issue."[14] He scorns any idea that Marshall is to be credited with statesmanship, vision, or even originality for his handling of the *Marbury* case. The opinion was purely "a political act,"[15] an occasional tract written for partisan purposes in the midst of a partisan dispute and without relevance to John Marshall's most enduring contributions to American constitutionalism"—fashioning the constitutional tools for the establishment of an effective national government.[16]

B. ROBERT LOWRY CLINTON

At the opposite end of the spectrum, Robert Clinton praises Marshall unstintingly for his unfailing judiciousness, a judiciousness manifested with particular clarity in the *Marbury* decision. Commentators have frequently noted the unusual sympathy that Albert Beveridge, author of the massive and classic *Life of John Marshall*,[17] displayed toward his subject, describing him as "Marshall's adoring biographer,"[18] but Clinton's worshipful treatment of Marshall the judge makes Beveridge appear downright captious. Whereas Beveridge characterizes the *Marbury* opinion as "a coup as bold in design and as daring in execution as that by which the Constitution had been framed,"[19] Clinton takes the position "that *Marbury* was not a political decision but was based on sound constitutional doctrine and existing legal precedent."[20] In Clinton's view, the power of judicial review that Marshall claimed was not the broad power to invalidate an act of Congress whenever a court was convinced that it did not comport with the Constitution, but nothing more than the authority "to disregard laws *only when such laws violate constitutional restrictions on judicial power*,"[21] as § 13 of the Judiciary Act of 1789,[22] declared invalid in *Marbury*, violated con-

---

[14] Id.

[15] Id at 221.

[16] Id at 260.

[17] Albert J. Beveridge, *The Life of John Marshall*, 4 vols (Houghton Mifflin, 1916–19).

[18] Donald O. Dewey, *Marshall versus Jefferson* 130 (Knopf, 1970).

[19] Beveridge, 3 *John Marshall* at 142 (cited in note 17).

[20] Clinton, *Marbury v. Madison* at 79 (cited in note 5).

[21] Id at 18. (Emphasis is in original.)

[22] Act of Sept 24, 1789, 1 Stat 73, 80–81.

stitutional restrictions on judicial power by giving the Supreme Court original jurisdiction in a case in which it was restricted to appellate jurisdiction by the terms of Article III, § 2. Clinton insists that it was the fault of future generations, particularly lawyers anxious to magnify judicial power for the protection of the interests of business and property, that Marshall's minimalist conception of judicial review was transmogrified by the late nineteenth century into its modern form, in which courts not only rule on the constitutionality of acts of Congress in matters unrelated to restrictions on judicial power, but undertake to assert final and unreviewable authority to invalidate both federal and state laws for policy considerations disguised as constitutional reasoning.[23]

Clinton appears to have aligned himself with an eccentric school of constitutional historians who, in the words of Leonard Levy, advance a theory—Levy terms it a "legal fiction" that is "particularly popular with conservatives"—that "romanticize[s] Supreme Court history" and, in the interest of "portray[ing] as satanical the modern Supreme Court," conjures up the idyllic notion that "the subjectivity of the Court used to amount to little, because the Justices, out of respect for the traditions of the bench, suppressed their own policy preferences and impersonally decided as the law told them to, without exercising private discretion."[24] Because this theory is charming, even if phony, and serves an ideological purpose to which it may appear justifiable to subordinate reality, Levy adds that "[a] lot of malarkey receives currency nowadays about the differences between Supreme Court decisions of the Court's classic early years and its decisions in recent constitutional history."[25] Robert Clinton has added considerably to the available quantity of malarkey.

C. SYLVIA SNOWISS

Sylvia Snowiss agrees with Clinton in perceiving a vast difference between judicial review as conceived at the time of *Marbury*, and judicial review as it is understood and practiced today, and, although she is not entirely consistent on this point, she seems to

---

[23] Clinton, *Marbury v. Madison* at 161–75.

[24] Leonard W. Levy, *Original Intent and the Framers' Constitution* 54 (Macmillan, 1988).

[25] Id at 55.

come down by arguing, like Clinton, that Marshall's *Marbury* opinion was a logical application of previously accepted views about the role of courts in a constitutional system. For Snowiss, as for Clinton, the changes in the institution of judicial review came later. Snowiss, however, does not see the pre-*Marbury* conception of judicial review as limiting it to use only in cases involving restrictions on judicial power. She does not even mention the possibility of such a restriction. Unlike O'Fallon, who is repelled by Marshall's faithfulness to the Federalists' distrust of the people, or Clinton, who is dismayed by the wholesale judicial involvement in policy evaluation that he sees as following necessarily from the modern form of judicial review, Snowiss does not seek to advance any causes or to propose a return to an earlier and happier day. To "reestablish the original distinctions," she writes, "is no longer possible or particularly desirable."[26]

For Snowiss, the changes that occurred were a result of the *legalization* of the Constitution, that is, the development of the conception of the Constitution as law (albeit supreme law) to be interpreted and expounded by the courts in the same way as ordinary law. Judicial review up to the time of *Marbury*, she contends, did not involve the courts in interpreting the meaning of specific constitutional provisions. While specific provisions were sometimes invoked, review by the courts involved only a consideration of whether the challenged legislation violated basic constitutional principles drawn from natural law and common law, and was not looked upon as a legal act, but as "a political act, a peaceful substitute for revolution," in that it provided a means by which the people could escape the operation of egregiously unjust laws.[27] That is, if the legislature should pass a "publicly verifiable, concededly unconstitutional act," appeal to the courts provided an opportunity for redress that was at once more efficacious than petitioning for repeal and less drastic than revolution.[28] Because review was a political, rather than a legal, act, courts in deciding constitutional cases might "resort to" the Constitution, or "regard" it, or "take notice of" it, but not expound it, and, she contends, they were careful to describe their actions in those terms.[29]

---

[26] Snowiss, *Judicial Review* at 10 (cited in note 6).

[27] Id at 50.

[28] Id at 51.

[29] Id at 58.

But, after *Marbury*, Snowiss argues, review under Marshall became a legal act, and the Constitution came to be treated as "supreme written law," subject to judicial interpretation just as any
ordinary law. Whereas Clinton sees Marshall as resolutely adhering
to a narrow conception of judicial review throughout his long tenure as Chief Justice, Snowiss sees him as the progenitor of the
modern form, who "single-handedly transformed judicial review
from enforcement of explicit fundamental law against conceded
violation into the open-ended exposition of supreme written law."[30]
Because Marshall based his constitutional decisionmaking on analysis of the words of the Constitution, and because the critical words
are generally ambiguous, this approach necessarily meant that, although Marshall never admitted it, declarations of unconstitutionality could no longer be limited to laws that were concededly and
verifiably invalid,[31] and would necessarily involve the courts in
choosing among competing views of public policy.[32] There is, of
course, a tremendous irony here. Contemporary opponents of judicial activism demand that courts restrain themselves from employing constitutional adjudication as a means of establishing public policy by adhering faithfully to the words of the Constitution
as those words were originally understood by their framers.[33] Yet,
as Professor Snowiss sees it, it was Marshall's insistence on "pain-
stakingly defin[ing] constitutional words"[34] that opened the door
for the modern form of judicial review in which judicial policymaking is inextricably intertwined with constitutional adjudication.

III. IN DEFENSE OF THE TRADITIONAL WISDOM REGARDING MARBURY

A. ON SNOWISS AND THE LEGALIZATION OF JUDICIAL REVIEW

Professor Snowiss's discussion of the significance of *Marbury v
Madison* in the development of judicial review may be dealt with

---

[30] Id at 123.

[31] Id at 122.

[32] Id at 103.

[33] See, for example, Robert H. Bork, *The Tempting of America* 143–46 (Free Press, 1990);
Gary L. McDowell, *Judicial Activism: Toward a Constitutional Solution*, in Gary L. McDowell,
ed, *Taking the Constitution Seriously* 139, 143–44 (Kendall/Hunt, 1981). Compare Leslie
Friedman Goldstein, *In Defense of the Text* (Rowman, 1991).

[34] Snowiss, *Judicial Review* at 121.

in advance of an examination of the political context in which that case arose because Snowiss never even alludes to the politics surrounding the *Marbury* decision, and it may be dealt with prior to a discussion of the arguments of Professors O'Fallon and Clinton because, in sharp contrast to those commentators, both of whom focus their attention on that decision and analyze Marshall's opinion in great detail, Snowiss speeds by it, providing only a brief and sketchy discussion. She obviously regards it as a case which, although possessing enormous symbolic importance, is only of secondary significance in the history of the development of judicial review.

Somewhere in the course of her study, she appears to have changed her mind about whether *Marbury* is to be regarded as an example of old-style or modern judicial review. Before she discusses the case, she suggests that it is the first decision of the modern era, and states that *Marbury* calls for "authoritative judicial application and interpretation of fundamental law."[35] She later reiterates that view, declaring that, in clear distinction to the understandings of the eighteenth century, *Marbury* derives judicial review "from a uniquely judicial relationship to supreme written law"[36]—the very hallmark of the modern approach as she describes it. But when she comes to her discussion of *Marbury*, her previous statements seem to have been forgotten, and the case becomes, with minor modifications, fully representative of eighteenth-century understandings.

Snowiss ignores all facets of the *Marbury* case except the concluding segment of Marshall's opinion in which he explains why courts must refuse to enforce unconstitutional laws. Her discussion of that segment both illustrates her argument and demonstrates why it is unconvincing. Marshall's case for the logical necessity of judicial review is essentially contained in the following celebrated passage, on which she focuses:[37]

> It is, emphatically, the province and duty of the judicial department, to say what the law is. Those who apply the rule to particular cases, must of necessity expound and interpret that rule. If two laws conflict with each other, the courts must

---

[35] Id at 49.

[36] Id at 55.

[37] *Marbury*, 1 Cranch at 177–78.

decide on the operation of each. So, if a law be in opposition
to the constitution; if both the law and the constitution apply
to a particular case, so that the court must decide that case,
conformable to the law, disregarding the constitution; or conformable to the constitution, disregarding the law; the court
must determine which of these conflicting rules governs the
case: this is of the very essence of judicial duty. If then, the
courts are to regard the constitution, and the constitution is
superior to any ordinary act of the legislature, the constitution,
and not such ordinary act, must govern the case to which they
both apply.

Despite Marshall's categorical statement that "[t]hose who apply
the rule to particular cases, must of necessity expound and interpret
that rule," Snowiss incredibly contends that, while this passage
asserted a judicial power "to expound ordinary law," it only
claimed for the courts the authority " 'to regard' the Constitution,"
but not to interpret or expound it, and that Marshall merely "used
the conflict of laws analogy to justify refusal to enforce a concededly unconstitutional act."[38] Snowiss does not deny that a constitution was universally regarded as fundamental or supreme law, or
that Marshall insisted that it was to be applied to decide particular
cases. What she does deny is that "the constitution and ordinary
law were cognizable in the same way or that the judicial responsibility to them was comparable."[39] She states that she is "convinced
that none of Marshall's contemporaries" understood the word "law"
to include the Constitution, and that it is only because of the mis-
understandings implanted in the minds of twentieth-century read-
ers by their familiarity with judicial review as practiced since *Marbury* that it is wrongly assumed that Marshall meant to include the
Constitution in his conception of the word "law."[40]

But that cannot be a misunderstanding. Marshall's argument is
not coherent unless the Constitution is included within the meaning of the word "law"—except where the words are used in contra-
distinction to emphasize the difference in status between fundamental and ordinary law. Snowiss's claim rests on her contention
that it was commonly understood in 1803 that judicial invocation
of a constitution was not a legal act, but "a political act, a peaceful

---

[38] Snowiss, *Judicial Review* at 111.

[39] Id at 49.

[40] Id at 111.

substitute for revolution."[41] However, Marshall does not suggest that the Court is performing a political act. He begins his argument by stating the premise that courts must "say what the law is," and then moves systematically to the conclusion that where a law is in conflict with the Constitution, the latter "must govern the case to which they both apply." Courts decide cases by "say[ing] what the law is," and if the Constitution is to "govern the case to which [it] appl[ies]," it must be because it is law. Nothing in Marshall's opinion provides a basis on which to conclude that he was claiming that courts must "say what the law is," and also must perform certain other important political acts. Indeed, in the political climate of 1803 (about which Snowiss is completely silent), where the dominant Republicans viewed the Federalist judiciary with great distrust because they recognized that the Justices possessed a penchant for acting politically rather than legally,[42] it would have been politically suicidal for the Court to claim a power to perform nonlegal political acts in order to protect the people against their popularly elected government. Moreover, in an earlier part of his opinion, Marshall pointedly noted that the Court had no power to engage in political acts.[43]

Had Snowiss paid the slightest attention to the earlier parts of Marshall's opinion, she would have noted that he arrived at his judgment that § 13 of the Judiciary Act of 1789 was unconstitutional not merely by giving "regard" to the Constitution and its overarching principles, but by doing exactly what she said he claimed no power to do in this case—deciding on a question of constitutionality by expounding the words of the Constitution. His conclusion was based on an intricate, and distinctly dubious, interpretation of the meaning of Article III, § 2, describing the scope of the original and appellate jurisdiction of the Supreme Court.[44]

The fundamental difficulty with Snowiss's overall argument is that she has tried too hard, to return to Alan Westin's phraseology, to "carry off a coup from the library stacks" and to "fashion a new thesis which will resolve this dispute once and for all."[45] Westin

---

[41] See text at note 27.

[42] See, for example, Richard E. Ellis, *The Jeffersonian Crisis* 30–35 (Oxford, 1971).

[43] *Marbury*, 1 Cranch at 165–66.

[44] Id at 173–76.

[45] See text at note 7.

predicted that it wouldn't be done, and Snowiss hasn't done it. And in her valiant effort to carry off her coup, she has stretched the evidence for her argument past the breaking point. The case cannot be made, as Snowiss tries to make it, that federal or state courts prior to Marshall, when they invoked their constitutions to provide a standard for determining whether they were obligated to give effect to a legislative act, did not regard themselves as interpreting law. Obviously, constitutions were not just like any ordinary law. For one thing, they were supreme, and thus were always to be preferred to legislative acts when they were cognizable in court. More significantly, constitutions, unlike ordinary acts, are addressed to governments, and thus a court, in invoking the constitution as a basis for refusal to enforce an act of the legislature, is necessarily exercising power over another branch of the government. But to state the obvious truth that courts act politically whenever they declare a legislative act unconstitutional is not to say that these political actions gain legitimacy as political actions. Legitimacy has been accorded to judicial review only because it is viewed as the application of law. Snowiss provides no examples of cases in which courts, in disregarding legislative acts, openly acknowledge that they are performing political acts. They always invoke the constitution as supreme law, although initially they might also have invoked natural law or common law principles reflecting fundamental requirements of natural justice. But the standard that is invoked is regarded as a rule binding on government, and therefore as a form of law. Courts can claim no other authority.

This has been recognized since the first stirrings of judicial willingness to disregard legislative acts. Sir Edward Coke's renowned dictum in *Dr. Bonham's Case* in 1610 asserted that "when an act of Parliament is against common right and reason, or repugnant, or impossible to be performed, the common law will controul it, and adjudge such act to be void."[46] The act may be "against common right and reason," but it is the fact that it thereby runs afoul of the common law that enables courts to declare it invalid.[47] As Coke explained to James I when the King suggested that he, too, pos-

---

[46] 8 Coke's Reports 107a, 118a (1610).

[47] See Edward S. Corwin, *The "Higher Law" Background of American Constitutional Law* 47 (Great Seal, 1955).

sessed common reason, the possession of outstanding reason is insufficient because cases that come before courts "are not to be decided by natural reason, but by the artificial reason and judgment of law."[48] Coke then added that "the law was the golden met-wand and measure to try the causes of the subjects."[49] Similarly, American courts were not about to abandon the advantages provided them by "the artificial reason and judgment of law" in order to make avowedly political decisions invalidating legislative directives, particularly since legislatures, as the elected representatives of the sovereign people, could rally substantial public support for their own political choices.[50] Snowiss suggests that when James Iredell noted in 1786 that the opportunity to present constitutional issues to the judgment of courts provided the public with a far less drastic alternative to revolution, he was tacitly acknowledging that judicial review was a political act.[51] However, with commendable candor, she also quotes a subsequent passage in Iredell's argument in which he states that the duty of courts "is to decide according to the *laws of the State*," and adds that "the constitution is a *law of the State*."[52]

Even if one concedes that Snowiss is right and that courts in this period (roughly 1787 to 1803) refrained from expounding their constitutions, but merely "resorted to" them, that distinction is

---

[48] *Prohibitions del Roy*, 12 Coke's Reports 63, 65 (1609). Coke noted that "the King was greatly offended" by this message. Id.

[49] Id.

[50] As Edward Corwin has noted, courts sought to deflect challenges to their authority to invalidate legislative acts by turning the concept of popular sovereignty around and treating the will of the people, as expressed in constitutions, as "the *highest* governing power." Edward S. Corwin, *The Doctrine of Judicial Review* 62 (Princeton, 1914). (Emphasis is in original.) He added that "the result of [this] development was to impart to the constitution the character, not simply of an act of revolution, but of *law*, in the true sense of the term, of a source of rules enforceable by the courts." Id. (Emphasis is in original.)

[51] Snowiss, *Judicial Review* at 50, citing a newspaper essay published by Iredell at the time he was, as an attorney, urging the courts of North Carolina to declare a state law unconstitutional. See Griffith McRee, ed, 2 *The Life and Correspondence of James Iredell* 145–49 (Appleton, 1857). The case about which Iredell was writing was *Bayard v Singleton*, 1 Martin 42 (NC 1787), in which a state law requiring courts summarily to dismiss claims brought against subsequent purchasers by persons whose property had been confiscated during the Revolutionary War was held to violate the constitutional right of a citizen "to a decision of his property by a trial by jury." Id at 45. This case is widely discussed as "the first reported state case in which an act was held void, as contrary to the terms of a written constitution." Charles Grove Haines, *The American Doctrine of Judicial Supremacy* 120 (U Calif, 2d ed 1932).

[52] Snowiss, *Judicial Review* at 48, quoting McRee, ed, 2 *Iredell Correspondence* at 148 (cited in note 51). (Emphasis is Iredell's.)

inherently unstable and could not be maintained for an extended period as long as courts regarded constitutions as a form of law relevant to the decision of cases before them. Ultimately, whatever law is going to govern a case before a court is going to have to be expounded by that court. Indeed, several of the defenders of judicial review in the pre-*Marbury* period whose work she cites seem to assert that courts are responsible for expounding the fundamental law of the constitution as well as ordinary law, but she is so determined not to let that defeat her argument that she tries very hard to show that these statements do not really mean what they say, and are actually compatible with the distinction that she insists was implicitly understood and accepted by everyone. For example, Judge St. George Tucker of the General Court of Virginia stated that because the constitution is "the first law of the land," it "must be resorted to on every occasion where it becomes necessary to expound *what the law is*."[53] Perhaps, as Snowiss contends, all that means is that knowledge of the constitution is necessary before judges can properly interpret legislative acts,[54] as called for by the canon of statutory construction that directs that statutes should be construed to avoid conflict with the constitution.[55] But, in the absence of a more explicit indication of this meaning, a more likely reading is that courts, who are expected to expound the law, must also have the responsibility for expounding, not merely ordinary laws, but also that which is "the first law of the land." And, although it would be hard to imagine a more express statement of the view that the judiciary has the duty of expounding the constitution than is provided by Alexander Hamilton in *Federalist 78*, Snowiss feels certain that he meant something other than what he wrote, which was: "A constitution is in fact, and must be, regarded by the judges as a fundamental law. It therefore belongs to them to ascertain its meaning as well as the meaning of any particular act proceeding from the legislative body."[56] Although she concedes that she is "not confident" that it can be demonstrated as surely as

---

[53] Snowiss, *Judicial Review* at 54, quoting the opinion of Judge St. George Tucker of the General Court of Virginia in *Kamper v Hawkins*, 1 Va Cases 20, 78 (1793). (Emphasis is Tucker's.)

[54] Snowiss, *Judicial Review* at 55.

[55] See, for example, Federalist 78 (Hamilton) in Jacob E. Cooke, ed, *The Federalist* 525–26 (Wesleyan, 1961).

[56] Id at 525.

it can be with regard to the statements of others,[57] Snowiss still insists that any "conclusion that Hamilton . . . was claiming authority for authoritative judicial exposition of the constitutional text as we know it today would . . . be premature."[58]

Underneath all of the rationalizations Snowiss throws up in support of her thesis there is a solid point. It is a modest point; it does not qualify as a coup, and certainly would not seem to require all of the elaborate theoretical trappings that are jerry-built around it and which serve only to obfuscate it, but it is an important point nevertheless. In insisting that Hamilton's statement that it was the duty of judges to ascertain the meaning of constitutions did not mean that it was the duty of judges to ascertain the meaning of constitutions, she noted that "Supreme Court justices before and through Marshall's tenure who sanctioned judicial authority over legislation routinely coupled this sanction with enunciation of the doubtful case rule, a rule that is a denial of judicial authority to expound the Constitution."[59] As a statement of fact that the Justices at that time "routinely" expressed the belief that laws should never be held to be unconstitutional in a doubtful case, Snowiss's observation is perfectly accurate. On the other hand, the assertion that "the doubtful case rule . . . is a denial of judicial authority to expound the Constitution" grossly overstates and distorts the element of truth that her statement contains. If the frequent invocation of the doubtful case rule is the basis of her conclusion that the judges of that period were not considered to have the authority to interpret constitutions, it is an unsound basis. The solid point that is contained in her argument is that the doubtful case rule was an important element in the legitimation of judicial review at the turn of the nineteenth century. But it does not follow that legitimation of the practice also required judges to deny that they possessed the authority to interpret the provisions of a constitution.

That the two points that Snowiss mistakenly conjoins are in fact unrelated is evident in that the very same Justices that Snowiss correctly identifies as articulating the doubtful case rule in their opinions also proceeded to expound the Constitution in the very same opinions in which they declared their adherence to the rule.

---

[57] Snowiss, *Judicial Review* at 81.

[58] Id at 79–80.

[59] Id at 80.

For example, in *Hylton v United States*,[60] involving a constitutional challenge to an act of Congress levying a tax on carriages,[61] Justice Chase stated that, whether or not the courts possessed the power of judicial review over acts of Congress (it remained for Marshall, seven years later, to pronounce that they did), he was "free to declare, that [he] will never exercise it, but in a very clear case,"[62] but he reached the conclusion that this was not a clear case only after examining the meaning of the relevant provisions of Article I, §§ 2, 8, and 9, to satisfy himself that they did not clearly prohibit Congress's imposition of the tax.[63] In *Calder v Bull*,[64] in which the Court responded negatively to the question whether the constitutional prohibition against ex post facto laws[65] prohibited a state legislature from enacting a law setting aside a decree of a probate court, or from generally enacting retroactive civil legislation, Justice Chase, in the sentence immediately preceding his reiteration of his declaration that he would "not decide any law to be void, but in a very clear case,"[66] declared that "I am under a necessity to give a construction or explanation of the words, '*ex post facto* law,' because they have not any certain meaning attached to them."[67] In the same case, Justice Iredell, who stated in his opinion that the power to declare a legislative act unconstitutional should never be exercised "but in a clear and urgent case,"[68] arrived at his judgment that the challenged law should be sustained only after examining the Constitution and concluding that "the true construction of the prohibition extends to criminal, not to civil cases."[69] Justice Paterson, concurring in the judgment of his colleagues, declared that decision of the case required "ascertaining the meaning of" the term *ex post facto* law,[70] although in *Cooper v Telfair*,[71] two years later, he

---

[60] 3 Dallas 171 (1796).

[61] Act of June 5, 1794. 1 Stat 373.

[62] 3 Dallas at 175.

[63] Id at 173–75.

[64] 3 Dallas 386 (1798).

[65] US Const, Art I, § 9 (prohibiting the enactment of ex post facto laws by Congress); Art I, § 10 (prohibiting their enactment by the states).

[66] 3 Dallas at 395.

[67] Id.

[68] Id at 399.

[69] Id.

[70] Id at 396.

[71] 4 Dallas 14 (1800).

maintained that "to authorize this court to pronounce any law void, it must be a clear and unequivocal breach of the constitution, not a doubtful and argumentative application."[72] Plainly, the doubtful case rule is not "a denial of judicial authority to expound the Constitution."

The significance of the doubtful case rule is not that it prevents judges from expounding the provisions of a constitution, but that it calls upon them not to ask *what is the true meaning of the constitution, but whether legislation is sustainable or not.*[73] This quotation, of course, is from the classic 1893 article by James Bradley Thayer urging courts to defer to the judgment of the legislature whenever a constitutional question was doubtful. Poor Thayer is treated pretty shabbily by Snowiss,[74] along with Edward Corwin,[75] and others among the most respected constitutional scholars of the past century and a half, down through Alexander Bickel[76] and John Hart Ely.[77] Since all of these scholars may be presumed to have read whatever Snowiss has read (she does not claim access to any new material), and some devoted their whole lives and careers to the study of the material that Snowiss relies on, it would be quite remarkable if all of them had misunderstood these writings and that she alone possessed the acuity to grasp the simple reality that no one before her had been able to perceive.

In the course of criticizing Thayer, Snowiss comments that his

---

[72] Id at 19.

[73] James B. Thayer, *The Origin and Scope of the American Doctrine of Constitutional Law*, 7 Harv L Rev 129, 150 (1893). (Emphasis is in original.)

[74] Snowiss describes Thayer's conception of the role of courts in constitutional adjudication as "a contradiction in terms." Snowiss, *Judicial Review* at 191. She characterizes his error as a simple failure to understand the distinction she has discovered between the coherence of the doubtful case rule where courts do not seek to expound the meaning of constitutions, and its incoherence where courts actually undertake to interpret them. Id at 188–94. See text at notes 78–83.

[75] She describes Corwin's explanation of the development of the theory and practice of judicial review as being "based on incomplete understanding." Snowiss, *Judicial Review* at 71.

[76] Bickel's analysis of the problems with modern judicial review—see Bickel, *Least Dangerous Branch* (cited in note 8)—suffers, Snowiss notes, because he undertook it "[w]ithout recognizing the depth of the differences between fundamental law and ordinary law, the unacknowledged legalization of the former, and the novelty of the mature practice." Snowiss, *Judicial Review* at 211.

[77] Ely's effort to legitimize judicial review where the political process has broken down to the disadvantage of inadequately represented groups—see John Hart Ely, *Democracy and Distrust* (Harvard, 1980)—Snowiss states, is regrettably reflective of the fact that "we persist unthinkingly in bringing to the Constitution the inappropriate enforcement conceptions of ordinary law." Snowiss, *Judicial Review* at 104.

"solution failed because the doubtful case rule is neither practical
nor internally coherent when applied to modern judicial review.
. . . Indeed, it was devised precisely because there was no judicial
authority whatever to apply or interpret the Constitution."[78] But,
in rejecting Thayer, Snowiss rejects herself. For the doubtful case
rule that she regards as incoherent in the modern era was no more
or less coherent when it was articulated by the Supreme Court in
Calder v Bull than it was when it was urged upon the courts by
Thayer. All that had changed was the willingness of the courts to
take the rule seriously. Between the time of *Calder* and of Thayer's
article, courts had abandoned the rule in favor of the practice of
deciding constitutional questions for themselves, but that did not
render the rule incoherent. It is perfectly circular to say, as Snowiss
does, that the rule can no longer be employed because courts are
no longer willing to employ it, and her assessment that if the rule
were "conscientiously followed it means the end of judicial review"[79] would not seem to be any more applicable today than in
1800. Snowiss bases that assessment on the belief that, nowadays,
given the courts' insistence on interpreting constitutions as if they
were ordinary law, all cases are doubtful and there is no such
thing as a concededly unconstitutional act,[80] whereas, in the years
immediately after independence, there was a period of revolutionary instability during which state legislatures took clearly unconstitutional actions such as confiscating the property of individuals
remaining loyal to England and denying them trial by jury.[81] (Since
then, the only acts that she would see as clearly satisfying the
doubtful case rule were those involved in the sweeping denial to
blacks of equal justice and the rights of citizenship in the years
prior to the civil rights revolution, and those providing for the
internment of Japanese during World War II.)[82] Without challenging the accuracy of her judgment that concededly unconstitutional
laws were more likely to be enacted 200 years ago, it is difficult to
understand why that should be relevant. The coherence and practical applicability of the doubtful case rule surely cannot turn on the
number of undoubtful cases that may be expected to arise.

---

[78] Id at 190.

[79] Id at 191.

[80] Id at 190–91.

[81] Id at 35.

[82] Id at 103.

It may be unlikely that judges, having experienced the heady satisfactions of deciding constitutional questions for themselves rather than deferring to the judgments of the legislature, would be willing to give up the practice, but they could certainly do so without logical inconsistency or incoherence. Among the things that "Thayer did not understand," Snowiss argues, was that the judges of the postrevolutionary era who asserted a power of judicial review "were in fact ready to abandon the practice if conditions warranted it. As an additional political responsibility outside the judiciary's assigned function, it could easily be abandoned. By Thayer's time, however, constitutional law was an established branch of law."[83] It is certainly true that novel practices are more easily abandoned than those that have become traditional and are looked upon as an integral part of the governmental system, but that has nothing to do with the question of whether the scope of the practice could be limited without logical incoherence. Moreover, it is not clear that when Thayer wrote in 1893, the practice of active judicial scrutiny of acts of Congress by the federal courts was so well established that application of the doubtful case rule would have been impracticable. (It may be that Snowiss is the one who has been led into misunderstanding by her familiarity with current practice.) In fact, when the Supreme Court in 1937 abandoned its activist stance of the previous fifty years, it adopted the doubtful case rule,[84] and maintained adherence to that rule with regard to acts of Congress for about twenty years without the slightest trace of logical incoherence.[85] When the rule was again discarded, it was

---

[83] Id at 191.

[84] See, for example, *West Coast Hotel Co. v Parrish*, 300 US 379, 399 (1937) (upholding the constitutionality of minimum-wage legislation): "Even if the wisdom of the policy be regarded as debatable and its effect uncertain, still the legislature is entitled to its judgment."

[85] In the eighteen years between 1937 and 1955, the Court declared acts of Congress unconstitutional in only three cases: *Tot v United States*, 319 US 463 (1943) (striking down § 2 (f) of the Federal Firearms Act of 1938, 52 Stat 1250, 1251, which provided that possession of a firearm by a convicted felon or fugitive from justice "shall be presumptive evidence" that the firearm was transported in interstate or foreign commerce); *United States v Lovett*, 328 US 303 (1946) (striking down as a bill of attainder § 304 of the Urgent Deficiency Appropriation Act of 1943, 57 Stat 431, 450, which provided that no appropriated funds be used to pay salary or compensation to three named individuals); *Bolling v Sharpe*, 347 US 497 (1954), a companion case to *Brown v Board of Education*, 347 US 483 (1954) (holding congressional authorization of racially segregated schools in the District of Columbia to be a violation of the Due Process Clause of the Fifth Amendment). These three decisions—declaring unconstitutional an irrational statutory presumption establishing an element of a criminal offense, a legislative act summarily removing three named individuals from the federal payroll, and a perpetuation of racial injustice—would all seem to qualify

not because it could not be logically or practicably maintained, but because the new majority of the Warren Court concluded that continued adherence to it would result in the denial of judicial protection essential to the preservation of civil rights and civil liberties. As a matter of logic, or even of practice, coherence is not a sometime thing. If the rule could have been applied coherently yesterday, it could be applied coherently today.

In any event, what is truly incoherent is Snowiss's claim that the doubtful case rule is inconsistent with the practice of judicial interpretation of constitutions because a case cannot be without doubt if some interpretation of the constitutional text is required. For if a constitution is to be applied by courts, judicial interpretation of it is unavoidable.[86] A law cannot be declared unconstitutional unless some meaning is assigned to the constitutional provision it is said to violate, and giving meaning is the definition of interpretation. In the clearest cases, an explicit act of interpretation may be dispensed with as superfluous, but interpretation occurs all the same. An argument in Judge Gibson's opinion in *Eakin v Raub* helps illuminate the error in Snowiss's assertion that "the doubtful case rule . . . is a denial of judicial authority to expound the Constitution." "[T]he abstract existence of a power," he wrote, "cannot depend on the clearness or obscurity of the case in which it is to be exercised; for that is a consideration that cannot present itself, before the question of the existence of the power shall have been determined."[87] In other words, unless a court can interpret a constitution, and thus provide an authoritative definition of its meaning, it cannot say that a law is *clearly* unconstitutional, just as it cannot say that it is clearly constitutional or that the question of

---

as instances in which invalidation of the challenged laws would be proper under the doubtful case rule as described by Snowiss. See Snowiss, *Judicial Review* at 34–38, 102–6.

[86] The classic statement of this proposition is, of course, John Marshall's in *Marbury v Madison:* "Those who apply the rule to particular cases, *must of necessity expound and interpret that rule.*" 1 Cranch at 177. (Emphasis added.) In this regard, one may also wonder whether the framers of the Constitution, who drafted the document at a time when, according to Snowiss, no one conceived that judicial interpretation of constitutions was permissible, could possibly have believed, when they conferred on state courts (and, by implication, federal courts, see text at notes 386–88) in Article VI the duty to invalidate state laws or constitutional provisions that conflicted with provisions of treaties, acts of Congress, or the United States Constitution in order to insure the primacy of federal law, that these courts could effectively discharge that vital responsibility, so critical to the success of the federal system, without expounding the meaning of the national Constitution (or, for that matter, the state constitutions).

[87] 12 Sergeant and Rawle 330, 352 (Pa 1825) (dissenting opinion).

constitutionality is doubtful, because the ability to draw any such conclusion is entirely dependent on a pre-existing recognition of its possession of a power to engage in interpretation.

What Snowiss's case boils down to, therefore, is nothing more than the unremarkable conclusion that courts used to profess adherence to the doubtful case rule (with apparent sincerity), but now do not adhere to the rule or even claim to. That is certainly an accurate observation, and it provides a major part of the explanation of why judicial review is such a different institution today than it was perceived to be in the concluding years of the eighteenth century. But Snowiss did not need to tell us that; we already knew it. The remainder of her argument is at best misleading. The doubtful case rule did not, as she contends, demonstrate that judicial review was a political act rather than an act of legal interpretation. The effect of the rule was to determine the outcome of most challenges to the validity of legislation, and its abandonment did not change the character of judicial review from a political to a legal doctrine. Judicial review, of course, *is* a political act, but it is a political act carried out through legal devices, including the interpretation of constitutional provisions. The original political act was the assertion of power to refuse to enforce an unconstitutional law in the first place. The moment that was done, the application of that power to the decision of a specific case became a legal act—in that it necessarily and absolutely inescapably required the courts to ascertain the meaning of both the challenged law and the constitutional provision it was said to violate. The legal nature of the decision (and the need for interpretation) cannot depend on the clarity of the case or the fact that there may or may not be universal acceptance of the soundness of the court's judgment.

Thus, the heart of Snowiss's thesis—that decisions on constitutionality were not regarded as legal acts requiring interpretation until the time of John Marshall, who was "single-handedly" responsible for the legalization of judicial review by his insistence upon interpreting constitutional language and who thus established the basis for modern judicial review—is simply wrong. Marshall's accomplishment was not to make interpretation a part of the process of judicial review, for judicial review and constitutional interpretation are inseparable, but was successfully to proclaim the judiciary's possession of the power in *Marbury v Madison* and then to abandon the doubtful case rule that had previously been regarded as an essential ingredient of any legitimate use of the power. Snowiss is correct in noting that under the Marshall Court the character of judicial review changed both qualitatively and quantitatively, and that Marshall was able to bring about these changes without admitting that any changes had occurred—a mark of his extraordinary political acumen—but she attributes the changes, not to the demise of the doubtful case rule, but to the incorporation of constitutional interpretation into the practice of judicial review. In so doing, she goes beyond making the worthwhile, but relatively undramatic, point that her study should have led her to, in an attempt to fashion a thesis about the historical development of judicial review that no one before her had been able to discover. It appears that they were unable to discover it because it wasn't there. She has striven "to carry off a coup from the library stacks," but, in the end, her coup fails.

B. THE POLITICAL CONTEXT OF MARBURY V MADISON

A serious deficiency in Snowiss's study is her attempt to analyze Marshall's opinion in *Marbury v Madison* without any reference to the political context in which the case arose, for it is impossible to understand that decision without recognizing that it was inextricably linked, historically and politically, with the intense partisan struggles that surrounded the Republican ouster of the Federalists from control of the presidency and Congress in the election of 1800, and, more directly, with the Republican ouster of Federalist judges from the circuit courts created by the Judiciary Act of 1801[88] through the Repeal Act of 1802.[89] Robert Clinton also does not attribute any significance to these historical circumstances in the shaping of Marshall's *Marbury* opinion, but he at least admits that there was a political struggle taking place at the time. On the other hand, a great strength of James O'Fallon's essay lies in his perception that the *Marbury* decision is a creature of the politics of the period. For to discuss *Marbury* without placing it in its political

---

[88] Act of Feb 13, 1801, 2 Stat 89.

[89] Act of March 8, 1802, 2 Stat 132.

context is exactly like trying to analyze Hamlet's behavior without attaching any significance to his father's murder.

The *Marbury* decision, as has often been observed, grew out of the unhappy embroilment of the federal judiciary in the angry political disputes that wracked the constitutional order at the turn of the nineteenth century.[90] By 1800, as Charles Warren has aptly summarized, the disagreements between Federalists and Jeffersonians were becoming increasingly rancorous, and "[i]nto this boiling political caldron, the Court had been drawn [between 1798 and 1800], by reason of the fact that all the delicate questions on which the Federalist and the Anti-Federalist parties were so sharply divided—neutrality, Federal common law criminal jurisdiction, the right of expatriation, the constitutionality of the Alien and Sedition laws—had been presented in cases arising before the Judges of the Court sitting on Circuit, and on each of these questions the decisions had been invariably adverse to the view held by the Anti-Federalists."[91] Federalist judges, and particularly members of the Supreme Court, most notably Samuel Chase, who was ultimately to become the target of an impeachment attempt, had outraged the Jeffersonians by the partisan nature of their charges to juries in Sedition Act cases and by their willingness also to invoke a federal common law of crimes against outspoken critics of Federalist policies.[92] The Republicans, therefore, had reason to be dismayed when, after their electoral defeat in 1800, the lame-duck Federalist Congress enacted a law, originally proposed prior to the election,[93] creating new circuit courts and sixteen circuit court judgeships to

---

[90] See Ellis, *Jeffersonian Crisis* at 36–68 (cited in note 42); Charles Grove Haines, *The Role of the Supreme Court in American Government and Politics, 1789–1835* 223–58 (U Calif, 1944); George L. Haskins and Herbert A. Johnson, *Foundations of Power: John Marshall 1801–15*, 2 *History of the Supreme Court of the United States* 183–86 (Macmillan, 1981).

[91] Charles Warren, 1 *The Supreme Court in United States History* 158–59 (Little, Brown, 1922). See also a dramatic cataloguing of the Republicans' grievances over the actions of the Federalist judiciary in John Bach McMaster, 2 *A History of the People of the United States* 533 (Appleton, 1885).

[92] See, generally, James Morton Smith, *Freedom's Fetters* (Cornell, 1956). When the House of Representatives voted to impeach Justice Chase in 1804, among the articles of impeachment were charges of prejudicial misbehavior at trials, the issuance of a partisan charge to a jury in a trial of a Republican editor, and an effort to coerce a grand jury to return an indictment against the editors of a newspaper hostile to the Federalist administration. See Ellis, *Jeffersonian Crisis* at 76–82 (cited in note 42).

[93] See Haskins and Johnson, *Foundations of Power* at 109–10 (cited in note 90); Kathryn Turner, *Federalist Policy and the Judiciary Act of 1801*, 22 Wm & Mary Q (3d Ser) 3, 32 (1965).

which President John Adams could and did appoint loyal Federalists putatively guaranteed tenure during good behavior by the
terms of Article III.

This law, the Judiciary Act of 1801, is often dismissed as a
purely partisan measure with no virtues except in terms of the
political interests of the Federalist party,[94] but careful historians
have demonstrated that the law, in fact, "was not conceived in the
exigencies of defeat to compensate for that catastrophe."[95] The key
provisions of the act—eliminating the highly onerous circuit-riding
duties of Supreme Court Justices and creating separate circuit
courts in order to end the unfortunate arrangement under which
the same judges who presided at trials would be responsible for
participating in the review of their own decisions on appeal—had
been urged upon Congress by members of the Court[96] and by the
Attorney General[97] almost as soon as the federal court system created by the Judiciary Act of 1789 went into effect, but Congress
apparently did not place court reform high on its list of priorities
until political realities underscored its desirability for the Federalists. However, the Federalists' hearts were hardly pure in 1801,
and, even though the law had more than ample merit to justify
its enactment without regard to its political advantages,[98] only a

---

[94] See, for example, Haines, *Role of Supreme Court* at 180–81 (cited in note 90), citing
William A. Sutherland, *Politics and the Supreme Court*, 48 Am L Rev 390, 394 (1914): "[I]t
is perfectly clear that it was a pure case of political intrigue, of a defeated party striving to
retain some semblance of power by intrenching [sic] itself in the Judiciary."

[95] Turner, 22 Wm & Mary Q at 32 (cited in note 93). See also Haskins and Johnson,
Foundations of Power at 108–10 (cited in note 90).

[96] Haskins and Johnson, *Foundations of Power* at 111. A letter to Congress in 1792, signed
by all members of the Court, asking for a modification of the existing system, is reprinted
id at 112–13.

[97] For a lengthy summary of the report of Attorney General Edmund Randolph to the
House of Representatives in 1790 urging Congress to remedy the defects in the Judiciary
Act of 1789, see id at 116–20.

[98] Professor Turner's detailed analysis of the act demonstrates that, in addition to improv-
ing the organization of the federal judiciary, in § 11 it expanded the jurisdiction of the lower
federal courts, provided the circuit courts with general federal question jurisdiction that the
federal courts then lacked (and, following repeal, were to continue to lack until 1875), and
made the federal courts generally more accessible to litigants, particularly in diversity suits
and land disputes. See Turner, 22 Wm & Mary Q at 21–31 (cited in note 93). Gouverneur
Morris wrote at the time of its passage that the law "answers the double purpose of bringing
justice near to men's doors, and of giving additional fibres to the root of government." Jared
Sparks, ed, 3 *The Life of Gouverneur Morris* 153 (Gray & Bowen, 1832). But, of course, from
the standpoint of the Republicans, that was one of its most glaring defects. By expanding
federal jurisdiction and making it easier for litigants to take their cases to federal court, it
threatened to expand federal authority at the expense of the states. See O'Fallon, 44 Stan
L Rev at 223 (cited in note 4).

desperate concern for political gain can explain the frantic rush to pass it after the 1800 elections[99] and the frantic rush of the Adams administration to fill the newly created circuit court vacancies with Federalist judges before the inauguration of Thomas Jefferson.[100]

It was less the creation of circuit judgeships than the "midnight" appointment of Federalist judges to these positions, raising the specter of a bench filled with partisans of the ilk of Samuel Chase, that particularly infuriated the Republicans and made it unlikely that they would decline the opportunity to retaliate. John Bach McMaster, the outstanding nineteenth-century historian, has persuasively commented that, "[h]ad the appointment of these officers been left to Jefferson, the Republicans would undoubtedly have found little fault with the law. Twenty-three well paid places [including district court judgeships] would thus have been added to the list of offices within the President's gift. But they would have gained what they valued far more than places: a control of the inferior United States courts."[101] But, as it was, control of the inferior courts was in the hands of the Federalists, and, since the Judiciary Act reduced the number of Supreme Court Justices from six to five,[102] Jefferson would also have to wait until two Federalists left the Court before having the opportunity to make his first appointment.[103] Thus, when control of the political branches of the government changed hands less than a month after the Judiciary Act became law, it was only a matter of time before the Republi-

---

[99] After its passage by the House of Representatives on January 20, 1801, the bill was pushed through the Senate without amendment for fear that the delay that would have been created by returning it to the House of Representatives for subsequent reconciliation would leave insufficient time to fill the judgeships with Federalists prior to Jefferson's accession to office on March 4. See Turner, 22 Wm & Mary Q at 19–20 (cited in note 93).

[100] See Kathryn Turner, *The Midnight Judges*, 109 U Pa L Rev 494 (1961).

[101] McMaster, 2 *History* at 533 (cited in note 91).

[102] Act of Feb 13, 1801, § 3, 2 Stat 89.

[103] After Oliver Ellsworth resigned as Chief Justice in December, 1800, and John Jay declined reappointment to that office, news of which reached President Adams in mid-January, 1801, while the Judiciary Act was approaching passage, the selection of John Marshall to be the new Chief Justice had to be hastily made, and had to be confirmed by the Senate without extended delay (even though the Federalists in the Senate delayed as long as they could in the vain hope that they could persuade Adams to appoint Marshall as Associate Justice and elevate William Paterson to the position of Chief Justice), or else the ironic effect of the act's reduction of the size of the Supreme Court would have been to deny an appointment to Adams, rather than Jefferson. See Kathryn Turner, *The Appointment of Chief Justice Marshall*, 17 Wm & Mary Q (3d Ser) 143, 153–60 (1960).

cans reacted, and it only remained to be seen what the character of that reaction would be.

Because the new Republican Congress did not convene until December 1801, no immediate legislative response was threatened, and Jefferson's inaugural address displayed a remarkably conciliatory tone.[104] Even on such fundamentally partisan matters as removing Federalist officeholders to assign their positions to loyal Republicans (for which no precedent existed to establish a standard of behavior), Jefferson disappointed many of his supporters by adopting a moderate policy rather than engaging in wholesale removals. He was prepared to remove all civil officers serving at the pleasure of the President whose appointments were made after the results of the presidential election were known, as well as those who had abused the authority of their offices, and, because a Republican presence in the judicial system was seen as essential, all federal attorneys and marshals were to be replaced by Republicans, but, aside from that, Federalist appointees could remain in their positions.[105] Nevertheless, one quite minor element of Jefferson's policy with regard to Federalist officeholders was to take on enormous significance, both in its impact on immediate political developments and in its historical consequences.

Two weeks after the passage of the Judiciary Act of 1801, the Federalist Congress enacted legislation providing a judicial system for the District of Columbia, creating a circuit court to be composed of three judges who would serve during good behavior,[106] and authorizing the appointment of "such number of discreet persons to be justices of the peace, as the President of the United States shall from time to time think expedient, to continue in office five years."[107] When this act became law, only four full days remained in the tenure of the Adams administration, and the scramble to take the necessary formal and informal steps to fill these positions before the allotted time of the administration expired must have had something of the flavor of a Keystone Cops chase.

---

[104] See Dumas Malone, *Jefferson the President: First Term, 1801–1805*, 4 *Jefferson and His Time* 17–28 (Little, Brown, 1970).

[105] See letter to William B. Giles, March 23, 1801, in Andrew A. Lipscomb, ed, 10 *The Writings of Thomas Jefferson* 238–39 (Thos Jefferson Mem Assn, 1904).

[106] Act of Feb 27, 1801, § 3, 2 Stat 103, 105.

[107] Id, § 11, 2 Stat 107.

But, within three days, Adams had sent the names of the three circuit court judges that he had selected and no fewer than forty-two justices of the peace to the Senate, which acted promptly to confirm them in the brief time remaining before its adjournment.[108] It fell to John Marshall, who remained on as Secretary of State after his confirmation as Chief Justice, to insure that the commissions of the substantial number of last-minute presidential appointees were authenticated by the Seal of the United States and delivered to the individuals concerned, but several of the commissions of the newly appointed justices of the peace were undelivered, although signed and sealed. Failure of delivery was to prove more of a legal than a practical issue since Jefferson treated all forty-two justice of the peace appointments as null whether or not the commissions had been delivered, although, in accordance with the conciliatory spirit manifested at the outset of his presidential term, he promptly reappointed twenty-five of the forty-two individuals that Adams had selected, together with five persons of his own choosing, evidently in the quite reasonable belief that thirty was an ample number of these officers to serve the needs of the District of Columbia.[109] Among the seventeen who were denied office by Jefferson's action was William Marbury who, together with three others, commenced litigation in late December 1801 to seek restoration to these offices.

The immediate political significance of Marbury's attempt to obtain a judicial resolution of his dispute with the administration was that it cemented Republican resolve to repeal the Judiciary Act of 1801. Repeal was certainly a course favored by many Republicans,[110] and that it was also on the mind of Thomas Jefferson is attested to by passages in his correspondence during the spring of 1801. In a letter to Archibald Stuart in April requesting suggestions for the names of good Republicans to replace the Adams appointees as attorney and marshal for the western district of Virginia, whose appointments he regarded as "nullities," he wrote, distinguishing between the removal of these appointees and Adams's judicial appointments: "The judge, of course, stands till the law shall be repealed, which we trust will be at the next Con-

---

[108] See Turner, 109 U Pa L Rev at 517–19 (cited in note 100).

[109] See Malone, *Jefferson the President* at 73 (cited in note 104).

[110] See Warren, 1 *Supreme Court History* at 193–94 (cited in note 91).

gress."[111] And, in the same month, he wrote to James Monroe that it was "highly probable the law [would] be repealed at the next meeting of Congress."[112] But Jefferson's December 8 message to Congress upon its reconvening barely alluded to the federal courts and made no recommendations for any specific action. All he said on the subject was that the federal judiciary "and especially that portion of it recently erected, will of course present itself to the contemplation of Congress," and, to assist Congress in its contemplation, he announced that he would separately present data on the workloads of the federal courts so that it "may be able to judge of the proportion which the institution bears to the business it has to perform."[113] However brief and unspecific these remarks may have been, they can certainly be understood as a broad hint to Congress that it might want to think about removing unneeded judges from the federal payroll for reasons of economy if not of politics,[114] one obvious way to do that being to repeal the Judiciary Act and thereby eliminate the judgeships it created.[115] George Haskins, who makes no effort to disguise his antipathy to Jefferson, has no doubt that he was determined to secure the repeal of the Judiciary Act well before the time Congress convened.[116] Other historians, however, believe that Jefferson had not firmly committed himself to repeal even at the time of his December 8 message.[117]

---

[111] Lipscomb, ed, 10 *Writings of Jefferson* at 257 (cited in note 105).

[112] Quoted in Haskins and Johnson, *Foundations of Power* at 152 (cited in note 90).

[113] Lipscomb, ed, 3 *Writings of Jefferson* at 337 (cited in note 105).

[114] Bringing economy to the federal government was a major element of the Republican program; see Malone, *Jefferson the President* at 99–106 (cited in note 104). But, then as now, considerations of economy were not separable from considerations of politics; spending, or not spending, money has political effects. As Malone notes, economy was essential to Jefferson's "concept of a limited federal government." Id at 102.

[115] Albert Beveridge was certain that Jefferson's "lieutenants in House and Senate understood their orders and were eager to execute them." Beveridge, 3 *John Marshall* at 51 (cited in note 17).

[116] Haskins and Johnson, *Foundations of Power* at 152 (cited in note 90). Albert Beveridge, equally antipathetic to Jefferson, seems to take the same view. See Beveridge, 3 *John Marshall* at 18–22 (cited in note 17). In addition to the references to repeal in his April correspondence, Haskins understandably finds persuasive the fact that Jefferson was able to present Congress, at the time it reconvened, with data on the workloads of the federal courts. "These statistics," he observed, "could not have been collected overnight, as their detail indicates." Haskins and Johnson, *Foundations of Power* at 105. In any event, it appears that the data were, to a large extent, erroneous, and Jefferson was obliged to offer a correction, albeit "too late to have any effect on the strictly party vote by which the 1802 Bill was passed." Id.

[117] For example, Charles Warren wrote that: "Although on December 8, 1801, . . . Jefferson . . . had made a mild reference to a reform of the judicial system, no final decision had been reached as to a repeal of the Circuit Court Act of 1801." Warren, 1 *Supreme Court*

In any event, if Jefferson had not been absolutely committed to repeal in early December, he became committed as soon as the Supreme Court indicated its willingness to hear Marbury's complaint.

Although, as Dumas Malone has noted, "there was no doubt whatsoever in [Jefferson's] mind about the desirability of repealing the judiciary law,"[118] there is a difference between perceiving an end as desirable and concluding that it would be politically prudent or constitutionally proper to try to bring it about. The President may still have been vacillating in mid-December, but the act after which he no longer harbored any thought of pursuing a moderate course and forgoing repeal was the Supreme Court's preliminary response to Marbury's suit demanding delivery of his commission. At that point, any doubt that the Federalist judiciary constituted a grave enough threat to warrant direct action against it appears to have vanished.[119]

On December 16, just one day over a week after Jefferson's message to Congress, Secretary of State James Madison was served with notice that a motion would be made on the following day in the Supreme Court for a rule requiring him to show cause why a writ of mandamus should not issue directing delivery of the commissions as justices of the peace that, although signed and sealed, had been withheld from Marbury and his co-plaintiffs.[120] As an unidentified member of Congress explained to a friend in a letter, part of which was published in the Philadelphia *Aurora*, Madison "took no notice" and "an ex parte argument before their honors"[121]

History at 204 (cited in note 91). Jefferson's biographer, Dumas Malone, has suggested that rather than systematically working to carry through a carefully orchestrated plan to achieve a desired end, "[i]t seems more likely that [Jefferson] took one step without being sure of or necessarily committed to the next one," Malone, *Jefferson the President* at 115–16 (cited in note 104), adding that "[w]e may doubt if anybody knew, or if the President had determined his future course." Id at 119. Richard Ellis has similarly concluded that Jefferson "had not really made up his mind as to what he wanted to do about the federal judiciary," Ellis, *Jeffersonian Crisis* at 34 (cited in note 42), for "he had no fixed or definite policy." Id at 35.

[118] Malone, *Jefferson the President* at 119.

[119] Another action that did much to convince the Republicans that the judiciary was a continuing threat occurred when the two midnight appointees serving on the District of Columbia circuit court—William Cranch and Marshall's brother, James—sought, although unsuccessfully, at the first term of this court in June, 1801, to institute a common-law prosecution of a Republican publisher for criticism of the activities of the courts. See Warren, 1 *Supreme Court History* at 195–98 (cited in note 91).

[120] National Intelligencer (Dec 21, 1801).

[121] Philadelphia Aurora (Dec 30, 1801).

was conducted the next day[122] on the motion for the rule. On the day after this argument, the Court granted the rule and directed Madison to show cause on the fourth day of the Court's next term why a writ of mandamus should not issue.[123]

The Republican reaction to the Court's temerity in ordering the Secretary of State to appear before it to show cause why it should not rule on the legality of the actions of the President was explosive. Although the editor of the *Aurora* could see that the Court's action was an empty threat, "all *fume* which can excite no more than a judicious irritation,"[124] others were less prepared to be so cavalier in dismissing what the unidentified member of Congress described as "a high-handed exertion of Judiciary power" whose "true intention . . . is to stigmatize the executive."[125] It was now absolutely clear to Republican leaders that the Federalist judges were prepared to make mischievous use of their powers to frustrate wherever possible the achievement of Republican policy goals, and that direct action against them was therefore mandatory.

It is an interesting question why the Federalists should have undertaken a course of action so well calculated to outrage the Republicans and to invite a hostile reaction over an issue so utterly unimportant. In view of the pettiness of the office of justice of the peace, there is little reason to believe that even the litigants themselves were terribly concerned.[126] Since no other explanation seems

---

[122] The argument before the Court on Marbury's motion was held on December 17, 1801. Charles Warren erroneously sets the date of this argument as December 21, Warren, 1 *Supreme Court History* at 202, which would place it after, rather than before, the angry statements made by Jefferson quoted in text at notes 132–33, and Donald Dewey, apparently following Warren, makes the same mistake. Dewey, *Marshall versus Jefferson* at 96 (cited in note 18). Irwin Rhodes comes closer, unaccountably setting the date as December 18, see Irwin S. Rhodes, *Marbury versus Madison Revisited,* 33 U Cin L Rev 23, 29 (1964), but that is still a day off. Richard Ellis cites the correct day. Ellis, *Jeffersonian Crisis* at 43 (cited in note 42). That the date could not be December 21 is shown by the fact that the letter from the unidentified member of Congress, cited in text at note 121, is dated December 21, and identifies the proceedings as having taken place "a few days ago." That the date was in fact December 17 is shown by the accounts in both the *National Intelligencer* and the Philadelphia *Aurora.* The *Aurora* story is datelined December 17, and speaks of the argument on the motion for a rule to show cause as having taken place "this day." Philadelphia Aurora (Dec 22, 1801). The account in the *National Intelligencer* of Monday, December 21, 1801, describes the notice to Secretary of State Madison as having been given "[o]n Wednesday last," which would be December 16, and the argument on the motion as having occurred on "[t]he next day," which would be December 17.

[123] National Intelligencer (Dec 21, 1801).

[124] Philadelphia Aurora (Dec 22, 1801). (Emphasis is in original.)

[125] Id, Dec 30, 1801.

[126] See Dewey, *Marshall versus Jefferson* at 81–83 (cited in note 18).

credible, the perception that the Court's acceptance of the suit was intended to create an opportunity "to stigmatize the executive" would appear to be sound, and it is also likely that, as Richard Ellis has surmised, the Federalists "hoped a show of determination would deter the Republicans on the court issue."[127] Charles Warren regarded as well founded the Republicans' assumption that the institution of the proceedings was "a purely political move on the part of the Federalist Party . . . to scare off their opponents from attempting to repeal the Judiciary Law."[128] But, rather than scaring the Republicans off, the effect of the Court's action was to end any chance that repeal of the Judiciary Act could be avoided. A Republican leader, Senator Stevens Thomson Mason of Virginia, declared that the effort "to assail the President (through the sides of Mr. Madison) . . . has excited a very general indignation and will secure the repeal of the Judiciary Law of the last session, about the propriety of which some of our Republican friends were hesitating."[129] Robert McCloskey, commenting on the failure to convict Samuel Chase on impeachment charges in 1805, suggested that a principal reason for the failure was that, in the years between 1801 and 1805, the Supreme Court had chosen a very cautious and circumspect course so that it was no longer regarded as a serious threat to Jeffersonian democracy.[130] But that was a lesson that John Marshall, the new Chief Justice, and his colleagues on the Court had not yet learned in the closing days of 1801, and, in all likelihood, the federal judiciary paid a price for its brief moment of aggressiveness.

On December 19, the day after the Court issued its show cause order,[131] Thomas Jefferson made clear how much of a danger he then regarded the courts to be, writing that the opponents of his party "have retired into the judiciary as a stronghold. There the

---

[127] Ellis, *Jeffersonian Crisis* at 44 (cited in note 42).

[128] Warren, 1 *Supreme Court History* at 205 (cited in note 91).

[129] Quoted id at 204. Warren concluded that the hesitation was due to concern over the constitutionality of repeal. Id.

[130] Robert G. McCloskey, *The American Supreme Court* 47 (U Chicago, 1960).

[131] O'Fallon states that this letter was written "on the day that the Supreme Court issued its show cause order in *Marbury*." O'Fallon, 44 Stan L Rev at 222 (cited in note 4). Richard Ellis also states that the letter was written "on the very day" that the Court issued the order. Ellis, *Jeffersonian Crisis* at 44 (cited in note 42). However, the letter is dated December 19, and the Court's order was issued on Friday, December 18.

remains of federalism are to be preserved and fed from the treasury, and from that battery all the works of republicanism are to be beaten down and erased."[132] He then added, in direct reference to the Judiciary Act: "By a fraudulent use of the Constitution, which has made judges irremovable, they have multiplied useless judges merely to strengthen their phalanx."[133] On the following day, he noted that altercations were to be anticipated when Congress set about the task of "lopping off the parasitical plant engrafted at the last session on the judiciary body."[134] Senator John Breckinridge[135] of Kentucky, who described the Court's show cause order as "the most daring attack which the annals of Federalism have yet exhibited,"[136] announced that his response would be to introduce a bill to deal with the judiciary,[137] which he did by moving for repeal of the 1801 Judiciary Act on January 6, 1802.[138] After a vigorous and impressive debate over principles, politics, and the Constitution that Albert Beveridge was to describe as "one of the permanently notable engagements in American legislative history,"[139] the bill squeaked through the Senate (where the Republican majority was precarious because only one-third of that body had turned over in 1800) by a single vote in February[140] and then passed the House by a more comfortable margin one month later on a virtually strict party-line division.[141]

Before the end of April 1802, Congress had enacted another bill related to the judiciary. It amended the now revived court system established by the Judiciary Act of 1789[142] and also provided that

---

[132] Lipscomb, ed, 10 *Writings of Jefferson* at 302 (cited in note 105).

[133] Id.

[134] Id at 304.

[135] In O'Fallon's article, as in much, if not most, of the literature, and, indeed, in the *Annals of Congress*, the Senator's name is incorrectly spelled Breckenridge. The biographer of Senator Breckinridge's grandson, John Cabell Breckinridge, who became Vice-President of the United States under James Buchanan and was the South's candidate for President in the election of 1860, notes that the family name had originally been spelled Breckenridge, but that, "for some unknown reason," the Senator changed the spelling while a young man. William C. Davis, *Breckinridge* 7 (LSU Press, 1974).

[136] Quoted in Warren, 1 *Supreme Court History* at 204 (cited in note 91).

[137] Annals of Congress, 7th Cong, 1st Sess c 21 (1802).

[138] Id at c 23.

[139] Beveridge, 3 *John Marshall* at 50 (cited in note 17).

[140] Annals of Congress, 7th Cong, 1st Sess c 183 (1802).

[141] Id at c 982.

[142] Act of Apr 29, 1802, § 4, 2 Stat 156, 157–58.

the Supreme Court would have only one term each year—to be held in February.[143] The effect of this provision was to delay the next session of the Supreme Court until February 1803, and the Federalists naturally saw this as a transparent effort to deny the Court the opportunity to declare the Repeal Act unconstitutional "until the act has gone into full execution, and the excitement of the public mind is abated."[144] But they could not prevent its passage.[145] Not only did the new law prevent the question of the constitutionality of the Repeal Act from coming before the Court for almost a year, it similarly postponed further proceedings in the case of *Marbury v Madison*.

The Federalist judges were thus left to contemplate whether and how to respond to these legislative assaults. The dilemma was particularly acute for the circuit court judges who were apparently to be judges no longer after July 1, the effective date of the abolition of their courts.[146] Alexander Hamilton, the acknowledged leader of the Federalist party, wrote to James Bayard, the Federalist leader in the House of Representatives, in April 1802, urging that the necessary steps be taken "to bring as soon as possible the repeal of the Judiciary law before the Supreme Court."[147] Oliver Wolcott, former Secretary of the Treasury, who had been appointed by Adams to the new Second Circuit and thus was soon to be without an office, suggested a potentially quicker way of bringing matters to a head. If the Justices of the Supreme Court regarded repeal as unconstitutional, they could refuse to serve as circuit judges (which revival of the 1789 system was again to require them to do), leaving the way open for the pre-existing circuit judges to continue to serve.[148]

Of course, any attempt to solve the problem by obtaining a judicial test of the law was doomed to failure unless the Justices of the Supreme Court were prepared to take the risks necessary to

---

[143] Id, § 1, 2 Stat 156.

[144] Annals of Congress, 7th Cong, 1st Sess c 1235 (1802) (remarks of Representative James A. Bayard of Delaware).

[145] The Republicans denied that their rearrangement of the Court's schedule was infected with any devious motivation. See, for example, id at c 1229 (remarks of Representative Joseph H. Nicholson of Maryland).

[146] 2 Stat 132.

[147] Harold C. Syrett, ed, 25 *The Papers of Alexander Hamilton* 609 (Columbia, 1977).

[148] Letter of Oliver Wolcott to Roger Griswold, March 23, 1802, quoted in Wythe Holt, *"[I]f the Courts have firmness enough to render the decision:,"* in Wythe Holt and David A. Nourse, *Egbert Benson* 9, 11 (2d Cir Bicentennial Comm, 1987).

declare the repeal void. Representative John Rutledge, Jr., of South
Carolina (son of the momentary Chief Justice), who was sent to
visit John Marshall in Richmond to find out if the Federalists could
expect support from the Court, reported to Bayard on March 26
that "the firmness of the Supreme Court may be depended on
should the business be brought before 'em."[149] But, as Marshall
pondered the Republicans' willingness to delay the Court's next
term until 1803, he began to have understandable reservations
about a confrontation. He wrote on April 5 that "[t]he power which
could pass [the repeal] act can fail at nothing."[150] On April 19,
Marshall apparently wrote letters to all of his colleagues on the
Court, seeking their opinions on whether they could, consistently
with the Constitution, undertake the duties as circuit judges which
would be reverting to them.[151] To Paterson, he added the unnecessary reminder that "[t]his is a subject not to be lightly resolv[e]d
on. The consequences of refusing to carry the law into effect may
be very serious."[152] Wythe Holt has persuasively contended that
Marshall's decision to focus the attention of the Justices on the
issue of the validity of their taking on responsibilities as circuit
judges (which had been settled practice between 1789 and 1801)
rather than on the issue of the validity of terminating the appointments of federal judges who, under the Constitution, are to "hold
their Offices during good Behaviour,"[153] led to a result which
"while not preordained was predictable. Having in mind the extreme personal and political dangers which confrontation would
place them in, and given no encouragement by their new young
politically astute Chief," the Justices capitulated.[154]

Samuel Chase did not. He asked Marshall to bring the members

[149] Quoted id at 10.

[150] Letter to Oliver Wolcott, Apr 5, 1802, in Charles F. Hobson and Fredrika J. Teute,
eds, 6 *The Papers of John Marshall* 104 (U North Carolina, 1990).

[151] The letters to Cushing and Paterson have been preserved. See id at 108–9.

[152] Id at 109. Just how serious they may have been is suggested by the ominous remarks
of Caesar Augustus Rodney of Delaware, soon to be Attorney General of the United States,
who wrote in early 1803 that the judges should understand "that there is a boundary which
they cannot pass with impunity. If they cross the Rubicon, they may repent when it will
be too late to return. Judicial supremacy may be made to bow before the strong arm of
Legislative authority. We shall discover who is master of the ship. Whether men appointed
for life or the immediate representatives of the people agreeably to the Constitution are to
give laws to the community." Quoted in Warren, 1 *Supreme Court History* at 228–29 (cited
in note 91).

[153] US Const, Art III, § 1.

[154] Holt, *"[I]f the Courts"* at 14 (cited in note 148).

of the Court together in Washington during the summer so that they could have a face-to-face exchange of views and decide on a common course, for "an individual Judge, declining to take a Circuit, must sink under" the burden of having to make such a decision alone.[155] But Justices Washington, Paterson, and Cushing were content to follow Marshall's lead and to serve as circuit judges on the ground that that was a practice whose constitutional validity was settled.[156] Justice Cushing wrote that Chase could have his summer meeting by himself.[157] With this decision, the fate of the circuit judges was sealed, for, as Chase had correctly noted in his letter, if a member of the Court "executes the Office of Circuit Judge, I think he, thereby, decides that the repealing was *constitutional*,"[158] and Marshall advised Bayard that the circuit courts should close up their business and quietly adjourn,[159] advice that they apparently heeded. Eleven of the deposed judges submitted a memorial to Congress, pointing out their constitutional entitlement to serve during good behavior and asking for continued compensation and the assignment of appropriate duties, but they were not given the courtesy of a response.[160]

When the Supreme Court finally reconvened in February 1803, one of the cases it had before it, in addition to *Marbury v Madison*, was *Stuart v Laird*,[161] a case that Federalists had hoped would be a vehicle for a Supreme Court declaration that the Repeal Act was unconstitutional. The case involved an order issued by Chief Jus-

---

[155] Letter of Samuel Chase to John Marshall, Apr 24, 1802, in Hobson and Teute, eds, 6 *Papers of Marshall* at 116 (cited in note 150).

[156] Haskins and Johnson, *Foundations of Power* at 177 (cited in note 90).

[157] Id.

[158] Hobson and Teute, eds, 6 *Papers of Marshall* at 114 (cited in note 150). (Emphasis is in original.)

[159] See Morton Borden, *The Federalism of James A. Bayard* 125 (Columbia, 1954). Bayard promptly apprised Hamilton of Marshall's advice, writing to him on April 25, 1802, to report that he had learned that "the Chief J. . . . considers the late repealing act as operative in depriving the Judges of all power derived under the act repealed. . . . It has been considered here [in Washington] that the most adviseable course for the Circuit Courts to pursue will be at the end of their ensuing Session to adjourn generally, & to leave what remains to be done to the Supreme Court." Syrett, ed, 25 *Papers of Hamilton* at 614 (cited in note 147). Charles Warren cites this letter, but identifies it as being from Hamilton to Charles Cotesworth Pinckney on April 25. See Warren, 1 *Supreme Court History* at 224–25 n 1 (cited in note 91).

[160] Haskins and Johnson, *Foundations of Power* at 178–80 (cited in note 90). The memorial is quoted in full, id at 178–79.

[161] 1 Cranch 299 (1803).

tice Marshall, sitting as circuit judge, to execute a judgment of the
old circuit court that had been abolished by the Repeal Act. The
defendant argued that the new circuit court had no authority to
issue the order because the Repeal Act's abolition of the old court
was unconstitutional, and, therefore, jurisdiction remained with
it, and Marshall was improperly sitting.[162] Marshall rejected this
argument, and his decision was appealed to the Supreme Court,
where he recused himself because it was his ruling that was under
review. Charles Lee, a former Attorney General, who was also
Marbury's counsel, argued the case for the plaintiff in error, his
principal contention being that the Repeal Act was void because
Congress had "displace[d] judges who have been guilty of no misbehavior in their offices."[163] However, the Court refused to deviate
from its insistence upon dealing with the question of the constitutionality of repeal only in terms of whether Supreme Court Justices
could be assigned duties as circuit judges. Justice Paterson, writing
for the Court, disposed of this enormously important case in an
opinion consisting of only three short paragraphs, without even
alluding to, let alone addressing, the issue of the constitutionality
of the summary removal of Article III judges. After stating the
facts of the case, he declared only that Congress had the power to
reassign jurisdiction over a case from one court to another, and
that it was too late to challenge the validity of the practice by
which Supreme Court Justices could sit on circuit courts since this
had become an accepted practice under the first Judiciary Act.[164]

Of this decision, Charles Warren has written that: "No more
striking example of the non-partisanship of the American Judiciary
can be found than this decision by a Court composed wholly of
Federalists, upholding, contrary to its personal and political views,
a detested Republican measure."[165] No more striking example of
silliness can be found in commentary on the American judiciary
than this statement. *Stuart v Laird* was manifestly not an example
of nonpartisan fairness, but of a craven unwillingness on the part
of the Court even to admit the existence of the principal constitutional issue presented by the case. The Court refused to consider

---

[162] Id at 300–02.

[163] Id at 303.

[164] Id at 309.

[165] Warren, 1 *Supreme Court History* at 272 (cited in note 91).

this constitutional question even though the author of its opinion had earlier categorically written that he believed the law to be invalid for precisely the reasons that he here chose not even to mention.[166] The Court acted out of a fully justified fear of the political consequences of doing otherwise, not out of an overriding compulsion to reach the correct legal result at whatever sacrifice of their own political preferences.

The decision in *Stuart v Laird* was handed down exactly one week after Marshall delivered the opinion of the Court in *Marbury v Madison* on February 24, 1803. As can be seen from the nature of the *Laird* decision, the Court's sensitivity to its political environment had changed dramatically from the previous term (a full fourteen months earlier) when it seemed willing, even eager, to do battle with the Jefferson administration. But events had shown that the consequences of such rashness could be dire. The Court's readiness to inquire into the conduct of the affairs of the executive, and to intervene in those affairs, as manifested by its order to the Secretary of State to show cause why a writ of mandamus should not be issued to direct him in the performance of the duties of his office, had spurred the Republicans to enact legislation repealing the Federalists' Judiciary Act and keeping the Supreme Court out of session for over a year. Federalist circuit judges were required to yield their offices without effective protest despite their constitutional guarantee of life tenure, and Federalist Supreme Court Justices were obliged supinely to return to circuit riding and to refrain from raising a constitutional challenge to the law that brought these ends about. As Professor O'Fallon properly observes, "*Marbury* was born out of political defeat."[167] Furthermore, to add to the apprehensions of the Justices, the Republicans began to brandish the weapon of impeachment. On February 4, just prior to the commencement of the Court's term, President Jefferson transmitted information to the House of Representatives so that it could consider whether to bring articles of impeachment against John Pickering, district judge for the district of New Hampshire.[168] Pickering had become mentally ill and utterly incapable of dis-

---

[166] Holt, "*[I]f the Courts*" at 14–15, 71 n 35 (cited in note 148).

[167] O'Fallon, 44 Stan L Rev at 259 (cited in note 4).

[168] Annals of Congress, 7th Cong, 2d Sess c 460 (1803).

charging his judicial responsibilities,[169] but impeachment was the
ultimate power that Congress could use against the courts, and any
precedent for its use was an overhanging threat to the Justices. The
Marbury case was thus argued and decided under that additional
cloud.[170]

The Supreme Court turned to its consideration of the *Marbury*
case on the third day of its February term.[171] Ominously, just as
Madison "took no notice" of the Court's proceedings in this matter
in the previous term, he did not deign to acknowledge the propriety
of the proceedings at this stage either. Although the Attorney General, Levi Lincoln, appeared as a witness[172]—he had been interim
Secretary of State after Marshall left the office until Madison could
assume it[173]—he explained that he had no instructions to participate as counsel, and no one was present to argue on Madison's
behalf.[174] The administration manifestly regarded the entire proceeding as a nullity. It paid no heed to it while it was taking place,
and clearly had not the slightest intention of paying heed to any
order or writ that the Court might issue. Unfortunately, because
the Justices were together in Washington, there is no record of the
deliberations leading up to their decision—as there was with regard
to their decision not to challenge the Repeal Act by refusing to
resume their duties as circuit judges. The editors of Marshall's
papers confirm that "[t]he only documentary evidence of the justices' motives in deciding the case in the manner they did is the
opinion itself."[175] But, given the Justices' keen awareness of the
possible political consequences of their actions, as reflected in their
discussions of strategy in the aftermath of the passage of the Repeal
Act, and their knowledge of their own vulnerability and that of
the entire judicial branch in the face of the hostility of Congress
and the administration, it cannot be doubted that they fully understood, even before the case was called on the docket, or even before

---

[169] See Haskins and Johnson, *Foundations of Power* at 211–14 (cited in note 90).

[170] See id at 213–14.

[171] See Rhodes, 33 U Cin L Rev at 31 (cited in note 122).

[172] *Marbury*, 1 Cranch at 143. The testimony of the witnesses, including Attorney General
Lincoln, regarding the existence of the commissions and how they were handled, is summarized id at 141–46.

[173] See Dewey, *Marshall versus Jefferson* at 103–4 (cited in note 18).

[174] See Warren, 1 *Supreme Court History* at 237 n 1 (cited in note 91).

[175] Hobson and Teute, eds, 6 *Papers of Marshall* at 162 (cited in note 150).

the term began, that they could no more issue a writ of mandamus to Secretary Madison than they could declare the Repeal Act unconstitutional and order the circuit judges restored to their offices. If necessary, they could have decided the case in Madison's favor on the merits by ruling that Marbury and his co-plaintiffs had no legal entitlement to the delivery of their commissions, but that would have been to concede too much to the authority of the executive and was therefore unacceptable unless no other alternative was available.

The way out must have been immediately obvious to all of the members of the Court. Judges understand that they can, by refusing jurisdiction, escape the necessity of deciding a case in which any ruling on the merits would have unfortunate ramifications. It would therefore have been simple, and sensible, to hold that § 13 of the Judiciary Act of 1789, authorizing the Supreme Court to issue "writs of *mandamus* . . . to any courts appointed, or persons holding office, under the authority of the United States,"[176] conferred no jurisdiction on the Court in this case, on the ground that that provision only gave the Court authority to issue such writs in cases in which it otherwise had jurisdiction, and that this case, which presented an instance of original jurisdiction, was not properly before it because Article III only allows the Court to take original jurisdiction in cases involving states or emissaries of foreign governments.[177] But it was probably not immediately obvious to all members of the Court that they might also escape jurisdiction by the more complicated, and more dubious, route of ruling that the statute *did* authorize the Supreme Court to issue writs of mandamus in cases of this sort, but that it was unconstitutional in that it improperly sought to confer original jurisdiction on the Court. By choosing this way of avoiding the assumption of jurisdiction, the Court could assert the power of judicial review.

It may be argued that there was no need for the Supreme Court to go out of its way to assert the authority to declare acts of Congress unconstitutional because the existence of this power was all but universally conceded. O'Fallon makes precisely this point.[178]

---

[176] 1 Stat 73, 81.

[177] For a brief but trenchant discussion of this point, see Levy, *Original Intent* at 82 (cited in note 24).

[178] O'Fallon, 44 Stan L Rev at 227 n 30 (cited in note 4).

But such an argument does not take adequate account of the political situation in which the Federalist judiciary found itself in 1803. Even though it is true, as Charles Warren has demonstrated, that "in every Congress from 1789 to 1802, the power of the Court to hold Acts of Congress invalid was not only recognized but endorsed by members of both political parties,—Federalist and Anti-Federalist alike,"[179] and that the Republicans had hoped that the courts would invalidate congressional legislation that they particularly opposed[180] — particularly the national bank,[181] the excise tax on carriages,[182] and the Alien[183] and Sedition[184] Acts—the hostility between the judiciary and the political branches that had developed as a result of the midnight appointments and the repeal of the Judiciary Act of 1801 made the climate for an exercise of judicial review far different than it had been in the preceding decade. It was one thing for Republicans to call for the invalidation of Federalist legislation, but it was quite another thing for them to contemplate courts comprised of Federalist judges gutting Republican policies on questionable constitutional grounds.

As Charles Warren also pointed out, many Republicans in the Repeal Act debate answered the Federalists' assertions that the courts would declare unconstitutional a law that would strip federal judges of their offices with a flat denial that courts had any authority to set limits on the powers of Congress.[185] Marshall obviously recognized that an attempt on the part of the Court to declare the Repeal Act unconstitutional would have brought terrible retribution, and almost certainly concluded that at a time when the dominant political forces of the nation stood vehemently opposed to any exercise of judicial authority that could affect the direction of public policy—opposition that was likely to remain obdurate for the foreseeable future—it was important to invoke the power of judicial review in order to establish a precedent for its later use and to

---

[179] Warren, *Congress, Constitution and Court* at 97 (cited in note 12).

[180] Id at 105–22.

[181] Act of Feb 25, 1791, 1 Stat 191.

[182] Act of June 5, 1794, 1 Stat 373.

[183] Act of June 18, 1798, 1 Stat 566. Act of June 25, 1798, 1 Stat 570. Act of July 6, 1798, 1 Stat 577.

[184] Act of July 14, 1798, 1 Stat 596.

[185] Warren, 1 *Supreme Court History* at 215–16 (cited in note 91).

include in the Reports of the Supreme Court a statement of the reasoning by which the power could be shown to be absolutely necessary. Thus, since judicial review could not safely have been used to invalidate a law that the Republicans cared about, it was necessary to find a law that the Republicans did not care about. And what more perfect law could have been found for this purpose than § 13 of the Judiciary Act of 1789? Here was a law that no one cared about. It was of any interest only to lawyers, and, while its invalidation might be thought to be a denial by the Court of some of its own authority,[186] it was not even that to any significant extent because § 13 was only held to be unconstitutional as applied, and the Court retained full power under the law to issue writs of mandamus whenever it found it proper to do so in a case within the scope of its constitutional jurisdiction. So the Court did not merely declare itself to be without jurisdiction. While it was about it, it seized the opportunity to declare an act of Congress unconstitutional. Small wonder that the *Marbury* opinion has been described as "a masterpiece of political strategy."[187]

At no point in *Marbury* does the Supreme Court settle for good enough when it can have it all. In at least three respects, it could have contented itself with half a loaf, which would have been ample for its immediate needs, but in each instance it gathered up for future use much more than it needed at the moment. First, as noted above, it could have escaped the political dilemma that the case presented by simply ruling that no jurisdiction had been conferred on it, but it chose to accomplish this purpose by declaring an act of Congress unconstitutional. Second, the power of judicial review that it claimed for itself could have been merely the power to disregard acts of Congress that authorize or direct courts to take action inconsistent with the Constitution's directives to the judiciary. This is the least controversial use of the power of judicial review,[188] and was the basis of the judgments of three separate circuit courts in the one previous instance in which federal courts had refused to comply with an act of Congress—an act which

---

[186] See McCloskey, *American Supreme Court* at 42 (cited in note 130).

[187] Carl Brent Swisher, *The Growth of Constitutional Power in the United States* 55 (U Chicago, 1946).

[188] In *Eakin v Raub*, Judge Gibson noted that he fully accepted the authority of courts to employ judicial review in that context, even in the absence of a grant of power in the constitution or laws. 12 Sergeant and Rawle at 353. See text at note 434.

sought to confer upon the courts the nonjudicial function of assessing the eligibility of disabled Revolutionary War veterans for pensions, subject to review by the Secretary of War and Congress,[189]
a duty that the courts declined to perform because it conflicted
with the Constitution's grant to the judiciary of only judicial
power.[190] Since § 13, according to the Court's interpretation, assigned jurisdiction to the Supreme Court that it was not constitutionally authorized to accept, Marshall could have contented himself with claiming a power to review acts of Congress only in this
context. But not a word in Marshall's opinion expresses or implies
any such limitation on the power of review that he there asserts as
belonging to the judiciary, and, of the three hypothetical examples
he gives of situations in which judicial review would be essential
to protect against legislative abuses, two have nothing to do with
legislation in conflict with constitutional restrictions on the powers
of the courts.[191]

Third, the Court was not satisfied with having escaped the necessity of ruling on the merits by holding itself to be without jurisdiction, even though it did so by declaring an act of Congress unconstitutional, for, had it merely announced itself to be without
jurisdiction and dismissed the suit, it would have passed up an
opportunity to proclaim to the country that Jefferson and Madison
were acting unlawfully and in disregard of the vested rights of
individuals. Therefore, instead of following the ordinary course of
ruling first on the threshold question of its jurisdiction, the Court
first ruled on the merits, declaring that the withholding of the
undelivered commissions was "not warranted by law, but violative
of a vested legal right,"[192] and adding that courts were not forbidden "to issue a *mandamus* [to the head of an executive department],
directing the performance of a duty, not depending on executive
discretion, but on particular acts of congress, and the general prin-

---

[189] Act of March 23, 1792, 1 Stat 243.

[190] See *Hayburn's Case*, 2 Dallas 409 (1792).

[191] See 1 Cranch at 179. The first example was an export tax enacted in disregard of the
prohibition of such taxes in Art I, § 9. The second was a bill of attainder or ex post facto
law, both of which are forbidden to Congress in Art I, § 9. Only the third example, where
Congress would "declare one witness, or a confession out of court, sufficient for conviction"
of treason, id, despite the requirement of Art III, § 3, that treason convictions be based
"on the Testimony of two Witnesses to the same overt Act, or on Confession in open
Court," involves the violation of a constitutional provision addressed to the courts.

[192] Id at 162.

ciples of law."[193] Such a bold assertion of judicial authority to issue orders to cabinet officers directing them to take action contrary to presidential instructions was quite remarkable given the political climate of 1803, but Marshall and the Court could make these extraordinary pronouncements in this case with relative impunity because they were secure in the knowledge that they would later excuse themselves from having to back up their words with an order by finding themselves to be without jurisdiction in the case they had just decided.

In his excellent analysis of the *Marbury* opinion, William Van Alstyne charitably suggests that the Court's action in putting the jurisdictional question last may have been justified because, as the Court dealt with it, the jurisdictional question involved a ruling on the constitutionality of an act of Congress, and the decision on this constitutional question (which is to be avoided whenever possible) would have become unnecessary if the Court had found, on the merits, that the writ of mandamus could not or should not be issued.[194] That suggestion, which Van Alstyne does not in fact endorse, was not made for the first time in his article; it has also appeared in the dissenting opinion of Justice McReynolds in *Myers v United States*,[195] and was emphatically rejected at that time by Andrew McLaughlin, who noted that it could hardly be sound doctrine "that a court, rather than declare an act of Congress void because the act is beyond the constitutional competence of Congress, may go itself beyond its competence" by discussing and deciding on rights and duties in a case in which it was without jurisdiction.[196]

There is the puzzling comment of George Haskins that Marshall's discussion of the merits in *Marbury* was not "an 'excursus' unnecessary to the opinion" because "[t]o Marshall and his brethren then on the Court, this part of the opinion was probably the more important of the two portions. Carefully read, it can be seen not as a skewing round of the case in order to preach at Jefferson, but rather as a statesmanlike justification both of the decision that

---

[193] Id at 170.

[194] William W. Van Alstyne, *A Critical Guide to Marbury v. Madison*, 1969 Duke L J 1, 7–8.

[195] 272 US 52, 217–20 (1926).

[196] Andrew C. McLaughlin, *Marbury v. Madison Again*, 14 ABA J 155, 156 (1928).

Marbury had acquired a vested right and of the extent of judicial power to protect individual rights."[197] But that comment is not worthy of being taken seriously. No doubt Haskins was right in identifying the discussion of the merits as the more important part of the opinion for Marshall and the Court, for it was more important to the Court at that moment in its history to undermine the legitimacy of the actions of its powerful political opponents than to invoke the power of judicial review, however useful and prudent it may have been to create an early precedent for its exercise when opposition to it was beginning to find vigorous expression. But to argue that it was "statesmanlike" and not unnecessary for the Court to issue pronouncements on significant constitutional questions relating to the separation of powers without first pausing to determine whether it had jurisdiction in the case at hand is to argue that it would be "statesmanlike" and proper for the Court to announce an advisory opinion whenever it has anything important to say.[198] Surely it would have been at least as "statesmanlike" and important for the Court, in *Stuart v Laird*, one week later, to have announced a judgment on the vital issue of whether Congress could abolish Article III courts and strip federal judges of their offices, especially as that question had been argued by the parties[199] and was ripe for decision in a case in which the Court clearly had jurisdiction. That particular "statesmanlike" ruling, however, would have led to the political imbroglio that the Court wanted to avoid. What the Court in *Marbury* perceived is that it was better to be "statesmanlike" when doing so would not require the acquiescence of its political enemies.

In any event, it is entirely misleading to think of the Court in *Marbury* as being faced with a dilemma in which it had to make

---

[197] Haskins and Johnson, *Foundations of Power* at 193 (cited in note 90).

[198] For the classic statement of the contrary position, see Felix Frankfurter, *A Note on Advisory Opinions*, 37 Harv L Rev 1002 (1924). In the summer of 1793, almost ten years before Marshall's opinion in *Marbury v Madison*, Secretary of State Jefferson, on behalf of President Washington, asked permission of the Court to refer to them for their advice questions of law that were faced by the executive but that were "presented under circumstances *which do not give a cognizance of them to the tribunals of the country.*" Henry P. Johnston, ed, 3 *The Correspondence and Public Papers of John Jay* 486 (Putnam, 1891). (Emphasis is in original.) The Court responded regretfully that it felt it should not do so since considerations of separation of powers "afford strong arguments against the propriety of our extra-judicially deciding the questions alluded to." Id at 488. See also David P. Currie, *The Constitution in the Supreme Court: The First Hundred Years. 1789–1888* 11–14 (U Chicago, 1985).

[199] 1 Cranch at 302–8.

the painful choice of either looking at the merits in order to avoid the constitutional question that would be presented if it turned first to the jurisdictional issue, or else deciding the jurisdictional question in order to avoid the sensitive issues that a ruling on the merits would make it necessary to address. For the point is that the Court made no choice; it did both. It avoided neither issue. Even if, in its deliberations, it had reflected on the merits in a sincere belief that a decision on those grounds might obviate the need to face a constitutional question, once it had determined that the constitutional question could not be avoided in this way, it was under no obligation to include its conclusions on the merits of the case in its final opinion, particularly since the discussion of the merits involved the Court in the resolution of constitutional questions scarcely less vital than those involved in the jurisdictional issue.[200] The Court ruled on both questions because it was to its political advantage to do so. As Wythe Holt has observed, by ruling on both questions, Marshall was "upholding the authority of the federal judiciary over *both* other branches of government,"[201] Marshall and the Court seized every opportunity for political advantage that the case offered, those that were not easily seen as well as those that were. The only step that the Court refrained from taking was the issuance of the writ, for that was the one step that political reality foreclosed.

C. ON O'FALLON AND THE UNIMPORTANCE OF MARBURY V MADISON

James O'Fallon begins his analysis of *Marbury* with an examination of the debate over the Repeal Act of 1802 in order to demonstrate that Marshall's opinion was directly derived from the Federalist arguments articulated there.[202] The Republicans argued for repeal on grounds of economy and efficiency.[203] Surely, they con-

---

[200] See McLaughlin, 14 ABA J at 156 (cited in note 196). See also text at note 280.

[201] Holt, *"[I]f the Courts"* at 21 (cited in note 148). (Emphasis added.)

[202] O'Fallon is in complete agreement with Albert Beveridge, who concluded that "an understanding of Marbury *vs.* Madison is impossible without a thorough knowledge of the debate in Congress which preceded and largely caused that epochal decision." Beveridge, 3 *John Marshall* at 75 (cited in note 17).

[203] While economy and efficiency were convenient and attractive reasons to justify repeal, and while curtailing the size of the federal government was undoubtedly seen as an additional happy incident of undoing the Federalists' judicial plan, it is hard not to believe that the principal motivation underlying the Republican effort was that the repeal would remove Federalists from the judiciary, not that it would reduce the total number of federal judges. For a cogent statement of that view, see McMaster, 2 *History* at 533 (cited in note 91),

tended, the framers of the Constitution did not mean to require
the retention of judges for whom there was not enough work, and,
since it was conceded that Congress could abolish courts—as the
Federalists had abolished the circuit courts constituted under the
Judiciary Act of 1789—there could be no constitutional obligation
to continue to pay the salaries of judges of nonexistent courts.[204]
As John Randolph stated the case in the House of Representatives,
the constitutional guarantee of judicial independence protects
judges against being removed for political reasons so that they
could be replaced with others of differing political views, but, if
the removal is intended to serve "the general good by abolishing
useless offices, it is a Constitutional act."[205] While the Federalists
responded to these arguments by citing the inefficiencies associated
with requiring Supreme Court Justices to travel to assigned circuits
in order to sit as circuit court judges, as well as the potential for
unfairness created by a system in which the same judges who presided at trials could participate in hearing appeals from their own
trial rulings,[206] their principal response was to mount the obvious
challenge to repeal—that it ignored the constitutional guarantee of
life tenure for federal judges.

The dispute over the constitutionality of repeal led directly to
the question of how such disagreements were to be resolved, and
thus to the issue of the legitimacy of judicial review. As O'Fallon
points out, the "Federalists claimed that judicial review by an independent judiciary was necessary to protect the people from their
own worst enemies—themselves—[and] they also appealed to the
people as authors of the Constitution that established limits on the

---

quoted in text at note 101. Congress could have prevented the federal courts from taking
over an undue amount of state judicial business simply by restricting their jurisdiction—and,
as O'Fallon points out, Samuel Chase, seeing the danger of this, argued that Congress is
required to vest in some federal court or other all of the jurisdiction that Article III authorizes
the federal judiciary to assume. O'Fallon, 44 Stan L Rev at 254 (cited in note 4), citing
Chase's letter to Marshall of April 24, 1802, quoted in Hobson and Teute, eds, 6 *Papers of
Marshall* at 110–11 (cited in note 150).

[204] See O'Fallon, 44 Stan L Rev at 226.

[205] Annals of Congress, 7th Cong, 1st Sess c 658 (1802), quoted in O'Fallon, 44 Stan L
Rev at 226.

[206] Id at 224. See, in particular, the comments by James Bayard, Federalist leader in the
House of Representatives, Annals of Congress, 7th Cong, 1st Sess cc 616–27 (1802), and
by Gouverneur Morris in the Senate, id at cc 37–38. Bayard also noted that the data
presented by Jefferson to show that creation by the Federalists of additional judicial offices
was uneconomical and inefficient because of an insufficient federal judicial workload were
erroneous. Id at cc 627–28. See note 116.

authority of their agent, the legislature."[207] On the other hand, Representative Robert Williams of North Carolina stated the Republican view, which categorically rejected the claim that judicial power was needed to protect the people from themselves: "Are the people to be told that they are so lost to a sense of their own interests, so ignorant and regardless of them, that they must take fifteen or twenty men to guard them from themselves?"[208] If so, he continued, "the sovereignty of the Government [is] to be swallowed up in the vortex of the Judiciary. . . . [T]he people [will] be astonished to hear that their laws depend upon the will of the judges, who are themselves independent of all law."[209] Republicans also used the example of the enthusiastic enforcement of the Sedition Act by Federalist judges as evidence of the futility of the hope that the judiciary can be counted on to protect individual rights against government attack, and warned that an unchecked judiciary prepared to employ a common law of crimes—as federal judges then were—as a vehicle to suppress public expression of discontent was at least as likely to abridge the rights of the people as to protect them.[210]

Whatever the merits of these competing arguments, the Republicans had the votes to pass the Repeal Act and the political strength to discourage any effort by the Federalist judiciary to prevent the law from taking effect, either by ruling that it was unconstitutional or by a refusal by the Justices of the Supreme Court to resume their circuit riding duties.[211] The only remaining opportunity for a judicial response was the case of *Marbury v Madison*, but circumspection was essential here also. The effrontery of the Marshall Court in calling on Madison to show cause why a writ of mandamus should not be issued against him, and thereby suggesting that the judiciary had the authority to direct the conduct of the affairs of the executive branch, had played a major role in convincing the

[207] O'Fallon, 44 Stan L Rev at 235. See the remarks of Gouverneur Morris, Annals of Congress, 7th Cong, 1st Sess c 41 (1802).

[208] Id at c 532, quoted in O'Fallon, 44 Stan L Rev at 236.

[209] Annals of Congress, 7th Cong, 1st Sess c 532.

[210] These points were made with great force and effect by John Randolph of Roanoke in the House debate. See Annals of Congress, 7th Cong, 1st Sess cc 661–62, quoted in O'Fallon, 44 Stan L Rev at 237–38.

[211] See text at notes 146–60.

Republicans that it was essential to strike at the courts through repeal of the lame-duck Judiciary Act, and, in the repeal debate, they had made it clear that any attempt to follow through on that suggestion would not be received with equanimity.[212] But, as *Marbury* was the only basket that the Supreme Court possessed, Marshall and his colleagues decided to put all their eggs in it. If the Court did not actually do anything in *Marbury* that could be defied, nullified, or repudiated by the executive or Congress, it might be able to make an authoritative (although empty) assertion of judicial power both to command Congress to comply with the Constitution and to command the President to comply with the Constitution and the laws. From the standpoint of the Court, given the political situation in which it found itself, assertion of authority over the executive branch was no less vital to its purpose than the assertion of the power of judicial review.

O'Fallon is therefore plainly correct in ascribing great importance to the first part of Marshall's opinion in *Marbury*, in which he concludes that the administration had acted wrongfully in withholding the commissions and that the courts have power to compel executive officers to carry out duties required of them by law. But he is not correct in dismissing as insignificant the second, and more celebrated, part of the opinion, in which Marshall makes his case for judicial review.[213] *Both* aspects of the opinion were of crucial importance for the Court's political purposes, and the fact that many Republicans conceded the existence of the power of judicial review did not make the establishment of a precedent for its exercise less essential given the hostility toward the judiciary then being exhibited by the dominant political forces in the nation.[214]

O'Fallon demonstrates how the reasoning of the first part of

---

[212] See Warren, 1 *Supreme Court History* at 207 (cited in note 91).

[213] O'Fallon's entire discussion of this aspect of Marshall's opinion is limited to one brief dismissive paragraph, O'Fallon, 44 Stan L Rev at 256–57, and a footnote in which he observes that "[t]he weaknesses in Marshall's argument are notorious" and require no further elaboration. Id at 256 n 129.

[214] Although O'Fallon suggests that the Court's assertion of the power of judicial review was without particular significance, id at 227 n 30, Charles Grove Haines, for one, has persuasively argued otherwise: "Marshall, who was an ardent Federalist, was aware of a rising opposition to the theory of judicial control over legislation, and he no doubt concluded that the wavering opinions on federal judicial supremacy needed to be replaced by a positive and unmistakable assertion of authority." Haines, *American Doctrine* at 202 (cited in note 51). See also Beveridge, 3 *John Marshall*, at 118 (cited in note 17).

Marshall's opinion tracks the Federalist arguments in the repeal debate. Marbury's entitlement to his commission, in Marshall's view, flowed from the fact that, once the commission had been signed and sealed, the discretionary political aspect of the appointment process had been completed, and Marbury was vested with a property right to hold the office of justice of the peace for the prescribed five-year term.[215] But if Marbury had been denied a property right by the refusal of the administration to deliver his commission to an office with a five-year term, then, even more emphatically, the circuit judges were invalidly stripped of property rights when they were deprived of their lifetime appointments by congressional fiat.[216] Framing the issue in terms of individual rights served to call attention to the public need for judicial protection against abuses of their authority by the political branches,[217] a protection that could only be provided if there were adequate judicial remedies for breaches of the law by government officials. Unless "the act of delivering or withholding a commission [is] to be considered as a mere political act, belonging to the executive department alone," Marshall declared that a judicial remedy must be available to vindicate personal rights to "offices of trust, of honor, or of profit" that would be denied by refusal to deliver a valid commission.[218]

If the delivery of a commission were a political act, the decision as to its performance would rest entirely in the discretion of the President, who would be "accountable only to his country in his political character, and to his own conscience."[219] But not all acts of executive officials involve the exercise of political discretion; some are mandated by law, and, in such cases, the official is not the agent of the President, to be controlled only by the President, but "the officer of the law; [and] is amenable to the laws for his conduct."[220] Since, in this case, once the commission is signed and the political act of appointment thereby completed, "the subsequent duty of the secretary of state is prescribed by law, and not

---

[215] 1 Cranch at 155.

[216] O'Fallon, 44 Stan L Rev at 247.

[217] Id.

[218] 1 Cranch at 164.

[219] Id at 166.

[220] Id.

to be guided by the will of the president,"[221] "a refusal to deliver [it] . . . is a plain violation of [Marbury's vested legal] right, for which the laws of his country afford him a remedy."[222]

Despite the Court's acknowledgment that it could not interfere with the discretionary political actions of the President, O'Fallon maintains that Marshall was not deviating at all from Federalist doctrine because "[t]he line between discretion and duty was to be drawn by law, and law is the province of the judiciary."[223] He sees no evidence in Marshall's opinion "that the Court appreciated that it was examining the conduct of a coordinate branch of government,"[224] and his point is not without merit. The issue of whether delivery of the commission was essential to consummate Marbury's appointment was at least arguable,[225] and thus the Court was asserting here, as in its discussion of judicial review, the authority to treat its own conclusions on debatable issues as final and definitive. Similarly, the Court's conclusion that it had the authority to determine which actions of the executive were discretionary and which were controlled by law, as well as the authority to compel executive compliance with the law as it was understood by the judiciary,

---

[221] Id at 158. The "subsequent duty of the secretary of state [which] is prescribed by law" was the act of affixing the Seal of the United States to commissions signed by the President. The Secretary was assigned that duty when the Department of Foreign Affairs was redesignated the Department of State. Act of Sept 15, 1789, § 4, 1 Stat 68, 68–69. But the performance of that duty was not involved in this case since Marshall himself apparently carried it out while he was the occupant of the office of Secretary. The duty that the Court in this case held to be a duty required by law was the act of delivering the commission, which is not a duty imposed by statute. Marshall conceded this, 1 Cranch at 172–73, but dismissed it as irrelevant, for, if the appointee had a legal right to the commission, it could not lawfully be withheld from him by the government official who was in physical possession of it. Id. O'Fallon, however, regards the distinction as significant because given "both the potential for unconstrained executive officers trampling the rights of innocent citizens, and an unbridled judiciary insinuating itself in executive matters, limitation of the mandamus remedy to violations of statutorily prescribed duty might appear an inviting solution." O'Fallon, 44 Stan L Rev at 251. But Marshall did not settle for half a loaf here, either. (See text at notes 188–201.) As O'Fallon saw it, he "gave not one inch as he insisted that the determination of rights was the special prerogative of the judiciary." Id at 251–52.

[222] 1 Cranch at 168.

[223] O'Fallon, 44 Stan L Rev at 250.

[224] Id at 244. O'Fallon's argument here tracks the discussion in Van Alstyne, 1969 Duke L J at 9–10.

[225] Jefferson maintained at the time that delivery of the commission was essential before any right to hold an office was vested in an appointee, a position from which he never receded, see Warren, 1 *Supreme Court History* at 244–45 (cited in note 91), and Edward Corwin was of the opinion that Jefferson's "is probably the correct doctrine." United States Senate, *The Constitution of the United States of America*, 82d Cong, 2d Sess 454 (Edward S. Corwin ed, 1953).

and its further conclusion that federal officers serving in offices with statutorily prescribed terms were not removable by the President, represented gratuitous judgments on major issues of constitutional law that were arrived at without the benefit of any argument on behalf of the executive in a case in which the Court was to declare itself to be without jurisdiction.

But that is not to say that Marshall's conclusions were wrong. On the issue of whether delivery of a commission is an essential element of the right to hold office, Jefferson, whatever the merits of his position, was not very well situated to argue the importance of the act of delivery, since he had treated all of Adams's appointments to the post of justice of the peace as null, without regard to whether the commissions had been delivered, and proceeded to nominate an entirely new slate (including most of Adams's original appointees).[226] And the Court's judgment that Congress, by establishing a fixed term of office, could place limits on the removal power of the President was a notable starting place for the development of the salutary doctrine that, notwithstanding *Myers v United States*,[227] Congress may limit the power of the President to remove at will even officers performing executive functions in order to be able "to vest some among the broad new array of governmental functions in officers who are free from the partisanship that may be expected of agents wholly dependent upon the President."[228]

Moreover, the idea that courts can order executive officers to comply with the law even when compliance would be contrary to express presidential instructions[229] is a constitutional concept of

---

[226] See text at note 109.

[227] 272 US 52 (1926).

[228] *Bowsher v Synar*, 478 US 714, 762 (1986) (White, J, dissenting). The restrictions on the reach of *Myers v United States*, 272 US 52 (1926), began with *Humphrey's Executor v United States*, 295 US 602 (1935), which held that Congress could require the President to have good cause before removing an officer performing quasi-legislative or quasi-judicial functions, and perhaps culminated in *Morrison v Olson*, 487 US 654, 689–90 (1988), which held that the Constitution does not guarantee the President unlimited power of removal over every official performing executive functions. The case for allowing Congress to place restrictions on presidential removal power in *Marbury* was even stronger, for the officials involved there were to perform judicial rather than executive functions. The decision of the Supreme Court that most squarely reaffirms *Marbury* on this point is *Wiener v United States*, 357 US 349 (1958), holding that, in the absence of statutory authorization for removal, the President could not remove without cause a member of the War Claims Commission, a body of limited duration, because the duties of the commission were adjudicatory in nature.

[229] In *Kendall v United States*, 12 Peters 524 (1838), shortly after Marshall's death, the Court rejected the claim that executive branch officials were subject to no directives except those of the President. The Court concluded that "it would be an alarming doctrine, that

vital importance in the age of the imperial presidency,[230] marked
by instances of official lawlessness such as Watergate[231] and the
Iran-Contra affair.[232] It establishes the indispensable principle that
neither the President nor the President's agents can be above the
law,[233] and helps to guarantee that the constitutional duty of the
President to "take Care that the Laws be faithfully executed"[234] is
not used as a pretext for insuring that the laws are not executed at
all.[235] For these reasons, Leonard Levy was not right when he
declared of *Marbury* that "[o]nly the passages of the opinion on
judicial review survive . . . ; all else, which preoccupied national
attention in 1803, disappeared in our constitutional law."[236] Nevertheless, the fully justified appreciation for the virtues of Marshall's
"excursus" on the imperative of presidential respect for the law
must be tempered by the realization that he was able to deliver it
only by failing to respect accepted limits on judicial authority in
order to address, for reasons of political advantage, the merits of a
case in which the Court, according to his own ruling, was without
jurisdiction. As Irwin Rhodes noted, a "balanced appraisal" of
Marshall's performance must take note of "his unnecessary temerity and his use of the judicial office for strategic ends."[237]

O'Fallon regards the discussion of judicial review in the *Marbury*
opinion—which is the aspect of the case that makes it universally
recognized as perhaps the most historic landmark of American constitutional law—as barely worthy of notice. He accepts as "cer-

---

Congress cannot impose upon any executive officer any duty they may think proper, which
is not repugnant to any rights secured and protected by the constitution; and in such cases,
the duty and responsibility grow out of and are subject to the control of the law, and not
to the direction of the president." Id at 610. Such duties can be enforced by writs of
mandamus. Id at 614.

[230] See Arthur M. Schlesinger, Jr., *The Imperial Presidency* (Houghton Mifflin, 1973).

[231] See, for example, Philip B. Kurland, *Watergate and the Constitution* (U Chicago, 1978).

[232] See, for example, Harold Hongju Koh, *The National Security Constitution* (Yale, 1990).

[233] In *United States v Nixon*, 418 US 683, 703–5 (1974), a unanimous Court, citing *Marbury
v Madison*, held that authority to determine when the President could validly claim executive
privilege in withholding information sought by a subpoena *duces tecum* rested with the
Supreme Court. The Court flatly rejected any idea "that a President is above the law." Id
at 715.

[234] US Const, Art II, § 3.

[235] In *Kendall*, 12 Peters at 613, the Court emphatically repudiated the proposition "that
the obligation imposed on the president to see the laws faithfully executed, implies a power
to forbid their execution."

[236] Levy, *Original Intent* at 83–84 (cited in note 24).

[237] Rhodes, 33 U Cin L Rev at 37 (cited in note 122).

tainly a plausible account of Marshall's strategy," the commonly held view that he unnecessarily interpreted the statute as conferring jurisdiction on the Court so that he could assert the power of judicial review and declare the law to be unconstitutional, but he denies that this "require[s] that Marshall be credited as a visionary."[238] And, of Marshall's discussion of judicial review, it suffices for him to comment that "[t]here is an abundant literature on these matters" and to leave it to any interested reader to consult that literature.[239]

O'Fallon's contemptuous omission of judicial review from the list of issues he regarded as worthy of discussion in an article entitled *"Marbury"* appears to reflect his resentment of the praise that commentators have accorded Marshall for the genius of his decision. He rejects any notion that the *Marbury* opinion proved him to be "a judicial statesman fit to stand alongside Washington and Lincoln, Webster and Clay."[240] Instead, in O'Fallon's view, he was, in *Marbury*, just an ordinary politician espousing the party line of the Federalists that a strong judiciary was necessary to protect the people against the abuses inevitably to be anticipated from a legislature and an executive driven by factional passions to ignore the vested rights of individuals safeguarded by the Constitution or by common law.[241] But, unlike most politicians, he got lucky when future historians, enamored of judicial review, reached back to praise the great man for having enshrined the doctrine in the official reports of the Supreme Court and articulating the reasons why the existence of this power was indispensably necessary. According to O'Fallon, the standard reading of the *Marbury* opinion "caricatures Marshall and impoverishes our understanding of the clash of political beliefs that underlay the conflict over the Judiciary."[242] But an account of *Marbury* that treats judicial review as an unimportant element of the decision likewise "caricatures Marshall and impoverishes our understanding."

O'Fallon's particular *bête noire* among the commentators is Robert McCloskey, whose admiration of Marshall's political acumen[243]

---

[238] O'Fallon, 44 Stan L Rev at 252 (cited in note 4).

[239] Id at 256 n 129.

[240] Id at 220.

[241] Id at 249.

[242] Id at 220.

[243] See McCloskey, *American Supreme Court* at 40–44 (cited in note 130).

seems to have enraged him.[244] Much praise of Marshall does confuse clever political tactics with visionary statesmanship, as, for
example, the ridiculous statement of George Haskins crediting
Marshall with "statesmanlike" behavior without regard to the fact
that the lecture to the administration on its lawless behavior that
Haskins so admired was delivered in a case in which the Court had
no jurisdiction.[245] Moreover, Marshall is not entitled to credit for
genius or originality for his reasoning in defense of judicial review,
for, as even his enthusiastic biographer recognized, "[i]n establishing this principle Marshall was to contribute nothing new to the
thought upon the subject."[246] But the one thing that it is impossible
to deny is Marshall's extraordinary political acumen, and O'Fallon's criticism of McCloskey therefore seems entirely misplaced.

O'Fallon charges McCloskey with effecting "the marriage of history to doctrine"[247]—that is, with misinterpreting the history of
Marbury v Madison in order to make the doctrine of judicial review
the central focus of the case when in fact the central focus was
the ongoing political battle over the Republicans' efforts to curtail
judicial power. Such a view, he states, "is inconsistent with Marshall's timorousness regarding conflict with the other branches, as
reflected in his cautious action respecting repeal of the Judiciary
Act."[248] But McCloskey did not state a position that was "inconsistent with Marshall's timorousness." In fact, he declared that *Marbury* "confirms" Marshall's "sense of self-restraint."[249] He recognized that Marshall knew that the Court was, politically, in a very
vulnerable position, and that its decision not to upset the repeal of
the Judiciary Act was important in creating the "impression of a
non-aggressive bench," against which retaliation would be unnecessary.[250] Moreover, he denied that *Marbury* was not fully representative of that cautious attitude, or that it should be read as "sug-

---

[244] See O'Fallon, 44 Stan L Rev at 219–20.

[245] See text at note 197.

[246] Beveridge, 3 *John Marshall* at 116 (cited in note 17). But Beveridge nevertheless maintained that "Marshall's acts and words were those of a statesman of the first rank," id at
143, in that he had the "vision" and "courage" to proclaim the power of judicial review in
the difficult political circumstances of the time. Id at 142.

[247] O'Fallon, 44 Stan L Rev at 280.

[248] Id at 242–43.

[249] McCloskey, *American Supreme Court* at 40 (cited in note 130).

[250] Id at 47.

gesting that Marshall was rash or even very bold in exercising judicial supervision."[251]   Any appearance of difference between Marshall's "timorousness" in the repeal controversy and his apparent aggressiveness in claiming the power of judicial review is, of course, to be explained by the fact that an appearance of aggressiveness, although not without risk, was politically possible in *Marbury*. The opinion in *Marbury* was simply an opinion, and did not alter the status quo—the Court was without jurisdiction and issued no order—whereas any judicial effort to undo the effectiveness of repeal would emphatically have altered the postrepeal status quo and would almost certainly have generated retaliatory action. But, in any event, it is difficult to understand O'Fallon's point. If treating judicial review as the principal issue in *Marbury* would be to take a position "inconsistent with Marshall's timorousness" in avoiding a political confrontation over repeal, then treating the attack on presidential authority as the central focus of the case would be even more inconsistent with a basic posture of timidity, for that aspect of Marshall's opinion was far more likely to have prompted political retaliation than the assertion of the power of judicial review. Any inconsistency rests with O'Fallon.

The passage in McCloskey's excellent brief history of the Supreme Court that O'Fallon most particularly takes exception to is one that displays McCloskey's characteristically arresting style. The *Marbury* decision, he wrote, "is a masterwork of indirection, a brilliant example of Marshall's capacity to sidestep danger while seeming to court it, to advance in one direction while his opponents are looking in another."[252] That is a perfectly accurate observation, one that captures Marshall's approach precisely and insightfully, and O'Fallon's disagreement may simply reflect a misunderstanding of its meaning. He assumes that the cited passage expresses McCloskey's view that "Marshall used the potential conflict between Court and President to draw attention away from his real objective—the establishment of judicial review."[253] But that is not what McCloskey was saying at all. He nowhere stated or even suggested that his reference to Marshall's "advance in one direction while his opponents are looking in another" meant that the advance

---

[251] Id at 43.

[252] Id at 40.

[253] O'Fallon, 44 Stan L Rev at 242.

was in the direction of judicial review while the Republicans were looking in the direction of Marshall's diversionary attack on the administration. Indeed, a careful reading of McCloskey's argument demonstrates that his reference was to something quite different.

The courting of danger was surely the pronouncement that Jefferson had violated Marbury's legal rights and that a judicial remedy for such a violation was properly available, which danger was sidestepped by the denial of jurisdiction. The attack on Jefferson was "a masterwork of indirection" because it involved no direct confrontation in the form of an order that could and would have been disregarded.[254] And the description of an "advance in one direction while his opponents are looking in another" relates entirely to Marshall's discussion of judicial review and judicial remedy, and does not refer to any distraction that may have been created by Marshall's discussion of the administration's misbehavior. McCloskey states: "The attention of the Republicans was focused on the question of Marbury's commission, and they cared very little how the Court went about justifying a hands-off policy so long as that policy was followed."[255] Thus, his observation was that while the Republicans were looking in the direction of the writ of mandamus that they anticipated might be issued, Marshall proceeded to confound their expectations by asserting the power of judicial review. As he concluded, "[t]he moment for immortal statement was at hand all right, but only a judge of Marshall's discernment could have recognized it."[256] McCloskey's analysis emerges unscathed from O'Fallon's attack.

O'Fallon's essay enhances our understanding of *Marbury* by stressing that the Court's opinion was an integral part of a political battle with life-or-death implications for the principle of judicial independence, and that the constitutional ideology that Marshall there articulated was a Federalist ideology repeatedly reiterated in the remarkable congressional debates over repeal that were conducted in the opening months of 1802. It is also useful to be reminded, as O'Fallon reminds us, that judicial review was not the only issue addressed by the Court in *Marbury* and, from the standpoint of the Court in 1803, was probably not the most important

---

[254] See McCloskey, *American Supreme Court* at 41–42.

[255] Id at 42.

[256] Id.

one. The Court was profoundly distrusted both by the Jefferson administration and by Congress, and the distrust was heartily reciprocated. Political power being firmly in the hands of the Republicans, the Court was cowed and unable to moderate or modify their actions, as clearly demonstrated in its abject acquiescence to the repeal of the Judiciary Act of 1801. But when the *Marbury* case arrived and the Court denied itself jurisdiction, and thus freed itself from any need to back up its pronouncements with decrees that would have been ignored by the government, it found itself with an unparalleled opportunity to make an authoritative expression from the bench of the Federalist position that an independent judiciary was essential to protect the people against abuses of authority destructive of vested rights, to assert for future use the doctrine that the judiciary has the power to compel administrative officials to comply with the law whether or not they wanted to, and to seek to erode public support for Jefferson and his administration by proclaiming to the nation that the President and his Secretary of State had acted in a way that was heedless of personal property rights for narrowly partisan political purposes.

The Court's discussion of Madison's unfulfilled duty to respect Marbury's legal right and of the existence of judicial power to compel such respect was thus not an incidental part of the *Marbury* opinion. On this point, O'Fallon is absolutely correct. But judicial review was also not an incidental part of the opinion; it, too, was a key element of what the Court was seeking to accomplish. The Court wanted *both* to assert the power (when the issue was properly presented in a legal dispute) to compel executive officers to comply with the law as judicially construed *and* to compel Congress to conform its legislative actions to the Constitution as judicially construed. As O'Fallon himself observes, the Republicans' recognition that the judiciary was an institution controlled by the Federalists had led several members of Congress to deny completely the legitimacy of judicial review.[257] Marshall evidently perceived the need for prompt establishment of a clear precedent for its exercise, but also realized that the law to be chosen for sacrifice for this purpose had to be one that could be invalidated without political cost. Section 13 was perfect in this regard, and the fact that Marshall was required to give a strained interpretation both of it and of the

---

[257] O'Fallon, 44 Stan L Rev at 227–30.

Constitution to make it unconstitutional is clear evidence that he did not see this aspect of the case as a mere trivial incidental, as O'Fallon would have it, but as a crucial part of the Court's complex strategy in designing its opinion. O'Fallon is right in maintaining that an exclusive concentration on the issue of judicial review obscures what Marshall and the Court actually did in *Marbury*, but what Marshall and the Court actually did is equally obscured by dismissing as unworthy of attention the Court's assertion and exercise of the power of judicial review. That, regrettably, is what O'Fallon has done.

D. ON CLINTON AND MARSHALL'S FLAWLESS OPINION

Robert Lowry Clinton contends, incredibly, that politics played absolutely no part in the Court's opinion in *Marbury*, which he refers to as "a precedent for all seasons."[258] He admits there was some sort of "political squabble between President Jefferson and Chief Justice Marshall" that was going on at the time,[259] and that when the Court convened for its long-delayed February Term in 1803, "it found itself in a problematic situation" for "reasons [which] were primarily political."[260] Moreover, he recognizes that the Republicans had launched "an unprecedented attack on the federal judiciary,"[261] and that "the federal courts were under siege throughout the entire period in which Marbury's case was before the Court," a siege marked by the repeal of the Judiciary Act of 1801, the impeachment of a federal judge, and the elimination of Supreme Court terms between December 1801 and February 1803.[262] But, he insists, undue focus on these political events "has obscured so many other important aspects of the case,"[263] and he portrays Marshall as unaffected by this turmoil and capable of rising above it to produce an opinion uncontaminated by the slight-

---

[258] That is the phrase Clinton uses as the heading of the section of his book dealing with the *Marbury* opinion and its reception. Clinton, *Marbury v. Madison* at 79–138 (cited in note 5).

[259] Id at 13.

[260] Id at 81.

[261] Id.

[262] Id at 88.

[263] Id at 13.

est trace of political concern and resting exclusively "on sound constitutional doctrine and existing legal precedent."[264] Uh-huh.

Whereas O'Fallon demonstrates the extent to which the *Marbury* opinion is a direct outgrowth of the Repeal Act controversy, any commentary on that controversy is entirely absent from Clinton's discussion. He does provide the barest passing reference to the fact that the Judiciary Act of 1801 had been repealed by the newly elected Republican Congress,[265] but he does not bother to go into any of the details of this struggle or to assess its implications in shaping the political context in which the *Marbury* case arose. He finds it sufficient to note that the Republicans had been behaving badly by placing the federal courts "under siege," but the possibility does not seem to have occurred to him that the Federalists might have considered a political response to the political attacks they were enduring, or that, in developing that response, they might have sought to take advantage of the one constitutional weapon—control of the federal judiciary—that they still possessed, or that John Marshall and his colleagues on the Supreme Court, all loyal and committed Federalists, might have been prepared to do their bit to defend the just cause of their party against what they undoubtedly perceived as the unprincipled Republican onslaught. Certainly Marshall's colleagues on the Court were not particularly renowned for their scrupulous nonpartisanship—the nonpartisanship that Clinton insists they meticulously displayed in *Marbury*. They were among the "few Federalist judges" who, as even Clinton concedes, were guilty of "improper behavior" in their "attempt[s] to enforce the Alien and Sedition Acts"[266]—behavior that was as partisan as it was improper.[267] Indeed, Wythe Holt has demonstrated that the Federalist judges, including Marshall, were involved in an attempt to orchestrate an effective response to the Repeal Act,[268] which collapsed only after the Justices of the Supreme Court (except Samuel Chase), fully cognizant of the cer-

---

[264] Id at 79.

[265] See text at notes 260–62.

[266] Clinton, *Marbury v. Madison* at 81–82.

[267] Charles Warren described as "surely justified" Jefferson's charge that Federalist judges enforcing the Sedition Act had been "converted into political partisans." Warren, 1 *Supreme Court History* at 165 (cited in note 91).

[268] Holt, "*[I]f the Courts*" at 10–15 (cited in note 148).

tainty that retaliatory action would be taken against them, "got cold feet."[269]

Having divorced Marshall's *Marbury* opinion from its political setting, Clinton proceeds to argue why, in all its particulars, it reflected the only conclusions that fair and dispassionate judges could properly have arrived at. He is fully aware that virtually every scholar who has preceded him in the study of this case has come to the opposite conclusion, and that they have examined the same materials he has—he, too, has not "uncovered a crumbling diary or set of letters"[270]—but he has a perfectly simple explanation for the disparity: he is right, and they are wrong.[271] One reads Clinton's work with something of the wonderment with which orthodox geneticists must have read the writings of T. D. Lysenko—acceptance of which was enforced in the Soviet Union by Stalinist terror—which rejected the conclusions of biological research and substituted for them a fanciful theory based on "practical intuition."[272]

Clinton's contention is, of course, preposterous, and his analysis is embarrassing in its shoddiness, but nowhere more than in his discussion of the first part of the opinion, in which Marshall addresses the issues of Marbury's entitlement to his commission and the availability of mandamus to compel senior executive branch officials to carry out their legal responsibilities. Clinton either fails to understand or chooses to ignore the objections leveled against this part of the opinion, which go to the issues of why the Court was addressing these questions at all, given the fact that it was subsequently to hold that it was without jurisdiction in the case, and why the Court went directly to them without first examining the threshold question of its own jurisdiction.[273] Nothing in *Marbury* demonstrates more clearly the political character of this opin-

---

[269] Id at 15.

[270] See text at note 7.

[271] Barbara Tuchman has written of a naval historian who resolved discrepancies between his own version of a naval battle and the versions of others "by saying other accounts 'are all incorrect.'" Ms. Tuchman added: "('That's the spirit!')." Barbara W. Tuchman, *The First Salute* 4 (Knopf, 1988). Professor Clinton's spirit is equally indomitable.

[272] David Joravsky, *The Lysenko Affair* 130 (Harvard, 1970).

[273] See, for example, Currie, *Constitution in the Court* at 66–67 (cited in note 198); Levy, *Original Intent* at 82–83 (cited in note 24); J. A. C. Grant, *Marbury v. Madison Today*, 23 Am Pol Sci Rev 673, 675–76 (1929); Van Alstyne, 1969 Duke L J at 6–7 (cited in note 194); McLaughlin, 14 ABA J at 155–57 (cited in note 196).

ion than its gratuitous pronouncement on the failure of the Jefferson administration to respect the vested legal rights of individuals and its equally gratuitous assertion of judicial authority to compel specific actions by executive branch officials. One would have expected Clinton to have been especially sensitive to this difficulty in light of his emphasis on the fact that the federal courts have no authority to make constitutional declarations at all except in "cases of a judiciary nature,"[274] a term whose core meaning must include a limitation on the exercise of judicial power to those cases in which courts have jurisdiction.[275] But Clinton exhibits no awareness that such a problem even exists.

He begins his evaluation of the first part of Marshall's opinion with a statement that is entirely beside the point: "Under normal circumstances, where the law is considered settled, it is appropriate for the Supreme Court to dismiss a claim for want of jurisdiction without expressing opinion on the merits of the dispute."[276] Nothing could be more erroneous or irrelevant. Needless to remark, even if the law were settled, the Court's jurisdiction would be unaffected, but, in any event, it could hardly be contended that the legal and constitutional questions pertaining to Marbury's rights and the President's powers were settled. These issues were, as Marshall correctly noted at the outset of his opinion, ones of "delicacy," "novelty," and "difficulty."[277] It is clear that Clinton was somehow trying to fit *Marbury* into the category of cases in which the Court has discretion to deal with or pass over an issue as it deems wise. He proceeds to argue that Marshall's exercise of discretion in choosing to deal with these questions was justified,

---

[274] At the Constitutional Convention, Madison noted that the jurisdiction given to the federal courts by Art III, § 2, over "all Cases . . . arising under this Constitution" should be understood as being limited to "cases of a judiciary nature," a proposition to which there was no apparent dissent. James Madison, 2 *Journal of the Federal Convention* 617 (Scott, Foresman, 1893). See Clinton, *Marbury v. Madison* at 18 and passim.

[275] In a classic non sequitur, Clinton declares that *Marbury* was "a case of a judiciary nature in the strongest sense" because it involved an attempt by the executive to interfere with the proper functioning of the judicial branch by not allowing an individual who was "potentially a judicial officer of the United States" to occupy his office. Clinton, *Marbury v. Madison* at 94. But even if Marbury were "potentially a judicial officer," that would not make this "a case of a judiciary nature" in any sense unless the term can be thought to include cases in which a court is without jurisdiction. In any event, "cases of a judiciary nature" would not appear to mean cases affecting judges or courts, as Clinton seems to suggest, but, rather, those appropriate for judicial resolution.

[276] Id at 88.

[277] 1 Cranch at 154.

and that his discussion of them was appropriate and fully warranted.[278] The wisdom of a decision to address these matters, had
the Court had discretion to do so or not as it thought best, may
well be arguable, but that is surely not the point. Marshall's constitutional fault was not that he chose to discuss issues not absolutely
necessary to the resolution of a case properly before the Court.
That would have been a venial transgression—one that the Court
frequently commits. It was, instead, to pronounce its conclusions
on the merits of a case over which, according to its own judgment
in that very case, the Constitution prohibited Congress to grant
the Court, or the Court to assume, jurisdiction. The decision to
rule on the merits was therefore as much a violation of the Constitution as anything Jefferson or Madison or Congress may have done.
It was a deliberate flouting by the Court of the constitutional limits
on its authority that were specifically identified by the Court in the
very same case in which it ignored them. It is, therefore, perfectly
understandable that Clinton would have wanted to overlook this
issue completely, but the fact that he did so does not say much for
the fairness of his commentary.

Because Clinton is absolutely silent on this matter, he does not
mention some possible justifications for Marshall's decision to address the merits of Marbury's case against the administration before
ruling on the question of its own jurisdiction. These justifications
are without merit, but at least they are relevant to the proper issue.
First, as William Van Alstyne suggested for the sake of argument,[279]
and as Justice McReynolds actually argued,[280] it could be contended that Marshall properly began by inquiring whether Secretary Madison had acted illegally and whether a writ of mandamus
could be directed to a cabinet officer, because, if either of these
questions could have been answered negatively, Marbury's request
for the writ could have been denied on its merits without necessitat-
ing a decision of the question of whether Congress could constitutionally empower the Court to issue it. But the problem with this
argument is that, as noted above,[281] Marshall was not choosing on
a prudential basis which constitutional questions to decide and

---

[278] Clinton, *Marbury v. Madison* at 90.

[279] Van Alstyne, 1969 Duke L J at 7–8 (cited in note 194).

[280] *Myers v United States*, 272 US 52, 217–20 (1926) (McReynolds, J, dissenting).

[281] See text at notes 194–201.

which to avoid; he very carefully and deliberately decided them all—those relating to the President's appointing and commissioning powers, his removal power, and the amenability of executive branch officials to judicial order, as well as the question of the constitutionality of Congress's power to enlarge the original jurisdiction of the Supreme Court, and the existence of judicial power to declare an act of Congress unconstitutional.

Second, it might be argued that the rule that courts must first ascertain the existence of jurisdiction before ruling on the merits of a case, which is so firmly established today, might not have been so clear a principle at the beginning of the nineteenth century.[282] But that contention cannot be sustained in light of the Court's action in another case, two years after *Marbury*, that happened also to involve the office of justice of the peace in the District of Columbia. In that case, the government appealed the dismissal by the District of Columbia circuit court of an indictment brought against Benjamin More who, unlike Marbury, actually received a commission and took office. More had been indicted for accepting a 12½-cent fee for his official services, despite an 1802 act[283] in which Congress, following repeal of the Judiciary Act of 1801, repealed the provisions of the laws passed by the lame-duck Federalist Congress authorizing justices of the peace in the District of Columbia to collect fees for their services.[284] The case raised the interesting question of whether justices of the peace for the District of Columbia, despite the fact that their offices were created by Congress under its delegated power to legislate for the capital district[285] rather than the power "to constitute Tribunals inferior to the supreme Court,"[286] and that they served a specified term and had duties beyond those to which the judicial power of the United States was extended under Article III, were nevertheless judges of the United States the compensation for whose services cannot constitutionally be diminished.[287] But Marshall, probably not eager

---

[282] As David Currie has written, "[o]ne must be cautious in evaluating early materials by modern standards." Currie, *Constitution in the Court* at 66 n 14 (cited in note 198).

[283] Act of May 3, 1802, § 8, 2 Stat 193, 194–95.

[284] Act of Feb 27, 1801, § 11, 2 Stat 103, 107. Act of March 3, 1801, § 4, 2 Stat 115.

[285] US Const, Art I, § 8, cl 17.

[286] US Const, Art I, § 8, cl 9.

[287] The Circuit Court of the District of Columbia divided, 2–1, in answering these questions affirmatively and thus sustaining the demurrer to the indictment. The two Adams appointees to this court, William Cranch and James Marshall (the brother of the Chief Justice), constituted the majority; William Kilty, a Jefferson appointee, vigorously dissented.

to enter into another altercation with the administration over the status of the justices of the peace, raised, on his own motion, the issue of whether Congress had given the Supreme Court jurisdiction over appeals in criminal cases from the District of Columbia circuit court.[288] When Marshall delivered the opinion of the Court, he began by noting that "doubt has been suggested, respecting the jurisdiction of this court . . . ; *and this question is to be decided, before the court can inquire into the merits of the case.*"[289] Marshall and the Court were thus fully cognizant of the fact that it was improper for the Court to rule on or even discuss the merits of a case before resolving any unsettled questions as to its jurisdiction. It simply chose not to heed that rule in *Marbury*.

Clinton seems to suggest that the Court's decision to discuss the validity of the administration's actions was justified because of the refusal of Jefferson and Madison to recognize the authority of the Court to rule on the legality or propriety of the activities of the executive branch. He writes: "The separation doctrine of the Federal Convention surely enabled the Court to defend itself against brazen attempts by coordinate branches of government to impair the capacity of the judiciary to perform its functions properly."[290] No doubt the Court perceived that the administration was seeking to impair the capacity of the federal judiciary, but that serves only to demonstrate that the Court, in fashioning a response to a political challenge, was itself acting politically—the very point that Clinton is seeking to disprove. Except in political terms, it does not justify the Court in deciding the merits of a case over which it had no jurisdiction. In any event, if the Court's purpose

---

The majority and dissenting opinions appear in full as a footnote to the report of the case in the United States Reports. See *United States v More*, 3 Cranch 159, 160 n (b) (1805). See also the discussion of the constitutional issues presented by the *More* case in Currie, *Constitution in the Court* at 78–79 (cited in note 198).

[288] *United States v More*, 3 Cranch 159, 169 (1805). The act providing for a judicial system for the District of Columbia, probably through inadvertence, gave the Supreme Court jurisdiction to hear appeals from "any final judgment" of the District of Columbia circuit court "wherein the matter in dispute, exclusive of costs, shall exceed the value of one hundred dollars." Act of Feb 27, 1801, § 8, 2 Stat 103, 106. This qualifying language seems to limit the Supreme Court's appellate jurisdiction over that court to civil cases, and the Court so held. *More*, 3 Cranch at 172–73. It was called to Marshall's attention that the Supreme Court had heard an appeal from that court in a criminal case—*United States v Simms*, 1 Cranch 252 (1803)—but he replied that as the jurisdictional issue had not been argued in that case, the Court did not regard its action there as a binding precedent on that issue. 3 Cranch at 172.

[289] Id. (Emphasis added.)

[290] Clinton, *Marbury v. Madison* at 88–89. See also id at 94.

had been, without regard to political considerations, to do what was necessary to defend the integrity of the judiciary against brazen challenges by the coordinate branches, it is difficult to explain its refusal, in *Stuart v Laird*[291] the following week (a case conspicuous by the total absence of any substantive reference to it in Clinton's book), to say anything at all about the constitutionality of the Repeal Act of 1802, which was certainly a direct and brazen attempt by the political branches to undermine the integrity of the judiciary, despite the fact that the Court had jurisdiction in that case, that the issue of the constitutionality of the act was squarely before it and was, in fact, the issue principally urged by the plaintiff in error,[292] whose most serious constitutional contentions were left unaddressed by the Court's silence. And, in the *More* case, if the Court were following the course that Clinton described, it should not have quietly allowed Congress to disqualify individuals performing judicial functions from continuing to receive the fees for their services that had been previously authorized by law.

Finally, because Clinton's omissions speak so loudly, it is interesting that he never mentions the fact that Marshall did not decline to sit in *Marbury*, although he declined to sit in *Stuart v Laird* because he had served as circuit judge when the case was at that level. After all, Marshall was a central actor in the events that resulted in the dispute before the Court in *Marbury*. He had been Secretary of State when the appointment was made, and had been responsible for sealing, and for failing to deliver, Marbury's commission.[293] Now he was sitting in judgment in a case that presented the questions of whether his act in sealing the commission had given Marbury a legal right to hold office, and whether his act in failing to deliver the commission had destroyed that right. Indeed, Marbury had difficulty providing evidence of the existence of his commission because the person who should have been his principal

---

[291] 1 Cranch 299 (1803). See text at notes 161–66.

[292] These arguments, presented by Charles Lee, who was also counsel for Marbury, are described in 1 Cranch at 302–6.

[293] Although Clinton's silence regarding Marshall's willingness to sit to hear this case is loud, his silence on Marshall's personal involvement in the case as Secretary of State is deafening. In his discussion of the background of the case—Clinton, *Marbury v. Madison* at 82–83—he makes no mention of the fact that Marshall was a central player in the creation of Marbury's problem. He does note that Marshall's brother "had acted as a courier for the State Department in the delivery of several of the commissions," id at 85, but he does not mention that James Marshall was acting as a courier for his brother.

witness was the presiding judge of the court that was hearing his
case.[294] As William Van Alstyne has observed, the question of the
propriety of Marshall's serving as a judge in this case was the one
issue that should have had precedence even over the question of
the Court's jurisdiction.[295] That Marshall chose to sit, let alone that
he wrote the Court's opinion, is itself powerful evidence that
"sound constitutional doctrine and existing legal precedent" were
not controlling factors in the Court's decision.

After satisfactorily accomplishing his purpose of "branding the
President and the Secretary of State as law-breakers,"[296] Marshall
turned to the question of whether the Supreme Court had authority
to issue the writ of mandamus that Marbury had requested. He
read § 13 of the Judiciary Act of 1789 as conferring jurisdiction on
the Court, and then held it unconstitutional because it enlarged
the Court's original jurisdiction beyond that specified in Article
III, § 2. Neither the Court's reading of the statute nor its reading
of the Constitution was obvious, and commentators have generally
concluded that Marshall adopted strained constructions of both in
order to be able to invalidate the act.[297] Clinton sets out to demonstrate that these commentators have been wrong, and that Marshall's interpretation of both the statute and the Constitution was
sound. It is a formidable task, and he does not succeed.

On the issue of the interpretation of § 13, Marshall does not give
Clinton much to work with because his argument is so cursory.
His discussion is essentially confined to one short paragraph in
which he simply quotes that part of § 13 that provides that the
Supreme Court may "issue 'writs of *mandamus*, in cases warranted
by the principles and usages of law, to any courts appointed, or
persons holding office, under the authority of the United
States,' "[298] and, because he had in the preceding paragraphs concluded that a writ of mandamus was warranted by the principles
and usages of law to "direct[ ] the performance of a duty, not

---

[294] See Dewey, *Marshall versus Jefferson* at 101 (cited in note 18).

[295] Van Alstyne, 1969 Duke L J at 8 (cited in note 194).

[296] McLaughlin, 14 ABA J at 157 (cited in note 196).

[297] See, for example, Currie, *Constitution in the Court* at 67–69 (cited in note 198); Corwin,
Doctrine at 3–10 (cited in note 50); Levy, *Original Intent* at 80–82 (cited in note 24); Van
Alstyne, 1969 Duke L J at 14–16, 30–33 (cited in note 194); McLaughlin, 14 ABA J at
157–58 (cited in note 196); Grant, 23 Am Pol Sci Rev at 676–78 (cited in note 273).

[298] 1 Cranch at 173, quoting Act of Sept 24, 1789, § 13, 1 Stat 73, 80–81.

depending on executive discretion, but on particular acts of congress, and the general principles of law,"[299] he felt it necessary in this paragraph only to note that the Secretary of State was an officer covered by the language of the statute, and to conclude that "if this court is not authorized to issue a writ of *mandamus* to such an officer, it must be because the law is unconstitutional."[300]

That was the sum total of Marshall's discussion regarding the meaning of § 13, and, of course, it was not enough. Granting that he was correct on the two points of interpretation that he mentioned—that this was a case in which the issuance of a writ of mandamus would be warranted by the principles of law and that the Secretary of State is an officer of the United States within the meaning of the statute—and also granting Marshall's later point that the issuance of the writ to a federal official would be an exercise of original jurisdiction,[301] it is a huge leap to go from there, as Marshall does, directly to the conclusion that either the Court is authorized to issue the writ or the law is unconstitutional. For the relevant portion of the statute, which Marshall correctly quotes, says nothing about jurisdiction. It emphatically does not say what Marshall implies it must be understood to mean, that the Supreme Court is authorized to issue writs of mandamus, as appropriate, to federal courts or federal officials whether or not the matter at hand is otherwise within the Court's jurisdiction. Other parts of § 13 relate to the original or appellate jurisdiction of the Supreme Court, but these portions are not grammatically linked to the language of the passage authorizing the issuance of writs of mandamus by the Court. The most sensible interpretation of this language, therefore, would be that it does not authorize the Court to assume jurisdiction that it would not otherwise possess in order to issue writs of mandamus, but that it authorizes the issuance of such writs, when appropriate, in cases properly within the Court's jurisdiction on other grounds. Indeed, as Andrew McLaughlin has noted, "any other ruling seems forced."[302]

Clinton, however, is dauntless. He rejects this interpretation, arguing that Marshall "tend[ed] to read legal provisions literally,

[299] 1 Cranch at 170.

[300] Id at 173.

[301] Id at 175.

[302] McLaughlin, 14 ABA J at 158 (cited in note 196).

at least whenever language is relatively unambiguous,"[303] and concluding that since, literally, § 13 says nothing about jurisdiction in
the passage relating to the issuance of writs of mandamus, a literal
reading would have the provision apply to "*any*" federal officer and
be applicable to "*both* appellate *and* original jurisdiction." The literal reading therefore "enlarges the Court's jurisdiction" and "is
thus unconstitutional."[304] Even putting aside the insurmountable
problem of why Marshall's interpretive tendencies, whatever they
may be, should control the meaning of an act of Congress, Clinton's
contention that a literal reading would render the statute unconstitutional is logically impossible. Because, as he notes, and even
emphasizes, there is no reference to jurisdiction in that part of § 13
that pertains to the issuance of writs of mandamus by the Supreme
Court, the statute, read literally, cannot confer any jurisdiction. It
must, therefore, apply only in cases where the Court already has
jurisdiction, and thus, by definition, cannot enlarge the Court's
jurisdiction.

But, in keeping with his practice of simply ignoring the principal
arguments against Marshall's opinion, Clinton is completely silent
regarding the most telling criticism of Marshall's interpretation of
the statute. Given the absence of any reference to a conferral of
jurisdiction in the language of § 13 pertaining to the issuance
of writs of mandamus, the very most that can be said is that it
is ambiguous on the question of whether it adds to the original
jurisdiction of the Supreme Court. In light of the accepted rule of
statutory construction that an interpretation of an ambiguous statute that raises constitutional questions is not to be adopted if an
alternate interpretation that would not raise such questions is reasonably available,[305] the "interpretation [that] would have eliminated any question regarding the constitutionality of the section
. . . should have been made."[306] To be sure, constitutional adjudication was still in its infancy in 1803, but this principle of construc-

---

[303] Clinton, *Marbury v. Madison* at 92.

[304] Id at 92–93. (Emphasis is in original.)

[305] See, for example, *Parsons v Bedford*, 3 Peters 433, 448–49 (1830) (per Story, J): "No
court ought, unless the terms of an act rendered it unavoidable, to give a construction to
it, which should involve a violation, however unintentional, of the constitution." See also
Rust v Sullivan, 111 S Ct 1759, 1778 (1991) (Blackmun, J, dissenting); id at 1788 (O'Connor,
J, dissenting).

[306] Van Alstyne, 1969 Duke L J at 16 (cited in note 194). See also Corwin, *Doctrine* at
7–9 (cited in note 50); Levy, *Original Intent* at 81–82 (cited in note 24); McLaughlin, 14
ABA J at 158 (cited in note 196); Grant, 23 Am Pol Sci Rev at 676 (cited in note 273).

tion had already been recognized and employed by the Supreme Court, which, in order to preserve its constitutionality, had given a limiting construction to § 11 of the Judiciary Act of 1789, granting circuit courts jurisdiction over civil suits in which "an alien is a party."[307] This grant, if read literally, conferred jurisdiction in excess of that authorized by Article III, § 2, which extended the judicial power of the United States to cases involving aliens only when the opposing party was "a State or the Citizens thereof," but the Court construed the statute to confer only that jurisdiction that was constitutionally authorized, on the ground that § 11 "can and must receive a construction consistent with the constitution."[308]

This rule of construction was widely understood and broadly applied. In *Federalist 78*, Alexander Hamilton had spoken of the need for choosing interpretations of laws that would avoid conflicts with other laws or the Constitution,[309] and it is true that "the general principles of statutory construction, where a statute seriously alters the common law, were very old in 1803."[310] Clinton himself notes, although in an entirely different context, that the year after *Marbury*, Marshall declared for the Court that "an act of congress ought never to be construed to violate the law of nations, if any other possible construction remains."[311] Even if this principle had been less well known at the time, common sense and appropriate respect for the legislature should have induced any court to avoid the possible necessity of invalidating a legislative act by choosing a plainly constitutional interpretation of ambiguous language over an interpretation that could render the law unconstitutional. There was no reason for Marshall not to have invoked that principle in *Marbury* except that doing so would have denied the Court the opportunity to establish a precedent for judicial review. Certainly, it cannot be argued that the Court could not have invoked this principle in *Marbury* because, prior to that decision, it had already accepted cases on original jurisdiction involving requests for writs of mandamus. Given the choice between adherence

---

[307] Act of Sept 24, 1789, 1 Stat 73, 78.

[308] *Mossman v Higginson*, 4 Dallas 12, 13 (1800).

[309] Federalist 78 (Hamilton) in Cooke, ed, *The Federalist* at 525–26 (cited in note 55).

[310] McLaughlin, 14 ABA J at 158 (cited in note 196).

[311] *The Charming Betsy*, 2 Cranch 64, 118 (1804), cited in Clinton, *Marbury v. Madison* at 49.

to a prior construction of an ambiguous statute that was now, for the first time, understood to make the statute unconstitutional, or abandonment of that prior construction to avoid declaring it invalid, the latter alternative is surely the one to be preferred.

Even if one accepts Marshall's unwarranted interpretation of § 13 as conferring original jurisdiction on the Supreme Court to entertain petitions for writs of mandamus, there is no constitutional problem unless the Constitution prohibits Congress from giving the Supreme Court original jurisdiction except in the cases specified in Article III, § 2—those "affecting Ambassadors, other public Ministers, and Consuls, and those in which a State shall be Party." There is no question that the power to issue writs of mandamus is within the constitutional authority of the federal courts; therefore, it could constitutionally be assigned to the Supreme Court as part of its appellate jurisdiction. Thus, the only question was whether Congress could constitutionally take matters legitimately within the appellate jurisdiction of the Court and transfer them to its original jurisdiction. The case that it can validly do so is obvious and rests on the express language of the Constitution, which declares, after specification of the cases in which the Supreme Court is to have original jurisdiction, that: "In all the other Cases before mentioned, the supreme Court shall have appellate Jurisdiction, both as to Law and Fact, with such Exceptions, and under such Regulations as the Congress shall make."[312] Why could that language not, with perfect reason, be interpreted to mean that Congress may except matters from the Court's appellate jurisdiction by assigning them to its original jurisdiction? Commentators have repeatedly noted this in the course of arguing that the Court's conclusion that § 13, even as Marshall interpreted it, was invalid was by no means compelled by the language of the Constitution.[313]

---

[312] US Const, Art III, § 2.

[313] See Levy, *Original Intent* at 81 (cited in note 24), citing a draft version of Article III prepared in the Committee of Detail that would have provided that the Supreme Court was to have "appellate [jurisdiction] only, except in . . . those instances in which the legislature shall make it original." Max Farrand, ed, 2 *Records of the Federal Convention of 1787* 147 (Yale, 1923). See also, for example, Currie, *Constitution in the Court* at 68–69 (cited in note 198); Corwin, *Doctrine* at 4–7 (cited in note 50); Van Alstyne, 1969 Duke L J at 30–33 (cited in note 194); Grant, 23 Am Pol Sci Rev at 676–77 (cited in note 273). Compare William Winslow Crosskey, 2 *Politics and the Constitution in the History of the United States* 1040–42 (U Chicago, 1953), where it is argued that while Marshall's interpretation of § 13 as conferring original jurisdiction on the Supreme Court to entertain petitions for writs of mandamus was correct, that created no constitutional problem because Congress had full constitutional authority to enlarge the Court's original jurisdiction.

Confidence in the fullness and fairness of Marshall's analysis of the constitutional issue can only be shaken by the fact that when he begins his discussion of it by quoting the relevant language of Article III, § 2, he puts a period in the middle of the critical sentence, and completely omits the exceptions clause, which is the clause that casts the most serious doubt on the soundness of his interpretation.[314] But, two paragraphs later, he alludes to the clause as offhandedly as possible, and presents an argument to counter the case that rests on it, contending that if Congress could move matters at will from the Court's appellate to its original jurisdiction, it would have been sufficient merely to have identified the cases that must fall within its original jurisdiction, and then left it to Congress to divide the remainder of cases between original and appellate jurisdiction as it saw fit. However, since Article III went on to declare that "[i]n all the other Cases before mentioned, the supreme Court shall have appellate Jurisdiction," "further restriction on the powers of congress [must have] been intended." Yet if the exceptions clause were read to allow Congress to transfer matters from the Court's appellate jurisdiction to its original jurisdiction, there would be no further restriction because Congress could still divide the remainder of the Court's jurisdiction between appellate and original at its discretion. Therefore, he concluded, the power granted under the exceptions clause cannot include the power to transfer cases from the appellate to the original jurisdiction of the Court.[315]

Marshall's interpretation of the exceptions clause stands or falls on his assumption that the inclusion of the reference to the appellate jurisdiction of the Supreme Court in Article III, § 2 was intended to limit the discretion of Congress to move matters at will between the Court's original and its appellate jurisdiction. But that is a questionable assumption. The reference to appellate jurisdiction need not have been intended to prevent any inference that the original jurisdiction of the Court could be expanded beyond the cases expressly placed there by the Constitution. The purpose of the reference might, instead, have been merely to provide a context for the exceptions clause—that is, its purpose may have been solely to announce that Congress would have power to make exceptions to

---

[314] 1 Cranch at 174.

[315] Id at 175.

the Court's appellate jurisdiction. That would insure that Congress would have authority to protect the fact-finding prerogative of juries against appellate review by the Supreme Court, which might, if left unregulated, decide to undertake *de novo* examination of facts found by a jury. Raoul Berger's study of the exceptions clause led him to conclude in 1969 that its proponents among the framers were "solely concerned with review of matters of 'fact,' "[316] and that discussion of the clause during the ratification debates "revolved almost exclusively about the retrial of facts found by a jury."[317] In support of this view is Hamilton's argument in *Federalist 81*. Hamilton contended that in some cases, but not others, review of facts by an appellate court might be appropriate for the preservation of justice and the public peace, but the large number of different circumstances and distinctions among state procedures pertaining to juries would have made it difficult to define the proper scope of the appellate jurisdiction of the Supreme Court over matters of fact in a simple statement suitable for inclusion in a constitution. He thus concluded that, "[t]o avoid all inconveniences, it will be safest to declare generally that the supreme court shall possess appellate jurisdiction, both as to law and *fact*" and to "enable the government to modify [that jurisdiction] in such a manner as will best answer the ends of public justice and security" through the power of Congress to make exceptions and regulations.[318]

Marshall's interpretation of the exceptions clause served to prevent it from defeating his contention that Congress cannot add to the original jurisdiction of the Supreme Court. That contention was also based on the idea that specific reference to the Court's original and appellate jurisdiction in Article III, § 2 demonstrated that Congress was without power to reassign cases between the two categories. If it could, the constitutional language describing the scope of the Court's original and appellate jurisdiction "is mere surplusage—is entirely without meaning."[319] But, as Edward Corwin long ago replied, "this is simply not so." Even if the Court's original jurisdiction can be enlarged by Congress, the specification

---

[316] Raoul Berger, *Congress v. the Supreme Court* at 286–87 (Harvard, 1969).

[317] Id at 289.

[318] Federalist 81 (Hamilton), in Cooke, ed, *The Federalist* at 552 (cited in note 55). (Emphasis is in original.)

[319] 1 Cranch at 174.

of cases in which the Court is to have such jurisdiction is not made meaningless, for that specification creates a category of cases that must be in its original jurisdiction, and thus "place[s] the cases enumerated by [it] beyond the reach of Congress,—surely no negligible matter."[320] And David Currie has recently pointed out that "Marshall himself was to reject the implications of the *Marbury* reasoning in *Cohens v. Virginia*,[321] where he declared that Congress could grant appellate jurisdiction in cases where the Constitution provided for original."[322]

Clinton takes on the task of defending Marshall against both of these criticisms. He begins by rejecting Currie's assumption that there is an equivalency between enlarging the Court's original jurisdiction (which was not allowed in *Marbury*) and enlarging (or contracting) its appellate jurisdiction (which was allowed in *Cohens*). He asserts that the Court must have understood this distinction at the time of *Marbury* because the first part of § 13 of the Judiciary Act of 1789 specifies that some of the Court's original jurisdiction is not to be exclusive, the effect of which is to enlarge the Court's appellate jurisdiction.[323] (It, of course, also subtracts from the Court's original jurisdiction—which is surely far more questionable constitutionally than adding to it—and thus undermines the distinction that Clinton was trying to make, but he seems not to have noticed that.) He then bolsters his conclusion that Marshall was fully conscious in 1803 of the need to give the Supreme Court appellate jurisdiction in cases within its constitutional grant of original jurisdiction by quoting Marshall's unanswerable argument in *Cohens* in 1821 that, unless that is constitutionally permissible, a case falling within the Court's original jurisdiction would not be reviewable on appeal in the Supreme Court if original jurisdiction had been improperly given to or assumed by a lower federal court, or if the case originated in a state court,[324] with the result that "a

---

[320] Corwin, *Doctrine* at 5 (cited in note 50).

[321] 6 Wheaton 264 (1821). *Cohens* involved the Supreme Court's acceptance of an appeal from a state criminal conviction despite the provision of Art III, § 2, that the Court shall have original jurisdiction "[i]n all Cases . . . in which a State shall be Party."

[322] Currie, *Constitution in the Court* at 69 (cited in note 198).

[323] Clinton, *Marbury v. Madison* at 96.

[324] Id, citing *Cohens v Virginia*, 6 Wheaton at 396–98. The absolute necessity of allowing the Supreme Court appellate jurisdiction in cases within its original jurisdiction where original jurisdiction was assumed by a lower federal court, or where the case was heard in a state court, does not settle the constitutionality of a specific assignment by Congress to a

clause inserted for the purpose of excluding the jurisdiction of all other courts than this, in a particular case, would have the effect of excluding the jurisdiction of this court, in that very case, if the suit were to be brought in another court, and that court were to assert jurisdiction."[325]

After defending his conclusion that Marshall must have known at the time of *Marbury* that there had to be flexibility in Congress's power to grant the Court appellate jurisdiction, but not original jurisdiction, he turns to the sentence in *Marbury* that seems to contradict it: "If congress remains at liberty to give this court appellate jurisdiction, where the constitution has declared their jurisdiction shall be original; and original jurisdiction where the constitution has declared it shall be appellate; the distribution of jurisdiction, made in the constitution, is form without substance."[326] The exact parallelism of this statement would appear to demonstrate that Marshall in *Marbury* did *not* see the distinction between the two types of jurisdiction that Clinton insists he did see, but Clinton provides an extremely clever reading of that sentence to show that its apparent meaning was not its real meaning. The problem, Clinton declares, is that Marshall carelessly failed to express himself clearly. What he really meant, Clinton claims, is that the specific identification in Article III, § 2 of cases within the original jurisdiction of the Supreme Court would be "form without substance" if Congress were free *both* to change appellate jurisdiction to original *and* original jurisdiction to appellate. Since it was understood that Congress *can* do the latter (as Marshall must have known from the terms of § 13 and as he later made clear in *Cohens*), it must follow that it cannot also do the former and transfer matters from the Court's appellate jurisdiction to its original jurisdiction. For, if it could, both types of transfer would be allowable, and the constitutional "distribution of jurisdiction" would be "form without substance."[327] Therefore, contrary to Corwin, the specifi-

---

lower federal court of original jurisdiction to hear a case within the scope of the Supreme Court's original jurisdicion, and the assignment to the Supreme Court of authority to review that court's judgment on appeal. Yet Congress, in § 13 of the Judiciary Act of 1789, 1 Stat 73, 80–81, provided that some of the Court's specified original jurisdiction need not be exclusive, but may be shared with the lower courts, and the Supreme Court has affirmed the constitutionality of the practice. See *Ames v Kansas*, 111 US 449, 463–69 (1884). That is still further evidence of the doubtfulness of the Court's constitutional judgment in *Marbury*.

[325] *Cohens*, 6 Wheaton at 397.

[326] 1 Cranch at 174.

[327] Clinton, *Marbury v. Madison* at 97.

cation in Article III of the cases to be within the original jurisdiction of the Court *does* become meaningless if the constitutionality
of § 13 is upheld, and, contrary to Currie, Marshall's reasoning in
Cohens supports, and does not repudiate, his reasoning in *Marbury*.
(Indeed, if one accepts Clinton's argument, Corwin is hopelessly
wrong, for the one thing that he agrees that the constitutional
specification of the Court's original jurisdiction *does* do is to "place
the cases enumerated by [it] beyond the reach of Congress," which
is the very thing that, according to Clinton, Congress remains constitutionally free to do.)

Although Clinton merits high marks for ingenuity, his argument
is unsuccessful. The fact that the Court must be able to exercise
appellate jurisdiction over cases specified in the Constitution as
falling within its original jurisdiction when those cases properly
or improperly originate elsewhere, as Marshall soundly argued in
Cohens, does not render the constitutional specification meaningless
if Congress is allowed to add to the Court's original jurisdiction.
And, despite his commendable effort to reconstruct the meaning
of Marshall's parallelism in *Marbury*, it is simply not believable
that Marshall did not mean what he said, but rather meant what
Clinton now says he meant. In the first place, as anyone with a
passing familiarity with his style of opinion writing will immediately recognize, when Marshall sets out to make a logical argument,
he proceeds step by step, and hammers home the point he wishes
to make at each stage of the process of reasoning. He would never
leave out the critical explanatory steps in developing a subtle point
of logic—particularly if that were to leave his reasoning so opaque
that his point would be lost for almost 200 years until it was finally
deciphered by an unusually keen analyst near the close of the twen-
tieth century. But there is even better evidence than that to show
that Clinton is mistaken, for when Marshall in *Cohens* undertook to
reconcile that decision with *Marbury*, he did not identify Clinton's
interpretation as the proper meaning of a previously misunderstood
sentence. Instead, he conceded that the result in *Cohens* was contrary to some of the language in *Marbury*, and declared that the
statements in *Marbury* that were inconsistent with *Cohens* were to
be regarded as *obiter dicta*, in that they went beyond what was
necessary to decide the case at hand, and as stating a principle "in
terms much broader than the decision, and not only much broader
than the reasoning with which that decision is supported, but in

some instances, contradictory to its principle."[328] He then added that "general expressions" in the *Marbury* opinion "must be understood, with the limitations which are given to them in this opinion."[329] Surely, the general expression in *Marbury* most clearly limited and thus repudiated in *Cohens* is the very same sweeping statement that Clinton tries so hard to use as proof of the consistency of the reasoning of the two cases.

Marshall's conclusion in *Marbury* that it was unconstitutional for Congress to vest the Supreme Court with original jurisdiction to issue writs of mandamus was also at odds with the Court's past practice. The Supreme Court had already been asked to issue writs of mandamus and prohibition under its original jurisdiction prior to *Marbury*, and no constitutional concerns had been expressed.[330] Albert Beveridge noted that, before *Marbury*, "[n]obody ever had questioned the validity of that section of the statute which Marshall now challenged."[331] The Judiciary Act of 1789 had been drafted by the First Congress under the particular guidance of Oliver Ellsworth, its main author, and William Paterson, both of whom were important participants in the Constitutional Convention and both of whom were later to become members of the Supreme Court, and the act had been warmly supported in both houses of Congress by other prominent members of the Convention,[332] which strongly suggests that there should have been no striking incompatibility between the provisions of the act and the stipulations of Article III, although, as Maeva Marcus and Natalie Wexler have wisely cautioned, there were many complications and compromises in-

---

[328] 6 Wheaton at 401.

[329] Id. Clinton quotes the Court's language here, Clinton, *Marbury v. Madison* at 97, but appears not to understand what it means. Because Marshall states that the limitations imposed by the *Cohens* opinion on the statements made by the Court in *Marbury* "in no degree affect the decision in that case, or the tenor of its reasoning," 6 Wheaton at 401–2, Clinton seems to believe that this is a reaffirmance of the *Marbury* opinion rather than a repudiation of its reasoning to the extent that the opinion contains overly broad statements—notably the statement that Clinton strives so valiantly to reinterpret, see text at note 327—that are inconsistent with *Cohens*.

[330] Charles Lee, Marbury's counsel, identified three cases in which, prior to *Marbury*, the Supreme Court had accepted original jurisdiction to consider petitions for writs of mandamus, and one case in which it granted a writ of prohibition—the issuance of which was also authorized by § 13 of the 1789 Judiciary Act. See 1 Cranch at 148–49. See also text at note 339.

[331] Beveridge, 3 *John Marshall* at 128 (cited in note 17).

[332] Id at 128–29.

volved in the drafting of the act, and "thus it is hazardous to rely on the Judiciary Act as evidence of the 'original understanding' of Article III."[333] Charles Lee, arguing the case for Marbury before the Supreme Court, declared that "there has been a legislative construction of the constitution upon this point, and a judicial practice under it, for the whole time since the formation of the government."[334]

The Supreme Court was certainly aware of its own precedents. The cases that Lee identified had arisen in 1794 and 1795, and two members of the Court at the time of *Marbury*—Paterson and Cushing—had been on the Court when they were decided (although Cushing was ill and apparently did not participate in *Marbury*). But a recent article by Susan Low Bloch and Maeva Marcus has demonstrated that the Marshall Court did not treat its precedents responsibly in *Marbury*,[335] thus providing further evidence— if further evidence was needed—that the Court regarded that case as a political, rather than a legal, event. In establishing his point that a writ of mandamus could be issued to an executive branch officer to compel performance of a duty mandated by law, Marshall referred to, but did not identify by name, a precedent in which the Court had been asked to direct the writ to the Secretary of War requiring him to place an individual on the list of those eligible for veterans' pensions.[336] He explained the outcome of that case as follows: "When the subject was brought before the court, the decision was, not that a *mandamus* would not lie to the head of a department, directing him to perform an act, enjoined by law, . . . but that a *mandamus* ought not to issue in that case."[337] Bloch and Marcus point out that no case that had come before the Court precisely fits the Court's description of the facts and the outcome, but that Marshall had apparently combined parts of three separate cases to create a fictitious precedent that made just the points he wanted to make.[338] These points could validly have been made if the individ-

---

[333] Maeva Marcus and Natalie Wexler, *The Judiciary Act of 1789: Political Compromise or Constitutional Interpretation?* in Maeva Marcus, ed, *Origins of the Federal Judiciary* 13, 30 (Oxford, 1992).

[334] 1 Cranch at 149.

[335] Susan Low Bloch and Maeva Marcus, *John Marshall's Selective Use of History in Marbury v. Madison*, 1986 Wis L Rev 301.

[336] 1 Cranch at 172.

[337] Id.

[338] Bloch and Marcus, 1986 Wis L Rev at 311–18 (cited in note 335).

ual cases had been accurately described, but reliance on three cases instead of one would have required a more convoluted set of explanations that would have cramped Marshall's rhetorical style.

But if that rearrangement of the facts can be excused as artistic license, it was much less excusable for Marshall to ignore this precedent, whether it be in the form of one case or three, when it became convenient to do so for the sake of his constitutional argument.[339] For while the precedent established, as Marshall stated, that a writ of mandamus can be directed to the head of an executive department, a conclusion that he cited because it supported his argument, it also established that the Supreme Court could issue the writ in the exercise of original jurisdiction, a conclusion that he did not cite because it did not support his argument. Marshall nowhere acknowledged or discussed or tried to explain away Lee's demonstration that precedents for the issuance of the writ existed, nor did he acknowledge, discuss, or try to explain away, in the course of that part of his argument, the "precedent" that he himself cited at the point in his opinion when it was to his advantage to do so. He was too determined to reach his desired end.

Having proved, to his own satisfaction at least, that § 13 was unconstitutional—even his "adoring biographer," Albert Beveridge, does not take him seriously on this point and concedes that the holding of invalidity could only be understood as a "pretext" for the exercise of judicial review[340]—Marshall turns to the most famous part of his opinion, the brief concluding section in which he seeks to prove that courts are obligated to disregard unconstitutional legislation. It is Clinton's explanation of that argument—the core of which is contained in the passage quoted in full earlier[341]— that constitutes his major distortion of Marshall's position. He notes that Marshall did not claim for the judiciary an exclusive authority to interpret the Constitution, and that the authority that he did claim was grounded in what he saw as the inescapable necessity of doing so in deciding cases in which a law and a constitutional provision may be in conflict.[342] That much is certainly true, but then, suddenly and without a shred of explanation or justification, he leaps to a conclusion that cannot be derived from

---

[339] See id at 322.

[340] Beveridge, 3 *John Marshall* at 133 (cited in note 17).

[341] See text at note 37.

[342] Clinton, *Marbury v. Madison* at 98–99. See 1 Cranch at 177–78.

anything in Marshall's opinion: "In other words, the power of review claimed by the Court in *Marbury* is merely a power of discretion to disregard existing laws, provided that the constitutional and
statutory provisions involved are, like those in Article III and the
Judiciary Act, *addressed to the Court itself.*"[343] One searches Marshall's opinion in vain for any words that would support Clinton's
proviso, for Marshall never comes close to asserting that judicial
review is only to be exercised when the challenged law and the
constitutional provision it is said to violate are "addressed to the
Court itself." His language is sweeping in its generality, and, moreover, he provides three hypothetical examples[344] of instances where
judicial review would be essential to prevent the Constitution from
being "reduce[d] to nothing" by a legislature willing to ignore its
provisions,[345] two of which—those relating to export taxes and to
bills of attainder or *ex post facto* laws—obviously have nothing to
do with laws or constitutional provisions addressed specifically to
the courts.

Clinton's attempt to force Marshall's argument into the mold he
designed for it appears to rest entirely on the words "of necessity"
in Marshall's statement that "[t]hose who apply the rule to particular cases, must of necessity expound and interpret that rule."[346] He
writes: "If the provisions are *not* addressed to the Court itself, then
the court is not *compelled*, as a matter of *logic*, to choose between
them *in order to decide the case.*"[347] In other words, in such circumstances, they would not do so "of necessity." But note where the
words "of necessity" appear in Marshall's statement. Marshall does
not say that those "who, of necessity, apply the rule to particular
cases, must expound and interpret that rule." That language might
have provided support for Clinton's contention, for it suggests that
the courts should only apply constitutional rules where they *must*
do so—*viz.*, in cases where the relevant rules are addressed to the
courts. But what Marshall actually wrote is something entirely
different. His actual statement assumed that the Court was properly applying the relevant rules to the case at hand, and he then

---

[343] Clinton, *Marbury v. Madison* at 99. (Emphasis is in original.)

[344] 1 Cranch at 179.

[345] Id at 178.

[346] Clinton, *Marbury v. Madison* at 99, citing 1 Cranch at 177.

[347] Clinton, *Marbury v. Madison* at 99. (Emphasis is in original.)

declared, unremarkably, that to do so, it "must of necessity expound and interpret" those rules, including the provisions of the Constitution where they are involved. That statement provides no support at all for Clinton's conclusion. Marshall was specifically equating the function of deciding a conflict between a law and a constitutional provision with the judicial function of deciding a conflict between two legislative acts,[348] and the latter function obviously requires the courts to reach a judgment regardless of whether the laws are addressed to the courts. Indeed, in the vast majority of cases, they will not be. As Clinton reads Marshall's statement, there would be no *necessity* to reach a judgment unless each of the relevant rules involve directives to the courts, but there is no way to match that interpretation with Marshall's own words except by brute force.[349]

To be sure, Marshall was making no claim for judicial power to decide constitutional questions except in the course of deciding cases or controversies properly before the courts for adjudication. In putting forward his hypothetical examples of unconstitutional legislative actions that could be frustrated by the exercise of the power of judicial review, he was careful to place the judicial declarations of unconstitutionality that he saw as vital for the protection of the Constitution in a context in which an exercise of judicial power would be appropriate. Thus, in Marshall's examples, a court would declare an export tax unconstitutional in "a suit instituted to recover it," or invalidate a bill of attainder or *ex post facto* law when "a person should be prosecuted under it."[350] But disclaiming authority to exercise the power to declare acts unconstitutional except in a case or controversy is not the same thing as disclaiming authority to do so except where the constitutional provision said

---

[348] 1 Cranch at 177–78.

[349] Clinton also tries to argue that his conception of judicial review as being appropriate only "in that relatively small number of instances where the Constitution furnishes a direct rule for the courts" was the same conception held by the Court in *Marbury*, as reflected "in its reference to the idea of political questions." Clinton, *Marbury v. Madison* at 99. This, too, is nonsense. Marshall argued that the courts could not interfere with the executive branch in matters in which the executive possessed discretion to act as it chose. 1 Cranch at 165–66, 169–70. But the President does not have discretion to violate the Constitution, and so Marshall's discussion of political questions has no relevance to the scope of judicial review in cases involving constitutional limits on the powers of the political branches of the government.

[350] 1 Cranch at 179. See Robert A. Burt, *Inventing Judicial Review: Israel and America*, 10 Cardozo L Rev 2013, 2092 (1989).

to be violated concerns the power or jurisdiction of the courts. It is true that the constitutional question decided in *Marbury* involved a law and a constitutional provision that were addressed to the Supreme Court, and that the holding in that case thus could have been carefully confined to the assertion of the narrow principle that courts can disregard acts of Congress that call on them to take actions inconsistent with constitutional limits on judicial power. But, as Robert Burt has observed, "Marshall did rely on this principle but with his characteristic masterful ambiguity he did not disclaim the possibility of more extensive judicial review authority."[351] Marshall's opinion was not carefully crafted to have only a narrow application; it espoused a broad vision of judicial review, and, in drafting it, Marshall avoided (and, one must assume, carefully avoided) the use of any language that would have limited the range of applicability of the power of judicial review that he claimed for the courts in the execution of their responsibilities in deciding cases or controversies.

Apart from his analysis of the content of Marshall's opinion, Clinton turns to the subsequent history of the treatment of *Marbury* by courts and scholars in an effort to prove that it was not regarded until late in the nineteenth century as establishing broad judicial authority to invalidate legislation that did not contravene a constitutional provision addressed to the courts. He notes that, as constitutional historians have long recognized, the decision did not evoke a storm of controversy upon its announcement,[352] and concludes

---

[351] Id at 2053. To serve the purposes of the argument in his recent book, Professor Burt downplays the breadth of the claim for judicial authority in Marshall's opinion. See Robert A. Burt, *The Constitution in Conflict* 119 (Belknap, 1992). But his earlier statement, cited above, is more accurately descriptive. See also Louis B. Boudin, 1 *Government by Judiciary* 232–33 (Godwin, 1932), where it is noted that, although "nothing had been *decided* in *Marbury v. Madison* that in any way countenanced the Judicial Power as we know it today . . . considerably more than was *decided*, was *said* in the opinion accompanying the decision." (Emphasis is in original.) Boudin, who was a vigorous opponent of judicial review, agreed that the formal precedential value of *Marbury* is limited to the precise question that was presented for decision and actually decided—that courts may disregard an act of Congress unconstitutionally altering the powers of the judiciary. But he understood that that was not the full reach of the power that Marshall claimed, because "in deciding upon those facts a general rule had been laid down which goes beyond those facts," and, indeed, that the "rule is laid down by Marshall in the broadest terms imaginable." Id at 230.

[352] Clinton, *Marbury v. Madison* at 102, citing Dewey, *Marshall versus Jefferson* at 135–36 (cited in note 18). See also Haines, *American Doctrine* at 232–321 (cited in note 51); Haskins and Johnson, *Foundations of Power* at 215–17 (cited in note 90); McCloskey, *American Supreme Court* at 43–44 (cited in note 130); Warren, 1 *Supreme Court History* at 231–32 (cited in note 91); Beveridge, 3 *John Marshall* at 153–54 (cited in note 17). As Beveridge observed, "the first of Marshall's great Constitutional opinions received scant notice at the time of its

that that demonstrates "the general acceptability of the decision itself and the opinion that justified it."[353] It may be conceded that the absence of controversy is evidence that the conception of judicial review embodied in *Marbury* was not controversial, but that does not prove that that conception was Clinton's. Indeed, the copious evidence collected by Charles Warren with regard to the views repeatedly expressed in Congress and elsewhere during the 1790s shows beyond much doubt that judicial review was generally conceived of as a broad authority to refuse enforcement of any unconstitutional law.[354] But, beyond that, there is a further obvious reason why *Marbury* should not have elicited much immediate hostile reaction. The case was universally understood, by participants and observers alike, to be a political event, rather than a legal event. And, as a political event, it did little to threaten the power of the incumbent Republicans. Their view of the case as a political event was made clear by the administration's refusal to acknowledge the jurisdiction of the Court or to offer a legal argument at any stage of the proceedings. They were undoubtedly anticipating the issuance of the writ of mandamus, and were prepared to ignore it and to engage in some form of political retaliation. The expected judicial assault fizzled, however, when no order was issued. The assertion of the power of judicial review was not itself an occasion for consternation. There had been a general consensus that such a power should rest with the judiciary,[355] and although that consensus was beginning to fall apart—as reflected in the congressional debate over the Repeal Act of 1802—because of the Republicans' perception that a Federalist judiciary might use that power to thwart the achievement of the goals of their party,[356] its use to invalidate § 13 of the Judiciary Act of 1789 was of no concern to anyone, least of all the Republicans. A political war over judicial review would surely have erupted had the Court attempted to invalidate the Repeal Act, but the Court, well aware of its political defenselessness, was relieved to be able to let the occasion for that

---

delivery. The newspapers had little to say about it. Even the bench and bar of the country, at least in the sections remote from Washington, appear not to have heard of it, or, if they had, to have forgotten it amid the thrilling events that filled the times." Id.

[353] Clinton, *Marbury v. Madison* at 103.

[354] Warren, *Congress, Constitution and Court* at 95–127 (cited in note 12).

[355] See, for example, id at 95–99.

[356] See, for example, Warren, 1 *Supreme Court History* at 215–16 (cited in note 91).

go by in *Stuart v Laird*,[357] one week after *Marbury*. As Leonard Levy has noted, in *Stuart* the Court "refused to hold unconstitutional an act of doubtful validity, while in *Marbury* it held unconstitutional an act of undoubted validity."[358]

The sole temerarious aspect of Marshall's opinion was its wholly gratuitous pronouncement that the President and the Secretary of State were acting in disregard of the vested legal rights of individuals in failing to deliver the signed and sealed commissions to Marbury and his co-plaintiffs. It is hardly surprising that this was the only aspect of the opinion that was particularly perturbing to Jefferson and the Republicans.[359] Even here, the criticisms were relatively muted because Marshall's use of the judicial forum to attack the administration was not backed up by any concrete judicial demands. Thus, the absence of a powerful antijudicial response to the *Marbury* decision seems readily explainable. While judicial office was used for the delivery of a lecture to the Court's Republican opponents, that lecture, although provocative, was merely words. There was nothing in the opinion that demanded any form of action, and it was therefore easy to turn attention to other concerns where some form of action might be required.[360]

But Clinton insists that the Supreme Court "must have agreed, throughout most of the nineteenth century, with the view of *Marbury v Madison* advanced in this study."[361] The evidence he presents in support of this proposition consists of the failure of the Supreme Court, prior to *Mugler v Kansas*[362] in 1887, to cite *Marbury* "as precedent for the idea that courts may enforce constitutional limitations on legislative bodies,"[363] the fact that the Court did not, after 1803, exercise the power of judicial review aggressively until late in the century, and did not declare another act of Congress uncon-

---

[357] 1 Cranch 299 (1803). See text at notes 161–66.

[358] Levy, *Original Intent* at 87–88 (cited in note 24).

[359] See, for example, Ellis, *Jeffersonian Crisis* at 65–66 (cited in note 42); Malone, *Jefferson the President* at 149 (cited in note 104); Warren, 1 *Supreme Court History* at 264–66 (cited in note 91).

[360] See Beveridge, 3 *John Marshall* at 145–53 (cited in note 17), for a summary of the pressing political concerns of the moment that diverted the Republicans' attention away from the *Marbury* ruling.

[361] Clinton, *Marbury v. Madison* at 117.

[362] 123 US 623 (1887).

[363] Clinton, *Marbury v. Madison* at 120.

stitutional until *Dred Scott v Sandford*[364] in 1857 (which also did not cite *Marbury*), and, finally, that most of the relatively few citations of *Marbury* prior to *Mugler* relate to jurisdiction while none relates to judicial review.[365] Various conclusions can be drawn from this evidence, but one of them is not that the Court embraced Clinton's view of *Marbury v Madison*. The failure to cite *Marbury* as a precedent for judicial review suggests that the Court understood the basis for judicial review to lie in the Constitution, and that the power does not depend on *Marbury* for its legitimacy. In any event, the absence of citations of *Marbury* says nothing about what particular theory of judicial review had been advanced in that case. The fact that when *Marbury* was cited, it was usually cited with regard to jurisdictional issues is not surprising given the fact that the holding of that case pertained to the jurisdiction of the Supreme Court. Nor is it possible to draw any conclusions about the theory of judicial review espoused in *Marbury* from the fact that frequent exercise of the power did not occur until over fifty years after Marshall's opinion was written. Clinton's evidence is purely negative. He presents no affirmative historical evidence to support his thesis—no statements by judges, lawyers, or commentators expressing an understanding or belief that courts had final authority to invalidate legislation that they found to be in violation of the Constitution only where constitutional directives to the courts were involved.

It does not follow from the fact that the Court exercised judicial review sparingly, and generally did not appear "desirous of expanding its authority at the expense of either Congress or the states,"[366] that it took a narrow view of the scope of its power. The power may be broadly applicable even if it is not often exercised. Clinton is certainly correct that the impact of judicial review on the governing process changed dramatically in the final years of the nineteenth century, with the onset of a fervid judicial commitment to protect businesses against regulatory legislation, and, with the development of substantive due process, the practice reached proportions that Marshall could not possibly have imagined.[367] In

---

[364] 19 Howard 393 (1857).

[365] Clinton, *Marbury v. Madison* at 117–20.

[366] Id at 118.

[367] See Walton Hamilton, *The Path of Due Process of Law*, in Conyers Read, ed, *The Constitution Reconsidered* 167 (Columbia, 1938).

this period, as reluctant Justices warned, judicial review became a means by which acts could be struck down because of the views of judges as to "the merits of the legislation."[368] But although Marshall could not have contemplated what would occur almost a century later, there was nothing in his opinion in *Marbury* (except for the limitation that it can only be exercised in a case or controversy) to preclude the expansion of judicial review, in practice, to the fullest extent that society is prepared to tolerate. It is interesting in light of Clinton's insistence that *Marbury* expressed only a narrow conception of judicial review, and provides no sanction for the institution in its modern form, to consider the statement in *Mugler v Kansas* that Clinton identifies as marking the Court's departure from Marshall's position: "[T]he courts must obey the Constitution rather than the lawmaking department of government, and must, upon their own responsibility, determine whether, in any particular case, these limits have been passed."[369] There is nothing in that statement that would not fit comfortably in Marshall's opinion in *Marbury*. It does not alter, it simply restates, Marshall's argument.[370]

Clinton obviously did a great deal of research in the preparation of his book, and he provides a useful compendium of précis of many references to *Marbury* over the years. But his efforts were squandered in his determination to make Marshall's opinion into something it was not. Clinton's goal was to prove that, in contrast to judges who adhere to the activist principles of modern judicial review, John Marshall was a jurist who never presumed to deviate from the course dictated by faithful adherence to pure legal principle. In the service of that goal, there was no fact that could not be overlooked, no language that could not be distorted, no idea that could not be misconstrued, no criticism that could not be misunderstood. It was necessary to misread or wantonly misinterpret Marshall's opinion, to disregard the significance of the political

---

[368] *Davidson v New Orleans*, 96 US 97, 104 (1877).

[369] *Mugler*, 123 US at 661, quoted in Clinton, *Marbury v. Madison* at 120.

[370] The statement in *Mugler* (by Justice Harlan) is entirely compatible with Marshall's assertion in *Marbury* that if "the courts are to regard the constitution, and the constitution is superior to any ordinary act of the legislature, the constitution, and not such ordinary act, must govern the case to which they both apply," for to hold otherwise would be "prescribing limits, and declaring that those limits may be passed at pleasure." 1 Cranch at 178. Note also that Marshall declares that the constitution must take precedence over "*any* ordinary act of the legislature," not just those that affect the powers of the judiciary.

context in which the case arose and was decided, and to dismiss the accumulated understandings of generations of historians and constitutional scholars, whose conclusions were cavalierly pushed aside as confused or misguided. What Clinton presents is a form of constitutional lysenkoism,[371] in which all that we have learned about *Marbury* to date is to be rejected in favor of a pseudo-theory dictated by a commitment to a false belief that yesterday's judges were lawyers while today's are politicians. His work pulls forward the frontiers of knowledge. The effect may not be serious because the book seems destined to receive the inattention it deserves. Our understanding of *Marbury* is not, therefore, likely to be seriously diminished, but the effort is nevertheless to be deplored.

IV. JOHN BANNISTER GIBSON AND THE LOGIC OF JUDICIAL REVIEW

Because the principal significance of *Marbury* lies in the concluding passages of Marshall's opinion in which he seeks to make the case for judicial review, and because the nature of his argument there seems rarely to be adequately examined, it may be worthwhile to reconsider it here. A century ago, James Bradley Thayer wrote that "much the ablest discussion of the question [of judicial review] that I have ever seen" was presented in the dissenting opinion of Judge John Bannister Gibson of the Pennsylvania Supreme Court in the 1825 case of *Eakin v Raub*.[372] Gibson's opinion was essentially a response to Marshall's argument for judicial review, and, to this day, it remains "much the ablest discussion" of that argument. To appreciate fully the case that Marshall made, and to understand why it fails, it is important to scrutinize it in light of Gibson's critique.

After finding § 13 of the Judiciary Act of 1789 to be inconsistent with the Constitution, Marshall turned to "[t]he question, whether an act, repugnant to the constitution, can become the law of the land," a question which he found "deeply interesting to the United States; but, happily, not of an intricacy proportioned to its inter-

---

[371] See text at note 272.

[372] Thayer, 7 Harv L Rev at 130 n 1. The dissent appears in 12 Sergeant and Rawle 330, 344–58 (Pa 1825).

est."[373] The question was not intricate, as he saw it, because only one answer was logically possible. If a constitution limits the legislature, and legislative acts that ignore those limits are nevertheless valid and enforceable, "then written constitutions are absurd attempts, on the part of the people, to limit a power, in its own nature, illimitable."[374] Therefore, "the theory of every . . . government [with a written constitution], must be, that an act of the legislature, repugnant to the constitution, is void."[375] So far, so good. As Gibson declared, it "is conceded" that if the constitution "were to come into collision with an act of the legislature, the latter would have to give way."[376] Or, as Alexander Bickel has noted, from the incontrovertible fact that constitutions are intended to limit governmental power, "[i]t follows—and one may grant to Marshall that it follows as 'a proposition too plain to be contested'—that the Constitution is a paramount law, and that ordinary legislative acts must conform to it."[377]

But, as Bickel further noted, Marshall's argument to that point had "begged the question-in-chief, which was not whether an act repugnant to the Constitution could stand, but who should be empowered to decide that the act is repugnant."[378] Of course, Marshall clearly recognized that the existence of the power of judicial review does not automatically follow from the mere acknowledgment of the invalidity of a legislative act,[379] and so turned to the next step in his proof by framing the issue in these terms:[380]

> If an act of the legislature, repugnant to the constitution, is void, does it, notwithstanding its invalidity, bind the courts, and oblige them to give it effect? Or, in other words, though it be not law, does it constitute a rule as operative as if it was

---

[373] 1 Cranch at 176.

[374] Id at 177.

[375] Id.

[376] 12 Sergeant and Rawle at 347.

[377] Bickel, *Least Dangerous Branch* at 3 (cited in note 8), quoting *Marbury*, 1 Cranch at 177.

[378] Bickel, *Least Dangerous Branch* at 3.

[379] Clinton correctly points out that "Marshall clearly distinguishes between a law *being* null due to incompatibility with the Constitution, and a court having the *power* to nullify such a law. He does not . . . attempt to derive his second conclusion *by implication* from premises that will support only the first conclusion." Clinton, *Marbury v. Madison* at 16. (Emphasis is in original.)

[380] 1 Cranch at 177.

a law? This would be to overthrow, in fact, what was established in theory; and would seem, at first view, an absurdity too gross to be insisted on.

The problem is that the argument, stated in that way, proves too much. If the word "executive" is substituted for the word "courts" in the first sentence of the quoted paragraph, the absurdity described would seem no less gross. The executive is responsible for ensuring that the commands of the laws are observed, and is empowered to use force to do so if necessary, so, if the executive is obliged to give effect to an unconstitutional law, and must arrest those who disregard it, that would also seem to make a rule that was void "as operative as if it was a law" and equally "to overthrow, in fact, what was established in theory." But it cannot be doubted that if the word "executive" were substituted, Marhall would expect the question to be answered affirmatively. Thus the power of a governmental body to refuse to carry out the requirements of a legislative act in the course of performing its official duties must depend not on the absurdity of making an invalid law operative, but on the nature of the responsibilities of that body that would make it appropriate for it, but not for other governmental bodies, to make a decision as to the constitutionality of the law.

Therefore, the task that Marshall faced was to demonstrate that the responsibility for ruling on the constitutionality of legislation should or must belong—and belong uniquely—to the judicial branch of the government. There are various ways of making such an argument. One possibility would be to defend the assignment of this responsibility to the judiciary as a matter of policy—to show why it would be a good idea to allow courts to resolve constitutional controversies. Gibson suggests a basis for such an argument, noting that a case could be made for "vest[ing] the power in the judiciary; as it might be expected, that its habits of deliberation, and the aid derived from the arguments of counsel, would more frequently lead to accurate conclusions."[381] Or an argument of this sort could have been developed from Hamilton's observation that the judiciary was the weakest branch of the government, "the least dangerous to the political rights of the constitution,"[382] and therefore the safest repository of the power to decide on questions of constitu

---

[381] 12 Sergeant and Rawle at 355.

[382] Federalist 78 (Hamilton), in Cooke, ed, *The Federalist* at 522 (cited in note 55).

tionality. But, for Marshall's purposes, the immediate difficulty with such an approach was that arguments based on policy and practicality are necessarily subjective, and, given the distrust with which the judiciary was regarded by the dominant political forces in the country at that time—forces which enjoyed broad public support—the subjective conclusion of judges that it would be a good idea that they should be given this power was not likely to prove very persuasive.

A related argument could have replicated the Federalists' argument in the Repeal Act debate of 1802, which, as O'Fallon demonstrated, was focused on the need to protect vested rights to property and liberty against abuses of legislative authority.[383] The Federalists in Congress had argued that: "Legislatures will, in violent times, enact laws manifestly unjust, oppressive, and unconstitutional. . . . Such laws, it is the business of the judges, elevated above the influence of party, to control."[384] However, the Repeal Act debate demonstrated that the argument based on abuse could be turned around and directed against the courts by the Republicans, who were not so certain that they were "elevated above the influence of party." Judges could abuse the power of deciding constitutional questions in order to thwart the implementation of policies of which they disapproved: "Give the Judiciary this check upon the Legislature, allow them the power to declare your laws null and void . . . and in vain have the people placed you upon this floor to legislate; your laws will be nullified, your proceedings will be checked."[385]

Still another argument might have been based on specific provisions of the Constitution, but, of course, there is nothing in the Constitution that clearly and unequivocally confers authority on the federal courts to adjudge the constitutionality of the acts of the political branches of the government. Herbert Wechsler claimed to have found such a grant of authority in the Supremacy Clause of Article VI, which bound state judges to adherence to "the supreme Law of the Land"—that is, the Constitution, "the Laws of

---

[383] O'Fallon, 44 Stan L Rev at 227–36. See also Beveridge 3 *John Marshall* at 58–92 (cited in note 17).

[384] Annals of Congress, 7th Cong, 1st Sess c 728 (1802) (remarks of Representative Calvin Goddard of Connecticut).

[385] Id at cc 552–53 (remarks of Representative Philip R. Thompson of Virginia).

the United States which shall be made in Pursuance thereof," and treaties—"any Thing in the Constitution or Laws of any State to the Contrary notwithstanding."[386] Professor Wechsler was undoubtedly correct in concluding that whatever power was conferred on state courts by Article VI must also be possessed by federal courts.[387] (Federal law would not be supreme if state courts had unreviewable authority to decide whether state laws conflicted with the Constitution, laws, or treaties of the United States.) Thus, it can properly be concluded that the Supremacy Clause vests authority in the Supreme Court to declare *state* laws or *state* constitutional provisions invalid because they are inconsistent with "the supreme Law of the Land."[388] But the problem that Wechsler never surmounts is that this clause does not, either explicitly or implicitly, confer any authority on any court, state or federal, to review the constitutional validity of federal law.[389] The requirement of Article VI that acts of Congress must "be made in Pursuance" of the Constitution in order to qualify as "the supreme Law of the Land" does not in terms confer any power on courts to decide if a law has been "made in Pursuance" of the Constitution,[390] and, in any event, the fact that this provision applies only to laws, and not to treaties (which become "the supreme Law of the Land" merely

---

[386] Herbert Wechsler, *Toward Neutral Principles of Constitutional Law*, 73 Harv L Rev 1, 2–5 (1959).

[387] Id at 3–4.

[388] See § 25 of the Judiciary Act of 1789, Act of Sept 24, 1789, 1 Stat 73, 85–87.

[389] In § 25 of the Judiciary Act of 1789, 1 Stat 73, 85–86, Congress authorized the Supreme Court to "re-examine[] and reverse[] or affirm[]" state court judgments declaring invalid "a treaty or statute of, or an authority exercised under the United States" (as well as state court judgments sustaining state laws against supremacy clause challenges or rejecting claims based on federal law). It has been argued that, by giving the Court power to *affirm* state court decisions invalidating federal statutes, Congress implicitly acknowledged that the Court possessed the power to declare national legislation invalid on constitutional grounds. See, for example, Warren, *Congress, Constitution and Court* at 104 (cited in note 12). Leonard Levy, however, has canvassed the difficulties with such a conclusion, and has rather conclusively demonstrated that this part of § 25 could only be the result of clumsy drafting, and that, while the power to *affirm* state court judgments applied to the other two categories of state court decisions over which § 25 gave the Supreme Court appellate jurisdiction, only the power to *reverse* was applicable to Supreme Court review of state court judgments declaring federal law invalid and refusing to enforce it. See Levy, *Original Intent* at 111–13 (cited in note 24). If Congress did intend to confer on the Supreme Court a power to declare federal laws unconstitutional, it does seem strange that the power to do so would be limited to cases in which these laws had first been invalidated by a state court.

[390] See Corwin, *Doctrine* at 14 (cited in note 50); Van Alstyne, 1969 Duke L J at 21–22 (cited in note 194). But compare Berger, *Congress v. Court* at 228–34 (cited in note 316).

by having been made "under the Authority of the United States"), rather clearly demonstrates that, unless treaties are to be valid whether or not they are consistent with the Constitution, the term "made in Pursuance" of the Constitution has nothing to do with whether acts of Congress are constitutional, and would appear to mean nothing more than that federal laws passed under the Articles of Confederation are not supreme law, but only those laws passed by the two houses of Congress established by the Constitution and signed by the President or passed over his veto, whereas treaties qualify even if made before the adoption of the Constitution.[391]

Another constitutional provision that can arguably be employed to provide a textual basis for judicial review is Article III, § 2, extending the judicial power of the United States "to all Cases, in Law and Equity, arising under this Constitution." But the fact that federal courts may take jurisdiction over cases "arising under" the Constitution does not necessarily imply the existence of the power of judicial review because cases may arise under the Constitution which do not involve any question as to the constitutionality of an act of Congress.[392] Questions involving the constitutionality of state laws would surely fit in this category, as would cases in which the Constitution provides specific rules for courts to follow—as, for example, the provision of Article III, § 3 requiring "the Testimony of two Witnesses to the same overt Act, or . . . Confession in open Court" to sustain a conviction for the crime of treason. Therefore, it is not surprising that Marshall does not seek to establish the existence of the power to declare acts of Congress unconstitutional directly from the text of the Constitution. To be sure, he refers to the language of Article III, § 2, and to two provisions of Article VI—the Supremacy Clause and the oath of office requirement—in the course of his opinion;[393] however, he does not do so to make

---

[391] For a thorough discussion of this point, see Crosskey, 2 *Politics and the Constitution* at 996–99 (cited in note 313). A vigorous rebuttal of Crosskey's analysis is in Berger, *Congress v. Court* at 234–36 (cited in note 316).

[392] See Bickel, *Least Dangerous Branch* at 6 (cited in note 8); Van Alstyne, 1969 Duke L J at 27–28 (cited in note 194). In *Federalist 80*, Alexander Hamilton, describing the meaning of the phrase "arising under this Constitution," explained that it referred to cases involving "restrictions upon the authority of the state legislatures." Federalist 80 (Hamilton), in Cooke, ed, *The Federalist* at 539 (cited in note 55). An historical case for concluding that the grant of "arising under" jurisdiction implies a grant of judicial review is made in Berger, *Congress v. Court* at 198–222 (cited in note 316).

[393] 1 Cranch at 178–79 (reference to Art III, § 2); id at 180 (references to Art VI). Marshall's reliance on the oath of office required by Art VI is discussed in text at notes 455–59.

his case, but only to bolster a conclusion he has already arrived at.[394] Indeed, his only reference to the "made in Pursuance" language of Article VI comes at the very end of his opinion, and he uses it for no substantive purpose. His only comment on it is that it is "not entirely unworthy of observation" that this phrasing was employed by the framers.[395]

Marshall could not, in 1803, rely on anything other than the text as evidence of the intent of the framers. Even if the use of extratextual material to supplement the language of a written law were not then regarded as a questionable practice,[396] no legislative history bearing on the framing of the Constitution was then available. The meetings of the Convention were held in secrecy, and its records remained closed until 1818.[397] And, given the fact that the debate over the intention of the framers with regard to judicial review continues to rage even today,[398] it is hardly likely that Marshall could have constructed an argument based on the framers' intent that would have satisfied the Republicans, whose determined opposition to the existence of a powerful judiciary was vigorously articulated in the Repeal Act debates. Senator John Breckinridge of Kentucky, who introduced the repeal bill in Congress, for example, expressed great skepticism about the constitutional legitimacy of judicial review: "If it is derived from the Constitution, I ask gentle-

---

[394] Marshall is quite explicit about this. In the concluding paragraph of his opinion, he states that "the particular phraseology of the constitution of the United States *confirms and strengthens the principle, supposed to be essential to all written constitutions*, that a law repugnant to the constitution is void." 1 Cranch at 180. (Emphasis added.)

[395] Id.

[396] In *Sturges v Crowninshield*, 4 Wheaton 122, 202 (1819), Marshall wrote that "although the spirit of an instrument, especially of a constitution, is to be respected not less than its letter, yet the spirit is to be collected chiefly from its words." For an outstanding examination of the uses of legislative history in constitutional interpretation, see the series of articles by Jacobus ten Broek, *Admissibility and Use by the United States Supreme Court of Extrinsic Aids in Constitutional Construction*, 26 Cal L Rev 137 (1938); 26 Cal L Rev 437 (1938); 26 Cal L Rev 664 (1938); 27 Cal L Rev 157 (1939); 27 Cal L Rev 399 (1939).

[397] See Farrand, ed, 1 *Records* at xi–xii (cited in note 313).

[398] Compare Berger, *Congress v. Court* at 335 (cited in note 316): "[T]he Framers, I consider, made reasonably plain that [judicial] review was part of the Constitutional scheme," with Levy, *Original Intent* at 100 (cited in note 24): "The evidence seems to indicate that the Framers did not mean for the Supreme Court to have authority to void acts of Congress." The judgment expressed by Edward Corwin, in testimony before the Senate Judiciary Committee in 1937 during its consideration of Franklin Roosevelt's "court-packing" plan, was that: "These people who say the framers intended it are talking nonsense; and the people who say they did not intend it are talking nonsense. There is evidence on both sides." Reorganization of the Federal Judiciary, Hearings Before the Committee on the Judiciary, United States Senate, 75th Cong, 1st Sess 176 (1937).

men to point out the clause which grants it. I can find no such grant. Is it not extraordinary, that if this high power was intended, it should nowhere appear? Is it not truly astonishing that the Constitution, in its abundant care to define the powers of each department, should have omitted so important a power as that of the courts to nullify all the acts of Congress, which, in their opinion, were contrary to the Constitution?"[399]

Another possible way in which Marshall could have constructed his argument for judicial review would have been to rest it on precedent. Charles Grove Haines, half a century ago, collected and comprehensively examined the state and federal cases prior to *Marbury* in which the power of courts to disregard unconstitutional legislation was assumed or exercised.[400] The relevance and reality of many of these precedents has been seriously questioned,[401] and Edward Corwin expressed the view that any argument for judicial review to be drawn from the precedents "was a shadowy one at best,"[402] but certainly precedents were available that could have been cited. Marshall's unwillingness to use them, however, is certainly understandable. The majority of the precedents, having to do with state court, or even federal court,[403] invalidation of state laws as violative of state constitutions, would have offered scant help in proving that the United States Constitution conferred power on the federal courts to declare an act of Congress unconstitutional. To be sure, the Supreme Court, in *Hylton v United States* in 1796,[404] had entertained a constitutional challenge to an act of Congress (imposing an excise tax on carriages), and thereby implicitly acknowledged a power to declare federal laws invalid, and, four years earlier, members of the Court, sitting as circuit judges, declined to serve, in their judicial capacities, as commissioners to determine the eligibility of Revolutionary War veterans for pensions, on the basis of their belief that Congress could not constitutionally assign them nonjudicial functions,[405] but the probative

---

[399] Annals of Congress, 7th Cong, 1st Sess c 179 (1802).

[400] Haines, *American Doctrine* at 88–121, 148–203 (cited in note 51).

[401] Levy, *Original Intent* at 92–99 (cited in note 24).

[402] Edward S. Corwin, *Court over Constitution* 25 (Princeton, 1938).

[403] See *Vanhorne's Lessee v Dorrance*, 2 Dallas 304 (1795).

[404] 3 Dallas 171 (1796). See text at notes 60–63.

[405] See *Hayburn's Case*, 2 Dallas 409 (1792).

value of these examples was limited. On the other hand, the precedents could have been used not to make an argument specific to
the United States Constitution, but to establish that the institution
of judicial review had such widespread general acceptance that it
would have been unnecessary to have made express provision for
it in the Constitution. Such use of precedent would have been
analogous to the effort to establish framers' intent, and, for the
same reasons that other indicia of the framers' intent would have
been unlikely to convince the Court's political opponents, citation
of these examples would not have satisfied the Republicans that
the institution of judicial review was given to the courts by implicit
consensus.

Marshall's decision not to rest his argument for judicial review
even partly on precedent was to some extent probably a reflection
of his personal style of opinion writing—which tended to ignore
precedent and to rely instead on his genius for powerful argumenta-
tion[406]—but, in *Marbury*, that inclination was almost certainly rein-
forced by the recognition that invocation of precedent would have
been of no use in persuading those who did not already accept
the wisdom and desirability of judicial review. In addition, he
undoubtedly also realized that the question of whether judicial
review was a proper part of the American constitutional system
was too fundamental to be decided on the basis of precedent. Either
the practice was justified in terms of basic principles of constitutional governance or it was not, and, if it was not, the mere fact
that the power had been unjustifiably exercised at various times in
the past would provide no warrant for its acceptance. As Judge
Gibson declared, "in questions of this sort, precedents ought to go
for absolutely nothing."[407]

In the absence of any clear grant to the federal courts in the

---

[406] See, for example, Robert K. Faulkner, *The Jurisprudence of John Marshall* 220 (Princeton,
1968). In his entire opinion in *Marbury v Madison*, Marshall mentions only two precedents—
one of which he does not identify by name, and which proves to be a fictitious composite
of three different (and nonfictitious) cases. See Bloch and Marcus, 1986 Wis L Rev 301
(cited in note 335). See also text at notes 335–39.

[407] 12 Sergeant and Rawle at 346. Similarly, Edward Corwin has observed that to rest
the case for judicial review on precedent "is plainly illogical," and thus *Marbury* alone
provides no authority for judicial review. Either it "was based upon the Constitution or it
was not. In the former case, however, it is the Constitution that is the real basis of power,
while in the latter the decision was erroneous by the court's own premises." Corwin, *Doctrine*
at 3 (cited in note 50).

Constitution of power to declare acts of Congress unconstitutional, the lack of solidly convincing evidence of the framers' intent to convey such a grant by implication, the inappropriateness of reliance on precedent for the resolution of such a fundamental constitutional question (and the scarcity of relevant precedents), and the existence of a hostile political climate that made it impossible for the Court to employ subjective arguments regarding the desirability of maintaining a judicial check on legislative abuses, Marshall chose to rest his case for judicial review on the one approach that would be politically unassailable—pure deductive logic. If it could be shown by objective logic that a written constitution *required* judicial review, political opposition to the institution would be rendered impotent. Politics would have to yield to the syllogism. Marshall was justifiably confident that he possessed the rhetorical and argumentative skills to make this case, and history has proved him right. Even today, one reads this part of Marshall's opinion and is all but helplessly swept along to its conclusion. Thus, when Chancellor James Kent described Marshall's argument as "approaching to the precision and certainty of a mathematical demonstration,"[408] or when Edward Corwin observed that the argument "marches to its conclusion with all the precision of a demonstration from Euclid,"[409] they were not merely employing figures of speech. Marshall's argument was designed to be just that—a Euclidian mathematical demonstration of the proposition that the institution of judicial review follows ineluctably from the fact of a written constitution. But he who lives by the sword, dies by the sword. Had Marshall made a subjective argument based on the wisdom of having a judicial check on political authority, one could argue with his conclusion, but could not prove him wrong. However, an argument resting on deductive logic, while not vulnerable to subjective criticism, can be proved erroneous if any part of the reasoning rests on a fallacy. For this reason, it can be said with certainty that Marshall's argument for judicial review in *Marbury v Madison* was wrong.

Marshall's logical syllogism is contained in a single brief passage of his opinion, which was earlier quoted in its entirety.[410] The

---

[408] James Kent, 1 *Commentaries on American Law* 424 (O. Halsted, 1826).

[409] Edward S. Corwin, *John Marshall and the Constitution* 67 (Yale, 1919).

[410] 1 Cranch at 177–78, quoted in text at note 37.

syllogism, which closely tracks the virtually identical reasoning in the argument for judicial review put forward by Alexander Hamilton in *Federalist 78*,[411] is based on an analogy with the inescapable responsibility of courts to resolve conflicts between two contradictory acts of the legislature:[412]

> If two laws conflict with each other, the courts must decide on the operation of each. So, if a law be in opposition to the constitution; if both the law and the constitution apply to a particular case . . . [then, because] the constitution is superior to any ordinary act of the legislature, the constitution, and not such ordinary act, must govern the case to which they both apply.

Thus, the elements of his syllogism are plainly laid out. Major premise: It "is of the very essence of judicial duty"[413] to decide cases involving conflicts between laws by choosing which of the conflicting laws is to be given effect. Minor premise: A conflict between a law and the constitution is merely a special case of a conflict between laws. Conclusion: It "is of the very essence of judicial duty" to decide a case involving a conflict between a law and the constitution by disregarding the inferior rule, the act of the legislature. It should be noted that there is nothing here that in the least respect depends on any specific constitutional provision. It follows regardless of what the United States Constitution, or any constitution, may say about judicial power, or even if it were completely silent as to the powers of courts. The only condition, which Marshall earlier posits, is that the constitution be written.[414] This condition was important in Marshall's argument, and was probably included in minor part because a written document has a specificity of content that would make it more amenable to judicial interpretation, and, in major part, to provide a contrast with the practice in England, whose constitution is unwritten and whose courts have felt no logical compulsion to disregard legislative acts. But, even with that qualification, Marshall's conclusion was simplicity itself. If there are courts, and if there is a written constitu-

---

[411] Federalist 78 (Hamilton), in Cooke, ed, *The Federalist* at 525–26 (cited in note 55).

[412] 1 Cranch at 177–78.

[413] Id at 178.

[414] Id at 177.

tion, then there must be judicial review. No other conclusion is logically possible.

Because Marshall's argument rests on pure logic, it necessarily also proves the power of Pennsylvania courts to declare invalid acts of the Pennsylvania legislature that conflict with the Pennsylvania constitution. Therefore, although John Gibson was a member of a state supreme court, his discussion of that argument is as relevant to the power of his court as if he had been one of Marshall's colleagues. In *Eakin v Raub*, Gibson examined Marshall's syllogism, and demonstrated that it is fallacious because the minor premise is unsound. A conflict between a law and the constitution is *not* merely a special case of a conflict of laws. It is an entirely different matter. Resolution of a conflict between laws is a matter involving the performance of the ordinary duties of courts; resolution of a conflict between a law and the constitution is not. A conflict between a law and the constitution, Gibson pointed out, does not occur "before the judiciary,"[415] whereas a conflict between legislative acts necessarily occurs there. To argue otherwise is to ignore the fundamental difference between laws and constitutions.

Constitutions are directed to governments—they establish the structure and the interrelationship of the institutions of government and place limits on governmental authority, but they normally contain no rules to govern or direct individual behavior. Individual behavior is controlled by laws. In Gibson's words, "[t]he constitution . . . contains no practical rules for the administration of *distributive justice*, with which alone the judiciary has to do; these being furnished in acts of ordinary legislation."[416] In the ordinary situation involving conflicting laws, different rules enacted by the legislature create inconsistent duties, obligations, or privileges for individuals or other legal entities, and the courts, whose function it is to apply the law in individual cases, *must*, when a dispute involving such a conflict is brought before them, choose to give effect to one of the conflicting rules to the exclusion of the other (or others) because it is essential that it do so in order to be able to adjudge the legal rights and duties of the parties. Not to do so would make it impossible to decide the case. However, in the situation where a law is said to conflict with the constitution, there is no similar

---

[415] 12 Sergeant and Rawle at 347. (Emphasis deleted.)

[416] Id at 348. (Emphasis is in original.)

necessity that the court resolve the conflict in order to be able to decide the case. The disputants are not claiming that the laws are giving them contradictory instructions to direct their behavior. Instead, the requirements of the law are clear, but the court is being asked to rule on the question of whether the legislature had the constitutional authority to establish those requirements. Thus, as Gibson explained, "the constitution and act of assembly . . . do not furnish conflicting rules *applicable to the point before the court;* nor is it at all necessary, that the one or the other of them should give way."[417]

Thus, a court need not look to see whether a law is constitutional in order to decide a case before it any more than the executive would need to look to see whether a law was constitutional in order to decide whether to enforce it. If the courts, but not the executive, are to be expected to examine the constitutionality of a legislative act, that can only be because the responsibility to engage in such an examination is uniquely judicial. But since the entire purpose of Marshall's syllogism is to *prove* that this is a judicial responsibility, it is clearly improper, as a matter of logic, to assume the conclusion in the premises. That is Gibson's precise point:[418]

> It is the business of the judiciary, to interpret the laws, not scan the authority of the lawgiver; and without the latter, it cannot take cognisance of a collision between a law and the constitution. So that, to affirm that the judiciary has a right to judge of the existence of such collision, is to take for granted the very thing to be proved; and that a very cogent argument may be made in this way, I am not disposed to deny; for no conclusions are so strong as those that are drawn from the *petitio principii.*

Whatever the merits or desirability of judicial review, and it was not Gibson's purpose to address those, the power cannot be logically derived from the unquestionable existence of judicial power to choose between conflicting acts of the legislature in deciding cases before the courts. But Marshall's argument, like Hamilton's, seeks to prove the necessary existence of the former from the necessary existence of the latter. Therefore, since the analogy fails, Marshall's minor premise is invalid, and his syllogism is false. Nor

---

[417] Id. (Emphasis is in original.)
[418] Id.

does the fact that a constitution may be written alter the merits of Marshall's logical case in any way. The act of putting a constitution into writing does not convert its provisions into rules to govern individual behavior that are to be applied by courts, nor does it give the judiciary (any more than it would give the executive) power that it would not otherwise have to go beyond the rules of law established by the legislature and to determine whether the legislature had the authority to make those rules in the first place. Thus, Gibson noted that, even "where the government exists by virtue of a *written* constitution, the judiciary does not necessarily derive from that circumstance, any other than its ordinary and appropriate powers."[419]

As soon as it is perceived that Marshall's syllogism collapses, his next argument becomes a *non sequitur*. His point was that persons "who controvert the principle, that the constitution is to be considered, in court, as a paramount law, are reduced to the necessity of maintaining that courts must close their eyes on the constitution, and see only the law."[420] But nowhere in Marshall's opinion does he maintain that courts may look to the constitution and make pronouncements regarding its meaning except for the purpose of deciding cases before them.[421] If, therefore, the decision of a case does not require a judgment as to the meaning of the constitution, and—given the invalidity of Marshall's and Hamilton's equation of constitutional cases with cases involving conflicts between legislative acts—it normally would not, then denial of the power of judicial review would not require courts to "close their eyes on the constitution" any more than would the accepted understanding that courts are to remain silent in the face of any constitutional violation that does not present itself in the form of a case or controversy that demands judicial resolution.

But, said Marshall, if courts cannot refuse to apply a law that is expressly forbidden by the constitution, the result would be that the legislature, although limited by constitutional restrictions, would be free to ignore those restrictions, "thus reduc[ing] to nothing, what we have deemed the greatest improvement on political

[419] Id at 346. (Emphasis is in original.)

[420] 1 Cranch at 178.

[421] See text at note 350.

institutions, a written constitution."[422] Since, as previously noted, Marshall is not troubled by the obligation of the executive unquestioningly to enforce unconstitutional laws, his argument becomes nothing more than an assertion that unless *courts* (and only courts) can declare legislative acts unconstitutional in cases coming before them, then written constitutions are utterly worthless—"absurd attempts, on the part of the people, to limit a power, in its own nature, illimitable."[423] A written constitution, however, would certainly not be utterly worthless in the absence of judicial review. If one can concede a modicum of integrity to the legislature, a written constitution would serve to inform legislators as to whether the actions they wish to take or the means by which they would like to achieve their goals are constitutionally permissible. Moreover, even if the legislature were to choose to disregard the restrictions on its authority, a written constitution would still provide a standard by which the people could measure the conduct of their representatives, and, if one can concede that the people should possess a sincere desire to preserve the integrity of the constitution, would enable them to exercise their democratic power to bring the government within constitutional bounds.[424]

These real advantages of a written constitution, which would be retained even if there were no judicial review, are noted in Gibson's response to this part of Marshall's argument. The fact that the constitution is written, he declared, makes its principles "more fixed and certain, and more apparent to the apprehension of the people, than principles which depend on tradition and the vague comprehension of the individuals who compose the nation." It also gives the legislature more precise guidance than "vague comprehension" could supply by "answer[ing] the end of an observation at sea, with a view to correct the dead-reckoning."[425] But if, in fact, these concessions are not justified, and the legislature does not possess a modicum of integrity and the public has no desire to preserve the principles of the constitution, then judicial review could not save the constitutional order, for "let public opinion be so corrupt, as to sanction every misconstruction of the constitution,

[422] 1 Cranch at 178.
[423] Id at 177.
[424] See Van Alstyne, 1969 Duke L J at 18–20 (cited in note 194).
[425] 12 Sergeant and Rawle at 354.

and abuse of power, which the temptation of the moment may dictate, and the party which may happen to be predominant, will laugh at the puny efforts of a dependent power to arrest it in its course."[426]

To dramatize his argument that a written constitution would be "reduce[d] to nothing" in the absence of judicial review, Marshall posited hypothetical examples of blatant constitutional violations that could occur if courts were without power to nullify unconstitutional legislative acts. His examples were (1) an export tax passed by Congress in direct disregard of the prohibition of Article I, § 9; (2) a bill of attainder or *ex post facto* law passed despite the prohibition in the same section; and (3) legislation providing less stringent standards for a conviction for treason than the testimony of two witnesses or confession in open court that are required by Article III, § 3.[427] It is virtually impossible to contemplate such outrageous legislative actions without immediately embracing Marshall's conclusion that there must be power in the courts to prevent them. Indeed, if one perceives the issue of judicial review exclusively in the terms in which Marshall sets it out—a legislature contemptuously ignoring express and specific prohibitions on its authority and a court heroically intervening to protect the constitution against flagrant attempts to render it meaningless—one can only enthusiastically agree that it is essential that the courts possess this power. But if judicial review is so obviously vital in the type of situation that Marshall posits, what about a situation in which the legislature has passed a law well within the scope of its constitutional authority, only to have it struck down by a court prepared to distort constitutional meaning to prevent the implementation of a policy it disfavors? Or, what about the less extreme case in which the legislature's judgment that the law it has enacted is constitutional is just as defensible, given the ambiguity of the constitutional text, as the judiciary's conclusion that it is invalid? Why should the courts' view of the constitution prevail over that of the elected representatives of the people when it is not clearly right? Although the situations in which there is no plainly correct answer should, in practice, greatly outnumber the situations in which the courts reject a patently unconstitutional law, Marshall never allows the reader of his opinion to consider for an instant that the power of

---

[426] Id at 355.

[427] 1 Cranch at 179.

judicial review could ever be exercised when the legislature was
not clearly wrong and the courts not clearly right—and that is why
the reader is swept along so relentlessly by the apparent force of
his logic.

Hamilton was more candid in *Federalist 78*, perhaps because he
was writing fifteen years earlier at a time when courts were not
viewed with such great distrust by the dominant political forces.
He conceded that abuse of power by the courts was theoretically
possible, but dismissed this concern as a ground for the rejection
of judicial review because the possibility of judicial abuse in constitutional cases is no different from the possibility of abuse in cases
of statutory interpretation, and could only be avoided by the elimination of judicial independence.[428] Marshall, however, never admitted that such a possibility could exist, and was therefore able
to make a much more convincing argument than he could have
had he admitted the existence of considerations that would have
introduced cross-currents into the analysis. Thus, Robert McCloskey's comment was both pithy and extremely cogent:[429]

> These [considerations] are not met at all in the argument of
> the *Marbury* case, and by ignoring them Marshall succeeds in
> beclouding them. . . . The *Marbury* opinion is justly celebrated,
> but not the least of its virtues is the fact that it is somewhat
> beside the point.

Because Gibson was discussing Marshall's logical case for judicial
review rather than providing a detailed critique of the construction
of the *Marbury* opinion, he did not comment on how Marshall's
examples confuse the issue. He did point out, contrary to the suggestion that the examples were intended to convey, that questions
of constitutionality may "require for their solution the most vigorous exertion of the higher faculties of the mind."[430] And, more
importantly, he noted that since the attempt to prove the existence
of judicial review through syllogistic logic fails, it fails no less for
the decision of the clear-cut cases described in Marshall's examples
than for the decision of those cases which "require for their solution

---

[428] Federalist 78 (Hamilton), in Cooke, ed, *The Federalist* at 526 (cited in note 55). Instances
of judicial abuse in cases of statutory interpretation, however, can be corrected legislatively;
instances of judicial abuse in cases of constitutional interpretation may require resort to the
process of constitutional amendment. See text at notes 438–39.

[429] McCloskey, *American Supreme Court* at 43 (cited in note 130).

[430] 12 Sergeant and Rawle at 350.

the most vigorous exertion of the higher faculties of the mind."
For courts cannot look to see whether an act is clearly unconstitutional if it is not their business to determine whether legislative acts
conform to the constitution. In his words, "the abstract existence of
a power cannot depend on the clearness or obscurity of the case in
which it is to be exercised; for that is a consideration that cannot
present itself, before the question of the existence of the power
shall have been determined."[431]

But Gibson would certainly have agreed with regard to one of
Marshall's three examples. He would have agreed that a federal
court could nullify an act of Congress that authorized a conviction
for treason based on lesser evidence than "the Testimony of two
Witnesses to the same overt Act, or on Confession in open Court"
that is required by the provisions of Article III, § 3. His agreement
would not have been based on the clarity of the constitutional
violation, which was Marshall's reason for giving the example, but
on the fact that the constitutional provision that would be violated
by this hypothetical law is directed to the courts. In each of Marshall's other two examples—export taxes and bills of attainder or
ex post facto laws—the constitutional directive was addressed to the
legislature, which, by passing the law at issue, had evidenced its
judgment that it possessed the constitutional authority to do so.
For a court to undertake to reject that judgment and to substitute
its own by refusing to apply the law in cases coming before it
would be to rule on whether the legislature correctly interpreted
the constitution which would not seem to be "a legitimate subject
for judicial determination."[432] If it were, Gibson noted:[433]

> the judiciary must be a peculiar organ, to revise the proceedings
> of the legislature and to correct its mistakes. . . . Viewing the
> matter in the opposite direction, what would be thought of an
> act of assembly in which it should be declared that the supreme

---

[431] Id at 352.

[432] Id at 348. As William Van Alstyne noted, "it was 'emphatically the province and duty'
of *legislative* departments to say what the law is, and the customary duty of judicial departments was merely to apply the law to the case once the meaning and formal authenticity of
the law were established." Van Alstyne, 1969 Duke L J at 24 (cited in note 194). (Emphasis is
in original.)

[433] 12 Sergeant and Rawle at 348. Gibson makes specific reference to the United States
Constitution in this passage because, under the express terms of Article VI, state courts are
instructed to exercise judicial review over state laws which are challenged as violating the
United States Constitution. See text at notes 478–80.

court had, in a particular case, put a wrong construction on the constitution of the *United States*, and that the judgment should therefore be reversed? It would, doubtless, be thought a usurpation of judicial power. But it is by no means clear, that to declare a law void, which has been enacted according to the forms prescribed in the constitution, is not a usurpation of legislative power.

But the treason example is a different matter. The Constitution, in Article III, § 3, speaks to the courts, and instructs them not to adjudge a person guilty of treason in the absence of specified evidence, while the hypothetical law, which is also addressed to the courts, directs them to accept a lesser evidentiary standard as the basis for a conviction. Here the judiciary is given two conflicting directives, one from the Constitution and the other from Congress; in that circumstance, it would plainly be obligated to obey the Constitution and to disregard the act of Congress. "In the very few cases," Gibson explained, "in which the judiciary, and not the legislature, is the immediate organ to execute its provisions, they are bound by it, in preference to any act of assembly to the contrary; in such cases, the constitution is a rule to the courts."[434] Had Marshall limited his argument for judicial review to this category of cases, his "conflict of laws" analogy would have been pertinent and his logical argument would have been sound. Certainly he would have had no argument from Gibson.

The case for judicial review that is based on the fear that Congress would be able to abuse its authority if it is not subject to an external check founders with an appreciation that the powers of all the branches of the federal government are limited by the Constitution, and, therefore, if unreviewable authority to interpret the Constitution is given to any branch, the courts included, that branch will be able to ignore or interpret away whatever restrictions the Constitution may place on its power.[435] The argument can be saved if it is accompanied (as Hamilton's argument was, but Marshall's argument was not) by the inclusion of subjective considerations— for example, "the judiciary . . . will always be the least dangerous to the political rights of the constitution"[436]—that would support

---

[434] 12 Sergeant and Rawle at 353.

[435] See Bickel, *Least Dangerous Branch* at 3–4 (cited in note 8).

[436] Federalist 78 (Hamilton), in Cooke, ed, *The Federalist* at 522 (cited in note 55).

a conclusion that the possibility of judicial abuse is less to be feared than the possibility of legislative abuse, but all such considerations would have been out of place in Marshall's purely logical argument.[437] In any event, Hamilton's claim that the judiciary is the best place to put unreviewable authority to interpret the Constitution is certainly vulnerable to counterargument. As Alexander Bickel observed, "[i]t is, indeed, more absurd" to give such authority to the courts than to legislatures "because courts are not subject to electoral control."[438] Or, as Judge Gibson noted, if the legislature is given this authority, its mistakes could be more readily corrected than judicial mistakes:[439]

> the judiciary is not infallible; and an error by it would admit of no remedy but a more distinct expression of the public will, through the [amending process]; whereas, an error by the legislature admits of a remedy by an exertion of the same will, in the ordinary exercise of the right of suffrage.

One thing that our experience with Vietnam, Watergate, and Iran-Contra has taught us is that the one branch of government that must not be vested with unreviewable authority to interpret the Constitution is the executive—given its control over military and intelligence operations and its capacity and penchant for operating in secrecy and thus beyond the reach of immediate public or political scrutiny.[440] The principle that the President does not have the power to determine unilaterally the scope and extent of the constitutional or legal authority of the executive branch is one that John Marshall fortunately, even if inappropriately, proclaimed in *Marbury*.[441]

The notion embodied in Marshall's *Marbury* opinion that unreviewable authority to interpret the Constitution cannot be located where it might be abused is not only one that is incapable of practical application, it is one that Marshall and his colleagues had not the slightest interest in applying outside the political context that shaped the *Marbury* decision. As noted above, this notion can be

---

[437] See text at notes 381–82.

[438] Bickel, *Least Dangerous Branch* at 4 (cited in note 8).

[439] 12 Sergeant and Rawle at 355.

[440] See, for example, Abe Fortas, *The Constitution and the Presidency*, 49 Wash L Rev 987, 1011 (1974).

[441] See text at notes 229–36.

turned against the judiciary by noting that courts, too, can ignore the constitutional limits placed on them if their interpretation of the Constitution is unreviewable, and the Marshall Court faced just such an argument in *Martin v Hunter's Lessee*[442] in 1816, when the Virginia Court of Appeals declared unconstitutional § 25 of the Judiciary Act of 1789 giving the Supreme Court appellate jurisdiction over state court decisions on federal questions.[443] In response to the argument that if the Supreme Court had final decisional authority, it could abuse that authority, Justice Story, speaking for the Court (Marshall having recused himself because of a possible pecuniary interest in the outcome), replied: "It is always a doubtful course, to argue against the use or existence of a power, from the possibility of its abuse. . . . From the very nature of things, the absolute right of decision, in the last resort, must rest somewhere—wherever it may be vested, it is susceptible of abuse."[444] In *Gibbons v Ogden*[445] in 1824, Marshall indicated that it was not cause for concern that Congress could determine the extent of its own constitutional authority because political checks were the appropriate safeguards to be relied on by a democratic society to prevent legislative abuse.[446] And in *McCulloch v Maryland*[447] in 1819, Marshall, defining the extent of congressional power under the "necessary and proper" clause,[448] conceded to Congress the authority to select any appropriate means not prohibited by the Constitution to achieve an end within the scope of its delegated powers,[449] despite the warning of Thomas Jefferson that such a concession would have the effect "of instituting a Congress with power to do whatever would be for the good of the United

---

[442] 1 Wheaton 304 (1816).

[443] See id at 323–24.

[444] Id at 344–45.

[445] 9 Wheaton 1 (1824).

[446] See id at 197:

> The wisdom and the discretion of congress, their identity with the people, and the influence which their constituents possess at elections, are, in this, as in many other instances, as that, for example, of declaring war, the sole restraints on which they have relied, to secure them from its abuse. They are the restraints on which the people must often rely solely, in all representative governments.

[447] 4 Wheaton 316 (1819).

[448] US Const, Art I, § 8, cl 18.

[449] 4 Wheaton at 421.

States; and, as they would be the sole judges of the good or evil, it would also be a power to do whatever evil they please."[450]

Robert Faulkner, in his thoughtful analysis of Marshall's legal ideas, maintained that "Marshall is not inconsistent in holding that the legislature must keep within the political sphere apportioned by the Constitution, the great theme of the last part of his opinion in *Marbury v Madison*, and in also insisting that within that extensive sphere its discretion is vast."[451] But that misses the fundamental point of the inconsistency, which goes to the issue of abuse. In *Marbury*, Marshall asserted that to allow Congress to be the judge of the constitutionality of its own acts "would be giving to the legislature a practical and real omnipotence, with the same breath which professes to restrict their powers within narrow limits. It is prescribing limits, and declaring that those limits may be passed at pleasure."[452] Yet, in *McCulloch*, with regard to the only limits on congressional power that were of serious concern during the Marshall years—those whose purpose was to prevent it from encroaching on areas of state authority—Marshall announced a doctrine the practical effect of which, as Jefferson recognized, was to allow Congress to draw (and redraw as the occasion arose) the line marking the extent of its powers as against those of the state legislatures. Certainly, if Congress may choose any appropriate means to a legitimate end, and it is the sole judge of necessity,[453] it can abuse its authority in precisely the same way that Marshall in *Marbury* pronounced to be intolerable. It can, in effect, do what it believes it needs to do.[454]

The framers' expectation that courts would hold the other

---

[450] Thomas Jefferson, *Opinion Against the Constitutionality of a National Bank*, in Lipscomb, ed, 3 *Writings of Jefferson* at 148 (cited in note 105). In the quoted passage, Jefferson was warning against the danger of allowing a latitudinarian construction to Congress's power to tax and spend, US Const, Art I, § 8, cl 1, but he explained later that the same reasoning applied to the "necessary and proper" clause. Id at 149.

[451] Faulkner, *Jurisprudence of Marshall* at 80–81 (cited in note 406).

[452] 1 Cranch at 178.

[453] See *McCulloch v Maryland*, 4 Wheaton at 423: "But were its necessity less apparent, none can deny its being an appropriate measure; and if it is, the degree of its necessity, as has been very justly observed, is to be discussed in another place."

[454] As Jefferson put it: "If such a latitude of construction be allowed to this phrase [the "necessary and proper" clause] as to give any non-enumerated power, it will go to every one, for there is not one which ingenuity may not torture into a *convenience* in some instance or other, to *some one* of so long a list of enumerated powers." Lipscomb, ed, 3 *Writings of Jefferson* at 149 (cited in note 105). (Emphasis is in original.)

branches in check, Marshall contended, was also reflected in the requirement of Article VI that judges (including state judges, as well as members of Congress and state legislators and federal and state executive officers, although Marshall took no note of the breadth of coverage of the constitutional requirement) "shall be bound by Oath or Affirmation, to support this Constitution." Then, in specific reference to the oath prescribed by Congress which required judges to swear to discharge their duties "agreeably to the constitution and laws of the United States," he asked: "Why does a judge swear to discharge his duties agreeably to the constitution of the United States, if that constitution forms no rule for his government? if it is closed upon him, and cannot be inspected by him."[455]

Marshall's reliance on the judicial oath of office is the most transparently fallacious aspect of his opinion. Even those students, encountering *Marbury* for the first time, who are not able to find any other fault with Marshall's reasoning recognize immediately that this argument proves nothing—or at least not what Marshall wants to prove. Alexander Bickel remarked that, "[f]ar from supporting Marshall, the oath is perhaps the strongest textual argument against him."[456] William Van Alstyne and David Currie, in their analyses of Marshall's opinion, do not even bother to provide their own explanations of the difficulties with this argument. They merely quote from Judge Gibson's response and then go on to other points, apparently in the perfectly correct belief that this response is so self-evidently sound that, once it is stated, nothing more need be said.[457] Gibson merely noted that an oath to support the constitution "is taken indiscriminately by every officer of the government," and, since not every officer is expected to disregard legislative acts that he or she deems to be unconstitutional, the oath itself cannot confer any power to refuse to enforce unconstitutional laws, but "must be understood in reference to supporting the constitution, *only as far as that may be involved in his official duty;* and consequently, if his official duty does not comprehend an inquiry into the authority of the legislature, neither does his oath."[458] Since the oath "re-

---

[455] 1 Cranch at 180.

[456] Bickel, *Least Dangerous Branch* at 8 (cited in note 8).

[457] See Currie, *Constitution in the Court* at 73 (cited in note 198); Van Alstyne, 1969 Duke L J at 25–26 (cited in note 194).

[458] 12 Sergeant and Rawle at 353. (Emphasis is in original.)

lates only to the official conduct of the officer, [it] does not prove that he ought to stray from the path of his ordinary business, to search for violations of duty in the business of others; nor does it, as supposed, define the powers of the officer."[459]

Because Marshall's argument is wholly an attempt to prove by deductive logic that judicial review is objectively necessary where there is a written constitution, Gibson appropriately and pointedly noted that here, too, the argument rests on a logical trick. In the "conflict of laws" analogy, Marshall claimed that the conclusion that the courts have a duty to decide on conflicts between a law and a constitutional provision necessarily followed from the conceded· existence of a judicial duty to decide cases involving conflicts between different acts of the legislature. That conclusion, however, only follows if one assumes at the outset that questions pertaining to the constitutionality of legislation are as proper subjects of judicial inquiry as questions of statutory interpretation—which means that the proof is dependent upon an assumption of the thing to be proved. Gibson explicitly pointed out that, similarly, the oath argument is dependent upon an initial assumption of the matter to be proved. For just as the oath to support the constitution taken by executive officers does not confer a power to disregard legislative acts deemed to be unconstitutional because making judgments as to the constitutionality of laws is not part of the executive's responsibility, the same oath would not confer this power on the judiciary unless it is initially assumed that making judgments as to the constitutionality of laws *is* a judicial responsibility—the thing to be proved. "It is worthy of remark here," Gibson observed, "that the foundation of every argument in favor of the right of the judiciary, is found, at last, to be an assumption of the whole ground in dispute."[460] At best, Marshall's argument based on the oath proves what he does not want to prove, for, unless one begins by assuming that constitutional decisionmaking is a uniquely judicial function, then the oath, since it is taken by all government officers, would, as Bickel commented, extend the power of constitutional decisionmaking to every officer,[461] or, worse, as Charles Grove Haines

---

[459] Id at 354.

[460] Id at 353.

[461] Bickel, *Least Dangerous Branch* at 8. It is for this reason that Bickel maintained that the oath provides "the strongest textual argument against" Marshall's position. Id. See text at note 456.

noted, it would lead to the conclusion that "the members of Congress and the Executive could refuse to accept a decision of the Supreme Court with which they disagreed."[462]

It is important to understand that the debate, if it can be called that, between Marshall in *Marbury* and Gibson in *Eakin* was *not* over the wisdom or desirability of judicial review. Whether or not judicial review is a good idea was not the issue. Marshall did not argue that it is a good idea—that would have been to inject subjective evaluation into a logical demonstration. Gibson did not argue that judicial review is not a good idea—at one point in his opinion he made clear that he was of the view that it might well be a good idea, inasmuch "as it might be expected, that [the judiciary's] habits of deliberation, and the aid derived from the arguments of counsel, would more frequently lead to accurate conclusions" on questions of whether governmental actions conform to constitutional requirements.[463] The issue was whether judicial review is deducible, without more, from the mere existence of a written constitution. Marshall insisted that it is; Gibson demonstrated that it isn't. Since Gibson's sole task was to show the logical unsoundness of the arguments seeking to rest judicial review on an objectively provable base, his was the easier task, and, because it is entirely a matter of objective logic, he can be proved right merely by noting the flaws in Marshall's logical argument.

This is not to say that Marshall did not believe that judicial review was a good idea. As Robert Faulkner has properly warned, despite the fact that Marshall's opinion in *Marbury* was shaped by the political context in which it was written, one should resist "the tendency to reduce Marshall's thoughts to his politics in a narrowly partisan sense,"[464] and to assume that his invocation of judicial review was merely a tactic designed to gain an advantage over his Republican opponents at a particularly critical moment in American political history. It is not to be doubted that Marshall truly believed that judicial review was not only a good idea, but, as Faulkner shows, was also "an integral part of a government designed in good part to minimize the people's vices."[465] The fact that

---

[462] Haines, *Role of Supreme Court* at 255 (cited in note 90).

[463] 12 Sergeant and Rawle at 355.

[464] Faulkner, *Jurisprudence of Marshall* at 201 (cited in note 406).

[465] Id at 210.

the Supreme Court in the remaining thirty-two years of Marshall's service as Chief Justice never again declared an act of Congress unconstitutional demonstrates persuasively that Marshall did not claim the power for the purpose of frustrating the policy goals of Republican administrations,[466] but, on the other hand, the fact that in thirty-four years the only act of Congress invalidated by the Marshall Court was an innocuous piece of Federalist legislation whose constitutionality was clearly defensible demonstrates beyond any real doubt that it was not the egregious invalidity of this law that prompted the Court's action, but the perception of Marshall and his colleagues that it was politically essential to establish very quickly a precedent that would demonstrate the legitimacy of judicial authority to declare legislative acts unconstitutional.

While there is no question that Marshall believed in the wisdom of allowing courts to determine the constitutionality of legislative acts, and could conscientiously have written an opinion defending the advantages of judicial review over a system in which legislative sovereignty would prevail, the fact remains that that was not the opinion he wrote. And it would be difficult to contend that his decision to eschew reliance on subjective considerations was not a rational one. Given the manifest hostility of a Republican Congress and a Republican administration toward the one institution of government still controlled by the Federalists, whose members were protected by a constitutional guarantee of life tenure—a hostility characterized by Jefferson's expression of fear that "all the works of republicanism are to be battered down and erased" by the Federalist judiciary[467]—any argument by the Supreme Court that the welfare of the polity would be best promoted by granting the judiciary power to check legislative depredations on the Constitution would not, in all likelihood, have been accorded a terribly gracious political reception.[468] So Marshall chose to make an objective case for the logical necessity of judicial review, and, while his case can

---

[466] Robert McCloskey has cogently argued that Marshall's fundamental purpose in asserting the power of judicial review over an act of Congress in *Marbury* was to provide a precedent that would help lay the theoretical groundwork for a claim of judicial power to invalidate state laws—which was Marshall's real objective. McCloskey, *American Supreme Court* at 44 (cited in note 130).

[467] See text at note 132.

[468] See, for example, O'Fallon, 44 Stan L Rev at 257 (cited in note 4).

be proved wrong by logical standards, it has been resoundingly triumphant as measured by the standards of history and politics. Whether judicial review gained its acceptance as an American political institution because the Court seized the occasion to proclaim it in *Marbury* is problematic. Thomas Reed Powell, for one, believed that the *Marbury* opinion was not a decisive factor, and "that in due season the power would have been exercised even had not Marshall made his affirmation in 1803."[469] Yet it is hard to conclude that the path to acceptance of the institution of judicial review was not made enormously smoother by virtue of having its case set forth in Marshall's remarkable opinion, the exceptionally effective rhetoric of which more than compensates for the illogic of its argument.[470]

For Gibson's part, he was not an opponent of judicial review on principle. It is certainly true that he regarded with perfect equanimity a political order in which judges would not possess the power to declare legislative acts unconstitutional. He recognized that the legislature could not validly exceed its constitutional powers, but he could find no warrant, in the absence of a grant of authority to the courts in the constitution or laws, for a judicial assumption of power to keep it in check. Questions of constitutionality did not, in the normal case, come before the courts for decision, for the function of courts was to apply the rules of the common law or of statutory law pertaining to the conduct of individuals for the purpose of deciding the controversies presented by the parties before them, and was not to "scan the authority of the lawgiver."[471] This would not mean that the legislature would be unchecked, but merely that the responsibility for checking it "rest[ed] with the people, in whom full and absolute sovereign power resides,"[472] a responsibility that they might choose to exercise themselves, or that they might choose to delegate to the courts through a constitutional provision or through a legislative enactment by their elected representatives. Nor, in his view, was it permissible

---

[469] Thomas Reed Powell, *Vagaries and Varieties in Constitutional Interpretation* 21–22 (Columbia, 1956).

[470] Robert Faulkner holds this view. See Faulkner, *Jurisprudence of Marshall* at 212 (cited in note 406).

[471] 12 Sergeant and Rawle at 348.

[472] Id at 355.

for courts to arrogate this authority to themselves on the ground that the people could not effectively exercise it, for the theory of democracy is "that the people are wise, virtuous, and competent to manage their own affairs: and if they are not so, in fact, . . . [that] would not justify those who administer the government, in applying a corrective in practice."[473]

Gibson's objection was to the judiciary's willingness to assume the power of review without having been given it by the framers of the constitution or by an act of the legislature. He divided judicial power into two categories—political and civil. Civil powers are those that necessarily belong to any body that is a court, such as the power to hear and decide cases within its jurisdiction through the application of existing rules of law. Such powers need not be explicitly conferred; they are automatically possessed by every court.[474] On the other hand, political powers, which would include judicial review, are those "by which one organ of the government is enabled to control another, or to exert an influence over its acts."[475] They are not inherently judicial, and courts do not possess them in the absence of a specific grant. Gibson clearly recognized that the people might wish to assign to the judiciary the power to decide on the constitutionality of legislative acts;[476] however, "[t]he grant of a power so extraordinary, ought to appear so plain, that he who should run might read."[477] But if the power is clearly and expressly given to them, Gibson did not deny that courts may—indeed, must—exercise it. Thus, when the issue facing the Pennsylvania Supreme Court on which Gibson sat was not the validity of a state law under the state constitution, but the validity of a state law (or state constitutional provision) as against "the supreme Law of the Land"—the Constitution, laws, or treaties of the United States—Gibson saw his court's duty "to be exactly the reverse,"[478] for Article VI of the United States Constitution expressly binds state judges (and, as previously noted, this authority necessarily extends to federal judges as well)[479] to adhere to the

---

[473] Id.

[474] Id at 346.

[475] Id.

[476] Id at 355.

[477] Id at 352.

[478] Id at 356.

[479] See Wechsler, 73 Harv L Rev at 3–4 (cited in note 386).

commands of federal law "any Thing in the Constitution or Laws of any State to the Contrary notwithstanding."[480]

This, then, and not any dispute over the wisdom, desirability, or necessity of judicial review, was the basis of the disagreement between Marshall and Gibson. For both Marshall and Gibson, the merits of judicial review were entirely irrelevant to the question of whether courts possess this authority. Gibson acknowledged the potential merits (as well as the potential drawbacks) of judicial review, but insisted that courts have no inherent authority to exercise it, and must wait until the sovereign people—through a constitutional delegation—or the people's representatives in the legislature decide that this power should be granted to them before they can undertake to rule on the constitutionality of legislative acts. For Marshall, there was no need for the courts to wait for a specific grant of authority in the constitution or laws, for it was demonstrable through deductive logic that this power necessarily resides in the judiciary in any political system with a written constitution. Subjective evaluation, through the political process, of the desirability of vesting the courts with the power of judicial review would be out of place, for either courts possess this authority or the constitution is rendered a worthless absurdity. It was this conclusion that Gibson regarded as patently fallacious. On the battleground that Marshall himself selected, it is Gibson who, beyond cavil, was victorious.

But James Bradley Thayer reminded us that Gibson apparently recanted his position twenty years later.[481] In 1846, when he was sitting as Chief Justice of the Pennsylvania Supreme Court, he interrupted oral argument after counsel had asserted that the fact that "the courts possess the power to declare an act void is settled [citing *Eakin v Raub*, in which Gibson's dissent appeared] though it is said it must be a very clear case,"[482] to say: "I have changed that opinion for two reasons. The late Convention, by their silence sanctioned the pretensions of the courts to deal freely with acts of the legislature; and from experience of the necessity of the case."[483]

---

[480] 12 Sergeant and Rawle at 356, citing US Const, Art VI.

[481] Thayer, 7 Harv L Rev at 130 n 1 (cited in note 73).

[482] *Norris v Clymer*, 2 Pa St 277, 281 (Pa 1846).

[483] Id. It is not altogether clear from that snippet, which is all that appears in the report of the case, what opinion it is that Gibson has changed. From the immediate context, it would appear that the opinion he no longer claimed to hold was the opinion he expressed in *Eakin* that where courts *are* granted authority to rule on the constitutionality of legislation, they should refrain from exercising that authority "except in cases free from all doubt." 12

Of these two reasons, the first was consistent with his *Eakin* dissent, the second was not. Under the rule of interpretation that legislative acquiescence by silence in the courts' interpretation of legislation implies approval of that interpretation, the failure of the state constitutional convention to withdraw this power that the courts had undertaken to exercise could be understood as the equivalent of the affirmative conferral of authority that Gibson regarded as the necessary precondition for judicial review. If the second reason, "experience of the necessity of the case," is a subsidiary of the first, there is still no inconsistency with his *Eakin* opinion— judicial review is a good idea as well as being constitutionally authorized. If, however, the second reason was to stand alone as a justification for the exercise of judicial review, independent of the first, it contradicts Gibson's contention in *Eakin* that judgments as to the desirability of placing such authority in the courts would not warrant judges in assuming the power, for "the existence of a defect [in the constitution] which was not foreseen, would not justify those who administer the government, in applying a corrective in practice, which can be provided only by a convention."[484]

If Gibson had intended by his brief remark to espouse the view that experience and necessity dictate that courts should exercise the power of judicial review even where such a power has not been expressly conferred upon them, he was abandoning a logically impeccable position for one that must have then seemed to him to be more consistent with the promotion of the public welfare. That is a perfectly understandable basis for change. It would be, in fact, a marvelous example of Oliver Wendell Holmes's celebrated observation that "[t]he life of the law has not been logic: it has been experience. The felt necessities of the time, the prevalent moral and political theories, intuitions of public policy, avowed or unconscious, even the prejudices which judges share with their fellowmen, have had a good deal more to do than the syllogism in de-

---

Sergeant and Rawle at 357. That would mean that he was abandoning the doubtful case limitation on the exercise of judicial review where that power was properly vested in the courts. There is nothing in his brief statement that is inconsistent with such an interpretation. But it is perhaps more likely, in light of the fact that no express authority had been given to the courts of his state to declare acts of the state legislature void for violation of the state constitution, that the view he had changed was the general position he maintained in his *Eakin* dissent that the courts of Pennsylvania lacked such power.

[484] Id at 355.

termining the rules by which men should be governed."[485] It has not been logic but what Holmes called "intuitions of public policy" that has led to American society's embrace of the institution of judicial review. It was these "intuitions," plus, of course, the fact that Marshall was extremely judicious in his selection of the law to be invalidated, that muted the opposition to the Supreme Court's assertion of this power in *Marbury*, not any misconception that Marshall was only claiming a power to invalidate laws in situations where both the law and the relevant constitutional provision were addressed to the courts. And it was these "intuitions" that preserved the power of judicial review and the integrity of the judicial branch itself in 1937, when the public and a New Deal Congress could not be brought to support Franklin Roosevelt's plan to undercut the independence of the federal judiciary through his plan to "pack" the courts,[486] even though, for the preceding fifty years, the Supreme Court, interpreting the Constitution as "enact[ing] Mr. Herbert Spencer's Social Statics,"[487] had been engaged in the invalidation of much state and federal legislation that was well within the constitutional authority of these governments and that was aimed at ameliorating the social harshness of the industrial revolution and the rise of capitalism by imposing regulations on business and industry.

Today, the remarkable increase in the number of countries throughout the world that have adopted the institution of judicial review in their own constitutional systems is a clear reflection of the "felt necessities of the time," particularly the need to prevent the resurgence of totalitarian regimes and to provide an effective means for safeguarding the civil rights and civil liberties of individuals, even though, as Mauro Cappelletti has noted in his study of these developments, the legitimacy of judicial review in a democratic society cannot be established "by the force of syllogistic argument."[488] Thus, while Judge Gibson's opinion in *Eakin v Raub* is not, and was not meant to be, decisive on the question of the merits

---

[485] Oliver Wendell Holmes, Jr., *The Common Law* 1 (Little, Brown, 1881).

[486] See William E. Leuchtenberg, *Franklin D. Roosevelt's Supreme Court "Packing" Plan*, in Harold M. Hollingsworth and William F. Holmes eds, *Essays on the New Deal* 69 (U Texas, 1969).

[487] *Lochner v New York*, 198 US 45, 75 (1905) (Holmes, J, dissenting).

[488] Mauro Cappelletti, *The Expanding Role of Judicial Review in Modern Societies*, 58 Revista Juridica U Puerto Rico 1, 13 (1989).

of judicial review, it remains a brilliantly conclusive demonstration that of all the arguments that can be presented in defense of the institution of judicial review, the one that cannot be sustained is the one John Marshall made in *Marbury v Madison*.

V. Conclusion

The study of jurisprudence and legal history in the United States has over the past century attracted many outstanding scholars whose works continue to provide guidance and illumination for contemporary students. The list of such scholars, even if restricted to those no longer living whose work has been cited in this article, is an extremely impressive honor roll—Alexander Bickel, Edward S. Corwin, Charles Grove Haines, Robert McCloskey, Andrew C. McLaughlin, Thomas Reed Powell, Carl Brent Swisher, James Bradley Thayer, Charles Warren. Each of these individuals was human; each was therefore capable of error, and, undoubtedly, each made his share of errors that need to be corrected by the efforts of students of law and history who come after them. Any of them may be found to have had an idiosyncratic perspective or a particular point of view that they wished to propound even though all the evidence was not supportive of that view. Their work is thus properly subjected, despite their stature, to skeptical criticism. But it is unlikely that all of them, together with their co-workers and contemporaries and later scholars down to the present day, fundamentally misunderstood the subject they were studying and in which they had immersed themselves for a lifetime. We have a right to be dubious, therefore, when a present-day author, not in possession of any new material to which previous scholars lacked access, retraces the same ground as they, and claims to have discovered the true interpretation of judicial decisions or legal writings that had simply been missed or misunderstood by all those who had gone before, even though, in some cases, they were much closer in time to the events they supposedly failed to comprehend. And our doubts should be considerably strengthened when we compare the writings of these present-day authors and find out that each has discovered a true interpretation that is quite different and entirely incompatible with the true interpretation discovered by the others. At the very least, that demonstrates that all but perhaps one of these authors can be no less befuddled than the

great scholars of the past whose work they now so patronizingly
dismiss on the ground that they did not know what they were
talking about.

Part of the problem undoubtedly lies with the expectations created by current standards for measuring academic achievement.
To build on, refine, or magnify the understandings of the past is
likely to be viewed with a condescending tolerance, but to demonstrate that past scholarship has been grounded on fundamental error, and to repudiate it in favor of newly revealed truths that had
previously been shrouded from view because of the misconceptions
of all of one's predecessors, is surely an impressive achievement.
New is distinctly better than old, and even if the new is wrong,
its creator can still enjoy the satisfaction of generating momentary
interest in a novel, even if soon to be forgotten, theory. The problem is, of course, compounded if there are ideological goals to be
served by reinterpretation of the past, for then the willingness to
be fair and judicious in assessing the conclusions of others whose
views do not comport with one's ideological preconceptions is cor-
respondingly diminished. This problem feeds on itself when those
who share the ideological purposes of the new theory rush to ap-
plaud it and thus provide it with credentials that, on its merits, it
does not deserve. Thus did the genetic theories of T. D. Lysenko
win acceptance in the Soviet Union, and American legal scholarship is not entirely immune from this phenomenon—either on the
right or the left of the political spectrum.

The three authors whose works have been examined here are
dramatically different from one another in their outlooks and approaches. They have in common only a belief that previous scholars have been seriously wrong in their assessments or understandings of the meaning and purpose of John Marshall's opinion in
Marbury v Madison or of the conception of what we now call judicial
review that prevailed in the years before and after the *Marbury*
decision. James O'Fallon obscures *Marbury* when he goes beyond
making the perfectly proper points that it was a political opinion,
and that the aspects of it that are unrelated to judicial review warrant more scrutiny than they normally receive, and dismisses Marshall's discussion of judicial review as essentially irrelevant to the
case. Sylvia Snowiss tries to construct a grand theory of the origins
of judicial review in which the practice was initially thought not
to involve the interpretation of constitutional texts, but her theory

grossly outsweeps the evidence on which it is based. Robert Clinton presents a fraudulent argument that is not even superficially defensible, attempting to show that Marshall only claimed a power to invalidate laws that transgressed constitutional provisions relating to judicial authority.

At least part of the problem with the work of all three rests on their unwillingness to credit the competence of scholars of past generations or of contemporary scholars whose writings build on and do not reject the conclusions based on almost 200 years of analysis of the *Marbury* opinion. Current students of *Marbury* and the origins of judicial review who are sifting through the same historical materials as their predecessors and who have not discovered any new evidence, perhaps in the form of "a crumbling diary or set of letters," to which past scholars did not have access, would be far less likely to find themselves skating on thin ice if they were more reluctant to conclude that they had suddenly discovered the true meaning of these materials, a meaning that had simply escaped the grasp of all past scholars, whose minds, they now ask us to believe, were clouded by confusion. Those who have preceded us in the study of *Marbury* and the history of the development of judicial review in the United States have left behind a rich heritage of knowledge and insight. We must be prepared to reexamine it, to add to it, to emphasize aspects of the subject to which insufficient attention may have been given, and to disagree, where appropriate, with the conclusions of even the most respected and thorough scholars. But any approach that dismisses all previous understandings as misconceived, and starts afresh with a new theory that everyone else was supposedly too benighted to perceive even though the evidence was before them all along, is more likely to lead to a dead end than to a new horizon.